Jonava On the Banks of the Vylia;
In memory of the destroyed
Jewish community of Jonava
(Jonava, Lithuania)

Translation of

Yanove oyf di breges fun Vilye; tsum ondenk fun di khorev-gevorene yidishe kehile in Yanove

Original Yizkor Book Edited by: Shimon Noy

Published in1972 in Tel Aviv, by the Jonava Society, (Yiddish and English)

JewishGen

מרכז עולמי לגנאלוגיה יהודית

The Global Home for Jewish Genealogy

A Publication of JewishGen, INC
Edmond J. Safra Plaza, 36 Battery Place, New York, NY 10280
646.494.5972 | info@JewishGen.org | www.jewishgen.org

Jonava On The Banks Of The Vylia
In memory of the Destroyed Jewish Community of Jonava, Lithuania

Translation *of Yanove oyf di breges fun Vilye, tsum ondenk fun di khorev-gevorene yidishe kehile in Yanove*

Copyright © 2017 by JewishGen, Inc.
All rights reserved.
First Printing: December 2017, Shevat 5778
Second Printing: March 2019, Adar II 5779
Third Printing: May 2022, Iyar 5782

Translation Project Coordinator: Susan M. Goldsmith
Layout: Joel Alpert and Sharon Grosfeld
Cover Design: Rachel Kolokoff Hopper

Published by JewishGen, Inc.
An Affiliate of the Museum of Jewish Heritage
A Living Memorial to the Holocaust
36 Battery Place, New York, NY 10280

"JewishGen, Inc. is not responsible for inaccuracies or omissions in the original work and makes no representations regarding the accuracy of this translation. Digital images of the original book's contents can be seen online at the New York Public Library Web site."

The mission of the JewishGen organization is to produce a translation of the original work and we cannot verify the accuracy of statements or alter facts cited.

Printed in the United States of America by Lightning Source, Inc.

Library of Congress Control Number (LCCN): 2016944514
ISBN 978-1-939561-59-6 (hard cover: 850 pages, alk. paper)

About JewishGen.org

JewishGen, an affiliate of the Museum of Jewish Heritage - A Living Memorial to the Holocaust, serves as the global home for Jewish genealogy.

Featuring unparalleled access to 30+ million records, it offers unique search tools, along with opportunities for researchers to connect with others who share similar interests. Award winning resources such as the Family Finder, Discussion Groups, and ViewMate, are relied upon by thousands each day.

In addition, JewishGen's extensive informational, educational and historical offerings, such as the Jewish Communities Database, Yizkor Book translations, InfoFiles, Family Tree of the Jewish People, and KehilaLinks, provide critical insights, first-hand accounts, and context about Jewish communal and familial life throughout the world.

Offered as a free resource, JewishGen.org has facilitated thousands of family connections and success stories, and is currently engaged in an intensive expansion effort that will bring many more records, tools, and resources to its collections.

Please visit https://www.jewishgen.org/ to learn more.

Executive Director: Avraham Groll

About the JewishGen Yizkor Book Project

Yizkor Books (Memorial Books) were traditionally written to memorialize the names of departed family and martyrs during holiday services in the synagogue (a practice that still exists in many synagogues today).

Over the centuries, as a result of countless persecutions and horrific atrocities committed against the Jews, Yizkor Books (Sefer Zikaron in Hebrew) were expanded to include more historical information, such as biographical sketches of famous personalities and descriptions of daily town life.

Following the Holocaust, the idea of remembrance and learning took on an urgent and crucial importance. Survivors of the Holocaust sought out other surviving residents of their former towns to memorialize and document the names and way of life of those who were ruthlessly murdered by the Nazis. These remembrances were documented in Yizkor Books, hundreds of which were published in the first decades after the Holocaust.

Most of these books were published privately, or through landsmanshaftn (social organizations comprised of members originating from the same European town or region) that still existed, and were often distributed free of charge. Sadly, the languages used to document these crucial histories and links to our past, Yiddish and Hebrew, are no longer commonly understood by a significant percentage of Jews today. As a result, JewishGen has undertaken the sacred responsibility of translating these books into English so that the culture and way of life of these communities will be preserved and transmitted to future generations.

In 1986, a group of farsighted JewishGenners started a project to pool their efforts together in groups based upon their ancestors from each town and donate money to get the Yizkor books of their ancestral towns translated into English. As the translated material became available, it was made accessible for free at www.JewishGen.org/Yizkor. Hardcover copies can be purchased by visiting https://www.jewishgen.org/Yizkor/ybip.html (see below).

It is our hope that the translation of these books into English (and other languages) will assist the countless Jewish family researchers who are so desperately seeking to forge a connection with their heritage.

Director of JewishGen Yizkor Book Project: Lance Ackerfeld

About the JewishGen Press

JewishGen Press (formerly the Yizkor Books-in-Print Project) is the publishing division of JewishGen.org, and provides a venue for the publication of non-fiction books pertaining to Jewish genealogy, history, culture, and heritage.

In addition to the Yizkor Book category, publications in the Other Non-Fiction category include Shoah memoirs and research, genealogical research, collections of genealogical and historical materials, biographies, diaries and letters, studies of Jewish experience and cultural life in the past, academic theses, and other books of interest to the Jewish community.

Please visit https://www.jewishgen.org/Yizkor/ybip.html to learn more.

Director of JewishGen Press: Joel Alpert
Managing Editor - Jessica Feinstein
Publications Manager - Susan Rosin

Acknowledgements

The translation of the Yanova Yizkor Book into English from Yiddish and Hebrew was a ten year effort. I am immensely grateful to the loyal Yanova landsleyt who generously contributed, many of them contributing repeatedly, so that our excellent translator Jerrold Landau of Toronto, Canada could produce a translation reflective of the joys and sorrows of the Shoah survivor authors of the Yizkor Book. Thank you to Joyce Fields who helped the translation get underway and to Lance Ackerfeld for his continuing enthusiasm and support to see it through.

Words cannot express the deep gratitude I feel toward Sidney Iwens z"l of Sarasota, Florida who was born Shaiah Ivensky in Yanova in 1924. I read Sidney's moving book, How Dark the Heavens, about his experiences as a young man during the Shoah and turned a page to see the names of two Goldsmith family members from whom my family had been separated because of the War. I did something I have never done before or since: I found a telephone number for Sidney in Florida and called him. We spoke for hours that first time. He was so kind and generous in sharing his knowledge. It was from Sidney that I learned that two Goldsmith cousins, Meir Leib and Avraham had survived the War, one in the Resistance and one as a child in hiding. Not only was Sidney responsible for my finding my family in Israel, he told me he had an extra copy of the Yanova Yizkor Book and wanted to send it to me. It was truly *bashert*. Sidney was the inspiration behind my serving as Translation Coordinator. Sidney passed away in 2010, but I know how thrilled he would be that more people will be able to read and learn from the Yizkor Book.

In addition to the translation efforts of Jerrold Landau, I was also assisted at early stages by the enthusiasm and insights of Sonia Kovitz of Columbus, Ohio. Danielle Thompson of Berkeley, California also contributed to the translation.

Thank you especially to my family who supported the translation efforts with encouragement and contributions and even accompanied me to Lithuania to visit Yanova (Jonava), Shat (Seta), Kovno (Kaunas) and Keidan (Kedainiai). And I must mention my unbounded gratitude for and appreciation of my paternal Goldsmith/Gittes, Shliomovich/P[F]ilvinsky family who made everything possible.

Special thanks to the National Yiddish Book Center in Amherst, Massachusetts and the New York Public Library for supplying the high resolution images used in this book.

Our sincere appreciation to Helen Rosenstein Wolf for typing up the English text

Susan M. Goldsmith
San Francisco Bay Area, California, USA
November 7, 2017

Yanova Yizkor Book

*Yanova on the Vilia,*Yizkor Book in memory of the Jewish Community of Yanova, is a tribute to a community; to its members, whose lives were extinguished by the Nazis and their willing Lithuanian collaborators; and to its survivors, who generously contributed chapters to the book and/or provided inspiration, support and aided in its publication. Edited by Shimeon Noy, with materials collected by Itzchak Burstein, and illustrated by Larissa Bolnik, the book is more than 460 pages in length, filled with many captioned photos. The book is written in Hebrew, Yiddish and English. Irgun Yotzei Yanova (Organization of Jonava Landsleyt in Israel) with the assistance of Jonava Landsleyt in the United States and South Africa, published the book, under the imprimatur of Arieli Co. in Tel Aviv in 1972.

As movingly explained in the Introduction, by Itzchak Ben David Burstein on behalf of the Book Committee, it was on January 17, 1967, when approximately thirty survivors met to unveil the memorial plaque for the martyrs of Jonava, that they decided to publish a book that would perpetuate their town Yanova for future generations.

> An opinion was expressed not to publish a book. The
> reasons were that the end of the elders who remember
> Jonava will be death, and the younger generation, the
> children of those who came from the town, born
> in Israel, America, or Russia are not interested in such
> a topic. Therefore, it would be a shame to invest so
> much energy and money into this. The majority stood
> firmly on their opinion with the hope that the 350
> natives of the town, scattered in the Land [of Israel]
> and throughout the Diaspora, would leaf through the
> book and read it with feelings of honor and love.
> Their town would spread out for a second time
> before the eyes of their spirit – with its cultural
> and social institutions, buildings, activists, and
> common folk. They claimed that no small number
> of the second and third generation of our town
> would take an interest in the book, in order to research
> their ancestral heritage....
> *   *   *
> The reader will certainly discover ... [Yanova's] unique
> characteristics, about which he had not yet learned, as he
> reads through the book. To the Jewish residents of this
> town, to its youth who were educated with Mapu's novels

and who dreamed of the Land of Israel, to those who have
a part in what transpired and what is transpiring here in the
Land, and to the scattered natives of Jonava wherever they
are – to you this book is dedicated.

This Yizkor Book is a unique source of information on a once vibrant
town, once within the Russian Pale of Settlement, now in the center of
Lithuania, whose Jewish population was destroyed in the Holocaust.
Written after World War II by émigrés and Holocaust survivors, this Yizkor
Book contains narratives of the history of the town, details of daily life,
religious and political figures and movements, religious and secular
education, and gripping stories of the major intellectual and Zionist
movements of the 20th century. The necrologies and lists of residents are
of tremendous genealogical value, as often the names of individuals who
were taken to extermination camps or shot in the forests are not recorded
elsewhere. Written in Hebrew and Yiddish, this important book has until
now not been accessible to most users, who cannot read these languages.
Thus, the translation of this Book into English unlocks this information to
many more researchers all over the world.

Jonava, as it is currently known, developed on the Vilia River; Jews
began to settle there in the 18th Century. By 1897, 3,975 Jews resided in
Jonava, constituting 80% of the population. Jews were shopkeepers and
skilled craftspeople, providing virtually all supplies and services needed by
the area's peasant farmers. Jews also participated in the timber industry
and furniture-making for which Jonava was noted. Jonava was
distinguished by the fact that although Jews were expelled from Jonava by
the Russians during WW I, many returned after the war. As many as two-
thirds of the municipal council were Jewish as were the Mayor and Deputy
Mayor. By the 1930s however, Lithuanians in Jonava agreed to boycott all
Jewish businesses, thereby enabling their own fledgling shops and services
to become established without competition. The Jewish population in
1940 was 3,000, 60% of the total. Many Jonava Jews had emigrated to the
United States, South Africa and Palestine; Jews fleeing Poland had arrived
in Jonava.

On June 22, 1941, the Nazis invaded Lithuania. On that day, the
Deputy Mayor was killed by a Lithuanian; the following day, 70 Jews were
killed by a battlefield explosion. On June 26, Jews were rounded up and
forced to the market square where Lithuanians stood ready to murder
them. A mortar exploded in the square, disrupting the annhilation plan,
but only for a few days. From June 29, 1941 on 2,108 Jewish citizens of
Jonava were shot in the Girelke Wood just outside Jonava. Although many
Lithuanian shtetlach were not able to publish their own Yizkor Book due to
the fact that even before the Nazis entered Lithunian towns, the
Lithuanians had already slaughtered close to 95% of the Jews, we are

fortunate that Jonava did have survivors, who, as noted above, took on the task of remembering their lost families and town.

Jewish researchers with Jonava ties will find crucial genealogical information about their families, unlikely to be found in any other source. In many cases they will be able to read what an ancestor has written, see a photo, and learn firsthand how their ancestors lived and their fate, thereby making the Yizkor Book's treasure of information and insights readily accessible. We are the future generations for whom this book was published; it is we who will remember and pass on the memory so carefully set out for us in this book.

Notes to the Reader:

Within the text the reader will note "{34}" standing ahead of a paragraph. This indicates that the material translated below was on page 34 of the original book. However, when a paragraph was split between two pages in the original book, the marker is placed in this book after the end of the paragraph for ease of reading.

Also please note that all references within the text of the book to page numbers, refer to the page numbers of the original Yizkor Book.

The original book can be seen online at the NY Public Library site:

http://yizkor.nypl.org/index.php?id= 2236

It can also be seen on the Yiddish Book Centers web site either with a reader or downloaded in pdf form:

https://www.yiddishbookcenter.org/collections/yizkor-books/yzk-nybc313801/burstein-itzchak-noi-shimon-sefer-yanovah-le-hantsahat-zikhram-shel-yehude-ha-ayarah

In order to obtain a list of Shoah victims from Jonava, the reader should access the Yad Vashem web site listed below; one can also search for specific family names using family name option. These lists are continually updated by Yad Vashem, so it is worthwhile to periodically search these lists.

There is much valuable information available on this web site, including the Pages of Testimony, etc.

http://yvng.yadvashem.org

A list of this book and all books available in the Yizkor-Book-In-Print Project along with prices is available at:

http://www.jewishgen.org/Yizkor/ybip.html

Special Acknowledgement

A special group of volunteers helped processes all the images for the book, each processing a large number of images. Special thanks to them:

Frank Adler	Errol Genet
Marlene Bishow	Sharon Grosfeld
Fran Cohen	Kenneth Pack
Linda Epstein	Gerald Simon
Sondra Ettlinger	Jill Ullman
Martha Forsyth	Michael Weisman
Larry Gaum	Mary Zucker

Geopolitical Information:

Jonava is located at 55°05' North Latitude and 24°17' East Longitude

Alternate names for the town are: Jonava [Lithuanian], Yanove [Yiddish], Ianovo [Russian], Janów [Polish], Janova, Janovo, Janowa, Janowo, Yanova, Yonava, Ionava, Janów nad Wilią, Jonavos Miestelis

Period	Town	District	Province	Country
Before WWI (c. 1900):	Ianovo	Kovno	Kovno	Russian Empire
Between the wars (c. 1930):	Jonava	Kaunas		Lithuania
After WWII (c. 1950):	Jonava			Soviet Union
Today (c. 2000):	Jonava			Lithuania

Nearby Jewish Communities:

Žeimiai 7 miles NNW

Vandžiogala 13 miles W

Šėta 14 miles N

Kaišiadorys 16 miles SSE

Rumšiškes 16 miles S

Gelvonai 17 miles E

Čiobiškis 17 miles ESE

Siesikai 17 miles NNE

Kėdainiai 19 miles NW

Pagiriai 19 miles NNE

Bagaslaviškis 19 miles E

Babtai 19 miles W

Siauliai

Rokiskis

Klaipeda

Lithuania

Taurage

Jonava

Kaunas

Vilnius

Marijampole

Map of Lithuania showing Jonava

Cover Design

By Rachel Kolokoff Hopper

I created the cover for this Yizkor book with four symbolic images:

First is the hand drawn map of Jonava (found on page 4 & 5) which serves as the ba[s]
for the cover. Lovingly created by survivors, it shows us the daily existence of a vibra[nt]
village full of Jews, active in their everyday religious and domestic life.

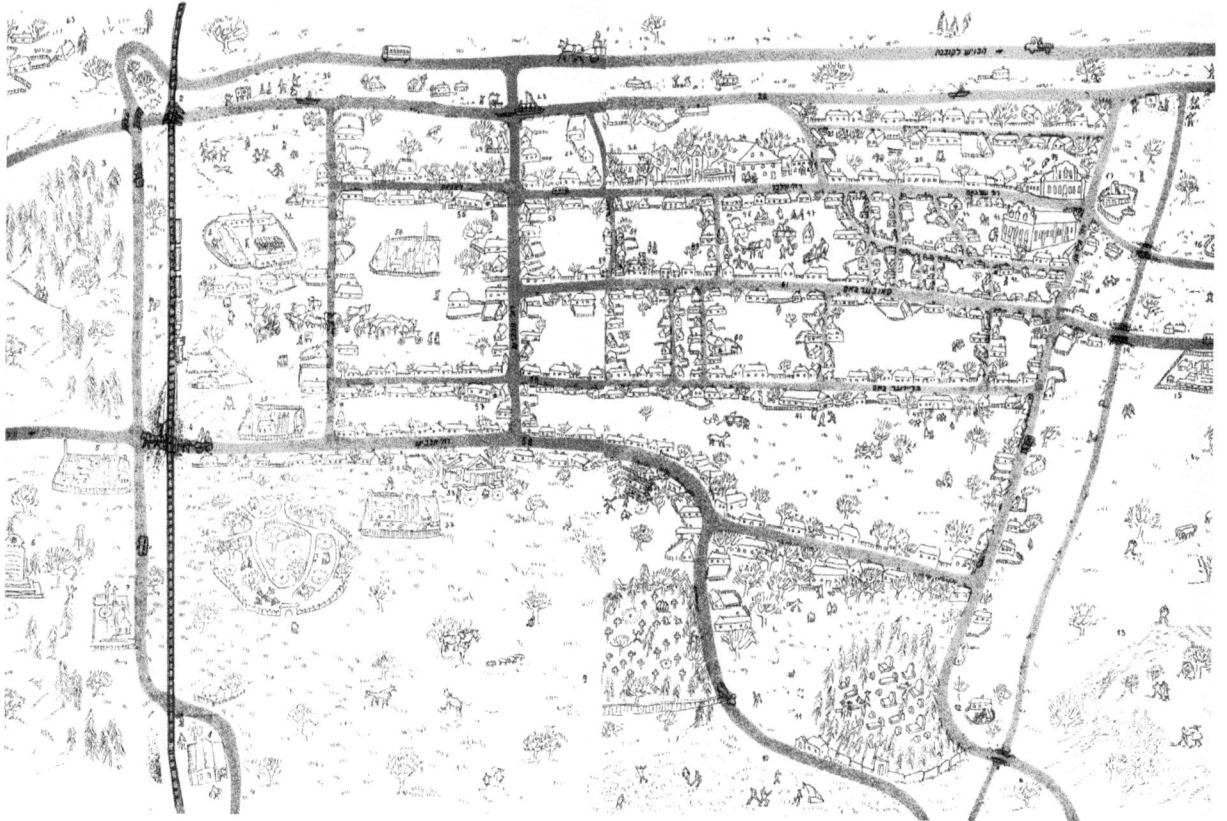

From page 41:
"...Here is the house of Yona Katz, the grain merchant. He was an intelligent Jew, a
scholar, and a Zionist...
...Here is the house of the grain merchant Abba Solsky and Gordon...
...Here is the wooden house and granary of the grain merchant Chaim Perlstein. He was
tall, quiet, intelligent, and a scholar...
...Here is the house and granary of Mota Feliks the miser...
...Here is the house of Yerachmiel Shachor, the tall cobbler...
...Here is the house of Reb Shlomo Zisel Blumberg, who was tall, thin and handsome. He
had four sons like cedars, and a beautiful daughter Henia...
...Here is the butcher shop of Itzik Nochimovich, strong and mustached...
...Here is the iron shop of Shmerl Stern. There is a small flour mill in his yard..."

"Second is the image of fire superimposed on the village (cover image depicted here in black & white). Fire is a recurring theme throughout the history of Jonava until the final burning and destruction of the town at the hands of the Germans and Lithuanians.

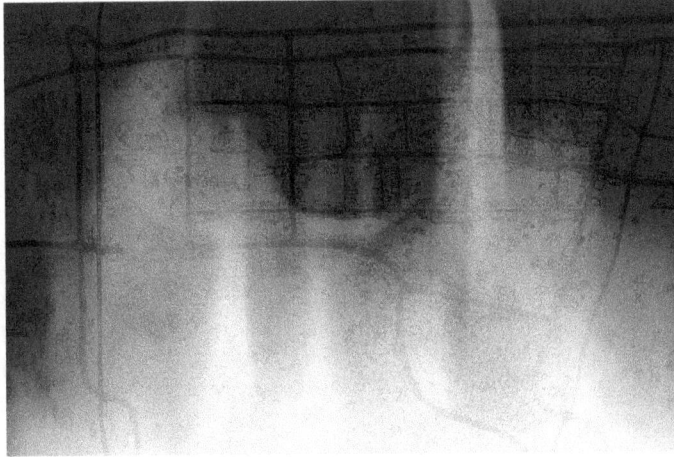

"Jonava -- the city of our birth, where we spent the years of our childhood -- is no longer. It was burned and destroyed. Empty fields with white heaps remain. These are the latticed chimneys that stick out from the ruins as monuments in memory of the martyrs who were murdered by the Lithuanians, may their names and memories be blotted out." (page 149)

Through the third image, a barren and bent tree left standing in Jonava after the destruction of the town (page 685), we feel the sorrow of the survivors who return to a burned and shattered place that they do not recognize.

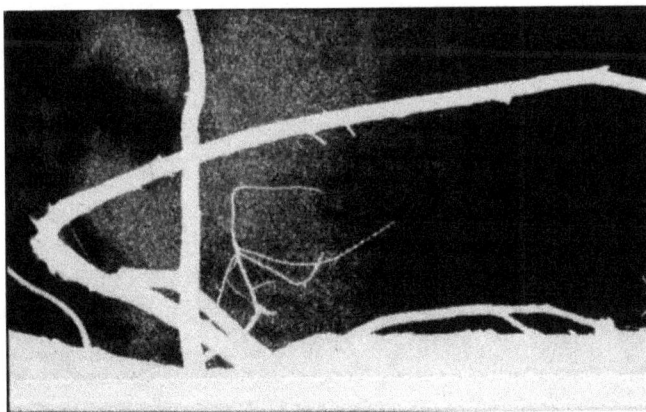

"With a heavy heart, I continue my steps along the wild grass that grows on the street. The old shul (synagogue) stands before me as a naked stump whose branches have been cut off, as if it is immersed in slumber, as a monument shouting Heavenward." (page 105)

And finally, on the back of the cover, is an unsigned drawing (page 3) that depicts what life in Janova looked like before all was lost. It is a stark reminder to us that the lives, families, and the community that were destroyed were of real people with jobs, homes and families they loved.

It is my sincere wish that the cover of this Yizkor Book faithfully represents loving memories, as well as the horrific losses, and deep, searing pain of the Jewish Community of Jonava, on the banks of the Vylia.

Yiddish or Hebrew Title Page of Original Yiddish or Hebrew Book
{Note: this title page is in Hebrew, the one on the following page is in Yiddish. That explains the duplication. It repeats some of the material on Yiddish, once again in Hebrew.}

ספר ינובה

להנצחת זכרם
של יהודי העיירה
שנחרבה בשואה

הוצא על-ידי ארגון יוצאי ינובה בישראל
בעזרת יוצאי ינובה בארצות הברית ודרום אפריקה

דפוס אריאלי בע"מ, תל אביב   תשל"ג, 1972

יאנאווע

אויף די ברעגעס פון וויליע

צום אנדענק פון די חרוב־געוואָרענע

יידישע קהילה

אין

יאנאווע

מאטעריאל געזאמלט ביי   רעדאגירט ביי

יצחק בורשטיין   שמעון נוי

אילוסטראציעס :

לאריסא באלניק

אַרויסגעגעבן דורכן אַרגון יוצאי ינובה בישראל

ביי דער מיטהילף פון יאנאווער אין אמעריקע און דרום אפריקע

תל־אביב, 1972

ינובה

על גדות הווילה

עריכה :	איסוף החומר :
שמעון נוי	יצחק בורשטיין

איורים :

לאריסה בולניק

Translation of the Above Pages of Original Yizkor Book in Hebrew and Yiddish

YIZKOR BOOK
in memory of
the Jewish Community of

YANOVA

Collector :
ITZCHAK BURSTEIN

Editor :
SHIMEON NOY

Illustrator :
LARISSA BOLNIK

Published by "Irgun Yotzei Yanova"
Tel-Aviv, 1972

Table of Contents

[1]

Translated by Jerrold Landau

{First pages}　　　　　　　　　　　　　　　　　　　　　　　　　　　1
A Word from the Editor　　　　　　　　　　　　　　　　　　　　　　　12
List of Pictures and Drawings　　　　　　　　　　　　　　　　　　　14
List of Pages of Pictures and Drawings　　　　　　　　　　　　　　18

Know From Whence You Came
Our Vibrant Town　　　　　　　　　　Yisrael Yaakov Pogir [USA]　　　19
These are the Generations　　　　　　• • •　　　　　　　　　　　　22
Foster mother　　　　　　　　　　　Shimon Noy (Gorfein) [Kibbutz Amir][2]　24
A Town of Working People "Common Folk"　Yitzchak Ben-David [Burstein]　29
My Jonava　　　　　　　　　　　　Shmuel Goldshmid [London]　　　33
During the First World War　　　　　Aharon Gazit (Zisla) [Ramat Gan]　40
Tours of our Town in Reality and Imagination　Yitzchak Burstein　　　48
Sabbath Eve on the Vylia (poem)　　　Noach Stern [Israel]　　　　　　75
Before and After the War　　　　　　Meir Tzoref (Goldshmid) [Tel Aviv]　96

Our Parents Home
My Parental Home　　　　　　　　　Moshe Shamir　　　　　　　　122
The House on the Street of the Road (Rechov Hakvish)　Rachel Soloveitchik (nee Janosevich) [Tel Aviv]　123
He Preferred the Interpersonal Commandments　Shimon Noy (Gorfein)　125
The Story and Annals of One Family　Sara Burstein [Tel Aviv]　　　128
Friday in my Town (poem)　　　　　Dov Blumberg [Cape Town]　　143
They are all Dear to me　　　　　　Ala Daltitsky (nee Abramovich) [Tel Aviv]　148
Years that I Will Never Forget　　　Aryeh Solsky　　　　　　　　152
"I am not Owed Payment for that which G-d Granted me"　Shoshana and Mordechai Rashkes　154
Father was also Like a Mother to us　Freda Khasid　　　　　　　159
"Your Wife is Like a Fruitful Vine, Your Children are Like Olive Shoots"　David Rubin [Bnai Brak]　161
With Torah, Service and Good Deeds　T.[oybe] B.[en Paz] (Goldshteyn) [Jerusalem]　164
The Abridged Code of Jewish Law [The Shulchan Arukh] on the Work Table　Menachem Levin　165
Links in the Chain of Generations (a poem)　AAvshalom Tzoref (Goldschmidt) of [Kibbuz Ginosar]　168
In my Parents Home　　　　　　　Dr. Shimon Zak　　　　　　　172
Grandfather is Also Remembered for the Good　Tikva Katz [Givataim]　175
I Loved to go to Grandmother　　　Chaya Grabersky [Tel Aviv]　　178
My Grandfather Reb Mashel　　　　Baruch Lin (Jalinovich or Ilinevits) [Ramat Gan]　179
But...　　　　　　　　　　　　　Dina Rikless (nee Perlstein)　　184

Journeys to the Land
In the Achva Group with the First Chalutzim of Lithuania　Aharon Gazit (Zisla)　186
Something About My Parent's Home　Aharon Gazit (Zisla)　　　　193
His Entire Essence Was Firmly Rooted　Friends tell about Chaim Chermoni (Munits)　195
...And the Straw Pierced our Flesh　Dvora Garber (nee Zlonker) [Petach Tikva]　197
Four Who Were Among the First Pioneers　Dov Blumberg [Capetown]　198
I Snuck Out the Window　　　　　Batya Tauba Opnitzky [Tel Aviv]　202
About an Orange　　　　　　　　Tzvi Khasid [Tel Aviv]　　　　207
A Pioneering Family　　　　　　　Rachel Ben-Yehuda (Mintz)　　220
Fortunate With a Dual Meaning　　Zelig Even (Stein) [Kibbutz Gavat]　223

From the Cheder to Hechalutz   Eliezer Kokhavi (Stern) [Kibbutz Netzer Sereni]   225
A Carpenters Journey to the Land   Daniel Rikless [Tel Aviv]   227
On the Heels of the First Ones   Baruch Lin (Ilinevits)   232
A Town of Chalutzim (Pioneers)   Shimon Shapira   235

Personalities and Events
Some Jewish Lithuanian Scholars   From The Book of Lithuanian Jewry   237
Rabbi Chaim Yitzchak Silman   The sisters Sara Pinta and Mina Markusevich (nee Silman) 257
His Entire Life Was Dedicated to His Art   Yeshayahu Kulviansky   258
One of the Dear ones of Jonava (M.[oshe] Ivensky)   Yitzchak Ben-David Burstein   265
I Learned a Great Deal from Him: More on Ivensky   Sara Burstein   270
Shmuel Goldshmid   (Autobiographical article)   274
Noach Stern   276
A Portrait of the Young Poet (poem)   Noach Stern [Israel]   278
About Two Brothers who Dedicated their Lives to Those in Need   Tovia Ben-Pazi (Bronznik) [Jerusalem] 280
Rabbi Yisrael Yaakov and his Son the Artist   Golda Sirek (Saker) [Givataim]   283
Inside and Outside   Golda Sirek (Saker)[3]   284
With Mixed Feelings   Chaya-Rivka Feinberg (nee Aharonson)   288
A Little of This and a Little of That   Shmuel Ben-Menachem (Deitz) [Khadera]   289
Between Water and Fire   Esther Tilmun (nee Novikhovich)   291
Dvor'ka the Divorcée {Y: 341}   Israel Yaacov Pagir [USA]   293
Mosheke the "Moldy"   Yitzchak Ben David   295
Tales and Exaggerations   Sara Burstein   296

Activist Youth and Social Awareness
Maccabee   Yitzchak Ben-David Burstein   298
"Halpoel" and the Youth   Eliahu Kagan [Tel Aviv]   301
The First National Youth Organization   Y[itzchak]. B[urstein].   327
The Hashomer Hatzair Chapter   Shimon Noy (Gorfein)   338
The First Hebrew Kindergarten   Golda Sirek (Saker) [Givataim]   340
The Tarbut Hebrew Elementary School   Chana Zimrani (Granevich)   341
The Or Noga Yeshiva   Shmuel Ben-Menachem   359
Institutions and Social Activities   Y[itzchak. Ben David. (Burstein)   360
A Note on the Communal Council   Baruch Kursik   364
The Firefighters   Baruch Lin (Ilinevits)   365

Personalities and Events
The Beginning of the Destruction {Y: 376}   Menachem Levin   370
The Last Day {Y:382}   Reizl David (Rashkes)   372
Days of Torment   Yerachmiel Garber   380
My Town (a poem)   Nachum Blumberg [Tel Aviv]   383
We Were Saved From the Talons of the Murderers {Y: 387}   Dov Blumberg [Capetown]   396
How I Survived {Y: 384}   Tovia Garber   400
My Paths of Suffering {Y: 389}   Leah Druker (Manusevich)   402
Thus Was I Saved {Y: 395}   Leah Hellerman (Kronik)   405
We Fled From Our House {Y: 392}   Lipa Berzin   408
In the Talons of the Enemy   Chana Leah Gutler (Kravchok)   411
                                                Meir Tzoref (Goldshmid) [Tel Aviv]   414

A Hymn of Jewish Faith (poem)   Noach Stern [Israel]   436
What I Endured – A Little of the Large Amount…   Ala Abromovich–Dalitsisky   438
The Shaulists Were Worse than the Germans   Shmuel Tepper [Ramat Hasharon]   459
In the Ghetto and the Camp   Nachum Blumberg [Tel Aviv]   462
From the Vale of Tears and the Valley of Murder   Sinai Persky [Tel Aviv]   475
In the Path of Suffering {E: 19}   [Sidney Iwens] Yeshaya Ivensky [USA]   479
With the Townspeople of Jonava on the Front and the Hospital {Y: 400} David Friedman   482
My Activities in the Kovno Ghetto {Y: 402}   Tzvi Levin   485
The Straight Path that We had to Follow   -- More on the Work of Tzvi Levin   488
With a Clear Conscience   In memory of Yehuda Zopovich   490
People of Jonava in the Fight Against the Nazis   David Rubin   491
Miriam Lan   493
A Veteran Partisan and Commander   In Memory of Shmerke "Valonas" (Namiot)   494
A Pistol and Tefillin   Shmuel Ben-Menachem   496
The Stubborn People of Starovir   502
Illegal Mail in the Kovno Ghetto {Y: 404}   Efraim Zilberman   503
I Was a Partisan for Three Years   Zalman Rochman   507
Marching Song   Noach Stern   514
Townspeople of Jonava in Siberia   Y[itzchak]. [Ben-David] (Burstein)   515
15 Years and One Day   Batya Goldshmid, (nee Perevoznik) [Israel]   547
One Day in the Siberian Taiga   Batya Goldshmid, (nee Perevoznik) [Israel]   556
To Those who are Making the Effort - Be Strong and of Good Courage!   559
A Small Room that Contains So Much   Riva Shalovich   566
Impressions…   At the Memorial Ceremony   567
In Memory of the Fallen   569
   Yitzchak Pogirsky   Dr. Shimon Zak from the book "Banim" ("Sons")   569
   Yerubaal and Hillel Lavie, Rachel Zisla   Published by Ein Harod   571
   Mordechai Herman   Shoshana and Gershon Vilan   574
   Eliahu Hagalili (Galanreichik)   577

Jonava[4]
A Backward Glance   578
Our Big–City Shtetl   Yisrael Yaakov Pagir (United States)   578
Productivity, Cultural, and Peculiarities   Efraim Zilberman   583

Our Parental Home
My Incarnations   Yisrael Yaakov Pagir [USA]   587
My Life Stopovers   Mari Winton (Moshe Vinitzky)   597
Through America to Israe   Tzipora Winton (nee Shaham)   603

Characters and Personalities
The Excommunication Declared by Rabbi Silman   Frank Sirek (America)   609
Rabbi Silman the Stringent   Frank Sirek (America)   611
A Series of Personalities   David Friedman [Vilna]   612
Areh Yankel   Yisrael Yaakov Pogir   623
With his own Traits   Yitzchak   627

A Gallery of Personalities   Meir Tzoref (Goldschmid)   632
Episodes and Events   Ella Daltitsky (Abramovitch) of Tel Aviv   638
Two Poems   Avraham Yitzchak Abramovitch   642
Meita the Baker   Frank Sirek   645
One Relates   Sara Burstein   647
"Labas" the Lithuanian Policeman   Yerachmiel Garber   648
Noach the Roof Layer   Yerachmiel Garber (Tel Aviv)   652
Where is Father   Rachel Dushnitzky   653
My First Year of Working at Filvinskys   Yisrael Yaakov Pogir   654
From the Series of Folk Songs   656
Nicknames   658
Our Talmud Torah   Yisrael Yaakov Pogir   661
On Separate Paths   Y. Y. Pogir   673
My Native Village of Siesikail   Shmuel Balnik   674

To Hell and Back
Untitled Poem   Batya Perlstein   684
At the Large Mass Grave   Efraim Zilberman   686
The Beginning of the Destruction {H: 167}   Reizl David (Rashkes) [USA]   690
The Last Day {H: 171}   Yerachmiel Garber   698
Fortunate to Remain Alive {H: 185}   Leah Drucker (Monosevich) [Tel Aviv]   701
We Were Saved from the Talons of the Murderers {H: 187} Tuvia Garber [Tel Aviv]   701
My Way of Suffering {H: 186}   Leah Helerman (Kronik) [Melbourne, Australia]   704
We Fled from the Home {H: 189}   Chana–Leah Gutler (Kravchok) [Tel Aviv]   704
Thus Was I Saved {H: 188}   Lipa Berzin [Tel Aviv]   705
I Was With Them At Night   R. Spigler (Mankovski), Melbourne   708
Songs from the Ghetto   710
With the People of Jonava on the Front and in the Hospital {H: 241} Dovid Friedman of Vilna   713
My Activities in the Kovno Ghetto {H: 243}   Tzvi Levin   713
Illegal Mail in the Kovno Ghetto {H: 252}   Efraim Zilberman   715
Two Good Friends   Yitzchak [Ben–David (Burstein)]   715
List of those Killed   719
List of Those Who Fell on the Battlefield   759
Jonaver (Yanover) Organization in New York   761
Efraim is No More!   765

Contents of the English Part
Glimpses at Janova {H: 8}   Miriam Zakhary (Lomiansky-Wulf)   767
Beginning, Growth and Destruction {H: 19}   I. Judelevitch   774
My Years of Agony {H: 229}   [Sidney Iwens] Jesaiah Ivensky [USA]   779

Index   804

Translator's Footnotes

1   When an article appears in translation in a different section (Hebrew, Yiddish, or English), I added an annotation of correspondence. Thus, H: 229 means that the article appears in Hebrew on page 229 in the original Yizkor Book.

2   When the Israeli or American name differs from the original Yiddish name, the Yiddish name is included in parentheses.

3   The order of last names of this entry and the previous was transcribed from the text (I suspect one ordering is in error).

Family Notes

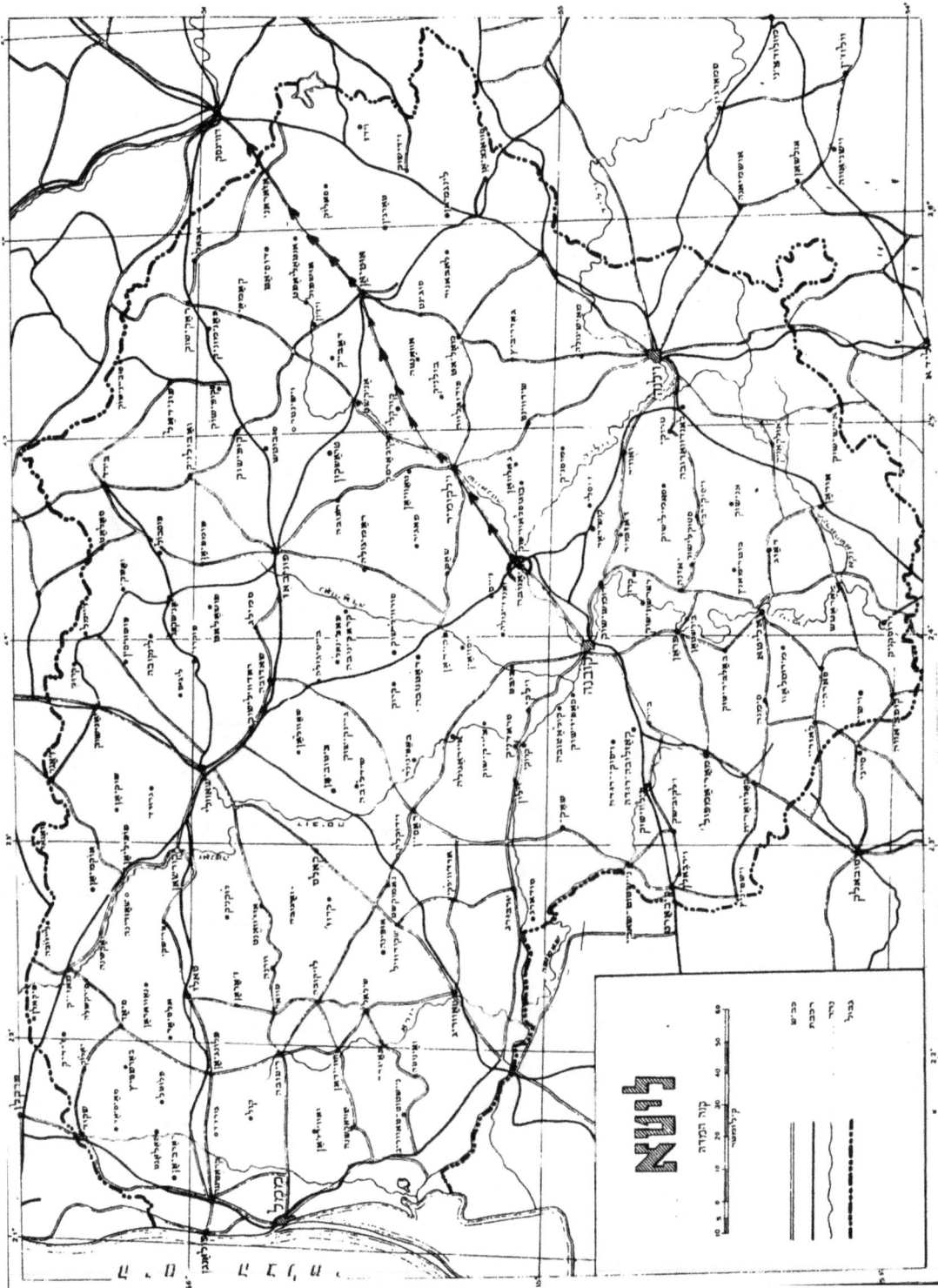

A map of Lithuania, with Yiddish captions. Jonava is circled

Uncaptioned drawings of scenes in the town.

{Image 5} – Map of Jonava by memory (Map follows on next two pages – several streets are listed on the map itself in Yiddish rather than on the key.

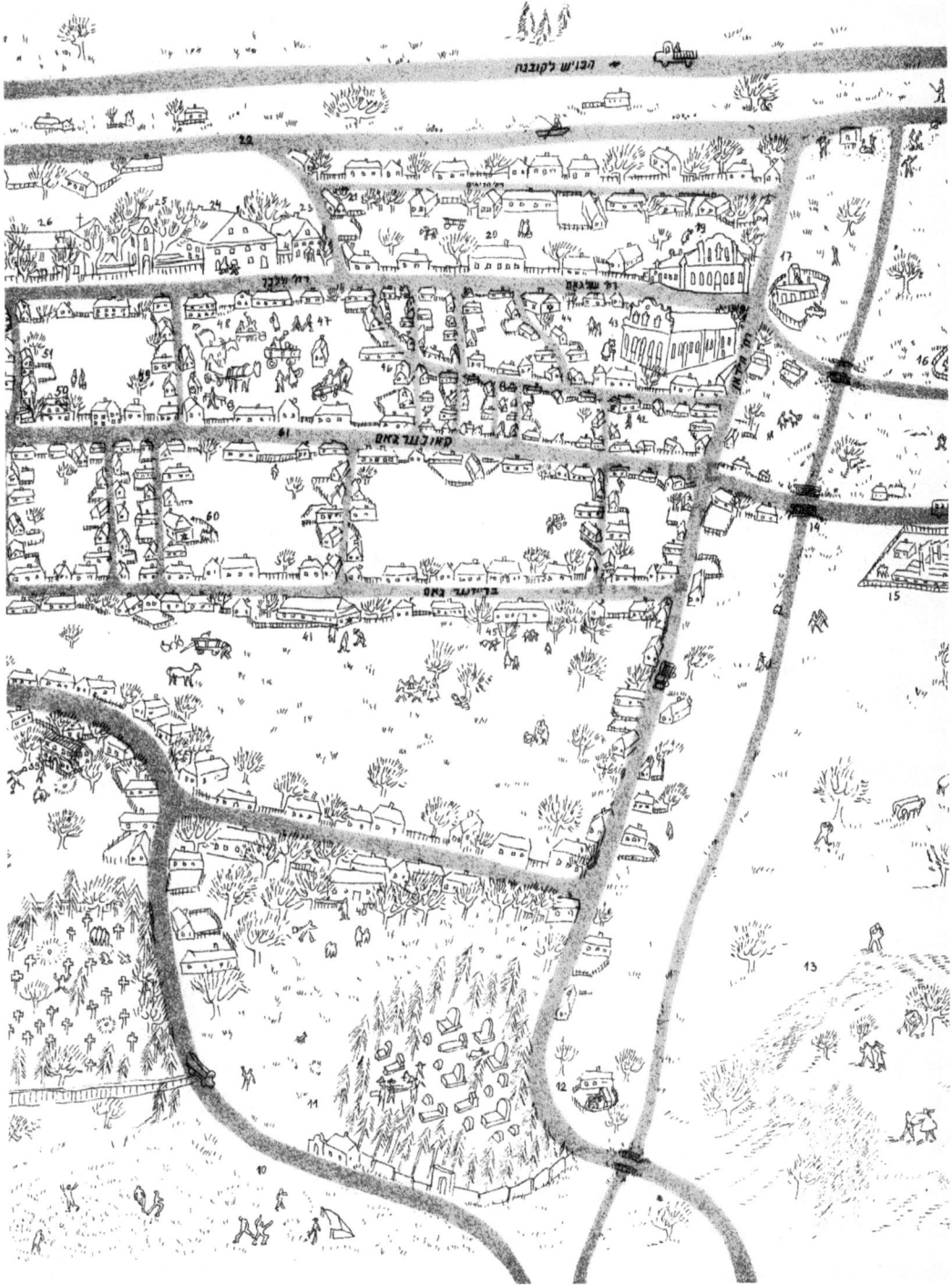

Map of Jonava

The key to the map.

Places, structures, communal institutions

1. Bridge
2. Train bridge
3. Forest
4. Train pass
5. Sawmill and flourmill
6. Memorial monument
7. Oran match factory
8. Train station
9. Christian cemetery
10. Basketball field
11. Jewish cemetery
12. Water mill
13. Swirling Mountain (Hebrew: *Har Hasecharchoret*)
14. Small bridge
15. Brick kiln
16. Slaughterhouse
17. Fire station
18. Beach
19. Synagogue
20. Hospital
21. Maccabee Hall
22. Vylia
23. Cooperative store
24. Pharmacy
25. Hospital
26. Pro-gymnasium
27. Bus station
28. Passageway
29. Billiard hall
30. Beach
31. Apportioned field
32. Barracks
33. Town hall
34. Horse and cattle market
35. Sawmill and flourmill (Opnitzky)
36. Park
37. Sawmill and flourmill (Segalovsky)
38. Post office
39. Lithuanian school
40. Lithuanian culture hall
41. Synagogue
42. Synagogue
43. Synagogue
44. Synagogue
45. Tarbut School
46. Jalinovich house
47. Market
48. Two story house
49. Movie theater
50. Two story house
51. Two story house
52. Two story house (Burstein)
53. Hall
54. Two story house (Weiner)
55. New Beis Midrash
56. Madis sawmill
57. Synagogue
58. Street of the Road
59. Breizer Street
60. Synagogue
61. Kovno Street
62. Residence
63. Village

Book of Jonava

To perpetuate the memory
Of the Jews of the town
That was destroyed in the Holocaust
Published by the Organization of Jonava Natives in Israel
With the assistance of Jonava natives of the United States and South Africa

5733, 1972

Published by Arieli Co., Israel

Jonava
On the Banks of the Vylia

In memory of the destroyed Jewish community of Jonava

Material collected by Yitzchak [Ben-David] (Burstein)
Edited by Shimon Noy [(Gorfein)]
Illustrations: Larisa Balnik

Published by the Organization of Jonava Natives in Israel
With the assistance of Jonava natives of the United States and South Africa
5733, 1972

Material collected by Yitzchak Burstein
Edited by Shimon Noy
Illustrated by Larisa Balnik

[Page V]

On January 17, 1967, we unveiled the memorial plaque for the martyrs of Jonava that had been set up in the Holocaust Cellar. On that winter day, when snow covered the streets of our capital with a white blanket, about 30 natives of our town gathered for a modest ceremony to honor our martyrs of the Holocaust after 26 years. Those who were present will never forget those moving moments of unity.

At that gathering, the members of the organizing committee decided to publish a book that would perpetuate our town for future generations. An opinion was expressed not to publish a book. The reasons were that the end of the elders who remember Jonava will be death, and the younger generation, the children of those who came from the town, born in Israel, America, or Russia are not interested in such a topic. Therefore, it would be a shame to invest so much energy and money into this. The majority stood firmly on their opinion with the hope that the 350 natives of the town, scattered in the Land and throughout the Diaspora, would leaf through the book and read it with feelings of honor and love. Their town would spread out for a second time before the eyes of their spirit – with its cultural and social institutions, buildings, activists, and common folk. They claimed that no small number of the second and third generation of our town would taken interest in the book, in order research their ancestral heritage. There are some among them who know about the life of the town very well, and who know many of the typical stories of their parents and events that took place in the town.

Miriam Zakhary (Lomiansky-Wulf) wrote to us from California: In response to your request, I have decided to write memoirs. In this I wish to fulfil the request of my son Morton, who was born in America, who asked me: "Mother, write your memoirs. I want my children to know about your roots."

Riva Shalovitz lives in Bat Yam. She is a teacher in the Geulim School, and a native of Jonava. She came here as a child. Her mother is Yentl Solomon. When the schools began exercises about destroyed communities, she recalled Jonava. How much effort did she put in to gather together the natives of the town, and to make contact with us! How much interest did the teachers and students display in their meetings and sharing of ideas with Zeev Ofek, Sara Burstein, Eliahu Kagan, Mordechai Rashkes, Chana Zimrani, and Yitzchak Burstein. The school dedicated a special corner to our town, and this served also as educational material.

A meeting of the book committee. October 20, 1968. From right to left, from top to bottom: Hasia and Baruch Kursnik, Moshe Barron, Zeev Ofek, Daniel Rikless, Menachem Levin, Shimon Noy, Baruch Lin, Rabbi Aryeh Lipshitz, Panirsky, Yitzchak Burstein, Dina Rikless, Shmuel Bolnik.

June 2, 1971. B Lin., Mordechai Rashkes, Shoham, Yitzchak B.[urstein], Bolnik, M. Levin, Z. Ofek, Eliahu Kagan, D. Rikless, Batya [nee] Goldshmid (Perevoznik), Meir Tzoref (Goldshmid), Rabbi Lipschitz, Sh.[imon] Noy, Dina R. Zahava Saker (Sirek), Leah Segalovsky (Burstein)}

As we began our efforts, we were astonished at the required monetary sums and the great effort involved in the gathering of material and fundraising. The Society of Jonava Natives of New York, founded in 1906, should be mentioned for praise. The chairman of the organization Yisrael Goldberg and the secretary Efraim Zilberman answered us positively and promised us their full assistance. They thereby strengthened our hands. We also received a warm and positive response from the Vinitzky brothers – Julius and Maurie Vinton from Hartford, U.S.A. They aroused their wide-branched family to activity, including the second and third generations. Sara Baker (Solomon) and Alan Salkan (Bin) of Johannesburg must also be singled out for praise. Without the spiritual and material support of all of these and others, perhaps our hands would have weakened.

Unlike other towns of Lithuania, Jonava had something unique. The reader will certainly discover its unique characteristics, about which he had not yet learned, as he reads through the book. To the Jewish residents of this town, to its youth who were educated with Mapu's novels and who dreamed of the Land of Israel, to those who have a part in what transpired and what is transpiring here in the Land, and to the scattered natives of Jonava wherever they are – to you this book is dedicated.

In the name of the Book Committee
Yitzchak Ben-David [Burstein]

[Page VII]

A Word from the Editor

I commenced the work of editing with awe and trepidation, and I conclude it with mixed emotions; from seeing what this book has and does not have.

Those who toiled and labored to bring the book to print realize that the material is not balanced. It is possible that we elongated where we should have shortened, while other subjects came out brief and truncated. However, this matter was not dependent on us, but rather on account of the response to our request that we received from no small number of people, who for some reason did not pick up their pens and give of their time to write chapters, segments of life and memories of days gone by. If we had to visit all of these people to record what they had to say, the publication of the book would have been delayed for too long. For the most part, the lacunae are due to the fact that some of those who could relate a great deal about the life of the Jewish community of Jonava are no longer alive.

We attempted to fill in the lacunae with many pictures, which also tell a great deal. As the Chinese motto says, a picture is worth 2,000 words.

More than sixty people participated in the book.

You will not find literary works in the content of this book, but rather material dredged from loving and sorrowful hearts, which were glancing backward with anger and longing. Each person has his own style. As much as possible, we attempted to leave the material in the manner that it was written, as well as to make it easy to read, and to remove extraneous material that bogs down the reading, and repeats material that others, who wrote earlier, had already dealt with.

We could not provide too much material in Yiddish and English, for we were restricted by budgetary constraints that restricted the dimensions of the book.

We included in English the three articles that were given to us. These were fine, broad and exhaustive articles. They have also been translated into Hebrew. English speakers will be able to make up the lacunae in the long Yiddish section, provided that they have not forgotten that language. With regard to the second generation of our natives overseas, as their interest increases they will have to learn Hebrew.

In 1968, when the idea of the book was first presented in a meeting that was called for that purpose, we were of small faith. What before what – material or "material", that is to say, articles or money, or vice versa? Now that we have come to give our blessings to the completed task, we must first and foremost thank the dedication of Yitzchak Burstein who was the living spirit in this matter, and dedicated all of his free time and great effort to this endeavor.

All of those who answered us and assisted us must be thanked – and these are not few. We must primarily thank Daniel and Dina Rikless, who gave over themselves, their home and their car to the activities on behalf of the book. Even though not everything is in it, one can turn it over again and again, and the years of our lives from our common past will be revealed once again.

First and foremost, this book should serve as a memorial to our dear ones, who were prematurely cut off from the land of life.

[Page VIII]

Bitter Events in the History of the Jewish Community of Jonava
    1895 – The first great fire.
    1904 – The second great fire.
    1915 – The expulsion (on the eve of Shavuot).
    1941 – The day of murder in the forest, 20 Av, 5701, August 13.

[Pages IX-XII]

[Pages XIII– XV]

List of Pictures and Drawings[1]

Page numbers are the page numbers in the original Yizkor Book

Y[israel] . Y[aakov]. Pogir and his wife Chana [USA]	3
Sh[imon]. Noy (Gorfein) [Kibbutz Amir]	6
Miriam Zakhary (Lomiansky-Wulf) [USA]	8
Sholem the Balagole, wagon driver	9
Youths on a raft	11
Y[itzchak Ben-David] Burstein	12
Blacksmiths	13
Sh[muel]. Goldshmid [London]	15
Noach Stern	22
The cemetery	24
Yitzchak B[en-David (Burstein)]. and Zelig Epstein	33
Meir Tzoref (Goldshmid)	38
At the play "Yankel the Blacksmith"	41
Students of the Culture League	49
Summer holiday in Sponenai	52
The Street of the Road (Hakhvish Street)	55
Gorfein's house	56
Mendel Gorfein	57
Sara Burstein	58
David Burstein (Drawing)	61
The Burstein family	67
Dov Blumberg	68
Ala Daltisisky-Abramovich	70
Zelig prepares sulfur	71
Zeev and Beila	72
Rabbi Yehuda Movshovich, Aryeh Solsky	73
Shoshana and Mordechai Rashkes	74
Rachel Rashkes	76
Father (drawing)	77
David Rubin	78

The Rubin family	79
The Levin family	81
The Goldshmid family	83
Baruch Lin (Ilinevits) [Ramat Gan]	88
Moshel	89
Perlstein's parents	90
Zisla's parents	97
Chaim Khermoni (Munits)	98
Leib Opnitsky, Batya Tauba Opnitsky	102
Rachel Ben-Yehuda (Mintz)	106
D[aniel]. Rikless [Tel Aviv]	109
Rikless family	111
Shimon Shapira	114
Reb Chaim Mratchk	117
Morris Vintshevsky	117
Yisrael Davidson	118
Dov Zisla	120
Y[eshiyahu. Kulbiansky	122
M[oses]. Ivensky	125
Gordonia	128
N[oach]. Stern in Kibbutz Amir	130
Golda Sirek (Sakar) (Givataim)	134
Moshe David Mar (drawing)	140
Maccabee Sportsmen	143
Eliahu Kagan (Tel Aviv)	144
Members of Tzeirei Tzion – Hitachdut	148
With soldiers, the "Brit Hakhayil" organization	149
Members of the Hashomer Hatzair Chapter	150
The teachers Yoselevich and Dov Zisla	152
Shlomo Ber Meirovich	156
Reb Menachem Mendel Deitz, Hashomer Hadati	157
Memorial Plaque	165
Yerachmiel Garber	171
Nachum Blumberg	173
"I took up an axe.." (drawing)	177

As the shepherd sees life…	179
Lipa Berzin	188
Chaya Leah Kravchok[2]	189
Miriam Lan	197
In the destroyed cemetery	201
Shmuel Sofer	218
Sinai Persky	227
[Sidney Iwens] (Yeshayahu Ivensky)	229
Dovid Friedman	241
Shlomo Berzin	242
Tzvi Levin	243
Chana the partisan (drawing)	246
David Burstein (drawing)	263
Yitzchak and Miriam [Ben-David] (Burstein) in Siberia	271
Eidel Burstein (drawing)	273
Batya Perevoznik (nee Goldshmid)	276
The girls of the Geulim School on the memorial day	280
The students of Geulim at the identification event	282
Yitzchak Pogirsky and his family	283
Yerubaal and Hillel Lavie	284
Mordechai Herman	285

In the Yiddish Section

Y[Israel]. Pogir	291
Efraim Zilberman	294
A Maccabee March in the Girelka Forest	295
Mari Vintman (Moshe Vinitsky)	307
Yudel and Tzipora Vintman	309
Avraham-Yitzchak the Shochet	310
Make Hamotzie, child (drawing: A. Kanan)	314
Dovid Friedman	317
Shacharit Service (illustration)	318
The Wagon Driver (illustration)	327
Leiba the Water Carrier (illustration)	328
The Fine Singer, Yosel the Tzimes (illustrations)	329

Mende the Head of Hair (illustration)	333
The Water Carrier (illustration)	335
Avraham Yitzchak Avrahamovich	337
Meita the Baker (illustration)	339
The Policeman (illustration)	344
Shmerl Stern	359
Shmuel Balnik	362
A Wedding in Siesiki	364
At the Monument	371
Reizl David (Rashkes)	376
Yerachmiel Garber	382
Chana Leah Gutler (Kravchok)	392
Rachel Spigler-Mankovsky	397
Hershel Levin	402
Shaultufer and Greenblatt with Tzeirei Tzion	409
A share of the Jewish Colonial Bank in the name of Basha Tartak (Perlstein), 1901	410
Memorial script in the Holocaust Cellar	412
Managing Committee of the Jonava Organization of New York with the participation of Y[Israel]. Pogir	427

In the English Section

Miriam Zakhary (Lomiansky-Wulf)	5
Pretty girls at the waterfall of the mill	6
Yoska Ablaz (illustration)	6
Menda the Head of Hair	10
Tarbut School, teachers and students	12
The water carrier (illustration)	14
[Sidney Iwens] (Y[eshiyahu]. Ivensky	15

[Page XVI]

List of Pages of Pictures and Drawings
Page numbers of the page numbers of the original Yizkor Book

General views on the Vylia	8
On the Street	24
People of various ages and generations	32
A party of the carpenters	36
The Shapira family and the grandmother	86
With the Achva Chalutzim, Hechalutz and Hechalutz Hatzair	104
Drawings by A Kagan and [Yeshiyahu] Kulbiansky	120
Drawings by Shifra Lomiansky	124
Images	128
Floods	136
Organizations and parties	144
Young Zion, Hashomer Hatzair, Revisionist Zionists	148
Schools: Tarbut, Yavneh	152
Fire in the Town, Smiths	160
Jonava in flames	168
Next to the memorial monument	240
In Siberia	272
Batya [Perevoznik (nee Goldshmid)] in Siberia	276
Those making efforts, and the room of perpetuation	280
Shmidan	298
The four Voves and Pogir	308
Siesiki	364
With A. Zilberman	428

Translator's Footnotes

In all the pictures, the people are to be identified from top to bottom, from left to right.

In the table of contents, this was 'Chana'. One of them is obviously a typo.

Know From Whence You Came

Our Vibrant Town

by Yisrael Yaakov Pogir
Translated by Jerrold Landau

Yisrael Yaakov Pogir and his wife Chana [USA]

Our native town, the place where we enjoyed our childhood, where we saw the light of the world for the first time -- You remain etched in our memory, in your young minds, from the time we looked out at you from atop Har Hascharchoret (Dizzy Mountain).

Your houses spread from Keidain Street until the road, from the Vylia river until the hill of the cemetery. There was even a part of our town on the other side of the river. At first Velvel Frumer and later Shneur Sesitzky, the government appointed rabbi, operated the ferryboat with the long rope that linked the other side of the river to the town. The ferry boat floated back and forth, each time with different passengers.

Before my eyes stand your streets and alleyways, your synagogues and *Beis Midrash*, your Hassidic *Shtibel* -- and on the other hand, the Russian church and the Catholic church. The merchants of Jonava waited for the Christian holidays when the villagers would come to make their purchases.

I heard the ringing of their bells. On Sabbath eves before candle lighting, I heard the proclamation in a loud, melodious voice summoning the people to the synagogue. I saw your weddings and heard your musical instruments. I saw the bride and groom being led to the wedding canopy, with the faces of the parents beaming with joy.

I saw your funerals and heard your eulogies and chapters of Psalms. The lads of the Talmud Torah would call out "Righteousness walks before him" before the bier, and the sexton would clang his charity box and declare, "charity saves from death." I saw your *Simchat Torah* filled with heartfelt joy, and I was wary of the fear of pogroms.

Jonava! I saw your youth preparing to protect the lives of the Jews and all their property. Eight youths waited in each of the eight synagogues, and not with empty hands. Therefore, the evil gentiles forgot the day that they had designated for the pogrom. Not one gentile was seen that day in the town. It was almost entirely Jewish:

The miller and the bakers, --- Shlomo the barber is giving a haircut

Even the tree cutters, --- and Leizer the chimney sweep,

The smiths and the carpenters, --- Bentza the deaf, the night guard

All are dear Jews, --- and Izak Segalovsky -- with one son and eleven daughters

The town is beautiful, with Jewish charm, everyone is a beautiful daughter of Zion.

Itzik Dembo the wood engraver and Itzik the tinsmith / who tread carefully upon the roofs / were the head of the firefighters / all of them together and others / were the group of shooters.

[Page 4]

Keidain Street

It was supposed to be called the Russian Street, for Russians lived in the houses sprinkled with gardens and fruit trees. Flowers with many colors decorated the lower houses. The house of the Pristov (police chief) stood out. There was also a girls' school in that house. No small number of Jewish girls also studied there, girls of age 14-15, from well-to-do homes, wearing black dresses with white aprons, well-combed, walking and speaking Russian. These were the charming girls of the community.

Whoever has not seen Keidain Street on summer Sabbaths has not seen an amazing sight in his life. The road was straight, long and unpaved -- which are three beneficial qualities for a stroll. In addition, there were cherry trees on both sides of the street. They were adorned with their white flowers in the warm spring, and when the cherries ripened, the branches turned green and were covered with red.

This road led to the water mill that ground the flour for the Sabbath challahs, and from there to the ascent to Har Hascharchoret.

Har Hascharchoret

The fields and forest cast their shadows. The air was clear, and the aroma of spruce and strawberries brought enjoyment to the hearts of the strollers. In the mountain, everyone found what they were looking for in terms of joy and beauty.

The bashful bride and groom / are wary of the evil eye / -- the bride is walking with her friends on that road / and the groom with his friends turned aside from nearby. / and when the groom, the bride / "suddenly" sees on the stroll / he takes her hand. / The friends -- following the groom and bride / all walk with joy and mirth. / the bashful boys and girls / run to avert the eyes of the women / and hasten their steps. / Next to Har Hashcharchoret the girl finds her beloved / and the boy returns full of hope. / And at evening when they return -- they are all happy with their lot.

The youth of Jonava was also idealistic, wanting to do something for their nation and for humanity. Har Hascharchoret was the place where the factions would meet. The spruce forest covered everything.

The teacher of the Talmud Torah, Yachnowitz, spoke at the meeting of the parties. Even though Shmuelke Brandwein, the son of the teacher, and Davidka who worked in the store of Chaim Levin the pharmacist, belonged to the S.S.[1] Youth, they were not removed from there. Guards stood on guard to watch if the police were approaching. At that time, there were six policemen and a supervisor in the town, who also did not succeed in stopping the distribution of illegal signs written in red ink.

At evening, they began to return home. Each person saw their town from the heights of the mountain, with the roofs sparkling with the last rays of the sun / whether the houses were high or low / whether they were straight or leaning to a side / the sun rays lit them all up.

Keidain Street witnessed the parade of boys and girls / who accompanied the Sabbath / in their fine Sabbath clothes / and the people of Breizer Street would also look at them.

Happy is the eye who saw all this.

From Yiddish by Sh.[imon] N.[oy] [Gorfein]

[Page 5]

These are the Generations
Translated by Jerrold Landau

Jonava -- a town in the district and region of Kovno. The population of the town was 813 in 1847. According to the census of 1897, its population was 4,993, including 3,975 Jews

Brokhod-Efron Encyclopedia of 1907

In the middle of the 18th century, Duke Koskowska took possession of the Skarol farms that belonged to Duke Skarolski. A town was founded not far away. Its name was later changed to Jonava after his son Jonas. In 1864, the population was 4,933, and in 1939 -- 5,400. The area of the town reached 528 hectares before the Second World War. Three percent of the buildings of the town were brick, and the rest were made of wood. Approximately 70% of the buildings were destroyed during the Second World War.

From the Lithuanian Encyclopedia, Vilna, Volume I, pages 693-694

Jonava was destroyed in the year 1750. Duchess Maria Koskowska, the owner of the Lyukani farm, set up a small house of worship next to the private family cemetery, not far from the Lipniak farm. Later, one of her sons decided to found a city on the right bank of the Neris (Vylia) River. The first residents were mainly fishermen, ferrymen, and craftsmen of various types, especially carpenters. The city was named after the Polish King and great Lithuanian Duke Jan Sobieski, who had won the war against the Turks.

The first Jews who congregated in Jonava in 1775 were Jews from the village of Skaroli on the other side of the Vylia, whose population had been 300 prior to this. The development of the city took place thanks to the paving of the long Peterburg-Warsaw-Berlin road, which passed through Jonava. The paving was completed in the year 1852. The development was also due to the building of the Libau-Romana railway, which was completed in 1873 and also passed through Jonava. Trade in grain and fruit increased. The merchants took advantage of the train and were able to send their merchandise in railway cars from the Jonava station directly to eastern Prussia.

In 1877, the Vylia River flooded the city and brought great damage. Jonava was destroyed twice by fires, in 1895 and 1904. On the eve of the festival of *Shavuot* 1915, the Czar and his security advisors issued an edict to expel all the Jews from the region of Kovno within a 24 hour period. The residents of Jonava passed through Žasliai and Vilna. Most traveled by train to Ukraine and central Russia. The latter returned to Jonava only in the years 1917-1921.

From amongst the Lithuanian residents of Jonava who dedicated themselves to social and cultural activity, we should mention in a positive fashion Dr. Reiles who translated the Iliad and the Odyssey into Lithuania. From amongst the Jonava personalities we should mention the poet Morris Winchevsky, and the artists Yeshayahu Kolbiansky and DavidCohen.

The region of Jonava was populated by Russian villages of the "Starovarit" sect. Because of them, the people of Jonava were nicknamed Burliaks. The relationship between the Jewish, Lithuanian and Polish communities were good enough, and there were never any disturbances. During the first years of Lithuanian rule, the Jews earned their livelihood in a sufficient manner, but in the latter period, due to government pressure on the sources of livelihood through providing support to competitors such as the Lithuanian cooperatives and banks -- their economic situation declined, except for isolated individuals. During the 1930s, there were tradesmen of the following types in Jonava: 30 tailors, 25 shoemakers, 3 watchmakers, 20 blacksmiths, 2 locksmiths, 5 engravers, 6 wooden door makers, 9 scribes, 5 sewers, 2 strap makers, 1 slipper maker, 3 rope makers, 3 builders, 5 dyers, 26 carpenters, 3 tuft joiners, 10 bakers, 3 sausage makers, 1 photographer, and 3 tinsmiths. Aside from this, there were butchers, porters, wagon drivers, and barge floaters. The tradesmen were organized into a trade union that had 140 members.

From the Book of Lithuania [Lita] by Dr. Mendel Sodarsky, published in 1951 in Yiddish in the United States. The writer was Pesach Janover. The details were collected through the archives of the Lithuanian priest Vytkonas.

[Page 6]

Foster Mother

by Shimon Noy (Gorfein) of Kibbutz Amir
Translated by Jerrold Landau

Shimon Noy (Gorfein)

"... Only Keidain Street remains. All of the houses and factories were destroyed and covered with grass. There is not one Jew in Jonava. The Jews of Jonava were already murdered in 1941. They murdered them all one in one day in the Girialki Forest, on August 13, a day designated for disaster. Before they left the city, the Nazis opened the communal grave and burned the bodies day and night, so that there would be no remnant of their atrocities. Of all the Jewish residents of Jonava, only about ten remained." (from a letter that was received around the time of the end of the war).

It was not a city and mother of Israel[2] -- rather it is a town and step mother. Furthermore, the community of Jonava is apparently not particularly ancient. The oldest gravestones in the cemetery are from about 100 years ago. It is not famous amongst the great ones, and did not give rise to famous people. Once a Jonava resident was asked if their town ever gave rise to great people. He answered, "No, only young children were born with us." Indeed, there was once among them an artist and sculptor whose works were exhibited in the world capitals. One or two poets were born there. However, these were not the pride of the Jewish population of Jonava, which numbered ¾ of its residents.

Jonava was an anonymous town, immersed in toil. First and foremost there were its carpenters. Approximately 800 workers, a significant number of whom were Jews, worked in dozens of furniture factories. There was almost no young couple, even from afar, who did not come to town before their wedding to choose their furniture. Just as there was the alley of the carpenters, there was also the alley of the blacksmiths, which was filled with the echoes of the sledge hammers all day, hammering on the anvils, accompanied by the singing of the blacksmiths. And the butchers? Their fear was upon everybody. During the time of the draft, the draftees from the villages of the area would create disturbances on the main road when they were drunk. They would remove poles from fences or shelves from wagons, and dish out blows that their victims would remember for the rest of their lives. Above all were the wagon drivers of the town. Once, a certain rabbi who was visiting Jonava was asked for his opinion on its people. He responded,

"G-d should save me from the exile and from the wagon drivers of Jonava..."

[Page 7]

While they were still standing, chatting on the main road and exchanging words with the porters -- their voices could be heard from one end of the road to the other. Even when they modernized themselves and exchanged their wagons that were hitched to "eagles" (that could make the 30 kilometer trip to Kovno in 6 hours) with cars and buses, they still remained wagon drivers as they were. Now, nobody was afraid of them.

The many porters and tradesmen, and especially the water-men, who went down to the rivers and floated barges!

Indeed, there were many "common folk", the "burliaks" as they were nicknamed by the residents of Jonava -- since the villages of the region were populated by farmers from Russia.

Once someone asked a Jonava native who had immigrated to America, had become involved in film making, and could only sign his name with difficulty -- which university he had completed. He responded, "What difference does it make? -- the University of Skaroli." This is the name of a tiny village near the town. Indeed, the first Jews who had moved to Jonava at the end of the 18th century were from Skaroli, where there was a small community. However, take it easy! The *Haskalah* was not foreign to the townsfolk, especially to the younger people. The old and the new were intermixed, and the new had the upper hand.

Jonava -- a crossroads of railways and roads. International trains would transfer nearby. It was in the center of the areas of the three cities of Kovno, Keidain and Wilkomir. Cultural activities were carried out to no small degree through local talent, but were also helped by talent brought in from Kovno. From time to time, symposiums (before the concept was known) were conducted, as well as literary and communal debates on various topics with the participation of writers and communal activists from Kovno. There were three schools in Jonava -- Tarbut, Yavneh, and Culture League. The youth was for the most part Zionist, with all the organizations being represented. No small number belonged to the ranks of Hechalutz, went to *Hachsharah*, and awaited their *aliya* to the Land. The aliya came in trickles, however, and people managed somehow while they wearily waited for their permits and certificates. Certain exceptional individuals later reached the ranks of the Red Army and Lithuanian Division; they conquered, they came and saw -- woe to the eyes that saw! They quickly surveyed the scene, and moved onward with hardened heart, thirsty for revenge over what was perpetrated against their dear ones who remained behind in the large mass grave.

And now -- now let us arise, overcome, and record the memory of your townsfolk in the past tense: They once were, they existed, and are no longer. For us, Jonava no longer exists. It was wiped out and will not arise again.

The atrocity took place in the pleasant grove, in the place to which we were attracted on the Sabbath walks of your youth. This was the place where the Hashomer Hatzair group organized its meetings, games and activities; the place where the "Genuzia" and "Syuniut" organized their parties on moonlit May evenings, and where mixed couples would dance to the sounds of the band of wind instruments. On that bitter and violent day of 1941, a Satanic dance was organized by human beings, and the evergreen trees witnessed hellish scenes and absorbed the bloodcurdling screams.

The gentiles did not stand aside. They did not wait for the arrival of the Nazis.

In this book, we hope to give expression to that which took place on those terrible days, as well as in the life that preceded it.

Translator's Footnotes

S.S. Was a Zionist Socialist youth movement.

A poetic biblical term for a major Jewish city. See Second Samuel 20:19. I would not have translated it literally, but a literal translation was needed in order to understand the title and following sentence

Sholem, the Wagon Driver

Youths on a raft

Yoshke der Meshugener

Mende di Kop Hoor

[Page 12]

A Town of Working People

by Yitzchak Ben David
Translated by Jerrold Landau

Yitzchak Ben David

The Jewish settlement in Jonava grew with the paving of the Petersburg-Warsaw road that ran through the city. During those days, the stonecutting trade developed, and a stonecutters' synagogue was founded.

The city grew further on account of the decree of the Czarist ruler in 1882 which restricted the bounds of [Jewish] settlement by forbidding the settling in villages and purchase of land outside the bounds of the cities and towns. Hundreds of Jewish families were forced to leave the villages of the region, where they occupied themselves with the growing of fruit and vegetables, dairying and flour milling. People of the nearby villages moved to Jonava. The great fires and the expulsion on the eve of Shavuot 1915 reduced the number of residents. Many did not return and many immigrated to America and Africa[1]. On the eve of the Holocaust we estimate that there were approximately 4,000-4,500 Jews in Jonava.

The geographical conditions of the town and its district were favorable for economic development. There were communication arteries – a main road, railways upon which international trains traveled, the Vylia River, forests and other things. On account of this, the lumber industry developed. Before the Holocaust, there were four midsize sawmills whose annual output exceeded 50,000 cubic meters, the large "Oren" match factory, the Farkt Factory[2], three flour mills and two brick kilns. All of these were founded through the initiative of Jewish manufacturers. Thanks to this, furniture manufacturing also developed. There were approximately 15 large, mechanized, carpentry shops in Jonava, and many other average sized ones. Most of them were owned by Jews. This manufacturing provided almost all of the furniture of Lithuania.

During the barge season (May-November), hundreds of barges laden with all types of trees floated day and night. Some remained in Jonava and were dismantled for local manufacturing, and others continued their journey to Kovno, Jurburg (Jurbarkas) and Tilzit. A large proportion of the professional barge floaters were Jews of Jonava. These were courageous people who had a strong connection with the powerful forces of the rivers already from their youth. Great strength was needed in order to transport the barges through the sandbars and waterfalls, especially during the spring during the tide season. Some of them [the barge floaters] transported the barges for two weeks.

Blacksmiths in 1911: Moshe Ritz (Moshe Feiga Leah's), Yisrael Pogir, Tevka, Shlomo (of David-Elia the Karetnik).

Some of those working in assembling and dismantling were Jews. Most of the wagon drivers were Jews. These were characters like Noach Pandra of Zalman Shneour[3]: muscular, solid and strong, who did their work easily and diligently, and earned their livelihood by the sweat of their brow.

The fishermen were bound to their light boats day and night in order to provide carp for the upcoming Sabbath. Jonava was also noted for light manufacturing that was concentrated in dozens of workshops where the owners worked with several employees. There were workshops for tailoring, smithies that manufactured wagons, sleds and all types of household and building utensils, sawmills, cobblers, harness makers, tinsmiths and brick kilns. There were also builders, plasterers, painters and watchmakers. All of these employed hundreds of Jewish workers and tradesmen. Grain warehouses were concentrated along the length of the Street of the Road. Dozens of Jews worked in this business, including large scale exporters. Three hotels served the passers by. There were male and female shopkeepers of all types – large and small – of iron implements, textiles, fancy goods, groceries, hides, and the like.

Along with the economic activities, with the passage of time, activities in the realm of culture, society and sport arose. In Jonava there were seven synagogues, groups for Talmud study and Psalms recital, a Talmud Torah and a Yeshiva. Later, a Tarbut school was founded, headed by the principal Shaul Keidanski. There was a Yavneh school and a Yiddish school of the Culture League. Youth groups also arose – Hechalutz Hatzair, Hashomer Hatzair, Gordonia, Beitar, the General Zionists, Young Zion – Hitachdut, Socialist Zionists, Culture League, Mizrachi, and the Revisionists. There were the Maccabee and Hapoel and Culture League sports organizations. There were dramatic groups, choirs and bands. Through the initiative of the community, a public bank, a hospital, a bathhouse with a modern section, and slaughterhouses were set up.

The Tarbut school used the "Hebrew in Hebrew"[4] teaching methodology. The teachers came from Hebrew seminaries in Kovno. The schools and youth organizations with their cultural and educational activities imprinted their stamp on the majority of the youth, who for the most part were Zionist. There were those who continued their studies in the Hebrew gymnasiums of Dr. Carlebach and Dr. Schwabbe in Kovno or the Hebrew gymnasium in Wilkomir [Ukmerge]. The Hebrew library was founded to provide spiritual sustenance. It was under the supervision of members of the Young Zion – Hitachdut.

On Sabbaths and festivals, presentations on various topics, symposia and literary and public discussions were organized. Between the two world wars, along with the stream of immigration to various continents, the number of immigrants to the Land, especially from among the youth, increased. They quickly became accustomed the life of the settlement in cities and kibbutzim. They paved roads, worked the land, built houses, and were active in defense. They composed the kernel of the group of survivors of Jonava, and they were joined after the war by those who survived the Holocaust, from the various concentration camps and from the vast expanses of Soviet Russia.

Translator's Footnotes

South Africa.

Farkt (Feh Alfph Resh Kuf Tet) seems to be some product. I am not familiar with this word. However, the name Prakt appears elsewhere in the book (see 12th unnumbered photo page following page 144, NYPL scan 230), so it is conceivable that this term may refer to the owner of the factory (although the presence of the 'of' ('le') preposition would make this interpretation grammatically awkward.

Zalman Shneour is a Yiddish writer (see http://www.ithl.org.il/author_info.asp?id=251) and Noach Pandra would be one of his characters.

Hebrew in Hebrew (Ivrit beIvrit) is a teaching methodology whereby the language of instruction of the Hebrew language is Hebrew (i.e. the vernacular is avoided in the classroom to the extent possible).

[Page 15]

My Yaneve

by Samuel Goldsmith [London]
Edited by Jerrold Landau

{Editor's note: This translation was produced by Samuel Goldsmith, the author of the original Hebrew article, and provided to me by his daughter Tessa. The book translator, Jerrold Landau, has performed some very superficial editing of Goldsmith's translation. Jerrold also notes that the translation is not 100% literal – there are some minor embellishments and changes, but none change the meaning of the article in any substantial fashion. They were left intact for the most part.}

Samuel Goldsmith

Rome was built in Latium, on the left bank of the River Tiber, in the eighth century before the Christian Era. Yaneve was built in Lithuania, on the right bank of the River Viliya, in the eighteenth century of the Christian Era. The details are not quite clear. It seems nobody has ever bothered to investigate the origins of Yaneve in a scholarly manner. At any rate, I have never seen anything in writing relating to the history of Yaneve. Mind you, we did have in Yaneve a historian and folklorist by the name of Nathan Yanosevich, but he could not devote any time to research. He was the secretary of the Jewish Community Council (Kehilah) in Kovno, the capital city. He had some notes, and some early documents in his possession, but never came to writing his book.

The Non-Jewish Yaneve

There were, as a matter of history, two Yaneves: the Jewish one and the non-Jewish one. Those two never truly amalgamated. The non-Jewish Yaneve was faceless – half Lithuanian, half Polish, with a group of Russians dwelling over the hill. The Lithuanians tried hard to make of Yaneve a Lithuanian town, but they failed. The place had no high school. The symbol of Lithuanian nationalism in Yaneve at the time was the Roman Catholic cemetery. In it stood the monument to Dr. Juozas Ralys. He was a doctor of medicine but also a fine writer and one of the pioneers of Lithuanian culture in the new state. It was he who translated Homer into Lithuanian. Dr. Ralys served as the local doctor for many years. At the turn of the century, he was among the Lithuanian patriots who smuggled Lithuanian books into Czarist Russia from East Prussia. He used to hide those books in Jewish homes until it was safe to distribute them among the population. My father told me that he used to hide Ralys' smuggled-in books in my grandfather's warehouse. My father was not quite sure whether he had done it in order to please a friend or in order to give progressive neighbors a hand.[1]

The local bishop, Juozas Vaitokunas, was a fascist, a member of the party that had ruled Lithuania between 1926 and until the end in 1940. He was not a pious man at all, and ignored even the Lithuanian Bishops, representatives of the Pope. Some of the Poles in the town tried to pander to the new masters. All in all, gentile Yaneve was a place without Lithuanian tradition, without genuine Lithuanian culture, without a religious leader, and without a civic leader of stature.

The Jewish Yaneve[2]

The Jews of Yaneve were of a totally different breed. The survivors, and there are very few, still bear the stamp of Jewish Yaneve upon their personalities. This despite all the water that has flowed under the bridges of the Viliya since then.

A significant part of the Jews of Yaneve drew their livelihood from the river and the dense forests in the district. The trees used to be cut, rolled into the river, tied together into rafts with special ropes, and navigated downstream to Germany. For the Viliya flows into the Nieman, which flows into the Baltic Sea on the German side[3]. There were several specialties in this trade: the merchants, the navigators, and the middlemen. Some of this timber used to be bought by local Jewish furniture makers. Yaneve was – and still is – a world center of the furniture industry. Many other Jews made a living in subsidiary trades. There were leather merchants, smiths – gold and black -, cobblers, tailors, and grain dealers. My father was a leather merchant. The people of the timber trade needed sound boots. Thus, he was well-off, importing leather and selling it to local cobblers. The bustling trade gave Jewish Yaneve a prosperous aspect. There were some poor Jews, of course, but it was not a "Shtetl" as described by American Jewish novelists. Nobody opened up a shop and hoped that the Almighty will send him customers. The Jews in Yaneve knew what they wanted to do, and the craftsmen were well trained. The furniture made in Yaneve used to be sold all over the world.

Best of all I remember the expert navigators, who took the rafts down to the Baltic Sea. They were not unlike British seamen or Norwegian fishermen. It is the influence of long hours on the river or at sea. They used to eat and drink on the rafts. To be a good navigator, you had to have physical strength, agility, powers of observation and endless patience.

Jews Who Hail from Yaneve

It is true to say that Yaneve was never a center of Jewish learning. Some Lithuanian towns, Volozhin, Telzh, Lyda, Slobodka near Kovno (I refer to "Classical Lithuania") used to be famous as places of Jewish learning. And then there was Vilna. Yaneve claimed no such fame. There were one or two great Talmudic scholars in the place, but they had come from other places and brought their learning with them. There was no Yeshiva in Yaneve. Nor was there a Jewish high school. All Jewish Yaneve had was a Hebrew primary school and a Yiddish school of rather low standing. The rabbis came from outside and so did the teachers. The children of Yaneve usually continued their education in larger towns.

It would be difficult to name a world-famous Jew who hailed from Yaneve. Here and there a scholar; here and there a painter. Neither of them very well known. But the Jews of Yaneve as a group made a profound impact upon Jewish life in the Diaspora. They were profound, devoted to Eretz Israel, stubborn fighters for Jewish rights. Every Jew within this group was a man and a brother. I cannot recall a really bad Jewish character in the town. I still like to say, "We men of Yaneve…"[4]

As to Jewish institutions, I must issue a caveat at this point: I am writing all this from memory. I have no documents with me. It is a personal picture, though my memory is not bad…

The Library

As far as I was concerned, the most important Jewish institution in Yaneve – and there were only five thousand Jews in the place – was the Jewish Library. It was called "The Hebrew Library" but it also stocked Yiddish books and was thus a bilingual institution. There was never a rivalry between Hebrew and Yiddish in Yaneve, not even at the time of the tremendous battles between the Zionists and the Bundists. Everybody knew both languages. In fact, only those who knew Hebrew well also knew Yiddish well. The others knew neither properly…

The Hebrew Library of Yaneve was established in the last years of the Enlightenment (Haskalah) era in Jewish history (c. 1880). It contained only secular books. Religious tracts and books were to be found in the synagogues. Each of them had a large collection of Seforim, and they were available to all comers. In the days before radio and television were heard of, the library made life tolerable. But, of course, it also had a decisive civilizing effect. Generations of Yaneve Jews, who had no chance to acquire secular knowledge, looked on the library as their "alma mater." It was not an orderly and planned education, but it was an education. There was a very small fee for the use of the books, and the poor paid nothing. The librarians, some of them great experts, were all volunteers. They not only handed out the books; they also advised "clients" what to read. The library belonged to the Jewish Community, of course.

I was never a real citizen of Yaneve after the age of twelve. I went to high school in Kovno, and only spent my holidays in Yaneve. After high school, I went to university – again in Kovno. Nevertheless, I made good use of the library during the long vacations. I still harbor a sense of gratitude to this institution. Yiddish literature was not taught at my Hebrew school. I learned it from the library in Yaneve…

Let me tell you a story here. A few weeks ago, British Television screened "Daniel Deronda" by George Eliot (Mary Ann Evans). The hero of this novel by an Englishwoman – she was not Jewish – is a Sephardi Jew. The authoress uses her hero as a mouthpiece for a powerful plea for decent relations between man and man. She even qualifies as an early Anglo-Zionist. It is necessary to remember that she lived between 1819 and 1880, and her Zionism preceded the Balfour Declaration by forty-one years. As soon as the first pictures of the Eliot play appeared on the screen, I remembered the story in all its details, and Daniel seemed an old friend, who prays in the Sephardi synagogue… I even knew the monologues. Where did I come across "Daniel Deronda"? In the library of Yaneve. I read it for the first time in Hebrew. I don't remember who the translator was, but I remember the binding – black cloth with a brown leather back. When I told an English friend about this total recall, he could not get over the miracle of George Eliot in Yaneve in the Twenties…. George Eliot was not the only famous author in our local library. She was one of a series which also included Dickens, Shaw, Zangwill, Jerome K Jerome, and Mark Twain.

We all know of Sholem Aleichem, Bialik and their likes. But I also discovered in our local library such obscure Hebrew authors as Mordechai David Bransteter, Eliyahu Meidanek, Reuven Asher Broides, Menachem Mendl Dolitzki, Adam Hacohen Levinson, Micha Yossef Levinson, Moshe Leib Lilienbaum, and Peretz Smolenskin.

Who knows what would have happened to my literary education without our local library?...

The longing for Zion also drew upon the books available at this library. Yaneve was no forsaken place. It had the river, a railroad and a highway. But our window to the world was our library.

Maccabi

The Yaneve branch of "Maccabi" was no great shakes as a sporting center. Yaneve never played "Hacoah" of Vienna, to be sure. We never produced world champions in athletics, swimming or cycling. But this was unimportant. We had enough fresh air and wide, open spaces for exercise.

But "Maccabi" gave us three other important treasures. A) An appreciation of sport and a knowledge of its various branches. Until this day I meet in various parts of the globe former members of "Maccabi," and they all love sport and are very knowledgeable about it. And do not treat such knowledge lightly. Experts in sports are as good as any other experts – at least in the West. Even ordinary people are expected to understand at least some of the games that are being played nowadays, otherwise they are "poor fish," second-rate people … Society will sooner forgive those who are ignorant of, say, opera than those who are ignorant of football…

B) In "Maccabi" we learned to have a straight back, metaphorically as well as physically, the secret of fair play, and Jewish pride. C) "Maccabi" did away with boredom. The club was a social meeting place, and not only a place for physical exercise. The use of free time was a new discipline, and we learned it in "Maccabi," long before it was introduced into the curriculum of high schools.

The Stage

There is no generation without its clowns, according to our sages. Most people like to dress up and play on stage. It gives them a chance to escape from the part which life has forced upon them. We had such people in Yaneve, and some of them were gifted actors and actresses. I knew myself two generations of amateur actors in Yaneve, and I heard from my elders about actors of previous generations. I remember Elchanan Katzenberg, an actor and producer of great talent. He was also a humorist of some stature. He would have gone very far in different circumstances. In Yaneve, he was the head of the local troupe.

Over the years, I saw in Yaneve plays by Sholem Aleichem, David Pinski, Zvi Hirshkan, Shalom Ash, but above all by Jacob Gordin. I know Gordin to the present day thanks to those Yaneve productions… Some years ago, I saw Ida Kaminska in the title role of "Mirele Efros" by Gordin. I suddenly discovered that I knew the dialogue by heart…[5] I told Ida I had seen the play before – in Yaneve. She knew exactly what I was talking about.

All the productions were in Yiddish, for some reason. It was the local custom to have the plays in Yiddish. Nobody had to convince his friends that he knew Hebrew… That was taken for granted.

The Synagogues

There were seven synagogues in Yaneve. In other words, a synagogue for every seven hundred souls, more or less. This was a high proportion of synagogues, since women attended services only on the Sabbath and High Holidays, and there was no problem of travel on the Sabbath. All synagogues were within walking distance from any spot. The Jews of Yaneve were not pious Jews who worshipped frequently. The high proportion of synagogues merely testified to the social strata in the place.

There was a "Choral" synagogue, a kind of representative house of prayer. It was a very handsome building which belonged to the community as a whole. But only sophisticated people prayed in it. Opposite the "Choral" synagogue was the "Great Beth Medrash." The "Choral" was a red brick building; the "Beth Medrash" was painted white. The "Beth Medrash" was not only a house of prayer, but also a house of study.

Then we had "The Old Shul," patronized by shopkeepers and skilled craftsmen. The poor prayed in the synagogue known as "The Shul of the Wandering Salesmen." The name is self-explanatory. An interesting institution was the smallest of them all: "The Shul of the Stone Masons." It was a small, square structure, spotlessly clean and beautifully appointed. It always smelled of polished oak. It was patronized by wealthy merchants and landowners (among them my great-uncle), bakers and blacksmiths, for some reason. They all got on very well, despite the disparity.

There was also a tiny Hassidic house of prayer which a few of the Lubavitch Hassidim – we had some - had built for themselves. But they never behaved like "Galitzianer" Hassidim. They used their spare time to study the Torah rather than indulge in endless devotions.

I left the "New Synagogue" for the end of the story. It was the one my father patronized. It was relatively new, and differed from the rest in that it stood in isolation outside the town, where the fields opened up. Its neighbors were non-Jews… On both sides grew tall pine trees. There were no outside ornaments on this one. It must have been an attempt to avoid the jealousy of the gentiles. But it was very beautiful inside. On its west wall, there were twelve painted symbols of the twelve tribes. It was the work of a gifted painter who did not sign his name. I wish he did. Reuven was symbolized by a fast stream (his temper). Simon had a sword as his symbol. You had there the donkey of Issachar, the wolf of Benjamin, etc. The lion of Judah was the pride of this permanent "exhibition." I remember best the snake of Dan, because it faced our seat at the east wall. It was yellowish, with the face of a gangster in a Western – vile, ruthless, and ready to bite innocent people for no reason at all…

Our synagogue was a very democratic institution. Among its worshippers were the local rabbi, the local recluse, and the "millionaires," the navigators of the rafts, horsemen and inn-keepers. I never prayed too much, but I was connected with this particular house of prayer through my father, who was Chairman of the Board (Warden). In fact, I liked all the seven synagogues, especially on weekdays, when they were empty…

Translator's Footnotes

The following sentence was provided in Goldsmith's translation, and is not in the original Hebrew: I assume he was motivated by both these considerations.

In the original Hebrew, this section is entitled "Bread from Trees". The author significantly reworked this entire section in his translation, adding in many details including a note on his own father's livelihood. I left this intact.

The German province of East Prussia bordered on Lithuania prior to the Second World War. That area is now part of Russia.

In the original Hebrew this reads as follows: "If I had to describe the typical Jew of Yaneve, I would say that he was a brother and a man, according to the English adage. This is a great level. It is not for naught that one can hear on occasion in Tel Aviv, London, Johannesburg, and New York: "as it was in Yaneve". The words are understood only by Yanevers.

In the Hebrew, this reads as follows: I told Ida that I had once seen the endearing actress Miriam Nachumovitch on stage, and this left a greater impression upon me than Ida herself in that role... I recall Yitzchak Burstein in "Grine Felder" (Green Fields) of Pinski; Aryeh Raging in the role of Uriel the Demon in Gordin's "God, Man and the Devil"; and Hinda Levitz in the leading role in Gordin's "The Slaughter". These were actors and actresses of stature.

[Page 21]

During the First World War
by Aharon Zisla-Gazit of Ramat Gan
Translated by Jerrold Landau

The First World War broke out on Tish B'Av, the day designated for disasters.

I was then a 14 year old lad, a student of the Yeshiva in Jonava that was headed by Rabbi Yehuda Gorfinkel of blessed memory.

My elder brother Dov of blessed memory had studied in that Yeshiva earlier. The Rosh Yeshiva was a genius in Talmud and didactics, an exacting teacher, but not an obscure fanatic. He dreamed and desired to go the Land of Israel. His wife was from a family of rabbis and Torah scholars to whom Zion was at the head of their dreams. Her father Rabbi Nisan Ovadia Rosenson served as the rabbi of Wendziago³a [Vandziogala]. Her eldest brother Rabbi Avraham Mordechai Rosenson of blessed memory was born in Jonava and made aliya to the Land already prior to the outbreak of the First World War. However, after the outbreak of the war he returned as an alien citizen, first to Egypt and then to Russia. He was exiled to Siberia during the era of the revolution. He returned to the Land after many tribulations.

He served as a successful teacher in the Tachkemoni School of Tel Aviv. His son David who was born in Smargon arrived along with his family when he was approximately three years old. He later became well known as David Raziel, the commander of the Etzel[1].

Rabbi Yehuda Gorfinkel and his second brother-in-law Tzvi Raziel also succeeded in coming to the Land after the First World War.

At the time of the declaration of war, many of the youth of Jonava were drafted into the army as well as a significant number of heads of families who were called to the reserve army. At that time, a senior cutter and two young apprentices worked in my parents' hide shop with the adjacent sewing shop. One of them was drafted immediately and the second was in danger of being drafted. My father decided to stop my Yeshiva studies and take me on as an assistant in the store and sewing workshop. Even though I was not as studious as my brother Dov, I regretted the cessation of my studies. However, the contingencies of the times were decisive.

The chief commander of the Russian army, Nikolay Nikolevitch, blamed the Jews for the failures in the battlefield by accusing them of spying for the benefit of the Germans. Approximately ten of the community notables of Jonava were imprisoned as guarantors for good behavior of the Jews. My father and my uncle Eliezer Judelevitch of blessed memory were among the imprisoned.

In the meantime the front approached. The city was filled with fleeing soldiers. Many began to uproot themselves and move in the direction of Vilna and its surrounding towns.

My mother, who was responsible for the family, decided to move all of our family to ¯asliai. Only I remained with her to guard the store and to wait for Father's liberation.

Two days before the Festival of Shavuot 1915, the chief command issued a decree of the expulsion of the Jews from the Kovno region within 24 hours. This decree caused a great panic. We had some relief, since on account of this Father was freed from his imprisonment along with the rest of the prisoners.

[Page 22]
{There is an interlude of a poem on page 22, and the above article resumes on page 23}

Exile
by Noach Stern
Translated by Jerrold Landau

Noach Stern

(In memory of the disturbances of 1919)
The vision of wandering still poisons my blood,
Its grey flags still hover over my head,
Oh, orphanhood, oh, the cry of hearts that are bound
Between the cruel vistas, closed and clouded –

… The last bird of the area in the leaden sky already melted away..
And in the desolation a train wailed the howl of a bereaved mother,
Burning up in despair in the deep, opaque vista,
To provide escape from the yawning abyss for desperate people…

-- -- And once again the smoke of the trains enveloped me with the odor of fire and exile
billowing with steam before me, as the furrows in the autumn fields.
Oh, my self, my soul, once again wings hasten you
On your great journey…

5693 (1933)

[Page 23]

The decree of expulsion came so suddenly that people were at a loss as to what to do. My mother demonstrated at that time that she was a woman of valor who controlled her nerves. She encouraged my father to start packing the merchandise from the store and the most necessary clothing and belongings. She got in touch with farmers who were our customers, and obtained wagons to transport the merchandise, sewing machines, and many belongings that remained.

Thus did thousands of Jews, uprooted from Jonava and its environs, set out to wherever fate would take them. Our family traveled to ‾asliai to join up with the rest of the family. Along the way, in the forest, we stumbled into bands of Cossacks who beat the travelers to the left and the right and tortured some of them – in one case to death. Beaten, persecuted and frightened, we arrived in ‾asliai for Shavuot. We celebrated the festival in a crowded environment and with tears, but also with thanks that we succeeded in arriving in peace and being all together. After the festival we moved from ‾asliai to Vilna, where my parents opened a hide shop with the merchandise that they had brought with them.

Vilna was crowded with tens of thousands of refugees. Its citizens were drafted to take care of those who came almost empty handed. My brother Dov and I volunteered to take turns guarding the mentally ill people who gathered together from all the towns and were concentrated in a large yard until they were able to be placed in closed quarters. We also volunteered for other acts of assistance.

As the front approached Vilna close to the time of the High Holy Days, my parents decided to travel to the interior of Russia after the holidays, to the family of my uncle and grandmother. We sent a portion of our merchandise there. In the meantime, the Germans decided to bombard Vilna, and they conquered it on the night of Yom Kippur.

Their relationship to the Jews in those days were particularly good, for the Jews were the only people with whom they were able to communicate.

After the Festival of Sukkot, several heads of families of Jonava gathered together and decided to travel to the city [Jonava] to see what the situation was there. Due to the mass movement of the army on the roads, we were permitted to travel only by river. There were no steamboats. Therefore it was decided that at first only the men would travel in ordinary boats. Among them were Leib Opanitzky, his son Eliahu, my father and I. I seem to recall that Eliezer Judelevitch was also with us. We hired gentile boat owners, and with their assistance, we floated along the current of the river. Along the way we stumbled upon bridges sunken in the water that had been bombarded by the retreating Russian army. We carried the boats over land to the other side.

This journey lasted a few days until we succeeded in arriving in Jonava. The city appeared dead. The houses and the streets were quiet. The farmers of the region avoided coming to the city for fear of confiscation of their merchandise and animals by the army.

The arrival of the first Jews was received in a friendly manner by both the Germans and the gentile residents, except for those whose houses were filled with the property of the Jews who left. Slowly, the Jews began to return. Life began to organize itself. The distress was great due to the lack of merchandise and foodstuffs. Most of the merchandise was rationed, and the military government forbade free trade.

Since the sources of livelihood were virtually sealed off, a black market began to develop, in which most of the residents worked. They purchased goods from farmers in the villages, and brought them to town, under the constant danger of fines and confiscation. As is said in the prayers of Yom Kippur: "He earns his bread at the risk of his life".

Coffee and tea houses were opened for the soldiers by proper families who had charming daughters. Through the connections with the German soldiers, they succeeded in purchasing from them leftovers or merchandise that could be obtained from the military canteens.

The rest of our family returned along with all those who retuned from Vilna, except for my brother Dov, who remained in Vilna to study at the teachers' seminary in the conditions of lack that pervaded then. My parents once again opened the hide shop with the sewing workshop. The cutter remained in Russia, so one young person worked there along with me as the assistant.

Houses of prayer were opened. The returnees did not have intellectual prowess. A unique personality who stood out was Nathan Janosevitch, the son of well-to-do parents, with a pleasant appearance and general education, a Zionist by conviction, and concerned about raising the cultural level. Through his initiative, the library in the Wiener house was reestablished. When my brother Dov returned from Vilna, he was appointed along with Nathan and the teacher Joselovitch to open up the Tzeirei Zion hall as well as the Hebrew public school, in which Dov served as the principal and teacher along with his friend Joselovitch who was brought from Wilkomir [Ukmerge].

At that time, a young actor from Vilna, Germanisky, lived in Jonava. With his help and initiative, the play Yankel the Smith was performed, in which among others, Rikla Janosevitch and my sister Rachel of blessed memory performed. Later, with the expansion of the activities of Tzeirei Zion, plays on Israeli topics were performed, and the income was donated to the Keren Kayemet.

Translator's Footnotes

Irgun Tzvai Leumi (often known by its acronym Etzel) – a pre-1948 Zionist military faction.

[Page 24]
Tours of our Town in Reality and Imagination
by Yitzchak Burstein of Neve Sharet
Translated by Jerrold Landau

In the photo list, it is captioned, 'the cemetery'.

Already from my early childhood, Jonava was like a major, central city for me. I was born and raised in the village of Kaplice, 17 kilometers north of Jonava. The 15 families were tightly tied to Jonava in their cultural, religious and material life. From there we brought study textbooks, books to read, the mail, and merchandise. We turned to the rabbi of Jonava with questions on *kashruth*, and the dead were buried in the cemetery there. We would travel there in festive clothes for theatrical performances. In 1916, when I studied in the Carlebach Hebrew Real Gymnasium in Kovno, I would pass through Jonava, sleep over there, and continue the next day to Kovno.

In 1922, we moved to the town itself, as residents in the house of Wiener the builder. I lived there until 1940 with brief interruptions when I studied in Vienna. In 1941, a short time before the war, the Soviets deported me to Siberia. I returned to Jonava for a visit 16 years later, on my long journey from the city of Frunze, through Siberia and Central Asia, in the autumn of 1957.

A group of Jonavers traveled from Vilna for a memorial day. We arrived at the edge of Wilkomir and entered the Girialka grove. This was the place where dancing parties took place in the spring, and now it was the resting place of our martyrs after the mass slaughter. The Jonavers from Vilna and Kovno set up a large monument with an inscription in Lithuanian and Yiddish next to the main mass grave. The monument was enclosed with a chain.

Behold, here was the recognizable grove. Here were the fir trees, trees that bore silent witness to the days of atrocities. We were together -- some in silence, and some with sighs and tears. We were photographed, and then we saw the old cemetery before us. From it remained only a small part that was opposite the water mill, as well as the stone fence in its foreground. Here is the monument atop the grave of Rabbi Silman, and here are the graves of Itzik Segalovsky and of many others. The fence was broken on the other side, and the monuments were scattered. Cows and horses were milling about.

{Translator's note: At this point, there is an interlude of unnumbered photo pages, that are not listed in detail in the "List of Pictures and Drawings", but are noted with a single entry in "List of Pages of Pictures and Drawings."}

The Market Street

Jonava in 1914

A general view from the roof of the church. 1, 3 -- The Great Synagogue and Beis
Midrash. 2. Goldman House and the "Maccabee" Hall. Right background -- Har
Hascharchoret

Vilna Street -- Granevich's house and the public bank.

The second side of the street

A section of Kovno Street

Top: On the Vylia: The ferry
Middle: The wooden bridge
Bottom: "The water men" on the rafts

Scenes on the Vylia

Shimon Gorfein (Noy), Leah Yudelevich, Zeev Opnik, Rachel Lipschitz, Shifra Stoller, Izak Reibstein, Tzvi and Levi Perevoznik.

Shimon Gorfein, Yitzchak Nochimovich, Eliahu Koper, X., Yitzchak Solsky, Chaim Teitelbaum, Zeev Opnik, Yehuda Zopovich, Baruch Shabtai's, Tzvi Perevoznik.

Yosef Riklansky, Chana Davidovich, Golda Sirek, X., Shlimovich, Libertal, Aryeh Stern, Tzipa and Leah Wiener, Yerachmiel Teitelbaum, Miriam Nochimovich, Shlomo Meirovich.

Yitzchak B.[urstein], Shimon Zak, Sara Burstein, Efraim Frakt, Miriam Burstein, Tzvi Levin, Mitzel Pogirsky.

Groups of bathers (1927-32)
{Series of 5 photos, all captioned together -- the names going from left to right, top to bottom.}

X, Grunia Kaplan, Yitzchak B.[urstein], David Pogirsky, Roza Kagan, Alter Sandler, Moshe Baron; X, Sheva Segalovsky, Bluma Pogirsky, Chana Segalovsky, Yesha Epstein, Yaakov Miltz; Zelig Epstein, Moshe Miltz.

Zeev Kerzner, Moshe Baron, Eliahu Kagan, Chaviva Goldshmid, Efraim Frakt; Mina Zak, Rachel B.[urstein], Shifra Lomiansky; Leva Koper, Yitzchak B.[urstein], Batya Zandman, Aryeh Stern, Yosef Fridland, Pesia Dembo, Miriam Levin, Yaakov Dembo, Chana Goldshmid.

Mitzel Pogirsky, Miriam B.[urstein], Tzvi Levin, Sara and Yitzchak B.[urstein], Shimon Zak;

Efraim Frakt
Yosha Epstein and Yaakov Dembo

Rachel Levin, Mitzel P.[ogirsky], Roza Kagan, Feitza Levin, Miriam Nochimovich; Tzvi Levin, Sara Burstein, Sheina Levin, Efraim Frakt; Anna Kagan, Rachel and Miriam B.[urstein], Bluma Pogirsky.

Bridges and Youths

Dvora Zelonker and Miriam Nochimovich

Mendel Dobiansky; Hinda Perlstein, Chana Davidovich, Chaya Katz; Dina Perlstein, Charna Baron, Liba Stern. Yaakov Dembo, Shlomo Perlstein, B. Kremenitzin; Dvora Goldshmid

The Segal family next to the train bridge.

The post office

On Lithuanian Independence Day

The Great Beis Midrash

The Synagogue

The train bridge "Tshigunka"

With scenery in the background: Yaakov Klibansky, Chasia Fridland, Malka
Unterschatz, Chana Goldshmid, Shifra Lomiansky, Shmuel Goldshmid

The train bridge

Next to the Flaks home on the Street of the Road (1925): Moshe Solsky, Rachel Levin, Mitzel Pogirsky, Malka Kaplan, Sara Burstein, Eliezer Goldshmid, David Pogirsky.

Walking on   vin, Miriam Burstein, Eliezer Goldshmid, Rachel Levin, Yitzchak Burstein.

Next to the "Kemach" (1932): Levi Koper, Chasia Fridland, Shifra Lomiansky, Malka Unterschatz, Chana Goldshmid, Yaakov Klibansky, Avraham Zuchovsky, Shmuel Goldshmid, Moshe Baron.

Right to left: Izak Segalovsky and his wife Chaya. Chana Segalovsky, Sara and Yitzchak Burstein, Masha Segalovsky.

Beila Apatkina, Menashe Wiener, Surka Ziman, Etka Segalovsky, Yona Saltuper, Chaya Morr, Rita and Esther Bulnik, Chaya Kapol; Meir Zopovich, Pesach Shachor, Eliezer Goldshmid, Moshe Epstein, Sheva Segalovsky, Tzipora Kapol, Breina Yaffa, Sonia Epstein.

Yitzchak B.[urstein], Dina Kapol, Sheina Segalovsky, Berl S., Ruth Hencha, Chaya Segalovsky, Alter and Mina Sandler, Zelda Solsky, Moshe Bulnik, Slumin, Henia Segalovsky, Chana Sandler, Blima Pogirsy-Epstein, Grunia Kaplan, Moshe Miltz.

Yaakov Klibansky, Yehuda Katzenberg, Rachel Unterschatz and her sons Binyamin and Menashe.

The cart from 1920. Tzvi Liberman, the lawyer Avraham Yudelevich, Tania Yudelevich, Ela Pogirsky (Segalovsky), Binyamin P. On top -- Shlomo Dragatsky.

In the yard of Abba Pogirsky. Next to the scale -- Avraham Liberman and Zalman Abramovich.

[Page 25]

A few days later, I returned here from Kovno. I continued to the city of murder. The town went up in flames and was destroyed along with its Jewish residents. As you come from the direction of Kovno, there is an iron and concrete bridge before your eyes. The road is covered with a wide layer of asphalt. Here is the post office building, remaining as it was, a reminder of the days of Nikolai. From both its sides and the center -- everything is empty. I can only identify with difficulty the place where our two-story house stood at an intersection. There is no sign or remnant of the houses. The only identifying landmark is the Catholic church. Houses remain on the continuation of Kovno Street behind the market square; on the right is the alley where Rabbi Silman lived. They appear poor and abandoned, and strange faces peer from their windows. I move over to Breizer Street. On the right is an empty field, and on the left the street remains whole until Keidain Street, which was also not harmed. The two synagogues at the edge of the Synagogue Street have turned into warehouses, and stand desecrated and defiled. Thus was also the appearance of the Synagogue of the Merchants (Krabliniks). The alley that leads from the market square to the Street of the Fisherman was also burnt. No remnant remains of the home of the Opnitzky family.

I wend my way through the road. No remnant remains of the Segalovsky house as well. All of the houses along the road were consumed by fire. Only the house of Yitzchak Levin remains. The sawmills of Opnitzky and "Madis" have disappeared from the horizon. New, gentile houses have taken their place. The foundations were built from the monuments of the cemetery. The building of the cooperative remains standing. The new marketplace and all of its houses remain intact, as they were. As you pass below the railway bridge (Tshigunka) and move further along, it becomes clear to you that no remnant remains of the Kemach enterprise. The "Oren" match factory remains. The cooperative of the furniture manufacturers also remains. The train station -- has passed through a furnace. On the left is the house of the Kaplan family. Next to it is a kiosk. I tarry there for a moment, drink something, and snatch a conversation with the woman, a survivor of the family. Her eyes exude deep sadness.

Jonava in the years 1916-1920

Let us present the Jonava of bygone days, as is etched in our memories. Many people, myself included, remember it from the time of the German occupation during the First World War. As I passed from Kaplice through the Markortishk estate, I would meet Jonava women who were walking to go to the German commander who lived there "for assistance". When the Jonava refugees who were deported returned to occupied Jonava, Chaim Levin was appointed as the mayor. A Jewish police force was put at his disposal, whose members included Chone Katzenberg, Chone Perevoznik, and others. Do any of you remember that the first modern coffeehouse was opened by the daughters of Itzik Segalovsky?

Do you remember the smugglers, the *malinshitzikim*, of those days? Shmerl, Bina and Avraham Shapira, Itzik Nochimovich, Itzik Dans, the Gershoviches (the "Turks") and others. They smuggled everything, especially grain, and caused a grain shortage in town. Therefore, Rabbi Silman imposed a ban of excommunication upon them. There were some brave, strong, and energetic Jews who would sneak away from the German guard at night, setting out for Kovno and Vilna. They were considered to be the wealthy people of the town. A smuggler with a leather coat was a desirable guest during parties of that time, which included confetti, buffets and "air mail". They scattered money right and left at the buffets, and with raffles.

Do you recall the vehicles, the *diliznases*, on the road to Kovno? The monopoly was held by Shulem with the long, white beard, who was nicknamed "Methuselah", the son of Avraham Lukman, Gershon Asher Itzkovich, and the three Yudelevich brothers -- Izka, Hirshka and Shaulka. Shmerl Dragatzky held an important place. They would sit at their stalls like angels on their thrones. Important and honored travelers would sit inside on soft seats. Those less important sat opposite them, and next to them at the stalls were the simple folk. If a very important traveler came at the last minute, Shmerl would not be embarrassed to ask one of the travelers to give up his space.

[Page 26]

No protests would help. They would go out at night in order to arrive in Kovno in the morning. First, they would recite the wayfarers prayer (*Tefillat Haderech*). When the wagon reached the forbidden forests that stretched for 10 kilometers on both sides of the road, they would awaken from their sleep and recite verses of Psalms as a protection against demons. They would reach the inn at Davalgonys, about 12 kilometers from Kovno, early in the morning. The family of Uncle Rom was there. They would drink a hot drink and eat fresh rolls that had just been taken out of the oven.

Jonava 1922-40

I once again ascended the mountain and turned my head toward the mass grave in Girialka. Jonava came to my memory, full of vibrant Jewish life.

The "Gaguzina": parties took place in that grove. People would dance to the sounds of a military band. Our acquaintances Puzitzer and Abramovich would bring cold lemonade and soda in a wagon. Yisrael Namiot, Persky and others would set up buffets. Hundreds of youths would be attracted to the direction of the grove. At midnight, they would descend the mountain, some alone and some with their partner, full of impressions from the party in the bosom of nature. The echoes of Hebrew and Yiddish songs filled the air of the warm summer night.

Now we pass by the "Kemach", a combination of a sawmill, a flour mill and parquet factory. The enterprise occupied both sides of the street. Its owners David Burstein and Leiba Wolfovich were nationalist Jews. The name of the enterprise attests to this. Fifteen Jews worked there as experienced officials: Yona Saltuper, Grinblat-- avowed bachelors during the 1930s and active members of Young Zion; Moshel Beker the hunchbacked bookkeeper -- a great joker, with whom one was always happy in his presence; Moshel Baron -- a young sportsman and member of "Maccabee". The work in the mill went very quickly under his hands. However, at the end of the workday, he would suddenly appear clean-shaven, dressed in etched trousers, a silk shirt and a tie, as he hurried to spend time in the company of women; the brothers Leibel and Pinia Burstein of Wilkomir -- one of them was a member of Young Zion, and the other, with *peyos*, was a Revisionist; Hershel Wolfovich, short, was also a Revisionist. He was the first person in town to own a radio. He played the mandolin in the Maccabee band, had a sense of humor, and played comic roles in the Maccabee dramatic group; Shmuel Bulnik of Siesikai appeared on Sundays from the forests. His penetrating gaze would quickly attract the attention of anyone standing next to him, who would then successfully imitate him; Shimon Murbiansky -- with left leanings, who found favor among the women of the town; Micha Baron -- approximately 55 years old, the lessee of the mill, with a small beard and mustache. He was a great expert, with a sense of humor. He was always covered in flour dust; Dovil Dudak -- who would cook for the bachelors, and do her work quietly and with dedication.

All of them were like a collective unit, and they were bound to each other in life.

You can imagine for yourselves the attractive force that this enterprise had for the youth of the town, especially of the prettier sex. Toward the end, two lovely girls worked there: Masha Namiot and Chana Sesitsky. On Sabbaths, the youths would literally lay siege at the enterprise. The Grossman family lived close by in the house of Petrosovich. He was a grain merchant. Both he and his sister Rivka were members of Young Zion. Due to their proximity, they were also numbered among the "Kemach" collective. On the other side was the granary of Nachum Blumberg and Grossman. On market days, Nachum would stand on the road and examine the wagons of the farmers to find out what merchandise they were bringing with them.

Here are the railway tracks. We would walk along the railway tracks on Sabbaths and festivals, and thereby shorten our journey to the mill. From there, we would go to the Geizon station and eat to our fill in the restaurant, especially on Yom Kippur.

The sawmill and flourmill of Leiba Opnitzky were before the train station. A large staff also worked there. Leiba's four sons worked alongside him: Eliahu, Abba, Tzvi, and Ezriel. The first were members of Young Zion and the latter was a Revisionist. Eliahu and Abba were among the first pioneers in the "Achva" group who made aliya to the Land. At the request of his father he returned from there after he got married, and brought his two young Sabra sons with him. They all perished.

Here is the "villa" of Leiba Wolfovich -- a wooden structure with a garden in front and a fruit orchard in the back. He was nicknamed Leiba Taroker since he was born in the Tarok inn between Kaplice and Siesikai. He had a calm personality, was always satisfied and was slightly haughty. I see him in the eyes of my spirit sitting with a pipe in his mouth, playing a difficult game of chess with his neighbor Yitzchak Levin.

[Page 27]

Here is the house of Yona Katz, the grain merchant. He was an intelligent Jew, a scholar, and a Zionist. He was tall, with glasses, spoke with pathos, was a general Zionist, was never satisfied, always imbued with discomfort and trembling. He conducted a battle against the bank and its director Chaim Abramson. His wife Ethel was the opposite. She was calm and deliberate. Her maiden name was Stern. Their daughters Tikva and Chaya, educated in a Zionist home, made aliya to the Land as *chalutzot*, and work today for Kupat Cholim. Yona and Ethel also came to the Land, where they died and were buried at a ripe old age.

Here is the house of the grain merchant Abba Solsky and Gordon. They were considered to be the largest of the grain merchants. They would purchase geese and export them to Germany. Opposite this is the house of the grain merchant Yisrael Buz. There is a field next to the granary, which the Maccabee rented for light athletics. Yisrael would intermingle with the landowners and the farmers, and his appearance was like one of them. His daughter Lipsha, one of the prettiest girls in the city, was active in Gordonia.

Here is the wooden house and granary of the grain merchant Chaim Perlstein. He was tall, quiet, intelligent, and a scholar. It was not easy for him to compete with Abba Solsky, Chaim Blumberg, and others. His intelligent son Yosef was the best chess player in Maccabee, and won games against the chess players of Kovno. There were three daughters in the household: Chaya who was married to Meir Zuchovsky, Hinda who was married to Mendel Dobiansky, and Dina who was married to Daniel Riklis, an activist of Tz.S.[1] The two latter made aliya to the Land, as well as his brother Shlomo Perlstein. They were the only survivors of the family.

Here is the house and granary of Mota Feliks the miser. The house stood out with its unique shape, its garden, and the well in the front -- definitive signs of being well off. Reb Mota was one of the wealthiest of the grain merchants. He also engaged in profiteering. He refused to give donations and gifts. It is said that he was once asked to give a gift to a householder who had lost his means, and who had been a great philanthropist in his day. Mota turned to his wife with the following statement, "Did you hear what has happened to so-and-so, who used to be prominent among his people, and used to disburse many gifts?!..."

Opposite it stood the house of the Sluman family, with its blue shutters, and surrounded by a garden. Shlomo Nota was tall. He always went on trips for the purposes of the grain trade, and he befriended the landowners of the area. His wife was short and always sickly. The porch of the house served as a meeting place for the youth. The sounds of the piano and mandolin could be heard from the house. The three daughters, Shifra, Yentl and Sara, played the piano, and Chaim Moshe the dwarf and hunchback played the mandolin. He played music to accompany the silent films in the movie theater of Tovia Yaffa Wasgal. The sisters would sing romances to the accompaniment of the mandolin. Shifra and Yentl made *aliya* to the Land, and Sara immigrated to South Africa. After time, the house and the porch were abandoned.

Here is the house of Yerachmiel Shachor, the tall cobbler. He was a lazy person who earned his livelihood with difficulty. His son Pesach became a student in the Lithuanian university after he concluded his studies in the Hebrew high school of Wilkomir. He was active in Maccabee, and participated in the string instrument band and the dramatic club. Later he was active in Tz.S. His younger sister Sara was a member of Hashomer Hatzair.

Here is the hotel and tavern of Yisrael Rikliansky. His son Yosef married Rashel Davidovich, the writer and member of Young Zion. The stepdaughter Roza lives in the Land. She is married to the Jonaver Yerachmiel Garber.

Here is the first enterprise of Jonava, the flour mill, sawmill and electric station of Itzik Segalovsky. The house and garden are in the front, and next to it are two houses for officials and their families. For years, the mill provided electric light for the town. At midnight, the light would slowly dwindle. People would rush to find matches, "Hurry, hurry, Itzik is crushing!" The siren of the mill would announce the advent of the Sabbath. Itzik was handsome, and hard hearted, but treated his employees well. He had eleven daughters and one son from his two wives: Ella, Sheina, Esther, Pesil, Feiga, Henia, Sheva, Chana, Masha, Ethel, Saraka, and Berko. One daughter was prettier than the next. Masha was once crowned as the beauty queen of Lithuania. Many boys were attracted to this house. However, most of the daughters would be "Yatzuh"[2]. They would play cards and social games, and dabble in love.

[Page 28]

Before the outbreak of the war, Ethel, Genia[3], Chiletz and Berl, who was married to Leah Burstein, remained in the house. The only one who tied her lot to the Land was Chana, who married the teacher Alter Sandler. They lived in Tel Aviv, where they died. Ella, who married Binyamin Pogirsky, also made *aliya* to the land with him. The mother Chaicha with the two daughters Ethel and Genia perished in the Kovno ghetto. Four daughters survive, two in the Land and two in the Diaspora. The official Grundman who worked in the factory for many years and fell in love with all the daughters, also arrived in the Land.

Here is the post office, which was already in existence in the days of the Czar. There was a building such as this every few kilometers. They would exchange their horses and continue hauling the mail. At holiday times, the mail would distribute letters that included checks from America and South Africa.

Opposite is the house of Chaim Goldshmid with its hide store. He was learned, bespectacled, and blessed with three sons and a daughter Dvorale. The eldest Shmuel, a graduate of the Hebrew gymnasium, worked in "Di Yiddishe Shtima" (The "Jewish Voice" newspaper). Nisan and Moshe Yitzchak were members of Beitar. Nisan was deported to Siberia and died in a camp there. Moshe escaped to Russia, enlisted in the Lithuanian division on the Kursk front, and died from an enemy bullet.

Here is the bench in front of the house. On summer evenings, this served as a place to idle away time, headed by Shmuel Goldshmid and Pesach Shachor. They would sing songs in Hebrew that were composed in the tune of the opera Rigoletto, "Tempo Allegreto / Figure Nito / places at his own pace / to the maiden Shmukleretto."

From the corner of the house, a lane leads to the mountain, on the old path to the train station. There is a basketball court there. Opposite it was the house, called Beit Hechalutz, where the *chalutzim* from Jonava and other towns were housed. They received their training through working in the enterprises and workshops, and prepared themselves for aliya. The cultural activities were helped by Moshe Ivensky, Menachem Mines, the teachers Shaul Keidiansky, David Rosenberg, Leibel Stern, and others.

Here is the building of Yankel Weitzstein, who was a partner in the match factory. He would drink cups of liquor before the meal. He would face the mirror and say, "*Lechayim, Reb Yankel!*" He got married late and took pride in his two daughters.

Here is the new two-story building of Chaim Dobiansky. This was a family of builders. Whoever did not see Chaim and his sons at work, with their mastery of the plastering tool and the level, and with no compromise on speed or quality -- would not know how to appreciate this. His wife Sara-Eidel and his son ran a grocery store. The three sons were members of Maccabee. Mendel excelled in light athletics.

Here is the house of Reb Shlomo Zisel Blumberg, who was tall, thin and handsome. He had four sons like cedars, and a beautiful daughter Henia. Dov was one of the first *chalutzim*. Moshe, Chaim and Henia were active in Young Zion. Nachum was a Revisionist. Dov is in Africa, and Nachum is in the Land.

The Lopianski house was next to Blumberg's. One daughter was married to Mula Shpilansky, and their second daughter Perla, a graceful Maccabeeist, was married to Petrikansky from Kozlowa Ruda. Mula was a joker and a cynic, but was always ready to help anyone in need.

Going further, there is the house of Lipa Klotz, a nice man, who was a baker and store owner. On the eve of the Sabbath, he would take the pots of hot victuals from the housewives and place them in the oven[4]. Their daughter Feiga who was active in Young Zion and their son Alter both perished. Menachem Mines inherited the house and set up a wholesale store there.

Menachem was a political person, one of the heads of Young Zion in the town. He was active in the community, in the public bank, and the national funds.

Here is the building and store of Reb David Ginzberg and his two unmarried sisters. He was a measurer and later a treasurer at Kemach. He got married at a late age to Malka Wolfovich. He was a miser like Mota Feliks.

Here is the house of Nathan Wolchokovsky. He was short. He was active in the communal institutions, from which he earned his livelihood. He was active in the national funds, and served as director of the bathhouse and slaughterhouse. The young couple Chaya and Meir Zuchovsky lived with him. The four eyes of Chaya and Mrs. Wolchokovsky would peer out from the open door. From them, one could hear the latest news on matters between them.

[Page 29]

Here is the house of Yudel Rashkes, a scholar, *maskil*, and active Zionist. He was a member of the directorship of the public bank and the *gabbai* of the new *Beis Midrash* in Lipniak. For a time, his house served as the meeting place of Hashomer Hatzair. His son Mordechai made *aliya* to the Land. His daughter Shoshana survived the Kovno ghetto. She lives in the United States today, where she is a Hebrew teacher.

Here is the wooden, two-story house of Gershon Kagan. His daughter Rachel and her husband Moshel Kolbiansky lived on top. Gershon was tall, a scholar, intelligent, and cynical. On *Simchat Torah* he would be jubilant, drink, sing and dance. He was a kerosene merchant.

On the other side of the street is the house of Nusoviches. He was a merchant of forestry products. The teacher Rosenberg, who married Yosef's daughter Zlata, lived there. The house was full of books. The three daughters received a Jewish and general education. The son Nathan, who was active in cultural life, moved to Kovno and served as the secretary of the community. He founded the ethnographic-historical society.

Now I am tarrying next to the houses of my acquaintances Yechiel Davidovich and Yosef Munitz. They were cobblers. Yechiel's son Moshe-Hirschka, a member of Maccabee and Tz.S., helped him with his work. As has been previously noted, his daughter Chana was active in Young Zion and the Library. Even Feiga, the daughter of Yosef the cobbler, was active in Young Zion. The son Alter was active in Tz.S. Feiga was deported with her family to Siberia. All the rest of them perished.

Here are the wooden houses of Avraham Lukman and Shmerl Dragatzky, which served as class 3 inns. Since they were owners of carriages, they concerned themselves with hosting travelers. Entertainment groups that came to play in the town were forced to stay there due to the low prices.

Shmerl, broad shouldered, fat-bellied, red faced, would walk like Noach Pandre[5], with his hands behind him, giving instructions to his sons Shmuel and Shlomo as they were hitching and unhitching the horses. On warm summer evenings, after he ate fat, tasty *tzimmes* to satiation, he would lie down to rest in the fresh air in front of his house. His snoring, carried by the wind, could be heard from afar.

When the wagons went out of style and the pace of life quickened, Lukman and Dragatzky were the first one to obtain buses. They operated the Jonava-Kovno route.

The home of Reb Moshe-David Morr, with its large porch, stood out on the opposite side. Merchants, agents and matchmakers would come there. The house was clean and first class, all thanks to his wife Sara Batya. Moshe David was large in stature. He was formerly a "water man" who floated rafts. There was always a pipe in his mouth. With his black pipe, he always looked like the captain of his ship-home. He excelled as a host. He knew how to tell stories and tall tales to the satisfaction of his guests. The stories of Moshe David accompanied them as they ate their gefilte fish with fresh rolls. A home-style atmosphere existed. Moshe David himself had a large appetite. At night he would polish off the roasted ducks and leave money on the table. Sara Batya wondered:

"Moshe David, where did the ducks and fish disappear?"

"There were guests here at night. Here is the money that they left."

I remember their two sons and two daughters. Yosef built a workshop near the grove and later sold it to Wolfovich-Burstein, who set up the "Kemach". Their daughter

Chaya graduated from the Carlebach Hebrew gymnasium in Kovno. She studied in a university in Germany and married the son of Intriligator from Kovno. The sons are in the Diaspora. The daughters Chaya and Reizl perished.

Yisrael Namiot lived near the banks of the Vylia after he gave up the inn on the other side of the river. He was brave. There was a bus stop in his yard. Jewish refugees from Poland were put up in his inn. Yisrael and Petrosovich received a permit to construct a wooden bridge on the Vylia in place of the ferry. They put up the bridge when the ice melted, and took it apart when the first ice blocks appeared. The buses from Ezsharni to Kovno would stop there for a light meal and to pick up passengers. The gefilte fish of Yentel Namiot and her sister Shula was well known. Shula, who married Manosovich, would treat us with roast ducks, potatoes, and sauerkraut that restored the soul. There was a smile on her face, and it seemed to us that the ducks were also smiling at us. Her husband Yisrael also smiled a lot. Their daughter Masha survived and lives in Vilna, and their daughter Leah lives in the Land.

[Page 30]

Opposite was Avraham Persky's inn with the billiard table. The youth would come there to enjoy a light beer after bathing in the Vylia. They would lick their fingers from the fresh buns that were filled with lung, the splendid handiwork of Frumel Perevoznik. Their daughter Chaviva is in the Land, as well as a son who has recently arrived from Vilna.

Next to the Vylia is the large house in which the sisters Zelda Solsky and Chaya Dina Epstein, two widows, lived. Zelda had a lovely daughter and three sons, Moshke, Itzke, and Leibka. The latter lives in Israel. Chaya Dina had three sons like cedars. She lived in the Land with her son Zelig, but returned and perished with her family.

The Vylia, Water Men, Raft Floaters

The Vylia played an important role in the life of our town. The fishermen, headed by Yosef Katzenberg and Suntochky ("Garbatzki") earned their livelihood from the river. Carp would appear on the tables of the wealthy every day, and of the regular people only in honor of the Sabbath. The gentiles would mine rocks from the bottom of the river with pans. Earlier, Jewish quarriers would earn their livelihood from hewing rocks for various purposes. They even set up a synagogue of rock hewers.

"Water men" with long rafts would float with the current. This was a group of strong men. The rafts would float to Kovno, and even to the descent of the Neman. They would spend days and nights on the rafts, in the rain and the wind. They would light bonfires at night. The typical command was heard from afar:

"Father, break your head in the direction of the shore!"
"Shimon-Feitel, strengthen the rear in the direction of Skrol!"

Here is the gallery of the raft floaters:

There were four strong brothers, Nachum-Leizer, Shmuel, Yankel, and Yona Berzin. The four sons of Nachum-Leizer were Arka, Shlomoka, Luka and Lipaka (even their sister, who was a Maccabeeist, was nicknamed Marka Kozak). Yechiel (the Turk) Gershovich, David Kagan, the brothers Leizer and Lozer Levitt, the brothers Mendel and Shimon Suntochky, Avraham Morr, Chaim Kapiner, Moshe Yaffa, Koshka Snunit-Zelmanovich, Binyamin Kapliansky, and Yisrael Handler.

You certainly also knew the two brothers Hirshe and Abba "Veriker" Fridman, who were expert at riding the rafts. They would float on isolated blocks of wood and transport them to designated places on the raft. Outside, they would break apart parts of the raft and bring the parts to the ground. Then a group of wagon drivers would appear who would load the blocks with the help of cranes and their muscles, and bring them to the rafts. Everything was done quickly, and if you stood on the side, it would seem to you that it was even done with ease. However, their shirts were dripping with sweat, and droplets dripped from their foreheads. Before us is: Hirshe Klotz with his beard, the son of Menda with the long hair and strong body, Itzka Dudak, Hirsh Leizer Micha's Alter Micha's, Shepsl Droskin, Yudel Bereznikov, Nachum "Aho", Chaim Elka Steinkert, Shaya Leib Heiman, and Leizer Shabtai's the "Kushi".

Before there were connections with buses, steamboats would float on the Vylia. The travelers would enjoy the scenery. The boats would transport bricks from the brick kilns of Perevoznik, Meirovich, and Ricklis to Kovno. The boards from the "Kemach" would be transported by large boats to Tilsit.

On Sabbaths, the youth would sail on sailboats and sing songs of Zion accompanied by the mandolin.

They enjoyed bathing in the river, especially on the beach at the downstream of the current, between the willow trees. Persky's cabins were there. Some people would show their prowess by swimming to the other side, demonstrating various swimming strokes. At times there were competitions with lengthy immersions...

Images from those days, when there were still ferries, pass before my eyes. They would gather on the shore in order to cross to Namiot and Itza-Meir the Warsawer and arrange the "Drala" -- parties gluttony. However, the ferry was on the other side. They would shout loudly:

"Rafael, Davai Parum!

The ferryman finally woke up. After some time, they already saw the flickering of the lantern from the ferry. We would go aboard and disappear into the darkness of the night.
[continued on page 87]

[Page 31]

Sabbath Eve on the Vylia
-- A poem of memories -
Translated by Jerrold Landau

The Vylia was proud on Sabbath eves
Its thin belly rose up
Without a sound, the water flowed through the entire breadth,
Very easily,
Touching -- and not touching the high shore, strewn with houses,
The houses of the fisherman
Who know the life of the river.

As the day ends, to greet the Sabbath
The Vylia silences,
Its breathing stops,
A veil of silence falls upon it.
It was enveloped with the soft beauty of the Sabbath eve.

... And a child who would then wander to the high bank of the Vylia
(Far off, opposite, between the fields, the dirt path leads,
To the abandoned white palace,
Linked in its paleness to the horizon),
Would hear in the silence the advent of the ministering angels.

[Page 32]
(Was this light melody actually heard,
Or just imagined?)

He would see the celestial brilliance kissing the Vylia:
Murmuring:

> Sabbath
> Wonderful Sabbath
> The holy Sabbath of the river of childhood
> Enveloping the Diaspora

> With the light of the far-off Holy Land --
>   *

... From the house of prayer hidden somewhere
Among the trees in the fields, in another moment
The sound of the hymn will be heard
"Come my Beloved..." (Lecha Dodi)[6]

5718 / 1958

———

Various generations of youth:

Tz.[vi] Perevoznik, Y. Kotler, Tzvi Ulpasky, N. Shapira, M.[oshe] Yaffa, Rivka Simkovich; Itzik Reibstein, Batya Gorfein, Dova Dobiansky, M. Kremenitzin Reuven Yudelevich, Levi Perevoznik.

A. Chasid, Y. Teitelbaum, Sara Shachor, X., Perchik, X., Eliahu Baron, Breina Reibstein, Leah Klibansky, Rachel Rashkes; B. Gorfein, Yenta Nochimovich, X., Esther Novichovich, Yaakov Dembo, Ruda Klibansky, Chasid.

X,. X., X., Elimelech Klotz, Avraham Pimstein

Yaakov Yaffa, Moshe Slomin, Tzvi Suntochky, Moshe Segal, Tovia Kolbiansky, Shmuel
Klotz; Meir Wolfovich, Zelig Wender, Moshe Shapira, Yerachmiel Garber, Reuven
Yonatan, Hirsh Yankele Stein

Moshe Yaffa, Y. Kremenitzin, Meir Pogir, Asher Gorfein; Notake Fridman, Fridman, Yaakov Grun

Zelig Abramovich, X., Tzadok Yudelevich; Moshe Klachman, Motel Yudelevich

Generations of Students:

Mina Zak, Nadia Granevich, Feicha Levin, Chasia Fridland; Shifra Lomiansky, Chana Goldshmid, Malka Unterschatz, Lena Kagan

Hadassa Fridman, Henna Granevich, Sara Goldberg, Leah Yudelevich, Pesia Kazansky; Rachel Rashkes, Gita Felkser, Bunia Wolfovich, Rachel Lipschitz; Sheinka Klibansky, Leah Grodsky, Shifra Stoller

Batya Gorfein, Esther Shaposhnik, Sheinka Fridland, Anna Kagan; Rachel Lukman, Freda Wilkomirsky; Leah Klibansky, Sarka Segalovsky, Chaya Dobiansky, Yenta Nochimovich

Chana Marka Unterschatz, Moshe Chaim and Batya Novichovich, Sheina and Mirka
Landman, Leah Kronik; Etka and Freda Landman, Binyamin and Rachel Unterschatz,
Leah Landman, Feiga Klibansky

Tzipa Leah Wiener, Moshe Baron, Nadia Granevich, Pesach Shachor, Shmuel
Goldshmid, Meir Wolfovich, Rachel Burstein, Chasia Fridland; David Pogirsky, Shifra
Lomiansky, Miriam Nochimovich, Yitzchak B.[urstein]; Leva Koper, Feicha Levin

Zelig Epstein, Shifra L.[omiansky], Yitzchak B.[urstein], Reizel Aronovsky, Leah B.;
Levi Koper, Rachel and Miriam B.[urstein], Mordechai Wolfovich

What is the joy? They escaped from class: Yitzchak Solsky, Netanel Shapira,
Mordechai Yaffa; Hirshka Yudfas, Zeev Opnik

Elimelech Perchik, Yudel Katzenberg, X., Avraka Unterschatz

{Bottom photo: Rachel Burstein, Shimon Rubinstein, Feicha Levin, Yitzchak and Miriam B.[urstein], Eliezer Goldshmid, Chaya Zuchovsky, Apatkina

{Translator's notes -- There are three photos on top, and one on the bottom. It is assumed that the single caption runs from top right to bottom.}

Various groups of youths:

Lula Wilkomirsky, Yosef Rikliansky, Yudel Winitzky, Moshe Lantzman; Yosef Levin, Hershel Levin, Avraham Zuchovsky.

Zelig Epstein, Moshe Solsky, Mitzel Pogirsky, Menashe Wiener, X.,

Velvel Sesitsky, El.[iezer] Goldshmid, Yona Saltuper, Grunia Kaplan, Yitzchak B[urstein], Grundman; Bluma Pogirsky, Shimon Zak, Sara Burstein, Rachel Levin. Mitzel P.[ogirsky], Roza Kagan.

Elka Namiot, Zamka Kaplan, X., Elka Fridman; Lula V.[ilkomirsky], Moshe Baron, Nisan Goldshmid, Yitzchak B.[urstein], Shmuel Goldshmid, David Fridman

Boys during the years of girls:

Yitzchak Solsky, Velvel Abramovich, Mordechai Yaffa, Yechezkel Kotler; Shimon Gorfein, Yitzchak Nochimovich, Baruch Shabtai's, Eliahu Koper, Yaakov Katzav; Chaim Teitelbaum, Yisrael Shneid, Alter Chasid

Y.[itzchak] Nochimovich, Shmuel Teper, X., Avraham Portnoy, M.[ordechai] Yaffa,
Elimelech Perchik, Perchik, X., V.[elvel] Abramovich, Y.[echezkel] Kotler, Y.[aakov]
Katzav, X., X., B.[aruch] Shabtai's; Z. Yudelevich, Tzvi Yudfas, Ch.[aim] Teitelbaum

[page 33]

Yitzchak B.[urstein] and Zelig Epstein. The wooden bridge is in the right background
The wooden bridge took the place of the ferry.

The corner of Kovno Road and the Street of the Road served as a center and meeting point for the common folk. The wagons parked there. From among their owners, Leiba Gershovich (the "Turk"), Shlomo Dragatzky and others stood out.

Here is Itzka "Bul", tall, physical, and a porter. When a guest appeared, two people would take hold of his suitcase -- one would pull one way, and the other would pull the other way. The Dragatzkys and Leiba Gershovich became bus owners. They continued to transport passengers from the train station to town.

Another group of wagon owners was involved in hauling merchandise on the Kovno line, especially iron cargo for Pogirsky, and furniture. They would set out at night and sleep on the platform. One could depend on the following people: Hirshe Fridman and his son Reuvke, Moshe Handler and his sons Leizer and Yisrael, Berl Sesitsky, Abba Wender, Yisrael Wender, Abake, Yosa Leizer and Hirshe Leizer Manosovich, and the sons of the latter -- Yisrael and David -- who later became drivers.

Those who lacked vehicles, the porters, "street men" with muscles also gathered on that corner:

Moshe Itzka Bauer, Alter Zilber, Alter Gershon Itzikovich, Walza Shoub, Feiska, and others. They always wore sackcloth belts and sacks over their heads and backs, covered with flour dust and permeated with the odor of herring.

Kovno Street

Here is the butcher shop of Itzik Nochimovich, strong and mustached. The farmers were afraid of him. In his neighborhood was the butcher Shlomo Yudelevich the Muscovite. He was also strong.

Here is the barber shop of Chaim Kobliansky -- a meeting place for the leftist circles, thanks to his bookish, prima donna daughter who was a member of the dramatic club of the Yiddishist cultural league.

Here is the wholesale store of Liber Farber, a general Zionist and philanthropist.

Here is the iron shop of Shmerl Stern. There is a small flour mill in his yard. He was the agent of "Di Yiddishe Shtime" (The Jewish Voice). He was an intelligent scholar, and a Mizrachi activist. Glasses were always perched at the tip of his nose. He would frequently peer into a book. He had three sons and a daughter: Eliezer is in Kibbutz Netzer Sereni. There was also Leibel, Noach and Liba-Chana, who was married to the artist Kagan, who was also a teacher in the Yavneh School. Noach the poet died in the Land. The others perished.

Here is the inn of Alter Zuchovsky, permeated with the smells of liquor, herring, and onion. Drunks would sleep by the tables. Reb Alter was a Hassid who was able to study *Gemara*. He was blessed with a pleasant voice and was sought after as a prayer leader. He had two sons and a daughter, Meir, Avraham and Rivka. Rivka made *aliya* to the Land and established a family. Avraham is also in the Land.

Here is the store of Chatzkel Fried. He was able to study, but he was a miser. The store was filled with sacks of flour, sugar and salt. His wife was a greater miser than he was. This is what the neighbors would hear:

"My wife, please give me a bagel with sausage to eat."

"Bundles of sorrows are upon your head. Is this all that you are lacking. He always complains that he has pressure from under his heart -- and now he desires a bagel with sausage!"

"If that is the case, then please give me a cup of tea with jam."

"A sickness I will give you. An entire night, he does not stop running to the ..."[7]

[Page 34]

Their son Moshe was active in Maccabee and Gordonia. They all perished.

Here is the barbershop of Nachum Vidutzky. He had a Yiddishist outlook. He would put makeup on the actors.

A bit further on is the building of Mina Wilkomirsky, the daughter of Menda Tzemach's. They had two sons and a daughter: Lula, who was a Maccabeeist, Yosha, and Freda, who was a member of Hashomer Hatzair.

Here is the two-story house on the corner of Kovno Street and the Street of the Shore, belonging to Shlupsky the strong. He owned an electrical goods store. His wife was sickly, and walked with a cane. They perished.

The manufacturing shop of Zelig Kapol and his wife Chaya was in that shop. He sported a mustache, and there was always a smile on his face. He had a proud gait, dressed impeccably and was therefore nicknamed "the Lord". Their daughter Feiga arrived in the Land at the end of the war as a concentration camp survivor. She built her family here. Their son Yosef is in South Africa. Another daughter Dina, as well as the mother, perished.

The Street of the Shore

In that same building, on the side of the Street of the Shore, was the pharmacy of Chaim Levin. Do you remember the peal of bells when the door opened? As you entered, you would be awestruck from the aromas that reached your nose from the medications and perfumed water. The shelves were laden with plates with etched letters. With the ring, Chaim appeared, wearing gold spectacles. He was a Yeshiva student and an autodidact. He was a Zionist activist, who was involved in the communal institutions. He was the first mayor during the German occupation at the time of the First World War. Later, he ran the Oren match factory, even after it passed over to Kriger's concern. He had a pleasant character. He was an initiator in the establishing of the hospital and the modern bathhouse. He was known as a Don Juan. His wife Hashil was also a Zionist activist, who concerned herself with orphans, widows, and the poor. They had three daughters and a son: Sheina, Rachel, Feicha, and Hershel. The son was married to Miriam Burstein. He survived in the city of Frunze in Russia. Today he is in the Land.

Yosa Levi Itziks's and Tzipa (the epicene) were their neighbors. They were both intelligent, and got along well with people. They were willing to give assistance to others, but... with interest.

A bit further on is the house of Meita Levin the baker and her son Leizer the intelligent, a member of Poale Zion. He got along well with people and was a bachelor for many years. He later married Tzipa Leah, the sister of Yona Katz, who was a shoulder length taller than he was. They perished.

Here is also the large store of Moshe Zak and his wife Feiga. The haberdashery store was always clean and well ordered. Reb Moshe had a small, gray beard, and always sported a collar and a necktie. Both of them had an easy disposition, and were prepared to help those in need. Yisrael Pogir of America describes him as he knew him in 1913, as follows:

"Avraham of Shaty had a son, Moshe Zak, who owned a paper store. I loved to buy from him notebooks with Yiddish poems printed on their covers. These poems included: A Letter to Mother and G-d is True and His Judgment is True. He dressed splendidly. My father would send me to purchase buttons, needles and a stamp from his store, all for one kopeck.

At night I would see them strolling, he with a proud gait, and she waddling like a duck. In 1963, when my sister Sara came to Moscow from Israel, we went to look for their daughter who remained there. We had not seen her in 48 years. We did not find her at home, so we waited for her arrival. We saw from afar a woman approaching, waddling like a duck, similar to her mother. We realized that this was her. Indeed, this was their daughter."

Here is the house with green shutters and the large iron shop with a sign above, belonging to Reb Avchik Pogirsky and his wife Sarahl. Reb Abba was tall, proud, with a small beard, a mustache, and spectacles. He knew Torah, Russian and German. He had nationalistic sentiments, but he was not involved in communal affairs, aside from charitable activities.

About his wife Sara, people used to say: A woman of valor who can find. She had a good heart, and gave many donations to orphans and windows. As opposed to Abba, she moved gracefully. She ran the business, and purchases would come from afar. They raised four daughters and two sons: Freda (who died recently in the Land), Tania and

Bluma -- who live in Lithuania, Mitzel -- who lives in the Land, and enlisted in the British Army as a doctor during the Second World War, from which she did not return. Davidl, who ran the store along with his brother-in-law the engineer Yosha Epstein, perished with his wife in the Kovno Ghetto.

[Page 35]

The Street of the Market and the Street of the Fishermen

Here is the large house of Leiba Opnitzky. Before my eyes, I see the owner of the house standing bareheaded, with a pipe, and wearing a belt below his belly. The house attracted many young people. There were four sons and a daughter, and the pioneering spirit pervaded in the house.

On Vilna Street, on the other side of the market, lived the family of tailors -- Naftali Senior and his sons. He was thin, and his glasses were at the tip of his nose. He had a sense of humor, and was always smiling. His sons Tovia and Chaim were jokers. Tovia excelled in the dramatic club of the culture league. One could hear the latest jokes in their house.

In their neighborhood, near the market, was the workshop of Chone Strum and the two Baron brothers -- Leibel and Hershel. Leibel immigrated to South Africa, and Chone ran the sewing workshop.

Itzik Dembo lived in the front of the market. He was a wood engraver, as well as a barber. A bell would ring as the door opened. Itzik would then leave his engraving and start cutting hair. One profession was not sufficient to sustain the family. Many pieces of furniture that were manufactured in Jonava were adorned with his engraving. He was expert in Hebrew and Yiddish literature. He was a popular man, with a sense of humor, who wrote many verses. His son Yankel had broad education, and knew Esperanto. His daughter Pesele concluded gardening school in Riga, and set up a kindergarten along with Batya Zandman. The younger son was Moshe. They all perished.

[Page 36]

The owner of the lemonade enterprise, Moshe Yalinovich, lived in their neighborhood. He quenched the thirst of the residents on the hot summer days.

Moving on -- is the two-story house of Silberman. As far as I recall, the two brothers Efraim and Shlomo, and their sister Sara lived there. Since the parents were no longer around, the Maccabee youth ruled over the house. They would come there straight from the meeting place. The sports counselors also lived there.

Opposite was the large house of Meir Goldshmid. He had three daughters and a son: Liba, Sara, Chana, and Leizer. The haberdashery store was in the hands of the men. Meir, who limped, was a scholar and lover of Zion. He excelled as the Torah reader in the large *Beis Midrash*. The son Leizer obtained higher education. He studied chemistry at the University of Strasbourg. He married the teacher Beila Apatkina. Chana arrived in the Land. The rest perished.

At the side of Kovno Road, opposite the market, stood the house of the government appointed rabbi (in his time) Rabbi Shneur Sesitsky. He was intelligent and sharp. After his death, the house served as a meeting place for the Zionist youth: Maccabee, Young Zion, Tz.S. Hashomer Hatzair, and Gordonia. All of them remained in harmony thanks to Rivka Sesitsky, who inherited the traits of her father. You could have a conversation on any topic with her. She was active in Young Zion. She was intelligent, understood innuendoes, was pleasant, and had beauty marks. She set the tone at meetings. Velvel Sesitsky, who was Pogirsky's bookkeeper, had leftist leanings. He was a good friend to everyone. The house was full of youth, and people who arrived late had difficulty finding a seat. Matches were made there: Rivka got married to Yerachmiel Teitelbaum (the "lantern"), Velvel married Pesil Kerzner, and the youngest, Chana, married Leibel Stern.

Moving on from there is the home of Eliahu Frakt. He was a grain wholesaler, and a former Yeshiva student. He would talk on the telephone in Lithuanian, of course with a Gemara melody: "Fanile, Fanile, Dakit Devinta." His son Efraim, a member of Maccabee and Tz.S. had a weakness -- to stroll until 2:00 a.m. Leah Kerzner ensured that he had a group to walk with when they left the Sesitsky house. Due to his nighttime strolls, he would often sleep for an entire day. The situation was as follows: The siren at Itzik's sounded at 4:00 p.m. He got up and thought that it was 7:00 a.m. He turned over to his other side, and woke up the next day.

Alleyways

Here is the house and the carpentry shop of Yankel Leib Landman in the alley that leads from Kovno Road. Yankel Leib attained the status of a wealthy man. He was not a great scholar, but was haughty. He was attracted to leading prayer services, either *Shacharit* or the Welcoming of the Sabbath. He was broad shouldered, always with a pipe in his mouth, blowing smoke incessantly. He donated generously to the funds and charities. His two sons David and Menashe, and his three daughters Sheina, Marka and Hindaka received a Zionist education. They all perished.

Here is the alleyway that leads from the Market Square to the Synagogue of the Merchants on Breizer Street. On that alleyway, Rabbi Chaim Yitzchak Silman lived and adjudicated matters of Jewish law. He, the genius of Siesikai, is before my eyes. Short in stature, thin, with a long beard, wearing a long frock. He was full of Torah and rabbinic decisions. He never stopped learning. You could always find him sitting with an open *Gemara*, *Mishna*, or *Ein Yaakov* in front of him. The house was full of bookshelves with religious books. He was modest, and charitable. He was stringent in his rabbinical decisions. The court of law (*Beis Din*) was in a small room. Monetary and business issues were debated there, and issues on kashruth were decided. His enterprise was also there: a charitable fund and bank for widows and orphans, who entrusted him with their few coins. He would speak quietly, with a hoarse voice, but his influence was great. He would lead the *Neila* service on Yom Kippur in the large *Beis Midrash*. It was an unforgettable experience to hear him. It seemed that he stood with his full authority before the Creator of the World in order to earn a good verdict for his community and the entire Jewish people. When the prayers and supplications would reach their summit, he would bang his hand on the podium and call out "And Seal!" His helpmate in his good deeds was his modest wife Chana Leah.

A party of carpenters. X., Chasid, Kaminsky, Meniuk, X., X., Mongin, -- the murderer of the Jews, Tovia and Chaim Kobliansky, X., Chana the wafer maker, Rivka Kobliansky, Aharon Tovia, X., Avraham Pimstein, Rachel Kolbiansky, Yitzchak Dembo, Fancevich, Mashil Kobliansky, Daniel Ricklis, Zeev Opnik, Yaakov Dobiansky, X., Binyamin Kopilansky, David Garber

[Page 37]

The families of Meir Riklis, Baron, Desent and David Ginzberg after his marriage also lived nearby on that lane.

Shlomo the Shochet, tall, and with a black beard similar to that of Herzl, lived on the continuation of the Synagogue Street. He excelled as a prayer leader. He was literally like a cantor, with a sweet voice. The youth would come from all of the *Beis Midrashes* to hear his *Musaf* services on the High Holy Days. He was very careful with his voice. It was said that if anyone opened a window on the street, Shlomo would freeze on the Street of the Synagogue.

Blacksmiths

I loved to wander on the alley of the blacksmiths. I would go to the smithy of Yisrael Kremenitzin. He was of strong build, and his face was covered with sweat and soot. His muscular hands would hold the smoldering iron anvil as he would forge an image with a heavy mallet. He had leftist leanings, and loved to converse about politics.

Here is the large smithy of the brothers Yudel and Yitzchak Beten. Its yard is filled with wagons, winter carriages, and wheels. The two brothers belonged to Young Zion.

Similarly, I remember the smithies of Lande and the Winitzky brothers. The latter was one of the largest. The wagons that were manufactured were sold in Kovno, Žasliai and other cities. The brothers immigrated to the United States. Only Yudel remained, and he also immigrated there in 1935.

Vilna Street

Here is the red brick building on the corner of Vilna Street and Shore Street, where our family lived. Here is the balcony on the second floor, surrounded by flower pots that were tended to by Mother. Here is the doorbell on the entrance, which was an innovation at that time. As children passed by, they could not restrain themselves from ringing and disturbing the residents of the house.

Nearby was the house of Zelig Kapol. Chaya, a widow with three sons and a daughter, remained. She had a difficult life. A son immigrated to South Africa. Two daughters survived the Holocaust and are in the Land. The rest perished.

Here are the two two-story red brick buildings of Shimon Wiener the builder. We lived on the second floor for more than a year when we arrived from Kaplice. His son Menashe Wiener graduated in chemistry from the Lithuanian University and married in Kovno. There were two daughters, Tzipa-Leah and Yehudit. They all perished.

The dentist Eida Katz and her lame husband lived and worked in that building. They were nice people.

Further on is the house of Leibka Gershovich (the "Turk").

Here is the house of Mendel Gorfein. He was of medium height with a small beard. He had a calm personality. He was modest and scholarly. He would sit for long periods writing his impressions about the wide world, and express his opinions about important matters. This was a sort of diary of intimate matters, and was like his friend. His back was slightly hunched from all the writing. He was active in the general Zionists and in the parent committee of the Tarbut School.

Leizer Levitt and his wife Chaya-Bayla lived across the street. He was a raft floater, and she was a seamstress. They were quiet, upright, working folk. These traits beamed forth from their faces.

Here are the houses of Kopel Reznik. The Wolfovich family used to live in one of them. Later, the carpentry shop moved there, equipped with new machines by Kopel and his son Hershel. Kopel was a member of the town council during the 1920s. The mayor was Dr. Reiles. Kopel would doze during the meetings. When the chairman would ask for his opinion on a matter, he would wake up and say in Polish, *"Niech bedzie jak pan doktor mowi".* Let it be as your words.

I left Jonava forever with a broken heart. I traveled to Kovno, and from there to central Asia, where I tarried for a number of years in the city of Frunze in Kyrgyzia.

I lived and worked there until November, 1965. At my mother's sickbed in 1964, I promised to fulfill her last wish before her death - that I would do everything in order to get to Israel. I fulfilled that promise on November 11, 1965.

On the way, I visited my sisters in Vilna and Kovno. I met Jonava friends and acquaintances who arranged a fine farewell party for me. In December, I arrived in Vienna after taking a train through Minsk, Moscow, and Warsaw[8]. From there, I arrived in Lod by airplane on December 23.

My arrival here has enabled me to put my thoughts and feelings in writing for the book of Jonava. If someone is disappointed about my article, I offer my apologies.

Translator's Footnotes

Probably Young Socialists.

I am not sure of the implication of this sentence. I suspect it means that they played "hard to get".

An alternate spelling of Henia.

Since it is forbidden to cook on the Sabbath, the Sabbath daytime meal is generally left in the oven or on the stove from the preceding late afternoon. This hot dish is often a stew called *'cholent'.* In many locales, the town baker would keep the *cholent* pots of all the townsfolk in the baker's over until noontime on Saturday.

"Noach Pandre" is the lead character in a five volume epic of the same name by the beloved Yiddish author Zalman Schneor, published in 1938-1939.

http://www.yivoencyclopedia.org/article.aspx/Shneour_Zalman.

"Come My beloved to greet the bride, let us welcome the Sabbath." -- the refrain from the main hymn of the Friday evening service.

It seems that the missing word here, of which only the first letters are given in the Hebrew, is the "washroom". In this conversation, it seems that the wife is talking to her husband in the third person.

The unusual sequence of cities could be explained by the need to visit the Israeli embassy in Moscow prior to departing.

[Page 38]

Before and After the War
by Meir Tzoref (Goldshmid), Tel Aviv
Translated by Jerrold Landau

Meir Tzoref

It was May 1945 – the biggest event in the annals of the 20th century. What was thought to be impossible had actually occurred. Cruel Germany, victorious and full of power, having conquered and occupied all of Europe with its talons – was finally defeated and crushed.

The bloody mighty men of yesterday, who perpetrated terrible atrocities on millions of people for five years, were scampering around like mice, searching for a hole in which to hide until the wrath and the desire for revenge of the victims would pass. The beasts of the S.S. and Gestapo dressed up in the clothes of concentration camp prisoners. The roads and paths were filled with refugees. Baby carriages were used as means of transport, and there were the same sacks over the shoulders – almost the exact picture that was etched in our memory when we left Jonava in 1941 – except this time those fleeing were the Germans and the children of the Germans. However, there was one difference: they were not awaiting concentration camps, crematoria, Auschwitz, Paneriai, Fort Nine, Girelka…[1]

The German mothers, who with their milk sustained the bloody murderers, the most evil, depraved human beings that humanity has ever seen – were returning to their homes along tortuous routes. If the bombed out house had been destroyed, it would be rebuilt without disturbance, for it was their house. We were indeed jealous of them. They had houses, grandmothers, grandfathers and children. But where were our houses, children, parents, and grandparents? We felt our terrible forlornness.

Despite this, we were attracted to our old houses with bonds of enchantment, not only to catch a glance of destroyed Jonava. We streamed on through the paths of Europe among the masses of liberated people – home! How pleasant and warm was the word – homeward…

Homeward?

My house in Jonava was a wooden house next to the sidewalk on Breizer Street. When it was old, its structure bent to the point that the children were able to touch its roof. In the winter, we were able to take down icicles and lick them like ice cream. Its garden overlooked the cemetery with its pines and crows, whose cawing frightened us children. It was as if they were informing us of the bitter fate that awaited us. The cemetery was part of my childhood; it aroused thoughts of life and death. There, my friend Berka Aiker and his sister Chavale lived. Their father was a stone engraver. They lived in the same lobby as the tahara room,[2] into which we were not permitted to enter. In the summer, we would sleep there on the aromatic hay in the attic. We would tell stories of spirits and shades, which we had heard on Sabbaths during the time between Mincha and Maariv in the Synagogue of the Peddlers. Even though I was afraid in my heart, I maintained my stance that I did not believe these stories, so that I could present myself as brave to pretty Chavale. Later, my friend Berka became a captain in the Soviet Army, and perished in the battles near Uriol. He was decorated posthumously with highest excellence for his bravery and strength of heart. Chava was murdered along with her family by the murderer Lyubka Zachar.

[Page 39]

We, a few youths, wandered through towns and villages, with each one thinking about his own home – Jonava, Keidani, Vilkomir (Ukmerge). Would anyone find his dear ones? We were filled with the desire to rebuild Communism on the land of Lithuania that had absorbed our blood.

We left accursed Germany, with its cold castles, ornate villages and gothic churches, as bands of surviving brothers. With joy mixed with sorrow, we greeted the familiar landscape of forests, wheat fields, cottages with straw roofs, and wells. We arrived in Kovno. To my good fortune, I found my child and sister alive. My brother had arrived in the Land of Israel. I also found my aunt. I continued on to Jonava.

I was crowded among gentiles on the train to Jonava. I searched for Jewish faces in vain. However, I saw a familiar face, red from an abundance of pork fat, the face of

Vansovitch. Did he recognize me or not? I was happy that he disappeared from my eyes. By coincidence he did not turn me in during his time, but how many Jews did he murder…

We reached the train station. There, the Beitar members arranged a reception for Jabotinski when he passed through our town. There, the merchants of the town would load up apples to export to Germany, as we children would pilfer large Antonovka apples from trains and at times receive beatings. We would often sit on the rear hinge of the wagon of Itza the "Bul" who was able to eat a chicken and remain hungry. It was said that he once made a bet that he could eat 50 cakes, and they took him to the hospital after 30. These were the same wagons, but the drivers were different. When one of them offered me his services, I refused. I wanted to go on foot.

Here is the match factory, but where is the guard Avraham the mason? There were new houses on high foundations. From up close, I was able to make out the Hebrew letters on the monuments that were used for building. (I later stumbled upon these on the sidewalks, pavement, stairs, etc.) My heart ached from sorrow and anger. On second thought, what is the use of stone monuments when the people had been cut off, from young to old… I also saw Torah parchments covering the walls of the farmers' houses on the way to Skaruliai.

The Dance of the Demons in the place of Sioniot

Here is the train crossing, under which is the road to Girelka.[1] People would stroll there on Sabbaths, and the children would go for Lag Baomer excursions there with their bows and arrows, and hard-boiled eggs kept warm in onion rinds. The Maccabee Organization would arrange a group of riders dressed in blue and white. The road to Girelka, where the Sioniot (Gaguzionot) took place – which was a dance celebration with the firefighters band. Couples would disappear among the trees during the dancing…

Those same trees and bushes served as camoflauge for secret meetings of the youth, including the writer of these lines, who wished to change the world with social justice, equality and brotherhood… Forgetting that these were not requested, and they themselves were indeed undesirable guests.

The Jews of Jonava were led to their frightful deaths along that same street.

Their teacher Henka Yudelevich, along with Roza Mar, the teacher in the Yiddish school, marched first in the row. They went without tears. "The Red Army will avenge our blood," "Long live Stalin" – these were their last words. This was related by one of the murderers, who hung himself on one of the trees next to the mass grave in 1943, at the time that the Germans were attempting to cover their trail of iniquity by burning the bodies.

I did not enter the forest. The army was there. I turned back with the feeling that I was the sole survivor from the valley of death and weeping.

As I was walking, the face of the tortured crucified one peered before me from the large cross.

[Page 40]

"For 200 years you have been staring at us, the son of our unfortunate Miriam[3]. Today you have won, but the price was great… and perhaps you are not guilty. Perhaps everything was done in your name without your agreement… May our spilled blood be a stain upon your head and upon all those who perpetrated such in your name throughout the dark generations! Again, what could you do more than remain a silent witness. You too they crucified."

Recognizable Images Flutter About

Behold I am inside you, Jonava. Here is the bus station that bustled with Jews, former wagon drivers. The horse market, the town hall, the post office. The street of the grain merchants, the craftsmen, and the lumber merchants – wiped out without a trace, covered with grass.

I am looking for any recognizable house. Here are the barracks. Here is the skating rink, and there, the new Beis Midrash. Its holiness has fled. People live in it.

Here is the Vilia to which we children were so attracted. Elia the fisherman drew his livelihood from it. He caught fresh fish to supply the housewives in honor of Sabbaths and festivals. The barges of the boatmen Levit, Dabol and others floated through it. As children, we sneaked free passages without paying. That river took our sins from us during Tashlich on Rosh Hashanah. Its waters continue to flow even without all this.

Here the church stands alone, as the wind of giants, with its steeples and crosses. As a victor, it looks over the destroyed Jewish town and the old synagogue and its competitor, the old synagogue, which stands whole, as if to irritate the gentiles – a memorial to the destruction.

Here is the alley where Silman of blessed memory lived. The basketball player Berka Rikless also lived there. We would wait for him before games so that we could have the honor of carrying his gear. We would climb over the low roofs of stables and barns, playing hide and seek, and conducting battles. Here in the small store one could buy haberdashery, whereas we would by our main provisions from Bluma the Golden, whom Grandmother nicknamed "Bluma the Thief", for she always erred in the calculations to her benefit. However Mother claimed that a shopkeeper must be a thief, for if not, she could not sell on credit. Mother would send us with full payment to purchase small items from Feiga, the second wife of Avraham the mason. His son from his first wife, Davidka Dezent, was an active Communist who immigrated to

Birobidzhan. He was imprisoned there and exiled to Siberia for 20 years, where he is today. His second wife had two daughters, Reizka and Itka. The first was very pretty, and the second was a talented student. Feiga also had a son and daughter from her first husband.

The Bird that Flew From the Next

The son – "Yoske the Bird"[4] was a shoemaker. Like all shoemakers, he would lick the soles with his tongue. His wife was the daughter of Hirshe Minde, who had a wild head of hair. She was a quiet woman and dedicated mother, until one day a young gypsy woman appeared in the shoe workshop, and predicted Yoske's future with cards. Our "Bird" removed his apron and disappeared with the gypsy. The family spared no effort to track down the "shoemaker under a spell", but it was in vain.

However our hero did not become a gypsy. One muddy autumn day, he returned to his wife and his work. Since he was a member of a large family of wagon drivers, he succeeded in escaping to Russia.

Here is the house of the Kopans family, relatives of Father. Hershel was a wood engraver. His talented hands produced artistic ornaments. Through his work, he endeared himself to G-d, man and nature. He loved art and literature. He was an avowed atheist. His wife Pesl was very friendly. She was burdened with the care of her two daughters and a son. The daughters studied with Balsher in school, and the son in Yavneh, so that he would be able to recite Kaddish.

An Event that Caused a Storm

The house in which we lived was owned by the widow Liba Bracanski and her only son Leibke. He was a hired carpenter. Even though he had completed the army, girls were not interested in him. However, we once saw him strolling with the daughter of Mottel the smith in the civic garden. She was a solid girl. She did not excel in beauty or wisdom. One eye was squinty, but she was upright. After their first walk – she became pregnant…

[Page 41]

The town was brewing. Her father and uncles were all puffed up. In their hands, it was like a crazy horse and a pure lamb. They threatened to break his bones as one breaks an old horseshoe if he does not marry the daughter whom he violated. He tried to deny it. After a Torah judgment with Rabbi Ginzberg, the couple got married, and Breizer Street breathed easily. They had two children. The widow swallowed the disgrace and was a good grandmother. She fattened ducks, fried fat for Passover, plucked feathers, and occupied herself with Jewish sources of livelihood until the bitter end.

Here is the house of an acquaintance, with green shutters. There, I would visit my older friend Motka Dudak. There were older girls in their house, and their friends would come to visit them – all pretty and joyous. They were very nice, and sometimes one of them caressed my cheek with a white, perfumed hand and said: "What a nice boy. It is too bad that you are so young, you were born so late." In my heart I agreed with her. It was good for me. Sara was prettier than all of them. She performed in plays better than all of them, and indeed, she got married before them all...

The Dramatic Circle

Thanks to my friendship with the members of the Dudak family, I later found my way to the theater circle of the culture league. Shmuelke Dudak was the living spirit of this club. He participated in all areas of culture: library, night courses, the club, the Communist party and "Meafar". He was a tailor by profession. For ten hours a day he worked with needle, thread, irons and scissors, and after that – in communal work and the acquisition of knowledge. He knew how to play any acting role very well. Woe to anyone who stumbled over a sentence or a movement. He would find himself in the crooked lens of Shmuel at the first opportunity. He concerned himself with everything: He brought the carpenters who were fond of theater – Chaim Katz, Chaim Praboznik, Berka Mar and Itzik Kalinski – with their work tools and materials. They all stood in the cold hall of the firefighters, sawing, cutting and building scenery. The actors rehearsed the text, the teacher Balsher supervised over the differentiating of the pronunciation of Shin and Samech – which was no small matter for a Lithuanian Jew, especially for older ones such as Hilka Epstein, Shmulke Milner, Abake Kotkas and others.

Tailors, shoemakers, carpenters, after a day of work, rehearsed their roles under the stage direction of the teacher Yosha Epstein. He was assisted by Pesach Kremenitzin the smith.

At the play "Yankel the Blacksmith"

[Page 42]

Then came the great day of the first performance. Eliahu Mar was near the entrance. Nobody could enter without a ticket, even his children. He arranged a full price ticket for his wife in the first row. Shmuelke Dudak sat at the cash, and Mosheke Odoskes, in his firefighter uniform, presided over order. Thus did everyone do his part voluntarily, for all income was for "Meafar." The teacher Balsher was not "kosher" in the eyes of the authorities. Even most of his students tended to be active Communists, such as Tzalka and Mosheke Glazer. Moshe was lame – he is now a judge in Vilna. Tzalka was a member of the N.K.V.D. He died in a mysterious manner in an auto accident in 1952 near Memel.

We should note that the teacher Balsher also conducted classes in Hebrew, Bible, and Jewish history in a free spirited manner. Even for this little matter he had to stand on guard from the opponents of Hebrew, who saw this as a diversion from the straight path. We, the former students of Yavneh, where education was based upon maintaining the distance between teacher and student, were particularly influenced by the warm and friendly relations between the teacher and the principal Balsher.

The young engineer Yaakov (Yosha) Epstein, the son-in-law of the Pogirsky family, played a special role in the dramatic club. He was the spiritual father of the club. He was busy all day with his business in the iron store. He dedicated his evenings to study with those who desired to learn. He broadened the activities of the club and added classes about movement and choreography by Bunia Wolfovich, the daughter of Leib. (They were exiled to Siberia in 1941. The intervention of Yosha Epstein did not help. On the contrary, this hurt him, and he was dismissed from his job as mayor of the city.)

Yosha Epstein invited us into his house for lessons and rehearsals. We felt at home in the large rooms of his house. At first we were perplexed because of our small homes in which we slept in cramped quarters – with an interlocking of arms and legs, and in the winter – on the oven.

Pogirsky's house was a symbol of excess and wealth for the Breizer Street neighborhood. I remember that when I was still a child, the "Leftist Group" used to come to my grandfather's home: Shmuelke Dudak, Chaim Weichko, Shmuel Silber (the two latter ones married my aunts and became my uncles. Chaim Weichko perished in the Uriol Front, and Shmuel Silber in the Kovno Ghetto), Leizerke Shabses (the dark), Yoske Zelmanovich (the Swallow or the Bird), Davidka Dezent, Sarahke and Mina Shapira, and others. When I went to grandmother to get fresh bread, one of them took me on their knees and asked: "Do you want to be a Communist?" To my negative question: "What is that?," they answered that we will live in the home of Pogirsky, and he in our house… That of course enchanted me, and I waited for Communism…

Now I am sitting in that same house, drawing knowledge from Pogirsky's son-in- law, Yosha Epstein, a teacher, friend and pal. We were also friendly with Yosha's wise wife Bluma, who apparently was not too thrilled with the proximity of the pretty "prima donna" Henka Yudelevich. We were also friendly with Dudia and his wife Maya, and I am embarrassed that during my childhood I dreamed of taken their home from them…

Yoshe Epstein drew us near to professional theater. Rashel Berger, Sidi Tal, and Yaakov Sternberg were our constant guests. This enabled us to appear in Beit Haam, which Rashel Berger directed. On occasion we visited the Lithuanian theater. We translated plays and successfully performed them. The Zionist tribune with the Herzlian elder Ivenski presented to us world and Jewish history. The accountant of the popular bank, Yankel Opnitzky, was laid up in bed. We came to him to discuss literature and theater. His wife Tzvia had pity on him lest he not regain his strength, but he would say, "let me enjoy the time that I still have left…" Indeed, he instilled optimism in us with his faith in the human spirit, as he would also do to those in distress who turned to him at the bank. He assisted everyone with a good word, with advice, with the goodness of his heart. Many accompanied him on his final journey.

On Breizer Street

Behold I am now standing on Breizer Street and attempting to review this portion of the town in my mind. Here was the alleyway of Yankel Leib, which coiled like a snake. Here lived the "Frantic Kravitz," the speedy tailor. He made the rounds to the villages and sewed there. He loved to tipple. When a farmer came to him, he would take the measurements, and send him off to get a bottle of liquor. The garment was ready by the time he returned.

[Page 43]

Yankel Leib indeed provided a livelihood to many families, but he was not well liked by people: both because he had changed from a simple worker to a big shot, and because his pretty daughter made her way among the gentiles.

His wayward daughter was a travesty to him. Were there too few Jewish boys that she had to spend her time with the Jew haters?!

Thus did the women of Breizer Street curse her when the pretty Itka Landman walked with Simon Dulgatz in the direction of Keidani Street… Apparently, they had premonitions about the future executioner… Even her former friend Lyubka Zachar was soaked with Jewish blood and pillaged Jewish property. That Simon Dulgatz presented himself as a Folksdeutsche during the German occupation and became an executioner of the Jewish community of Jonava, perhaps as well because of his knowledge of the Yiddish language. Thus was also the layer of snares, Jan Pinkovsky. He came from the same place, became a Sabbath Goy[5], laid snares, and learned to speak Yiddish. This made him valuable in the eyes of the Germans.

Here is the house in which Moshe Reiza-Leah's Josef the baker lived. I would go there at times to purchase fresh, aromatic, black bread. On the way back, I would devour approximately half the loaf. On account of this, I would get a curse rather than a blessing from Mother, such as, "A cholera should not take you!" This formula would arouse Father's anger: "Do not open up an opening for the Satan!" Better the belt than a harsh word. Indeed, that is how he acted.

We would bring our hot Sabbath dishes to the oven in the bakery.[6] Women would say about Chaim's father Moshe that he would peer into the pots and equalize them – that is he would transfer some food from a pot that had lots of meat into a poorer pot that had no meat at all – or he would even switch pots. Today the oven is orphaned – no hot dishes, no bread, no Jews…

Here is a small house, as if it was stuck to a regular house. Here lived the shoemaker Taffer – thin, short, and with many children. His wife was also thin. Even though they had older children, they continued to live as a couple in love. He sat by the shoe last and she peeled potatoes. Without stopping his work, he explained to her world events. After all of his explanations, it became clear to her that there was nothing to put in the cooking pot and nothing with which to pay the rent.

Her brother Leibel Shoub lived with them. He was thin, even though he wasn't tall and had long hair. Nobody was fond of him and nobody befriended him even though he belonged to the leftist circles. His external appearance was also repellant. He immigrated to Birobidzhan, and, as is related by those who returned from there, became an informer and provocateur of the N.K.V.D. He is responsible for the deaths of no small number of Jews. To this day we run into the name of L. Shoub of Birobidzhan who castigates the "Israeli strongmen."

Wells

Here is Rashel's well, overflowing with cold, fresh water. Even though the well of the yellow Itel was closer, Mother would send us specifically to Rashel's well. Itel was a gossiper. If she saw a child with a torn shirt or a hole in his pants, all the neighbors would know that Sara, Chaim Shimon's wife does not look after her children properly. She did not lack free time. Her husband, a water man, would go with their eldest son to float barges, and would return only for Sabbaths.

My father did not want me to go there because her children were busy all day with doves. They would use all means and enticements to attract a male or a female. They would send forth a fine male, and he would attract a female with his enchantment. The opposing side would employ various tactics to disturb them – they would whistle and throw stones until a battle would break out, with stones thrown from windows, curses, beatings and shrieks – a literal war on account of a dove… the symbol of peace. Finally they would make an agreement: two males for a female.

The primary competitor was Mota-Itzka, the son of Eliahu the fisherman, who lived on the alleyway of Shimon the teacher. Even though Shimon was already in the world of truth[7] and all that is left from his room was Yenta with the goat, with whom she never parted day and night for she even brought her to her room to sleep – the alleyway still bore the name of Shimon the teacher. This alleyway was always full of mud because of the water that lazy women poured out from their window. This served as an arena for the battle of the doves…

The word "Yonai"[8] rang in my father's ears like, for example, the word "meshumad" (apostate). Indeed, we had one such person on our street, behind the Tarbut School: Fabian Kolbiansky – Feivka the Apostate. He would go to church on Sundays, and work in his apiary during the week. I would sneak into his garden. I had a net with me, and he would give me little cups. I would help him raise smoke in order to chaise away the bees, and collect the honey. Of course, this was all without Father knowing. I was not able to withstand the temptation of studying the wonders of nature, for the bees lived like humans, with a queen, bridegrooms, loafers, guards, and regular "masses" of workers… Above all, I enjoyed the sweet, aromatic honey.

[Page 44]

Hautriner lived in my neighborhood. He was a medic who distributed pills for free. He was popular with the residents of the street. It was said that his son committed suicide because of his love for a Jewish girl, and the girl also committed suicide on that same day – a Romeo and Juliet in Jonava.

Jews would greet him with "good morning." When he died, many people accompanied him to his eternal rest. He was indeed worthy of this, for he related to the Jews with patience, and he was a true friend of the Jews. I was also among those who went to his funeral. My Lithuanian friend Ratni took my hands and led me to the church. Before I was able to think about it, he succeeded in removing my hat. I broke out in a cold sweat out of fear and trepidation. I was afraid of a punishment from Heaven, but nothing happened. The priest sang before the casket, lehavdil, [9] like our "Kel Maleh Rachamim."[10] My friend was standing beside me. I calmed down and continued to accompany the casket to the cemetery.

My Friend the Shiksa[11]

There was one more well on our street, next to the third house from our house – a well belonging to gentiles in a closed courtyard with a guard dog. I would go there to get water. I was friendly with their daughter from my childhood, and of course also with the dog. My father did not know about this. Mother pretended not to know: "So what, if they are gentiles – is their water not kosher? And the fact that he talks to the shiksa, 'nothing bad will happen to him'"…

I would take advantage of the absence of her father and the fact that her mother was always busy, and I would come to draw water. Their daughter would also come then to draw water. We were not short of anything to talk about. I was interested about what takes place in church, what foods they prepare for their holidays, and about the spruce tree.[12] I would taste a cookie in order not to embarrass my hostess, feel bad that I sinned, and worry lest someone saw me in my disgrace and would tell my father. Whiplashes would fly atop my young body, and as they increased, the persistence increased to endeavor not to cry. Passover drew near, and my Christian friend waited for matzos. She also had lots of questions: Why do the Jews not believe in Jesus? Indeed he loves everyone. Is it correct that when one sees a rabbi, one must close one's mouth, otherwise one's teeth will fall out… When I told her that we say the same thing about the priest, she was astonished: "Why? He is so good"…

Thus did we come to the agreement that G-d is equivalent for everyone, and that it is people who are evil. It was divided up between the Jews and Christians, Lithuanians and Poles to conduct wars… Our secret friendship continued until the outbreak of the war.

Today I am to her as an unexpected guest who came from the other world. Their house did not change. There was no addition of Jewish furniture and property – not even Jewish candlesticks in front of the icons. I am sitting and hearing about the suffering of our dear ones. She tells me about our neighbors, that they were prepared to give everything for bread, flour, or grits. But nobody wanted to purchase from them, for they waited for the day when they could take everything without payment.

She told me with an open heart that she very much wanted to help with something, but she was afraid of her husband who was an anti-Semite – perhaps because she loved Jews… I leave her house with a broken heart.

And These Are My Neighbors on the Street

Here is the house of Recha the miller. Her husband Moshe worked in Izak's mill. She was always white from the flour dust. She enjoyed letting children smell tobacco, and she burst out laughing when they would begin to sneeze. Recha was always angry. She cursed and castigated us and the chickens who wreaked havoc in her garden. During the summer, she would let me lead her cow out to pasture, under the supervision of the shepherd Jan with his bugle and puppy. This Janek learned how to read and write from me. He later became a Comsomolitz, the sole Lithuanian among Jews.

[Page 45]

I could not find my house any more. The gentiles dismantled it. I was particularly distressed about the oven. On cold days we would spend time atop of it, reading books secretly and weaving childhood dreams about a bright future. Here, next to it, my uncle Shmuel Pogir, and later my uncle Eliahu, would twist ropes. I would assist them in turning the wheel, and in other tasks. My aunt Sarale, Eliahu's wife was not pleased with this. She complained to him that he liked us better than his own children. My uncle Eliahu did not lose his composure, and he returned – part in seriousness and part in jest
– "my nephews take after me, and my children take after you…"

Here is the new house of Yechiel the potter. This was a low, depressing house. However, he cheated the authorities. He replaced rotting beams – one by one – until he reached the roof. Itzik Milner the builder was an expert in such matters. The new beams were covered on the outside with connecting boards, and on the inside with tar and pitch. My father built the ovens. Noach covered the roof. Behold, he had a new house.

I especially enjoyed seeing Itzik the builder at his work. He drew the form of a beam and put some moss between the beams, as he sang Kol Nidre, Ele Dvarim, and other cantorial pieces. Father told me that he was once a musician, and he had a voice like a harp.

We were afraid of Noach the roofer. It was said of him that in his anger he put an end to the life of his first wife. He had his own style of prayer during services. When we came to the word "shalom" (peace), he would get hysterical and shout out loud: "There is no peace, there will be a war, and one will bite the other in his throat and remove the bread from his mouth…" In the ghetto and the camp, I would remember the strength of his dark prophecy.

Yechiel the potter was also called "Chilka Tafus,"[13] for in addition to making pots, he was the undertaker along with his partner Alter the potter. During a funeral, in the midst of the weeping before taking leave of the dead, one would hear the voice of Alter: "Women to the side, Chilka – tafus (grab hold!)." From this came his nickname.

Yechiel renovated his house with money that he received from America on account of his son who fell during the First World War. The house was designated for his daughter Chanake with golden teeth. Women would say that she does not remember which month it is, and therefore a wooden piece was placed under her bed each month. Since she was pregnant, a pile of wooden pieces piled up under her bed…

Nisan Kapol the shoemaker lived a bit further on from there. Women nicknamed him "Nisan with Hazeh"[14], since he would add "zeh" to every thing. I took of "zeh" from you, from your child; "zeh," means a measurement of "this thing," i.e. shoes…

His wife Perel was apparently pretty, but they did not have an easy life, for he devoted his whole life to the pair of shoes: he would purchase good and expensive leather, work for a week, and at the end – the shoes were not appropriate… He had to sell them at cost, and sew other ones in their place. On one occasion, he sewed two right boots… When he succeeded in sewing shoes larger than the measure, and the purchaser was satisfied, for shoes that are too big are better than ones that are too small – he would get half price, and he would receive the other half when the shoes wore out. However, the shoes of Nisan did not wear out so quickly. They are shoes of iron,
Mother would say. Indeed they were as heavy as iron…

"You should use them in good health," Nissan would wish the purchaser, and would be happy when the child did not complain that the shoes were too tight… What does a woman of valor do when her husband does not earn enough livelihood? She occupied herself in selling fruits and vegetables. My mother would buy cucumbers from her to pickle for the winter, apples, pears, and other vegetables, as she would incidentally hear her utter her complaints against the world and its Creator.

The Kloiz of the Peddlers

Here is the synagogue of the peddlers, the pride of our street, especially after Meir the bath attendant, nicknamed the "consul," plastered it from outside and in. Our relative Hershel Kopans engraved a new amud (prayer leader's podium) with two cherubs spreading their wings, who inspired awe with their extended tongues, and simultaneously protected the amud, as if they were vigilant against a hidden danger… Hershel was a free-style artist, but he put a Divine spirit into the engraving of the amud.

[Page 46]

Meir the bath attendant became a painter by decree of the new mayor of the city, who decreed that every homeowner must renovate his house and paint the walls, blinds, roof, chimney and fences – everything! At first we sighed: Can you imagine? A decree such as this! From where will we get the money? But nothing helped. People waited until the last minute, and a panic ensued. They searched for tradesmen with candles. What did Meir the bath attendant do? He purchased a paintbrush and began to paint. He even demanded the fee of a true painter.

It was said of him that when he painted the synagogue, Rabbi Ginzberg, who replaced the late Rabbi Silman, came to inspect the quality of his work. He loved to inspect himself that which was done for communal affairs, and he would not be satisfied with nonsensical pictures in the synagogue, as there were lehavdil,[9] in the church. Apparently he told Meir that this would not be pleasing to him. Meir retorted to him from the top of the ladder: "Rabbi, one should not complain for nothing about half the work…."

He did not forego his post as bath attendant. On Friday he would serve the householders in the bathhouse.

I do not understand why our synagogue was called the Kloiz of the Peddlers. There was not even one peddler there, but rather shoemakers, tailors, butchers, smiths, carpenters, builders, wagon drivers, and ordinary Jews… Here, in the women's section, Chasia with her bundle would scream out at midnight and alert the neighbors that they wanted to steel her bundle. All that was in it were papers…

In that Kloiz, Yankel the vinegar maker would grab a lad, place a roll into his hand, and command him to make the hamotzie[15] blessing – as he would get the benefit of reciting Amen. It was said of him that he was one of the 36 tzadikim[16] in whose merit the world exists, whereas he himself would claim that the world exists in the merit of the Jews who study Torah. If Heaven forbid they would interrupt their studies, the world would be destroyed…

In that Kloiz, we would study the Talmudic discussions of the House of Hillel and the House of Shammai with Reb Mendel Deitz.

In that place, the extra soul of the Sabbath would envelop us after the Sabbath meal of tzimmes (carrot stew), gefilte fish, and challas, as we were all dressed in our Sabbath finery. We would listen to words of moral lessons from a local scholar or a preacher from outside the city – about the Garden of Eden for the righteous people, the preserved wine, the wild ox and leviathan, and about Gehinnom (hell) for the evildoers, with Lilith and Ashmadai…[17] We would constantly recite our chapters of Psalms in order to protect ourselves from the beautiful Lilith, who in my mind was impersonated by my Christian neighbor…

We would supplicate for a good year on the High Holy Days. There, we would collect money for the Keren Kayemet (Jewish National Fund), blot out Haman, praise the Creator for the wonders and miracles that were done through the Hasmonaeans, and weep over the destruction of the Temple as if it took pace yesterday before our eyes.[18] My father later started worshipping in Tiferet Barchurim, especially on the festivals, when the prayer leader was Shmuel Cohen.

The synagogue of the peddlers – my second home during my youth – is shamed, abandoned, and orphaned. There is no Yankel the vinegar maker, no Jewish children to study Torah – and the world continues on… the sun shines according its custom and sets in the distance behind Spinan– without the Shacharit, Mincha and Maariv of the Jews.

The Shul and the Poorhouse

With a heavy heart, I continue my steps along the wild grass that grows on the street. The old shul (synagogue) stands before me as a naked stump whose branches have been cut off, as if it is immersed in slumber, as a monument shouting Heavenward. The shul faces the church steeple with its shiny crosses, as if asking endlessly, "Where are my Jews?" Even though it had been turned into a storehouse and there was junk surrounding it, it seemed to me as if I heard the echo of prayers bursting forth from inside. I remember the Kel Maleh Rachamim of the cantor Shlomo Margolis. His powerful voice echoed from the dome and was carried on high. Next to it stands the old Beis Midrash, bereft of its holiness, embarrassed, as if asking, "Why and for what reason did I remain standing?"

Here is the guesthouse and the poorhouse. Half of it has been taken over by the local poor. Among them was Menucha who served in the wealthy homes. As she walked, she talked to herself. Her corner was clean, and there was a flower on her window. In the second half, poor from near and far found shelter for the night. They struggled for a good place, as if they were archetypes from Mendele Mocher Sefarim when he wrote "Pishke Hachiger"…

[Page 47]

Shneur Matei also lived there. This was apparently a corruption of Metatei,[19] for his work was cleaning out latrines. We kept our distance from him, because a bad odor emanated from him.

Here is the Yavneh School. There, the teacher Sheina Grodski zealously guarded the language of Bialik from the Sephardic pronunciation, which was used in the Tarbut schools. Sara Silman was there. She was a relative of Rabbi Silman. She enchanted us with her enthusiastic smile as she instilled in us grammar, with its rules and exceptions. There, the teacher Levinski influenced us with his noble appearance, and by playing basketball and handball with us during recess. There, the teacher Feldberg taught us Bible and Gemara in a way that was equivalent to everyone. There we would laugh about the calculations of the teacher Shoub. First, because he was short and looked like one of us. Second, since he was not licensed, whenever the government inspector came, he had to flee. At times, he even jumped out of the window at the last moment. We found this hilarious.

Here is the bathhouse. It has almost collapsed. There is nobody to tend to it. The person who took care of city hall matters, Valchokowski, is no more. Here, every Friday Jews ascended the tall steps, and thrust off their weekday concerns along with their sweat and dirt.

The streets of the gentiles were not damaged, such as a portion of the Fishermen's Street and Keidani Street, with its gardens, trees, flowers, whose pleasantness spread also to the adjacent streets.

Here is a house to which I often went. Here lived Bronius Walinchius. He worked as an assistant for my father. He learned how to make ovens, and became Father's partner. He loved to teach me to drink liquor. He did not succeed, for he would quickly get drunk himself. Or then his wife, a lovely village girl, would teach me from "the tree of knowledge."

I did not want to go to visit them. Why should I pour salt on my wounds? I was told that even before the Germans came, he went to my father to take his work tools. He already knew from the outset that Father would no longer need them…

Here lived the "Yellow midwife". It was said that she occupied herself with forbidden matters, and assisted girls who "transgressed" and who got "a little" pregnant. Her sons, Tzalka and Moshe Glazer, were under police surveillance. They would be arrested before May 1. Their house would be searched, and they would find nothing. They would be freed after a few days. Nevertheless, it was always possible to obtain a forbidden book from them, a booklet or pamphlet about the Garden of Eden in the Soviet Union, and about the liberty, equality and brotherhood that had already been achieved in the happy Soviet Union, where everyone worked "according to his ability" and received "according to his needs"… as well as other sharp reasons such as these, which were crafted against those who claimed that this was a foreign seedling, and that we must plant within ourselves a longing for our old, desolate homeland, lest we miss the opportunity…

Our Meeting Place

We gathered in the house of Tevka Graber, on the oven, on long winter nights. The kerosene lamp spread a cloudy, mysterious light. A yellow spot appeared on the ceiling like a full moon in a cloudy sky. Tevka's father, along with his friends and neighbors, were around the table immersed in games of cards. They were involved in passing time, discussing news, and deliberations, without paying attention to our presence. At times, the posterior of a young neighbor would appear as she came to Judith, Tevka's mother, to borrow something or to purchase sunflowers seeds, as she would tarry for a little while…

Judith did not sit idly. In addition to her housework, she would make ice cream in the summer to sell to children. In the winter, she would roast sunflower seeds, and prepare ginger candies or honey pastries. She would make delicacies for Passover or weddings – and everything was made with finesse. She would earn well on the eve of Passover by working in the matzo factory of Sonia Gans, the wife of the butcher. She would knead the dough. I would pour the flour and my sister Osnat would pour the water. My father also worked there next to the oven. Judith was a refined woman, quiet as a dove. When she was sure that the supervisor was not there, she would give us some rest or do our work: "So that the children can breathe easier a bit." She would also at times place an ice cream into our hands, saying, "Your mother already paid."

[Page 48]

As we have said, we would gather there when we were still children: Berka Aiker, the son of Yossi the son of Moshechik; and Mosheke Sharshab, the son of Alta the seamstress, who was orphaned from his father. Even though his mother was considered to be the best seamstress for women, and the women of Jonava required her sewing, her livelihood was meager. Why? She had three children. Her brother Avraham, the "perpetual womanizer" worked with her as well. He would pursue each girl that came to work with them. However, he did not get far. First, he stuttered slightly, and second, how could he leave his sister, a widow with three sons, alone…

Mosheke Sharshab had a rich imagination. He would tell drawn out stories, like a novel in the newspaper, and with a happy ending as in the movies in Tevchik Yaffa's movie theater. When did he compile them? When he prepared wooden skates for the group of friends, to be used on the railway tracks (he excelled at this), or by molding dreidels for Chanukah, as he helped his mother cook, bake and do the laundry – all this without missing attending the Beis Midrash three times a day to recite Kaddish… He continued thus until the general destruction. The future author of children's stories, drawn from the experiences of his living brothers, went to his eternal world. He had a Jewish joy of life for the home, and was suffused with justice and hope.

We also had our own "artist," Gershke the "Bas." His father was Reuven the "Bas." They lived in the guesthouse. His mother served in wealthy homes. Accompanied by her husband she claimed that a day before she had dreamed that she was sitting in the cellar and grating horseradish in the grater. He interpreted her dream: Itke, it will be bad and bitter for you…

This Gershke did not study at all and knew everything. He went to work only when he needed money to purchase a book about drawing, engraving or reproduction. He drew everything, including landscapes and portraits. He particularly enjoyed engraving on wood and molding clay. Even the handle of a toothbrush served as an image of a woman… He would engrave Moses with the tablets, and lehavdil, [9] Ashmadai [17]. He would also draw sets for our performances. He was ready to travel to Moscow to study in an art school, but he remained put, apparently, because of his mother. Thus did another one of our talented people perish at the outset of his blossoming.

An Exceptional Family

Keidani Street, as it was, had its flowers, trees, and benches for lovers – "legal" or forbidden, who hid in the shadows of the foliage and enjoyed the environment that fostered growth, along with the sweet aroma of spring love…

Here is the house of the old photographer Soloviov, with his white Tolstoy beard. During picture taking, it was like a drawn out religious service, with the echoes of his final warning: "Sani-ma-yo"[20]. Later, you would look at the photography without recognizing your face. It was said that in 1906 he was a representative in the Duma.

Across from him lived the only Jew on the gentile street, Keidanski, the teacher in the Tarbut School. In his home, he spoke with his wife and children only in Hebrew. Their names were also different and unusual: Shaul, Imanuel, Tziona, and Reuven (rather than Reuvke). In general, we never called a person named Ben-Zion by his full name, for example. He would be nicknamed Bentzka, such as the son of Shimon Elia the butcher. He was still nicknamed Bentzka the butcher even when he was the father of grown children. It was said that it was dangerous for a young woman to enter his butcher shop… He would be called by his full name only when he was called up for an aliya to the Torah.

The behavior of the teacher Keidanski was different than what was usual. He did not go on summer vacations. He worked in his garden along with his children. Even his means of combing his hair was unusual – a part in the middle of his curls that were black as tar. They called this: the Zionist hairdo of Elia Keidanski. He, like the teacher

Balsher, educated a generation, but in the opposite spirit: in the spirit of the love of Zion, the nation and the language.

[Page 49]

I Was Swept into the Vortex

The students went about on the streets and in the halls, immersed in fiery debates: Socialist Zionism, Revisionism, Grossminst, principles a and b – each one according to his ideas, and all together arraigned against the Communists, Folkists, Deists. The battles were conducted with zeal, as one even used one's fist to try to convince one's disputant about the correctness of the program – how to actualize the return to Zion, how to straighten the back and liberate it from the yoke of exile. Many of the townsfolk would escort the fortunate chalutz (Zionist pioneer) who received a certificate, and was going to build a home for his family and his nation. Thus would they also escort those who were immigrating to Birobidzhan in order to live there as a citizen with equal rights in "the great family of nations" and to benefit from the pride of the "father of the deprived"…

Thus was the vortex formed in Jonava – some to the right and some to the left, some partially, and some with all their might. Thus was I also swept into the vortex – to assist the redemption of the nation from its long exile. Since this path was very slow, I quickly found – with the help of secret books – the path in the opposite direction, with full and holy faith in humanity and the brotherhood of nations. We placed our hope in the "redeemer" with the red star…

A drastic change in my political orientation took place after the failure of my first love. The matter began with the reformation in the school, when boys and girls were seated together on one bench. The pure heart of a twelve year old boy was filled with pride and glee when a pretty and refined girl, with aromatic silken hair flowing in braids over her beautiful shoulders, sat next to him. Blue eyes peered bashfully through the hair as she attempted to gather it again into braids. Of course, she was my partner during school celebration, not without the jealousy of the rest of the children.

Students of the Culture League School. The teacher Balsher is on the right

Who could be compared to me when she came to visit my house so that I could explain to her something in arithmetic or history?! She recommended that I assist her younger brother in his studies, for already then he was more of a butcher than a student. It did not matter to me. The important thing was this was a good excuse to go to their home. My student was content that he did not have to sit and study, and he would leave us alone. I would sit and enjoy the beautiful form of the goddess sitting next to me, and I would feel the lovely heat of temptation. I would read to her constantly, and with feeling, in order to chase away the desire for wrongdoing.

[Page 50]

I had a desire to at least touch the princess of my heart, her developed form, her straight neck that was inviting caresses and kisses, as well as her partly opened lips, from which her teeth appeared as pearls… However, the fear that she might be hurt and I would lose the opportunity to gaze upon her beauty and sit next to her, kept me back. As if to vex me, as if the evil inclination itself was rubbing salt on the wounds, her father would state in the language of butchers, seriously or in jest:

"Why are you satisfying her with stories? Do not be a fool, grab her… lest someone else preempts you…"

In my heart I thought that he was right. But does a father speak thus about his daughter!

Not without pleasure did I hear mother tell grandmother that Bentzke the butcher gave her a piece of good meat for cheap, and hinted to her that she is his future in-law. My father was not happy with this: first, I had already studied in Yeshiva and he wanted his son to be a rabbi. Second, the butcher would also be concerned…

I was taken by longing also during the time of the study of Gemara. No Rashi and Tosafot (Talmudic commentaries) were able to remove her image from before my eyes. At night, I would wander around her house, stand beneath her window and listen to her breathing, even though the shutters were closed. I had nobody with whom to share my feelings. I was embarrassed before my friends. My Christian friend, to whom I revealed everything, was studying in Kovno. Thus my secret remained inside of me.

One spring night, as I passed by her window, I suddenly saw her in a nightgown with a sheet over her shoulders. Her beauty was as if it was engraved in marble – literal, but alive… The town was asleep. The moonlight was hidden behind the roofs of the barns and left the alley in which we were standing shrouded in darkness, as if deliberately. I stood astonished, not sure if this was a dream or reality… At that moment, I felt a kiss come forth from my lips, and disappear, like her mouth, with quiet and suddenness, as she appeared, leaving behind her aroma sweet as fresh honey. In vain did I attempt to utter her name and call her again. This was as if it was our goodbye kiss. From that time, she was embarrassed, avoided me, and refused to talk to me, even when I came to their house. My young mind was not able to grasp the sudden change that took place in her relations to me…

Because You Drowned Them They Drowned You[21]

I left the Yeshiva. I was now already among the wage earners. I worked with Benkkutzer the tailor. There the atmosphere was of the common folk. I would read the Folksblatt every day. "Di Yiddishe Shtime" was in the house. We received it all crumpled up from the partners, along with the leftovers of the chulent and kugel. Hershel Benkkutzer was active in the library, in the dramatic club and in the evening classes of the culture league. Shmuel Dudak would visit him sometimes, and alongside the needle, iron and scissors, the problems of the repertoire, roles, tickets and books would be solved. I read a great deal. I was not short of time. I was affiliated with all my heroes, with young Verter who contemplated suicide after his failed love with Gretchen. Like him, I found comfort with my Lithuanian neighbor, the gymnasium student, who came to visit from Kovno from time to time.

My disappointment with my own "Gretchen" pushed me to search for an outlet for my anger and anguish. I quickly found the path of the "truth seekers" without thinking about the dangers involved in this. I imbued my entire enthusiasm and youthful temperament into the struggle for a different Jonava, more just…without Jew and gentile – only free citizens, proud and content.

I must admit that not everything was clear and understood to me as it was to my comrades in this idea, Balsher's students. Particularly because we formerly believed with blind faith in the unique, omnipotent G-d, we were unable to believe with blind faith in the sole "leader of the downtrodden" who was always right. There was no shortage of reasons for this, such as – my court case of 1937. Overnight, the heroes of the revolution became "traitors and enemies" and even the judges of yesterday were declared as agents and subject to judgment themselves, as it is written: "Since you drowned others you were drowned, and at the end those who drowned you will be drowned"…

The newspapers wrote a great deal about this. The young mind struggled to understand what was transpiring – but in vain… Sworn Communists such as Tzalka Glazer, Yankele Magin, Marka Lon and others, explained this simply as: "The Capitalist smoke," "Yellow journalism," etc. Balsher, Yosha Epstein and others like them filled their mouths with water and were silent. This made our doubts greater.

[Page 51]

A special emissary appeared, the teacher Ziman from the Sholom Aleichem gymnasium in Kovno, today the editor of the official Lithuanian newspaper "Tiesa" and attempted to "explain" this with banal statements such as: "the petit bourgeois philosophy," "Talmudic didactics." The strongest reason was – the threat of being excommunicated and pushed out by the "progressive circles." This method, taken from the middle ages, used by the church and the rabbinate against apostates – had influence more than anything else.

Love that Began with a Slap

… And lest I was attracted there because of Henka Yudelevich… This or something else, and I was already, like other youths, smoking "Sapfu," wearing a suit, a silk coat, and lacquered shoes; performing in the theater, studying at evening courses, and a member of the leadership of the library. Girls were going around in scouting shirts, snug against their body so it seemed that they would shortly split open from the pressure… and they would appear in their full maturity before the eyes, like hot rolls from the oven… The hand stretches out to touch, to grab hold that the shirt does not split… and then you get a slap on the face…. As mother would slap on the hand when one grabs a roll from the dough trough:

"Don't grab them when they are hot. We are taking them out to sell. Let them cool down and make the Hamotzie blessing. Do not be a glutton!" And other similar chastisements that accompany us throughout out lives.

The slap did not interfere with our friendship. We began to spend time together. On one of our walks, we talked about the injustice in the world, the national problem, anti-Semitism and how to fight it, materialism and all sorts of other "isms" about which one could read in the Agura Library; We continued to talk about literature and theater, mentioning terms such as realism, futurism, cubism… as we got father from the town. She was under the influence of the words of the young "professor" who completed six grades with an excellent report, who knew how to explain everything well. The hot pride pushed him, as if he was afraid of losing her…

The pine trees wave silently as if they are keeping a secret. A bird chirps on a branch. Others chirp back, as if they are singing "Harei At"[22]. The skies serve as a chupa (wedding canopy). The lips join together, and the young couple becomes united with the scenery… The cool spring water flows gleefully, as if it sings a song of praise to the Creator. The large wooden wheel of the water mill marks the rhythm like the musician's drum. This is so heartwarming that there is a desire to join in the song.

The soft and delicate creation beside me looks at me with pure, gleeful, smiling and misty eyes… Her reddish-brown curls catch the last rays of sun that penetrate through the trees and roll over her muscular but delicate shoulders. How much understanding and tact does that girl have! She has no feelings of regret. On the contrary, it is clear to me that she was designated for me already when she was a student, and I was a scouting counselor. I was then in the clutches of the pretty Henka, and how can I measure up to her...

I found out how much she suffered with her domineering aunt Gittel and her uncle the shoemaker, who was coarse, although he was a good man and a warm Jew. She was born in Vilna. When she was still a child, she was taken from her mother, father, brothers and sister to spend a year as a guest with her aunt. Later the border closed, and family reunions in the Lingomiani Cemetery stopped. Thus, five or six years passed with Henka longing for her home, while in our Jonava, where the gentiles are here in "exile," and they require the Jews for their livelihood.

There were indeed experiences with disturbances, especially during the times of the army draft or the days of the Bulbars, when they would get very drunk and shout, "Beat the Jews." The shopkeepers had barely had a chance to lock the doors of their stores when the automobile owners, headed by the sons of Shmerl Dragachki, and the wagon drivers from Breizer Street appeared stormily. The butchers with Uncle Leibe, "Leibke the Bastard" would come – and the pillagers would flee for their lives. Later the policeman Labas would come to file a report, but he would find no witnesses. This would conclude with the drinking of a glass of liquor in the shoe store with that Leibke the "bastard," the uncle of my girl. He came from Vilna, and in Jonava they called all of the people from Vilna "bastards" or "thieves," just as they nicknamed people from Kovno, "Zhulikes," that is scoundrels; people from Keidani – thieves and hunchbacks, and people from Vilkomir – schnorrers;[23] people from Siauliai – empty paramours; people from Seta – little challas; and people from Anyksciai – prideful. This was because they used to pick their teeth after a meal of "fish and not fish" (potato soup with fried onion) as if they ate roasted duck… Even the people of Jonava were not without their nicknames. They were called "Burliaks," apparently because there were Russian villages around the town.

[Page 52]
My future wife ended up without choice in the town of Jonava, as opposed to the cultured Vilna, the Jerusalem of Lithuania…

The Gnawing Worm

Summer holiday in Sponenai

I was her protector and comforter. I studied drama in Kovno, and she studied in the conservatory. We came to Jonava on Sabbaths.

The Red Army entered Lithuania. Vilna united us. She returned to her home, which also became my home. The streets were filled with people. There were gatherings, speeches, concerts, pastimes, etc., for justice was victorious. There was a new life, and we were part of it. Farmers received land. However, deep in the consciousness, the worm gnawed away: perhaps not everything is as rosy as it seems… How come those celebrating the joy are only Jews… Perhaps the non-Jews see what we do not see, they sense the footsteps of the angel of death who is hiding behind the sea of red flags and waiting for his day to come. Perhaps they are already preparing the recompense for the assistance in nationalizing the private and government property. The expulsion of those who were called "enemies of the people" left a particularly difficult impression. These were Lithuanian nationalists, wealthy Jews and Zionists. They were sent off on sealed wagons. Even the fascist police of Smetona[24] were not so brazen as to do this.

The heart was pained over the cries of the innocent children, and you lacked the means of assisting.

And the punishment was not long in coming…

From Yiddish: Shimon Noy

Translator's Footnotes

Paneriai (Ponary) is a suburb of Vilna where mass killings took place during the Holocaust. Fort Nine, near Kaunas, was the site of imprisonment and murder of Jews. The Girelka Forest, near Jonava, was also a place of mass killings August 13, 1941, 20 Av 5701.

The room where the ritual purification of the body before burial took place.

Miriam is Hebrew for Mary.

Also known as "Yoske the Swallow" elsewhere in this text.

A gentile who turns on light, heat, or ovens for Jews on the Sabbath (which Jews themselves are forbidden to do).

It is forbidden to cook on the Sabbath, so the lunchtime food needs to be kept warmed in the oven from the beginning of the Sabbath on Friday night. In some communities, rather than each person keeping an oven lit in the home, the large oven in the bakery would remain lit, and everyone would place a pot of food for the Sabbath lunch there, and retrieve it at lunchtime.

I.e. he had died.

Dove person.

A Hebrew expression literally meaning 'to differentiate', and interjected in a sentence when the contrast between the two statements is extreme – in this case between a Christian prayer and a Jewish prayer.

Kel Maleh Rachamim is the prayer for the dead recited at funerals, yizkor, and other memorial occasions.

A derogatory (or semi-derogatory) term for a gentile woman.

I suspect that this is referring to the Christmas tree.

The meaning of the word here is apparently 'take hold' or 'grab'.

Hazeh, means "this".

The blessing made upon eating bread.

It is said in Jewish lore that each generation has 36 discrete tzadikim (righteous people).

In Jewish lore, the wine, wild ox and leviathan are delicacies to be enjoyed by the righteous in the world to come. Lilith and Ashmadai are names of demons

This sentence refers to Purim, Chanukah and Tisha B'av.

Hebrew for broom.

I am not sure what this phrase means.

A quote from the Mishnaic tractate of Pirke Avot, meaning, "you get what you deserve".

The first two words of the Jewish marriage ceremony, stated by the groom to the bride as he places the ring on her finger.

People who beg, but with a somewhat derogatory connotation.

A President of the inter-war republic of Lithuania.

See http://en.wikipedia.org/wiki/Antanas_Smetona.

[Page 53]

Personalities and Events
(Literally "House of Father and Mother")

[Page 54]

My Parental Home
by Moshe Shamir
Translated by Jerrold Landau

I wish to bring a recommendation to establish a full curriculum of study that would become obligatory in all of our schools: "My Parental Home".

The study material in this subject will be – the home of each student, his parents, their origins, history, work and way of life. As the course of study continues, it will broaden to include the grandfathers, grandmothers, their lands of origin, their cultural surroundings and their communities.

The coursework would primarily be independent work: essays on important topics in the annals of the parents and the family, collecting of photographs, documents, books, poems or drawings based on the material, etc. With the passage of time, the material would take on a more objective form and would encompass the arena of Jewish life from which the parental home stemmed.

… The issue of the "Jewish mission" would benefit from this new subject.

… It should be pointed out that the feeling of identification with the Jewish nation throughout its generations and in different places would be enhanced in the Israeli youth through occupying themselves practically and intimately in their family history – not as something imposed by other people (which can cause a distaste), but rather as an open enjoyment of a person who is increasing his sense of self…

(Moshe Shamir, Maariv, October 1, 1971).

[Page 55]

The House on the Street of the Road
by Rachel Soloveitchik (Janosevitch), Tel Aviv
Translated by Jerrold Landau

The Street of the Road: The first house is the Davidovitch house and the fourth is the Janosevitch house

Who of the Jonavers does not remember the large, brick house, with its green shutters and garden decorated with colorful flowers on the Street of the Road? The interior of the house was constructed of four large rooms with a kitchen, a small porch, and benches on the side of the street. I still recall my family home with all of its splendor.

My late father Yosef the son of Yaakov Janosevitch of blessed memory, was a great scholar and a Maskil, as I heard from his acquaintances. He was a merchant of forestry products by profession, and he spent most of his time on business trips. Despite this, he also found the time to sit and study a page of Gemara and Mishna. I recall the bookshelves along the walls, overflowing with sacred texts, which were considered by my father as treasures of silver and gold. He dedicated much time to educating his children, the only son and the four daughters. In particular, he invited praiseworthy teachers from outside to teach the children. My parents were observant of the religion and tradition. In the house, a cordial spirit of mutual dedication pervaded.

To my great agony, this ideal situation did not last long. At the outbreak of the First World War, we were forced to leave the house and the city in accordance with the decree of expulsion issued by the Czarist government, which applied to Jews of the Kovno region. My father, whose entire property went to the government treasury, suffered a heart attack and died suddenly in a strange place. My widowed mother and the children returned to Jonava in 1918, in mourning and lacking of means. My mother maintained herself with difficulty. The large home remained, but the breadwinner was missing. My brother Nathan, thanks to his education and intelligence, entered cultural life and became very active in our city. In order to ease the situation of our family, he moved with his wife to live in Kovno, where he obtained the position of communal secretary. He excelled in his dedication and his fruitful work, and reached the level of one of the renowned activists in Lithuania. He founded an organization for ethnography and Jewish history, and was very active for the national funds in the city. He established a family with three talented daughters. All of them – he, his wife, and his daughters – perished in the Kovno ghetto.

My eldest sister was married to the teacher Rosenberg, who was a veteran member of the teaching staff of the Tarbut School in Jonava for years. He educated hundreds of students in national tradition and Zionism. Many of these are today in the Land and remember him positively. My brother-in-law, my sister and their two children, our mother, and another sister and her family all perished in Jonava. I was fortunate, for I was able to escape to Russia with my husband. We endured a difficult period there, and my husband died. I remained alone. I arrived in Vilna in 1945, and what I feared was true. As I have stated, nobody from the family remained alive.

I had another sister in the land, one of the first chalutzim of Lithuania. From the first day, I decided to use all my means to leave Russia and join up with my sister. I succeeded, and I arrived in the Land in 1956. Here, I continued with my profession as a kindergarten teacher for ten years. Through this, I now receive a pension. Despite my small pension I do not complain about my lot, for I am among friends, and I am happy that my objective was fulfilled, and I am amongst my people in the Jewish State. In my thoughts I still live with all my dear ones, victims of the Holocaust. May their memories be blessed.

[Page 56]

He Preferred the Interpersonal Commandments
by Shimon Noy (Gorfein)
Translated by Jerrold Landau

The house of Mendel and Reizl Gorfein on Vilna Street.
At the door is the young son Asher

I am here in Israel, so I must first and foremost give thanks to my father Menachem Mendel for making sure to give me a Hebrew and Zionist education from my childhood.

It was already possible in those days to find within a single family of Jonava both Hassidim as well as members of Tarbut and the Culture League. Even though my father came from a large family in Kamenetz Litovsk in Poland that was meticulous in the observance of commandments, when we came within the bounds of Lithuania at the conclusion of the First World War, I recall him as a dedicated Zionist and a man who followed the spirit of the times.

When I was still below school age, at approximately 5 ½, he sent me to Pitkowsky, the fine teacher of young children. Pitkowsky sent his eldest son to the Yeshiva of Hebron, where he was slaughtered.

Later I transferred to Beisegoler and Shima-Meir until I turned 7. Then I studied in the Tarbut School. My father was a member of the parents' committee.

I recall that he used to come on occasion to remind the students to urge their parents to pay their tuition. He would issue his statement in the Hebrew language with the Askenazic pronunciation, of course. When we finished school our parents made sure to find teachers so that we could continue our studies locally for an additional year. After that, I was sent to study in the Real Gymnasium in Kovno.

Father was alert to what was transpiring in the Zionist movement. He would often contribute more than we could afford to the funds. Since our small grocery store did not occupy him greatly, his time was free to become involved in the matters of the world. He wrote articles as a form of a diary about events that took place during those times. As he analyzed the political situation in the world, he foresaw the outbreak of the war. Incidentally, he wrote these records in Hebrew.

We would often read information in the newspaper about what was transpiring outside the bounds of our city. I already began to read the Yiddishe Shtime from the age of 8. He subscribed to the newspaper in partnership with Moshe Jalinowitz.

My father was known as a kind hearted man. Our gentile customers especially praised him. He would issue them credit, for he trusted every person. There were certainly those people who took advantage of his trust, and remained indebted to him for large sums. It would seem that this spirit of winning over the hearts of his customers often led to losses, for what was good for the customers was not so good for the family. However, this is the way it was.

People would frequently visit us and engage in conversation. My mother Reizl was known for her handwriting, and many women would come to her so that she could write the addresses in the vernacular. They were certain that when she wrote the addresses, the mail would reach its destination… When they began to collect donations for the redeeming of the Land, my mother donated gold earrings.

My grandmother Rivka Yehudit is also remembered positively. She was known as Rav Yudis (a corruption of Riva Yehudit) perhaps because she was considered one of the scholarly and knowledgeable women of her generation. Through her frequent reading of Tzena Urena, Menorat Hamaor and other books of that genre, she amassed a comprehensive treasury of popular proverbs and stories, which she was able to fit into any topic that was being discussed with her. Therefore, I spread her name even when I was on hachshara, and I attributed statements to her that I was not sure if she really said, but that without doubt might have been said. These include, "better a wrinkle on the clothing than on the forehead", or similarly, "a spot on the clothing rather than on the soul"…

She had a great deal to say about marriage matches, brides and grooms. She also knew how to sing old popular songs. It is too bad that I did not have a feeling for folklore, and that I did not think of writing these things down. There was indeed much to record. These matters have been forgotten with the passage of time. The hand of time took its toll.

Before the festivals, she would send my sister with packages of money to distribute discretely to the poor people of the town on Breizer Street.

My father wrote on Sabbaths and also turned on the lights. He would go to the synagogue only on Sabbaths. Incidentally, as far as I recall, the atmosphere in the synagogue was quite liberal. People came to be seen, and retreated into the hall during the reading of the Torah to discuss various matters. They would torment people by hiding their tallis. On Tisha BeAv, the day of mourning for the Holy Temple, people would throw thorns as a joke in order to lighten the mourning… They would stick to the clothing of the important elders of the town, to the point where the mourning became a source of fun, Heaven forbid.

Apparently Shimon Gorfein Noy

My father apparently preferred the interpersonal commandments to those between man and G-d. Many people who recall him as a pleasant man will confirm this.

In the meantime, my mother was afflicted with partial paralysis. This tied down my father to the place, as well as my younger brother Asher, for they could not leave her alone. In this situation, and with the rest of the difficulties associated with aliya, they could not think about aliya to the Land of Israel.

Thus, they remained there in their difficulties. In the meantime, Mother died, and the bitter days came when both our brother and father perished in such a tragic manner.

They did not merit seeing the desired Land. We were not able to save them.

Kibbutz Amir

[Page 58]

The Story and Annals of One Family
by Sara Burstein of Tel Aviv
Translated by Jerrold Landau

Sara Burstein

Bringing forth memories from days gone by is like mining pearls from the depths of the sea. One is connected and delves into each and every memory, even the weakest one. Slowly but surely the tapestry broadens and a wonderful picture appears before one's eyes -- a picture composed of many details. The eyes of your spirit see it with wondrous clarity, and the ears of the spirit suddenly begin to hear the echoes of dear acquaintances, and the echoes of the sounds of loved ones that have been hidden away. Even the sense of smell does its part. You sense smells that have disappeared, absorbing them into yourself, and it seems that only yesterday they broadened your nostrils. Even the sense of taste is awakened, and you sense on your palate the taste of various dishes and foodstuffs from Mother's home, that had not been tasted since. Suddenly you sense a strong desire to return to that time, to relive those experiences, to be enveloped with the love and the concern of dear parents; but the reality slaps you on the face. What has passed will no longer return. You are left only with impressions in dreams, memories and visions, a sort of "from there you will see the Land, but will not enter it."[1]

A G-d Forsaken Town

The home of our father was in Kaplice. The Lithuanians changed its name to Panoteriai. This small town was 17 kilometers northeast of Jonava. To get there, you must travel 9 kilometers on the Jonava Road in direction of the city of Wilkomir. You turn northward on a dirt road, and then the remote town spreads out before you between the pastureland and the greenery, between the thickets of forest and the fruit orchards. There we were born and received our childhood education. We only moved to the "metropolis" of Jonava in the 1920s. However Jonava was always our center. We were tied to it with family ties. Jonava provided us with most of our provisions. Even the rabbi to whom we had to turn with questions of *kashruth* was the rabbi of Jonava. On a completely different topic, the cemetery of Jonava served Kaplice.

Kaplice -- this was a G-d forsaken town in the eyes of everybody, which in its best years only consisted of several quorums of Jews. When we left it, only two or three families of elderly people remained.

[Page 59]

There was no school, no library, no cultural center, and even no post office in the town. We had to travel several kilometers to the nearest post office. On the other hand, it had a synagogue, and also a Catholic church. Their cemetery was around us, and one side of it bordered our yard. There was a "monopol" (government liquor store) in Kaplice. It supplied those in "need" with the bitter drop, which was their daily bread especially on their holidays. The priest with a long frock, the spiritual leader of the Catholics, lived in the bowels of the house of prayer. From time to time, he would pass through the Jewish street with all of his splendor, his silver tipped cane flying in his hand.

For Us - The Center of the World

Indeed, our town was poor -- poor in population and in institutions. However, in our eyes, it was the center of the world. An exceptionally active, bustling life from all perspectives sprouted there. Everyone, both the Jews and the gentiles, worked like toiling ants without darkness. There were several people with trades among the Jews: Yossel the shoemaker, Yasi-Kanczeker the blacksmith, Peretz the tailor, and Chone the potter. We children spent long hours with the shoemaker and were always excited to see the "secrets" of his trade. Kaplice had several meager stores, and also several Jewish merchants who spent most of their time peddling their merchandise in the neighboring villages. There were also several "clergymen" concentrated into one man: "Yossel the Shochet" as we called him. He was also the cantor and the *mohel* (ritual circumcisor), and at times answered straightforward questions on *kashruth*. Aside from this, he was also involved in all types of other businesses, such as selling non-kosher meat to the farmers, leasing a fruit orchard in the summer, etc. in order to sustain his wife and children. There was even a *shamash* (beadle) in our synagogue, "Rafael the Shamash". Aside from serving as the shamash, he was also involved in the sale of Sabbath candles made of sheep fat, and several other such trades.

The main thing -- Kaplice was a Jewish town in the full sense of the term, albeit in miniature and with a small Jewish population. However, it was a town where even the Keren Kayemet (Jewish National Fund) was not forgotten. Campaigns would be conducted for it from time to time. I remember the blue ledgers of the Keren Kayemet upon which was written: "The town Kaplice, the names of the donors, and "collected by David Burstein". On holidays, especially the High Holy Days, the town would suddenly grow and reach large dimensions. Isolated Jews from all the nearby villages would come to celebrate the holidays in a Jewish environment and to get an *aliya* in our synagogue. Every Jew in our town would take in a guest, lovingly take care of these "villagers" and enjoy the experience.

When the holidays were over, the town would shrink once again to its usual dimensions.

My Father becomes a *Maskil*

We were five children, one son and four daughters. We were born and raised in the home of our parents in Kaplice. This was a large, spacious house, surrounded by a yard and all sorts of buildings such as stables, granaries, a store and rental houses. There was a paved yard in front of the house. On the other side, there were grass meadows and flowers surrounding a well of fresh water. Behind and on the eastern side was a cultivated fruit orchard, consisting of choice types of fruit. In the corner of the orchard was a synagogue that was built on our land. Behind it was a potato field, and our bathhouse was in the right corner. There was another field on the left side, in which our father planted alfalfa, grass and clover. In front of it there was a young fruit orchard that father planted, and that was already producing fruit. Mother's vegetable garden was between the trees. She tended to it with great love, and was very successful. In his youth, our father of blessed memory was a Yeshiva student and a *Maskil*. He went through all the incarnations of Yeshiva students in those days in various Yeshivas in Jonava and Wilkomir, including taking his meals on a daily rotation system. However, to the disappointment of Grandfather and Grandmother, he finally turned his back on holy studies, and did not earn his livelihood from his learning. He began to read secular books in Hebrew, and became fluent in that language. He even "transgressed" by writing articles and essays in a unique weekly humorous publication that was published by three *Maskilim* of the town for their own enjoyment in their own handwriting, and was called "Kaploria". Father, one of the three, signed his articles as DV"Sh (David the son of Shlomo). I was still able to read those few unique periodicals. They were hidden in a drawer, and at special times we would take them out, read them and enjoy.

[Page 60]

When father got older, he turned to business. Keeping with his family tradition, he was a merchant of forest products and wood. He succeeded because he was diligent and worked a great deal. He would arise before dawn every day, light the kerosene lamp, get a cup of tea from the samovar, and sit down to study *Gemara* and *Mishna*. He studied Torah by the light of a lantern with his sweet voice and soulful dedication, and turned into the pillar of fire from which we children "warmed ourselves" throughout our life. We all remember this, and we all yearn for this with the depths of our soul. His sweet voice and wonderful melodies would pour out with a quiet voice. Father learned while we were still in bed, dozing but not asleep, with our ears absorbing this wonderful sound, as the soul felt like it sprouted. We could never get enough of the sweetness and enjoyment. The water urn at the edge of the table hummed away, adding its own touch. I often dreamed that I was listening and absorbing the warm tunes into my soul, as my soul was departing. However, I woke up, and it was only a dream. After father concluded his learning, he would go to the stable. In the summer, he would hitch the horse to the four wheels of the wagon with a type of straight rod, and then ride away. In the winter, he would hitch the horse to a small, light sled. Thus would Father leave the house with its sleeping residents and travel to his business. He would tarry outside almost the entire day. On the way, he would pass the village of "Pagloz", seven kilometers from the town. The post office was located there, and he would bring the letters, and especially the newspapers from there. He subscribed to all of the Hebrew newspapers that were published in those days in the large Jewish centers, such as "Hatzefira" from Warsaw, "Hazman" from Vilna, and "Haolam" from London. He would read and write only in the flowery Hebrew that was customary in those days. When he arrived home toward evening, he would eat his only warm meal of the day, occupy himself in various matters related to day to day life, and go to his couch to lie down and read by candlelight, of course. He read newspapers and other secular writings. I do not know when he went to sleep and for how long he slept, but it was sufficient for him, apparently, and he did not suffer from lack of sleep.

Father -- Involved in Everything

Father was a dedicated and active Zionist. When I was still a girl, I found a copy of a letter from Father to a friend of his in America in a drawer. The letter was, of course, in flowery Hebrew (this was the Hebrew that I absorbed as well). I read it and devoured it like a ripe fig before summer. The letter was long, and I was of course unable to understand everything. The letter was filled with ideas and concepts regarding Zionism, Herzl, the Congresses, and other great Zionist leaders. It seemed to me that it was discussing some Zionist Congress. Father investigated and purified everything that he copied into his heart as his core beliefs. It is unfortunate that this letter has disappeared with the vicissitudes of time, and is not with the rest of his things. It contained a great deal of material that would help understand Father, who was one of a kind: a Torah scholar, a scholar in secular subjects, astute in world affairs, someone who knew how to express his ideas in clear language, a logical thinker, and possessing a refined sense of humor with which he would spice his general conversations.

Aside from his work in the forest business, he was expert in all types of other work. He was competent in all types of agricultural work, since we had large plots of land surrounding the house. Sometimes in the summer, Father would lease plots of land around us and work them himself. When the season came, he would plant, harvest, gather, and put the produce in storehouses. Sometimes he would also include the children, who were then still very young. Of course, there was an important reason to have the children work: the fear of rain that might cause the hay to rot. He would corral the adults and the children, and with all of our work, the matter would be settled very well, with Father standing at the head!

Father would even take care of our old and new fruit orchard faithfully. Thanks to him, his garden was very successful. After I left Kaplice, I never again tasted the taste of those types of fruits that we had in our garden. At the beginning of the spring, father would hoe around the trees, fertilize, prune the dry branches, tar the trees as a protection against worms and other pests, erect supports for the trees that were laden with fruit so that the branches would not break, and do many other such tasks. He would toil and work without stop, and without concern for his energy and time. His Zionist activities found a broad field of action in the narrow confines of our tiny town. In his capacity as the *gabbai* of the synagogue, he would canvas all of the worshippers for the Keren Kayemet. The donations were indeed modest, but he would collect every coin, and joined together they would add up to a reasonable sum. Aside from this, he participated in the Zionist committees that were set up in nearby cities, and thereby he would strengthen his Zionist faith.

I Too Learn in *Cheder*

Aside from its main role, our synagogue also served as a *cheder* for children. The women's gallery was on the same floor, and only a partition separated the men's section from the women's gallery. There were small windows in the partition through which the women could look into and pay attention to the men's section in order to follow after them in the prayers. A narrow walkway from the main street above the well-known bog led to the synagogue. It was full of dust in the summer and mud in the winter. We children did not like to use it, so we would pass through the fence that encompassed the entire yard and all of the buildings therein. With one jump, we were in the *cheder*. Along the way, we could still snatch some fruit and enjoy it. A non-local teacher always headed the cheder that was conducted in the women's gallery. All of the children who were in need of Torah, without differentiation by ages, would come to the cheder. The teacher would try to the best of his ability to impart Torah to students, either with pleasantness or with a sailor's rod -- all in accordance with the need. In this manner, I too was absorbed into the *cheder* at a young age. Suddenly, at the beginning of the period of study, I was left without my playmates. They were all in the *cheder*, and of course, without choice, I followed after them and spent my time together with them. It was more interesting than wandering about alone on the street. In any case, I also absorbed the studies.

[Page 62]

I was fortunate, for during the time frame that I am discussing here, the disseminator of Torah was a wonderful teacher -- a young man named Shmuel Brandwein, the son of the rabbi of Kaplice. He knew Hebrew well, and was also expert in the ways of the world. He was about 17 years old. The Torah that I absorbed from him served as the foundation to my future studies, and I will always remember him with love. When my parents saw that in any case, I was in the cheder as an onlooker from the sidelines, they decided to settle the matter officially. Thus was I counted in with the rest of the students. From that time, Father began to treat the matter of his children's education very seriously. He attempted to bring in the best teachers. To this end, he came into contact, in writing or face to face, with those who worked in the Hebrew newspapers, and asked for recommendations of good teachers. It was customary at that time for talented youths to travel to small towns to teach Torah to Jewish children. In the meantime, they would earn some money so that they could continue their studies. Since Vilna was the Jerusalem of Lithuania, where those who were prominent in the Hebrew language gathered, and where the "Hazman" Hebrew newspaper was published, Vilna was the prime locale for Hebrew teachers.

I remember that at the time when I was digging through Father's writing table, which was overflowing with all types of letters and papers, I found postcards from Chernowitz (the father of Yaakov Tzur of our day). In those postcards, they discussed a Hebrew teacher for Kaplice. In this manner, we gained two additional teachers -- a man named Huberman and a woman who had already learned at a modern cheder and knew the Russian vernacular language. These teachers laid the groundwork that later bore tasty fruit and led the way to the Hebrew gymnasium that was set up after many years. In the interim, years passed and a further group of our children joined the *cheder* and entered the yoke of studies. Thus were we hatched in the *cheder*, and were happy with our lot. As has been stated, the *cheder* was located at the edge of our garden. In the summer, the windows were opened, the air was clear, and the aroma of the flowers and fruit filled the room. Before my eyes, the large, intertwined pear tree with small yellow pears appears. Its foliage covered almost half of the roof the synagogue and the cheder. We would enjoy this fine fruit during recess. I will never forget that during recess, my brother and I would climb the cherry tree next to the cheder and collect and eat the sweet cherries that grew on the sunny side of the tree. In this way, our lot was better than that of other *cheders* in small towns, which were located in gray, unventilated rooms with stifling air. Approximately two years before the First World War, we got a "Rebbe" from Jonava. We called him the "Kaplicer Rebbe". He was an elderly man named Brandwein, who was a relative of our family. He gave the best of his energy to teaching and disseminating Torah. The best of the youths were his students. His hometown was Kaplice, and he had also been the rebbe of Father and other family members from the previous generations. In his old age, when he wanted to rest a bit and locate himself in the bosom of nature, he returned to Kaplice with his wife. His only son, who had been my first teacher, was already in America, and they remained isolated and alone. This wonderful rebbe was filled with Torah and general knowledge, and he also had the ability to teach with pleasantness. (His strictness had dissipated in his old age.) We all loved him, and thanks to this, we succeeded at our studies. His memory will not depart from us. We will also remember him with love and reverence. He would teach us to read, and also to write compositions on all types of topics. He imparted good manners to us. The first Hebrew book that we began to study during his time was "Hadibur Haivri" for beginners, and the second was "Hadibur Haivri" for advanced students. The last one of this series was "Hasignon Haivri", a very serious book as I still recall. I never saw these books again.

In those days, the Herzlia gymnasium in the sand dunes of small Tel Aviv was talked about a great deal. There were daring people who traveled to the land of Israel to study there, in the first and only Hebrew gymnasium. Our parents dreamed of this, and my brother and I aspired to this with all our might. The novelty attracted our interest, for we had no such concept of that yet. But the difficulty was as follows: we were too young, and the gymnasium only accepted students from the Diaspora at a much higher age than we were at that time. Therefore, this dream only materialized in my home many years later. To my dismay, the aura of that school was no longer the same as it had been in my childhood.

[Page 63]
Mother's Hands Were Also Full of Work

Thus did we grow up in Kaplice as if in a greenhouse, far from the wide world and its vicissitudes. Nothing impeded our spirit. Complete harmony pervaded between our parents, and this had a positive influence on us children. Mother of blessed memory was the ideal helpmate of her husband. She was a beautiful woman both inside and out, refined and graced with many fine qualities, healthy and radiant, with a good temperament and merciful heart. She had a developed sense of esthetics. She loved nature and its creations, enjoyed the beauty of nature and attempted to bring its beauty and charm inside the house. She loved cleanliness and order, and her work was done with full completion. She did not lack any energy and strength for her work. All of the wide-ranging housework was upon her shoulders. She would go out early in the morning to bring the cows to pasture. She loved that journey. As she returned, she would gather ripe berries to bring to her children, including wild strawberries, which ripened early. In the meantime, she turned her eye to a variety of wildflowers. She loved even the most modest flower. These flowers, along with the flowers that she grew in the garden at the side of our house, would be arranged in arrangements of various shapes. In our days, there are courses for flower arrangements. Our reverend Mother knew everything with her natural sense, and was no less proficient than the professionals of our generation. Aside from cows, we also had horses in the stable, chickens, and ducks in the winter, which were fattened up to provide fat and cracklings (*gribenes*). The vegetable garden also demanded a great deal of dedication and work. Mother was astute, and made a greenhouse for spring vegetables. The beds were covered with closed glass panes of the same type that were used in winter for the double windows that kept the house warm. Thanks to Mother, we had radishes, green onions, and cucumbers before their normal season. However, how much work and toil did Mother invest I this! Bread, challahs, biscuits, cakes, and everything else were baked by Mother in large quantities. What hard work this was! She had to light the oven, spend hours afterward cleaning it from the ashes and embers, and craft large loaves of bread with a faithful hand in such a way that one loaf looked exactly like the next. The baking took about three hours. In addition to the regular bread, mother would bake special bread -- challahs in boiling water -- which had a unique taste. The loaves were smaller, and their aroma came from the cumin and the fennel that were sprinkled upon them liberally. This bread was Mother's little secret. Today we call it a "patent".

All of these efforts succeeded exceptionally well for her, for she put a great deal of love and diligence into her work. In the summer, when the fruit began to fall from the trees, we would gather them, and mother would cut the pears and apples into small slices and put them to dry in the oven after the bread was removed. These dried fruits would then serve us through the winter as compote, or Mother would make them into a type of drink called "Kwass". We would drink it when it was still hot, and then later when it was cold, and we could never have enough of it. The taste was splendid. I never tasted such a tasty drink again, despite the many drinks with fancy names that are found in the stores. Mother was an exceptionally good cook. Her dishes and tasty foods earned her fame. Her handmade cereal and noodles were complete in their outer form, as if made by machine. How she knew how to do this -- only G-d knows.

Toil and Efforts -- and Enjoyment

Even the drawing of water from the well was fraught with a great deal of toil. The well was indeed in the yard opposite the kitchen windows, but it was very deep. One had to turn the handle manually for a long time until the chain with the bucket reached the bottom of the well and came up again. We required a great deal of water for our large house, and especially for the horses, cows, and other living "inventory" that required a great deal of water. During the cold, winter nights, when the area around the well was still frozen and the ice reached the height of the well itself, Mother would toil to draw endless bucketfuls and carry them to the stable and the barn. I would stand next to her at times and light her way with a flashlight. For me, even this small work was toil, for it took a long time, and going out from a heated house to stand in the freezing cold was difficult for me. I was always astonished that this work was not disparaged by Mother, and her spirit did not waver and she did not complain from the first bucket until the last one. What type of patience did she have! She accepted everything with a cheerful face. During her few free hours, she would embroider, occupy herself with other fine handiwork, sew, and mend. She taught herself how to do everything. I recall that when there was a clothing shortage during the First World War, and the children grew out of their clothes, mother did not hesitate. She removed the furniture covers in the salon, which were made of white linen with red, stiff, curled decorations, and sewed shirts for the children. She sewed warm covers for the shoulders and warm kerchiefs for the head from all types of material that was in the house.

[Page 64]

Mother especially loved her small flower garden opposite the windows of the house. The arrangements were professionally crafted, covering the other side of the well with a blaze of colors. Every section of earth was worked with a simple hoe, and every arrangement was different from the others. All types of flowers grew and flourished there. Every species had its own place, and one type was not mixed in with the other. All of them joined together to form a magic carpet. This was expert workmanship! There were no seeds for planting available for purchase in Kaplice, let alone the type that Mother needed for her creations. She did not hesitate to go to a distant village in order to obtain the type of seeds that she wished to plant in her garden. Her voice was sweet and clear. She would sing a great deal during her work, and loved all types of song and melodies. One of our teachers, a lad from Vilna, also knew how to play a violin. Mother loved to listen to his playing, and her soul would weaken from the sweetness. Finally, she also tried to play the violin with the assistance and guidance of the teacher. The tune that she succeeded in playing was, of course, "Hatikva". Our first teacher visited the Yiddish theater during his vacation and saw Goldfaden's "Hamechashefa". When he returned, he told about the wonders and miracles that he had seen in that play. He offered to perform it before us. I recall that night as if it were today. Father and the children were already sleeping. The teacher, mother, one neighbor and I participated. We sat down together in the narrow kitchen as he performed for us in accordance with his G-d given talents. He jumped, ran, and sang the known tunes. Mother's face was filled with happiness and joy. She did not miss even one of his movements. She meditated on this for many days, and her enjoyment did not diminish.

Aside from the routine work, mother had a store in the second wing of the house. She had owned this store even before her marriage. Father did everything he could to liquidate the store, but Mother did not agree. In general, the store was closed, but when a customer came to house, mother took the big key and went with the purchaser to fill his wishes, which was no small matter. During the long winter nights, Mother would occupy herself with plucking duck feathers for pillows and blankets. Of course, everyone helped her, especially Grandmother, her mother, who lived with us throughout her life. This was the coffeehouse, the cocktail party of today's times. Even the neighbors were would join together, and the conversation would flow. Jokes and pleasantness would fill the time. Mother was loved by everyone, even by the gentile population. When Mother would come across a drunk who was causing a disturbance on their holidays, she would quiet him down with pleasant words. She educated her children in pleasantness and uprightness, and especially desired that the children would study, without concern that they would not be able to help in the house.

When the teachers were no longer sufficient for the older students, they would be sent to Jonava and Wilkomir to continue their studies. Finally, after the First World War, they were sent to the Hebrew gymnasium in Kovno. She was very proud and happy about this.

Our Experience During the War

The First World War broke out in 1914. We children did not understand much about the tribulations that were taking place. On the contrary, in our eyes, this war brought changes and new matters in life. At the beginning of the war, The Germans expelled the Jews from the fortified city of Kovno, and the Jews spread in all directions. We also got visitors -- two aunts, sisters of Mother, came to us until the wrath would subside. The aunts came along with their large families, including children of our age. Aside from this, many Jewish families who lived in nearby villages where the Germans had already begun to invade began to stream to Kaplice as a waystation.

[Page 65]

Some of them lived in Kaplice during that time. Some moved on and continued their journeys into the vast expanse of Russia. There was confusion and tumult. However, we children felt only the joy of life. We gained new friends. New games that we had not known until that time interested us greatly. We were very happy. Our parents did not think the same way.

I recall a large fire in a nearby village that covered the evening skies of Kaplice with a mist. In the train station of that town, father owned a warehouse for treated lumber that was to be sent abroad. The Germans set it on fire, and everything was destroyed. Mother, Father and Grandmother were broken, agitated and fell into endless despair. However, we did not understand this exactly, or perhaps we were not given the facts so as not to upset our high spirits. After about a year, we too were expelled to the district of Vilna. Even there, we were not as despondent as the adults in the family. All of these new experiences, such as traveling in wagons hitched to horses -- six wagons as I recall, with all of the family members including Father's parents, and one aunt and her family -- were happy and interesting experiences to us. Their impression was very great. At first we lived in a wood bunker of a forest guard in the district of Vilna that was owned by our parents. However, after some time, we were deported from there as well, and we moved to the nearby town of Galon. Once again we packed up and hitched up the horses. It was joy and pleasure for us. Relative to Kaplice, there were many Jews in the town of Galon. There, we found many children of our age, and the joy was great for us children. We endured this "exile" with great ease.

When the Germans conquered our place of residence, and advanced further toward the capital of Vilna, we returned, with our youths and children, to Kaplice our birthplace. However, the problem was as follows: Kaplice had lost its charm in the eyes of us children, for we had already seen "the world". Our horizons had broadened, and we had grown up in the interim. The town had almost been completely liquidated. Some of the families had moved to Russia -- some died in exile, and others had not yet returned. Some of the young people had begun to immigrate to America and other places in the world. It was difficult to constitute a *minyan* for the synagogue. Great hunger pervaded in Vilna after it was conquered. People began to wander throughout Lithuania to search for food. Many refugees thereby came to Kaplice, and then wandered further. When these refugees joined the worshippers, we were able to arrange public worship. In the meantime, the studies of the children suffered. There were no children of school age aside from us. The older children were sent to study in the nearby cities. Our parents began to think seriously about leaving Kaplice. It was difficult for them, and they deliberated over the matter a great deal, especially Mother. However, at that time Father had a share in a match factory in Jonava, and he spent a great deal of time in travel back and forth. The three older children were already in the gymnasium of Kovno or were preparing to enter there, so it was no longer worthwhile to maintain a teacher for the two younger ones only.

We Move to the "City" of Jonava

In 1922, the house and all of its contents were finally sold, with the exception of the synagogue that was transferred to the Jewish community of Wilkomir along with one Torah scroll. The two others were returned to the families that had donated them: one to Father's family and one to Mother's family. With a broken heart, Mother took leave of the place that she had loved so much, especially from the bosom of nature that had been her lot throughout all the years of her life. She had to suddenly get used to a new life, with no garden around the house, no flower garden opposite the windows, and no forests growing on all sides. With the passage of time, she solved the problem of a garden in a miniature fashion. Mother succeeded in growing splendid plants and all type of aromatic flowers and even vegetables such as tomatoes, onions, and radishes grew in crates of earth on the small area of our porch. This was a "symbol" of what there was in the past. Slowly, we became absorbed into the new life of Jonava. Father of blessed memory struck roots very easily there. He found a broad arena for his Zionist activities in this large community, and gave of his energy to all types of communal affairs. He became the *gabbai* of the synagogue and conducted its financial matters. He was always bent over some sort of accounting ledger. He was also active in the public bank, and he served as its chairman for several years. He devoted the best of his energies to the building of the Land of Israel. He was the chairman of the general Zionist organization, the Keren HaYesod and the Keren Kayemet. He was a delegate to all types of conventions and meetings, and would often travel to the national center in Kovno. He slowly limited his business activities, and was no longer involved in the ways that he was in former years. His business dealings in Jonava were local. He was a partner in "Oran" match factory and in the "Kemach" factory. He had more time for communal affairs. However, no change took place in his pre-dawn studies. He would continue to study with the old melody, and all members of the household would listen to this with bated breath, and with the hope that this would only continue and continue.

[Page 66]
A Visit that Did Not Go Well

Most of the daughters had married in the interim, and everything continued calmly -- however, as is known, this was not to last. In 1935, Father finally decided to travel to the Land of Israel as a tourist. The Maccabia was taking place in the Land. He was accompanied by a nephew as he finally traveled to see the Land that he pined for all the days of his life, and which was the pinnacle of his dreams. He had a brother and other relatives in the Land, and he already owned some land. He set out to the Land with an exalted spirit. He liked the Land, of course, and traveled to all sorts of places. However, his luck turned sour, and there were two week-long heat waves that year in the Land. The conditions in his brother's house were very primitive in those days. There was no refrigerator, the water that came in from the pipes that rested on the ground was hot, and it was even impossible to take a cold shower. Father suffered very much, and his strength faded. The travels tired him, and he did not find rest in his brother's home when he returned. The mites and other insects vexed him greatly. In frustration he decided to return to Lithuania. He returned disappointed and full of bitterness. He would say that the spies did not exaggerate when they said that it is "a land that consumes its inhabitants"[2]. He further continued his activities for the Land with love. He would constantly repeat, "My children will get lost there if they go. They are so delicate and weak, how could they get used to so difficult a climate?"

Were it not for this unfortunate incident of his unsuccessful visit to the Land, all of his children, as well as Mother and himself would all be here. However, fate did not have it thus. Were he to have had the ability to divine the future and foresee the bitter fate that awaited his 'delicate' children and his wife in the frozen wasteland of Siberia, without anything, and with physical and spiritual tribulations -- he would certainly have hastened them all to make *aliya* to the Land. But who is wise, and who can know?

Fate Did Not Skip Us

In the meantime the cruel world events of the Second World War did not skip over Lithuania and Jonava. The Russians ruled over Lithuania and took revenge against their opponents with a strong hand. Deportations and expulsions to Asiatic Russia began, to a place of darkness and the shadow of death. To our sorrow, Father was not exiled, since he was sick at that time when they brought the rest of the members of the household to the train station to begin their wandering in the breadths of Russia. Mother's fate was better, for she was deported along with some of her children, and she was reunited with others during the time in Russia. Thanks to our wonderful Mother, her character, activities, and flowing energy, some of the sting of exile was removed. In a situation of great want and with the difficulties of nature, she was the pillar of support for her children. She assisted them with advice and with physical work. She encouraged and comforted them, so that their spirit would not fall. G-d only knows from where she drew such strength. Thanks to her, all of them maintained their stand during the darkest years of their lives.

Father was imprisoned in the Kovno ghetto, without any relatives aside from one son-in-law. He endured three terrible years. However, as I knew him at that time and always, he did not abandon his learning even there. Perhaps this helped him somewhat during those difficult times, and sweetened the bitter fate that came to him. What did he think about when he had no information about any of those who were so dear to him?

From the Kovno ghetto, he was transferred to the Stutthof Concentration Camp in Germany. The rest of the elderly, ill, and weakened survivors in that infamous concentration camp were sent directly to the furnaces, and Father was among them. I had two regards from him from people who saw him in that concentration camp while he was still alive. A good, faithful friend told me that he had chatted with Father in that camp. Father seemingly knew the fate that awaited him, but he did not speak at all about any physical matters, but rather about lofty issues. He held a small Bible in his hands as a small remnant from all that he has, and a faithful souvenir of his life.

The Burstein Family

The Survivors of the Family Get Back Together

My family and I were saved from the talons of the enemy while there was still time, even before the Russian invasion of Lithuania. One month after the outbreak of the Second World War, on the eve of *Sukkot*, 1939, we left our house -- my husband, I and our two young daughters -- leaving everything behind except for the four suitcases that we took with us. The papers had already been prepared, and we made *aliya* to the Land after much wandering.

After I got in contact with Mother and the family in Siberia, a constant exchange of letters ensued. When the time came we decided to send packages to support them, and of course also the needed papers to bring them to the Land. My luck was bad, and I was not able to take Mother out under any circumstances, despite her old age and her strong desire for the Land to be her final resting place. I only succeeded in traveling to Russia for a trip, and visiting mother and the rest of the family for a five day visit.

This was a heartbreaking visit, that is impossible to describe. Mother passed away at an old age approximately one year later. The worshippers at the synagogue that she used to attend when she was still healthy eulogized her. They said, "She was like her name -- Eidel, refined -- she was indeed like that."

About one year later I succeeded in bringing my only brother to Israel, and about three months later, my youngest sister. Now my family is all in the Land.

[Page 68]

Friday in my Town
by Dov Blumberg of Capetown
Translated by Jerrold Landau

Dov Blumberg

The Jew singles out Friday
And honors it more than the other days of the week.
This town and its Jewish residents,
From young to old, testify to this.
In the windows of the houses, the candles were already lit.
The fire in the oven was burning and flaming.
The dough was already mixed and rising,
The yeast and oil gave it zest.
It puffed up and dropped, puffed up and rose.

Zisla Brechkis washed her hands with the required volume of water

Whispered *Modeh Ani*[3] and recited the blessing upon washing.

Between the blessings and the prayers, she pinched off a piece

And threw it into the oven to burn the challah[4].

The hot, good dough was easily made into a round shape

On the noodle tray, white, clear, and round.

She prepared four intertwined challahs for her husband

For the angelic meal in the evening, which they will sanctify with song;

And ten small, simple challahs

For her five sons who would be around the table.

She boiled and salted the meat, cleaned the chickens.

Everything was prepared and rendered kosher according to the command of the
    generations.

The fish were spread out in a place, waiting their turn,

To be turned within a moment into stuffed fish.

Even the *kugel* was prepared for the next day,

And many dishes in honor of the Sabbath.

For the hand was steady, and the Divine sprit was resting on it,

Even the ministering angels participated in the work.

The market was full, people were hurrying,

Announcing their merchandise and summoning purchases.

Women by the tens were feeling and choosing,

Giving their money lovingly to the sellers;

For what is money with respect to the day --

That is a gift of G-d for the generations, the holy Sabbath.

From every place, men are streaming to the bathhouse,

One is taking his time while the other hurries.

All of them are carrying bundles, and wearing white cloaks.

Hastening to shake off the heavy yoke of the week.

To clean and purify their bodies from their toil.

Even the modest women, with their honorable discreteness.

Hasten to wash their bodies,

Cleansing their skin like the daughters of kings.

The bathhouse took in all who came.

The steam from the heat was dissipating through the cracks in the doors.

Yoske the bathhouse keeper went with an upright posture,

With the leaf brush in his hands, the work of a craftsman.

Raising his fans to a high level;

The heat pinches the skin, the brush beats and brushes,

Both of them groan, the cleaner and the person being cleaned.

[Page 69]

A long and pleasant, ta ta ta.

It was good and pleasant for the Jew in the bathhouse.

Naked, everyone is equal,

And the hot and cold water are so pleasant,

The men and women leave with their faces glowing

The tribulations of the week and the difficulties of livelihood have dissipated from
   their bodies.

In the house, the hot water urn receives them with love.

A sugar cube in the mouth -- and the tea is pleasant and satisfying.

The town is preparing to go to the lit up synagogue.

To greet the face of the Sabbath Queen in holiness and purity.

The maids hasten to the bakers, with pots in their hand,

To place the food for the next day into the oven,

Lipa sweats profusely next to the opening of the oven,

Every pot receives its proper place.

Many blessings fall upon the head of the baker,

If the oven succeeds in its important work.

The town was emptied of farmers and gentiles,

Who participated in selling and purchasing during the day.

The elderly Shmuel was walking with his long coat,

His beard was combed, and he was leaning on his cane,

He tarried at the intersection, and declared:

Jews, the Sabbath is arriving, come to the service of the Creator.

His voice thunders in the ears of the townsfolk.

Urging on the customers to leave the stores.

Indeed, every coin is important, but the Sabbath,

The holy queen, is above everything.

The shutters and the windows close, the street empties.

Twilight falls -- the Sabbath is at the threshold.

The appearance of the houses and the square changes.
Everything is wearing a new robe.
Father and the children, with prayer books in their hands --
Turn toward the synagogue to pray.
The mother, washed and dressed, lights the candles.
The candelabra is sparkling, the table is spread with a white cloth.
The challahs are covered with white covers, a knife between them.
Every corner, every place, participates in the holiness
The additional soul enters everybody[5].
The synagogue is lit up, everything is full of light,
The prayer leader's podium is filled with burning candles.
The light dances and sparkles upon the metal
Upon which the Ten Commandments are engraved.

Everyone is sitting in his set place
Leaning on his staff, and chanting the Song of Songs,
The expression of eternal love to G-d Almighty.

Enthusiastic warmth envelops everyone,
The spirits are calmed, and are communing with the creator.

The cantor is on the podium, with a silk mitre on his head,
He begins, *Lechu Neranena Lashem*,
And the congregation calls out after him, *Naria Letzur Yisheinu.*

The melodious prayer continues, and the honored guest is invited
Come, oh bride; come, oh bride...
The service concludes, people wish each other a good and blessed Sabbath.

The door of the house opens. We approach Mother and kiss her.
A peaceful Sabbath, Mother, a peaceful Sabbath, and we accompany --
Peace be upon you, oh ministering angels, angels of the Almighty.
And we feel that the Divine presence itself and the angels
Are participating in the purity of the holiness and rest.
Father recites *Kiddush* and cuts the challah, and the sons recite *Kiddush*.

The golden fish tastes like the Garden of Eden. And the soup --
Yellow and fat, with long, tasty noodles.

And the round carrots, in circles, and the roasted meat.

Mother is proud of the meal of angels, and with golden tears
Joins the chorus, a woman of valor who can find
And her worth is greater than pearls[6], and indeed
The heart of her husband trusts in her, and she is not lacking in treasure.

The Sabbath hymns - who can forget the pleasant hymns
Tzur Mishelo Achalnu, Barchu Emunai --
Finally the call to recite grace, and the grace after meals and the weekly Torah
    portion.

Father takes out books, and asks questions
About what his children learned during the week.

Everyone is rejoicing, everyone is happy, they are the sons of kings.

Friday and Saturday are partners with G-d;
And his children, the children of Israel, are his holy angels.

[Page 70]

They Are All Dear to Me
by Ala Daltitsky (nee Abramovich) of Tel Aviv
Translated by Jerrold Landau

Ala Daltitsky

My best, happiest and most joyous years -- without worries, without bitterness -- were the years of my childhood and youth, which are always preserved in my mind. Indeed, most of them were years of physical tribulation and meager livelihood, but these were my best years, about which I can talk endlessly. It is most unfortunate that these years passed so quickly, and were followed by years of war and inhuman suffering.

I decided to write some memories about my father's house, which will be for me a form of "*kaddish*" and perpetuation, that will always be found in the Book of Jonava.

My Parents' Home

I grew up along with my family on 118 Kaunas Street in the city of Jonava. My family consisted of my father Avraham Yitzchak, mother Rivka, older brothers Zelig and Velka, and my younger sisters Sara and Beila.

Our house was build of red bricks, and was more or less protected from the fires that frequently afflicted our town.

My Father, who was among the Maskilim of the city, belonged to the general Zionists. He educated his children with a Zionist education and love of Israel. He spoke a free and fluent Hebrew, Russian, and German, and of course Yiddish. I never remember a day when Father went to sleep without reading a Hebrew book before bed.

He had a thick book called "Jesus of Nazareth" which he read frequently, aside from the books of Shalom Aleichem and Mendele Mocher Seforim -- all in Hebrew. We children studied in the Tarbut Hebrew School. I concluded it and received a graduation diploma. My father was always a member of the parents' committee of the school. Aside from this he studied Torah books a great deal, for he had studied in a Yeshiva when he was a lad.

When we would go out in the evening to stroll or to go to the Hashomer Hatzair meeting place, of which I was a member, he would say, "It is better to sit at home and read -- this will give you much more in life."

Even when he was eating, he had to have an open book in front of him. Aside from this, he knew how to and loved to play chess. Every Sabbath afternoon instead of resting, my father would go to the house of Nathan Wolchokovsky to play chess. Yankel Weitzstein, Yosef Perlstein, Yehuda Rashkes and other *Maskilim* who loved to play chess would be there.

[Page 71]

My father would say that the game of chess kept him away from the worries that had gathered up during the week, and that it was good that he was free of them, at least on the Sabbath.

My father was also the *gabbai* of the synagogue. He served in that role for 25 years. Elections for the position of *gabbai* took place every three years, and they never found a person more suitable than my father. The position of *gabbai* caused him all sorts of concerns. The cantor of the synagogue was Alter Zuchovsky, who sang such sweet tunes, that the entire congregation sang together with him. When he was sick once, Father had to travel to search for a cantor for the High Holy Days. It once happened that a cow passed through the courtyard of the synagogue and, you should forgive me, she took care of her needs there. The policeman Labas then appeared and brought Father a "protocol" (ticket) to pay a fine of 15 Lit.

My father did not like the Lithuanian language, and was not interested in learning it. In order to speak with this Labas, he always had to call our neighbor Mordechai Gurwitz, who spoke a fluent Lithuanian. Mordechai would always persuade Labas to cancel the ticket. Aside from this, my father sang nicely. He had a good sense of hearing. It was sufficient for him to hear a tune once for him to be able to sing it. He taught us the songs of Goldfaden from "Shlomit", "Hamechashefa" and "Bar Kochba". He had seen these plays once, and was able to sing them completely. He also knew songs in Hebrew, Russian, and German, as well as modern music. We children inherited these traits from him.

On Sabbath evenings after the meal, Father would begin to sing, and we would help him. Our songs could be heard from near and far, and people would come out of their houses to listen. Father was then very happy, and he beamed with contentment. My brother Wolf sang especially well. He was a splendid tenor. My sister Sara also sang well. Father used to say that were he able to, he would send both of them to Kovno to study voice.

My mother was a quiet, goodhearted woman, who was very concerned with the education of her five children. I remember that she would milk our cow and give every child a half a liter of milk and cake and say, "Go compete among yourselves, who will finish first!" Of course even if we did not want to drink, we drank because of this contest, and Mother made sure that we would not leave even one drop. She took great care that we should be satiated and healthy. Perhaps this helped me to endure the great hunger during the war.

My brother Zelig got married and worked in a match factory.

Zelig prepares matches

As is known, there were many wagon drivers in Jonava. First they would travel on wagons from Jonava to Kovno, a distance of 35 kilometers. In later years, they purchased a bus. The wagon drivers chose Father to do their accounting. The accounting was performed in our house twice a week. The shouts of the bus owners were strong. They suspected each other of being dishonest and not putting all of the money into the pot. However, Father slowly calmed them and explained to them with great wisdom that they must trust each other and not be suspicious. They loved him very much and said, "Avraham-Yitzchak, there is nobody like you! In the company of elders you act like an elder, and with the youths, you are a youth among them."

[Page 72]

During his work with the bus owners, Father learned how to analyze their characters and their weakness. He even composed two songs about them that were sung by the entire city[7]. Father sang his songs to the drivers. They grabbed him and lifted him up due to the great surprise as to the degree that these songs were appropriate for their lives and personalities. These were the Goldman brothers (the *"chalulim"* as we called them), Shmuel Dragatzki and his sons, David Lukman, David Elia Yudelevich and his sons, Asher and Yitzchak Itzikovich, and others.

The Youth Were Exemplary

Sister Beila

Brother Zeev

When we grew up, the physical situation in the house was much better. I worked, sewed blankets, and studied the trade with Beila Yaffa, the wife of Avraham Yaffa. Later I married their son Tzvi. My sister worked as a saleswoman with Kafar, the large textile shop. We arranged large excursions during the summer in the Girialka Forest, which we loved. We would sail boats on the Vylia. In the summer we would swim in the river and enjoy ourselves on its banks. In the winter we would take long walks on it after it froze over and became a sheet of ice.

Aside from Hashomer Hatzair, to which I belonged, I would occupy myself in athletics at Hapoel. I must point out that the Jonava youth was, as is said, "a healthy soul in a healthy body." The youth were exemplary. Every Sabbath eve, we would gather in the Hapoel hall and conduct an Oneg Shabbat celebration. We would sing and recite. All of these events left an impression on me that I will never forget.

However, all did not last long. In 1940, the Russians conquered us, and all of our Zionist parties disappeared from the horizon. The Communist party took their place. This Communist regime only lasted for one year, for in 1941 the Second World War began[8]. The Germans conquered us, and took almost all of the 5,000 Jews who lived in Jonava out to be murdered. Of course, this healthy youth was not able to stand against the enemy with empty hands, so they perished -- these fine athletic youths along with their parents and families.

The Jonava youth who made *aliya* to the Land in 1933-34 spread out -- some in *kibbutzim* and others in the cities. When we Jonavers get together, I feel great closeness and warmth toward each and every one, for they are all dear to me.

[Page 73]

Years that I Will Never Forget
by Aryeh Solsky
Translated by Jerrold Landau

Reb Yehuda Movshowitz   Aryeh Solsky

Our family lived in Jonava for several generations.

We moved to Russia at the beginning of the First World War. We returned to the town in 1920 without Father, who had died of a heart attack due to the threats of the N.K.V.D.

I was then eight years old. My mother was the sole breadwinner. It was very difficult. I began to study in the Tarbut School.

The town was then in a period of flourishing, full of life. Every Jew felt as if it was his private home. Sabbaths are particularly etched in my mind. The youth would then go out to the fields or the villages and enjoy themselves in tranquility.

The majority of the youths dreamed of making aliya to the Land of Israel some day. There were often debates with those youths who were sympathizers of the Soviet Union. Indeed, a significant portion of the youth succeeded in making aliya to the Land prior to the Nazi invasion.

My grandfather Reb Yehuda Movshowitz served as vice mayor for several years. His mastery of the Lithuanian language put him in good stead. He participated in delegations to Kovno and in deliberations with government representatives. My sister Malka and my brother –in-law were active in Tzeirei Tzion and sang in the choir. I did not remain in the town for a long time. I came home for every festival in order to enjoy the atmosphere of the Jewish holiday.

The last time I saw Jonava was during the time of the Nazi occupation. I visited for a few hours. I was able to see the atrocities and terror of the occupation. I begged my sister Malka and her husband Tzvi Opanitzki to move to the Kovno Ghetto, but she preferred to remain where she was. After some time, she was murdered in a forest along with the members of her family.

Our family included three brothers and a sister. My younger brother Yitzchak made aliya in 1934, and died of an illness in 1965. My brother Moshe was a teacher by profession, and moved with his family to Kelme. They were murdered there by the Nazis. My mother and I moved to Kovno. Mother died in the Stutthof Concentarion Camp.

One of the experiences which is especially etched in my mind was the laying of the cornerstone of the university in Jerusalem. This was a festive day for the Zionist youth. We went out on a parade in the streets of the town with waving flags, and we sang the songs of Zion. A small group of Bundist youth gathered in the Yiddish school, stood against the walls and sang: (Dance, enjoy, evil spirits. Today is your time). The cruel fate later afflicted all of them: Zionists along with non-Zionists.

I was liberated from the Nazi yoke by the American army. My brother Yitzchak of blessed memory assisted me in coming to the Land. At first, my absorption was difficult. I finally became acclimatized, established a family, and today I am happy.

I will never forget the years that I spent in Jonava.

[Page 74]

"I am not Owed Payment for that which G-d Granted me"

by Shoshana and Mordechai Rashkes
Translated by Jerrold Landau

Shoshana and Mordechai Rashkes

Jonava -- the city of our birth, where we spent the years of our childhood -- is no longer. It was burned and destroyed. Empty fields with white heaps remain. These are the latticed chimneys that stick out from the ruins as monuments in memory of the martyrs who were murdered by the Lithuanians, may their names and memories be blotted out. Large families, well rooted, poor and rich, merchants and tradesmen -- from most of these families, not even one survivor remains.

Two people survived from our family: Mordechai made aliya as a *chalutz* (pioneer) in 1935, and Shoshana (Reizl) was the only survivor of the seven Lithuanian-German levels of hell.

Our father Reb Yehuda Leib was born in Kovno on the Yarok River and studied in the Telz Yeshiva under Rabbi Eliezer Gordon along with Rabbi Meir Berlin (Bar-Ilan) and Yisrael Rozenson. He was known there as the Kovno genius. He also studied in the Slobodka Yeshiva. He received his rabbinical ordination at the age of 16 from the Gaon Rabbi Yitzchak Elchanan Spector. He was a relative of the Baal Machshavot (Dr. Elyashiv) and Rabbi Izekl Charif.

Already in his youth, he was influenced by the *Haskala* movement and began to study on his own languages and mathematics. There was no mathematical problem that he could not solve. Within a year, he had passed his matriculation exams and became a teacher in Marijampole. He had mastered languages: Russian, Polish, German, Hebrew, Yiddish and Lithuanian.

Later he was influenced by Zionism and headed the group of intelligentsia who founded the Zionist organization in Kovno. From then, he dedicated himself to the ideal of the building of the Land and its life. He went from house to house, affixing the Keren Kayemet boxes to the walls. He helped establish the Avraham Mapu Library. He was sent to the sister of Mapu in Riga in order to get a picture of her brother for the library. Similarly, he was among the founders of the Hebrew schools and the "Di Yiddishe Shtima" (Jewish Voice) daily newspaper. For a time, we received that newspaper without paying.

He was among those who greeted Dr. Binyamin Zeev Herzl in his visit to Vilna. He was also sent to the congress in Basel by the Zionist center.

He was among the founders of the Tarbut School in Jonava, and a member of the parents' council.

Here, in Jonava, he married Fruma Caro, a fourth generation native of Jonava. Her father was nicknamed Ben-Zion Mordechai Reuven's -- for the name of his grandfather and great-grandfather. He received a present for his marriage from the Zionist council -- a rare, original picture of Herzl. The names of all of the members of the center were signed upon it. A wedding invitation was affixed to its broad, black frame that was plated with silver. We would take this picture to Zionist celebrations.

[Page 75]

Our mother was a descendent of Rabbi Yosef Caro, the author of the Shulchan Aruch (Code of Jewish Law). Her father was a large-scale merchant. He occupied himself with the manufacturing and export of tar. An entire village of farmers, Dumsiai, worked for him. They would burn dying trees, extract the oils, fill up barrels, and ship them by train to Koenigsburg, Moscow, and other cities. At that time, Grandfather Ben- Zion had the biggest house in Jonava. It was a brick house with a roof of tin sheet, with a yard, stables, and a store. Grandmother Rachel gave birth to 14 children, but most of them died in their childhood, except for our mother who was the youngest, and her sister Chaya who was married to Reb Herschel Peretz, a scholar and a teacher of children. After the death of the Rabbi of Rockiai, he was offered the position of rabbi of Jonava, but he declined due to modesty. Then Rabbi Silman, who had been his student, was appointed.

Our mother studied with private teachers. She studied Hebrew, Yiddish, Russian and German. She read books in three languages. She was a very intelligent woman. She participated in debates on various topics that took place in our house when Father's friends came to play chess -- especially Itzik Dembo and Yankel Weitzstein. As they played, they would debate problems of the world.

Mother toured various countries before her marriage. She loved theater and opera, and would sing to us pieces of opera that she had seen in Moscow and Vilna. After an eight year romance, Mother married Father around the time of the passing of her father, who did not support the match while he was alive.

Our mother was one of the prettiest girls in the town. She was refined, cultured, and educated. She also excelled in discreet charitable giving.

Before every theatrical performance of the dramatic club, Miriam Nochimovich and Golda Sirek would come to her to choose various dresses from her wardrobe that were appropriate for their roles in the play.

Father was not a merchant, but rather a communal activist. He was a scholarly Jew who often studied books.

During the expulsion in 1915, they moved to Russia. They wandered around from town to town. They tarried in Minsk, and knew hunger and want. When they returned, they found an empty building without windows or doors. Father then founded a cooperative to supply provisions at low prices to refugee families who had returned. He was also one of the founders of the public bank. He was also the representative of Keren Hayesod.

Along with Shmerl Stern, he would read and expound on *Gemara* in the new *Beis Midrash*. He would pose questions to Rabbi Silman, who would require several days of study in order to answer them.

Near the time of the outbreak of the Second World War, he helped establish the Kibbutz *Hachshara* in Jonava. He dreamed and hoped to settle in the land of Israel. After he would send the children, he and Mother would come.

He would walk in a room and recite verses of the Bible by heart. On Sabbaths, during the reading of the weekly portion, he would enter into debates with Yosef Intriligator, the son-in-law of Reb Moshe David Morr, who was a scholar.

Father was very fluent in the Lithuanian language. He would write requests to government institutions on behalf of Jews and gentiles -- to reduce the tax burden or to obtain all types of permits. He would travel to Kovno himself to arrange matters. Everyone depended upon him and trusted his honesty. At first, he did not want to accept payment, except for trip expenses. Later, people began to pay him for his efforts. They realized that he needed it, and it was appropriate. He did not take from everyone, just from those who could afford.

Once, a gentile asked him:

"You invest so much effort in this, and receive such a small payment -- only one Lit."
Father answered:

"Even that I do not need to take. I am not owed payment for the knowledge with which G-d graced me."

The gentile shrugged his shoulders.

[Page 76]

Jews and gentiles owed him a debt of gratitude. When the policeman wrote a "protocol"[9], they would come to Father. He would send a message to the police officer to attempt to have the fine canceled. (The fine at that time was 15 Lit, a reasonably significant sum in those days.)

Once Shima Meir the butcher came running to us with tears in his eyes.

"Woe, Reb Yudel, help please! The policeman Labas wrote me a protocol because he found a cigarette butt next to the sidewalk."

Father got up from the table in the middle of his meal, hurried to the Pristov (police supervisor), and proved to him with intelligence and clear logic that the fine must be canceled. That is indeed what took place. Shima Meir wished to pay him for his efforts, but Father refused to accept anything. Shima Meir pleaded:

"How can I express my thanks to you?"

Father replied:

"Go home, and buy 'good things' for your grandchildren."

Thus was our Father: A righteous intercessor for the Jews of the town, who never refused to help a gentile. Indeed, he was loved by everyone.

All of this did not stand in his stead during the great, terrible disaster that overtook us.

Amalek remains Amalek.

Pour out your wrath upon the gentiles who do not know you.[10]

We lament those who are gone and will not be forgotten.

***

Our brother Ben-Zion was the first in the family to break the tradition of the "philosophy of the middle class" -- to be embarrassed to be a tradesman. Father supported him, but Mother was not pleased with this. He studied upholstering with Motel Horwitz. Later, he became a first class tradesman. He had a workshop and a store in Kovno. He escaped to Russia, and was in the Lithuanian Division. We received news that he fell near Wilkomir.

Seemingly the sister Rachel

Our sister Rachel was an accountant for Kopel Runik and his sons. She married a member of the "proletariat", the carpenter Yitzchak Goldman. He owned two carpentry shops along with his parents and his brothers: in Jonava and in Raseiniai.

May their memories be blessed.

Translator's Footnotes

Referring to G-d's instruction to Moses to view the Land of Israel before his death. Numbers 13:32.

A prayer to be said upon waking in the morning.

The commandment to remove a certain amount of dough 'taking of the challah' from the dough used to bake bread. In Temple times, it was given to the priest. In post Temple times, the portion of dough is burnt.

Tradition has it that a Jew gains an additional soul on the Sabbath.

A quote from Proverbs 31, recited at the Friday night Sabbath meal.

There is a footnote in the text here: See the Yiddish songs that my Father composed in the chapter on folklore.

Referring to the Russian-German part of the war.

This is what we would call a 'ticket'.

Amalek is the first enemy that the Jewish people encountered after the Exodus, and is considered to be the archetypal enemy of the Jewish people. "Pour out your wrath..." is a quotation from the Passover Haggadah.

[Page 77]

Father was to us also Like a Mother
by Frida Khasid
Translated by Yosi and Svetlana Shneider and Hadassa Goldsmith
Edited by Jerrold Landau

{Photo page 38: Uncaptioned. Meir Tzoref.}

A tailor at his work

I was the youngest daughter of Rabbi Yisrael Yakov the teacher. We were two daughters and one son. Our mother died after the deportation from Janova [at the beginning of World War I]. Our best of the best father was also like a mother to us. He watched over us, and did not let us get sad. When our mother died, our father said at the open grave, "Chaya, I pass to your merit half of my Torah (learning), because without you, my precious wife, I would not have been able to devote so much time to my studies."

When he lectured at the synagogue, there were many young people among his students and they were always full of happiness. In the days of Simchas Torah, his students came to take him to the synagogue. On the return, they carried him on their shoulders with candles in their hands and songs on their lips. In the house the tables were covered with white tablecloths and were prepared with honor. Father would sit at the head of the table and say words of Torah. Afterwards there would be songs, and eating and drinking till late in the night.

In the winter and on Shabbos, Father would get up early and learn Torah. He would have a lot of conversations with us, and taught us Torah with derech eretz (means the proper way to behave in this world).

He was a very bright man, he honored all human beings. He was devoted to everyone, and was very humble. There are no words to describe fully the goodness of his heart, and the gentleness of his soul.

My brother Alter was a teacher in the school called Yavneh. He was a bright man, and had a lot of common sense. He particularly excelled as an artist and sculptor. My sister was a good and modest woman.

Father became sick with paralysis. He lay in bed for three years. I took care of him day and night. When he passed away, they carried his casket from one synagogue to another, in which he had disseminated Torah publicly. Many people accompanied him on his final journey and said that he was a good-hearted man and a scholar, with not many like him.

My sister was married to the son of Rabbi Shimon the teacher. They had four sons, knowledgeable in Torah.

My brother Alter was married to the woman Liba Chana, the daughter of Reb Shmuel Stern. They had twins - two beautiful and successful daughters.

All of them were killed by the Reshaim (wicked ones).

[Page 78]

Your Wife is Like a Fruitful Vine…, Your Children are Like Olive Shoots…

by David Rubin (Bnei Brak)[1]
Translated by Jerrold Landau

David Rubin

Grandfather RebYonah David Gordon, the teacher, was searching for a Yeshiva student as a husband for his daughter Fruma. The student should continue to study after the wedding, so what about his livelihood? He who sustains the entire world will also sustain the children. The realities prove that the request of Grandfather was accepted On High.

Reb Nachum, the Yeshiva student, married the daughter of the teacher, and luck shined its face upon the Rubin couple. The family grew to nine children. Grandfather rented a dwelling with a store in the Lomianski house on Kovno Street. Mother opened up a textile store, and the livelihood was sufficient to sustain her large family, which was blessed with Torah and greatness, and was not lacking in anything – a rare situation in the towns of Lithuania.

Our mother ran the business with great wisdom, and gained many customers, primarily gentile. When they would see that the "Rabin" was in her store on the market day, they honored her greatly. Nobody left without purchasing something. The gentiles called Mother "Fanny Nachumova." It was considered a great honor amongst the Russians to be called by the name of the husband.

On Wednesday, the market day, the store was very crowded. When father caught somebody shoplifting, he did not shout at him or publicly embarrass him, but rather spoke to him calmly…

We, the sons, were not in the store that much, because we were in *cheder* all day. When we returned home from our studies, everything, including food, was prepared, for Mother was a woman of valor.

Everyone admitted that success penetrated the Rubin home through the windows and doors.

When we returned from the synagogue on Friday night, Father would bless each of us individually. He would place his hands on the head of each person, give us a kiss, and seat us around the long table in order of age. Father would recite the *Kiddush* over wine, and we would listen with awe and respect to every word that emanated from his mouth. Father looked into Mother's eyes and whispered silently, as if he was saying:

"Your wife is like a fruitful vine in the bosom of your home, your children are like olive shoots surrounding your table."

The fare was delicacies of a king. Even the guests that Father had brought from the synagogue would leave satiated and full of enjoyment. Father would say that one who brings home guests brings blessing into the home.

He got along well with his fellow man. He dedicated his free time to the study of *Gemara*, but he did not make his Torah into a means of earning a livelihood. He was a modest, unpretentious man, careful in his speech to his fellow man, fulfilling both the easy and the difficult commandments, practicing what he preached, and instilling peace in his fellow man. He was a good friend of Rabbis Silman and Ginzberg, of holy blessed memory. If anyone was seeking advice regarding the founding of a vital communal or religious institution, Father would take upon himself the yoke of its maintenance.

[Page 79]

He taught the sons Torah over and above what they learned in school. The education of the daughters was Mother's task. His words were pleasant, fulfilling the adage that the words of the wise are heard calmly.

Father was a lover of Zion. His desire to make *aliya* to the Land of Israel was very great. He desired to settle the Land and work the holy soil. In 1928, he purchased a plot of land near Balfouria through the agency of Agudas Yisroel. In 1938, he sent our brother Zusman as a pioneer, and a good beginning to the realization of his aspiration.

However, bitter fate had something else in mind. Our parents, brothers and sister perished along with the rest of the Holocaust victims.

The Rubin family

Two years before the bitter end and the outbreak of the war, we moved to live in Kovno. We were imprisoned in the Slobodka Ghetto at the time of the Nazi occupation. We worked at various backbreaking tasks. We all lived in one room. Hunger afflicted us day and night.

Our brother Nissan was amongst the first group captured. The group was murdered in the Seventh Fortress near Kovno.

Father, our brothers Chanoch and Yehoshua-Izak, and our sister Rasha, were sent to death camps in Estonia.

Our mother perished in the childrens' aktion in the Shantsy Camp near Kovno. Our brother Berl was murdered by the Nazis in the Dabali Camp.

Today, our brother Zusman is an emissary in the United States. Our sister Sara Minda lives in Tel Aviv, and our sister Yenta lives in Givatayim.

Our dear ones, whose souls are on high! We will never know your final words, and where your bones are buried. Our ears did not hear your cries during your final agony. You passed through the seven fires of hell before you perished. We are pained by your terrible end, and will mourn for you throughout our lives.

We will remember you forever.

Translator's Footnotes

From Psalms 128:3.

[Page 80]

With Torah, Service and Good Deeds
Translated by Jerrold Landau

There was a lane in the center of town whose original name was Samargon. It led to the two large synagogues and continued to the bathhouse. Next to it was a well of cold, clear water, from which not only men, women and children drew sweet, living water. The horses of Reb David Elia, the owner of the wagons, also enjoyed the water. When he returned from a trip to Kovno, he would bring the horses to the well to quench their thirst.

The Bronznik family lived in a wooden house in that place. The head of the family, Reb Henoch Gelgiser, was a scholarly, G-d fearing man who was involved in communal affairs. He was a working man who earned his livelihood through the toil of his hands. He inherited this lifestyle from his father Reb Moshe, who worked during the day and occupied himself with Torah at night.

He would frequently leave his work to involve himself with communal affairs. He frequented the home of Rabbi Chaim Silman of blessed memory.

During his youth, Reb Henoch was among the regular participants of the Torah classes in the home of Grandfather Reb Shimon. This was started by the Vorzhblower Maggid of blessed memory, who would preach fiery sermons from the synagogue pulpits in the town almost every evening. His pleasant, interesting words attracted every heart, and the synagogues were filled to the brim. The Maggid took upon himself the task of disseminating Torah in public, and bringing the working youth near to Judaism, so that they would set times for Torah study. His aim was to eliminate boorishness and ignorance, and instill them with knowledge of Torah and the ways of the world, so that they could be Jews and proper human beings, toward their fellow man and toward Heaven. Thanks to him, the town was blessed with an exalted spirit rather than an empty, materialistic life.

One of the centers of Torah study, which were founded in various places in the city, was the home of Grandfather Reb Shimon the teacher. The youth Henoch Bronznik, who was one of the participants in the lessons, found his favor due to his diligence, desire for Torah, knowledge and understanding, so he chose him as the husband for his daughter Paia (Puah) of blessed memory, who was graced with fine traits. Thus did Henoch continue his life in Torah, service and good deeds.

We arrived in Ukraine during the year of the deportation, 1915. There, mother Paia died in her prime, leaving behind two sons who had been educated in the sprit of a

Torah home. When they returned from Ukraine, they first studied in the Yeshiva in Kovno, and later in the Yeshiva of Telz.

In the year 5686 (1926), the younger son Tovia Ben-Pazi (his current name) made *aliya* to the Land of Israel, with a certificate as a laborer. When he arrived in Jerusalem, he continued his studies in the Merkaz Harav Yeshiva, named for Rabbi Kook. He became involved in business after his marriage, and in the later years, he worked in the office of education and culture of the Jerusalem city hall. He worked in the branch of Torah culture, and directed and centralized initiatives and Torah classes.

His elder brother Reb Yitzchak left for the United States before the ascent of Hitler, may his name be blotted out. He served as a *shochet* (ritual slaughter), *mohel* (circumcisor) and cantor for approximately 40 years. He then made aliya to Israel, and also settled in Jerusalem.

Our younger brother Nachum Meir from our father's second wife Shifra of blessed memory arrived in the United States during his youth. He studied in Yeshiva University, and served as a rabbi in Brooklyn and a lecturer at the Yeshiva.

Our brothers Moshe and Yonah, and our sisters Shoshana and Yetta perished along with the entire family on the bitter, accursed day, may G-d avenge their blood.

Brought to publication by T[ovia]. B[en Pazi].

[Page 81]

The Abridged Code of Jewish Law [The Shulchan Arukh] on the Work Table
by Menachem Levin
Translated by Jerrold Landau

We were five sons and three daughters born to our parents Moshe–Nota the carpenter and Tzvia–Dvora. There was always an Abridged Code of Jewish Law or Mishnah on his carpenter's workbench. Father peered into them at any free moment. He was modest in all of his actions. He would speak little. On the Sabbath, he would not speak any Yiddish, but rather the "Holy Tongue" [1]. He would always conduct himself according to the adage: A person should always speak with terse language. He educated us to refrain from speaking the evil tongue [2], tale bearing, uttering a lie, or taking an oath or a vow.

Our grandfather Rabbi Zeev HaLevi Levin did not serve in the rabbinate. Rather, he owned a shop for metal utensils. When I was three years old, he dressed me in a *tallis katan* [3] and put a *kippa* [skullcap] upon my head. After he taught me to recite *Modeh Ani* [4] and other blessings every morning, he put his hands upon my heads and blessed me:

You will grow and grow

You will desire to learn in *cheder*

And you will stand under the <u>*chupa*</u> [marriage canopy].

Mother would tell us that Father was taken to the army right after their wedding. He served the Czar for five years, and throughout that time, he never ate anything non–kosher. His sustenance was bread and water. When he returned from the army, he began to build his house – part of it as a residence and part as a carpenter shop. The livelihood was meager, but Mother made efforts to ensure that no necessities were missing from the house.

Our parents' desire that their children would become scholars was only realized partially: Yitzchak–Reuven and Chaim–Yaakov studied at the Slabodka Yeshiva.

The Levin family

I was 12 when Father died from an ear infection, because there was no certified physician in Yanova at that time. When Mother sensed that Father had stopped breathing, she placed a feather near his nose in order to verify whether he was still breathing. When she realized that he was no longer alive, she did not scream or shout. She only groaned and uttered, "It is a decree from Heaven, blessed is the true judge."

[Page 82]

From that time, Mother bore a double burden: conducting the business and tending to her children.

Our home was always open to guests and people in need of advice, help, and charity.

My oldest sister Esther immigrated to the United States when she was still a girl, as did my sister Batya–Elka, who had served as a clerk for Pogirsky. She made *aliya* in 1965, but died in 1969 after a difficult illness. In her eulogy, her donations to the poor and dedication to institutions such as the old age home and others were noted.

My brother Yitzchak–Reuven, who married the daughter of Rabbi Tzvi Pass of Kelm, was an expert in Bible and grammar. He knew foreign languages, and served as a Torah reader. Thanks to this, the Yerushalmi – the son–in–law of Rabbi Moshe Mordechai Epstein of Slabodka [5] – selected him to prepare his books for print.

My brother Chaim–Reuven, who was nicknamed Chaim Yanover in Slabodka, served as a teacher in various places for many years. He taught a class in Tiferes Bachurim.

My brother Shalom–Meir worked in our carpentry shop, and immigrated to Cuba in 1929. From there, he moved to the United States. He was active in Young Israel, and was a philanthropist and charitable man. He visited Israel in 1964 and hoped to live there, but he died in 1965 after a difficult illness.

My sister Chaya–Rivka worked as a clerk for Granovich.

My brother Nachum–Mordechai married Ethel Farber from Breizer Street.

All of them stand before my eyes. I never forgot them and never will forget them. All of my memories of them are from the few years – mostly bad and painful – years that passed as a passing shadow and gusting wind.

Translator's Footnotes

Hebrew.

Lashon Hara – referring to derogatory speech, slander, or any other form of improper language.

The small *tallis* worn under or atop the clothing, as opposed to the large prayer shawl worn during prayers.

The brief prayer recited immediately upon arising from sleep. See http://www.chabad.org/library/article_cdo/aid/623937/jewish/Modeh–Ani.htm

See http://en.wikipedia.org/wiki/Moshe_Mordechai_Epstein

Links in the Chain of Generations *
by Avshalom Tzoref (Goldschmidt) of Kibbuz Ginosar, Israel
Translated by Daniella Thompson

…Avraham, the youngest brother in the Tzoref family,
Was the fifth born…
He was born the fifth–and four came after him,
And the eldest, Malka–the comely and black.[1]
Five were annihilated in the *Shoah*–with Ma and Pa.
He remained the youngest–and I the eldest.

As the family elder at Dalia's wedding
I have the honor of presenting our family tree.
To present their figures to the *shushbinim*[2] and entourage,
And to call their memory to our family's mind.

First to honor–Mother and Father.
In life as in death, united by fate.
In their memory, both *yad* and *shem* were erected here,
A family grew secure and without fear.

Mother Sara–her beauty unmarred by her burden of care.
A *Yiddishe Mame*, as if copied from the song;
How she bore and raised a brood of nine children
With *Shir Ha'Ma'alot*[3] pasted on the wall.

Reading and writing she did not know,
But she kept the *Mitzvot* like a learned woman;
Tzenah Ur'enah[4] had to be read to her;
She was purer and more upright than any rabbi's wife.

Chaim–Shimon, our father, son of Avraham the potter–
An honest and upright man,
Worships his God to his utmost with honor;
Earned his bread in the sweat of his brow.

[Page 83]

The Goldshmid[5] family: The parents, Chaim–Shimon and Sara, the eldest son
Avshalom (of Kibbutz Ginosar), the daughter Malka

Honest laborer, working with bricks and mortar,
Builds stoves, a construction tradesman.
He kept the 613 *mitzvot* scrupulously,
Was free of all sin–and of all possessions.

(In my childhood I didn't grow up in my parents' lap,
I left home before having reached the age of *mitzvot*.
Of all my teachers, from whom I have learned,
My parents appear as my models of virtue.)

Grandmother Feiga, industrious woman,
Watches over her household and is all–powerful.
She toils from dawn and labors till night;
I don't recall that she ever fell ill.

She raised her grandsons as a mother would her offspring;
A face lined with the care of rearing and a wrinkle of contentment.

My palate still guards the taste of her delicacies–
Barrels of pickles, Passover wine, and jars of preserves.

"Yosse der Schneider"–Grandpa Yosef the tailor
Sews furs and garments for the villages' peasants;
A poor and modest Jew who's content with but little,
Equally unschooled in letters and books.

Tall of stature, solid, with golden hands;
He pours out his wrath over God and Man.
Sews his grandchildren's clothes with concealed affection,
Cultivates his garden as a peasant does his soil.
Simple mind, healthy reasoning–and wonderfully wise;
Talks to himself as if Grandma had asked.
He would lecture aloud while sewing and mending,
And his words still resonate like *kohelet*[6] translated.

And with them, a gallery of figures whose names I omitted;
They are bundled below, in words and in phrases;
Big ones and smaller ones that I haven't known–
May the living be singled out for a long life.

A Jewish family in a typical township–
Like pictures in a painting and figures in books;

Under the yoke of kingdoms–Lithuanian and Russian–
It expanded and yearned for freedom from oppression.

A house poor and crowded–the lowest in the quarter,
A dirt floor and a ceiling that touches the head;
But the *sh'chinah* dwelt there and stood high and mighty,
There they waited for the *mashiach*, waited in vain.

Cord braiders, blacksmiths, bricklayers,
Tailors bent over their sewing machines,
Orthodox Jews–and revolutionary fanatics,
Taliths and flags–faith and heresy.

Honest laborers in a productive family,
Rabbis and moguls–none of them for show.
This I'll tell my sons objectively–
It's a healthy root and a source of pride.

Geographically remote are these figures,
In substance and bonds they're as far as the stars.
Therefore I sketched here only a lifeline
That stretches like a bridge between generations.

A linking bridge, like the one from roots to canopy,
Unseen veins that nourish the fruit on the branch;
A bridge of connections like links in a chain–
Links that are sons, grandsons, and great–grandsons.

* From the congratulatory address of Avshalom Tzoref to Dalia, the daughter of his brother, Avraham Tzoref, formerly Goldschmidt, on the day of her marriage to her intended, Shmulik Gringold. It was recited at the wedding celebration in Kibbutz Lohamei HaGeta'ot [Ghetto Fighters Kibbutz], where they were born.

Translator's Footnotes

"Comely and black" is a reference to Shir Ha'shirim (Song of Songs), stanza 5: "I am black but comely, O daughters of Jerusalem! Like the tents of Kedar, like the curtains of Solomon."

Best men.

Psalm 126.

A Torah–based Yiddish book, written for women by Yaacov ben Yitzchak Ashkenazi in 1616.

The Hebrew caption spells the name Goldshmid, although Avshalom Tzoref consistently spells the family name Goldschmidt.

Ecclesiastes.

[Page 84]

In my Parents' Home
by Dr. Shimon Zak
Translated by Jerrold Landau

Of my mother's parents, I only remember Grandfather Chaikl, (incidentally, his mother died in 1914 at the age of 96). Grandfather Chaikl was observant of the commandments; however, like most of the Jews of Lithuania, he was not a zealot. His grocery store in the market square was always organized with exactness and good taste. Among other things, he sold all types of spices and medical herbs. The farmers of the region believed in their effectiveness more than medicine from the pharmacy.

I knew my father's parents well. Grandfather Avraham was a native of the city of nearby Shaty and the son of its rabbi. He had a splendid face and solid body. He was a scholar as well as a *Maskil*. He spoke calmly and intelligently, and his conversation was spiced with humor. I was his oldest grandson, and most connected to him. He would explain to me things that he had reading a book or newspaper. He would take me to the synagogue on the weekdays when Father did not worship, and, to differentiate, also to the bathhouse.

Grandmother Riva-Yehudit was popular and loved by all members of the family. Her world was built upon fear of Heaven and good deeds. She would come early to the synagogue services on weekdays, just as on festivals. What she missed in her prayers, she would make up at home or even in the store. Her pockets were always filled with sweets, which she would distribute among her grandchildren or other children in the area. Through the goodness of her heart, she also fulfilled the commandments of giving charity discreetly and visiting the sick. She was expert at her prayers, blessings and customs. Her expertise was recognized among those who came to the women's gallery.

Father and Mother were born and raised in Jonava. The families lived in close proximity to each other. The children grew up, played and studied together. They fell deeply in love at a young age, and with the passage of time, they proudly expressed their tokens of love. Father – on the embroidered Tefilin bag that he received from Mother at his Bar Mitzvah, and Mother with the gold ring that Father bought her as a present with the first money he earned.

Mother was a pretty woman, filled with the wisdom of life, natural refinement and insight. Like most of the Jewish women of Lithuania, she was a woman of valor who always assisted Father at his work. However, along with this she found time to be a dedicated and loving Mother. We children revered her. I was always wondering from whence flowed the wellsprings of her wisdom, since she never studied in an organized school and all of her wisdom came to her from private teachers who were not among the best in the town.

As I explained, Father was a talented and well-educated from his youth. He was noted for his excellent memory. Despite the economic straits that prevailed in his family of many children, he was able to learn with the best teachers in town. He also studied in the Yeshiva of Slobodka for a period of time, and he remembered pages of *Gemara* by heart throughout the years. He read a great deal from his youth, and was an avid reader throughout his entire life. He mastered the fundamentals of the Hebrew Language, and also composed humorous poems as well as love poems. He studied Russian and German through his own powers and searched for a way out from the poor life of the town. For a period of time, he worked as a clerk on the estate of his grandfather's sister, Miriam Kamber in the region of Raseiniai. After some time, he lived for a time in Warsaw with his relative and friend Yosef Lichtenstein of Gelvonai. When they returned to Lithuania after both had started their families, they opened fancy good stores (galentaria) in partnership, one in Jonava and the second in Kedainiai.

Father did well at business due to his business acumen, uprightness, decency and good name. He also received the sole agency for the districts of Kovno, Vilna, Suwalki and Grodno from a German firm that manufactured dyes for textiles.

My three sisters and I were raised in an atmosphere of love and mutual understanding. We received a liberal free education. I began to study in the modern *cheder* that had been opened at that time in Jonava under the direction of the teacher Shaul Keidianski. My two older sisters studied in the Jewish-Russian school. My younger sister Mina, who perished in the Holocaust, was not yet of school age at that time. Our parents were immersed in their business, but they always found time to dedicate time to our education and to care for us.

In the homes and families there were often Jewish maids who came for the most part from the villages and towns in the region. The relationship to them was patriarchal, and they were like members of the family. I remember several of them positively.

[Page 85]

They spent most of their time with us. From their mouths we heard legends, stories and songs, and they drew us close to the popular folklore and the lives of the masses of workers.

With the expulsion of the Jews in the year 1915, the family traveled to the city of Aleksandrovsk (today Zaporozha) in Ukraine. Mother had an uncle there. We got used to the new conditions with the passage of time.

Father started to conduct business and was successful, as usual. Mother helped him. We studied in Russian schools. Father ensured that my elder sister Sara (today in Moscow) and I continue with our Hebrew studies that we had already started in Lithuania. He also made sure that we obtained an advanced general education, as well as progressive Zionist education.

At the end of 1921, we returned from starving Russia to the bountiful land of independent Lithuania. In the meantime, my two older sisters had gotten married to Jews from Russia, and remained there.

We were happy to meet our friends and relatives once again. In Lithuania, a golden era prevailed on the Jewish street: national-cultural autonomy with schools and organized communities. Father once again became involved in business, and succeeded this time as well. I began to study in the Hebrew Real Gymnasium of Kovno. I drew close to the Zionist workers' movement while I was still a student at the gymnasium. I studied for two years in the faculty of medicine at the Lithuanian university.

I continued my studies in France. I returned to Lithuania in 1932 after concluding my studies in Strasbourg. I prepared to make *aliya* to the Land. In Jonava, as in every place in Lithuania, wide-branched Zionist activity took place. Chapters of all of the parties existed there. Sports and literary groups existed, as well as schools of all streams. Wide-branched communal and cultural activity took place, which attracted hundreds of male and female youths. I took part in all of these activities. I lectured, studied Hebrew in the chapter of Hechalutz and Haoved, and participated in conventions. Before I made *aliya*, I was sent by the Hechalutz center to set up a small hospital in Siauliai, and I was appointed as a traveling consulting physician for the *Hachshara* locations in the region. I made *aliya* in 1934.

News of Holocaust and the annihilation reached me as I was serving as a physician in the British Army in Sudan. The British did not believe this news and thought that it was wartime propaganda against the enemy. For some time, I too refused to believe what was taking place, until believable and verifiable information reached me from the Land.

Everything that happened to European Jewry, including the Jews of our town Jonava, will remain with each of us as an indelible memory. With deep agony, we bear the pain that can never be expressed.

May the memory of the pure, dear martyrs be blessed. May the remembrance of their suffering, as well as their deaths and circumstances of their deaths, remain with us forever!

Moshe and Feiga Zak

[Page 86]

Grandfather is also Remembered for the Good

by Tikva Katz, Givataim
Translated by Jerrold Landau

Reb Alter Mottel lay sick on his bed…
He lay down and read the ledgers of the names of the children
Whom he had circumcised.

Sh. Y. Agnon from "Tmol Shilshom" (Yesterday and Before)

My grandfather, Moshe Yitzchak Stern, was a mohel (ritual circumciser) in Jonava. He was famous for his work. People invited him to all the towns of the area. These travels took much time from him. He did everything, of course, without intention of receiving recompense. He related to this calling of his with awe and diligence. His instruments were modern and shiny, and the odor of formulin wafted from the case in which they were stored. After every activity, he would take apart the case, and clean and polish the utensils. His young granddaughter (the writer of these lines) stood next to him and watched him with an open mouth.

He was always in good spirits after he circumcised a child. There were delicacies in his pockets that he had taken from the tables for his grandchildren. I stood next to my tall, thin grandfather, full of reverence. His face was broad, with a well groomed, long beard. His brown eyes exuded warmth and wisdom. In my eyes, he was a pillar of physical and spiritual strength. Every Sabbath morning, I ran to the great synagogue where my grandfather worshipped. I would hasten to the Women's gallery, from where I would look at my grandfather, enwrapped in his talis and worshiping with devotion. He stood in the "highest plane" to his grandchildren. I did not move or remove my eyes from him until the end of the service. My grandfather did not return home after services. He was involved in the Chevrat Shas (Talmud Study Group). All the members of the group would gather together for a light meal. My grandfather sat at the head of the table, surrounded by elderly Jews with holy books next to them. They would raise their cups in honor of the Torah, and partake of cakes and desserts. Nobody paid attention to the young girl who was wandering around at their feet, absorbing this spirit (which supported me greatly during all periods of my life).

My grandfather was always surrounded by a group. The elders sat around the table studying a page of Gemara in the Chevrat Shas in the synagogue, and especially in my grandfather's home.

These were days of splendor in the town. It was the calm era prior to the terrible wars that took place later. During that era, it was not only the elders who spent their time with a page of Talmud, but some members of the younger generation would frequent the nearby famous Yeshiva.

My grandfather's son Shmaryahu Stern was a personality in his own right. He was the force behind the construction of the splendid Talmud Torah building. He founded the school and taught the children Gemara. My uncle did not imagine that next to the open window stood the young daughter of his sister, feasting her eyes and ears attentively on everything that took place in the class.

This uncle of mine was the great enthusiastic Zionist of the town. My father, Yonah Pesach Katz, was a prominent Zionist activist. I still have the mandate that my father received as he participated in the congress of all Russian Zionists in Petrograd in 1917.

My uncle had three children: Eliezer (may he live), Aryeh may G-d avenge his blood, and the youngest who was the poet Noach Stern of blessed memory. My cousin Liba Chana was the wife of the artist Alter Kagan. I was bound to all of them with bonds of love and understanding, but my grandfather was to me a symbol and example. I always wished to be like him, to be religious, to occupy myself in mitzvot, etc.

Aside from his honorable image in Torah, and aside from being the renowned mohel of the entire region, my grandfather was also a working man. He invented the secret of preparation of light black beer (malt beer). I see the man wearing simple clothing, bending over a machine, cooking and mixing the beer into small containers.

My grandmother Sheina Chaya sold this beer in her tavern. Her tavern was not similar to the other taverns in the town. Only the old, solid farmers who did not use liquor entered, drank my grandfather's beer and ate the food that my grandmother prepared. The atmosphere was always calm and cordial there. The customers were all friends. At that time, we felt that we had friends among the gentiles.

The well-to-do Jewish women would come every Thursday, with a fine pitcher in each hand. My grandfather would pour his beer for them. It was the custom in Jonava that at the third Sabbath meal (Seuda Shlishit), people would drink the dark beer blended with cream. Everyone loved the drink that was prepared through the blessed and good hands of my grandfather.

One day ill fortunate overtook us. My dear grandfather took ill. He was very ill, at first in his legs, and later in his esophagus. Grandfather was lying in bed, unable to swallow, and talking with difficulty. He lay on his clean bed, with his son Shmaryahu and daughter Ethel tending to him. Ethel neglected her children and did not move from the bed of her father day and night. The young granddaughter ran after her, circled around the bed, and nobody sensed her. All the members of the Talmud study organization visited my ill grandfather. The pages of Gemara rustled, and the debate was in full strength. Grandfather did not speak, but he still remained as the living spirit of the group.

The bitter day arrived when my grandfather sensed that his end was near. He donned his white kittel and prepared himself to recite the confessional prayer. His son and daughter were weeping silently beside him. The young granddaughter was slinking in a corner. The final sunrays of the day were streaming through the open windows. All the members of the Talmud study group stood around…

After Moshe Yitzchak Stern passed away, the evil days began. The First World War broke out. After one year, all of the Jews of the Kovno region were expelled in shame.

Twenty-five more years passed. The face of the city changed, until the great destruction arrived.

[Page 87]

I Loved to go to Grandmother
by Chaya Grabersky (Tel Aviv)
Translated by Jerrold Landau

There was a wooden house on the street that descended to the Vylia. As you would go up a few stairs, you would enter a small grocery store. This was the store of Grandmother Leah. Grandmother loved to conduct business, despite the fact that Grandfather Moshe Shapira had a large carpentry shop in the same house, in which many employees worked.

The large family of 12 people was not short of livelihood. Grandmother also had cows and fowl. There was an abundance of milk and dairy products. Grandmother had her own "Tnuva" dairy[1]. She made cheeses and put them into heart shaped cloths. They were hung in the kitchen until they dried out. Then she would carefully remove them in one piece – many heart shaped cheeses. I would come to help her with the cream. I was then a seven year old girl. Grandmother would give me a wooden stick that was placed into a wooden churn. I would beat the cream with the stick until it turned into butter. There was a vegetable garden in the yard behind the barn.

I loved to go to my grandmother, for I always had something with which to occupy myself there. When we made aliya to the Land in 1925, I missed the place very much, for there I had spent the pleasant early years of my life.

Translator's Footnotes

Tnuva is the name of the Israeli dairy conglomerate, so I expect that the name here is meant to be descriptive rather than the actual name.

[Page 88]

My Grandfather Reb Mashel

by Baruch Lin (Jalinovich or Ilinevits) [Ramat Gan]
Translated by Jerrold Landau

Baruch Lin

Mashel was known as an unusual man. He was prone to anger and wrath, and he would enter into judgments with his neighbors. This stemmed from his strong character and his inability to tolerate injustice and wrongdoing. In such cases, he would not withhold his sharp tongue from anyone, even if he was important and honorable.

In accordance with the situation in the town, there were many such injustices which we would now look upon with a forgiving smile. For example, with regard to an aliya to the Torah, someone who received the fourth aliya may have felt slighted as he felt that he deserved the third aliya. In the *hakafot of Simchat Torah*, some worshippers would feel insulted if they were honored with the *hakafa* of " *Ozer Dalim*"[1]...

As is known, Jonava was burnt down twice. The city elders knew how to count years from the times of the fires. After each fire, the Jews of Jonava built better and finer houses. The new construction caused border disputes between neighbors. Surveys of the lots did not exist yet. Everything was determined by memory and confirmed by witnesses.

My grandfather was engaged in a legal dispute with two of his neighbors: Reb Avraham Yitzchak the *shochet*, his neighbor on the right side; and Reb Henech Bronznik, his neighbor on the other side. The border adjudications lasted for years. The claims were peculiar. They would dispute and recall childhood caprices of each person. My grandfather nicknamed Henech "Strajkenik", meaning the striker, for he had participated in strikes and demonstrations against the Czar in 1905.

My grandfather was involved in the wheat business. He was a simple Jew, knowing only how to read the *Siddur* [prayer book]. In the general thought of the householders of his era, he felt that a proper Jew must be a merchant, since the tradesmen had no status in his eyes at all. He took pride in the fact that there were no tradesmen in his family. He had eight brothers - merchants, scholars, and communal activists. None of them served in the army. They either bribed the officials of the Czar or changed their family nanes. Thus, he had family members in Jonava by the name of Goldschmid and Gold, even though he himself was called Shlomovitz. His younger son studied in *Yeshivas*, received his rabbinical ordination, and was appointed to the rabbinate in a town in the district of Bialystok. His daughter, my mother Taiba of blessed memory, married a *Yeshiva* student who was ordained for the rabbinate in the Yeshiva of Volozhin, and who was given a fine dowry by my grandfather. He is my father, Reb Moshe of blessed memory.

The Jews of Jonava took pride in special places. They were proud of their town. A person from outside who settled there was considered an outsider for the rest of his life. My father, a native of Poland, was also considered an outsider, and my family considered its lineage from Mother's side. Therefore, I was called Baruch

{*Unnumbered Photo page between 88-89*}

The Shapira family: Feivka, Feiga, Shimon, and - may they live - Surka and Minaka - who are in Vilna; Yosa Meir Itzkovich, Sheina, Leah and Moshe, Beila and Binyamin Shapira; the children: Chaya, and may he live - Yaakov; Tzvi and Shraga of blessed memory; Chava - may she live long - who lives in Kibbutz Maoz Chaim

Grandmother churning butter

[Page 89]

Seemingly Mashel and another man sitting on steps

Seemingly Mashel. The drawing has the same appearance and pose as the elderly man
on the steps

Taiba Mashel Nechemia's[2]. In contrast with the custom of those days, my grandfather engaged special tutors to teach his daughters to read and write in Yiddish and Russian.

Two pictures hung in his house - of the Vilna Gaon and of Moses Montefiore. He purchased the latter in a special sale, the proceeds of which went to charity.

My grandfather worked hard as a wheat merchant. He would run around a great deal, usually on foot. He would sell seeds to the farmers on credit. After the harvest, he would hurry to the villages to collect the debts. Therefore, he was known as a fast walker, and nicknamed "Mashel the Kanke" (pony). The symbol of speed in those days was the wagon hitched to a horse that would travel on rails in the outskirts of Kovno. At that time there was a joke that Mashel would say to his wife, "Put the soup on table, and before it gets cold, I will go to Rimkes (a distance of about four kilometers).

This was a village of Strobars, of the old religion, who fled from Russia due to the Czarist persecutions and settled in the vicinity of the town. Every Wednesday, during the winter market days, young members of this sect would come from near and far, walk through the streets, travel in winter wagons, and choose their mates. This was called the Bulbar. One of their young women worked in our house as a maid. Mother would lend her furs to her so that she too could go to the Bulbar.

Like the majority of the Jews of Jonava who were known as manly, Father was also a healthy man. When he was over 80, he still was engaged in the wheat business and dragged sacks like a young man.

He was indifferent to Zionism. He did not understand pioneering. He could not tolerate boys and girls going out to work like gentiles. During a business debate with Reb Yona Katz, who was also a wheat merchant and a relative, he uttered sharply: "I did not send my daughter to weed the gardens." He was referring to Tikva, who made aliya to the Land and was active there. However, when I made aliya to the Land, he bade me farewell in a heartfelt fashion and blessed me.

He died in 1933.

Translator's Footnotes

Lots of religious nuances here. An aliya to the Torah is the honor of being called up to the reading of the public reading of the Torah. The hakafot (circuits) on *Simchat Torah* are the seven circuits made around the synagogue in the evening and again during the day. Different groups of worshippers are honored with carrying the Torah scrolls during the *hakafot*. The hymn for the sixth *hakafa* starts with " *Ozer Dalim hoshia na*" (He who helps the poor, please save), and some people may have felt that being honored with this *hakafa* may imply that they are considered to be poor.

A common form of nickname, with the person being called by the name of his mother, and in this case the grandfather as well, in the possessive form.

[Page 90]

But...
by Dina Rikless (nee Perlstein)
Translated by Jerrold Landau

Chaim and Batya Perlstein

Our home was traditional and very Zionist. Father was about to make *aliya* to the Land more than 80 years ago, when he was only 17 years old, along with his uncle, who made *aliya* at that time. But… on account of the opposition of his parents, he remained in Lithuania and established his household in Jonava.

When the Fund for Jewish Settlement was set up, my parents purchased shares in 1901. These remain in our hands to this day as a souvenir. It was natural that their children learned Hebrew and dreamed from an early age of *aliya* to the Land along with their parents. But the parents did not have sufficient energy to take this step. My brother Shlomo made *aliya* in 1932, as I did with my husband in 1934. Our parents reached us in 1935; but my father got very sick here, and returned alone to Jonava in 1937 with the intention of regaining his strength there and returning to us. But, the borders were closed due to the accursed war, and my dear father remained there and perished in Jonava along with most of its Jewish residents and a large portion of our family. May their memories be a blessing.

My mother Batya Perlstein, of the Tartak family, who was with us, died at the age of 90 in Tel Aviv. But, she was also a victim of the Nazi executioners, for she was not able to forget for one moment the bitter end of her dear ones – her husband Chaim, daughter Hinda, and two grandchildren Eta-Rivkale and Yosef-Hershele, along with the rest of the families.

A poem (see in the section To Hell and Back[1] will testify to her great suffering. Peace to her remains.

Dina Rickliss-Perlstein

Translator's Footnotes

Page 372

[Page 91]

Journeys to the Land

[Page 93]

In the Achva Group
– With the First Pioneers of Lithuania
by Aharon Gazit (Zisla)
Translated by Jerrold Landau

During the era of German occupation of the First World War, when ties were severed with the general Jewish world, and even ties between the cities and towns of Lithuania were difficult due to the laws of German occupation, a Young Zion meeting place was opened in Jonava. My brother Dov Zisla who had returned from his studies in the teacher's seminary of Vilna, and the teacher Joselovich, were among the initiators and activists in the opening of the meeting place.

As far as I recall, it seems to me that Rachel Jonashevich (today Soloveichik), Rachel Mintz (today Ben-Yehuda), my sister Rachel Zisla (Lavie) among the girls; and Baruch Namiot, Dov Blumberg, my cousin Eliahu Opnitzky, and I were among the participants in the meeting place.

In 1917, we began to think that we must become accustomed to physical work, agricultural work in particular, in order to prepare ourselves for *aliya* at the first opportunity.

As a first step, we took upon ourselves to work in the fruit orchard and vegetable garden that belonged to the family of Hinda (Shoham, I believe). We worked in this garden, which was called the Zionist Garden, during all of our free time, and on the Sabbaths. It also served as a place for meeting and mutual gatherings.

At the end of the summer of 1918, we organized an ingathering celebration during the festival of Sukkot to conclude the season. This was before we hatched the plan for the following year. In the winter of 1918/1919, the members Baruch Namiot, Eliahu Opnitzky, and Dov Blumberg were involved in smuggling food from Jonava to Kovno. I utilize the word "smuggling" because such endeavors were forbidden under the occupation statutes. Nevertheless, anyone daring enough became involved in such, since there was no other source of employment for the youth who did not have a specific trade.

On one occasion, the aforementioned members found out that a group of pioneers existed in Kovno, consisting of the best of the eighth grade students of the gymnasium of Dr. Carlebach. These pioneers set two goals for themselves: 1) *aliya* to the Land of Israel, and 2) agricultural preparations until the possibility of *aliya* arises.

The members Baruch, Dov and Eliahu met with them, forged mutual acquaintances, and discussed remaining in contact, both for *hachshara* (preparations) and *aliya*. During that meeting, they learned several songs of the Land of Israel from them, such as "*Ya-Chay-Li-Li Am-Li-Li*," and "*Chushu, Achim, Chushu.*"

During that period, I worked in sewing, which was connected to the hide business of my parents. I recall that I was working late one night, when Baruch Namiot and Eliahu Opnitzky came to me, after they had just returned that evening from Kovno. They told me in secrecy, "Leave your work! We have important, interesting news to tell you." We went outside, and as we were strolling on the street, they told me about their meeting with the pioneers in Kovno. With great emotion, the three of us burst out singing, "*Ya- Chay-Li-Li Am-Li-Li.*" This was an unusual sight in the quiet streets of the outskirts of Jonava at midnight, and more than one door opened up to take a look at the mischievous people who were disturbing the night rest. They were very surprised to discover that the mischief makers were people of their ilk rather than regular troublemakers.

From that time, the contact between us Jonavers and the group of gymnasium students in Kovno was forged. My sister Rachel, who was studying in that class, was among them. We began to seek out a place for agricultural *hachshara* for the summer. In the spring of 1919, an opportunity appeared on the horizon. The Lithuanian Army began to organize itself, and the agronomist Charna, who knew the group of pioneers, served as a sergeant. Since he was an avowed Zionist, he found work for the group in growing vegetables in the large fields next to the army bunkers in Koviatiski near Mariampol, in order to provide vegetables for the army.

The members accepted his offer with joy, and immediately informed us in Jonava about the opportunity for *hachshara*. Without any hesitation, we also gladly accepted their news. Each of us told our parents about what was about to take place.

[Page 94]

After some discussions and arguments, we set out after Passover to join our friends in Kovno to travel to Mariampol. For the entire evening before the journey, we sat in my parents' sewing workshop, as I sewed four large backpacks to pack our personal belongings and clothing.

We should recall that this was at the end of the period of German occupation, and the beginning of the establishment of the Lithuanian government. Until that time, it was forbidden to travel from district to district without a permit from the district representatives. Our appearance in the towns along the way – a group of youths with backpacks, like draftees – aroused questions: for what and to where? The surprise was even greater when they found out that we were not going to the army, but rather, we were pioneers going to *hachshara* in order to prepare for *aliya* to the Land of Israel.

Before that time, the term "*chalutz*" (Zionist pioneer) had yet to be heard; and talk of *aliya* to the Land of Israel, before free movement had been opened up at all, was like a daydream. In any case, we reached Mariampol, and from there, we went to the army bunkers in Koviatiski. There, they had set aside a special wing as our residence. The agronomist Charna found amongst the soldiers an agricultural youth from a village settlement, who served as the army representative as well as our guide in work. We received guns in order to protect the vegetable fields. This gave us the opportunity to practice with weapons in a free manner, which would help us prepare for the tests in the Land.

Our appearance in Mariampol and our involvement in the work aroused great interest among the local youth. In general, Mariampol was a cultural town with a recently founded Hebrew gymnasium. Its youth had definitive Zionist leanings. The news of the group of pioneers nearby aroused great interest. Some of them expressed interest in joining us. Our work area was restricted, so we began to search for additional work areas. We made contact with two Jews who owned farms in nearby Ongrina and Karlina, and our numbers grew. At that time, my sister Rachel came to Mariampol and joined our group.

I must point out the complete cooperation between us and the *chalutzim* of Kovno. Most of them were talented youths, and we were able to learn a great deal from them in development, knowledge, theory and communal dynamics. We influenced them in the areas of Judaism and nationalism. Our member Baruch Namiot of Jonava had grown up in a Hassidic home. His father was a prayer leader with a sweet voice, who read the Torah in the *shtibel* in Jonava, in which we had grown up and been educated together. His home was permeated with the spirit of Hassidism, and Hassidic melodies were often heard in their home. Baruch himself was blessed with a good ear and musical talent, and he introduced Hassidic melodies into our group, which was called Achva, at any opportunity of a sublime, festive mood.

The summer of work and *hachshara* passed with great meaningfulness until the autumn arrived. The work ended, and each of us had to go to his home. Of course, we did not see this as a solution, and we began to seek out ways to progress toward *aliya*.

It was the end of 1919. A debate broke out in the movement even before the independence movement existed within the countries of Europe. Some claimed that we must move to Germany, which was close to Lithuania, and from there, strive for progression toward *aliya*. A small group was organized that decided to attempt this. Baruch Namiot and Dov Blumberg were among those. They moved to Germany with forged documents. Since they could not make progress, they remained there, working in the coal mines of the Ruhr District. The other portion remained to wait for an opportunity in Lithuania. In the interim, in order maintain the preparations and the connections, they found work in the forests around Kovno. I found a position as a work foreman in the Bafrur Shantz sawmill near Kovno. I attempted to meet my friends in Kovno once or twice a week.

In June 1920, we sent a member of ours to Berlin. On account of our connections that we had with good Zionists in Germany, we were able to arrange passports to remain in Germany for the remaining 11 people of our group. We snuck across the border in Kybartai, with the help of *chalutzim* friends, and we arrived in Berlin during the Zionist Congress in Germany, in which Eliezer Kaplan and Chaim Arlozoroff were participating as representatives of Ukrainian Jewry. We made acquaintance with Eliezer Kaplan, and through a plan that we hatched with his assistance and using his connections, we obtained forged passports in which we were registered as refugees from the Land of Israel who were being sent back. He made one condition

[Page 95]

with us – that we could use those passports only from Vienna. Therefore, we were forced once again to sneak across the German-Czech, and Czech-Austrian borders. We made a portion of the journey on foot and a portion by train until we arrived in Vienna, from where we succeeded in setting out and arriving at the coast of Jaffa in August 1920. We were the first group of pioneers from Lithuania to arrive in the Land of Israel after the First World War. Our friend Baruch Namiot preceded us. He succeeded in making *aliya* in a roundabout way. He was the only one of the original group that set out for Germany to succeed in doing so.

We worked in Degania Aleph when we first arrived, until we made arrangements to go to Har Kinneret for preparatory work for forestry. We worked there as an organized group for about four months. In the meantime, the rest of the group who had remained in Lithuania arrived, including my sister Rachel. During our work period at Har Kinneret, we made a unanimous decision to join the Trumpeldor Work Brigade, which was headed by Yitzchak Landsberg (Yitzchak Sadeh), Yehuda Koplovich (Almog) and Elkind. We were accepted with great appreciation as an organized, serious and astute group. We succeeded in obtaining an honorable position in the workplace and the organization. Here too, our friend Baruch Namiot managed to introduce Hassidic melodies during the meals, and at all types of festive opportunities.

It is not my wish to continue with the rest of the stories of the development of the group and its members. I only wish to recall the memory of the good friends who were cut off before their time and did not succeed in reaching our primary goal of witnessing the establishment of Israeli independence. These include:

Baruch Namiot. He returned to Lithuania on account of a bout of depression with which he was afflicted in 1926, where he perished along with the rest of the Jews of Jonava. He was an upright person who had great professional talent. He trained as a plasterer in the Land, and took part in important jobs that took place during that period.

Eliahu Opnitzky was my childhood friend. We spent time together in conversations and dreams of *aliya* to the Land. Together we provided the initiative for the founding of the Zionist Garden in Jonava. Together we suffered the tribulations of the journey to the Land, and the hard work under difficult conditions. Eliahu married when he was in the Geniger Group. There, he had a son and a daughter. It was difficult for him to withstand the harsh living conditions of that era as well as the economic difficulties. Due to his worries about how to support his family, he acceded to the request of his wealthy parents and returned to Lithuania along with his brother Abba, who had arrived somewhat later. Both of them perished along with their families.

My sister Rachel of blessed memory. She also went through the melting pot of difficult labor under harsh conditions. She worked in gravelling the Migdal-Tabacha Road. Later, she went to work as a nurse in the hospital of the Migdal work group in the Lower Galilee during the typhus and malaria epidemics. Her refined soul suffered greatly as she witnessed the suffering and affliction of the sick people. She was willingly freed from this position when we moved to Kfar Giladi. There she worked at building. When the work group moved to Ein Harod, she joined that group and started working in the nursery. She later married Shlomo Lavie, and they had three children, Yerubaal, Hillel, and Ilana.

The first period in Ein Harod was full of enthusiasm and meaning. However, the malaria that had been spreading in the valley at that time and the difficult nutritional situation affected her health, and she died before her time at the age of 32 during the severe influenza epidemic of 1930. Her children, whom she did not merit in raising and who were orphaned from her while they were still very young, were educated in the group by their father Shlomo Lavie of blessed memory and his niece Sheindela, who devoted a great deal of love and dedication to them.

Her son Yerubaal became a volunteer in the brigade when he grew up. He fell in battle on Mount Gilboa at the beginning of the War of Independence. Her second son Hillel was injured while evacuating the wounded from Kfar Darom.

The last person in this list is my brother Dov Zisla-Gazit of blessed memory. Like the rest of us in the town, he received his early education in the *cheder*. He later went to study in the *Yeshiva* in Jonava under the leadership of Rabbi Yehuda Gorfinkel of blessed memory, where he became known as one of the most talented students. He went to study in the *Mussar*[1] *Yeshiva* of Slobodka at the age of about 15. There too, he took his places amongst the best of the students. He returned to Jonava at the outbreak of the First World War. We moved to Vilna, the Jerusalem of Lithuania, at the time of the decree of expulsion of all Jews from the district of Kovno.

[Page 96]

Broad vistas opened before him. There, he began to think about his future direction. Our family returned to Jonava when Vilna was conquered by the Germans. However, Dov remained in Vilna, and began his studies at the teachers' seminary, under the conditions of hunger and actual want – just like during the time of occupation during the First World War. After about two years, he returned to Jonava, where he began to work in the field of education. He was one of the founders of the Hebrew public school in Jonava, where he taught along with his friend, the teacher Joselovich, whom he had brought from Vilkomir. Along with this, he was active in the Poale Zion meeting place, and in the organization of evenings and celebrations on behalf of the Jewish National Fund and other Zionist funds.

He moved to the town of Pilviskai in 1918, where he founded and directed the first public Hebrew school in the town. From there, he moved to teach in the Hebrew high school in Mariampol. After my sister Rachel and I made *aliya* to the Land, he decided that the duty of the call to pioneering was not open only to students, but also applied to teachers. He then joined the pioneering camp "Kibbush" near Kedainiai as a *chalutz*. From there, he attempted to make *aliya* to the Land through an uncharted path. He moved to Germany, where he began to work as a farmer. Then he studied biology and agriculture at university.

He made *aliya* in 1924. He joined a work group in El Yosef and started again at agricultural work. About a year later, our parents, along with my brother Aryeh, and our youngest sister Chedva also made *aliya* to the Land.

Dov and I then left our kibbutzim in order to help our parents to strike roots in the land in their chosen place of residence, Tel Aviv. At that time, Dov once again became involved in educational activities together with those who were laying the foundations for the first school for working youth, set up in the Hacholot district where Gan Meir exists today.

When the youth village was set up in Gan Shemen by Dr. Lehman, Dov transferred there to work in teaching under its auspices. After about a year, he married Rachel of the Dimant family from the town of Seduva, who had made *aliya* with a group of *chalutzim* in 1922 and became involved with a work group in Ein Harod. When a hospital was set up in Ein Harod under the directorship of Dr. Hershkovitz (today Harel), she began to work there as a nurse. She was a well-known personality in the hospital, beaming with light, wisdom and warmth toward all in need of her assistance.

Dov's marriage demanded a more regular order, so he transferred to work as the principal of a school in the Borochov neighborhood. There, he built his family. There Dov found a broad arena in which to invest his energy and plans. He ensured the establishment of a local chapter of the Working Youth. The home of Dov and Rachel was always open to anyone in need of advice and guidance, both parents and his many students. In 1940, Dov joined the supervisory network of the Educational Center of the Workers' Current. Later, he transferred to the educational division of the National Council, where he served as vice director.

At that time, he founded and directed the teachers' seminary of Hamerkaz Lachinuch, that later developed further and was called the Teachers' Seminary of Givat Hashelosha.

At the end of the Second World War, Dov went out as an emissary to Germany to organize educational activities amongst the Holocaust survivors and in the Displaced Persons Camps.

When we achieved our independence, he was called to serve as the director of the division of professional education. From this role, he transferred to the branch of agricultural education, where he worked in overseeing the supervision, and as the chief inspector. To his many achievements, we can add the addition of a fourth year in the agricultural schools in order to ensure that they received a full secondary school accreditation.

During his diligent work in the field of education, he published articles on issues of education and the problems of the young generation and its relation to agriculture. Among other things, he succeeded in writing and preparing for publication his two volume book "the Annals of Agricultural Settlement," that was meant as a study textbook in the agricultural schools, as well as his book "Furrows of Education."

He hatched many plans, but his voice was stilled on account of his illness, and he was not able to see them to fruition.

I have recalled four natives of Jonava who passed away before their time. May the memories of our dear departed ones be bound in the bonds of all those who fought to attain our independence and security.

[Page 97]

Something About My Parents' Home
by Aharon Gazit (Zisla)
Translated by Jerrold Landau

Tzvi Yaakov and Chaya Dvora Zisla

My father Tzvi Yaakov Zisla was a native of Jonava. He was raised and educated in the home of his parents, who were Chabad Hassidim. He received a full Torah education, as was customary in those days. He was expert in Bible and Talmud, got along well with his fellow man, and was accepted and liked by everyone.

My mother, Chaya Dvora of the Heiman family was a native of Vilkomir [Ukmerge]. They earned their livelihood from their hide business with the adjacent sewing workshop. Mother was the living spirit of the professional aspects, as she knew the work of hides from her parents' home. However, he was more active in the business aspects and in purchasing. Father, of course, was observant, but he was not a dark zealot. All of the children received a traditional, religious education, and the spirit of Chabad Hassidism pervaded the home. This was instilled into us from our childhood, and we spent a great deal of time on weekdays and festivals in the Shtibel. Father also taught the weekly Torah portion with "*Midrash Rabba*" to the congregation of Hassidim on Sabbaths. He was often carried on the shoulders of his students while sitting on a bench on the day of *Simchat Torah*.

My parents dreamed and longed for the Land of Israel as a secret desire. The spirit in the home served the children well, for they were among the first to make *aliya*.

In 1925, we were fortunate that my parents made *aliya* to the Land along with my brother Aryeh, who had been among the activists of Maccabee in Jonava, and my youngest sister Chedva. With the help and support of my brother Dov, she continued her studies in the Herzliya Gymnasium, concluded her studies in the teachers' seminary, and finally transferred to the Technion in Haifa where she received an engineering certificate.

Our oldest sister Keila, who married Yisrael Levin at the end of the First World War and moved to Mariampol, continued with the family tradition of Zionist activities, through the funds and WIZO [World International Zionist Organization]. Her four sons were educated in the national spirit, and studied in the Hebrew gymnasium there. The younger ones studied in the public Hebrew school.

In 1936, we succeeded in bringing them all to the Land. Two of her sons volunteered for the British Army and served in the Israeli Brigade. All four later served and participated in the War of Independence.

As the first to make *aliya* in my family, I see it as a great merit for myself that I was able to witness and assist in the *aliya* of all the members of my family, who participated in the building, establishment and defense of the Land.

The sorrow and agony is great regarding the bitter fate that overtook those who remained in Jonava, Lithuania, and the rest of the Diaspora of Europe. They perished in cruelty and hellish torment at the hands of the evildoers and filth of the human race.

[Page 98]

His Entire Essence Was Firmly Rooted
Friends talk about Chaim Chermoni (Monitz:1893-1955)
Translated by Jerrold Landau

Uncaptioned. Chaim Chermoni

-- He was the first among the first, the elder of the group of founders of Kibbutz Sarid. He was one of the few who had ploughed the first furrow and erected the first bunk.

-- He had the merit of the first. Being first was imprinted in his fate and character. He drove the first stake in the settlement in Givat Khuneifis, which is Sarid.

-- Even before the Hechalutz organization was founded in Lithuania, he, the veteran of the Achva group, and one of the first *chalutzim* of Lithuania, and his friends set out on the uncharted path to the Land of Israel at the end of the First World War. There, he suffered from all the wanderings and tribulations of travel of the days of the Third Aliya in Migdal, Ayelet Hashachar, Yavneel, Geniger, and Sarid.

-- He was a veteran farmer, an expert in plants with fundamental knowledge, a planter, with deep understanding and diligence – a man of the farm, a lover of the Hebrew books, who was an avid Bible student.

-- To us, the people of Bivracha, natives of Czechoslovakia, he served as a strong bridge for the vital passage from an ideology embracing the world to the gray, day-to-day farm realities when we came to Sarid. He was a pathfinder and work guide for us.

-- His entire essence was well rooted, for his roots were deep in the farm, the Kibbutz community, as well as in Jewish culture.

-- One of the most well-rooted members, one of the most honest and sincere people with regard to his way of life. One of the complete people, whose life example and continual daily conduct laid strong foundations for the building of the kibbutz.

-- He was completely opposed to the Diaspora atmosphere, and to the lost agenda of Jewish wandering.

-- No social difficulty was able to push him off the path in which he marched with sure, straight steps, without doubts, hesitation, or spin. He was whole with himself, without great torments or soft sentimentality.

-- Few like him continued to work in agriculture literally daily, with hoeing, pruning, harvesting, and heaping up the produce. He did not stumble even when the work was difficult. He was constantly at work, until his last day.

-- His work hours with others would be spiced with calm conversation about the issues transpiring in the world, about a book that he read, and even about his past, which he was able to describe to the extent that drew him close to me. He exposed a new world to me with his stories about his town Jonava. Thus, I got to know a reality that was strange and remote from me until that time.

[Page 99]

-- Chaim also played an honorable role in various defense activities during the years of disturbances, and in guarding the place.

-- During his time in Kovno, he did not prepare himself in the direction of farming, but rather in the use of weapons. To this end, he joined the Lithuanian police. He did not come to Hechalutz from the benches of the Hebrew gymnasium, but rather from the *cheder* and *Yeshiva*, which forged his connection with the treasuries of our traditional culture. He was an educated man, knowledgeable in our new and ancient literature, an avid reader, adept at critical understanding of the writers and their works. His internal consistency and great satisfaction in his path beamed forth around him.

-- He was overflowing with knowledge and wisdom of life. We enjoyed hearing statements from *Pirke Avot* or from the *Talmud* from him. He was infused with infective optimism that added meaning to our life.

-- During the days of El Alamein[2], when the enemy was hovering close to the entrance to our land, there were those among us who thought that all of our toil was lost, because our enemy would not leave even one survivor from among us. Self assured, optimistic Chaim rose up, mocked the news, and ordered with the stubbornness of a healthy farmer: "Let us gather up, heap up, and send the produce to Tnuva[3] – and it will be good." His words were fulfilled.

-- Thus did he live among us for 30 years. For more than 35 years in the land, he remained true to himself and stood his guard, without weariness and without intermission.

(From the booklet in his memory published by Kibbutz Sarid.)

[Page 99]

... And the Straw Pierced our Flesh
by Dvora Garnow (Zlunker) of Petach Tikva
Translated by Jerrold Landau

My path to the Land was paved with hopes and experiences.

We sang and danced with joy on the ship, for we were on our way to the Land that was so desired by us.

When we disembarked on the coast, we were disappointed that there was no welcome reception for us. But I do not wish to tell of the disappointment, but rather of one of the first days of my life in the Land.

After great effort, I succeeded in arriving at Kibbutz Degania Beit with a friend in order to work on a voluntary basis.

We did not understand agricultural work. Our work clothes were those of European girls of 1932, and our shoes had high heels. This is how we went out to work. The shoes were not comfortable, so we exchanged them for soft slippers.

We sat in the field the entire day. We picked weeds from the cabbage patch. The sun was scorching. We got more and more tired. Sitting on our knees throughout the work also took its toll. At the end of the work day, in the evening, we could not get up on our feet to walk. Our feet gave in. Our entire body was in pain.

This was our first introduction to field work in the Land.

Night fell. There was a special bunk for guests on Degania. It had two beds and a table. We were tired to death. We quickly got up on our beds to sleep.

But, woe, what type of beds were these! These were not the comfortable beds in Mother's house, but rather high straw mattresses, which sunk inward as soon as we got up onto them. The straw pierced our flesh… Instead of sleeping the sweet sleep of workers, we spent that entire night laughing, "dancing" upon the sharp mattresses and laughing…

That fun night, without sleep and full of laughter and joy – will never be erased from my memory.

Thus ended one of my first nice days in the Land.

[Page 100]

Four Who Were Among the First Pioneers
by Dov Blumberg
Translated by Jerrold Landau

My memory directs me to a time period of more than fifty years ago.

Jonava – this name is filled with charm, splendor and bitterness. There we grew up, were educated and lived. We can state that we were happy and fortunate with our lot. It did not seem that we were actually in the Diaspora. Life went on as in previous times, without great changes. We felt secure in the bosom of our parents, family, and other residents. The Jews comprised 90% of the population of Jonava. There were some wealthy people among the Jews, who strongly pushed forward its development.

Izak Segalovsky, the owner of ten fine buildings, was the first manufacturer. He set up a large sawmill to produce planks for buildings and to make furniture, as well as a modern flourmill. He was the first to bring electricity into the town in 1910, bringing light into the dark corners and residential houses. Other manufacturers included Leiba Opnitzky, Levin, the Bursteins of Jonava, Zisla, and Yankele Eliash Weitzman who established a large factory for matches. Jonava also excelled in its many furniture factories, which gained acclaim far and wide. There were also workshops for producing utensils, and implements of iron and steel. All of these were owned by Jews, and employed Jews. There were also many workshops for sewing and production of clothing. Among others, there were merchants for forestry and wood products: the Bursteins, the Levins, the Blumbergs. Abba Pogirsky provided iron utensils and other work implements, primarily to the villagers. Chaim Levin, the owner of the pharmacy, also served as the mayor during the German occupation. Shneur Sesitzky, who lived next to the Vylia was the general rabbi appointed by the government. The rabbi of the city, Rabbi Chaim Ratzker, was a gaon, great in Torah. He was followed by Rabbi Silman of Sesik. The head of the *Yeshiva*, Rabbi Yudel, had a red beard. He was a wise man, a genius, who also had secular knowledge. He read the Hebrew newspapers "Hazman" and "Hatzefira." Rabbi Hershel Peretz was the second *Rosh Yeshiva*. All of these injected color and life into the residents of Jonava.

The wagon and carriage drivers who carried passengers along the road to Kovno, Vilkomir, and other places, formed a noticeable component of the residents of the city. The youths of Jonava were known as brave people who knew no fear. When the gentiles came to the city with their produce to buy and sell at the market, there were many times when they were drunk, and performed acts of mischief. The youths of Jonava went out against them and beat them on the thighs. Day-to-day life was a struggle for existence: to establish large families, to send the children to *cheders*, schools and *yeshivas*. The food of the residents was simple: bread, potatoes, a bit of meat, soup and fish. They did not aspire to wealth. They aspired to the days of Sabbaths and festivals, to fill the well- lit synagogues, to attend public worship, to study a chapter of *Mishna* and a page of *Talmud*, and to recite Psalms. Thus, did they and their fathers live, and thus would they continue to live until the final redemption arrives with the coming of the Messiah.

The prayers, supplications, *cheders*, and schools elicit longing to the birthplace. This was like a dream, distant from the reality.

It was the end of the First World War; the Russian Revolution and removal of the Czar led to a chain of massive changes. Extreme nationalism overtook all of the Baltic States and Poland. All these areas, which had been under the Russian Czar, were liberated and gained their independence. They set up parliaments, chose a president, a national flag fluttered from the national buildings, Lithuanian schools and a university were opened, and a Lithuanian Army with national uniforms was formed. The language was revived, Lithuanian songs were sung, and rallies with great people were arranged to awaken national feelings. We, the Jews of Lithuania, were given the gift of national autonomy on a small scale. However, the experience of the thousands of years of exile foreshadowed a disappointing future. The Balfour Declaration regarding the establishment of a national homeland in the Land of Israel also did not arouse a sense of awakening. The Jews of the Diaspora continued to remain sunk in their somnolence.

[Page 101]

We were four youths from Jonava. We woke up, and felt our nakedness and embarrassment: Baruch Namiot the son of Shlomo Chaim, Eliahu Opnitzky the son of Leibe, Aharon Zisla the son of Tzvi Yaakov, and this writer Berl Blumberg the son of

Shlomo, Rachel Zisla the daughter of Tzvi Yaakov also joined in. We all decided to sever our connections with the Diaspora and to become *chalutzim*.

At that same time, a group of male and female youths also organized in Kovno. Most of them were graduates of the Carlebach Gymnasium. These included: David Kolka, Tzvi Golombek, Yosef Shukstaliski, Efraim Eliash, Chaim Monitz, Mordechai Bina, Yaakov Kark, Yosef Joselovich, Chana Kaufman, Sara (I forgot her family name), and Shlomit Goloskos. There were approximately seventeen or eighteen youths. I recall that we all sat together in a circle on the floor in a narrow room in the Zionist hall in Kovno, with a Bible open before us and candles burning. We took an oath to become *chalutzim* and to organize ourselves into a group. The name of the group was Achva [brotherhood] – as a sign that from that day on, we would be brothers and sisters, whose goals were to become workers who live from the work of their hands, to separate ourselves immediately from the fetters of the Diaspora, to leave behind all of our private and family connections, and to immediately go out to pioneering *hachshara* so that we could get accustomed to physical labor. This oath was in accordance with the oath of Achad Haam of the "Bnei Moshe" group:

"In the name of everything that is dear and holy to us, we hereby swear to become *chalutzim*, to be faithful and dedicated to the nation of Israel, the Land of Israel, and the Hebrew Language." The motto was: "Work is our life."

After we returned home, we packed a few belongings and took leave of our families in a simple fashion. Our parents were suspicious of us and strongly opposed this step. However, all obstacles were as nothing in our eyes. We got work in Koviatiski near Mariampol working in the gardens and preparing vegetables for the Lithuanian Army.

The group grew and broadened. We became connected, and forged the character of each individual. We aspired to personal fulfillment, to the creation of a different Jewish persona whose life is based on trust, honesty and truth, personal sacrifice for one's friend and self-sacrifice for the realization of the ideal that we placed before ourselves.

We set out on our journey after more than six months. Baruch Namiot and I arrived at the German border. We snuck across the border and continued to Stalopanen and Berlin. There I gave Hebrew lessons, and we earned our livelihood. From there we moved on to selling coal in the Rhine District, and we helped transfer over other friends, who worked on the railway and in other places. We left for France and worked in Vaudron. From there, we went to Paris and Marseilles. We snuck onto a ship that was setting out for China via the Suez Canal. We worked on the ship. I will not tell of all the trials and tribulations that we underwent. We arrived in Israel after about a year and a quarter. The other members went through the Alps, and reached Odessa and other places after a tortuous journey. Eventually, the entire group reached Israel.

I do not have sufficient space to describe the activities of the group in the land and the influence that it left behind in Lithuania. Hechalutz went in the same direction. In the meantime, the following additional members from Jonava arrived: Abba Opnitzky, Rachel Mintz, Batya Opnitzky, and others.

The emotionally laden letters that the *chalutzim* wrote to their parents had great influence, for their parents also left, liquidated their houses and property in Jonava, and made *aliya* to settle in the Land of Israel. The following were among those who arrived in the 1920s, 30s and 40s: Tzvi Yaakov Zisla with his entire family, Berl Zisla who contributed greatly to the development of education in Tel Aviv and was an important personality, Keila Zisla-Levin of Mariampol, Rachel Zisla who married one of the important, veteran works who contributed greatly to the founding of the large kibbutz – Shlomo Lavie (Levkovich). Their two sons fell in the war of independence. At that time, Elazar Judelevich and his wife Bashel, the sister of Tzvi Yaakov Zisla, also arrived.

During my last visit to Israel, at a wedding, I met many Jonavers who live in Israel. There, they live, exist, and continue to contribute to the building and development of the homeland. May they continue to multiply and strengthen within our blessed Land.

Capetown

[Page 102]

I Snuck Out the Window
by Batya Tauba (Opnitzky) of Tel Aviv
Translated by Jerrold Landau

Leibe Opnitzky   Batya Tauba Opnitzky

In memory of the martyrs: My father Yehuda Leib, my mother Sheina Leah, my sister Doba – the good, generous woman, and my brothers Eliahu, Abba, Tzvi and Ezriel with their families who perished in the Holocaust at the hands of the wild Germans and Lithuanians.

Our house on Fisher Gasse (The Street of the Fishermen) was spacious, splendidly built externally, and enveloped with a Jewish and Zionist reality internally. This house stood out in the background of the fine scenery of the banks of the Vylia River. During the summer, we would spend time floating in boats on its waters, and in the winter, skating on the ice. The ways of this house, with its rooms, its yard, and all of its living beings and objects, were forged by my father Yehuda Leib, Abba Yankel's of blessed memory.

There were two smaller houses, a barn, stable and warehouse for old objects and boards in the internal courtyard of the house. We called the warehouse "*balagan*" (bedlam). It also served as the venue for rehearsals for the performances directed by Chana Katzenberg. Sanitary fixtures did not yet exist at that time, and the large copper container that stood in the anteroom of the house was filled with water that "Yosef Tzimes" had brought from the well.

After my father of blessed memory lost his parents at the age of six, he strove tirelessly for both economic and spiritual independence already in his early childhood.

He finally managed to set up his own exemplary Jewish household, whose gates were always open wide for anyone in need or suffering from difficulties. Aside from the *Yeshiva* student who would eat at our table on a daily basis, my father would bring guests who were passing through our town to our home from the synagogue on Sabbaths and festivals. My father was a charitable man in the full sense of the term in those days, and provided significant support to those in need.

Before the outbreak of the First World War, my father was a partner in the match factory, along with Chaim Levin and Yaakov Weitzstein. However, during the war, before the retreat of the Russians, he, like many other honorable residents of the town, was forced to leave the place, and abandon all the property that he had built up through the toil of many years. Our family moved to Vilna, where we waited impatiently until the wrath would subside. When an opportunity to return presented itself, we did so without hesitation. After wandering in boats on the river for four days and spending the nights in villages next to the river, we finally returned to Jonava, where we found ruin and destruction everywhere we turned. Everything was burned: the match factory, the trees in the forest, and even those in the river. Only the residential dwellings remained standing, but there was also a great deal of destruction in them due to the searches for silver and gold that were conducted there. Of course, it was difficult to begin everything from scratch. However, a man such as my father would not give up. With double energy, he began to search for business, until, after great effort, he succeeded in returning the situation to its former state, and rebuilt his home with the tradition of having an open hand and a broad heart to everyone.

[Page 103]

We studied in the public school. The boys continued to study Talmud and holy subjects privately, for they were not included in the school curriculum. The girls learned languages: Russian, German and Hebrew. Our father taught us to be meticulous. During the time of *Kiddush* on Sabbaths, we were forbidden to open our mouths. We were forced to sit quietly at the table, seriously and in awe. When we became older, the band was loosened somewhat. He would even discuss politics, issues of factions, and current events with us. There were even times when he would request a cigarette from my brother Eliahu, who smoked secretly and discretely up to that point.

Our home was a Zionist home. Various newspapers filled up the house, and the children even spoke Hebrew among themselves. I, together with my friends Rachele Levin and Blumka Pogirsky studied Hebrew and Bible with the teacher Dov Zisla of blessed memory. I liked Bible the least, as if what happened thousands of years ago was of no interest to me. However, when I made *aliya* to the Land, the Bible stories became more understandable and realistic to me, for I often trod on the places that were discussed in the Bible, which used to seem so remote and legendary to me. I was prepared to ask forgiveness of our teacher of that time, and our friend now in the Land, Dov Zisla of blessed memory.

Despite the Zionist spirit that pervaded our home, my father opposed our eldest brother Eliahu joining Hechalutz, which preached and educated toward a life of labor. According to him, it was possible to find sufficient work in the forests that we owned, and it was not necessary to wander far off for that purpose. However, the ice finally broke, and my brother Eliahu joined Hechalutz and made *aliya* to the land with the first group of Lithuanian *chalutzim* – the famous Achva group. My second brother Abba also made *aliya* to the Land a few years later, and joined the same group. I then made the decision in my heart to also join Hechalutz. Despite the fact that my two brothers were already in the land, my parents opposed this and interfered in the strongest possible fashion. They hid the letters that arrived for me from Hechalutz in Kovno. I was forced to change my address in order to receive letters. There was a library directed by Menachem Mines in Jonava. There, we conducted our meetings, the invitations to which were brought to me secretly by Baruch Kursikishik. Mines also recommended that I read the new books that arrived in the package, and that still smelled like glue. We would sit and discuss their content during the evenings. At times, there were also debates on issues of the Zionist parties that attempted to win over the hearts of the youth to strengthen their ranks.

Leizer Levin and others were among the participants in these debates.

I especially recall one evening when a member of the Hechalutz headquarters appeared in our house. He came to interrogate us regarding the reasons that we wished to make *aliya*. I was very afraid. My friend Mara Simka (Miriam Lomianski) encouraged me, told me not to become emotional, and to go and do what had to be done. That member of the headquarters was Eliahu Tauba, who later became my husband, and remains so to this day.

The next day, I assisted Miriam Lomianski to escape from her home, and Eliahu transported her to Kovno. The next day, her father came to us and began to shout: "Where is your Bilka? Where did you hide my daughter?" At that time, I was soaping up my face, and I hid behind the oven with soap on my face. When I later left my hiding place, I was only able to remove the soap from my face with difficulty.

Since my parents objected to my going on *hachshara*, I decided to escape from the house. One morning, my friend Rachele came to me and helped me escape trough the window with my suitcase. I then took a wagon directly to Kovno. I sent a letter home a few days later. Until that time, I was very disturbed on account of the worry I caused my parents. My *hachshara* location was Karkline, an agricultural farm under Jewish ownership. Of course, male and female workers from the general population worked together with us. We too had to work with them and like them. The work was difficult, and it was not easy for me to get used to it. One of the female Lithuanian workers assisted me in bringing the grain from the wagons to the barn. In return, I lent her my ring every Sunday so she could wear it to church. In the winter, we would sit and prepare sacks. All of the work was accompanied by song. At night, there would be dancing and friendly conversation. My second *hachshara* location was in Memel. There, we worked weaving baskets. Mordechai Ish-Shalom (later the mayor of Jerusalem) and his wife Shoshana were also in this group. This work was also not easy for me. After completing a basket, I had to cut off the ends on the inside to the point where I bled. All of the work was performed with minimal food, to the point of deprivation.

[Page 104]

Despite my long sojourn in *hachshara* locations under difficult conditions, I had to fight with the Hechalutz center in order to obtain a certificate for *aliya* to the Land. Only after I agreed to fund the travel of an additional member did I succeed in obtaining a certificate for *aliya* to the Land in 1924 along with my fictitious spouse Yitzchak Goldberg. I recall the farewell party that was made for me in the home of Libe Chana Stern and the dear member Ivensky. After a speech, we sang *"Amul is geven a postechl"* (There once was a little shepherd). As we were in the midst of our enthusiasm, a knock was heard on the door. The police came and wanted to arrest us. We all dispersed, and continued on the next day in our homes, albeit quietly.

When I arrived in the Land, I immediately joined the Achva group, to which my two brothers, Eliahu and Abba, belonged. At first I worked in tobacco growing in the area of Rosh Pina, and later in Emek. When we moved to Sarid, I planted the first trees there. To my dismay, only a few of my friends of that time remain alive, but the memory of that work remains. There was' a large forest and a fine, well-based farm. From there I transferred to a work brigade. I married and established a fine family. All of this was thanks to my strong willingness to overcome all obstacles, physical difficulties and spiritual struggles. Indeed, nothing stands before desire. It is only unfortunate that my parents and all my family did not merit seeing this with their own eyes.

When I recall in the eyes of my spirit the past, and all that transpired in my life throughout the course of the decades, I shed a warm, honest tear for my family that was destroyed – that exemplary Jewish home that served as a wellspring from which I drew all the strength, power and energy to withstand everything and overcome everything until this day.

From time to time, the memory of my parental home comes before me and appears to me as if it still exists as in previous days, with its calm, warmth, charm, benevolence, charity, hosting of guests, dreams that were woven therein, and hopes that were awaiting actualization.

Let these lines, written with the blood of my heart, serve as a memorial monument for this guesthouse of the Jewish people – my Father's house in the town of Jonava in the Diaspora of Lithuania – which was attacked by bands of thieves and wild people until it was destroyed from the world, along with all the houses of Israel in the wretched Diaspora.

Translator's Footnotes

Mussar refers to the study of Jewish morality, and is the name of a movement which was founded in the *Yeshivas* of Lithuania, which placed a stress on the study of Jewish moral teachings. The famous Yeshiva of Slobodka was one of the prime *Mussar* style *Yeshivas*.

During World War II, when the Nazi Army, under Erwin Rommel, was approaching Palestine through Egypt, it advanced as far as El Alamein, west of Alexandria, before being repelled by the allies.

Tnuva is an Israeli agricultural company.

[Page 104]

About an Orange
by Tzvi Khasid [Nachalat Yiztchak]
Translated by Yosi and Svetlana Shneider and Hadassa Goldsmith
Edited by Jerrold Landau

My father was from the Lubavitcher Chasidim. My grandfather was one of the organizers of Chasidim in Jonava. As he was very busy in the organization, he spent most of the time in the shtibel of the Chasidim. Therefore, the Chasidim began to call him Khasid. This name took root and was inherited from generation to generation. Even until today, all of the family members have the surname Khasid.

The Russians drove out the Jews from this region of Lithuania at the beginning of the First World War. It was in 1914. The Jews were sent out to different areas of White Russia and the Ukraine. Some of them came to Vilna, including us. We were in Vilna until the Germans captured Vilna. The Jews from Jonava who lived in Vilna returned to their houses in Jonava. But it was not so simple, because the railway did not work and everything was in the hands of the German Army.

Our family and two other families from Jonava bought boats. Since my parents were once occupied with the transporting of logs on rivers, they were able to organize this ferry along the Viliya river to Jonava. There were temporary low bridges along way that were built by Germans. We had to unload everything from the boat, carry the empty boats along the land, and put them back in the water on the other side of the bridges. This journey would take 3-4 days until we arrived in Jonava.

We found destroyed houses, and pillaged, empty dwellings. Our house was occupied by gentiles, but after a short time, we got it back. There were horses kept by the Germans in our synagogue, which they turned into a stable. When the German army advanced into Russia, they emptied the synagogue. The worshippers repaired it, and began to gather for services.

My parents began to work in their bakery again and reopened their grocery store. We also had machines to make felt slippers from sheep wool. The gentiles would bring the wool, and we would make the shoes for their private use.

We immigrated to Israel in 1925[1]. What caused us to immigrate?

The Rabbi from Jonava obtained 200 dunams of land in Israel to sell to the Jews of our town. We were among the buyers. We purchased 10 dunams on the condition that we would settle in Eretz Israel. The story goes like this:

My father was ill. My mother was supposed to buy oranges for him on the advice of the doctor, so that he should eat them and become healthy. One day, the rabbi saw my mother through the window and called to her saying that she would have her own oranges if she would buy from him a plot of land in Eretz Israel. Indeed, after we bought the land, we decided to move to Eretz Israel.

There were other families that also bought land and prepared to move, but they had no one to whom to sell their house and property. The priest told the gentiles not to buy from the Jews, because if they did not buy from them the Jews would be forced to leave everything anyway. We also did not have a buyer. We gave our property to a member of a family from Kedainiai, on the condition that if we could not succeed in Eretz Israel we would return to Lithuania and receive our property back.

I and my parents made aliya to the Land at a propitious moment in 1925. The land that we bought was near Afula. Agudat Israel called this place Mahane Israel. We lived with four other families. In addition, there were thirty people whose wives and children were still in the Diaspora. Agudat Israel hired these people to build cottages, pave roads, and other such work. They earned thirty grush a day, which was enough to live on because everything was cheap.

In 1927, Agudat Israel did not have the funds to employ people, so the work stopped. Many people went to other places or returned to their original towns in the Diaspora. My parents and I remained. My mother got a job in a children's village near Afula. I worked in agriculture, primarily in the cultivation of crops.

The disturbances began in 1929. We had to leave the place. In our neighborhood there was an Arab who owned a great deal of land. The place was called Ein-Dor. Today, Kibbutz Davrat is located there, opposite Mount Tabor. This Arab was a friend of the Jews. We remained in constant contact with him. One day he came and warned us that there were Arabs who were preparing to kill us and burn down our houses. We dismantled our house, bought a plot in Afula, and moved our house to the new location. We began to set up a cattle stall and an auxiliary farm. In five years our farm grew to the point that we had 12 milk cows. We moved to Nachalat Yitzchak near Tel-Aviv, because we could no longer maintain ourselves in Afula. We had nobody to whom to sell milk, and prices were very low because the situation in the areas was difficult, and there was no employment in other areas of work.

We enlarged our farm in Nachalat Yitzchak. Finally, we had to liquidate our farm along with everyone else according to the demand of the Minister of Agriculture, Moshe Dayan.

To this day I live with my family in the environs of Tel-Aviv.

Jonavers in the Achva group. Aharon Zisla (4), Dov Blumberg (3), Eliahu Opnitsky (2), Baruch Namiot (1) – 1919.

B. Namiot (6), Opnitsky (4), D. Blumberg (10), A. Zisla (11) – Achva, 1920.

Batya Tauba (with a hat) 1923.

Hechalutz Organization of Jonava 5683 / 1923.

With Batya Opnitsky before her aliya in 1924: Zacks, Sara Slomin, Intriligator, Reizel Morr, Chasia Intriligator, Yentel Slomin, Menachem Mines, Zacks, Eliezer Levin, Rivka Grossman, Sara B., Moshe Solski; Chasia Friedland, Sheina Levin, Elka Wolk, Bluma Pogirsky, Chana Sandler, Miriam Lomianski, Shoshana Morr, Henia Segalovski, Batya O.[pnitsky], Ivensky, Liba Chana Stern; Zeev Epstein, Rachel Levin, Yitzchak B., Berl Antes.

Passover 5684 / 1924 at the goodbye party: Velvel Sesitzki, Shimon Zack, Bleiman, Shmuel Kaplan, X, Aryeh Zisla, Lyuba Katz, Bluma Pogirsky, Moshe Solski, Sara Slomin, Sheina Levin, Tzvi Opnitsky, Sara Burstein, Eliezer Goldshmidt, Rivka Sesitzky, Rachel Levin, Masha Segalovski, Tivka Katz, Beila Opnitsky, Shimkovitz, Faya Donat, Malka Kaplan; Chaya Morr, Alter Sandler, Chana Segalovski, Menachem Mines

Batten, Shoshana Troyush, Chaim Blumberg, X., Prakt, Tzipora Klotz, Velvel Kirzner; Tzvi Resnick, Reina Lea Kulbiansky, Menachem Mines, Nathan Grinblatt, Ivensky, X; Dov Zisla, X. Caption on photo says: In memory of the activity on behalf of the Working Land of Israel, Jonava, 20 Iyar, <year is hard to make out>

Eliahu and Abba Opnitsky carrying water in the first year of the aliya of the Achva group, on the Geniger land (1924). Next to the wagon is Rachel, Eliahu's wife, with their daughter.}

Batya Opnitsky-Taub in the civic garden in Kovno, on her way to the Land. Accompanying her is Rachel Levin. The suitcase contains all of her possessions.

Eliahu and Rachel (1925)

Mendel Dobiansky, Reizel Khasid, Zelig Stein, Mina Grodsky; Batten, Tzipora
Shoham, Epstein, Tzipora Klibansky; Barron, Grodsky

The committee of the Tarbut evening courses in Jonava, Adar 5688 / 1928.
Henia Blumberg, Alter Monitz, Chana Pesia Glazer, Shlomo Friedman; Sara Lea
Rikliansky, Ivensky, Z. Stein, Tzipora Grossman

The Hechalutz and Young Hechalutz organizations in Jonava, 5 Adar 5685 / 1925.
(Note, the 5s may actually be 8s, as the caption is somewhat cut off, and these look
similar in Hebrew
X, A. Batten, Rivka Atkatz, Sara Rikliansky, Alter Monitz, Lea Kronick, Tzipora
Shoham, Tzila Unterschatz, X, X; Stein, Tz. L. Weiner, Guttman, Baron, Epstein, Ida
Zochovsky, Sonia Kaplan; Moshe Unterschatz, Tzipora Klibansky, Batten, Tzipora
Grossman, X

A group of athletes from Maccabee, 1924: Tzvi Opnitsky, X., Reping, Shlomo
Friedman, Avraka Unterschatz, Feivka Shapira, X, X, Zelig Stein

: A group of members of Maccabee taking leave of Aryeh Zisla: Zelig Stein, X,
Yaakov Dembo, Avram; Shimon Zack, X, Ezriel Opnitsky; Libka Goldshmidt, Shlomo
Ber Meirovitch, Aryeh Zisla, Ivensky, Shlomo Friedman, Hinda Levitz

Left: A female chalutz making a partition
Right: Hope takes root in the reality of Mizrachi in the Land

My hands are stiff with calluses
And the sun beats down over my head
I take hammers in my hand
From 5689 (1929) to 5690
A road walks, a road does not run
My life, a partition a partition.
From a poem from those days

Dov Zisla on Hachshara in Kibush (1922)

Aharon, mother and Rachel

Aharon Zisla and Eliahu Opnitsky

A convention of the Lithuanian Hechalutz, 22-24 Elul, Kovno. The delegates from
Jonava: at the top Baruch Namiot (1), Rachel Zisla.

As a souvenir to our member Zisla before her aliya to the Land. The Hechalutz
organization of Kovno, 5683 (1923)

Shlomo Lavie and his wife Rachel Zisla, his mother and brother Aharon

Translator's Footnotes

This sentence was not in the original text, and was apparently added in by the translators.

[Page 106]

A Pioneering Family
by Rachel Ben-Yehuda (Mintz)
Translated by Jerrold Landau

Rachel Ben-Yehuda (Mintz)

My father Reb Yoel of blessed memory was an ordained rabbi. It is said that he was one of the geniuses of the *Yeshiva*. My father did not wish to make his Torah into "a spade with which to dig"[1]. After he married Sara Rivka of blessed memory, the daughter of Menachem Cohen, he joined the business of his father-in-law, who was a wood merchant, and was well-known for his honesty.

We lived in our private house in Jonava next to the new synagogue, located on Lipniak. There was a large *Yeshiva* in the synagogue under the leadership of Yudel Gorfinkel and Rabbi Hershel Peretz. The latter was a scholar, an upright man, and a *Tzadik*. Rabbi Yehuda Gorfinkel was very knowledgeable in Torah, as well as being a modern man in general. He thoroughly knew Torah, *Gemara* and *halachic* decisors. He would not look into books during his studies with *Yeshiva* students due to his poor vision. During a discussion of didactics or the explanation of a difficult section of Talmud, he would tell the students the page number in the Talmud, and point to the place with his finger. He would see the Jordan River in his imagination as he walked by the banks of the Vylia. At times, when he was pining for Zion he would stop a gentile on his way and ask, "Mr. Squire, where is the route that leads to Palestine?" He moved away from Jonava, then went to Kovno, from where he made *aliya* to the Land. He died there. Both of these *Rosh Yeshivas* frequented our house in Jonava. They always debated about a page of *Gemara*, issues of the day and politics with my father. Our mother, Sara Rivka, was also present in their company, as she was a wise woman. She knew Hebrew and foreign languages. My mother excelled in hosting guests, and offering assistance and support to those in need. She was the "writer" of addresses and letters for women whose husbands had emigrated oversees in search of livelihood.

Our family moved to Kovno in 1921, for the daughters had grown up in the interim and there was no high school in Jonava. In 1924, a group of middle class Jews was organized in Kovno, who purchased agricultural land in the Land. My father was the head of this effort. Our family left Lithuania, made *aliya* to the Land and settled on the land that we had purchased. The Moshava Magdiel was established on these lands. My brothers Dov and Yekutiel were among the first to go to that land. They dedicated themselves to agricultural work with all their might. They struggled with the pitted land with all their energy. They had great erudition. They worked during the day and studied and researched their new profession of agriculture during the night. They took interest in plants that would be fitting for the local terrain. To our bad fortune and great agony, they both died prematurely. May their memories be a blessing. Yekutiel left behind a wife Chana, and two sons, Avraham and Yoel, who continue on in our path. My younger sister Dvora Dror also worked on the farm with our brothers for many years. My lot unfolded in a different manner. I spent the first 15 years of my life in Jonava. The best years of my youth are connected with that town. When I grew older, a group of friends would gather in our house to study the history of the Jewish people. Our teacher was Natan Janusovich of blessed memory, one of the young *maskilim* of Jonava. A policeman standing at the corner of the street noticed that we were gathering without a permit, and therefore we were forced to stop the lessons. I loved to see the Yeshiva students dispersing and strolling on Lipniak during their recess. They would even continue with their didactic discussions on their section of *Talmud* during these moments.

[Page 107]

I also enjoyed going out to Lipniak, sitting under the trees, being alone with a book, listening to the songs of the birds and the sounds of the Vylia. When I finished the Real Hebrew Gymnasium in Kovno, I traveled to continue my studies at the University of Vienna. I decided to change the path of my life after the first year of studies. This was after the Balfour Declaration. A wave of nationalism swept over the nation in the Diaspora. I came to the realization that this was not the time to sit on the school bench. It was our duty to make *aliya* to the land and to participate in the building of the homeland for the nation. I joined Hechalutz, and made *aliya* to the Land after a brief period of *hachshara*, even before the *aliya* of the entire family. In the Land, I was accepted by Kibbutz Ein Harod. Incidentally, I arrived there on the heels of Rachel Zisla of blessed memory, a native of Jonava, one of the first and best known *chalutzim* of Lithuania and in the Land in her time. When the family arrived in the Land, I advised Father to join me in the Kibbutz. His soul and inclination did not tend toward Socialism. Therefore, as I stated above, he chose Moshava Magdiel. Only our oldest sister, Reizel Cohen, remained in Lithuania to our sorrow. She endured all the tribulations of the war along with her family as refugees in Russia. Her desire is to be united with the remainder of the family in the Land.

[Page 107]

Fortunate – With a Dual Meaning
by Zelig Even (Stein), Kibbutz Givat
Translated by Jerrold Landau

When we returned from Russia after the First World War, I decided to study in the Tarbut evening classes. Thus did I learn Hebrew. I joined the Maccabee group.

I discovered that youths from Jonava were becoming *chalutzim* and were going out for agricultural *hachshara* on the Kibbush[2] farms of Hechalutz, and some of them had already succeeded in making *aliya* to the Land. I began to take interest in how to reach actualization and *aliya*. However my young age – I was 16 at the time – prevented me from realizing that dream.

Hechalutz Hatzair (Young Chalutz) was founded in Lithuania at that time. We set up a chapter in Jonava as well, and after a half a year, I succeeded in going out to *hachshara* with the first group of Hechalutz Hatzair, to a Jewish farmer near Radvilishki who agreed to take on eight *chalutzim*. There I learned to sow, harvest, grow vegetables and spread chemical fertilizer – all by hand of course.

I had to travel home after the summer of work. But I stood my ground that they should send me to a *hachshara* group that continues throughout the entire year. There were about twelve such places in the farms in the area of the city of Memel. Thus did I get to the Dompen group, about ten kilometers from Memel. There were fifteen of us there. Every Sabbath, we would go to meetings of all the *hachshara* groups under the auspices of the Memel Beit-Hechalutz.

Then the fortunate time came: I was authorized for *aliya*[3]. I arrived in the Land in 1926, even before I was 18 years old. There was a serious depression in the Land, which we already sensed on the journey. When we passed through the port of Marseilles, we were greeted by people returning from the Land, who had worked there. They uttered to us: "New victims!" When we arrived at the red Histadrut building in Jaffa, we saw a long line of unemployed people. Each person received a 25 grush stipend per week.

Our group of new immigrants numbered twenty people. We were sent to Rechovot to join the Lithuanian group that had made *aliya* before us. There was little work. We received an allotment of eight or nine work days for our group of thirty-five members. We worked in the orchards and vineyards. The Lithuanian group earned a good name as workers. The farmers asked for workers from the Lithuanian group. The salary was low – 15 grush per day! We worked as contractors in "Bechar" – digging with our hands.

At that time, the plan of "Hityashvut Haelef" (Settlement of the Thousand) appeared: settling about 1,000 families near the Moshavot, who would be able to tend to a small independent farm, 10-15 dunam per family. The Lithuanian group joined with the Ein Harod group, and together with the Wolhyn group and the Italian immigrants headed by Enzo Sereni[4], we were given an area of settlement near Rechovot, which we called Givat Brenner. Members of the Lithuanian group laid the foundation. Later, we were joined by *chalutzim* from Germany from Kibbutz Chirot. In this manner, the group of Lithuanian natives, I among them, was given the merit of founding and creating, along with others, a kibbutz that today is the largest in the country.

With the passage of time, I moved to the Jezreel Valley, and I continued my life in Kibbutz Givat.

[Page 108]

From *Cheder* to Hechalutz
by Eliezer Kochavi (Stern) of Kibbutz Netzer Sereni
Translated by Jerrold Landau

From the distance of time, I see the life of the Jewish community, the life of generations of Jews in the town, which for a long period lived independently in most areas of life.

The town was surrounded by villages of the ruling nation, but the majority of the population of the town itself was Jewish. The Jews imprinted their stamp on life on week days and holy days, in economy, work, education and culture.

With respect to the civic situation, the internal government was independent, and everyone was subordinate to its institutions. The connection to religion and the surrounding organization drew the Jews of the town together into one community, with an air of simplicity, and a flowing of life.

The influence of the rabbi of the city spread into secular matters as well. Every court case between one Jew and his fellow was brought before the rabbi rather than being brought to the gentile court system. The authority of the rabbi was accepted, and nobody refused to accept the decision of the rabbi in accordance with the laws of the Torah.

The educational institutions that were under the independent authority of the community included the *cheder*, the *Yeshiva* buildings, and later, the schools.

Before the First World War, I began my studies in *cheder* at the age of five. At that time, a Talmud Torah Hebrew school already existed. It was a modern school at a high level. I entered the *cheder* on my own accord, as I went with a friend, and I remained there to learn. The rebbe was Pitkovsky. I studied with him for one year. The class took place in one room. We sat next to tables around the walls, and the classes were conducted in a good spirit. For the second year, I transferred to the Talmud Torah, a modern school of four grades.

The school was founded during the first years of the century by a group of communal activists with the aim of raising the level of study and providing education in the Hebrew/national spirit. Its aim was to select students from all strata of the community. The school was full, and it could not accept everyone who wanted to enter. The wooden building was surrounded by a spacious yard. Even the classrooms were spacious, with light, air, and good equipment.

My teacher was Keidanski, a man with a pleasant disposition, and pedagogic and organizational talents. He did not impose strict punishments. One winter day, a

Christian parade passed by. Curiosity aroused several students of the class to watch the "mystery" of the dipping of the symbols into the frozen waters of the river, beneath the ice. I was one of the curious ones. When we returned, the teacher called me and told me to come to his house that evening. There he ordered me to write several pages of "handwriting." I did thus feel the justice of the "punishment." The exercise indeed improved my handwriting.

I have positive recollections of my period of study. I continued there until the outbreak of the First World War and the expulsion. The Germans were approaching on the front. As if to obfuscate the disgrace of their retreat, the Russian command accused the Jews of the region of spying for the Germans. We moved to Zusli, where we remained for several months. From there we moved to Bobruisk near Minsk in White Russia. There, I entered the Hebrew school that had been opened for the children of the refugees. This was a modern school, and good, dedicated teachers taught there.

We endured the year of the Russian Revolution in that city. For me, this was also a school of a different type – for awareness of the political and national movements, as I saw the events as they unfolded before my eyes.

We hastened to return to the town at the end of the war. At that time of government and general unrest, the Jews of the town took independent action to conduct their matters. A city council with a Jewish mayor was established. My father, Shmarya Stern, served in that role at that time. Alongside the city leadership, a militia was set up to preserve order, in which Jews also took part.

I continued my studies with Rabbi Hershel Peretz. We studied *Gemara* in his home. Then we moved to study in the *Beis Midrash*. Rabbi Hersh Peretz had a good disposition. We studied with him for two terms.

Then I went to study in a Hebrew secondary school – the Real Gymnasium of Kovno, under the direction of Dr. Tzemach Feldstein.

On the same day as the matriculation exams ended, I enrolled in Hechalutz. I made *aliya* to the Land of Israel in 1926 after two years of agricultural *hachshara*.

[Page 109]
A Carpenter's Journey to the Land
by Daniel Rikless of Tel Aviv
Translated by Jerrold Landau

As if from the mist, my father's spacious, brick home flutters and appears before my eyes. It had four windows, all facing toward the street, the Rabbi's Alleyway.

What We Saw Through the Windows

The five young children, four brothers and one sister, would stare out the window during the long winter days. They each had enough panes to comfortably see all that was taking place on the street. Thanks to peering out at the alleyway and beyond, during our childhood we absorbed the entire Jonava reality, starting with the hustling of the men and women for existence. We witnessed many experiences, noticed the differences in dress, and realized that among those, there were rich and poor. I slowly digested all this, and my horizons continued to expand. These childhood impressions remain etched in my mind to this day.

We Absorbed the Atmosphere of the Home

My father Reb Meir was a member of the family of Yisrael, the owner of the brick kiln. That family consisted of five sons and four daughters. He possessed Torah education that he had received from one of the *cheders* in Jonava. Father was not able to continue his education, since from his early youth, he was forced by conditions to help Grandfather in the brick kiln. Through mutual powers, they were able to overcome the issues of livelihood for a family of 11. According to Father, the livelihood was very meager.

Father managed to persevere, and fell in love with the young lady Sara Reizel of the Landsman family of Jonava. He[5] was nicknamed *"Bina der taker"* (Bina the engraver). Thanks to this well-matched couple, both in their characters, their spirit and their youth, with time a family of four sons: Yaakov, Chaim, Nachum-Berke, and Daniel, and a sister Yudit arose. My father was a tall man. He was not a zealot, but rather a progressive man. My dear mother was the same height as Father, pretty, blond, and good hearted. She was a faithful housewife for her husband, and dedicated

[Page 110]

to the education and care of her dear children. Family life went well, and was ideal in the full sense of the term. All of this left its mark on the education of the children, who followed in the footsteps of the parents.

Livelihood was meager. Father continued to work in the brick kiln with Grandfather. He attempted to expand it. He worked at all types of physical labor for the brick kilns were primitive and "automated" only by horsepower. There were other partners in the brick kiln, Chaim and Mordechai Rikless. In order to make things easier for Father, after the children got older, mother decided to open up a bakery in the house. Thereby, she too participated in the yoke of livelihood.

In the *Cheder* with Shimon the Teacher

Like many of the children of the city, we also studied in *cheder* with Shimon the teacher. His *cheder* was located on a narrow lane on Breizer Street. Approximately twenty students studied in the cheder. The teacher was observant, a zealot, and prone to anger and wrath. We received only a Torah education there. We were required to worship together with him three times a day. The rebbe especially elongated his *Shmone Esrei* prayer. During this break we let ourselves go free – we caused trouble and pulled at his *kapote*. When he finished *Shmone Esrei*, it was as if he had taken hold of "amok." He ran after us in anger inside the *cheder* and gave us what was coming to us – to some a slap with the hand, to others a blow with the stick – and he thereby assuaged his anger.

During the Expulsion – Korolenko Saves us From a Pogrom

In 1915, in the midst of the expulsion by the Czar that decreed that the Jews must leave the District of Kovno, we too were forced to pack up some of our belongings and wander afar. We traveled in the same train wagon as other Jonava families and arrived in Poltava, Ukraine. These families were the Silberman, Kursk (Kosiksik), Judelevich families and others. We lived in Poltava until 1921, for there was no possibility of returning to Lithuania, which had received its independence in the interim, due to the civil war and chaos that pervaded at that time. My brother and I studied in a *Yeshiva* in Smolensk with a cultured rabbi, who had incidentally also come from Jonava, and settled there before the war. My brother Yaakov did not wish to study in the *Yeshiva*, so he transferred to a Byelorussian gymnasium. Our studies at that time were not especially fruitful, for the revolution and the civil war had their influence. There were many days when we had no classes.

We lived in the neighborhood in which the house of the well-known Russian writer Korolenko[6] was located. He was a good man, in fact exceptional, and he related to us refugees with great understanding and a good heart. He would often invite us to his house and treat us with all types of delicacies. To us, he appeared as a redeeming angel. A pogrom took place on our street in 1918. Korolenko hurried out to the street to influence the Cossacks to refrain from perpetrating a slaughter on us. Thereby we were saved.

Returning to our Brick Kiln

We were finally able to return to Jonava and our home in 1921. Father began to reconstruct the ruins of the kiln, and we, the sons, helped him. In a short period, Father was able to take pride in his first shipment to the market. We children continued our studies in the modern Tarbut School, under the leadership of the well-known, eminent principal Shaul Keidanski. My brother Chaim continued his studies in the renowned Slobodka Yeshiva. Every summer Friday after our studies, we all ran to our brick kiln on the banks of the Vylia. We waited an entire week for these hours. There, in the bosom of nature, we were able to give freedom to our desires – either by riding on the horses that were associated with our brick kiln, by floating on boats, by gleefully bathing together, or climbing the nearby mountain to collect and eat handfuls of wild berries. We did not assist Father with physical labor in the summer. However, in the winter, during the time of the baking of the bricks, father would assign us a task. We would transfer the bricks that had been prepared in molds beneath the screens during the summer to the large, underground oven. When it was full, Father would ignite the oven through the crater in the middle that was full of dry wood.

[Page 111]

The baking lasted for two weeks. At night, the crater of the oven was like hell. We stood afar, warming up and enjoyed this splendid experience.

Daniel and Dina Perlstein Rickless before their *aliya* with Alter Monitz

The Rikless family

Activities at Young Socialists and in the Community

A group formed in 1928, headed by Aryeh Stern, Yerachmiel Teitelbaum, Shlomo Meirovich, Alter Monitz, Dr. Shimon Zak, Naftali Gurvich and I, and founded a chapter of Young Socialists. The governments did not permit the Socialist party to organize and engage in politics, therefore it was organized under the name "Sirkin Society," for cultural work only. Of course, it engaged in undercover political activities. Our meeting place was located in Petarosovich's house. The chapter was active in the social and cultural life in Jonava until the day that it united with Young Zion-Hitachdut. Our representative in the Jonava city council was Yerachmiel Teitelbaum, and in the Keren Kayemet and Keren Hayesod it was Alter Monitz and I. All of the meetings of these committees took place in the home of David Burstein, who was the chairman of the two funds. Our two representatives to the general Sick Fund of the Kovno District were Yitzchak Burstein and I. I will mention a few of the young activitsts: Tzvi Josefs, Tzvi Perevoznik, Dov Rikless, David Friedman, the Perchik brothers, Zelig Judelevich, Zelig Abramovich, Chaim Teitelbaum, Yitzchak Nachumovich, Dina Perlstein, Tzipora Grossman, Batya Sandman, Eliahu Kagan, Eliahu Braun, and Mordechai Yaffa.

The Plans for Aliya Drag On

In 1925, I decided to actualize my philosophy and make *aliya* to the Land of Israel. I registered for the Hechalutz organization, which directed me to *hachshara* on the "Avoda" cooperative in Kovno. The director of the cooperative was Chaya Shragovich. I continued to study the carpentry trade for two years and I then received my permit for *aliya*. The gates of the land closed in 1927, and I did not receive a certificate. I was forced to return to Jonava. I worked in the carpentry shop of Moshel Klibanski and Chaim Solomin. Our family had another house, inherited from my maternal grandfather, on Breizer Street near the Josefs. Incidentally, he was known by the name: Chaim- Moshe, Reiza-Leah's, and his son was known as Hirshka, Chaim-Moshe, Reiza Leah's Josefs. Since the crowding of the carpentry shop was great, the owners of the carpentry shop allowed me to set myself up in that house and work for them. I joined my brothers Yaakov and Dov, and the three of us worked together. Thus did we become professional carpenters. Our father died in 1929, and we were orphaned. We did not want to work in the brick kiln, so we sold it and took the yoke of the family livelihood onto ourselves. I would work during the day, and be active in communal work as stated above.

[Page 112]
We Merited to Actualize our Aspirations

I married Dina Perlstein, a member of my party, in 1934. I received a certificate, bid farewell to Mother, the family, and all of our friends, and we made *aliya* to the Land as *chalutzim*. I continued to work in the carpentry trade in the Land. We set up a cooperative group. We were four *chalutzim* from Jonava: Menachem Levin, Baruch Kursk, Yaakov Katzav and I. Later, the group expanded to fourteen. The name of the group was registered as "Hamekashet." The group disbanded with the passage of time due to the recessions that afflicted the Land and that area of trade. I took possession of a carpentry shop to work independently with a partner. In the meantime, our family grew. We had a son Yosef and a daughter Meira. I continued with my family life and the traditions of my parents' home.

Thirty-six years have passed since I left Jonava, and I have never regretted that I bound my lot to the Land, despite the difficult times that overtook us. My wife Dina and I have seen in this a full realization of our aspirations. I owe gratitude to my parents and the party that educated me in this direction and brought me to this point. However, my heart is pained over my family and my wife's family who struggled but were not daring enough to make *aliya* to the Land. All of them perished in the Holocaust, including my dear mother, my sister Yudit and her family, my three brothers and their families, my two uncles Chaim and Mordechai and their families, as well as Dina's parents, her two sisters and their families. May their memories be a blessing.

[Page 112]
On the Heels of the First Ones
by Baruch Lin (Ilinevich)
Translated by Jerrold Landau

Jonava was infused with the spirit of Zionism. However, there were also many opponents to Zionism, such as the Bund. They had a Yiddish school under the auspices of the Culture League. There were also many Communists as well as very Orthodox Jews who opposed Zionism. However, most people sent their children to study in the Hebrew schools, such as Tarbut and Yavneh, and the youth regarded *aliya* to the Land of Israel as the goal of their lives.

The Zionist activities were centered around the many parties and youth organizations that operated during those years. Hechalutz incorporated youth from all parties. Hashomer Hatzair, which began as a scouting group, later turned into a youth movement with the aim of actualization, whose primary aspiration was *aliya* to the Land of Israel and Kibbutz life. There was also a Beitar movement, which also aspired toward *aliya* to the Land and sent their members to a separate *hachshara*, outside of the Hechalutz organization.

The parties and organizations had their own meeting places, most of them in small houses and rooms. However, they conducted intensive activity, infused with Hebrew culture and an honest desire to join the workers movement in the Land.

Aliya to the Land already started in the early 1920s with the *aliya* of the Achva group; including the children of the Opnitzky and Zisla families, and others. This *aliya* was symbolic of the idealism and served as an example for many youths. At the beginning of the 1930s, a large scale exodus to *hachshara* and *aliya* to the Land began. Dozens of youths from the town, members of various movements, would go to agricultural and city *hachshara*. The *hachshara* were primarily centered around German estates in the Memel area. The lads would live in group conditions, like the Kibbutzim in the Land, about which the emissaries who came from the Land would talk and direct them toward. Most of the youth, who were primarily academic youth, were not used to labor, and the *hachshara* literally prepared them for labor. Conditions on the farms were sufficiently harsh. The Germans demanded the same level of effort from these youths as they did from the veteran workers. The youths would try with all their might to overcome the difficulties and get accustomed to physical labor. Indeed, the youth who underwent *hachshara* turned into working youth. When they made *aliya*, they began to work in the orchards and in construction, and were considered to be good workers.

[Page 113]

A civic kibbutz was set up in Jonava as well. This kibbutz was comprised of youth from other towns who worked in the factories of the city and prepared for *aliya* to the Land. All of this created a veritable Israeli feeling in the town. Most of the youth would have come to the land had the Holocaust not come.

I was a member of Hashomer Hatzair. I joined Hechalutz at the age of 18 and went out to *hachshara* in the Burkenheim estate near Memel. We would receive food provisions, and the female members would cook. Life was very difficult, but we overcame, and at the end of the term we were already veritable laborers. Some of the youths were given horses and plows to plow. This was considered to be an increase in level. Despite all the hard work, the group conducted significant cultural activity. We would sit at night and discuss all types of issues. Sometimes, a delegate from the Land came and described the realities of the kibbutzim and the workers' movement to us. We would sing and dance despite our weariness. It seems to me that everyone considered that time to be the best time of our youth.

The *hachshara* term was considered to be from Passover to Sukkot. For the second term, most people went to a city-based kibbutz. I went to the city kibbutz of Hashomer Hatzair in Ponovich [Panevezys]. Life in the city kibbutz was more difficult than on the estate. Work was not always to be found, and the woman in charge of the kitchen would at times state that she had no money with which to purchase food provisions from the store. We searched for jobs. Among other things, we would chop trees for householders. However, the tree cutting trade was considered inferior, and did not bring much income. The merciful Jews could not understand how a Jewish youth from a good home would chop trees. Therefore, out of pity they did not give us work, and we did not have the means to sustain ourselves. We passed through the second *hachshara* term in the city, and I returned home for Passover. That year, 1933, there was a large scale *aliya* to the Land. Approximately 1,000 *Litai* was needed for the journey, but I did not have that sum.

Hechalutz also gave certificates to youths who had not been on *hachshara*, but who had the financial means to pay an additional sum toward the *aliya* of the *chalutzim* who lacked the means.

In order to conserve *aliya* permits, a boy and a girl would join together on one passport, as if they were a family. Thus, fictitious marriages were created which broke apart after the *aliya* to the Land.

I joined with Shifra Lomianski, of blessed memory, on my certificate. She had not been on *hachshara*. Since my mother of blessed memory and her mother were good friends, they trusted that no mishap would come from this, Heaven forbid. ..

The day of July 16, 1933 came. I left Jonava together with Leah Judelevich, Leah Grodski, and Yaakov Dubinsky. We bid farewell to our town in which we had grown up and been educated. Many people, especially family members, joined us on the bus to Kovno. I bid farewell to my mother, brothers and sisters, and did not realize that this was the final farewell. My father accompanied me to Kovno. I parted from him with blessings. He was imbued with a Zionist spirit already from his youth in the Yeshiva of Volozhin. He hoped all his days that he would have the opportunity some time to go to the Land. He did not merit such. He perished along with his entire family, the residents of our city, and all the fine youth who were imbued with the Zionist and pioneering spirit.

[Page 114]

A Town of Chalutzim
by Shimon Shapira[7]
Translated by Jerrold Landau

Shimon Shapira

I was the commander of the Beitar *hachshara* group in Jonava in 1933-1934. This pioneering unit was strengthened by members of Beitar and the Revisionist Zionists. From among them, we should note the following activists: The Kaper brothers, the Klibansky brothers, Reuven Keidansky, Nissan Goldshmid, Tzvi Wolfovich of blessed memory, and Avraham Jochovsky, may he live. Those people concerned themselves with finding workplaces, ensuring acceptable sanitary conditions, and everything necessary for the existence of the group.

The relationship of the work providers to the *chalutzim* was very humane. The owners of the enterprises were interested in the existence of the unit, and their intention was to support it. Since *hachshara* units of Beitar and Hashomer Hatzair existed, the owners of enterprises who had Revisionist leanings would take on *chalutzim* from Beitar for work, and those who belonged to the Socialist Zionists would take on *chalutzim* from the Hashomer Hatzair *hachshara* groups. Only one enterprise was an exception – Kemach – in which *chalutzim* from all *hachshara* camps worked.

The *chalutzim* worked in Kemach, with Opnitzky and Segalovsky, in Gordon's storehouses, and in Wunder's lemonade factory.

The *hachshara* units imparted a pioneering spirit and content to the city. Their existence was tied to the availability of workplaces, good relations with the community, and personal contact between each *chalutz* and admirers in the group of regular Jews.

In the evenings, discussions on political and other topics would take place in the *hachshara* units. Many of the residents of the city would come to see and listen, and become familiar with the pioneering life. On Sabbaths and festivals, city notables and regular Jews would invite the members of the *hachshara* places to meals, despite the fact that *cholent* and gefilte fish was prepared within the group.

The lives of the *chalutzim* in Jonava were different from their lives in other Lithuanian cities. Most of the residents were common folk such as tradesmen and factory workers, and including many carpenters. A sense of admiration developed between the residents and the pioneers. After the end of the *hachshara* period, most of the *chalutzim* made *aliya* to the Land, joined pioneering units and groups, and did their share toward the upbuilding of the Land. One can find those *chaluzim* scattered in many kibbutzim.

I had poor luck. I did not succeed in making *aliya* after two years of *hachshara*. I was imprisoned by the Soviet authorities in 1941 on account of my Zionist activities, and was deported to hard labor in Siberia. I finally made *aliya* to the homeland in 1966 along with my wife and three children who were born in exile in Siberia.

Fate had it that we live in the same neighborhood as Yitzchak Burstein and his sister Leah, of the veteran Zionist activist of Jonava. We often get together and discuss memories of those days, the days of pioneering that instilled into us energy, desire, hope and strength to overcome all the difficult obstacles that we suffered in Siberia – including hard labor, hunger, cold, frost, illnesses, degradation and oppression by the Soviet authorities. We were finally redeemed, and were able to reach our desired destination, and live together in the independent State of Israel.

Translator's Footnotes

A rabbinic idiom describing a situation where one earns one's income from Torah.

Kibbush means "conquest" in Hebrew.

The Hebrew word for 'fortunate' and 'authorized' are based on the same Hebrew root: *aleph, shin, reish*. This is the meaning of the title of this article.

See http://www.sazionism.co.za/hot-topics/76-enzo-sereni.html

I assume this is referring to her father.

See http://en.wikipedia.org/wiki/Vladimir_Korolenko

There is a footnote in the text here, as follows: "The writer of these lines is from Vilkomir[Ukmerge]."

[Page 117]

Some Jewish Lithuanian Scholars

From the Book of Lithuanian Jewry, Volume III, published by the Mutual Benefit Organization of Lithuanian Natives in Israel, Tel Aviv, 5727 (1967)

Translated by Jerrold Landau

Eliashzon (Elizon) Rabbi Yehoshua Heshel the son of Rabbi Baruch (from the Book of Lithuania)
(5559–5634; 1799–1874)

He was born in Yanova. He served as a rabbi in the communities of Sakiai, Yanova, ŽieŽmariai, Vilki, Švenčionys, and Seini. He was an opponent of the Musar movement[1]. He was a friend of Rabbi Leib Shapiro, the head of the rabbinical court of Kovno. A large dispute broke out during the time that he was serving as the rabbi of Yanova, and he was forced to move to Švenčionys. He was nicknamed "Rosh Barzel" (Iron Head) on account of his greatness in Torah and sharpness. He died in Seini.

Segal (Chazan), Rabbi Chaim the son of Rabbi Avraham (Rabbi Chaim of Raczki)
(5605–5674; 1845–1914)

He was born in Slabodka and studied in *yeshiva* there. He served as rabbi in Sudargas, Raczki (district of Suwalki), and Yanova (for 30 years). He authored the response book "Orach Chaim" (Vilna, 5639; 1879), and published articles in "Gathering Place of Sages" (of Rabbi Y. Ch. Deichus), and in other Torah periodicals. His own journals, the fruit of many years of labor, went up in flames during a fire that afflicted the town. He died in Yanova.

Shlomovitz, Rabbi Avraham–Abba the son of Rabbi Zeev–Mordechai
(5612–5666; 1852–1906)

He was born in Yanova, one of the honorable people of Rabbi Avraham Abli of Krozh, a student of Rabbi Shmuel–Naftali–Hirsch HaLevi Epstein (the head of the

rabbinical court of Girtakola, the author of the book "Imre Shefer" on the Song of Songs).
He was one of the *Perushim*[2] of Kovno. He founded a *Yeshiva* in Utyana and was a friend
of Rabbi Binyamin Eisenstat. He served as a rabbi in Svėdasai (5654; 1894). He wrote
the book "Noga Eish," which is glosses on the "Beer Heitev" book on Yoreh Deah[3]
(Vilna 5656; 1896). Similarly, he authored additions and notes to the book "Pitchei
Teshiva" as well as to the Talmud. He died in Vilna.

Winchevsky, Morris (Lipa–Ben–Zion) the son of Zissel Novokhovich[4]
(1856–1932)

Morris Winchevsky

Rabbi Chaim Segal (Chazan)

He was a poet. He was born in Yanova. When still a child, his family moved to Kovno,
where he received a traditional education and also attended the Russian government
school. He settled in Vilna in 1870 and prepared for his entrance examinations for the
rabbinical seminary. During that time, he also composed poems in Hebrew and Russian.
In the meantime, he obtained a position in a business enterprise in Kovno, and was sent
to Ural. There, he came in contact with radical circles and became familiar with the
Socialist literature of that generation. He moved to Konigsberg in 1877, where he began
Socialist publicity among the Jewish students who came from Russia. He founded the
"Asefat Chachamim" [Gathering of Wise Ones] monthly as a

supplement to the "Hakol" of M. L. Radkinson to clarify issues of the organization. He would sign his Hebrew articles with the name "Ben–Netz" [Son of a Spark]. He was expelled from Russia in 1879 on account of his Socialist activities. He went to Denmark, but he was also expelled from there. After a short sojourn in Paris, he moved to London, where he joined the Communist Workers Educational Society that was founded by Marcus Wanglass. He was a pioneer of Socialist journalism in Yiddish and English. He published the "Polish Ideal" newspaper. He wrote pamphlets on Socialism in Yiddish under the name "Yehi Or" [Let There Be Light] and also founded and was one of the first writers of the Arbeiter Freund. He immigrated to the United States in 1894 and edited "Emet" [Truth] – a family weekly of literature and culture. When the Forward[5] was founded, it became one of his principal occupations. He also served as the editor of the Zukunft weekly. He visited Russia in 1924 as a guest of the Soviet government, and was received there with great honor. An anthology of proletariat poetry "Kamfs Gezangen" was published in his honor in Minsk. He played an important role in Yiddish literature as a poet and a writer. Despite his Jewish topics and language, his creations had a cosmopolitan character. The primary principle was the idea of freedom of the group from the yoke of slavery. In his poems, imbued with deep lyric emotion, he presented the life difficulties of the worker. Many of his poems were translated into foreign languages. He wrote plays, parables, novels, and feuilletons. He translated some of the works of Koroleno, Ivesin, and Hugo into Yiddish. His anthologized writings were published in Yiddish in ten volumes in 1927–1928.

[Page 118]

Davidson, Israel
(1870–1939)

Israel Davidson

He was a researcher in Hebrew poetry. He was born in Yanova and educated in the Slabodka Yeshiva. He emigrated to the United States in 1888. He served as a Hebrew teacher and taught in the City College of New York and Columbia University. He was a Talmudic advisor in the Jewish Theological Seminary of New York. In 1910, he was appointed there as a professor of Medieval Hebrew literature. He was a guest lecturer at the Hebrew University of Jerusalem. His magnum opus was the "Otzar Hasira VeHapiyut"[6] in four volumes (New York, 5685–5693; 1926–1933), which includes 3,500 religious compositions of 2,843 poets, and encompasses the entirety of Hebrew poetry from the end of the Biblical period to this day, as well as secular poetry until 1740. He won the Bialik Prize in 1936. He discovered the Machzor Yannai[7] – the work of an ancient Hebrew poet — in a *geniza* [repository of worn holy books]. He published from splendid manuscripts research works on "Shalosh Halatzot" attributed to Rabbi Yosef Ibn Zabara (New York 5664; 1904); "Sefer Shaashuim" by Rabbi Yosef Ibn Zabara (New York, 5674; 1914); "Hymns and Poetry from the Geniza in Egypt" (New York 5681; 1921); "Milchamot Hashem" by the Karaite Salomon ben Yerucham (New York, 5694; 1934); the Siddur of Rabbi Saadia Gaon (Jerusalem 5701; 1941). He died in New York.

Silman, Rabbi Chaim–Yitzchak the son of Rabbi Moshe–Yechiel (5637–5690; 1877–1930)

He was born in ŽieŽmariai. He was the student of Rabbi Meir–Michel Rabinovitz of Seta. He served as a rabbi in Yanova, where he carried out broad and dedicated communal activity. People turned to him from all of Lithuania for Torah adjudications. He gave over all of his income to charity, and his household was sustained in a very meager fashion through the support of his father–in–law. During the time of the First World War, he served as a guarantor for any Jew who was suspected of treason. He moved to Vilna after the Jews were deported from Yanova in the year 5675 (1915). When he returned to Yanova, he found the city destroyed, and its *Beis Midrashes* and institutions in ruins. He put great effort into reestablishing communal life. He set up buildings for Bikur Cholim [tending to the sick], and for the Yavneh School. He also set up a charitable fund for the needy. He participated as a delegate in the Agudas Yisroel conventions. His book "Zera Yitzchak" with didactics and encores (Keidaniai, 5694; 1934) was published after his death.

Meirson, Avraham
(1881–1948)

He was a neurologist and psychiatrist. He was born in Yanova. He served as a professor of neurology at the universities of St. Louis and Harvard. He was the physician in chief at a hospital in Boston. He was the author of fundamental books that serve as textbooks for students. He was the joint author of "The German Jew – His Share in Modern Culture." He died in Brooklyn.

[Page 119]

Ginzberg, Rabbi Nachum–Baruch the son of Reb Tzemach–David(5642–5701; 1882–1941)

He was born in Ponovich (Panevėžys). His father was a baker. He was a student of Rabbi Herzl Krechmer, the author of the book Noam HaMitzvot. He served as a rabbi in Upyna, Kybartai and Yanova. He was the last rabbi of the community of Yanova. He was the author of the two volume book "Mekor Baruch" (Keidaniai, 5685–5691; 1925– 1931). He was the last president of the Rabbinical Assembly of Lithuania, was active in communal life. He was tortured by the Nazis, and died a martyr's death along with all the members of his community.

Chizka's, Pesach the son of Nachum
(1891–?)

He was a sculptor. He was born in Yanova to a glassmaker. He was orphaned during his childhood. He worked as a baker. While he was still a *cheder* student, he displayed a tendency to drawing and sculpting, and his work inspired interest. At the age of 13, he worked at a lithography painter in Kovno. The artist Leon Antokolski uncovered his talent and guided him in his work. With the assistance of the family of A. B. Wolf of Kovno, he travelled to Max Liebermann in Berlin, and was accepted for work in his studio. He studied drawing under Hermann Struk and sculpting from Hugo Kaufmann. He returned to Kovno in 1913 and worked there in sculpting and drawing. He returned to Berlin in 1919 and joined the circle of young artists, which had great influence upon him. His artistic personality crystallized in Berlin, and he returned to Lithuania in 1920. His drawings include Abraham Mapu, Torganiv, and Mordechai Antokolski. His sculptures include an elderly Jewess, the loafer, the water drawer, and the horse of Mendele Mocher Seforim.

Janosovich, Nathan the son of Yosef
(1892–1944)

He was an activist. He was born in Yanova and educated in the Knesset Yisrael Yeshiva (Slabodka). He later completed his education in Vilna and Libau. He was one of the finest of the intelligentsia in our city. He was modest by nature, and he avoided standing out in public. He directed the local youth. During the time of the First World War, he served for a brief time as the mayor of his hometown, but when his administrative character became known to the Germans, he was fired from his position. After the war, he served as the secretary to the Community Council (and later, "Azara") in Kovno. He worked with great dedication on behalf of the Historical–Ethnographic Society. He published articles under the pseudonym "Yannai" — the vast majority of which were dedicated to the history of Lithuanian Jewry. He published "Year In and Year Out" (1940) – an annual calendar dedicated to the folklore and history of the Jews of Lithuania. He perished along with his family in the Kovno Ghetto.

Gazit (Zisla), Dov the son of Tzvi–Yaakov
(1897–1960)

He was an educator. He was born in Yanova. He received a Torah education during his childhood and studied in the Knesset Yisrael Yeshiva (Slabodka) for four years. He completed his general studies and his teaching degree. He began to work as a teacher in Yanova in 1917. In 1919, he founded and directed in Pilvishok (Pilviskiai) the first Hebrew public school in Lithuania. He served as a teacher in the Hebrew Gymnasium of Mariampol, where he joined Hechalutz and became a member of its central organization in Lithuania. He also was involved with Kvutzat Brenner, and worked for two years in the "Kibush" cooperative group in Pelėdnagiai. He completed the upper school for agriculture in Berlin. He made *aliya* to the Land in 1924. He worked in agriculture in Tel Yosef, and served as the principal of a school for the children of workers in Tel Aviv. He served as a teacher in the Ben–Shemen Youth Village. Following that, he served for 15 years as the teacher and principal of the primary school in the Borochov neighborhood. In 1942, he set up and served as principal of the local high school. In 1943, he began to serve as a supervisor of higher education for the worker's stream, and served as vice chairman for the educational committee of the national council. He founded and served as principal of the teacher's seminary of the educational center, that later became the Seminary for Teachers and Kindergarten Teachers in Givat Hashlosha. From 1948 to 1950, he gathered together and directed the educational activities in the American Occupation Zone of Germany on behalf of the

Jewish Agency. When he returned, he served as the director of the professional education division of the Ministry of Education (1950–1951). From 1953, he served in the agricultural education branch as the chief inspector of agricultural schools. He published many articles in "Davar", "Haaretz", "Hed Hachinuch", "Hachinuch", "Orim", and "Chaklaut BeYisrael." His compositions were: "Principles of Sorting and Developing Plants" together with Chana Nemlich (Tel Aviv, 1959); "The History of Agricultural Settlement in the Land of Israel" (Tel Aviv, 1962). He died in Tel Aviv. An anthology of his articles was published posthumously under the name of "Talmei Chinuch" (Tel Aviv, 1962).

[Page 120]

Dov Gazit

Kulvianski, Yeshayahu the son of Tovia
(born in 1892)

He was an artist. He was born in Yanova to his father, who was a carpenter. He was educated in the *cheder* and the primary school in the town. He was raised in the atmosphere of the *Haskalah* era. He displayed a talent in sculpting while he was still a child. He studied in the government school for the arts in Vilna in 1908. His first creation, ("Scholars") was displayed at an artistic display there. He went to Berlin in 1912 and became a student of Hermann Struk and Hugo Kaufmann. He served in the Russian Army during the First World War. He returned to Berlin after the war where he continued his academic studies in art. He was a member of the "November Group"[8] of German artists. He displayed his pictures in various showings in Berlin, Prague, Vienna, Zurich, Amsterdam, and Kovno. He lived in Israel from 1933–1950. His pictures were displayed at various showings in Jerusalem, Tel Aviv, and Haifa. He won prizes from the Jewish Agency and the Tel Aviv city council. He lived in France from 1950. His art was displayed in the Salon Des Enfants and other places (Berlin, Vienna, Oslo, and Helsinki). His creations include: the Jewish Carpenter, the Death of a Carpenter, My Parents, and others. [also see page 122 of the original book for more on Kulvianski]

Left :R. Israel Yaakov, father of the artist Alter Kagan

Right: Artist Alter (David) Kagan and his wife Leiba Channah (born Shtern)

Leiba Channah and the twins- Sarah and Rivka

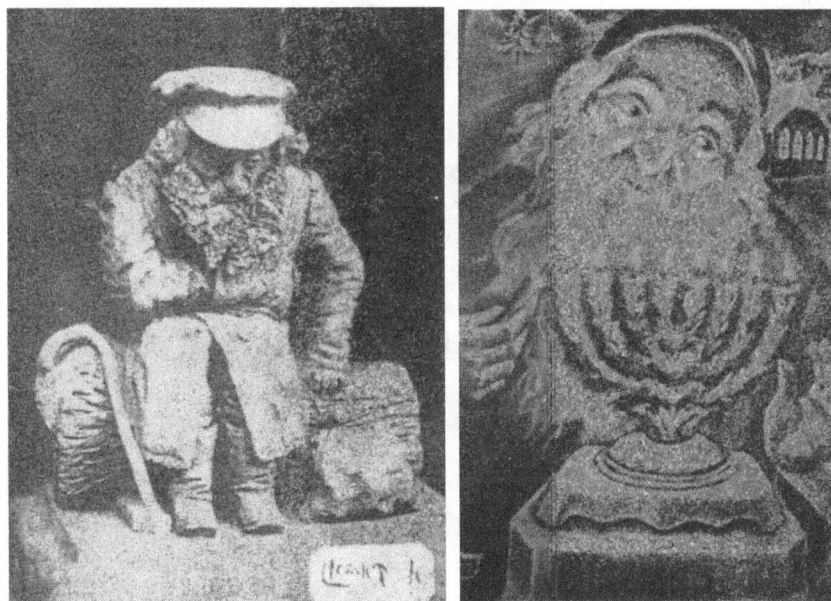

From the works of Alter Kagan:
Left- "The Wandering Jew" - (sculpture in clay). "The artist wrote- To my friend Aharon Zisele- Turn it over and you will see a typical figure of the Exile. You must be strong and seek freedom."

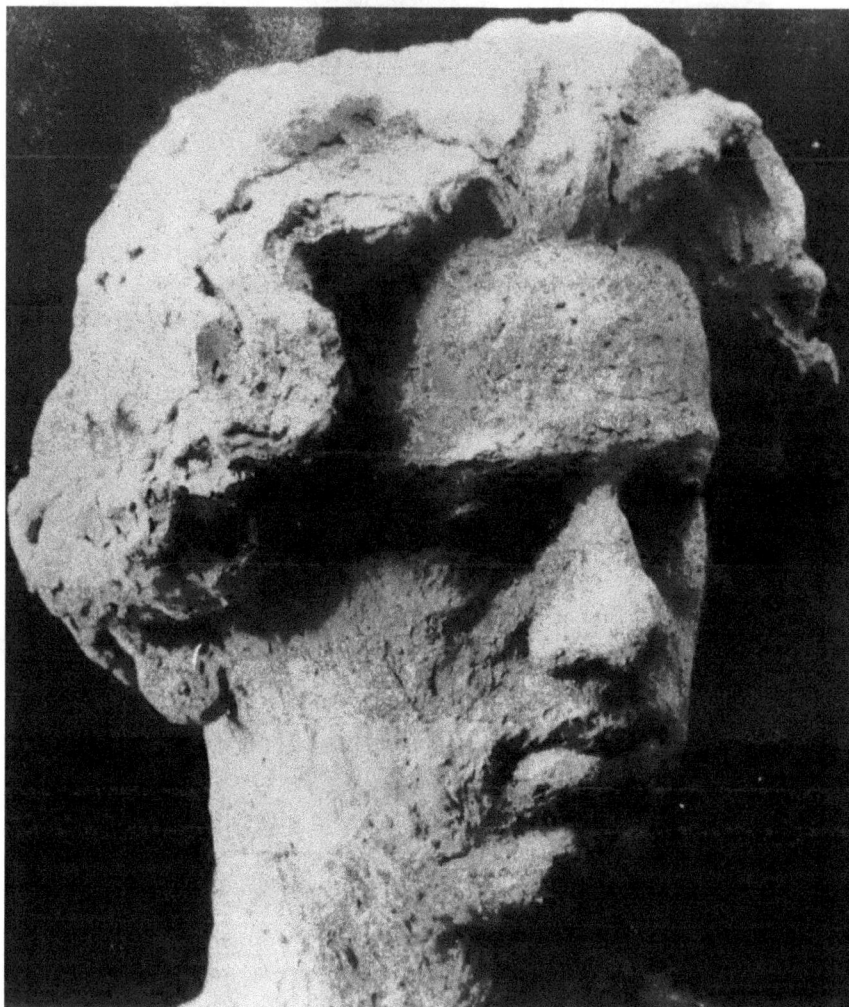

Sculpture. Self portrait of Kulvianski at the age of 14. Janowa 1904. Wood (?) Lost

Painting. "My Parents." Oil on Canvas 150 X 135 cm. Sgd middle below: Issai Kulviansky Bu Janowa 1925. Berlin. New National Gallary. Berlin-West. Tendency: "Neue Sachlichkeit."

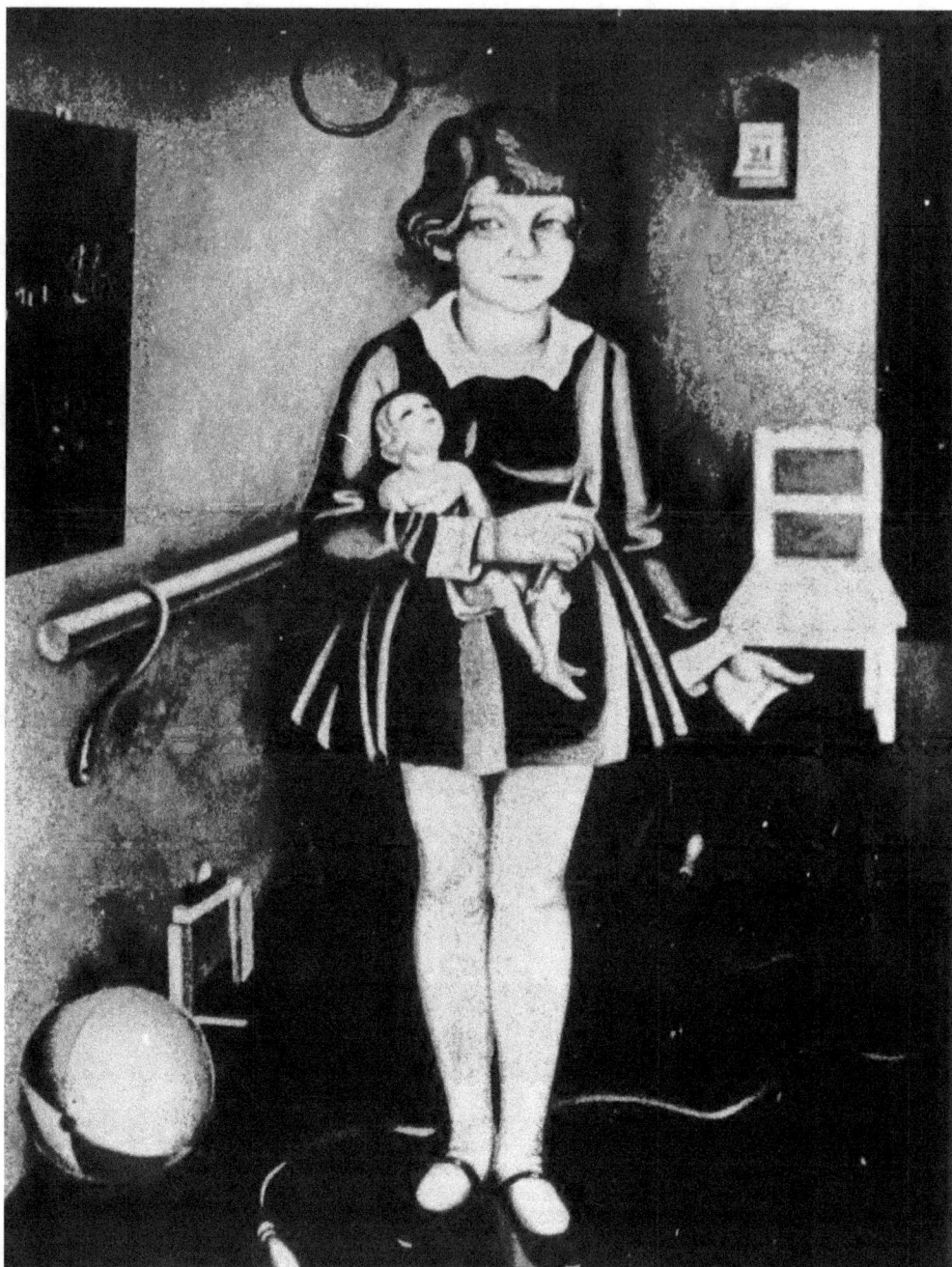

Painting. "My Daughter Kiki." Oil on canvas 127/96. Signed right below: Kulvianski 1927. Tendency: "Neue Sachlichkeit." In possession of Mrs. S. Kulcianski.

Painting. "Portrait of the actor Mischa Tschernoff" also called "The Fat Man." Oil on canvas 175X145. Signed right below: Kulvianski 1928. Tendency: "Neue Sachlichkeit." Lost after 1933.

Painting. "Death of a Jewish Carpenter." Oil on canvas 190.5 X 70. Signed right below: Kulvianski 1926. Tendency: "Neue Sachlichkeit." Bezalel – Israel Museum, Jerusalem

Painting. "Jewish Cabinmaker." Oil on canvas 82 X 65. Signed right below: Kulvianski 1927. Has been in possession of the Jewish Museum, Berlin. Tendency: "Neue Sachlichkeit." Lost after 1933.

Painting. "Old Jew." Oil on canvas. About 1940 In possession of Mrs. S. Kulcianski.

Sculpture. Steel. 1951. Tendency: Construction. In possession of Mrs. S. Kulcianski.

Painting. "Rabbi." Oil on canvas 120 X110. Signed right below:
Kulvianski 1952.   In possession of Mrs. Kulcianski.

Painting. "Composition ." Oil on paper, about 92 X 65. Signed right below: Kulvianski, Paris 1956. Tendency: "Neue Sachlichkeit." In possession of Mrs. S. Kulcianski.

Zisla (Lavie), Rachel the daughter of Tzvi Yaakov
(1899–1931)

She was a pioneer. She was born in Yanova. She was educated in the Russian public school and the Jewish–German Gymnasium of Kovno. When the pioneering movement arose in Lithuania, she stopped her studies and joined a *hachshara* group. She made *aliya* to the Land in 1919. She worked at planting in Hadera, with vegetables in Karkur, in building at Kfar Giladi, and in the hospital at Migdal. She became well–rooted in the Ein Harod Kibbutz, where she married Shlomo Lavie, and gave birth to two sons and a daughter. Her personality shone with light, love, joy, and faith. She was revered by all her friends and acquaintances. She died at a young age in Ein Harod. Her two sons fell in the War of Independence.

Kagan, David (Alter) the son of Yisrael–Yaakov
(1901–1941)

He was a painter. He was born in Yanova. He was educated in the *cheder* of his father the teacher, and grew up in a religiously Orthodox environment. He was a teacher in the Talmud Torah at age 20. He began to draw at an advanced age as an autodidact, and displayed serious talent within a short time. He travelled abroad for a brief time in 1927. Jewish artists in Berlin and Paris expressed great interest in his creations that he displayed there, and prophesied a great future for him. When he returned to Lithuania, he continued with his work in teaching, and continued to draw due to loneliness and a sense of being cut off from the outside world. Few saw his drawings. For the most part, the topic of his art was life in the *Beis Midrash* and his religious environment – the Talmud study group, Jews studying *Mishnah*, charity collectors, people of high moral standards, and simple Jews. He was noted for his simplicity and clarity. His style was realistic in form and color. He was one of the wonders of the artists of Lithuania of the latter period. He perished in Yanova during the Holocaust era.

Translator's Footnotes

See http://en.wikipedia.org/wiki/Musar_movement

See http://en.wikipedia.org/wiki/Perushim

Yoreh Deah is one of the four sections of the Code of Jewish Law.

See http://www.museumoffamilyhistory.com/yt/lex/W/winchevsky–morris.htm

See http://en.wikipedia.org/wiki/The_Jewish_Daily_Forward

Literally: The Treasury of Poetry and Hymns, but known colloquially as Thesaurus of Medieval Hebrew Poetry.

See https://archive.org/details/mazoryannaialit00ginzgoog

See http://en.wikipedia.org/wiki/November_Group_(German)

[Page 121]

Rabbi Chaim Yitzchak Silman

By the sisters Sara Pinta and Mina Markusevich (nee Silman) of Tel Aviv

Translated by Jerrold Landau

Rabbi Chaim Yitzchak Silman by the sisters Sara Pinta and Mina Markusevich (nee Silman) of Tel Aviv

The Rabbi and Gaon Chaim Yitzchak Silman the son of Rabi Moshe Yechiel was one of the famous rabbis of Lithuania. His fame spread beyond Lithuania, to the rest of Europe and overseas. He was chosen for the rabbinical seat of Yanova when he was still young. Before that, he was supported for some time at the table of his in–laws, the honorable resident Reb Bentza of Sesik [Siesikai]. In his home in Sesik, he continued to fill himself with Torah and rabbinical decisions, without differentiating between day and night.

In addition to his great knowledge in Torah, he had many other talents that he used to serve the Jews of his city with his heart and soul. Even the Christians related to him with honor on account of his just judgments between man and his fellow. In any dispute between two Jews, or between a Jew and a Christian that was brought before the local government judge, that judge would first turn to the rabbi. Rabbi Silman was known as a man who pursued peace. His verdicts were famous, and people came to him from all of Lithuania. He used his money for communal needs. He concerned himself with the religious education of the children of the city. The Yavneh School, in which about 200 students studied, was established through his initiative and money. He was active in building the civic hospital, and he took interested in the building of the new bathhouse (Panske Bad) and slaughterhouse.

His house was open to everyone from the early morning until the late evening. Any person with a bitter soul would find help and support with the rabbi.

The political libel from the 1930s, in which a youth who was a member of the Revisionist party, Aver Unterschatz, was accused of the murder of a Christian agent, is remembered by the natives of Yanova. Rabbi Silman, together with the rest of the community notables, dedicated himself completely to the aim of saving Unterschatz from the death that was awaiting him. He gathered a large sum of money, and enlisted a staff of well–known lawyers, headed by professor Bliatzkin of Kovno in order to defend the innocent youth. He himself appeared as a witness in the district court of Kovno. His words and appearance had a great influence upon the judges, and the youth finally was released.

During the First World War, when the Jews of Lithuania were deported, the rabbi concerned himself with helping the poor of Yanova. He was the last one to leave the city.

His wife, the modest rebbetzin Chana Leah, should be remembered positively. She was his helpmate in all of his blessed endeavors. She forewent a more comfortable life in order to enable the rabbi to provide the necessary money for communal needs. After his death, with the help of the rabbi's late brother, Rabbi Aharon Eliezer Silman, she published one of his books, "Zera Yitzchak." The rebbetzin perished in the Holocaust.

May their memory be blessed.

[Page 122]

His Entire Life Was Dedicated to His Art

by Yeshayahu Kulviansky

Translated by Jerrold Landau

"Yanova could be the pride of its sons" – thus writes Kulviansky's wife in her letter to us, in which she informs us that her unforgettable husband Yeshayahu passed away after a lengthy illness in London in November 1970.

In the continuation of her letter, she writes, "How fortunate could it have been if he were alive today and had heard about you and your intention to write a book on his beloved Yanova. You should know that Kulviansky had always been bound and faithful to his native town, in which he spent his childhood. There were many stories and depictions of his family, people of the town, its houses, its landscape, and its ways of life. He drew all of his influence from that place, which gave him the basis for his entire life in every place that fate took him. When, with the passage of years and his artistic development during various period of his life, he translated these impressions into the language of color and images, everything was influenced from the fruitfulness and richness of his beloved hometown."

"His personality was dynamic and gifted. He did not know any compromise with anything related to his art. He was a very proud Jew, an upright person, with a hearty, refined, and loving relationship to his friends and to everyone worthy of such."

"He wrote a great deal in Yiddish, particularly regarding Yanova. He would think and speak in a free manner and supple fashion."

She further writes:

"Despite the various styles in his creations, several themes stand out:"

"His dedication and faithfulness to Jewish life and his hometown; his feelings toward color; his connection to the avant garde in his conceptions; his ideas and aspirations; and with all that, he was free. He did not want to be bound into a specific niche, and he would work on different projects simultaneously."

"The following are some of his ideas on art:"

"Light is eternity, it is the primary source of color and form. It is the constant forger of spirit and physicality."

"The world of vision is different from the spiritual world; Art is the spiritual pinnacle of creativity."

"If we can do so, and pour richness onto creativity – we would decree upon you that you should find no rest, and that you would toil as long as your soul is within you."

"The secret of true art is bound up with the power of imagination that comes to actuality."

"The sole goal of art – spiritual truth."

"This comes from itself, as a spontaneous revolution, and becomes an independent investigation of creativity."

"Human creativity knows no bounds other than those of individual existence."

Yeshayahu Kulviansky

[Page 123]

Regarding his exhibit in Tel Aviv in 1938, Noach Stern writes the following, among other things:

"Anyone who claims that a Lithuanian Jew does not know the crown of colors and strong vitality – should go to see the paintings of Kulviansky. Like other Jewish–Lithuanian artists who stemmed from the working class or the common folk, he belongs to a group that is full of vitality and rich in power, suffused with full, meaningful life. This is the typical thread in his creations..."

"... Kulviansky barely gives over the form, but he does give over the essence, both physical and spiritual as one. His impressions minimize the physical and stress the ethereal; he does not present the optical, form–based impression, but rather the internal, psychological one..."

(From the book "Between the Clouds – songs, translations and articles on Noach Stern," published posthumously by Avraham Broides for the Writers Guild.)

From his many works, we will mention here the most prominent ones:

The Talmudist — in the Jewish Museum of Moscow.

My Parents — in the New National Gallery, West Berlin.

A Jewish Furniture Maker — in the Jewish Museum of Berlin until lost in 1933.

The Death of a Jewish Carpenter— formerly in the Jewish Museum of Berlin, today in Betzalel.

Silence — owned by the Giladi family of Degania Bet.

The Image of the Actor Mischa Chernoff — Lost in 1933.

The Houses of Kiki — owned by Mrs. Kulviansky, West Berlin.

The Image of a Woman — owned by Mrs. Kulviansky, West Berlin.

The Sea — owned by Mr. Strauch, Stockholm.

The Concern — presented by a Jewish organization to Bronislav Huberman, today owned by the Tel Aviv Philharmonic.

The Sand Wagon — in the Tel Aviv Museum.

Many works are found in private collections in Israel, Paris, London, West Germany, New York, etc.

Yeshayahu Kulviansky (November 5, 1892 – November 27, 1970)

1892 – Born in Yanova

1908 – Studied with Antokolski in Vilna. Sold some works. Befriended Soutine.

1912 –Studied at the Academy of Arts in Berlin under Professor Hugo Kaufmann. Worked with Liberman and Hermann Struk. Worked primarily at sculpting.

1913 – In Paris. Became acquainted with Chagall. Renewed his friendship with Soutine.

1914 – Participated in an exhibit in the Gurlitt Gallery in Berlin.

1914 – Forced to return to Lithuania. Served as a soldier during the First World War.

1918 – Returned to Berlin to complete his studies. Dedicated himself to painting.

1920 –Joined the November Group and was selected to the group of Judges (Klein, Kandinsky, and others).

1922 –1924 – A member of the Union of Berlin Artists.

1923 – Participated in an exhibit.

[Page 124]

1927 –1928 – An art teacher in a school in Berlin

1927 –1929 – Illustrator for the Radio Weekly.

1927 –Invited to participate in an exhibit, in which he exhibited "The Jewish Prayer Room".

1928 –Participated in an exhibit in Zurich on the occasion of the 16th World Zionist Congress (along with Pisarro, Libermann, Chagall, Modigliani, and others).

1929 –Participated in the "Humor in Art" exhibit in Berlin.

1930 –Participated in an exhibit in Prague: "Jewish Art in the 19th and 20th Centuries" – from Jozef Israëls until the era of modern art. He also participated in the "International Exhibit of Socialist Art" in a museum in Amsterdam.

1932 –A solo exhibit in Kovno.

1933 –Made *aliya* to the Land, leaving behind his works, which were lost.

1934 –1935 –Established an art school in Tel Aviv along with the sculptor Leshnitzer.

1934 – Among the founders and members of the "Professional Union of Artists of the Land of Israel."

1937 –1940 –A counselor and educator of art in the Teachers Seminary of the Kibbutzim, Tel Aviv.

1937 –A large solo exhibit in the Tel Aviv Museum.

1938 –A second solo exhibit.

1938 –1939 –Participated in the World Exhibition in New York, in the Jewish Pavilion.

1940 –Awarded an artistic prize from the Tel Aviv city council.

1941 –A third solo exhibit in the Tel Aviv Museum. Also a solo exhibit in the Betzalel Museum. Awarded an artistic prize from the Jewish Agency.

1940 –1950 –Participated in various exhibits. Worked with Habima in painting the sets for Tevye the Milkman, Fedora, Children to their Borders, and the Mallet, as well as the "The Bartered Bride" opera of Smetana. Forced to leave Israel for health reasons.

1950 –Lived in France, West Germany, and England. Dedicated himself again to sculpting.

1952 –1968 –A member of the Jewish Artists Guild in Paris.

1956 –1968 –A member of the Salon of Independent Artists in Paris

1960 –Participated in an exhibit in Berlin, as well as in Vienna, Oslo, and Helsinki. His works can be found in the Museum of Modern Art in New York, the Tel Aviv Museum, Betzalel, the Jewish Agency in New York, and the New Art Gallery of West Berlin. He stopped working in his latter years.

1970 –Died in London.

*

"First and foremost, he was a Jewish artist," Rabbi Y.D. Goldberg of London spoke about him in his eulogy. "He acknowledged his Jewish roots, and loved to recognize his childhood in Yanova, and life in the town, on canvas and in his words."

"He dedicated his entire life to art. If he demanded a great deal of others, this was because he demanded even more of himself."

"He was 78 when he died after 30 years of happy marriage. During his latter years, he was forced to abandon his work because of his illness."

"His personality, his good heart, and his creative talents will not be forgotten."

[Unnumbered page following 124]

Shifra – The Amateur Artist by Ida Braun

Four years have already passed since we lost Shifra. Her noble spirit, her modesty and straightforwardness float before our eyes.

Shifra Lamiansky was a native of Yanova, and studied in the Hebrew Gymnasium of Kovno. From a very young age, her desire was to attend an art school. However, to her great dismay, this never materialized, and she was forced to compromise on the pure art and to choose the vocation of professional photography. Having no choice, she dedicated herself to this profession with her entire soul and means, and completed her education in that profession in the school of the professional photographer Tallat– Kelpša.

Shifra made *aliya* to the Land in 1933. There, she created countless professional photographs. In addition, since she was an artist from birth and the womb, she did not forgo the brush. She took private lessons in painting with the artist Hendler, and also attended an art school.

Shifra's amateur artistic creations excelled in their delicate and calm colors. For the most part, these were pictures of flowers and various inanimate objects. We all were happy when we received one of Shifra's paintings as a gift. Lovely paintings brought by Shifra as a gift and an expression of her warm feelings to a person or a family adorn most of the houses of her friends. She bestowed upon them the fruits of her creative spirit.

Shifra's sudden passing during the prime of her life was a great blow to us – her friends and admirers.

May her memory be blessed forever! Woe over those who have gone and will not be forgotten!

A still–life painting by Shifra Lamiansky

A still–life painting by Shifra Lamiansky

[Page 125]

Personalities and Events

One of the Dear Ones of Jonava
by Yitzchak Ben-David

Translated by Jerrold Landau

Apparently Moshe Ivensky

Moshe Ivensky was born in 1897 in the village of Geguzine near Vilna, 14 kilometers east of Jonava, into a traditional Jewish family. His father Reb David, known as David the miller, was a simple villager, straightforward in his ways, fearing Heaven, with fine character traits. His mother was a cultured woman who read a great deal in Yiddish and German. She believed that she would earn her reward in the world of truth in reward for her good deeds in this world.

Childhood Landscape

This family owned a flourmill driven by water and machines for working wool. The farmers of the region would come to them, and all of them honored Reb David and his wife. Livelihood was found in abundance.

David had two children, Moshe and Shlomo. David attempted to bring teachers in for his children and the other Jewish children of the village. When the children got older, Reb David sent them to Vilna in order to obtain education in modern cheders. They also attended the Russian school.

Moshe was graced with great abilities. He studied diligently and constantly read Hebrew and Russian literature. He displayed a tendency toward communal work already from his youth. He would gather the children around him, and tell them legends and stories from reading or from the imagination. He would organize various games, and was considered as the leader of the children. In the calm village, surrounded by the landscape of forests, meadows, ponds and the Vylia, and under the influence of his honest parents, a refined, dreamy soul developed in him from his youth.

During the Expulsion

The family wandered to Vilna as a result of the decree of expulsion during the First World War. As the front approached, the family decided that Reb David would remain in Vilna until the danger passed, while the mother and the two sons would continue their journey with the stream of refugees to central Russia. Reb David returned to his native village after the Germans conquered Vilna. There, in Geguzine, he reactivated the flourmill and the wool working machines. Business flourished. There was no news from the family. Contact with Russia was severed due to the revolution and civil war.

During the years 1916-1919, a great famine pervaded in Vilna and its environs. Many Jews dispersed to the towns and villages in search of food and work. David the miller housed refugee families in his home. His home was open to every passerby and guest, and many people ate at his table. He fed and clothed all of them, and also gave them money and provisions for the journey.

His wife and two children returned in 1919 and found the house filled with all good things. The boys had grown up in the interim. In Russia they had studied in a Russian school, and they also had not forsaken their studies of Hebrew, Bible and literature.

Mother Struggles with her Share in the World To Come

After thee return of Reb David's wife, the women and men praised her husband to her ears, and told her of his many charitable deeds. After she absorbed these stories, jealousy took root within her. How? From the knowledge that her husband had amassed so many good deeds, and she was not a partner to all this?! Her husband was to be forced to divide his reward for his good deeds, which made him eligible for the World to Come, equally with her. These thoughts gave her no rest. One day, she turned to her husband and said:

"David, I want you to declare in the synagogue in front of the community that you are prepared to share with me your reward for your good deeds that you performed in my absence so that I can also enjoy them in the World of Righteousness."

Reb David was stubborn, and he was not willing to share. The peace in the home was disrupted. One Sabbath, when the Torah reader approached for the reading of the Torah, his wife girded herself with brazenness and interrupted the reading. She declared her claim with a loud voice and demanded the fulfillment of her demand. A long and tiresome discussion ensued. With the influence of the other householders, Reb David agreed to share, and to proclaim this in public. The Torah reading resumed, and the peace of the household returned.

Settling in Jonava and Immersion in Communal Affairs

Moshe Ivensky found the place too constricting, so he moved to Jonava in order to find work and communal activities. There, he had the opportunity to develop his talents and to broaden his knowledge by reading books and self study. He had the opportunity to sharpen his talents as an orator and public speaker. He had already demonstrated this talent in exile in Russia during the revolution. The young socialist was taken by the idea of the revolution, and he proclaimed his thoughts publicly with the enthusiasm of youth. The motto that he frequently stated with respect to those days was: "They wore a cloak for two weeks, but something was taking place." Despair came quickly. The Yevsektsia[1] became despicable to him. They fought against nationalist tradition and the Hebrew language and literature.

In Jonava, he was hired as an official in the public bank. When he arrived, he joined Tzeirei-Zion – Hitachdut, which at the time numbered approximately 100 active members and many other supporters. After a brief time he was elected as the chairman. He took interest in the sporting activities of Maccabee, and he was elected to the cultural committee. He was one of the important orators, and the youth was swept along with his fascinating words. He was elected to the community council, which in those days of the flourishing of Jewish autonomy in Lithuania, fulfilled an important role in social life. He was active on the committees of the national funds and lectured often at all Zionist organizations about the building of the Land and Zionism. He even preached fiery speeches about current events on Sabbaths from the synagogue pulpit. He would often debate with his Yiddishist and Communist rivals.

Moshe Establishes a Family

His mother's health weakened during the first years of his activities. His father came to Jonava to search for a Jewish woman who would take care of her. Along with the stream of refugees from places afflicted by famine came a young maiden from Mejszago³a, Mina Abramovitch. Since she was alone, his acquaintances recommended to him to take her to Geguzine. She agreed.

At first, Moshe traveled to visit his parents almost every Sabbath. There, Moshe met the beautiful girl Mina and fell in love with her. After a brief period, he became engaged to her, and then married her. The wedding took place in Jonava with great splendor. All of his friends and admirers participated in it. The members of the couple were not equivalent in the cultural and intellectual sense, but he admired her for her straightforwardness and dedication, and she was proud of the man, who was considered number one in Jonava, who chose her. They had two sons and a daughter – Yeshayahu, Reuven and Nechama.

The Spiritual Leader of the Youth

Concerns of livelihood, care of children, and spending time with his wife forced him to cut back on some of his communal work. However he rejoiced at every opportunity to appear on the stage, to do battle with his combatants, and to see the larger community who thirsted for his words and would take in the stream of his orations. For 15 years, he was the spiritual leader of most of the Jonava youth who were sheltered under the banner of Tzeirei-Zion – Hitachdut, Gordonia, Hechalutz, Maccabee, Tz. S., Beitar and Mizrachi. He did not know of compromise. He did not vacillate. He correctly evaluated the hidden threat of Nazism to the physical existence of the Jewish people, and fought against this impurity to the best of his ability.

Throughout the 1930s, the Jews of Lithuania declared a boycott against products of Nazi Germany. He was tirelessly bound to this endeavor. He was the chief of the spokesmen and the supporters.

When the Soviets entered Jonava, he "folded up" completely and waited for better days.

Like the Lot of Many Others

With the Nazi invasion, he decided to escape to Russia along with his family. Somewhere along the way, they were caught up in an air raid. The family dispersed in the confusion of the bombardment. We do not know of his fate, and that of his wife and his daughter. The two sons continued to flee in the direction of the Russian border. Only the eldest Yeshayahu was miraculously saved from the satanic talons. Today he is in America, and he describes everything that happened to him in his memoirs that are published in the book.

An Exemplary Image

The image of Moshe Ivensky floats before my eyes again and again. I see him sitting next to the counter in the public bank of Jonava, with a long, reddish-brown beard. His black hair with a part on the right side was slightly unkempt. The outline of his face was straight, good and refined. I always compared his visage to that of Herzl. I see him chatting with a customer or engaged in a fiery debate with a disputant. He was not at all concerned about his external appearance. His white cloak was without a collar, open, one sleeve was rolled up and the other moved with every motion of his hand.

He was a modest man in his life. In his opinion, concern about externals was superfluous. The most important thing which he stressed was matters of the spirit. I worked at his side in the party for many years. We operated the Maccabee and the Hebrew library together. He was always an example to me.

I will never forget him and we will never forget him.

These impressions from the father's house were recorded from the mouth of Frank Sirek, United States.

Translator's Footnotes

The Yevsektsia was the Jewish section of the Soviet Communist party, which wanted to eradicate the Bund and Zionist parties. See the following wikipedia article: http://en.wikipedia.org/wiki/Yevsektsiya

[Page 127]

I Learned a Great Deal from Him: More on Ivensky

by Sara Burstein

Translated by Jerrold Landau

In my first meeting with him, I was surprised and astounded at his external appearance and personal charm. He was still young, but he nevertheless had a flowing beard. He had black, disheveled locks of hair, a penetrating gaze, and refined, sculpted wrinkles on his face.

His entire body was in perpetual motion, especially his hands, which he moved to emphasize his words.

I was astounded that his physical appearance was so similar to Herzl.

The second and strongest impression came when he opened his mouth to speak and debate. I was enchanted and silenced by his words. At times, I had the impression that I was listening to the words of a prophet of yore, reproving and preaching in the gate, delivering his words with emphasis and logic.

He lectured on various topics - literature, arts, culture, and politics. He was intelligent and inspired. Everything was clear to him, even though he was an autodidact. His bountiful knowledge was gleaned from a great deal of reading, which he absorbed and digested thanks to his blessed talents. He was modest and upright to the point of innocence. He never wavered from his path, the path paved and forged with a good heart, dedication, faithfulness and diligence.

When I got to know him better and he used to visit our house, he once came to me with the recommendation that I take on the task of the accounting for the funds. He brought two large ledgers, once for the Keren Kayemet [Jewish National Fund] and the other for the Keren Hayesod, which had recently been founded. He also brought cards with the names of "householders" who were willing to donate with monthly payments. At the end, he recommended sincerely that I myself deal with the small expenditures, such as paper, ink, pens, and sponges [1]. Of course, I agreed.

[Page 128]

His words rang in my ears like the words of the living G-d. My awe and respect for him continually grew.

He led his private life discreetly. His low salary from the public bank was barely sufficient to meet his expenses. His wife was sickly, and his three children also had their requirements. He could have easily earned additional money outside his work hours, but his fruitful volunteer work for the land of Israel, that swallowed every free moment, prevented this. He did not want to turn this activity into a means of livelihood [2].

We would once again meet on occasion during my second winter in Jonava, during the vacation between study semesters in the Diaspora. One day, he appeared with a request, apparently in the name of the parents' committee, that I agree to give evening courses in English for the grade five students of the Tarbut School. I did not have the power to refuse, even though I was not a teacher or the daughter of a teacher.

I began as a "volunteer" teacher, and inexperienced teacher, who entered the classroom for the first time with trembling knees. However, Ivensky encouraged me and even offered me complements that I was successful, and that all my students were doing well…

Thanks to this, I benefited from my teaching experience when I came to the land. As a member of WIZO [3] in Kovno, I also joined WIZO and became a volunteer Hebrew teacher for new female immigrants. I did this for a few years until the Ulpan (school for new immigrants) stole my "livelihood."

At times, when the memory of Ivensky comes before me, I offer a blessing in my heart that I knew him. I learned a great deal from him.

I have a small picture of him as a memento. He wrote something on it, and it served as a symbol to me for everything sublime in the world.

Ivensky in the center. The Gordonia Youth Organization in Jonava

Shimon Zak, physician, in British Army fatigues

Aryeh Stern, lawyer

Menashe Weiner, chemist

Translator's Footnotes

Used for old fashioned pens.

Literally, "Into a spade for digging", a rabbinical adage referring to using a spiritual position to earn a livelihood.

Women's International Zionist Organization.

[Page 129]

Shmuel Goldshmid

(Autobiographical article)

Translated by Jerrold Landau

I was born in Jonava on the Road of the Street, number 33. With the passage of time, our street changed its named to Ralis Street, after Dr. Jeronimas Ralis,[1] the physician of our city, who was one of the founders of independent Lithuania and the translator of Homer into Lithuanian. If I have a single connection to famous people of Jonava, it is that Dr. Ralis himself delivered me. He would often say that of all his "deliveries," I was the only one who delved into the depths of his translation, and even knew some parts by heart. He told my mother: "Gita, you have a writer in the house. I hope that he will translate Homer into Hebrew." People bigger and better than me did this, and I do not even know Greek. However, I did become a journalist!

My father, Reb Chaim Goldschmid, was great in Torah and an expert in the literature of the middle ages. From him I studied topics on the Rambam, Yehuda HaLevi and Shlomo Ibn Gabirol. However, he was forced to earn his livelihood from a hide shop. To this day I love the smell of leather (for soles of shoes), and understand the quality.

From the Tarbut School, I transferred to the Hebrew Gymnasium of Kovno which was run by Dr. Moshe Shava. This was one of the best schools in the Diaspora. I graduated without undue effort, and I also was able to play basketball, sail on the Vilia and the Neiman rivers, ride horses – and write humorous articles in Yiddish. I also edited the student newspaper during my final year in the gymnasium. Two articles of mine about reading Shalom Aleichem and the joy of mathematics were published in Netivateinu. The latter demonstrated that I did not pay attention to the problems of the other during those days…

When I saw my name in print, I realized – no, I believed! – that I was already an expert on everything, a great writer, and a penetrating analyst. In any case, I entered the Vytautas Magna University and studied mathematics and law. I finished the course in law, and I excelled in criminology and criminal law rather than international law.

Throughout all my years in university, I worked as the night editor of the Yiddishe Shtime. Later, I became the editor of the night edition of the Shtime – Heintke Neies. I wrote the daily column and at times even the leading article.

In 1937, I traveled to the 20th Zionist Congress in Zurich. I do not know if I reported appropriately, but I learned how to size up all types of politicians and activists. To this day, I have had more than enough of them. At that congress I learned as well that we are in need of a country, and that equal rights alone is nothing other than deception.

Czechoslovakia during the time of the victory of the Nazis over the west, the bitter and hopeless days that were a second rung in my path as an international journalist. After this England – and the breadth of the war… I was a military writer throughout all the days of the Second World War. Fate had it that I was on site during the liberation of Belsen and Dachau. From that time, my heart turned to stone, and I do not react appropriately, for these scenes were beyond the pale of conception for a Jewish person. The time of the Belsen and Nuremburg trials were days of feverish work, with the descriptions of the hell that we heard, and meeting the war criminals face to face.

My four books, one of them in Hebrew, were published and sold – established a place for me in the world of essays, political writing. However at times it seemed to me that all of this – articles, essays, columns, books, editing for the Jewish News Agency (ST"A) of Europe – was performed in the light of a giant fire from which I was miraculously saved, for I stood a few steps outside of the bounds of the flames…

The first news that I reported on as a professional journalist was the telegram about the outbreak of the civil war in Spain. From that time there was no peace in the world… However, I am not complaining about my fate. I also wrote about the War of Independence, The Sinai Campaign and the Six Day War… and I still hope to report about the peace conference between Israel and the Arabs.

Then I will "return" to Jonava, to report about it in detail.

[Page 130]

Noach Stern

Translated by Jerrold Landau

On his visit to Kibbutz Amir

He was born in Jonava in 1912 to his father Shmerl and his mother Beila. He studied in the Real Hebrew Gymnasia in Kovno. He was among the first members of Gordonia. His poems and articles were published in Hed Lita and Netivot. He was influenced by the lyrics of Yaakov Pechman, the poems of reproof of Bialik, and the human strength in the poems of Tshernikovsky, as he said of himself. In 1929 he answered the invitation of one of his uncles. He went to the United States and was accepted to Harvard University, from which he graduated with distinction in 1934. He received a degree in English and general literature and won the gold medal. He spent close to a year conducting research at Columbia University. He published poems in the Hadoar weekly.

He arrived in the Land in 1935. He worked as the editor of Davar, served for a time as the literary advisor of the Ohel Theater, and taught and lectured at the popular university of the organization of workers of Jerusalem.

Noach was drafted into the brigade in which he served for four years. He worked as the editor of the Hachayil daily newspaper, and published some of his poems in it. He participated in the rescue work for the Holocaust survivors.

He was freed from the army in 1946 and returned to the land.

He was engaged to marry a woman, but it did not work out due to his instability. "I remained a bachelor, apparently because I did not attain sufficient harmony in order to make a permanent connection with a wife."

In his poems, we find clear steps to an internal life and his poetic style. At first, he dealt with topics of nature and scenery, and later, his poems took on the form of his Jewish essence and investigating the movements and trends of the world. In the background of the stormy and unfortunate era, man to him was symbolized by a dual visage: "as a Cohen and as Cain together"[2]. This poetry was at times infused "with amicability and despair". At times, the sober meditative spirit pervaded. Furthermore, the structure of his poems had free form, and they contained sections in the grey, day to day phraseology. In this style, he preceded our younger, new poets.

His poems expressed his actual response to the revolutions of the times, a form of prophetic voice to the happenings of the times: The events of 5696 (1936), Spain in flames, the Nazi atrocities, the ghetto revolutionaries, the growth of the illegal immigration, the War of Independence. His poems were full of feelings of sorrow and anger. He also wrote literary essays. He translated Eliot's "The Wasteland" and other works into Hebrew.

A severe depression took hold of him. After months of oppression, he wished to make peace with himself and occupy himself with ceramics, in which he saw the possibility of salvation and a source for extricating himself from manual labor. He was tired of teaching. He rose up against his own intellectuality. He wished to become less complex and simpler. However, this was not to happen.

He died on the 21st of Elul 5720 (1960) at the age of 48.

His works were collected into a book called "Among the Clouds" which was published in 1966 in Tel Aviv by the writers' guild. The book was edited by Avraham Braudes.

(Based on an article of Avraham Braudes).

[Page 131]

Portrait of the Young Poet
by Noach Stern
Translated by Jerrold Landau

He loves himself,
The spark within him:
He loves his fellow
The reflection of the pain,
His pain:
With the burning heat of the murderer
He is feverish from his own will
For with a parched soul
He clarifies and draws forth
The poem.
His words are weakened,
As if he is negating the general principle,
His mouth moves and does not move –
He is not afraid if
The hearer hears:
However – the poem within him enlightens
A tune that no person recognizes –
How enthusiastic! How sublime!
– and ironic.
The words were lost there
Then they too, but the echo of a letter
Returns still from the forest
And comes to him –
And to the poem.
And between poem and poem,
Between the village and the city
He walks slowly
And almost forgets
The world:
Thus does he live, he who loves
Only solitude and heat;
He who loves himself –

The spark within him –
And the joy lightens him up –
Only the poem.

5696 (1936)

[Page 132]

About Two Brothers Who Dedicated their Lives to Those in Need

by Tovia Ben-Pazi (Goldstein) Jerusalem

Translated by Jerrold Landau

During the years of about 5655-5686 (1895-1926), the town of Jonava had two outstanding holy men, great in Torah, G-d fearing, who were considered to be the righteous men of the generation. These were the brothers Rabbi Yaakov and Rabbi Shimon the sons of Yosef Goldstein of blessed memory. Each one excelled in his own realm, in the traits of kindness and mercy for one's fellow, as a scholar and a communal activist without any trace of self interest.

Rabbi Yaakov, known as Reb Yankel the vinegar maker, was involved in the selling of vinegar and other such products for his livelihood. Although it was not he who was occupied with his livelihood, but rather his wife (they had no children). He was busy all day with his holy work. He himself was satisfied with little. He was occupied with fasting and prayer for most of the day. He would offer help and support to those in need, and would give of his own money. The amount was modest, so he himself would visit all the houses of the residents on set days of the week to collect donations for those in need, such as householders who had come upon hard times and did not have a morsel of bread in their houses, and were afraid to ask for assistance. He found his way to them and offered them his assistance, whether through a loan or direct grant without setting a time for repayment. There were others whom he would assist with secret gifts.

The main part of his work was dedicated to supporting the children of the poor, of which there was no shortage in our town. He concerned himself with finding them lodging in various homes, and he would pay the fees. In his own home, not one day went by without some homeless children whom he would support with food and lodging. This was for their bodies. He concerned himself particularly with their souls, by arranging for them a place to study Torah and secular pursuits. He himself conducted this. Who does not remember the child Hershele, whom he took from the hands of his mother who had gone crazy on account of her many troubles. He did not let her hurt him. Reb Yankel, with his great wisdom and dedication to the commandment of raising orphans in his home and educating them to Torah and commandments, succeeded in bringing him into his own house and caring for him until he was ready to study in

Yeshiva. He became one of the top students. He also bore the yoke of many of the students at the elementary Yeshiva in the city. He also established and maintained the Tiferet Bachurim institution, an institution for young people and youths prior to adulthood, in which they could obtain torah knowledge. These young people came after a day of work to listen to classes on Torah, Jewish law, lore, morality, and proper direction. They enjoyed the splendor of Torah that was offered to them by Reb Yankel himself, and other lecturers who came to assist him. He would discretely pay the entry fee for those in need.

In this manner, he raised and educated a generation of youths to Torah and proper life. He expended great effort so that they would not spend their time for no purpose and their days in idleness. Thus was his manner in the holy work until his last days. May his memory be a blessing.

The second brother, Reb Shimon the teacher of blessed memory, was known as Reb Shimon the Melamed. Whoever had the privilege of studying with him in the cheder considered this to be an honorable and important matter. Most of the children and youths of the town from the more prominent strata studied in the cheder of Reb Shimon until they knew how to study a page of Gemara and were able to be accepted to the Yeshiva. He not only taught the children holy subjects such as Chumash, Bible, Gemara, etc., but also secular subjects such as arithmetic, grammar, and Russian reading and writing. Therefore, he was known as one of the important teachers of the town, and the parents appreciated this. They found him to be a person full of dedication and warmth, who toiled with complete dedication from morning until night on behalf of his students. They knew that here, the youths would have the proper influence in Torah and fear of Heaven, as well as in the ways of the world. They would understand their subjects completely. They knew that their children were found in the home of a prominent educator, who was filled with love and fear of Heaven.

Outside the walls of the cheder, in matters of interpersonal relations, the doors of his home were always opened wide to any guest who had fallen upon hard times, who was in need, and had a bitter heart. He would offer them lodging, food, and general assistance. Who did not remember the woman Freidel the deaf (Freidel Di Toibe)? In the latter times, she would wander around the town from place to place without knowledge, without a roof over her head. When she was tired, she found a place with Reb Shimon the teacher. She would sleep on a couch that was reserved for her. She would sleep this way for several consecutive days. People such as this frequented his house. He did not concern himself with his own meager livelihood, for he was raising a large family in a house that was not spacious enough. When the Rebbetzin would milk the goat in the morning, he would make sure that a glass of milk was offered first to the guest.

[Page 133]

After a day of hard holy work, he would go to the nearby synagogue in the evenings and deliver classes on Torah to the householders, who would enjoy his classes and discussions on law and lore very much. He would remain with several children who wandered about the synagogue in a childish manner, take them to a corner, give them candies or a coin, sit them down and discuss with them matters of spirituality, fear of Heaven, and proper behavior. When he returned home, he studied Torah himself until late at night. In the last years, when his eyes became dim and he had trouble seeing, he would sit and study with youths who were not his students. They would read to him, and he would explain and interpret. Thus was his was in holy affairs until his last days. About him one can apply the verse: and he expired and was gathered to his people[3]. He died in Nissan of 5686 (1926). May his memory be a blessing.

Rabbi Yisrael Yaakov
and his Son the Artist

by Golda Sirek (Saker)

Translated by Jerrold Landau

Rabbi Yisrael Yaakov lived across from our house. He was a teacher in the cheder and also the head of the yeshiva. Rabbi Yisrael was a righteous, good hearted man who sufficed himself with little. He always studied Torah and was an expert in it. He had three children. His son Alter was an artist and sculptor. I remember very well one of his sculptures – an elderly Jew full of wrinkles. Below was engraved: "From whence will my salvation arise?"[4] Once, after he finished painting a picture, he wished to show his creation to someone. He called me from my house to come to see his painting. It was a portrait of his father Rabbi Yisrael lying on the sofa, sleeping with a tallis. Alter saw his father taking his afternoon nap and decided to draw him. This was a very poignant picture. Alter's mother said that when he was a child, he would take the dough that she was preparing and mold it into all sorts of forms. They were Orthodox, and were not in favor of their child sitting and drawing. Therefore, Alter would hide in some corner, and draw away. Finally they parents made peace with the fact that their son loved to draw and sculpt.

Their daughter Alta married Yisrael Goldstein the son of Shimon the teacher. Yisrael was an intelligent Jew with a great sense of humor. Once I came to request a basin for kashering meat. Yisrael asked me: "Which basin do you want the dairy one or the meat one?" I, the girl, did not know what to answer him.

Rabbi Yisrael Yaakov studied Gemara during the evenings with simple Jews who toiled for their livelihood during the day, and went to the synagogue at night to study a page of Gemara. After they finished their studies, they made a celebration. They would take Rabbi Yisrael Yaakov on their shoulders, sing and dance in the street, and carry him home. There they ate and drank, and the joy was great.

In his old age, Rabbi Yisrael Yaakov was afflicted with paralysis. He could not speak or rise from his bed. Rabbi Yisrael lay in this situation for years. His good hearted daughter Freidka took care of him with dedication, as he deserved, until the day of his death.

May his memory be a blessing.

[Page 134]

Inside and Outside

by Golda Sirek (Saker)

Translated by Jerrold Landau

Apparently Golda Sirek Saker

I was born and raised in Jonava. I studied in the Tarbut School. This was the time of the Balfour Declaration. This was a great day, a great event, which was felt strongly within the walls of the school. Everyone spoke about the Land of Israel. The teacher Joselevich told us about the declaration. That day, the school arranged a parade that went out to the swirling mountain (Shvindel Barg). Henka Blumberg of blessed memory and I were responsible for carrying the flags, since we were the tallest in the class. To my great dismay, I was responsible for carrying the Lithuanian flag, whereas my friend carried our blue and white flag. I was very distraught about this. The teacher Joselevich noticed my sadness. As we sat at the foot of the mountain, we sang Hebrew songs and the joy was great. The teacher approached me and said: "Today is a great day for the Jews. We must be happy and festive." On the return trip to the school, I was given the opportunity to carry the blue and white flag. She said, "Hold the flag strongly in your hands. In order to rejoice with our flag, we must also carry a foreign flag."

Energetic Zionist Youth

There were Zionist factions of all orientations in Jonava. At night, the streets were filled with the youth, boys and girls. We walked through the streets of the city in groups, sometimes singing and sometimes debating. Everything was connected with the Land of Israel.

We had a large library that contained many books: Mendele, Bialik, translations of Tolstoy, Gorki and others – in Hebrew and Yiddish. The youth read a great deal and wished to acquire knowledge and education.

I remember the A. D. Gordon club on the Street of the Road. The youth would gather there to read, play damka[5] and chess, sing and dance. We could hear loud singing from the Maccabee club not far away. The headquarters of Hashomer Hatzair was located on the Smith's Alley. The noise was very great due to the work of the smiths, but this did not prevent Hashomer Hatzair and Hechalutz from debating and dreaming about the Land of Israel.

Moshe Ivensky was older than us. He was married and a father of three children. He was our teacher, educator, and friend. He was a great man with vast knowledge. He was good hearted, and he did not pursue honor. He was talented at the art of expressing himself strongly. He lectured to us a great deal about everything that was taking place in the world. He would say that in order to understand Herzl, one must understand the Dreyfus case. Moshe Ivensky was the living spirit of Jonava. He instilled in us a great love for the Land of Israel, and the desire to make aliya. He promoted the ideology of A. D. Gordon, and wrote about the state of "man, work, and nature." He was a disciple of Gordon. The Communists hated him. In order to understand why no benefit would come to the Jews from the Russian Revolution, we studied the doctrine of Karl Marx and Lenin. We did this to understand what was taking place around us, and why we had only one path to choose from – to make aliya to the Land of Israel.

[Page 135]

In Jonava, we spoke and read a great deal of Hebrew. The Zionist movement had penetrated into almost every home, and therefore, many chalutzim (Zionist pioneers) came from this town. My heart aches inside of me as I remember my friends who dreamed like me of making aliya to the Land, but whose dreams were not realized: Chana Raska Davidovich, Rivka Sesitzky, and many others whose memory will not depart from me forever. They were slaughtered by the Nazis and Lithuanians who joined forces with the murderers. We must be their mouth and tell this to the generations that follow, so that they will know about the roots that grew the many trees that are now fruitful in the Land of Israel.

Mother and Father's Home

I remember the home of my father. Many charity boxes were tied on the walls – for Bikur Cholim, orphans, and of course for the Keren Kayemet LeYisrael (Jewish National Fund). My mother Chaya Sara of blessed memory would put a few coins into each box before lighting candles on Friday. She never forgot to give her charity.

My father Pesach of blessed memory would go to the synagogue and return with a guest for dinner. They would discuss various matters. We children would listen quietly and would not dare to open our mouths.

A Yeshiva student would eat with us every Sunday and Monday – this is a custom that was common in the town. Everyone wanted to help their fellow.

I remember the large Beis Midrash in which my father of blessed memory worshipped, and the synagogue (shul) that was located opposite it, with the stained glass windows and wide steps. I also remember the Hassidic Shtibel. We loved to go to the synagogue on festivals. The atmosphere was festive. I loved to hear the cantor Shlomo the shochet of blessed memory. He had a wonderfully sweet voice. He worshipped with great feeling. He was handsome and good hearted. Everyone loved him. He earned his livelihood in a meager fashion, but he always donated to the Keren Kayemet.

There was anti-Semitism in Lithuania as in all lands of the Diaspora. In 1920, my father left the city on business. My 17-year old sister Dina accompanied him. They were murdered on their way by Lithuanian thieves, who stole their money and were not satisfied until they killed them also. My sister, who was wounded badly, said before her death that the murderers shouted "Death to the Jews," and did not let them escape.

This incident had a strong influence on my family and was the cause of our strong desire to not continue to live in that country. My brother Shraga traveled to the United States. I made aliya to the land, with the thought of bringing my mother here as soon as possible. My mother Chaya Sara did not make aliya. She was murdered by the Germans.

The Incident with Avraka

The Jews of Jonava were united and did not abandon one another during times of trouble and tribulation. I remember very well the incident with Avraham Untershatz (Avraka), who was a member of Maccabee and loved sports. One night, he left the clubhouse late at night. On his way, he chanced upon a place where a murder had taken place. A gentile had murdered another gentile. The police imprisoned Avraham without any reason and accused him of murdering the gentile. The town was in an uproar. People were not silent, and did not abandon Avraham in his time of distress. They hired famous lawyers for him. A long court case took place, filled with the spirit of anti-

Semitism. However justice prevailed this time, and it was proven that Avraham was innocent of any wrongdoing. He was freed. I will never forget the joy that pervaded in the city when he was freed. All the people of the town went out to greet him and wish him well.

Golda Seker (Sirek) of Givataim

[Page 136]

With Mixed Feelings

by Chaya Rivka Feinberg (Aaronson), United States

Translated by Jerrold Landau

I left Jonava on August 2, 1936, with feelings of both hope and pain. I was sure that I would never see it again.

These mixed feelings awaken in me the memory of my Jonava: A beautiful town between the forests and the Vilia, clear summer nights, snowy winters, well-heated houses, few large buildings, for the most part small wooden houses, good people, cordial friends, primarily – in our club, the Shomer Hatzair – the movement that gave me so much that will remain dear to me until the end of my life. The Shomer Hatzair and the Vilia – these two things saved me and removed me many times from my many personal and family sorrows. Amidst the waves I forgot my sorrows. Between the banks of the river, I revealed all the secrets of my youth to its flowing waters.

One summer night, the waters of the Vilia even overturned our boat under the new wooden bridge. With me in the boat at that time were Daniel Rickless whom we saw as an adult and advisor, Dovka Dobiansky, my friend Osnat Katzenberg, Alter Khasid and Shlomo Garber, who capsized the boat. At this time I forgive him for this.

I still sense the embarrassment and fear at this time. It is simply difficult for me to image that those same gentiles who saved us from the water that night were involved in all of the murders in which our dear ones were killed.

My father was Melech the smith. My mother Rachel had two other children: a young son Reuvele and my sister Shoshana who lives to day in Los Angeles, U.S.A. Uncles, aunts and cousins also perished along with my immediate family.

May their memories be a blessing.

A Little of This and a Little of That

by Shmuel Ben-Menachem of Hadera

Translated by Jerrold Landau

I alone survived of the nine children that my parents had.

Since my father Rabbi Menachem Mendel Deitz of holy blessed memory was the head of the Or Noga Yeshiva in Jonava, I was particularly close to the Orthodox circles.

Images of the teacher of the Yavneh School, in which I studied before I transferred to the Yeshiva, pass before my eyes: the teacher Levinsky, the teacher Grodsky who limped after she fell during her youth while wandering in a nearby village, the teacher Shoub and the teacher Alter Kagan who taught holy subjects in the small cheder of the shul. We would go there at night to capture doves from the attic. Rabbi Nachum Baruch Ginzberg would come to test us, accompanied by the city notables such as Reb Alter Jochovsky who had a tavern next to the market square.

Do you remember Noach the roofer, whom I called the crazy prophet? He lopped off his first wife's head with his axe. He got married a second time to a tiny woman. When the cantor would utter the word "Shalom" (peace), Noach would shake his head from side to side and say "nein" (no). We would paste the word "shalom" in large letters in the window next to his seat in the synagogue. A while ago I met a Jonaver, and when we recalled Noach, he stood still and said: "This Noach indeed prophesied the Holocaust!"

From among the wagon drivers and porters, I especially recall Itzele the Bul, who was large and fat. Once the wagon drivers bet him that he could not eat 25 rolls. After he ate 22, he felt ill and they took him to the hospital. He almost died.

Translator's Footnotes

See http://www.litnet.lt/lithuania/cities/jonav.html

In Hebrew, these terms almost rhyme, especially in the Lithuanian Yiddish pronunciation: "As a Caihen and Cayin together".

The verse in the Torah used to describe the death of the forefather Jacob. This verse does not mention that he 'died' – from which is derived the concept that Jacob did not die – i.e .that his influence remains forever.

A quote from Psalm 121.

A form of checkers.

The waters of the Vilia rise up to the porches of the houses

[Page 137]

Between Water and Fire

by Esther Tilmun (Novickovich) of Herzlia

Translated by Jerrold Landau

The greatest experience that I remember from my childhood was the days before Passover. This was connected with the Vylia.

When the spring came with the melting of the snow, the river would overflow its banks and the water would cover the entire area and flood the streets, the houses, and everything that was there.

We lived on a street close to the river. Every year as spring approached, we felt the great apprehension prior to the flood. When the noise of the breaking up of the ice was heard, the residents of the street would hastily pack up all the moveable belongings and bring them to the upper stories of the house.

For us children, this was a time of great joy. During the preparations for the flood, the parents were not particular about out behavior. We were able to perpetrate various tricks, to go to sleep late, and first and foremost, to stand for hours and watch the river as it rose and began to overflow. We would then run to tell enthusiastically how far the water rose and where it already started to penetrate.

A photograph that I have reminds me of one morning. It was very early. Someone entered our house and called out, "The ice broke, everyone come out to take a picture!" All the members of my family, the residents of the street and everyone who was present hurried outside to have our photograph taken with the background of the overflowing river.

This photograph is the only one that I still have from my childhood.

Most of the people in the photograph were murdered during the Holocaust.

Other experiences from those days are connected with the fires. Since almost the entire city was built with wood, the houses were very close to each other, and there were many carpentry shops, fires would often break out. There were so many that it seemed to me that not a week went by without a fire. For some reason it also seemed to me that Tuesday was the day designated for fires.

The shout, "Fire" spurred us children into action. We would run to see the burning fire. Many of the people of the town would come to the place of the fire. Most came to watch rather than assist.

I especially remember Sabbath eves from my childhood. We would sit at the table in our Sabbath clothes, having bathed, shampooed, and combed our hair. The house was filled with light and warmth, and father would recite Kiddush.

My father and my family members had studied in the Slobodka Yeshiva. I studied in the Culture League School. I was also a member of their youth group which was called "Wunderfoigl" (wandering bird). Most of the youths of our street were members of that group. We would go out on excursions a distance from the town even without the permission and knowledge of our parents. Then we would be afraid to return home.

Later on I transferred to Tz. S. However, I made aliya to the Land of Israel in 1935 with the group that was traveling to the Maccabiada. Six girls from Jonava, including myself, set out, and all remained in the Land.

[Page 138]

Dvor'ka the Divorcée

by Israel Yaacov Pagir

Translated by Daniella Thompson

Each time I remember Yanova, I am full of wonderment at her having been blessed with everything in abundance. Take, for example, the tailors: Naftali and his sons, Israel with his sons and daughters, Yossi–Moshe, or those two–story (and higher) name bearers, like Shlomo Batya Toleda's [I have no idea how this name is supposed to sound], Yossi Feiga Leah's, Shmuel Fruma Zlata's, and others.

The African Tailor

Ovadyah the tailor woke up one morning fresh and healthy… and made his way to Johannesburg, to rake up gold. What has gold to do with a tailor? Indeed, he found no gold. It's not in gold's nature to come of its own accord. He suffered hunger to the point of desperation.

In short, Ovadyah returned home thinner but also wiser than he had been. He went to Neta the painter, and the latter made him a sign illustrated with a headless and footless blue suit and a line underneath proclaiming, "African Tailor." He hung the sign in front of his house, in the Alley of Bentze the medic, across from the peddlers' *kloiz*.[1]

Our brethren, the Sons of Israel, laughed wholeheartedly: the *goys* won't be able to read what's written on the sign and, in any case, they weren't likely to show up near the *kloiz*, since there was no tavern there. So the sign was good for nothing except in serving as a scarecrow to the lads who used to return late at night from their sweethearts. When the wind blew the sign, banging it into the wall, and when candles for the souls of the departed shone on it through the kloiz windows, illuminating the headless, footless suit, it was as if a demon or a devil had appeared, and the boys were scared out of their wits.

Yossi Shimon's–Women's Tailor

Men's tailors there were more than could be counted; but for women's clothing, there was only tailor: Yossi Shimon's, unique in his generation. And if you think that he was happy with his lot, you are mistaken.

I ran into him once as he was carrying on his arm something wrapped in a white sheet. I understood that it was a woman's garment he was taking for measurements. His face looked worried.

Had it not been for his daughter, Dvor'ka, I wouldn't have paid him any notice. But since I knew his daughter–a beautiful, intelligent, charming girl with all the distinctions– I hastened to say "Good morning" to him.

That winter I traveled to America, never to return. After Passover I received a letter saying that Dvor'ka must obtain a divorce. She hadn't even been married, but they were telling her that she was the chimney sweep's wife. She didn't want to be a chimney sweep's wife.

How She Came to This

Here's how it happened. On a Shabbat after the kugel, a group got together to sing and dance as usual. Someone suggested that they hold a mock wedding and play at being bride–and–groom and in–laws. Dvor'ka agreed to play the part of the bride. Among the assembled was a lad–a new face. He took it upon himself to be the groom. It transpired like this: Leizer the chimney sweep had fallen from a roof and was badly injured. The new lad took his place.

They prepared a proper *chuppah* and *kiddushin*, with rings and witnesses. Then they dispersed.

Rumors of this event reached the ears of the religious circles. The Rabbi invited the bride, the groom, and the witnesses, interrogated them, and pronounced that, according to the Law of Moses and Israel, Dvora, daughter of *rebbe* Yossi Shimon, is the wife of Unknown, son of Obscure.[2]

But Dvora rejected this honor and also refused to obtain a divorce. The *shtetl* Yanova was in an uproar[3] until a flaw was found in one of the witnesses' testimony. They disqualified him for having been drunk. The marriage was nullified, but Dvor'ka was henceforth known as "The Divorcée."

Translator's Footnotes

Midrash house.

The Hebrew expression "Ploni ben Almoni" is similar to the English "John Doe."

"Yanova was on wheels" in the original Hebrew text.

[Page 139]

Mosheke the "Moldy"

by Yitzchak Ben David

Translated by Jerrold Landau

Who does not remember Mosheke "The Stale"[1]? He was a unique character - not an idler, but someone who toiled like most of the Jonava youth. His trade was a glassmaker, but he was short on work most of the time. Life did not pamper him.

The scoffers would say to him: "Mosheke, you have no work? Go and break the windowpanes of the wealthy people at night, and remake them during the day."

He lived with his mother in a dismal hut on Breizer Street. The smell of mould on his clothes accompanied him everywhere.

He stands before my eyes with his glassmakers sack on his back. His hands and clothes were soiled with putty - as a sort of advertisement of his handiwork.

He would debate hotly, with beads of saliva dripping from his mouth, as his anger was roused. In the library, he was known as a regular borrower and avid reader. He was particularly interested in criminological novels in Yiddish or Hebrew. He never missed one movie in the theater. With all this, it could not be said that he had an even temperament. Some small screw in his head was not tightened sufficiently.

"According to your outlook do you considered yourself a Zionist or a Communist?" I would ask him.

"I am considered more extreme than a Communist - I am a Trotskyite," he would respond with a sly smile.

He would go to the beach every Sabbath and tan himself from morning until evening. He would occupy himself with "making statues" in the soft sand. He would particularly make clumsy statues of women, as he would see them in his imagination as the symbol of femininity. Or he would then draw back a bit, set himself in the pose of Napoleon, and with blazing eyes and an opened mouth, he would attach himself to the image of Aphrodite that he had created with his own hands - as a replacement for the girls who kept their distance from him.

Translator's Footnote

The Hebrew in the title translates best as "moldy," whereas the Yiddish term here translates best as "stale." Both mean the same as a nickname, though.

Tales and Exaggerations

by Sara Burstein

Translated by Jerrold Landau

Who of the veteran Jonavers does not remember Moshe-David Mar, who would float barges along the rivers of Lithuania and outside of it? In addition to his profession, he owned an inn and a restaurant, which was run by his wife with great expertise, and was famous for its tasty delicacies. In the latter years of his life, when his difficult profession became burdensome for him, he helped his wife, especially in entertaining their guests during the evenings. He told them endless tales and stories.

Moshe David was a unique character: He looked like he was molded from steel. He was tall, fat, had the neck of an ox, a wide face, and hands and feet resembling ancient tree twigs. When he walked, it seemed as if the earth shook from the steps of his heavy feet that were covered in gigantic boots. He especially excelled in the huge capacity of his belly. This was a "stomach that knew no satiety." His healthy appetite was famous, and many jokes and tales were spread regarding it. He knew about this, but was not sad or distressed, for he was a calm man by nature. His face was always lit up with a pleasant smile, and the goodness of his heart was expressed from it. Furthermore, he loved telling jokes at his own expense. He would exaggerate to no small degree, and he enjoyed such. When someone was overly brazen and tread on his corns regarding his belly, which protruded from afar, Moshe David would say with a laugh, as he caressed his belly: "I wish that I had the money that this stomach cost; but I will not wish that you will have the present worth of this money." With this, he silenced the person who embarrassed him, and the friendship between them was not severed. His daughter Chaya of blessed memory, my good friend and schoolmate, was also a very intelligent and practical girl. She would follow his path and tell with a laugh all sorts of funny events about her father. Everything that I am going to relate here came from her mouth, and, as our sages have said, "Everyone who says something in the name of the person that stated it brings redemption to the world"[1]. Therefore, this "gossip" should be considered to me as a merit.

[Page 140]

One day, Moshe-David went to visit his daughters in Kovno. Chaya convinced him to see the wonders of the movies, something that he had never seen. He agreed and went with her. He was tired, slumber overtook him in the middle of the film, and the sound of his snoring was frightening. Chaya poked him on his side with her elbow, and he woke up confused and disoriented. He looked about and noticed a wide river on the screen. Moshe-David screamed, "Woe to me, where is my raft? Where did it disappear? Apparently it was ripped away from the shore."

On account of the girth of his neck, it was difficult for Moshe-David to purchase a necktie. One day, he entered a store along with his brother, who also floated barges, and requested a necktie. They measured all of the ties, and could not find even one that was appropriate for him. He turned to his brother and said, "Apparently, I need to buy two ties and join them, just like one joins two portion of a raft with twisted raffia rope. (This activity was known as " *Tzuzamenshver Teven*" in professional terminology.)

One day Moshe-David went to Naftali, the well-known tailor in Jonava, to order a suit. As usual, they had to take measurements. However, the problem was that taking measurements of Moshe-David was backbreaking work on account of his height and girth. The small Naftali figured out a solution. He took one end of the measuring tape, stuck it some place in Moshe-David's body and held it firmly. He gave the other end to his assistant, his son Meir, who walked around Moshe-David as he was measuring him. When Meir disappeared from his father's view because he was behind the customer, Naftali the joker began to laugh, "Meir, Meir, where are you? Where did you disappear?" Meir shouted back, "Don't worry father, I will return to you shortly…"

{Drawing page 140: Uncaptioned: Apparently Moshe-David Mar}

Translator's Footnotes

A quote from the sixth chapter of *Pirke Avot*.

[Page 141]

Activist Youth and Social Awareness

[Page 143]

Maccabee

by Yitzchak Burstein

Translated by Jerrold Landau

For many years its meeting place was located in the home of Nota Goldman. Maccabee had more than 200 active members. It was founded in 1920. Its founders included Aryeh Zisla, Dvora Shoham, Shlomo Ber Meirovich, and Zeev Kirzner. Later, I was appointed as the chairman of the committee, and I dedicated most of my time to physical and spiritual educational activities among the youth. I was assisted in my work by the committee members Avraham Jochovsky, Mordechai Wolfovich, Shlomo Ber, Kirzner, and David Friedman. Moshe Ivensky worked in the spiritual realm. The following groups took place within the meeting place: light athletics, ping pong, basketball, chess, cycling, a choir, a percussion band, and an active dramatic club.

Do you recall the conductor Shlomo Ber? He had a red face, was calm, and had nerves of steel. He is active in the field of music in Vilna to this day.

Recall our basketball players: Meika who was partially mute, Yitzchak Rikless, Levika and Elka Kaper, Berl Segalovsky, Feivel Shapira, Efraim Frakt, Leizka the Gingi [redhead], Meirka Mechnik, Moshe Untershatz, Hershel Levin, the defenseman Motele Yaffa, and Yankel Klibansky.

Hershel Levin, Leibel Stern, and Zelig Epstein formed the members' justice system.

The athletic parties in the halls of the movie theater and the firefighters attracted a large group of youths. Do you recall the party in the firefighters' hall with the participation of Stumpel's jazz band? When Stumpel and Nota were in good spirits from glasses of liquor in the tavern of Nota and his wife, they began to kiss, and Nota bit Stumpel's nose until it bled. Nota's nickname was "Chalulim"[1].

The first group of athletes in Maccabee bidding farewell to Meira Zisla: Tzvi Opnitzky, Avraka Untershatz, Feivka Shapira, Shlomo Drogetzky, Aryeh Zisla, Ezriel Opnitzky, Mendel Dobiansky, X, Shlomo Friedman, X

During the time of the Balfour Declaration and on Lag Baomer, Maccabee organized demonstrations on the streets of the town with the national flags, and riders on horses and decorated bicycles. They would walk with a show of strength, in the costume of the Maccabee organization, accompanied by Hebrew songs. Similarly, we organized gatherings and lectures on various topics through our own people as well as with the participation of people brought in from Kovno.

[Page 144]
The pride of the Maccabee was the dramatic circle under the stage direction of Chone Katzenberg: He was thin, clean shaven, enjoyed to tipple, always with a leather jacket. He was talented as a stage producer. He was assisted by Itzik Dembo in forging the characters of the actors. Our "prima donnas" were Miriam Nochimovich and Hinda Levitz. To this day, the image of "Mirale Efrat", as played by Miriam, is etched in the minds of many. Hershel Wolfovich, Abba Opnitzky, Yosef Chein "the wagon driver", Peiska Shachor, Velke Opanik, Reping, Tzipa-Leah Weiner, Shifra Lomiansky, Batya Zandman and others stood out in main roles and in other roles.

Our performances, such as Mirale Efrat, Green Fields, Yoshke Charlatan, the Miser and others were also performed on the stage of Vilkomir [Ukmerge]. Chone Katzenberg ensured that the actors would drink a glass of liquor prior to every performance, which would contribute its share to the success of the performance; and that there would be a party after the performance. Our trainers, such as Chone Katzenberg, Itzik Dembo and

Hershel Levin composed verses for our songs, which were heard from the mouths of the youths until the next party.

{The top of page 144 has an article entitled "About Hapoel and the Youth", starting in the top half of 144, above the line. After page 144, there is a hiatus in the text, with 16 unnumbered pages of photos. The article and pagination resumes at the end of the photos. I included that article at the end of the unnumbered pages, so as to ensure continuity and not break it by the unnumbered pages.}

Translator's Footnotes

Holes or cavities.

[Page 144]

About Hapoel and the Youth

by Eliahu Kagan, Tel Aviv

Translated by Jerrold Landau

Eliahu Kagan

In 1931, the Hakoach sports club of the Socialist-Zionist Youth (Hanoar Hatzioni-Socialisti) of Lithuania joined the Hapoalim sports movement and changed its name to Hapoel. From that time, Hapoel of Lithuania became an inseparable part of Hapoel in the Land of Israel. Its goal was to enable the community of workers to engage in sports, under the rubric of Eretz Yisrael Haoevedet (Working Land of Israel).

The practical connection with the youth in Lithuania was established after a representative of the Hapoel activists of that time from the Land of Israel came to Lithuania. This was Yosef Carmi (today a senior official in the office of labor in the employment department).

When Y. Carmi came for the duration of one year, the center of Hapoel was set up in Lithuania, and the main branch was strengthened in Kovno. At a later stage, chapters in the outlying cities were established.

The sporting activities were expressed primarily through common sports, football[3], basketball games, volleyball, gymnastics, weightlifting, boxing, swimming, ping-pong, and of course social-cultural activities based on Socialist Zionism. In order to facilitate the broadening of activities, a national course for sports leaders was organized. The writer of these lines, Eliahu Kagan, a native of the town of Jonava, was one of the participants in this course.

After the conclusion of the course, I became one of the activists and organizers of Hapoel in Lithuania, and a member of its center. Through my general activity on behalf of Hapoel in Lithuania, I dedicated some of my time to establish a chapter in Jonava, particularly during the summer, during the university vacation, when I resided in my home in Jonava. My parents lived in that home until their last day, at the beginning of the Second World War and the expulsion of the Jews.

A meeting with the Zionist orator, writer and activist Shmuel Chernovitz ("Safog")
1. Chaim Moshe Slomin 2. Chana Pesia Glazer 3. Rivka Dembo 4. Yosef Intriligitor 4a. Eidel Burstein 5. Avrum 5a. Sheina Abramson-Antes 6. Alta Rubin 7. Ethel Katz 8. Zlata Rosenberg-Janusovich 9. Alter Monitz 10. Tzila Untershatz 11. Henia Farber 12. Teibl Stein 13. Miriam Merbianski 14. Tzipora Shoham 15. Miriam Burstein 16. Henia Blumberg 17. Chaim Levin 18. Yatkonski from Kovno 19. Nadia Granovich 20. Nota Valchokovsky 21. Hershel Levin 22. Mordechai Itchikovich 23. the teacher Rosenberg 24. Kolbianski 25. Chernovitz 26. Yosef Abramson 27. Leib Wolfovich 28. Leiba Pogirski 29. Shimon Rubin 30. Pesach Shachor 31. Noach Stern 32. Shmuel Goldshmidt 33. Tzvi Yaffa 34. Moshe Fried 35. Moshe Ivensky 36. Shaul Keidanski 37. Dr. G. Ran 38. Lula Vilkomirsky 39. Chana Davidovich 40. Nechama Levin 41. Yitzchak Perevoznik 42. Moshe Sack 43. Shmerl Stern 44. Liber Farber 45. Yonah Katz
46. Menachem Mendel Gorfein 47. Meir Goldshmidt 48. Chaim Goldshmidt 49. Vilkomirsky

The card for the delegate to the Convention of Zionists in Russia
No. 212
Mr. Yosef Katz

הסתדרות הציונית בליטא
הועד העירוני ב יאנאווע

כרטיס חבר

№ 2

הציוניות, שואפת לרכש בטוח על ידי משפט גלוי לעם העברי
בארץ ישראל. (הפרוגרמה הבזילאית).

השם

העיר

יום לחדש תר פ

יושב ראש

מזכיר

בינומה

Right:

The Zionist Organization of Lithuania

The city committee in Jonava

Members Card

No. 2

Left:

Zionism. Aspiring to ensure a safe refuge through open justice for the Hebrew nation in the Land of Israel (The Basel Program).

Name: Mr. Yonah Katz

City: Jonava

22 of Tammuz 5686 (July 4, 1926)

Chairman {signature cannot be made out}

Secretary {signature cannot be made out}

The Organization of General Zionists in Jonava

Maccabee Jonava 1925

Yitzchak B, Miriam Berzin, Golda Friedman, Malka Untershatz, Grishovich, Shlomo Ber Meirovich, Sanel, Rabiner, Chana Goldshmidt, Perla Lopiansky, Miriam Burstein, Reibstein, Lantzman, X, Charna Goldshmidt, Yonina Gurvich, Anna Gurvich, Bogia Wolfovich, Miriam Levin

With the Maccabee athletes:

Yosef Rikliansky, Yitzchak Dragachki, Dina Perlstein, Yonina Gurvich, Moshe Baron, Lipsha Boz, Chana Shachor, Shoshana Friedman, Rabiner, Lantzman, Chaya Katz, Miriam Berzin, Shlomo Friedman

The Maccabee Football Team of Jonava

Shlomo Friedman, Moshe Untershatz, Yaakov Klibansky, Tzvi Levin, Aryeh Stern, Aryeh Zisla, Micha Mechnik, Meir Zopovich, Yitzhak Nuchimovich, Feivel Shapira, Aber Untershatz, Efraim Prakt

Shmerl Shapira, D. Friedman, Berl Segalovsky, Y. Klibansky, P. Shapira, Levi Kaper, M. Mechnik, G. Goldshmidt, Efraim Baten, Shoham, Shlomo Silberman, P. Shachor, Y. Nuchimovich, Z. Epstein, B. Shabtai's

Hershel Bankkutsher, Y. Klibansky, L. Kaper, M. Mechnik, B. Segalovsky, Berl Fein, Shaul Milner, P. Shapira, Elka Kaper, Shlomo Friedman.
Zelmanovich, Yaakov Novikhovich, Berka Aiker, Abba Fein

The Maccabee basketball team

Maccabee parade
The railway bridge to Chigonka
In the background, the "Kemach" (flour) factory and the Girialka factory

The parade on Breizer Street

The group of actors in the play "Green Fields" ("Di Grine Felder" by Peretz Hirshbein (in Yiddish)

The actors and members of the Maccabee with the set in the background.:
Y. Nuchimovich, B. Shabtai's, P. Shachor, Vidtzky, Sh. Goldshmidt, Avram, D.
Friedman, Efraim Prakt, A. Stern, A. Goldshmidt, B. Segalovsky, Moshe Sulsky.
Yitzchak B., Tz. L. Weiner, Abba Opanitzky, Ivensky, Chone Katzenberg – producer,
A. Kagan – the artist, G. Stern, Z. Opnik, X, N. Goldshmidt;
Shifra Lomiansky, Miriam Nuchimovich

Yitzchak Gurvich, Shlomo Silberman, Moshe Untershatz, Pesach Shachor, Reping, Tzipa
Leah Weiner, Miriam Nuchimovich, Elchanan Katzenberg, Hinda Levitz, Shifra
Lomiansky.

Four men around a table. The caption is superimposed on the photo and is unclear. It seems to refer to a gathering of the Jonaver chapter of an organization after the slaughter in Wilkomir [Ukmerge]

The Maccabee committee: David Friedman, Nisan Goldshmidt, Baron, Berl Segalovsky, P. Shachor, Shmuel Goldshmidt, Shlomo Friedman, M. Ivensky, Efraim Prakt, Moshe Baron

Yerachmiel Dobiansky, Bernstein, Z. Epstein, Yosef Grossman, Pinchas Burstein, Yosef Rikliansky, Yerachmiel Blumberg, Ezriel Opnitzky, Yaffa, Morr, Sarka Goldshmidt, Levi Kaper, Reping, Sh. Friedman, Avraham Jochovsky, Y. Klibansky, Moshe Lantzman, Moshe Untershatz, Etka Landman, Tzvi Wolfovich, Tzvi Levin, Hinda Levitz, Shlomo Silberman, Chona Kagan, Yosef Klibansky, Efraim Baten, Michel Mechnik, Avraka Untershatz, Feivel Shapira.

The flags of Hapoel in Jonava at a sporting gathering, 1935.

The leadership of Hapoel at a farewell gathering for A. Sirkin, Passover 1936: Avraham Klotz, Aryeh Perchik, Tz. Perevoznik, Dov Rikless, Elimelech Perchik, Zelig Yudelevich, Tz . Josefs, Aryeh Sirkin, Eliahu Kagan, D. Friedman, Yitzchak Goldman

A regional gathering of Hapoel, Jonava, 1938

The Tzeirei Zion – Hitachdut organization in Jonava at the fifth anniversary of its existence, Passover, 5686 (1926)

Greenblatt, Tz. Opnitzky, Malka Solsky, Leah Kronick, Chaim Blumberg, Trivish, Golda Sirek, Zev Kirzner, Feiga Klibansky, Baten, Leibel Burstein, Tzipora Klotz, Moshe Ivensky, Vinitzky, Freda Gold-Mines, Tzila Untershatz, Rivka Atkatz, Leizer Levin, Prakt, Yehudit Weiner, Yitzchak B., Riska Grossman, Chana Davidovich, Rivka Sesitzky, Tzvi Resnick, Freda Libertal, Yonah Shaltuper

Hitachdut chapter in Jonava, 20 Iyar 5787 (1927)

Greenblatt, P. Libertal, Mila Shpilansky, Y. Weiner, Nechama Levin, G. Sirek, Shliomovich, Tz. Klotz, Reizel Janusovich, X, L. Kronik, Shaltuper, Davidovich, Gold, Untershatz, Atkatz, Sesitsky, X, Ivensky

ביום פרידתנו מח' זלונקר לפני עליתו לארץ כ"ג אב אתתנ"ד

On the day we took leave of Ch. Zlonker before he made aliya to the Land, 23 Av {year is unclear}

(Four top people are not identified)

Epstein, Tzipora Klibansky, Tzipora Grossman, Yosef Klibansky, X, X, Baten, Tzipora Shoham, Michael Zlonker, Yaakov Dembo, Alter Monitz

Hitachdut Tzierei Zion in Jonava, 8 Elul 5685 (1925)

Sheina Tzipa Katz, Menashe Lantzman, Shlomo Meirovich, Strum, X, Moshe Klachman, X, Henia Blumberg, Chana Pesia Glazer, Zalman Kurskisik, Elchanal Glaz, Shmuel Kaplan, Alter Sandler, Yitzchak Zlonker, Menashe Weiner, Perchik, Yosef Shoham, Aryeh Stern, Golda Friedman, Yerachmiel Teitelbaum, Levin, Dvora Zlonker, Zelig Stein, Alter Monitz, Mendel Dobiansky, Tzipora Grossman, Hinda Perlstein, Yitzchak Resnick.

The Sirkin Group bids farewell to Tzvi Ulpasky, 1930.

X, Landsman, Reibstein, Strum, X, A. Monitz, X, Heiman, P. Shachor, Naftali Gurvich, Golda Glaz, Yehudit Rikless, Daniel Rikless, Y. Teitelbaum, Strum, Tz. Grossman, X, Tzvi Perevoznik, Miriam Berzin, Dov Rikless, Chaim Teitelbaum, Mordechai Yaffa, X, Zelig Yudelevich, Reizka Friedman, Tzvi, Chaya Portnoy, Mordechai Katz, Rachel Shabtai's, Elimelech Perchik, A. Khasid, V. Abramovich, Rivka Itzkovich, Yaakov Katzav, Yechezkel Kotler, Tzvi Josefs, Avraham Portnoy, Baruch Shabtai's, Yitzchak Nuchimovich

Members of the choir of Chevra Sirkin, including female members of Hashomer Hatzair. The conductor – Shlomo Ber Meirovich. Perevoznik, Perlstein, Gans, Yoska (the Schwalb)[2], Monitz, Rikless, Portnoy, N. Gurvich, Opnik, Abramovich, Tzvi Atkatz, Giga Plasker, Lantzman, Tzvia Berzin, Sara Opnik, Miriam Berzin, Malka Klotz, P. Shachor, Kazansky, Chaya Baten, Tz. Glinsky, Shlomo Ber [Meirovich], Sara Baten, Sh. Shachor, Golda Glaz, P. Kazansky, Chaya Portnoy, Dvora Berzin, Tzipora Zandman, Sh. Klibansky, L. Yudelevich

The Hechalutz chapter bids farewell to Shimon Sack and Daniel Rikless before they make aliya.

Young Zion – Hitachdut chapter in Jonava on the occasion if the aliya of our members
Perlstein and Sack. September 1, 1934.

Z. Yudelevich, D. Josefs, Berl Rikless, X, Breznikov, Strum, Heiman, Moshe Wolk,
Shanel, Perchik, Reuven Jurman, Ch. P. Glazer, Gurvich, Lantzman, Teitelbaum, Batya
Zandman, Zev Kirzner, Moshe Dembo, Sara Friedman, X,
Zuska Atkatz, Z. Abramovich, Y. Dembo, Ch. R. Davidovich, Shimon Sack, Dina
Perlstein, D. Rikless, A. Monitz, Avraham Pimstein, Golda Glaz, P. Kazansky, David
Friedman, Leibka Perchik, Yehudit Rikless, Yitzchak Goldman

Members of Young Zion and members of Hashomer Hatzair

Berka Rikless, David Friedman, Strum, Yechezkel Kotler, Sara and Chaya Baten, Zev Abramovich, Sara Opnik, Ulpasky, X, Daniel Rikless, Yitzchak Zlonker, Elimelech Perchik.

The "consul", Shlomo Ber, Rivka Itzkovich, X, X, Tzvi Perevoznik, Zalman Sesitzky, Moshe Friedman, Strum, Yerachmiel Teitelbaum, Tzipora Grossman, X, Shoshana Friedman, Glaz, Linda, X, X, Miriam Berzin, Leah Lantzman, Rabiner, Izik Reibstein, Alter Khasid, X, Shlomo Gerber, Pinchas Shapira.

Baruch Shabtai's, Baruch Jalinovich, Leah Yudelevich, Sheina Klibansky, Mordechai Yaffa, Yaakov Katzav, X

The mandolin band of Chevrak Sirkin, 1933

Alter Monitz, Rachel Kushilevich, Daniel Rikless, Chana Jalinovich, X, X, Yasha
Vilkomirsky, Avraham Portnoy, Mechnik, Yudka Katzenberg, X,
David and Hadassa Friedman, Rivka Kushilevich, Eliahu Baron, Meirovich – the
conductor, Chaya Portnoy, Aryeh Perchik, Nobichovich, Leah Klibansky, Lantzman, X

[Page 144 resumed]

In 1931, the Hakoach sports club of the Socialist-Zionist Youth (Hanoar Hatzioni-Socialisti) of Lithuania joined the Hapoalim sports movement and changed its name to Hapoel. From that time, Hapoel of Lithuania became an inseparable part of Hapoel in the Land of Israel. Its goal was to enable the community of workers to engage in sports, under the rubric of Eretz Yisrael Haoevedet (Working Land of Israel).

The practical connection with the youth in Lithuania was established after a representative of the Hapoel activists of that time from the Land of Israel came to Lithuania. This was Yosef Carmi (today a senior official in the office of labor in the employment department).

When Y. Carmi came for the duration of one year, the center of Hapoel was set up in Lithuania, and the main branch was strengthened in Kovno. At a later stage, chapters in the outlying cities were established.

The sporting activities were expressed primarily through common sports, football[3], basketball games, volleyball, gymnastics, weightlifting, boxing, swimming, ping-pong, and of course social-cultural activities based on Socialist Zionism. In order to facilitate the broadening of activities, a national course for sports leaders was organized. The writer of these lines, Eliahu Kagan, a native of the town of Jonava, was one of the participants in this course.

After the conclusion of the course, I became one of the activists and organizers of Hapoel in Lithuania, and a member of its center. Through my general activity on behalf of Hapoel in Lithuania, I dedicated some of my time to establish a chapter in Jonava, particularly during the summer, during the university vacation, when I resided in my home in Jonava. My parents lived in that home until their last day, at the beginning of the Second World War and the expulsion of the Jews.

[Page 145]

The Uniqueness of the Youth

The Jewish youth of Jonava were slightly different from the youth in other towns. Jonava was a town of about 4,000 people. The majority were Jews and the rest were Christian Lithuanians, Pravoslavs and Poles, who lived for the most part at the edges of town. The Jewish residents lived in the center.

Jonava, a town close geographically to the capital Kovno, is situated on the banks of the Vylia River. It is a wide river with a swift flowing current, with green meadows and forests on both banks. The beautiful surroundings, the river with strong, tall bridges, the railway line that passes close to the town – all bestow the character of natural beauty onto the region.

In Jonava itself there were many carpentry workshops, owned for the most part by Jews. There were also smithies, flourmills, and a significant number of stores and other businesses. The gentiles were primarily occupied with agriculture, cattle farming and fishing. In general, they were calm citizens. The town lived its life serenely and quietly, in full harmony with the beautiful surroundings. The forests of the regions, the green meadows, and the picturesque valley imbued the residents with calmness of the soul, mutual understanding, and orderly communal life.

Jonava was much better known in Lithuania, primarily due to the manufacture of furniture and its being a center of the furniture trade. This was also due to the unique trades related to floating barges along the Vylia and Neiman rivers. This was a unique trade, with family expertise passed from father to son. Its practitioners were known in Yiddish as "di vasser menchen", that is to say, "the water people". To this day, the echoes of those Jews who floated barges from the thick forests along the Vylia echo in my ears – commands issued from one side of the barge to the other side. This work demanded of its practitioners agility, knowledge, and great physical strength. These were simple, strong and brave Jews whose name went before them.

The Jewish youth were raised in this background, and became healthy, vibrant, and developed from both the physical and spiritual perspectives.

Thanks to the wide river, most of the Jewish youth knew how to swim, dive, and row in boats. This differentiated them from the youth in "dry" towns.

There were a number of Zionist youth organizations in Jonava as well as a longstanding sporting club called Maccabee, around which gathered primarily the general Zionist and revisionist youth. Most of them were from well-to-do families. Jonava was lacking a sport club that was appropriate for the working circles.

Upon looking back, it seems ridiculous when we mention today the political debates based on differences in outlook that pervaded the rival camps in the Jewish community. There was no shortage of political youth organizations in the Jewish towns of Lithuania, and the political wrangling was intense. Whoever lived during that time in the unique atmosphere of Lithuanian Jewry, Zionist in heart and soul, understands naturally the debates among the Zionist groups of the different factions in the background of the renewal that arrived from the Land of Israel at that time. This was the prime expression of cultural life in the town.

During that era, the Zionist activities of the various factions were overly provincial, but they imbued valuable content into the communal life of the local Jewish youth.

Two sports clubs, Maccabee and Hapoel, operated in this environment.

[Page 146]

The Organization in the Rubric of Hapoel

No small amount of struggle, deliberation and debate passed over the youth activists of Jonava during the time of the deliberating over the question of the establishment of Hapoel. There were those who were opposed to the establishment of an additional sporting organization over and above the longstanding Maccabee. On the other hand, others claimed that there was a need for a special sporting framework for the workers, so they went ahead with the establishment of Hapoel.

I recall the patrons of Hapoel in Jonava: Leibel Stern, Y. Monitz, Daniel Rikless (today in Tel Aviv), Tzipora Grossman (today in Haifa), Yerachmiel Teitelbaum, and me, who had an official position as the representative and member of the Hapoel headquarters.

Finally, a decision was made to establish Hapoel in Jonava. This was done with the support and assistance of the members of the Hapoel headquarters, especially Ben-Zion Moirer (who was among the first to be murdered by the Germans at the time of the liquidation of the Jewish leadership of Kovno at the Ninth Fort), and Aryeh Sirkin

(today Aryeh Sarig, a deputy director-general in the department of security [in Israel]).
An active committee was established, which later became the leadership committee of
the chapter. Members of the Tzeirei Zion youth organization participated, including:
Davidka Friedman, the Perchik brothers, Berl Rikless, Hershel Perevoznik, Elka
Abramovich, and Hershka Josefs.

The modest sporting activities began slowly. At first, a football team and gymnastics
team were set up. At a later time, when we rented a field (a large field on the outside of
the town), the members began to participate in light athletics, volleyball and basketball.

The youth became involved in these activities very willingly. Despite the meager
means at the disposal of the organizers, there was vibrancy and a great deal of activity.
The activities took place for the most part during the summer months, when the pleasant
weather facilitated the playing of sports in the open air.

At times, the members of Hapoel of Jonava took part in national and regional events
that were organized through the efforts of the Hapoel headquarters. The members
particularly enjoyed the trips to neighboring towns (Wilkomir, Keidani and others) for
football tournaments, joint regional gatherings, or friendly meetings. These events
introduced a competitive spirit and were challenging. They prepared for such gatherings
with great energy.

I recall the regional gathering of Hapoel in Jonava (1938) that took place in the form
of a camp outside the town, the regional gathering in Karmelava (1933), and the national
convention of all Hapoel chapters of Lithuania that took place in Kovno, in which Hapoel
of Jonava took part with a large representation of athletes and competitors in light
athletics and football.

The Importance of the Activity from a Social and Sporting Perspective

Indeed, we were not blessed with sporting achievements, but the meetings with the
Jewish youth from other towns provided a great deal of meaning for the youth. This
enabled Zionist crystallization, activity on behalf of Israel, training in pioneering, and
sublime aspirations for the building of the old-new homeland. Now we can note that many
of the youth of Jonava were saved by this blessed activity, for they succeeded in making
aliya to the Land of Israel under the rubric of Hechalutz, while there was still time, prior
to the destruction of Lithuanian Jewry, as well as at a later time as refugees from the
concentration camps or the remnants of the partisans.

This group of people arrived in Israel after various tribulations, after the ghettos, exile
in Siberia, or after participating in the war against the Germans in partisan units.

At this time we can state with certainty that thanks to that Zionist activity under the
auspices of Hapoel, Maccabee, and other Zionist organizations, we instilled a desire for

the Land of Israel into the hearts of the youth. Instead of scattering throughout the far reaches of the earth, they always desired to reach the Land of Israel. We had to fight strongly against the Communist propaganda that attempted to attract the Jewish youth to its ranks. All of those who joined the Communist youth were eventually lost. Most were murdered, and a very small number remain in Russia. In any case, they did not come to Israel.

Translator's Footnotes

The nickname "the Schwalb" means "the sparrow".

Probably in the European sense – i.e. soccer.

[Page 147]

The First National Youth Organization

by Y[itzchak] Ben-David (B[urstein])

Translated by Jerrold Landau

The chapter of Tzeirei-Zion—Hitachdut was the first nationalist youth organization that was founded in Jonava after the First World War. Its founders included Dov Zisla, Nathan Janusevich, the teacher Joselovich, Namiot and Dov Blumberg. The finest of the working youth, officials and youth of the middle class gathered into this organization.

The prime objectives which it stood for were: preparation of the youth for aliya, cultural activities, collection of money for the Keren Kayemet (Jewish National Fund) and knowledge of the Land.

The Hebrew library was founded in 1919 as a center for Hebrew culture. Alongside it was the meeting place in the Weiner home on Vilna Street. Meetings, lectures and social activities were organized in this place.

The chapter, which began in 1922, established itself and flourished through the efforts of Moshe Ivensky, and became a political factor in the life of the town.

Those days were the days of Jewish autonomy in Lithuania with the Jewish Ministry headed by Dr. Soloveitchik. Communities were established, headed by the national council. National banks and other organizations were founded. Tzeirei Zion had delegates to all of these.

The Tzeirei Zion party took first place in Jonava next to the General Zionists. It was the second largest in the community of Jonava and in the town council. Its delegates to the community council were Moshe Ivensky, Menachem Mines and Eliezer Levin.

Ivensky served as the chairman of the organization throughout many years. His second in command was Menachem Mines, one of the vibrant activists of the city. The writer of these lines served as the secretary.

During the years of 1922-1930, the chapter had more than 100 active members and more than 300 supporters who lent their support to Tzeirei Zion in elections to the community council and the Zionist congresses.

The Hechalutz organization was under the influence of the party, as was of course the Gordonia youth organization that was founded in 1927 and existed under the shadow of Tzeirei Zion. It was headed by Alter Klotz, Pesach Shachor, Shmuel Goldshmidt, Dina Perlstein and Leah Burstein. The members of Tzeirei-Zion also dedicated their time to tending to Maccabee.

During the 1930s, Tzeirei-Zion blended with the members of the Tz. S. (Young Socialists), and incorporated most of the national Socialist youth into their ranks.

Now, when we are far from that romantic era of the enthusiastic activities of the Jewish youth at gatherings, competitions and camps, we can properly value the great importance of that activity in forging the Jewish youth and creating meaning in their daily lives. This activity also gave them vigor, joy of life, and most importantly – the instilling of Jewish pride into their hearts.

Some of these Jewish youths of Jonava who succeeded in making aliya to the Land established large families, and took root in cities, towns and kibbutzim. Would it be that there were more of them, and that we did not have to weep over the many who perished at the hands of the German and Lithuanian murderers.

Thus concludes a pleasant chapter in the fruitful life of the youth in the exile of Lithuania, in a splendid town that was called Jonava – as if this was all a dream and not reality.

The beloved town remains far, far away – the town in which we spent our pleasant childhood. Nobody even visits the place, for no memory of the Jews remains there, and there is nobody to even say Shalom. This is the bitter reality.

[Page 148]

Members of Poale-Zion – Hitachdut

A group of members of Poale-Zion in the Girialka factory

The chapter of Hashomer Hatzair close to the time of its founding (1928). A meeting with the Keidani delegation.

Pesach Shachor, Zelig Yudelevich, X (from Keidani), Gila Plakser, Leah Grodsky, X, Alter Khasid, Shimon Gorfein, X, Leah Yudelevich, Moshe Fried, Shifra Stoller, Zeev Opnik, Yehuda Zopovich, Baruch Jalinovich, Pesia Konsky, Rachel Lifschitz, Sarah Shachor, Tvia Galinsky.

A group with Baruch Opnitzky from Keidani: L. Grodsky, R. Lifschitz, Chaya Rivka Aronson, Rachel Shapira, Beila Grodsky, Z. Opnik, Baruch, Batya Gorfein, Sheinka Friedland, Pinchas Shapira, Chana Josefs, Sheinka Klibansky, Rivka Simkovich, Dova Dobiansky, Osnat Katzenberg.

A group of older youths "Achduta" (with some youths):
Yitzchak Kremenitzin, Z. Opnik, Shlomo Perlstein, B. Jalinovich, Netanel Shapira, Izak Reibstein, Shimon Gorfein, P. Shapira, Chaya Dobiansky, Elka Untershatz, Sh. Shachor, Beilka Friedman, Batya Perchik, L. Grodsky, Mina Levitz, Hadassah Friedman, David Veps, Teibla Krabitzky, Freda Vilkomirsky, Tzvia Galinsky, M. Kremenitzin.

A group of Achva girls with Tzvi Ulpasky: Chana Josefs, B. Gorfein, Tzvi, Ch. R. Aronson, D. Dobiansky, R. Simkovich, Chaya Portnoy, Yenta Nochimovich, Sheina Friedland, Leah Klibansky, Dvora Berzin, R. Shapira, T, Galinsky, Feiga Zandman, A. Katzenberg.

Shevet Binyamin (Group Alef) with its counselors, photographs in the snow with the shul in the background. Passover 5681 (1921).

A group of Achduta prior to the aliya of Shimon Gorfein (Noy), at the beginning of 1933. A. Reibstein, Sh. Shachor, Sarah Goldberg, H. Friedman, Shimon, Alter Khasid, B. Jalinovich, R. Lifschitz, L. Grodsky, L. Yudelevich, P. Shapira, Sh. Stoller, Tz. Galinsky, S. Perlstein, Sh. Klibansky, N. Shapira, Z. Opnik.

A group of older girls with Tzvi Ulpasky

A group of scouts bidding farewell to Shimon [Gorfein (Noy)] D. Veps, A. Untershatz, B. Jalinovich, B Friedman, Ch. Dobiansky, B. Perchik, P. Vilkomirsky, Sh. Shachor, M. Kremenitzin, Sarka Segalovsky, Shimon, P. Shapira, X, A. Reibstein, Mina Levich.

חברת הסיוע לצופים העברים בליטא
הסתדרות הצופים העברים
„השומר־הצעיר"
ההנהגה הראשית

כרטיס צופה

1) כרטיס זה מעיד על בעלו, כי נמנה חבר של
הסתדרות הצופים העברים „השומר־הצעיר" בליטא.
2) הכרטיס נותן לצופים את זכות ללבוש תלבושת
הצופים, לשאת סימני צופים ולהלל במסודר את תפקידיהי הצופים.
3) כרטיס זה צריך להמצא תמיד בידי הצופה ובשעת
הצורך על הצופה להראותו.
4) אצל כל צופה יכול להיות רק כרטיס אחד.
5) אם יאבד כרטיס זה, אין הצופה יכול לקבל
כרטיס אחר כי אם ברשיון מיוחדת.

כרטיס № 703

השם ושם המשפחה

הקן　　　השכבה

הגיל　14　המדרגה

הבחנה

תפקיד

כמה זמן בהסתדרות　1929

התעסקותו

כרטיס זה כחו יפה עד 31.XII.193

יושב ראש חברת הסיוע

מזכיר חבּ"ר

ראש הקן

קובנה: יום　5　לחדש　193

Palestinos Žydų darb. bei jų
įstaigoms remti draugija
„Kapai"

חברה
למען ארץ־ישראל העובדת בליטא
»קפא"י«
פארבאנד
פֿאַר אַרבעטנדן אָרץ־ישׂראל אין ליטא

פּרטיס־חבר – חבר־קאַרטע
№ 1491/3

רפֿיס ס. יוסלוביץ, קובנה.

חברי, דואג אתה דאגת מחר בשביליך ובשביל אלפים מאחיך
עמד בחיל נאמן בין שורות העובדים בתרבות! שלם
בדיוק וגבה את חֹס מאה אחריֹם! כל פרוטה וגרוט: מצטרים
לחשבון.

הכרטיס נתן – די קארטע ארין ארױסגענו:
1932 4/תֹ

הועד המרכזי
צענטראל קֹמִיטֹעֹ

חתימה
סֹעקֹרֹעֹטֹאֹר'

הועד המקומי
אֹרֹטֹיֹקֹוֹם קֹמִיֹטֹעֹ

חתימה
אֹוֹטֹעֹרֹשֹרֹיֹבֹטֹ

יאַנאַסטא פֿאַר דיין צוקונפֿט אין די צוקונפֿט פֿון דיינע ברי:
מֹעֹר ברידער אין אֹיֹ: – סטאַרק דעם פֿאַרבאַנד אין פֿאַרגרֹעֹ:
דיינע רייהן! צאָל פֿינקֹטליך דיין קֹאָדמעֹל און העלֹף אירֹנ: –
גדן פֿון דיינע חברים.

כל מפעל ומפעל של הגועל העברי בארץ, כל קמדרה
חדשה הגרכבת שם על ידי ו – מגבירים את כח קליטתה של
הארץ ומרחחים את ספֹריה לפני מחנות צֹליֹם – עֹלוֹדֹם.

עיר

שטאם

שם

נאַמען

שם המשפחה

פֿאַמיליע־נאַמען

נכנס לחברה ביום

גֹעֹהֹעֹרֹט צום פֿאַרבאַנד זיים:

יעוֹדֹר נֹיֹע מֹאֹדֹרֹיֹח אֹרֹדֹעֹר אֹינֹסֹטֹיֹטֹוֹצֹיֹה פֿון דער אֹרֹץ
יֹשֹרֹאֹלֹדֹיֹקֹעֹר אֹרֹגֹעֹנֹעֹרֹ־שֹאַפֿט עֹמֹבֹט די מֹיֹליֹרֹן פֿון עֹרֹץ־ישׂראל
מֹעֹר נֹיֹע מֹחֹנֹוֹת עֹלֹוֹדֹם.

דער פֿאֹרֹבֹאֹצֹעֹר פֿאַרן אֹרֹבֹעֹיֹטֹנֹדֹן אֹרֹגֹעֹמֹיֹנֹזֹן אֹ־יֹ העלֹפֹט באֹמֹפֹעֹסֹטֹיֹקֹן
עֹלֹע אֹוֹמֹטֹעֹרֹנֹעֹמֹעֹנֹטֹוֹנֹגֹעֹן פֿון דער אֹרֹץ־ישׂראֹלֹדֹיֹקֹעֹר אֹרֹגֹעֹמֹעֹר־
סֹ־בֹ־ש.

{This page contains photocopies of pages of an organization membership card, and one letter.}

{Top right card photocopy}

The organization for the aid of Hebrew scouts in Lithuania

The Organization of Hebrew Scouts

Hashomer Hatzair

Central leadership

SCOUTING CARD

1) This card certifies that its owner is a member of the organization of Hebrew scouts, Hashomer Hatzair of Lithuania

2) This card gives the scout the right to wear the scouting uniform, to bear the insignia of the scouts, and to publicly fill its scouting tasks.

3) This card must be constantly found in the possession of the scout, and must be presented by the scout at a time of need.

4) Each scout may only possess one card.

5) If this card is lost, the scout cannot receive another card without special permission

{Bottom right card photocopy}

Palestinos Zydu darb bel ju

Istigoms remti draugija

KAPAI

The organization

For the Working Land of Israel in Lithuania

{Repeated in Yiddish}

Member card

No 19913

Printed by Sh. Joselovich, Kovno

{Top left letter}

The organization of Hebrew Scouts, Hashomer Hatzair, Kovno Chapter

March 1, 1928

Yente Nochimovich

We acknowledge the receipt of your request of February 14, 1928.

At a meeting of the council that took place on February 28, we dealt with your request, and the members of the council decided to accept you as a member of our organization.

For the first three months, you will be {cannot be made out}

The kibbutzim will be begin immediately after {cannot be made out}, and we will inform you of this.

With scouting greetings *{Signatures cannot be made out}*

{Middle card photocopy}

Card number 703

First name and Surname: Yente Nochimovich

Chapter: Jonava Class: D

Age: 17 Level: III

Surety: --

Role: --

How long in the organization: From 1929

Her task: --

This card is valid until: Dec 31, 1939 {last digit is overwritten and unclear}

Chairman of the support committee: {signature illegible}

Secretary: {Signature illegible}

Head of the chapter: {No signature}

Kovno, February, 5, 1932

{Lower center card photocopy}

Each and every activity of the Hebrew Hapoel in the Land, every new achievement attained by it – strengthens the ability of the Land to absorb, and opens it gates to the camps of pioneering immigrants.

City: Jonava

Name: Rachel

Family Name: Nochimovich

Joined the organization on: June 21, 1929

{Top statement repeated in Yiddish}

{Lower left card photocopy}

Member, you should be concerned about tomorrow for yourself and thousands of your brethren. Arise as a faithful soldier among the ranks of the workers in the organization! Pay your dues promptly and collect dues from others! Every penny is added to the account.

The card is given on:

June 4, 1929

{Signatures of the central committee, the local committee, and the card holder are illegible.}

[Page 149]

With soldiers: Efraim Baten, X, Yitzchak Gurvich, X, Levi Kaper, Chana Zopovich, X, Daniel Rikless, Aber Untershatz, X, Shlomo Friedman, Feivel Shapira

Members of Brit Hechail: X, Aberka, A. Kaper, Reping, Berl Segalovsky, Grossman, Reznik, Gurvich, Y. Klibansky, Baten, X, Vinitzky, N. Goldshmidt, L. Kaper, Friedman, A. Dochovsky, Mechnik

[Page 150]

Hashomer Hatzair Chapter

by Shimon [Gorfein] Noy

Translated by Jerrold Landau

Our town was graced with strong[1], vibrant youth – possibly in no small measure due to the influence of nearby Kovno. The youth were able to fill the ranks of all of the youth organizations that existed in the Jewish community. Some of the youth who did not find their place in other organizations joined together in part and founded the chapter of Hashomer Hatzair.

This took place on January 1, 1928. There were a few members of the movement among the students of the Hebrew seminary for teachers in Kovno, who had arrived on their winter expedition from Kovno. The guests were received by the graduating class of the Tarbut school. The members of the movement took the initiative, gathered the students and explained to them – that is to us – about Hashomer Hatzair.

No small number responded to these words of explanation, and organized themselves with the feeling that they would find an answer to their youthful desires within this movement.

Zeev Opnik, Sheinka Friedland, Shlomo Gerber, K., Pinchas Shapira, K., Shlomo Perlstein; K., Izik Reibstein, Elka Untershatz, Sheinka Klibansky, K., David Veps, Leah Klibansky, K., Leah Yudelevich, Chanka Jalinovich, Leah Grodsky, Shimon Gorfein, X, Netanel Shapira, K. (with people from Keidani who came for a visit – K. stands for someone from Keidani)

After some time, two groups crystallized: Achduta – the group for older youths and Achva – the scouting group. Females comprised a significant portion of the chapter. The chapter expanded and broadened, and attracted youth and children also to class A.[2]. They rented a hall, which roved from house to house, and made efforts to establish organized activities, or as we called our meetings – Kibbutz. We would say "Kibbutz kvutza, kibbutz kan"[3]. We conducted some of the activities with our own power, and we were helped by counselors from outside: Avigdor Opnitzky from the Keidani chapter, and the student Tzvi Ulpasky, a member of the Young Socialists, who conducted activities for us on the themes of Socialism, the worker's movement, the doctrine of Borochov, and other such topics.

Of course, the activities were conducted in Hebrew, for we were all students of the Tarbut school. The chapter and the meeting place were quickly filled with content, and filled our lives with great meaning. Sabbath parties were organized on Sabbath eves. Newspapers articles written by alumni of the chapter were read. We made contact with other chapters in Keidani, Wilkomir [Ukmerge] and Kovno. Our horizons broadened. Our spiritual and social world became richer. We gained friends and knowledge. Our lives were filled with experiences. We felt as if we had grown wings, and had been liberated from our fears and the mentality of exile. We frequently hiked, went on excursions, and conducted summer activities in the bosom of nature. We often went out to summer camps. We conducted many activities in that very grove [the Gerialka Woods] where our dear ones were later taken out to be murdered.

When we took matters seriously and prepared to go to hachsharah in preparation for aliya to the Land, it was not easy for our parents to take leave of us and permit us to leave them. There were those who refused to permit their sons and daughters to make aliya. It was hard to convince them that, upon analyzing the Jewish situation in the lands of the Diaspora according to the doctrine of Borochov as we had studied in our programs, we had no future in the Diaspora, and our existence there was fraught with danger. There were those parents who claimed that they were not short of any good thing there. It is most unfortunate that only a few of the youth succeeded in escaping from the vale of murder while there was still time.

There were only a few who continued the life of the movement in the kibbutzim. However the years of the lives of many of those who were members of the movement and the chapter were not only pleasant years, but also – as all would agree – in addition to the pleasant memories that remain in their hearts, there are also certain values, the fruit of the education of the movement. Without doubt these values will accompany them throughout their lives, wherever they are.

[Page 151]

The First Hebrew Kindergarten

Translated by Jerrold Landau by Golda Sirek (Saker)

Batya Zandman and Pesia Dembo were two friends who studied together and completed the Hebrew gymnasium in Kovno. After that, they traveled to study in the seminary for kindergarten teachers in Riga. When they completed their studies, they returned home to Jonava and opened a kindergarten that was exemplary, and the first of its kind in the town. They spoke to the children only in Hebrew. Of course, they sang Hebrew songs. Many parents requested that the kindergarten teachers speak to their children in Yiddish. However, Batya and Pesia stood their ground and only spoke in the Hebrew language.

I remember those children whom we ran into on the streets of the town, strolling and singing the songs of Bialik. This scene was always moving – hearing their sweet voices breaking out in Hebrew song, and seeing their pure and clear images.

Batya Zandman dedicated a great deal of her time to the town of Jonava. At night she sat in the library and exchanged books. She collected money for Keren Kayemet. Her father of blessed memory purchased land in Israel, but they did not succeed in benefiting from this.

[Page 152]

The Tarbut Hebrew Public School

by Chana Zimrani (Granevich) of Tel Aviv

Translated by Jerrold Landau

The teachers Yoselovich and Dov Zisla, the founders of the popular Tarbut Hebrew School.

Already during the era of Czarist rule, there were many parents in Jonava who possessed a Hebrew-Zionist culture, and who desired to establish a modern Hebrew school for their children. However Czarist Russia did not permit the teaching of general subjects in the Hebrew languages. The Germans, who conquered Lithuania in 1915, looked favorably upon the desires of the Jews to establish modern educational institutions in their language, for they regarded this as a good means against Russification. However, the depressed economic situation and poverty of the community of Jonava during that era did not make the establishment of a school feasible.

With the declaration of independence of Lithuania in 1918, a popular Hebrew school was established in Jonava in the wooden building of the Talmud Torah on Breizer Street. At first this was a school for girls, but after a short time it turned into a coeducational school for girls and boys. However, the sign "Hebrew School for Girls" continued to flutter over the building for a few years after it became a mixed school.

As is known, Lithuania issued a decree of autonomy for its Jews in August 1919. It recognized the Jewish national committee and established a special Jewish ministry that existed until 1924. This was very conducive to the development of Jewish schools in Lithuania in general, and of the popular Tarbut Hebrew school in Jonava in particular.

The number of students grew, as the refugees returned from Russia to Jonava. This created the need to open more classes, especially preparatory classes. The school building was only four rooms, and even the teachers' room was a small section of the first room on the left, in which a wooden partition was erected. Therefore, one or two classes had to study during the afternoon hours. When the children of the refugees joined in, a gap became evident between the knowledge of the veteran students and that of the newcomers, especially in the knowledge of the Hebrew language. Therefore, it is self evident that during those years of the early 1920s, classes were composed from different age groups.

{The article continues on page 352, after a series of eight unnumbered pages.}

The Tarbut school that separated from the Talmud Torah, 1919-1920. The teachers Kolbiansky, Joselovich, Liba Chana Stern, and Alter (David) Kagan

A visit from the Hebrew teachers' seminary in Kovno, January 1, 1928.

Among those standing: Shaul Keidansky, Alter Sadler, Rabinovich the principal of the seminary; to the left: Rosenberg. At the edge, Menachem Mendel Gorfein from the teaching staff. In the background is the cemetery.

A gym class and roll call with the teacher Alter Sandler

Some of the students of the Tarbut school:

Sara Silberman, Mina Sack, Estia Granevich, Malka Untershatz; Chana Goldshmidt, Peisha Levin, Libka Rosenthal, Etka Segalovsky, Nadia Granevich; Freidka Zisla, Peisha Heiman, Shifra Lomiansky.

Students of the sixth grade and their teachers: Jonava, June 27, 1928.

Sarah Shachor, Hadassah Friedman, Yitzchak Sulsky, Tzvi Josefs, Baruch Jalinovich, Netanel Shapira, Mordechai Yaffa, Sheinka Klibansky, Rachel Rashkes; Lipsha Buz, Dvora Goldshmidt, Miriam Levin, Yesha Vilkomirsky, Tzvia Galinsky, Shimon Gorfein, Gita Plakser, Rachel Lifschitz, Shifra Stoller; the teachers: Tabchovich, Sara Burstein, Keidansky; Zeev Opnik, Leah Grodsky, Yehuda Zopovich.

A photograph of the entire school. The teachers are Keidansky, Aptkina, Rosenberg, Sandler.

שעורי ערב "תרבות" ביונובה
פסח תרפ"ח

The Tarbut Evening Classes in Jonava, Passover 5688 (1928)

The Tarbut school:

Chana Margolis, Tzvia Galinsky, Chana Shachor, Chana Miriam Untershatz, Chana Sesitzky, Leah Burstein, Pesia Yaffa, Dvora Goldshmidt, Sarah Shachor; Eliahu Baron, Aryeh Perchik, Zeev Abramovich, Chaya Davidovich, Lipsha Buz, Dina Perlstein, Malka Untershatz, Tzvia Berzin, Miriam Lantzman. The service personnel: Zuska Atkatz. The teachers – Rosenberg, Keidansky, Tabachovich, Isser Gurvich, Sandler – Tzvi Yaffa, Aryeh Sulsky; Dov Segalovsky, Pesach Shachor, Reuven Keidansky, Yasha Vilkomirsky, Yosef Friedland, Nissan Goldshmidt, Moshe Fried, M. Wolk.

The Yavneh Hebrew School
Jonava, Lag B'omer, 5690 (1930)

Rabbi Silman with the teaching staff of Yavneh:
David Kagan, Sheina Grodsky, Alter Kagan, Rabbi Silman, Moshe Feldberg

Alter Kagan and his students

The performance of Kever David (David's Tomb) by the students of the Yavneh
School in Jonava, January 14, 1934

A photograph of Rabbi Silman (uncaptioned)

Rabbi Silman's grave

The Great Gaon the Prince of Torah

Expert in

The Babylonian Talmud, The Jerusalem Talmud, The Sifra

The Sifrei, Rishonim, Acharonim[4]

Pursuing Righteousness and uprightness

A merciful father to any person who is suffering or is in tribulation

{Line cannot made made out – but includes the phrase Bikur Cholim}

Our Rabbi

Rabbi Chaim Yitzchak

The son of Moshe Silman of blessed memory

13 Sivan 5690 (1930)

May his soul be bound in the bonds of eternal life

[Page 153]

Immediately after they returned, the refugees were not established from an economic perspective, and many were unable to pay the tuition. Even though the school received support from the communal council, its physical situation was difficult during the beginning of the 1920s. At times, there was not enough money to purchase firewood. One winter day, the chairman of the parents committee, Mendel Gorfein (the father of Shimon Noy) appeared in the classes and turned to the students with a request to volunteer and bring wood from their homes to light the fire in the school. The next morning, girls and boys with schoolbags on their shoulders and pine and birch twigs in their hands appeared on the streets of Jonava, walking in the direction of the school.

On a volunteer basis and with great dedication, the members of the parents' committee took care of all administrative matters: the collection of tuition, the payment of the teachers' salary, the purchase of provisions, maintenance, etc. Moshe Granevich, one of the founders of the school, served as the treasurer for many years. Later Sinai Shapiro filled the role of treasurer.

During the 1920s, the physical situation of the school improved, for many students transferred over at one time from the Yavneh school, and furthermore, there were changes for the better due to the improvement of the economic situation in the town.

All subjects were taught in Hebrew in the school. The Lithuanian language was only studied as a subject. Within a brief period of time, the Yiddish Language was also taught as a subject from the reader "Der Shul-Chaver" (The School Companion) of Bastomsky. During its first years, there was a dearth of teachers of certain subjects. There was also a shortage of textbooks. For these reasons, there was a lag in the teaching of nature for about ten years. On the other hand, the teaching of the Hebrew language was on a high level. The teachers had an excellent command of the Hebrew language. There was also no shortage of readers: Sfat Ami, Tal-Yaldut, Yaldut, Bikurim, and Lashon Vasefer in five parts. The teaching of Bible was also on a high level. Special care was exhibited in the teaching of grammar in all subjects that were taught in the school. During the first years, when the general educational network of the young Lithuanian Republic was still at its inception, there was no obligatory curriculum.

At that time, the Lithuanian language was still taught at a minimal level. It is no wonder that throughout the first year, the students did not learn how to read in Lithuanian. When the Lithuanian anthem had to be learned for February 16, 1919, the first year of Lithuanian independence, the teachers wrote the words of the anthem on the board in Hebrew letters. The students copied it and learned it by heart, barely understanding even one word.

As the years passed, the demands from the ministry of education increased, and the level of general knowledge increased appropriately. At around the end of the 1920s, official matriculation examinations were arranged in the presence of a representative of the ministry of education. Demands on teachers were also imposed by the ministry of education. Teachers who could not prove their mastery of the Lithuanian language were not permitted to teach in the school.

The Lithuanian government maintained the public schools on its own account. However, it would only retain a teacher for a class that numbered at least 32 students. Most of the classes in the public Hebrew school in Jonava did not have that number of students, so the parents had to hire teachers on their own account. However, this did not deter the teachers, for the vast majority of the Jewish population of Jonava was imbued with the Hebrew-Zionist spirit. The parents also made efforts to found additional classes. Primary schools in Lithuania consisted of four grades. (A reformation took place only in the middle of the 1930s, expanding the primary schools to six grades.) After completing the fourth grade, students were accepted into the gymnasium or the progymnasium. There was only a Lithuanian progymnasium in Jonava, but the Jews tended not to send their children to the Lithuanian progymnasium, and only a few Jews studied there. Since it was difficult to send a 10-11 year old child to study in the city, the Hebrew public school opened additional unofficial classes that were called "preparatory a", or "preparatory b", or "the fifth grade". During the 1927-1928 school year a sixth grade was opened, composed of approximately 20 graduates of the fifth grade. Boys and girls who finished the fifth grade one year or even two years earlier joined the class. Thus did the class reach 30 students.

The existence of the sixth grade was made possible primarily by finding an appropriate teacher. He was Tabachovich, who was brought in from the gymnasium of Wilkomir. The principal Keidansky and Mrs. Sara Burstein, who taught English according to the Berlitz book, taught along with him. After a year, most of these students continued on to the seventh grade. This year was also completed with success. Even though at first there was a month-long break in studies due to the switching of teachers, the curriculum of study in those following years, which was taught in the afternoons, became increasingly similar to the curriculum of studies in the gymnasiums. Many students succeeded in being accepted into the upper grades of the gymnasiums of Kovno or Wilkomir after additional preparation with a private teacher during the summer vacation.

The first teacher and principal of the Hebrew public school in Jonava was Yoselovich, who came from the outside and worked in the school for 2-3 years. The second principal was Shaul Keidansky, who also came from outside with his family (a wife, two sons and a daughter), and became a permanent resident of Jonava. Mr. Keidansky was also the last principal of the school. There were other teachers who came from outside and became residents of the city: the teacher David Rosenberg who married Zlata Janusevich, and the teacher Beila Apatkina who married Eliezer, the son of Meir Goldshmidt. There were also a few natives of Jonava itself who worked as teachers in the Hebrew public school: Alter Kagan (the artist) and his wife Liba Chana, nee Stern; and Alter (Yitzchak) Sandler who began to teach in this school in 1924 after he completed the Real Hebrew Gymnasium in Kovno. He worked there until he made aliya in 1925. Yitzchak Sandler died in Tel Aviv in 1954 at the age of 52. Other teachers who worked in the Hebrew public school of Jonava were Zeidel, Isser Horowitz, Mrs. Sheinyuk who is remembered by the students primarily for her playful songs such as "Do you want to know?", "The bird and the cat", etc.; the writer Eliezer Heiman, Mines from Wilkomir, and Achber from Pasvalys who today lives in Kovno

[Section in the box on page 154]

To this day I recall two typical Jewish anecdotes that I heard from the mouth of the teacher Isser Horowitz.

Once a childless Jew came to the rabbi to request his blessing.

The rabbi told him: return home, and next year at this time you will have a son, at a propitious time.

At the end of the year, the Jew returned again and complained to the rabbi:

"Rabbi, oh woe, what did you perpetrate on me? You promised me a son – and behold, two daughters were born to me!"

The rabbi answered him calmly:

"Indeed it is so my son, I did not err. In my head was the acrostic for "Two females"[5]

A Jew came to consult with the rabbi. He had a daughter who came of age, and she found herself a groom who was without fault. But what was the problem? His family – their pedigree is not top notch… and the talebearers tell that his brother is a stain upon the family. What should we do? Should we agree to the match or not?

The rabbi pointed him to the third volume of the Tur[6], where he would find his answer. The Jew got the hint. He took out the book of Exodus, and found the description of the breastplate of the High Priest, with the names of the rows of stones: "Leshem, Shvo Veachlama" (a jacinth, an agate and an amethyst).

He wrinkled his brow and struggled to understand the answer. He could not fathom the intention of the rabbi at all.

He returned to the rabbi, and asked: "What is the interpretation?"

The rabbi said to him: You did not read it correctly. You need to change the vowels as follows "Leshem Shebo, veach lama?" (To his own name, and why the brother?)

All of the teachers who taught in the school were imbued with a Hebrew-Zionist spirit, and had great influence on their students. How astonishing it was to the students when they heard their teachers speak Hebrew to their own children in their homes. The ring of the names of the children had a special enchantment – Yoel (Zeidel), Emanuel (Keidansky) --with the accent at the end of the word[7], as well as such a Zionist name as Tziona (Keidansky). The unique Hebrew environment that pervaded in the school and that was expressed by the traditional Lag B'omer excursions to Har Hascharchoret (Dizzy Mountain), the celebrations and festivities and later also through the activities at the meeting place greatly influenced the enriching of the souls of the students and their connection to Hebrew culture.

Already during the first days of the existence of the school, Zionist songs such as "Hatikva," "Sham Baaretz Chemdat Avot" (There in the Land that was dear to the patriarchs), "Seu Tziona Nes Vadegel" (Raise a banner and a flag toward Zion), and the songs of Bialik, Tshernikovsky, Maneh, etc. burst forth from it. During recess, one could see in the yard girls dancing and playing with the accompaniment of Hebrew words "Open up quickly, open, open the gate", or "you are a cat, you are black, you are evil and bad". These game-rhymes were brought to the school by several girls who learned them from the private teacher Bara-Moshe Kolbiansky before the existence of the school. He maintained a sort of kindergarten for a very small group of girls in his dwelling (in the house of Aba Lomiansky) already during the era of German occupation.

During the second year of the school, the teacher Joselovich prepared a performance by the students: the operetta "The Lamb and the Wolf". One of the prime roles was given to Avraham Yitzchak Opnik (the brother of Zeev Ofek), who had a good voice. The role of the lamb was given to Tzipora Levin (the daughter of Chaim Levin) because of her curly hair. This performance was canceled at the last minute due to the fire that broke out in the hall due to the lack of knowledge of how to use the carbide lamp ("luks") which was borrowed for the play from the store of Masha Granevich. (This was the time before electric lights in Jonava.) It was fortunate that the fire broke out before a large crowd had gathered, and everyone succeeded in escaping by jumping over the long, wooden benches. Klibansky's carpentry shop was completely burnt.

During later years, the school arranged the students' celebrations in the hall of the "Union" theater (earlier, the "Reinoa"). During one of the performances, the play "The Kidnapped" was performed. The role of the kidnapped child was performed by Noach Stern, who later became known as a poet. In that play, Reiza Leah Khasid also appeared in the song "A poor wanderer is knocking here", dressed up as an elderly Jew with a large staff in her hand. At the end of this play, they were supposed to make a "living pyramid", but the disappointment of those who had to build this pyramid was very great

– especially the disappointment of the younger ones who waited with their blue and white flags to jump to the top of this pyramid – when they were informed that this number was being dropped due to a lack of time. Most of the time was stolen by the very long intermissions between each act that were used to set up the scenery on the stage. It is appropriate to mention the names of other students who contributed of their talents to the student celebrations: the two Koshlevich sisters with their charcoal eyes, Ahuva Stern, and Zeev Opnik (Ofek). There were certainly other students who participated in the student performances, but their names never reached me. On Chanukah and Tu B'Shevat, for the most part, school celebrations were arranged only for the students and teachers. Chanukah celebrations of course began with the lighting of candles. Zeev Opnik would recite the blessing over the candles, and then the choir conducted by Liba Chana Stern (Kagan) would sing Chanukah songs. Later in the program, one of the students would recite a poem from the curriculum of studies. During the Tu B'Shevat celebrations as well, there were choir songs, recitations, and something special for that holiday – the distribution of bags of fruit of the Land of Israel

– boxer (carobs), almonds, figs and raisins. The income was dedicated to Keren Kayemet.

During the 1930s, the teacher Mines did a great deal for the success of the student performances. He would arrange student plays with the characteristics of operettas. He composed them himself, improvised the music, or wrote words for known melodies. When there were ballet performances, Bunia Wolfovich would prepare the students for these performances. The Jonaver musician Shlomo-Ber Meirovich organized the choir and conducted it.

A unique event in the annals of the Tarbut school in Jonava was the parade and celebration on the occasion of the opening of the Hebrew University in Jerusalem in the year 1925. As with all celebrations, people crowded into the school hall or the movie theater. This celebration was a form of demonstration to all the residents of the town, Jewish and gentile – a demonstration of our attraction to the renewed Hebrew culture of our Land. The students marched through the streets of the town in pairs (a few weeks before this, they received special marching lessons from Shlomo Friedman, who was one of the finest of the Maccabee athletes), with the Zionist flag raised high and fluttering before them. The students joined the celebrating crowds on Har Hascharchoret (Dizzy Mountain). The national joy and pride filled all hearts on that festive spring day.

It should be noted that specifically during the first ten or twelve years of the Hebrew public school, there was little room for alternative subjects such as art, craftsmanship and gym. Similarly, there were barely any clubs outside of the curriculum of studies. It is therefore no wonder that when Hashomer Hatzair was founded in Jonava during the 1927-1928 school year, most of the students of the Tarbut Hebrew public school joined that movement, which had in its power the ability to complete that which was lacking in a complete educational experience. An awakening and progress took place in the supplementary education of the school itself during the 1930s, thanks to the blessed activities of the teacher Mines. We have already discussed above the success of his performances. He founded the meeting place for students, whose activities took place on Sabbaths. These activities were imbued with an enthusiastic Zionist spirit.

Throughout the more than twenty years of its existence, our Tarbut school in Jonava bestowed education upon and instilled national spirit in hundreds of students. Many of its graduates made aliya, and their excellent Hebrew education helped them in their physical and spiritual absorption. It also helped them imbue Hebrew culture in their own children, and to influence their entire surroundings with that spirit.

שלמה בר מאירוביץ

Shlomo Ber Meirovitch

Translator's Footnotes

Literally rich, but not used in the monetary sense.

The group would have been divided into various classes, with class A. being the youngest group.

"A group (kvutza) is a kibbutz, a chapter (kan) is a kibbutz."

Sifra and Sifrei are Torah commentaries from the Mishnaic period. Rishonim and Acharonim are the early and latter rabbinic sages.

Beit Nekeivot means "Two females" (using the alphabetical formulation of numbers in Hebrew). Its acrostic is "B N", the letters for "ben" – a son.

The Tur is a precursor to the Code of Jewish Law (Shulchan Aruch). It is short for "Arba Turim" (Four Rows) – referring literally to the four sections of the Code of Jewish law – and homiletically basing its names on the "four rows" of precious stones in the breastplate of the High Priest.

In opposition to Yiddish, which generally puts the stress on the penultimate syllable.

[Page 157]

The Or Noga Yeshiva

by Shmuel Ben-Menachem

Translated by Jerrold Landau

Reb Mendel Deitz

One day, Rabbi Silman came to the Slobodka Yeshiva to bring my father, Reb Mendel, as the *Rosh Yeshiva* of Jonava. The Yeshiva wandered from one synagogue to another. Youths from nearby towns also studied there. It was a small *Yeshiva* that served as a preparation for the larger *Yeshiva*. Most of the students later became householders[1] who were knowledgeable in *Gemara*. Reb Menachem Mendel continued to serve as the *Rosh Yeshiva* until the Russians came. The *shochet* Reb Michael Lichtenstein also studied there.

The *Yeshiva* disbanded when the Russians entered.

{Given over by Shmuel Ben-Menachem Deitz.}

Level 1 of the Hashomer Hadati at the Yavneh School in Jonava

[Page 157]

Institutions and Social Enterprises

by Y[itchak]. B[urstein]

Translated by Jerrold Landau

The People's Bank

This institution, which contributed to the economic life in the town, was located on the second floor of the Kaper home (previously, the home of Masha Granvich). The small-scale savers would bring their savings there. Moshe Ivenksy was the first person to whom the borrowers would turn. The trust in him was very great. The bookkeeper, Yankel Opnitzky, was tall and skinny, an avowed member of the culture league, and the personification of honesty. The director, Efraim Abramson, was calm, and able to satisfy everyone. During discussions with him in his office, he would rest his spectacles on his forehead. He was a General Zionist. Avigdor Opnitzky also worked there as a bookkeeper. He was a Shomer Hatzair member from Kedainiai. He also served as the leader of the chapter. He was a modest, upright person. He married the dentist Feiga Motnik. Gittel Ritz (Lopiansky) was the secretary. The directors were elected in a democratic fashion at a meeting. The last members included David Burstein as chairman, Shmerel Stern, Yudel Rashkes, Nathan Valchokovsky, and Dr. Ran.

[Page 158]

The Hebrew Library

It was finally transferred to two rooms in the building of Baruch Izraelson (and his two daughters Chana and Esther) on Vilna Street opposite the Wiener building. This was an enterprise of Young Zion. Eighty percent of the thousand books were in Hebrew, and the remainder in Yiddish, either in the original or in translation. Its dedicated workers, who dedicated their evenings to this, were: Velva Kerzner and Chana Davidovich (later Rikliansky) who perished, Golda Sirek who lives in Tel Aviv, as well as the writer of these lines.

The Yiddish Library

It was directed by the Culture League. It was smaller than the Hebrew library, but had dedicated readers and activists who concerned themselves with left-leaning literature. Its activists included the teacher Blusher, Vicho, Kolbansky, Marka Lin, and others.

The Bikur Cholim Hospital

Its building was located on the street of the Synagogue. It was run by the community. It was later supported by the town hall. It was expanded with the assistance of the family of Leiba Winik from the United States. It had five beds. Its de facto director was Glaz, a tall man with a large beard. He was modern and tolerant even though he belonged to Agudas Yisroel. Dr. Grisha Ran was the physician.

The Bathhouse

It was situated behind the fire station. After taking a bath and a shampoo with the aid of special brushes, people would leave with reddened faces, having left behind the filth and sweat, and go home to don their Sabbath attire. At the end of the 1920s, it was decided, through the initiative of Chaim Levin, to build a modern bathhouse. A branch was added to the old bathhouses, with dressing rooms, a table, a mirror, a bathing room covered with white porcelain, and a special steam room. There was a cafeteria at the entrance, called the Console. It was run by Yudel, and sold lemonade, soda, and snacks. Its director was Nathan Valchokovsky.

Physicians

When Mordechai Wolfovich concluded his university studies as a physician in the 1930s, after a brief period of apprenticeship in Switzerland, he opened an office on the second floor of the Lomiansky building. His number of patients grew from year to year. He was considered to be a more modern physician than Dr. Ran. He followed the professional literature, and never stopped improving himself. His name was known in the villages of the district, and he was held in esteem in the town. He married Julia Garb from Vilkomir [Ukmerge], and they lived opposite Eizik Segalovsky. He was deported to Siberia with his family. Today he lives in Barnaul in the Altay region of Siberia. His wife Julia, who had remained by chance in Lithuania, perished.

The office (reception room) of Dr. Bumash, who had moved to Jonava from Vilkomir, was also on the Street of the Road. He was a tall, thick man. His wife, from the Weitzstein family of Vilkomir, was beautiful and intelligent, but she also became fat with the passage of time. They did not get along well with people.

The Town Council

For many years, the head of the town council was Dr. Reilis, an intelligent, democratic man. His assistant was the treasurer Yehuda Movshovich, the father of Chaya Dina Epstein and Zelda Solsky. He was tall, and had a proud gait.

[Page 159]

There was a great deal of activity during the elections to the town council. There were economic interests, tax issues, and the like. The town council concerned itself with improving the appearance of the town. A large garden was planted at the side of the Street of the Road. A new street was opened from the cooperative to the Vylia, which contained a row of tender trees. This street also led to Breizer Street. Sidewalks were built. The streets were repaved. The availability of electric lighting expanded. The electricity was obtained directly from Kovno at all hours of the day. The hospital, bathhouse and slaughterhouse were supported by the town council, thereby easing the budget of the communal council.

The Oren Match Factory

There was a modern match factory on the road not far from the train station. It had already been built prior to the First World War, and was expanded in 1922. It was equipped with automated machinery and an electric station. It was a company with shares, that was founded by Leibe Optnitzky, David Burstein, Yosa Burstein (Zisla), Elia Entes, Yankel Weitzstein, and Chaim Levin. More than 100 workers from the district worked there. The technical staff, foremen and directors were Jews from Jonava. The director was Chaim Levin, the treasurer – Yankel Weitzstein, the bookkeeper – Chaya Briman, the technical directors – Shimon Rubin, Katz, Berl Entes, Kramerman, and others. The three latter ones lived within the precincts of the factory. The guard was Breznat.

The first parties of the gymnasium graduates – those of the Carlebach Hebrew gymnasium and the Timinski Russian gymnasium in Kovno – would take place here, in the large packaging hall. The "golden youth" participated in these parties, including: Dora Zians, Zelig Epstein, Alter Sandler, Abba Opnitzky, Berl Antes, Mitzel Pogirsky, Leizer Goldshmid, Rachel and Sheina Levin, Sara Burstein, Miriam Lomiansky, Bluma

Pogirsky, Chana and Masha Segalovsky, Batya Opnitzky, Ela Wolk and Menashe Weiner.

Chaim Levin expressed his opinion that this was the finest garden, with boulevards and benches.

In 1930, the Lithuanian government forced the owners of the company of shareholders to sell the enterprise to the Kruger Swedish concern. However, Chaim Levin remained as the director, through the concern, until just before the Russians came.

The Medis Sawmill

With the expansion of furniture manufacturing during the 1930s, the owners of the carpentry shops decided to free themselves from the supervision of the sawmill owners, and to found a cooperative called "Medis" ("tree" in Lithuanian). Hershel Friedman, formerly an official at Kemach, directed the enterprise. The members of the cooperative included: Yankel Leib Landman, Kopel Reznik and his sons, Abba Reznik, Mones Klibansky and his sons, Moshel Kolbiansky and Chaim Slomin, Moshe and Zusia Klotz, Shmuel Chernman, Nachum Levin, Moshe Shapira and his son, Shmerel Shapira, Plakser and his son, Kozanovsky, Yankel Tauber, Adler the "bass", Yankelevich, Landman, and Goldman.

[Page 160]

A Note on the Communal Council
by Baruch Kursik

{Text below the line}

It was during the 1920s, the years of Jewish autonomy in Lithuania. The communal councils began widespread work. In Jonava as well, the communal council conducted a great deal of work. Everybody worked on a volunteer basis except for the secretary and his assistant.

The communal council consisted of 16 members who were chosen as representatives of the parties and organizations. Agudas Yisroel was represented by Rabbi Silman and Yaakov Shimshon Glaz. The representatives of Mizrachi were Shmerl Stern and Rubin. The General Zionists were represented by D. Burstein, Rashkes and Valchokovsky. Young Zion was represented by Menachem Mines and Ivensky. The Yiddishists were represented by Yankel Opnitzky. The representatives of the craftsmen (handworkers) were Benkocher and Yechiel Davidovich.

After Glaz, the chairman was Mines. Yisrael Goldstein was the secretary.

Income was primarily from shechita (ritual slaughter) permits.

The communal council looked after the slaughterhouse, the bathhouse, and visiting the sick (Bikur Cholim) and was very active in the realm of assisting those in need for Maos Chittin for Passover, providing care, tending to wayfarers, providing firewood for the winter. Leib Opnitzky excelled particularly in this area.

Given over by Baruch Kursik
Who worked as the assistant to the secretary in 1921-1922.

Translator's Footnotes

The term here refers to well-educated laymen as opposed to rabbis.

[Page 160]

The Firefighters

by Baruch Levin

Translated by Jerrold Landau

Jonava had primarily wooden homes. There were brick houses only on the main street, in the market, and on the street next to the Christian church.

"Moyer" (brick walls) – were a symbol of strength and stability. If one wanted to say that something was strong, one would say "shtark vi moyer", that is to say, as strong as a brick building.

As is known, Jonava was entirely burnt down twice before the First World War. The elder natives of Jonava recall the first and second fires. They also recall all sorts of events and dates based on the dates of the fires. For example, so and so was born after the second fire, etc. After the world war, the Maccabee organization established a firefighting organization in Jonava – "Faszarne Kommande" as it was called in the town. The Jewish residents of the city regarded the firefighters as their own institution. Almost all of the volunteer firefighters were Jewish, and the few gentiles found themselves under Jewish management.

The equipment was particularly paltry. There were large barrels (batchkes) that were brought in immediately after the outbreak of a fire, as a form of first aid. There were also water-drawing machines which were operated by hand. However, the firefighters did not have horses to transport the batchkes and the water-drawing machines, and during the fires, they tried to confiscate horses from the wagon drivers. Until the time a wagon driver could be convinced to give over his horse, and until they brought the batchkes and water drawing machines to a well or to the river – the fire had completely consumed the building. The firefighters arrived and sprinkled water on the neighboring houses. Later, the firefighters obtained a larger water-drawing machine, but it also required horses. Only in the 1930s did they obtain a large machine that was operated by an engine. This was the height of modernity of the firefighters.

The firefighters would conduct "reftitzius," that is to say, drills. These were a part of the experience of the town. The guard of the firefighters would wear a blue uniform, place a trumpet in his belt, pass through the streets of the town, stop in certain corners, and trumpet with pride, announcing that a drill was about to take place.

A Fire in the Town

Jonaver Blacksmiths in 1911

[Page 161]

The volunteer firefighters would wear their own uniforms, some with brass helmets from the middle ages, and others in blue helmets. They wore wide belts, to which were hitched an axe and a pick-axe, which was called a "kirke" in Yiddish. They would run to present themselves in the yard of the fire hall. There they would be enumerated. After long negotiations with the wagon drivers, they would obtain horses and go out to the center of town with the machines and barrels. They would connect the machines to a well or the river, extend the fire hoses, and begin to spray water in the market or on some random houses. The children would run between them with great curiosity and try to help. After they proved that the fire hose worked properly, and after they poured out the appropriate amount of water – for in our town things were not measured by a watch – they would begin to gather up their equipment. They would return to the yard of the fire hall filled with personal satisfaction that the maneuver had succeeded.

Then the real experience would come. There were no alarms in the town, so when a fire broke out, they would run and shout "fazer", that is "fire". There were those who excelled in shouting "fazer" with a unique clear voice. When Mendel the shoemaker shouted "fazer" I would awaken in the middle of the night, recognizing his voice.

When they shouted "fazer", everyone would run outside and begin asking where it is burning. The firefighters would be running to and fro.

Indeed, there were jokes in the town about the shouting of "fazer". The adage "Peshka, shrei fazer" (Pesia, shout fire) was known. Peshka's neighbor came to her quickly during a fire and requested, "Peshka, shout fire", for shouting would, Heaven forbid, hurt herself…

During such fires in the town, many wooden buildings burnt down and poor people lost everything that they had. The residents were very afraid of fires. If a fire broke out at the end of a street, the people on the entire street and nearby streets would pack up their belongings. In the middle of the night, one could see people running with sacks of pillows and blankets. In particular, they would pack the bedding, so that "there would be something upon which to rest the head".

There were buildings which were well insured, and after the fire the owner of the buildings would build a better home, for the most part made of bricks. There were also occasions where by chance, the fire did not spread to them, and they would say about them in the town that they made "borei meorei haeish"[1].

I remember Naftali the tailor, known as a big joker, wandering around on the night that a fire broke out at the home of Sara Eidl, groaning "oy oy." They asked him, "Reb Naftali, why are you groaning? Your house is not burning." He answered, "Oy, what a large brick house will stand there."

These firefighters, with all of their provincialism and lack of means, formed an independent Jewish kernel within the harsh, anti-Semitic Diaspora that pervaded at that time in the midst of enlightened Lithuania.

Translator's Footnotes

This is the benediction of "Who created the light of the fire", which is recited over a lit flame as part of the havdallah ceremony at the end of the Sabbath. The obvious reference here is that these people ignited the fire themselves in order to collect insurance.

[Page 163]

Personalities and Events

[Page 165]

by Menachem Levin

Translated by Jerrold Landau

In Eternal Memory
Of the martyrs of the community of
Jonava
(near Kovno, Lithuania), may G-d avenge their blood.
Who were murdered and destroyed by the Germans
And Lithuanians, may their names be blotted out
In the year 5701, 1941
They day of their memorial[1]
Their holy memory shall never depart from us.
May their souls be bound in the bonds of eternal life.
The natives and survivors of the community of Jonava in Israel and the Diaspora

[Page 166]

There was a Jewish town – Jonava – and it is no more.

Several generations carried the roots of Jewish life in Jonava, a variegated life: a life of toil, a life of physicality and the spirit, a vibrant life.

We, the few survivors who were saved from the infernos of hell, and who merited to join the builders of the homeland, bear in our hearts the memory of all those who fell, and the image of every person.

It is very hard to overcome the thought that our Jonava no longer exists. How can we forget it?

It appears again and again before our eyes: a town that nature blessed with all good, thanks to which its residents lived under better and nicer conditions that those of the Jews of other towns. Many earned their livelihoods from the toil of their hands. It was known throughout Lithuania that the Jews of Jonava were physically strong, and they were nicknamed "Burliakes." This was not wild strength, but rather strength that flowed from Jewish pride.

The Jews of Jonava fell with blood and fire, but their memories live in our hearts. This was the request of the martyrs:

"Remember us always!"

It is certain that there is not one of us who thinks in his heart, "My soul is at peace since I was saved from the valley of murder…"

We have come with awe and respect to establish a monument for them:

In Jerusalem, on Mount Zion – a memorial plaque;

In the Geulim School of Bat Yam – a memorial room;

And in the memorial book –

For eternal memory!

Translator's Footnotes

It seems like the date of the memorial day was omitted from this plaque. On the photograph of the plaque, it seems as if there was a place left blank for the date.

[Page 167]

The Beginning of the Destruction

by Reizl David (Rashkes) of the United States

Translated by Jerrold Landau

As an eyewitness, I will attempt to describe here the beginning of the destruction of Jonava on June 23-24, 1941.

Jonava was one of the army camps of Lithuania. The camp named Poligon was located five kilometers south of the town. When the Russians conquered Lithuania in 1940, they fortified this camp further with tanks and cannons. The Poligon Camp overlooked two large bridges over the Vylia. In Poligon, the Russians demonstrated their greatest opposition to the Germans. I say "Russians" for the Lithuanians immediately turned into collaborators with the Germans.

The opposition lasted for one day and one night.

On Sunday, June 22, toward morning, the roaring of airplanes at a high altitude was heard in Kovno. The airplanes innocently looked like tiny birds, flying calmly at the beginning of a lovely summer morning.

However, suddenly, those innocent birds began to drop bombs on Kovno (at that time, I was living in Kovno). People ran outside to see what was going on, but it became known immediately that these were German airplanes. The war had also reached Lithuania.

We Escaped from Kovno

My brother who lived in Kovno, Ben-Zion Rashkes of blessed memory, immediately arrived with packed suitcases. People ran back and forth without knowing where to flee, what to do, how to save themselves – the confusion was great. We also ran, but we knew to where we were escaping: home to Jonava, in order to be together with Father, Mother and our sister; to be together with our closest, most beloved relatives, whatever may happen.

Hundreds of Jews escaped. Gentiles, of course, did not escape. We fled via the mountain road. The roads were overloaded. Nobody knew how far they would succeed in reaching during their escape. Everyone ran with great fear in their eyes and with large packages on their shoulders and in their hands. However, they were unable to drag all those bundles for a long period; and the roads were filled with abandoned suitcases, with their contents scattered. Gentile farmers stood in the fields at the side of the road and waited for these treasures, as if they fell from the sky, and grabbed them immediately. However, nobody cared about this, because we only thought that if we were to survive, we would also have belongings.

My brother saw a wagon driven by the Manoshovitzes and loaded up all our bags onto it. He also sat on the wagon, and we never saw him again.

The Russian Army was also in a state of confusion. Soldiers went by foot or traveled on tanks or vehicles without knowing where they were going. We saw them driving in opposite directions, with frightened eyes. They did not know how to answer the questions we asked them. The generals fled first and left the soldiers to their own devices.

We traveled for a full day. In the evening, we reached to a point next to the wooden bridge over the Vylia near Jonava. The bridge was already broken and bombed out, for the Germans had bombed there too. My dear father and sister Rachel were already standing there waiting for us on the banks of the river. Gentile farmers would transport people across the river in boats (of course in exchange for payment). Gentile women joined them in the boats in order to collect the belongings that the Jews had abandoned due to being unable to carry them further. On the other side of the Vylia, that is in Jonava, my dear, beloved mother was standing there waiting for us. This image is etched in my heart forever. She was happy through the tears of her eyes. Simultaneously, a great fear was expressed through her beautiful cherry-like eyes: What would be the end of her endangered chicks?

[Page 168]

Jews ran to and fro: "Tell me, Jews, to where are you escaping? Perhaps we will escape along with you!" The response was: "We also do not know. We were in the train station but the train did not arrive. Thousands of refugees were sitting there waiting for the train, including Jews from Poland who came to Lithuania in order to save themselves from the German, may his name and memory be blotted out. Then we ran to Wilkomir Road. The Germans bombed the roads. Many people were killed."

In the Snares

We remained in Jonava. After one night, the cannons began to shoot over our heads. From one side, the Germans were behind Keidiani Street, and from the other side, the Russians from Poligon. We remained in the middle, as if in a trap.

Then, the Lithuanians began to act in a wanton fashion. They gathered in the bell tower of the church and shot with machine guns at the Jews who were running to seek refuge from the cannons. The young fascist Lithuanians also shot from the progymnasium at their Jewish fellow townsfolk, with whom they had lived in harmony until this time. The good neighbors turned into great, deadly enemies within a moment.

We fled from our house the Street of the Road to the parents of my sister's husband, The Goldmans (who owned a furniture factory). They lived on the Street of the Synagogue. Why did we specifically go to them? Perhaps because their house was close to the synagogue courtyard – who knows? We hid in a pit that was quickly dug by the men in the yard of their house. My father and mother did not want to leave their house under any circumstance, for the house was filled with all types of food provisions that they had stockpiled throughout the year, since the time of the Russian regime (for the Russians would send the foodstuffs to Russia). The household economy had been firmly established for many years already, and leaving the house would leave everything ownerless – something that the gentiles were awaiting.

In the morning, as we were lying in the pit, we heard a knock on the opening to the pit. We opened the wooden door, and saw Father standing pale. It was difficult to recognize him. With a trembling voice he asked that we give him a jar of honey. When we peered out from the pit, we saw a German in green fatigues. We had taken from the house jars of honey and jam, and other foodstuffs that we would be able to live on – as Mother said when she gave them to us. She promised to bring the rest the next morning, when she and Father would come to us. They said that during the day, they would not be suspected of leaving the house. These unfortunate people were na?ve: they had faith in human beings – they might come to pillage at night, but during the day, they thought, the gentiles would be embarrassed…

We gave Father a jar of honey and asked him if the house is still whole, and why do Mother and he not join us. Father answered quickly, with a trembling voice, "Mother is making coffee for the Germans," and he quickly disappeared with the German.

Jonava in Flames

In the meantime, the bombardments increased. A shell damaged the synagogue. It seemed to us that it fell next to our pit. We peered out with our heads and saw that a large portion of the synagogue was missing. We could not continue to remain in the pit, for Jonava was already in flames by the afternoon. We already felt the heat of the fire in our pit, and the smoke penetrated inside. When we exited the pit it seemed that the Street of the Road, upon which our house stood, Kovno Street, Breizer Street, and Vilna Street were all burning. We ran to the Vylia River. At that time, the Lithuanians were shooting at us from their hiding places with machine guns. We miraculously reached the shrubs behind the bathhouse. Some gentiles also fled there with us, for the cannons did not discriminate, and they too were in danger. The gentiles were very friendly to us during those moments, but as soon as the bombardment stopped, they no longer knew us. It was already impossible to run back; therefore we dug as deeply as possible into the ground so that the bullets and shells that were literally flying over our heads would not hurt us. During the bombardment, Monas Klibensky the carpenter got up suddenly and said that he thinks that he did not lock his back door, and he started to go. His son- in-law Avraka Unterschatz dragged him back to the ground with his foot. His daughter Feiga began to weep and pleaded, "Father, where are you going? Everything is burning." However Monas apparently foresaw the Holocaust and his nerves weakened. He again got up and said that he thinks that he forgot to close the windows. He felt it necessary to go to find out. Avraka once again dragged him to the ground, covered him with his body, and did not let him get up.

Jonava in flames. (The houses of Granovich and Zopovich in the foreground

[Page 169]

I saw the wife of Avraham the *shochet* lying there with my friend Feigcha, Berele the youngest of the children, and Hirshka. I did not see the daughters Rachel and Rivka, nor Avraham the *shochet*.

I lay down and wept, for nobody saw Father and Mother anywhere. Anyone we asked was not able to say anything, and I suspected that they all knew something but did not want to tell us. Father and Mother had remained with the Germans. Only G-d knows what they endured on that dark night. What did the Germans do to them? How can I live without Mother and without Father, heaven forbid? How is it possible?

The sight of Jonava that night was terrifying: a frightening sky, very red, and all of Jonava engulfed in flames like hell.

The shells flew over our head with greater strength. We were already able to tell if a shell was falling closer to or farther from where we were. Every time that a cannon was shot and its scream was heard above us, a gentile would be able to determine where the bullet was. (The bullets fell far away, whereas the shells rained upon us.) He would say, "A shell has fallen at a distance of ten feet, now a shell has fallen at a distance of five feet." He was right, apparently, for we did no hear him speak anymore. The cannons quieted somewhat, and at sunrise they were almost completely silent. Then, when we began to arise and get up, we saw dead bodies lying near us. We did not realize that we had been lying beside dead bodies all night.

We looked up to see whether Jonava was still burning, and we saw thick smoke bursting forth to the sky. We ran back to the house of the parents of the husband of my sister Rachel. The house was still whole, almost the only one in the entire alley. The Jewish hospital opposite the Goldman's house was burnt. The ill people were lying burnt in the iron beds.

Running About

We did not yet know what had happened to our parents. It was dangerous for women to leave the house. I sat and prayed to G-d, and the door at the side of the house opened. They entered quickly, short of breath, sweaty and panting – first Father and then Mother. The joy was great. We hugged, kissed, and all wept from joy. Once again, we were all united with an eternal connection. Mother was wearing only a dress, and Father a cloak and pants. They could not salvage any more of their property. Father told us what had happened to them. When they were left alone in the large house, they were unable to sleep at night. Father went out to the yard and dug a deep pit as a refuge from the shells. Father said that the shells were flying very low between the houses. Not a living soul was seen on our street (the Street of the Road). The appearance was terrifying, like a city of ghosts. Only shadows were seen here and there sneaking into the abandoned houses and pillaging, even in the midst of the bombardment. Therefore, Father and Mother were very afraid to remain in the house, lest the pillaging gentiles kill them. They then decided to escape to us, to the Goldmans. However, before they had time to pack various valuables, they heard knocking on the door. It was still dark. Father approached the door with trembling steps and asked who was knocking. They answered in German, "Open the door, Jew!" With great fear, father opened the door. A group of 30 German soldiers broke into the house. Apparently, these were the first soldiers -- scouts. The commander ordered Father to go through all the rooms with them, then to the cellar and the storehouses in the courtyard, and even the pit that Father had dug in the yard – all this in order to check that no Russians were hiding there. Then the commander ordered to bring water. Father brought them pails of water from the well that was in the cellar. They all washed up. As per their order, Mother brought them towels and underwear so that they can change. Then they ordered Mother to make them coffee and give them something to eat. The Germans drank from the cups from the fine dishware set that belonged to my sister. Then they put the dishes into their backpacks along with many other valuables, such as the silver candlesticks, the silver cups, silver boxes, and other such items. Then one of the Germans asked Father if he had any honey, for he loved honey. Since Father was naive and innocent, he told the German that his daughter had taken the honey with her. That is why they came to us to get the honey. All of this took place under the rain of shells, as Jonava was already burning and almost the entire Street of the Road was in flames. The Germans did not permit my parents to escape from the fire and bullets until our house was bombed and began to burn. In the meantime, they saw other Jews, who before had apparently been hiding in the cellars. They also ran. Among them were Gitel Klotz and Zusman Klotz, our maternal cousins. Suddenly shots were fired from some place behind the fleeing Germans. The Germans captured Father, Zusman Klotz and other men whose names I do not know, and stood them against a burning wall in order to shoot them, out of suspicion that they had been shooting at the Germans. They would have been killed within another second, but suddenly two Lithuanians with guns in their hands burst forth from behind the burning wall. They were searching for a refuge from the fire. The Germans caught them and shot them, and freed the Jewish men. The Jewish men continued to escape toward us, but they could not run through the Street of the Synagogue because everything around was burning. Burning houses became shaky, and the streets were filled with ruins and fire. All of Jonava was one large ruin. They ran to a place where it was still somewhat possible to save oneself from the hell, and they came to the brick kiln. They lay down all night. In the morning, when the shelling ended, they ran to us.

[Page 170]
Dangers Lurk

Father stood on his feet and said, "We do not have time now to speak a great deal. Let us go out to see what the situation is." He told my sister Rachel and I to not dare to go outside. We accompanied him to the rabbi of the town, Rabbi Ginzburg, who was apparently leaving some hiding place. We surrounded him with questions, "Rabbi, what will be?" His fine face was pale, and his appearance had changed greatly. He spoke in choppy words, with tears choking his throat: "We have to be careful with security. G-d will help. Jews, we must be strong." He himself was wailing like a baby. Everyone was weeping. We returned home in order to hide from the dangers that began to stalk us.

After a few hours, Father returned with a darkened face. He told us, "An entire group of Jews was burned in Liber Farber's basement." Father was the first one to open the iron door of the cellar – burnt skeletons were resting on the door. The first skeleton was the largest, and they realized that it was of Meir Wunder. The door of the cellar locked itself on them, and they were unable to exit and save themselves from the fire.

"Our house," Father said, "and the streets in general are unrecognizable, for the destruction was great and went to the foundations. Here and there, smoke was coming out of the ruins." Father recognized the lot in which our house had stood from the pit that he had dug. Father noted, "A smart cat hides in a pit, but I locked our cat in the house. Perhaps it too was hiding in the pit…"

In the meantime, the Jews began to search for food, for a morsel of bread. Hunger pervaded the city. One Jewish bakery that by chance remained intact at the end of Kovno Street was taken over by gentiles who chased out the former owners and baked bread for he gentiles. Jews stood and stuck out their hands for a morsel of bread, and the gentiles chased them away, saying, "Go ask the Communists. They will give you bread." My sister risked her life and left the hiding place. A gentile acquaintance gave her a piece of bread and told her, "Hide and do not go outside. They are plotting to rape the young women of Jonava." The Jews of Jonava began to feel that danger was waiting for them not only from the Germans, but also from their Lithuanian neighbors.

There used to be a pharmacy in our house in which a gentile woman had worked as a cashier. We were good friends. Father came running to me with fear in his eyes and told me that this woman was looking for me, and of course, she was not planning to do anything good to me. She had become an important leader and immediately began to threaten the Jews of Jonava. With his clear sense, Father suspected that a great danger was awaiting me, his youngest daughter: The gentiles were wandering around looking for Jewish girls to rape. When I later was in the Kovno Ghetto, a group of Jonava woman arrived.

[Page 171]

One of them was Chanka Rabinovich who told me that the *shkotzim* forcefully put young Jewish girls into a barn and tortured hem to death.

Return to Kovno

Father immediately decided that I was to return to Kovno. "There, the gentiles do not know you," he said with a trembling voice. He was about to part from his beloved daughter for who knows how long, perhaps forever. Mother was overtaken by convulsions, and Father began to plead with Mother to calm down. "This is the only way," he claimed. As has been said, we, that is my husband and I (I got married only a few months before to Wolf David from Kretingen near Memel), parted also from my sister Rachel, from my brother-in-law Yitzchak Goldman, and from the entire Goldman family, none of whom survived. The Goldmans had five sons and a daughter Batya. The sons were Yitzchak the eldest, Mordechai, Zerach, and two twins whose names I do not recall.

Father said that we must escape back to Kovno via the old path, for he realized that a large army would be passing through the main road, and that we would be safer on the old road that begins on the descent of Kovno Road, for it is an inferior road. That is indeed the way it was, as my wise father had known. Many refugees returned to Kovno. The refugees were from all over Lithuania and also from Poland, who had come to Lithuania a year earlier when the Germans entered Poland. They wanted to reach some safe place, perhaps to Russia, but they had remained in Jonava. We, a full camp, went back to Jonava. All of the family and many other Jonavers accompanied us to the brick kiln. Father pleaded to everyone to refrain from making this public farewell procession, for this might end badly, heaven forbid. Nevertheless, everyone wanted to give us a farewell blessing. Taibl, Rachka Jalinowitz' mother, hugged me, kissed me, and wished me good fortune. I asked her, "Where is Rachka?" and she answered: "Hiding."

This was the last time that I saw my family and that I set foot on the ground of Jonava, my dear birthplace with its dear, heartwarming Jews, may their memory be a blessing, may G-d avenge their blood.

The Last Day

by Yerachmiel Garber of Neve Sharet

Translated by Jerrold Landau

Yerachmiel Garber

In the morning of Monday, June 23, I went as usual to my workplace in the Oren match factory. The war had begun, but the work had to take place no matter what. In any case – where was Jonava and where was the front? We were given spades and told to dig protective ditches. Some of the diggers were immersed in thoughts, some tried to joke that there was no need for ditches. The jokers trusted that the Soviets would not let Hitler reach Jonava.

Suddenly, the noise of autos reached our ears. We put down the spades and ran to the road to snatch a glance. We saw the Red Army trucks covered in green branches, such as *Sukkot* covered with *Sechach*[1]. The faces of the soldiers were black with dust. We only saw white teeth and glittering eyes. We suddenly heard the sound of thunder, but the skies were clear without any clouds at all. It seems that this was the echo of an artillery battle. Everyone's face became serious. People were immersed in thought.

[Page 172]

I did not return to the spade. I hastened to town to see what was going on. It was the same town, but unrecognizable. We felt hasty movement. Everyone's face was serious and perplexed, as if they were seeking a refuge from a crazy situation. Hundreds of people were running on the ascent of the road. Others turned toward the wooden fence. Refugees from Kovno turned in that direction. I turned toward the bridge with large steps. It seemed as if Jews were gathering here for Tashlich[2], however we heard no prayers, but rather conversations between Jonavers and Kovnoites who were astounded at the situation. I could not understand, what was with them? Did they take leave of their senses – to run by foot from Kovno?

Among those who were coming, I met a lad who was an acquaintance, Shliten. I had studied together with him in ORT[3]. We turned aside, and I asked,

"Oh, what is taking place here?"

"Don't ask questions," he responded, "lift up your feet and get out of here as fast as you can. The Germans are already in Kovno."

I was still rolling my eyes, but the seriousness of the situation penetrated my consciousness. I returned home. I met friends along the way, and we decided to leave Jonava for a brief time and to go to Wilkomir, with the belief that the Germans would quickly receive a deathly blow from the Soviet Army…

I ran to my friend Hershe-Yankel Stein. I heard shrieks and screams next to the house, as if during a funeral. Taibl Katzav was taking leave of her son, who was about to leave on his bicycle. This was strange in my eyes: is this how one weeps for a living person? He told me that he and his friends were setting out on their bicycle, and that they would wait for me. I ran home quickly. I met Uncle David, who had moved in with us with his family until the storm would pass. I told my parents about my plan, and they accepted it with understanding. They gave me several rubles, and I went out of the house without even taking leave. We did not grasp the seriousness of the situation, that we would never see each other again.

As we passed by the post office, we ran into young Lithuanians who were looking at us with a bitter smile and gnashing their teeth. We were on the ascent to the mountain. The entire way was strewn with people and wagons. The wagon drivers loaded their belongings and families, and fled for their lives. We passed under the railway crossing. Suddenly, airplanes appeared low above our heads. They shot at us and dropped bombs. We were lying in the ditches at the side of the road. We were not injured. We continued to move. Bad thoughts went through the head. It seemed that we were separating ourselves from Jonava. The journey was not easy, even though we were young and healthy. The repeated running back and forth to search for a hiding place in the ditches drained our strength. The enemy did not stop sending his airplanes at us, shooting at the refugees. Along the way, we lost some people and met up with others until we reached Wilkomir.

It was night. It was dark. The Germans shot shiny bullets that looked like stars from the airplanes. In Wilkomir, I met Mosheke Goldschmid of Jonava immersed in worries: There was a puncture in his tire. I helped him with the repair, and we prepared for the journey. It was only possible to move at night. The question was, in what direction. Some advised to go to Vilna, the capital of Lithuania. It would not be easily captured by the Germans. There, they would break their teeth. Others felt that we should go toward Zarasai (Ezrani) at the Latvian border. I supported this, and the group agreed.

We travelled all night. At dawn, the airplanes appeared again, and everything repeated from the day before. At times, we ran to the ditches. The breaks between the air attacks continued to shorten. We turned away from the road, went up to the side road, and lay in the grass to rest. An army truck stopped next to us. We wanted to have a conversation with them, but they did not know Russian. One person succeeded in asking what was happening in Jonava. The response was: In Jonava – the Germans.

This oppressed us, and we did not ask further.

Translator's Footnotes

A *Sukka* (plural *Sukkot*) is the tabernacle of the holiday of *Sukkot*, and *Sechach* is the foliage covering of the *Sukka*.

A ceremony that takes place near a river or body of water on Rosh Hashanah.

Organization of Rehabilitation through Training, that ran (and continues to run) various trade schools within some Jewish communities.

[Page 173]

Days of Torment

by Nachum Blumberg of Tel Aviv

Translated by Jerrold Landau

Nachum Blumberg

On Sunday, June 22, when the German attack on the Soviet Union began, the road from Kovno to Jonava was full of army caravans and civilians already from the morning. Among them were thousands of people who were hurrying eastward to Wilkomir. The town bustled like a beehive. The opinion of most of the middle class was that there was nothing to escape from. We should note in agony that the thought was prevalent among them that things would not be worse under the Germans than under the Bolsheviks; that they should not escape to unknown directions, where it was uncertain that they would even reach anywhere. Many ran to the nearby villages in order to hide with farmers that they knew until the wrath would subside.

Haphazard Escape

Among those who escaped were the Soviet Aktiva, the Comsomol Youth, all those who served in civic and district offices, the directors of the nationalized factories, the carpentry shops and commercial enterprises, and police officials. Similarly, the wagon drivers and cargo transporters escaped.

The entire day, the town was shuddering from a cruel murder: the shoemaker Victor Botzinski, who lived on the street next to Vichna Dobianski, burst into the town and murdered the vice mayor, the teacher Rosenberg, who had been appointed to that office by the Soviets.

My wife and I decided to flee in the direction of Russia, in accordance with what we had heard from the Mir Yeshiva students, refugees from Poland who settled in the town. From three Yeshiva students who used to eat at our table, we heard about the atrocities that the Germans perpetrated against the Jewish population. I had a good horse. I prepared a carriage and was prepared for the journey. I hid all of my gold and documents in the pillow of the harness (" *Chamet*"). I hitched the horse, loaded some moveable property, and left the yard. At that moment, my brother-in-law Mendel Dobianski approached me and asked, "Where are you going?" I answered that I was setting out in the direction of Russia. He begged that I do not leave the family. My wife advised me to return, to hitch the horse to the wagon, and take us to the rest of the family. That is what I did. We loaded the wagon and the entire Dobianski family – the brothers with their wives and children, the brother-in-law and sister-in-law, and set out along the way.

We reached Mount Lekai, about 12 kilometers from town. There we found out from a Lithuanian acquaintance, Lukshovich, that the Germans were already in Wilkomir. He recommended that we come to him. We hid there for three or four days. When we found out that the Germans were already in Jonava, we decided to return. We sent Shmuel Dobianski as a scout to find out whether our house had been burnt. He returned and told us that our house was still standing.

[Page 174]

We ran into German soldiers along the way. When the saw my fine horse, they ordered me to unhitch it. In return, they gave me a significantly inferior horse. I took down the main thing, the harness, and then hitched up and we left. When we reached home, we found out the following:

On Monday and Tuesday, June 23 and 24, the Germans engaged in battle in the town against the soldiers of the Russian unit in Poligon. Jonava went up in flames on Tuesday and Wednesday. Liber Farber had a large cellar, where approximately 80 Jews were hiding due to the bombardment. An electricity post that had gone up in flames fell upon the door of the cellar and sealed off the exit. None of them survived. The dead included Yankel Pozitzer, Meir Wunder, Liber Farber, Shmerl Stern and their families. The Germans had already pillaged the town by Thursday. The S.S. troops issued an order that everyone was to gather in the market square. The Shaulists and Lithuanian elements from the riffraff assisted the Germans in gathering up the Jews. The agronomist Grigaliunas from Mount Lekai, Simuk Dolgatz, two sons of the builder Wansovich, Pinkovski, Mangines Vytautas, and others were prominent among them.

The entire remaining Jewish population gathered in the marketplace. A command was issue to kneel down. Among those gathered were Rabbi Nachum Baruch Ginzburg, Kagan the pharmacy owner, Leibe Opnitzky and his sons, the Shapira family with their mighty children. Machine guns were placed around, and everyone was sure that they would shoot with them. The weeping and screaming of the children, women and men was indescribable. At that moment, as a miracle from heaven, an attack of cannon shells hit the movie theater building. The Germans and Lithuanians fled from fear, and after them – the entire Jewish population. The Jews housed themselves in houses that had survived the fire: On Vilna and Kovno Streets from the market place until Keidiani Street, the Lane of the Rabbi, Breizer Street from the synagogue until the synagogue of the miners, on Keidiani Street, and in houses on the new horse market.

On Thursday night, a shell hit the house of L. Opnitzky. They were saved, but the house went up in flames. On Friday morning, I went out to the street to search for Jews. A frightening scene unfolded before my eyes. Motel Fleischman was running with his remaining strength, with Shemeinka the daughter of Machulis and a German behind him. He had told the German that the war was just beginning and that the Russians would return again. He escaped to the house of the teacher Shaul Keidansky on Keidiani Street. They were following him. She was shouting that they were all Communists. The German ordered them to get up and commanded Meinka to bring spades. Motel Fleischman, Shaul Keidansky and his two children were brought to the cemetery, with the gentiles looking on…

There, they were ordered to dig a pit. Then, the German stood three of them next to the pit and shot them. They fell forward. Shaul Keidansky was ordered to cover them. Then, they shot him as well.

Reima the Contact Man

I returned home broken and crushed, and decided that I could not remain there.

I had opportunity to get in contact with Reima the Lithuanian, who worked with Sliagris, the aide of President Smetana. He lived behind Mount Lekai and was considered to be my good friend. He came. I asked him to go to the cemetery to find out what was the fate of those who were shot. He verified that the gentiles had removed them from the pit and stripped them. I went with Nota Valchokovsky, accompanied by Reima, who was wearing a Shaulist[1] uniform, as if he was transporting us to work. We arrived there and buried the desecrated dead bodies. The decision that we must escape was further strengthened in me. My brother-in-law and sister-in-law, the Dobianski family, opposed this.

Our situation worsened on Sunday, one day after the outbreak of the war. Valdiva, Valshchiaus' secretary, came to us and ordered us to vacate the house without removing any object. I asked him where we should go, and he directed me to the railway station. Since he knew me from before, my pleas apparently had an effect on him, and he permitted us to go… to one of our former warehouses.

[Page 175]

The situation became even more serious on Monday. The Lithuanians decided to pillage, rob and chase out the Jews from their places. There was also a lack of food provisions. Anything that remained from the fire was pillaged. About 40 people were with us in the warehouse, including L. Opnitzky with his children and grandchildren, Alter Jochovsky, Nota Valchokovsky, Yeshayahu Shugas, Rabbi Ginzburg, the pharmacy owner Kagan and others. Since we grew potatoes in our garden, we would take them out, cook them, and eat them.

Reima, our contact person, would bring us news of the situation in the city. He told us that approximately 50 people were brought in and locked in the Hershel Opnitzky's cellar. The new market was not far from us. They were brought to the Girialka Grove, under the guard of the Shaulists, and given spades. They dug ditches there. Rumors spread that they were preparing the ditches for fuel tanks. According to Reima, they dug ditches 20 meters long, 3 meters wide, and 2.5 meters deep. They were dug in the same of ê, and Reima convinced us that they were not designated for fuel, but rather for Jews.

After a few days, Vansovich's two sons and Kretzmer came with guns. They ordered me to hitch up the horse, and brought me to the homes of the Jews in order to gather up anything that had been pillaged from them. They employed me at that task for three days. The property was piled up in the town hall in the new market. They did not take my belongings. Apparently, they left them for secretary Wilks of the district council who moved into our house. Kazlauskas, the town secretary, who lived near us and was apparently our good friend, calmed me, saying that there was nothing to worry about. He himself had given over a detailed list of the Jews to the murderer Grigaliunas, with notes indicating who was a Communist or a supporter. His hands were also not clean. He lives peacefully in his home in Jonava.

Once, Reima came to me and advised me to speak to the murderer Grigaliunas about giving me work in building his new house at his farm. I went to him and offered to work for free. He agreed and gave me a directive that I, my father-in-law and brother- in-law should go to work every morning in Lekai and return in the evening. We also took my brother Chaim to work.

Reima explained to me that in the work, Gineika, Pinkovski and others brought groups of Jews, men and women, to remove the bricks from the burnt houses. The murderers chose young, pretty girls, took them to ruins, and raped them. They also murdered a few of them. This left an oppressive impression upon us. Thus did we continue to work for four days.

Hiding Place in the Cave

I could not fall asleep due to the emotions. I got up in the morning, hitched the horse, and advised my family to escape, for my heart does not foretell good things. They all got dressed and travelled to work in Lekai. Reima came to me and said that at 7:00, the Shaulists came to our yard and took all the men that were in the storehouse. That morning, about two weeks after the fire, about 1,200 men and young women were gathered together and concentrated in the Lipniak barracks. My older brother Moshe was among them. I found out that on that same day, Moshe went to my wife Chaya in the storehouse and asked for better clothes, since the Lithuanians were saying that they would be sending us to work in Lublin.

I came to Jonava at night with suspicions, and I brought Reima with me. My goal was to meet with Moshe, for perhaps I might be able to extricate him from the barracks. My wife Chaya told me that she had told Moshe that we were with Reima in Lekai, and she advised him to join us. He did not agree. He was certain that they would send them to work, and even suspected that my wife was being stingy with the clothing. "Do as you wish," she answered him, and he disappeared…

It was impossible to meet Moshe next to the bunkers, for the place was under strict guard. The Shaulist guards shot in the air in order to frighten the prisoners.

I returned Lekai later in the night. We all decided to flee. Reima advised us to dig a cave in the mountain and next to the river. We dug there all night. We camouflaged the door well with shrubs. The advice to dig the cave was with the knowledge of the wife of Sliagris (the deputy of President Smetana) who proved herself to be a good person and a friend of the Jews.

Early in the morning, when work finished, she appeared with Reima and brought two full baskets of food provisions. She said that we did well to flee, for our lives were in danger. Similarly, she said that she had come from Kovno, where she had told her husband about the number of Jews under her protection and asked him what to do. He told her to assist them to the best of her ability, since he had been saved by the Jews from a Russian transport to Siberia.

[Page 176]

The Bitter End of the Prisoners in the Bunkers

This is what happened with my brother Yerachmiel, who lived on the other side of the Vylia. When the Jews were already placed into bunkers for the most part, Mangin Vytautas, the wagon driver Simanis, and Gineika came to his home. He was not home, and Gineika raped his wife. Yerachmiel entered at that moment, and when he saw what was happening, he grabbed a footstool, banged it directly on Gineika's head, and quickly escaped out the window. He hid among the bushes, and when he saw that the murderers were at his heels, he hanged himself on a tree.

The Jews were imprisoned in the bunkers for four days. In the meantime, others were added, and the pits in Girialka were prepared. A notice was posted through the bunkers that everyone should take with them good clothes and money, for they were being sent to work in Lublin. The intention was that they should tell those remaining in the houses to bring everything.

Reima told me that they brought groups of 200 people from the bunkers to Girialka. Motel Chasia's Levitz was in the first group. He was sick, and he was carried by Shmerl and Binka Shapira. They made them run, as they were well guarded by the Shaulists. Abba Solsky, Leibl Stern and Leizer Goldshmid were also in that group. The women were not taken yet, but some of them burst through to go together with their husbands: Chana Sesitzki, the wife of the lawyer Leibel Stern; and the teacher Opteikina, the wife of Leizer Goldshmid. The Shaulists attempted to chase them away with whips, but this did not help. They stuck to their husbands and went along with them.

When they came within 100 meters of the pits, they were ordered to strip, under the pretext that they would be given Russian clothes. They were given a command to walk in the direction of the narrow railway track. When they approached the pits, they were fired upon from all sides. The panic was indescribable. They fell into the pits while still alive and wounded. Berka Fein, Berman and my brother Moshe succeeded in escaping, and ran to the road. They were caught and shot. Gentiles from Skaroli, the children of Vansovich, Kretzmer, Mangin, and Jaska Mazolis were prominent among the murderers. They were headed by Simuk Dolgatz and Mangin. Spirits were distributed to the shooters to strengthen their "morale," and they were promised that all of the belongings of the Jews would be theirs. Farmers from Bzlisik, Godzion and Lokgal were called to cover the pits. The earth moved from the bodies that were buried while still alive.

Four groups were brought in this manner, and each time, the same scene of terror repeated itself. It is known that Hirshke Friedman and Shmerl Shapira displayed strong resistance. They were stabbed by knives. Before they were brought there, all of them were commanded to write to their families to send money with the bearers of the letter. Hostages were kept in the barracks on account of the women and children who were still in the town: Rabbi Nachum Baruch Ginzburg, the pharmacist Kagan, and Nota Valchokovsky.

The Fate of the Women and Children

After the women sent belongings and money with the letter bearers, they were calmed with the knowledge that the men were working in the peat mines at Pagloz (Pagele?iai). My sister-in-law, Moshe's wife, was so certain that I did not succeed in convincing her through messengers that she should come over to us in the cave at Mount Lekai.

In the interim, the women were taken to work. They received a half kilogram of bread each day. I knew what awaited them, for Reima told me that the same fate awaits them as well. He had heard this from the Shaulist command. Therefore, I wrote to all the women in the family – including my wife, my mother-in-law, my sister-in-law and their children – that they should sneak to us at night.

We men, aside from my brother Moshe and brother-in-law Yerachmiel, had already been in hiding for several days. I sent Reima in the evening with a wagon to fetch them. They told him that they were not in danger, that they were working and receiving bread, and that my imagination was envisaging darkness. The only one to come to me was my wife Chaya with the six year old daughter of Mendel Dobianski. She came only because Pinkovski the fireman had taken interest in her and attempted to rape her. The next day, Feinia, Chaim Blumberg's wife, came to us and pleaded for Chaya to return, for the committee responsible for all those on the list of women and children were liable to the death penalty. I did not permit her to go, come what may. I advised Feinia to return and bring the families and the children.

[Page 177]

The next morning, I sent Reima to find out what had happened. He told me that all the women and children had already been brought into the bunkers. A band of Shaulists ordered some hostages to travel to the Kovno Ghetto under guard in order to bring ransom money. They brought the money and were led to think that this would redeem them from tribulation.

Reima, in his Shaulist uniform, approached the bunkers. Then Hinda Dobianski (Perlstein) gave him a note written by the women from the Dobianski and Blumberg families requesting us to come to join them, and together bear the fate that was awaiting them. They were unable to escape, for the guard was intense. When this news arrived, Mendel, Yerachmiel and Shmuel Dobianski, and Chaim Blumberg got up and said: we must go.

I took up the axe and stated that if anyone dared to move, I will crush his skull.

When I saw that I could not convince them to remain, I grabbed the axe and stated that if anyone dared to move, I would crush his skull. We had to remain and take revenge when the time came. The mood was beyond description. The men could not forgive themselves for failing to convince the women to join them. Yerachmiel wanted to commit suicide. I only prevented this with difficulty. Reima informed us that he was on the list of Shaulists who were enlisted to be at the bunkers the next day. Indeed, the next day, they brought the women and children in groups along the same tribulation filled journey to the grove.

Reima was present. He told us that the atrocities that took place cannot be described in words. They separated the women and children. A terrible wailing broke out. Mothers and children cleaved to each other. When they were separated, the children attempted to return to their mothers, and they were shot before their eyes while running. Children were tossed into the pits alive. We heard the screams of the women from Lekai, five kilometers away, for the wind was blowing in our direction. The Pole Kasparowicz, who lived close to the grove and saw with his own eyes what had taken place, took leave of his senses the next day.

The turn of the women came. They were ordered to strip and stand next to the pits. They were shot in their backs and fell into the pits. Finally, the hostages were also brought –Rabbi Ginzburg, Kagan the pharmacist, and Nota Valchokovsky.

The clothing that was collected was distributed at the gathering place with the murderers having first rights. They also received large portions of spirits to take home. During the gathering, when they were drunk, fights broke out among themselves regarding the pillaged belongings. They also broke into chauvinistic songs for their victory over the women and children.

[Page 178]

The Murderers Pillage and Rampage

During the first day, men, women and children fled to old Gostynits, behind the town of Seisikai. They were later returned to Jonava. Many of those who had escaped to Kovno had not reached safe places. German soldiers from the Wehrmacht, whose behavior incidentally was not bad, ordered them to return. Lithuanian partisans stood next to the wooden bridge that leads to the road to Kovno, and directed them all to the town. There, they were pillaged and shot in groups in the horse market.

A group of rabbis and G-d fearing Jews were gathered in Nachum Levin's carpentry shop. Mangin guarded them. He promised Nachum that they would survive if they would turn over their money and property. They did as commanded, but they were shot.

After the murders, Jonava was declared Judenrein. Grigaliunas confirmed this in an official letter to the German occupiers. Mina, the daughter of the butcher Shlomo (the Muscovite), hid with a Russian in the village of Rimkes. When she learned that her husband had been shot, she went crazy. She and her children wandered around the ruins of the town for several days. One day, they were shot.

Grigaliunas arranged a large party for all the Shaulists and murderers. When he was tipsy with wine, he said among other things that he himself had destroyed a Russian brigade that had passed through his place of residence on Mount Lekai, he had killed the Jews of the town, and that he had a similar fate in store for the Germans. Simuk Dolgatz heard this, and, being a Gestapo man, informed the S.S. command. Grigaliunas was arrested that night. Weapons were found during a search of his farm. Reima told us that he was to be sentenced to death in a field court.

I Took an Axe and Left

The next night, Sliagris' wife ran to us and informed us that our lives were in danger, and that we must escape. She explained that since a death sentence was awaiting Grigaliunas, his wife had requested that Reima save him. He had to give testimony that the weapons belonged to a group of Jews hiding on Mount Lekai. She had heard this by chance when Reima returned drunk to his wife, who was working with her in the kitchen, and told her about this in secrecy. The next day, he was responsible for taking them out of the cave to a specific spruce tree, where the Germans would discover them.

Reima came in the morning and said that the entire area was surrounded by Germans searching for Jews. He told us to come with him to a specific place, from where he would later transfer us to a secure location. He brought us there and disappeared. I said that we should take some belongings with us, as well as axes, and run quickly to the Matzkovitz Forests that border the farm. We wandered in the bogs of the forest for eight hours, and arrived at the hill in the evening. We camouflaged ourselves with branches and lay down to rest. We spent a night and day there. We heard movement on the second day. Branches were breaking. Suddenly, we heard a voice in Lithuanian, "Oh, Jesus, where are they?"

When I heard the voice from up close, I recognized Reima's voice. I took an axe, came out of my hiding place, and shouted, "Reima!"

"Panes Blumbergas," he said. He was happy to see me, and asked why we fled? He had two baskets with food in our hands. I called out to all of them and informed them that if any suspicion would be aroused, we would have to do away with him. I warned him to refrain from approaching, and asked for an explanation why had had moved us from the cave to the tree. He kneeled down on his knees, crossed himself, and told us everything just as Sliagris' wife had told us. He told us that Grigaliunas' wife had hired him and ordered him to behave thus. He did not intend to harm us. The Germans had combed the entire Mount Lekai, including the cave, and had found nothing. They had even freed Grigaliunas, for it was proven that there were indeed Jews there. After he was freed, Grigaliunas' wife came to him and said that the hand of god was involved in this, for her husband had been freed on account of the Jews, so she must find us and thank us. She was the one who had sent us the best food products that she had in her possession.

[Page 179]

From the Pigpen to the Forests

"What do you advise now?" I asked.

"You must return to the cave," he replied.

"I do not agree to go there. I prefer being with you in the pigpen." My opinion was that if he was indeed our good friend, he must take responsibility. Since his pen was too small for us (me, Chaim Blumberg, my brother, Chaim Dobianski and his sons Shmuel, Yerachmiel, Mendel, my wife Chaya (Dobianski), and Mendel's daughter Etela) he promised to speak with Sliagris' wife to see if we can go to her large pigpen, where we would be more secure. She agreed the next day, and we returned from the forest, a distance of 25 kilometers, and spent the evening in the pen. We arranged ourselves there and felt that we were in a secure place under the protection of Sliagris, who was a commander in Kovno. W remained there for about two weeks. Sliagris' wife and Reima provided us with provisions.

In the evening, Mrs. Sliagris came to us and told us that it is being said that America warned Germany that if there were any more acts of murder against the Jews, they would gather all the Germans in America into ghettos and treat them as they are treating the Jews. This somewhat calmed our tense nerves. Early the next morning, my brother Chaim left the pen to go to the field to breathe some fresh air. A shepherd noticed him. While he was still in

When the shepherd saw Chaim with his full beard, he began to run and scream…

[Page 180]

in the cave, Reima had warned the shepherd to not take the flock far from the fields, for Jews who had gone crazy were wandering about. (His intention was that they should not circulate in the vicinity of our cave.) When the shepherd saw Chaim with his grown, unkempt beard, he began to run and shout, "Jesus!" Chaim wanted to catch him and calm him. He became even more flustered, and fled to the house of farmers. When Chaim returned, he told us this. We had realized that our situation had deteriorated. I told this to Mrs. Sliagris, who called Reima and told him to transfer us to another hiding place.

We again moved to the Matzkovitz Forests and waited for additional instructions.

We Returned to the Bunkers in Jonava

That same day, partisans came to Sliagris' wife and informed her that they have information about Jews in the area, and that she knows about them. They took Reima with them to assist in the searches in Mount Lekai. They went and shot gunshots for fear of surprises. Of course, they did not find anyone. When they returned, they told Reima and Mrs. Sliagris that the Jews will no longer be murdered, but will rather be sent to the Kovno Ghetto, and that approximately 190 Jews – women and children, Jonavers and others – are still concentrated in the bunkers. When we were informed of this, and that Captain Kolkovski had been appointed as the mayor, and that he did not permit the killings, but rather authorized the transfer to the Kovno Ghetto, our spirits improved somewhat.

We decided that Shmuel Dobianski will go to Jonava at night in the company of Reima and meet Kolkovski in his house. Kolkovski had been his customer, and they were friendly. When they arrived there, Reima hid, for he was afraid of being exposed as a helper of the Jews. Shmuel was wearing a Shaulist uniform. He knocked on the door and entered, but realized that there were guests there, so he remained standing near the door. When Kolkovski's wife approached, she recognized him, and apparently became confused and began to babble. In the meantime the captain arrived, recognized him, greeted him with "Labas"[2] and brought him into a private room. Shmuel explained to him that he and a group of his family members had been taken to work in the area of Seisikai. There, they found out about the mass killings, and he had come to listen to his advice. His response was that he did well by coming. In the next day or two, a large group of Jews who had been gathered from the area were to be sent to the Kovno Ghetto. There is nothing to worry about. He would ensure that nothing bad would happen to us.

The next evening, we all decided to return to Jonava. Reima accompanied us to the road in a wagon, and we set out on a tortuous path through the fields. We reached the bunkers. The guards did not permit us to enter. They first had to ask Simuk Dolgatz, the local S.S. representative. Reima went to inform Kolkovski of our arrival. The latter telephoned Dolgatz and requested that he allow us in. At first Dolgatz refused and wanted to interrogate us. However Kolkovski calmed him, assuring him that we were not Communists. After this, the gates opened, and we entered the yard of the bunkers.

To the Kovno Ghetto

There, we met Nachumke Zisla and my brother Moshe's wife Zelda, who was in Lukinel until that time. The wives of Binka Shapira and Manka Mines, who had hidden in the Pereboznik brick kiln, were also there. Our joy was indescribable. Most of those present were from different places. The next day, October 4, 1941, wagons were gathered. We were all placed upon them, and we set out in the company of a policeman who knew us, "Labas." We travelled slowly, and stopped on occasion to drink water and purchase something to eat. I must emphasize the good conduct of the policeman Labas. We arrived at the gate of the ghetto in Kovno late at night. This was to our good fortune. That day, there was an aktion in the small ghetto. Had we arrived earlier, we would have been brought to Fort Nine to be killed.

Since dwellings in the ghetto had become available, they took us, the members of the Blumberg and Dobianski families, to a house on Linkava 15, next to the police station. The following Jonavers were policemen there: the three Zopovich brothers, Meir, Moshe, and Yudel, who was the chief of the station. Alter Klotz was also among the policemen. It was indeed a miracle that we were still alive. The following people perished in Jonava: the wife of Chaim Dobianski, that is my mother-in-law; as well as the wife and children of Mendel, Yerachmiel, and Shmuel Dobianski, and of my brother Chaim. From among the women, my wife Chaya (Dobianski), as well as Dobianski's daughter Etela were still alive; and from among the men – all the aforementioned.

These were our victims to this point along our journey of tribulations until the Kovno Ghetto.

Translator's Footnotes

A nationalist Lithuanian rifleman association, whose members collaborated with the Nazis.
"Hello" in Lithuanian.

[Page 181]

My Town

by Dov Blumberg (Capetown)

Translated by Daniella Thompson

My heart goes out to the victims of Yanova, my little town
Man and woman, five hundred families,
Were wiped out in the spring of their life.
Some suffocated in the house cellars
And the rest expelled to the forests at the edge of town.
The murderers opened their mouths wide, and with mocking contempt
Shot bullets into the bodies of my brothers and sisters,
Who were buried in trenches that they themselves had dug.
The earth's supplication, the stifled cries of children's camps
Pierce the empty air
They were removed from their homes, where they were rooted
Generations upon generations, where their fathers' forefathers
Lived, yearned, and hoped for a day to come.
And here came the day, and with the clap of a cruel hand
They were wiped out with no trace, uprooted forever.
Their homes were pillaged, their goods looted
And the *mezuzah* at the portal was replaced with a cross.

Still the same chairs, the same tables and cloths.
Only the Shabbat is missing, the holy queen was raped.
Father doesn't slice the *challa*, the child doesn't repeat the Kiddush,
Nobody sings *zmirot*, nobody lights the candles.
The synagogues and the midrash houses were desecrated,
No Jewish children rejoice in the courtyards,
And there's no rabbi, no *rav*, no *cheder*, no book.
Desolation in the midrash house, the voices are silenced.
Muted the doleful strains of *tnu rabanan* and *Abayei ve–Raba*.

Damned is this earth that houses assassins,

Looters and robbers who murdered and pillaged

And filled their mouths with the laughter of plunder.

The Jewish street is dead, there's no Jew and no Judaism.

The trees grew and sent their roots deep into the earth;

There, underneath, lie my brothers, sisters, and their children.

The trees have matured, their color dark green, their branches have grown,

Since the soil was enriched with the blood of infants.

Tar drips from the trees like crystallized teardrops in wooden crevices,

Like tears that couldn't roll down to earth like dewdrops to moisten the soil.

Lord of the world, how are you not mortified and ashamed?

[Page 182]

Why did they naïvely believe in David's prayers, to praise

The God who had chosen his people above all others…

When the axe was hoisted over them, they still cried out for help,

Believing that their God would not abandon them in misery and need.

Capitulated, I stand before myself and spit in my face

For the stupid crime of superstition.

Where did all those prayers go,

The torments and supplications, the fasting and charity to the last coin?!

Why were all those killers saved,

While most of Israel went to its relentless doom?

My heart goes out to you, too, my saintly mother, wrapped in a white kerchief

Standing on her feet all day at Atonement;

Crying, pleading, fasting and praying innocently all day,

Reading for women a legend of martyrs who die for their faith

They all listen and cry, their faith is deep and clear as the sky.

They believe in a God up above who would never, ever abandon them.

All is silenced with no return, their father, too, was taken with them.

The Jews have died, so has Judaism, they had no chance to live,

They only hoped, dreamed, prayed and, in the sorrow of their suffering,

They didn't foresee their tragic, cruel end,

That one day will rise a murder that had never been known in the world,

Their neighbors, who lived with them, would bury them alive.

My heart bursts with tears on the *rav* of my town, Yanova,

The *rav* who made do with rough bread, who didn't know envy

Knew only his God, and watched over his flock like a shepherd.

I remember, when I was still a child, his tears as he preached to the assembly,

To awaken them to prayer, to purify the soul,

To prepare them to receive the Shekhinah and final redemption.

They lopped off his head, and he died a cruel death

At the hands of a murderer, a goy of my hometown.

Cursed is this earth, soaked in the blood of many thousands,

Whose entreaties scream for vengeance from the bowels of the earth.

From the distance, my eyes perceive that holy mountain, the cemetery,

That is seen descending toward the town, graves upon graves,

Rows upon rows, where my fathers' fathers were deposited,

Generations upon generations, who lived and died in their time, my parents among them.

With dread and respect we visited them on the 9th of Av or the 17th of Tammuz,

Placing wooden swords for the days to come–

The Resurrection and final redemption.

These gravestones were yanked from their places and used to pave the roads.

I will give no more prayers and supplications, since they are all for naught,

Since the best people's prayers did not help them.

I will spread my arms and call for vengeance, reprisal for thousands of Jews

Who were killed, buried, and burned alive with "Shema" on their tongue.

[Page 183]

Every Jew should swear and take an oath of vengeance, hate.

Not to enjoy anything by this abominable humanity.

Not to deal with them, spurn and excommunicate!

To my shame, this horror has still not been wiped from my memory–

I would stand shamefaced in front of shop windows,

Widows filled with the wares of Ashkenaz, made by assassins.

My brothers are bowing again to the idol of profit, buying and selling,

Adorning their homes with ornaments made by the hands

That spilled the blood of families and friends.

How have you sunk so low, without shame,

For yourselves, your children, and the members of your community?!

Have you been blinded and are senseless fo your actions,

You are enriching the same robbers who killed and looted,

Raped your daughters and consigned them to brothels–

They were subjected to all manners of indignity, were tried and defiled.

Blood drips from their merchandise, real blood,
Blood that screams from shame and cries for vengeance.

My heart goes out to the motherland struggling like a woman in labor,
To gather unto herself her infants from all ends of the earth,
Receiving reparations from the killers, to redeem and rebuilt them.
The reparations are the blood of her sons who were murdered,
Burned, strangled, looted and robbed.
These reparations are but a fragment of a vast Jewish wealth
That was built and acquired over thousands of years.
I forgive the motherland for receiving this blood money
To erect a home for the surviving refugees.

It's good and just to receive reparations from the murderers' land
Without the illusion that they compensate for murder.
They are ours, and we have the right to them, since we're the owners.
But forgiveness for the great murder of millions,
Is not possible for us Jews.

From generation to generation, father to son and son to son, will tell,
Until the end of time forever and ever,
The depth of the horrible tragedy, fathers lost sons;
Sons died before their mothers.
Skeletons upon skeletons lay sighing in piles,
Corpses–half dead and half alive.
They are piled up like mud and thrown into the furnaces.
Will such a thing be forgotten? And if forgotten, so will a Jew from his people!
For there's no right to exist for a people that eats its own vomit,
Forgetting and renouncing its honor, the honor of humans as humans.
It should be written and chiseled forever in Jewish homes
Memorial stones and eternal candles should be put up in midrash houses,
The sainted souls shall be remembered on holy days,
So that we don't forget nor those who come after us.

[Page 184]

We Were Saved from the Nazi Talons

by Tovia Garber, Neve Sharet

Translated by Jerrold Landau

Before the outbreak of the war, I worked in the carpentry shop of Koppel Reznik and his sons, which was nationalized under the directorship of one of the gentile workers as Government Carpentry Shop Number One.

On the day of the outbreak of the war, all of the workers were gathered together and assigned a rotation for guarding. I guarded the carpentry shop that night. We heard the roar of airplanes that were flying to bombard the Polygon.

On the second day, nobody thought about work. Our family, consisting of my father Melech, my mother Judith, my brothers Chaim and Hershel, my sisters Henia, Batya and Gittel and I, decided to escape to Russia. We spoke to our relative Shabtai Droskin, who owned a horse and wagon, in order to escape along with them in the direction of Wilkomir [Ukmerge]. We naively believed that we would be able to return easily from there. We left Jonava on the second day in the evening. When we reached the Kemach factory, I and my cousin Zamka Droskin decided to run to the railroad station where we might catch a train going in the direction of the border. Along the way we met many people returning from there who told us that there is no hope at all with a train.

On the third morning, we arrived in Wilkomir tired and crushed. A terrifying panic pervaded the city. There were dead and wounded people. Many had fled. We wished to rest at the exit of the city, but we continued in the direction of Lëteniai. Along the way, The Shaulists[1] shot at us from the forests. Utënai was also destroyed. After a brief rest in the grove outside the city, we traveled on and reached Airënai. The Shaulists shot at us from the church in the center of the city, but they did not hit us. Two Russian tanks shot at the church tower and destroyed it. As we passed through villages, there were farmers who brought us food and water. Along the way, we ran into Shaulists who threatened us with arms and ordered us to return. We were frightened when they told us that the Germans had blocked our way. Many of the refugees believed them and returned along the way that they came. We were not influenced by their words. We continued to travel quickly. We caught a lost horse along the way, harnessed it to our wagon, and continue to move onward.

We reached Dvinsk (Daugavpils) by the morning. When the people of Dvinsk saw the masses of refugees, they also took up the wandering staff and set out along the way. We had just left the city when we saw German airplanes bombing the bridges. We stopped in a village. A farmer gave us food and refused to take money. We rested there for a few days. Father approached the nearby town of Dagda to assess the situation. We saw the guards looking at us. We quickly returned and decided to escape to the border. Within a few days we arrived at the town of Zhivich next to the border. Thousands of refugees waited there for permission to cross. When we reached there, we received permits, and entered the Soviet Union.

We split up. Our family of eight traveled by train deep into Russia. Uncle Shabtai Droskin and his family traveled on their wagon. We reached a kolkhoz called "The Second Five Year Plan" in the Mordovian Autonomous Republic.

I was drafted into the Lithuanian division of the army on February 7, 1942. I was sent to the Otkorsk Pass in the area of Sartov. There, they cut off my left hand. I returned to my family in the kolkhoz in November. We returned to Vilna after the war. Uncle Shabtai Droskin and his family arrived in the Tatar Autonomous Republic, and at the end of the war they returned to Lithuania. To our good fortune, nobody in the family was killed.

Finally I arrived in Israel with my wife and two children.

Recorded by Y. B.

[Page 185]

How I Remained Alive

by Leah Drucker (Monosevich), Neve Sharet

Translated by Jerrold Landau

I moved to Kovno to live with my mother-in-law and father-in-law a few months after I married David Tzon.

On Sunday, June 22, when the war broke out, my father Yisrael arrived in Slobodka in the evening and informed us that the family would be escaping by truck to Russia. He took my husband and me to Jonava. An oppressive atmosphere prevailed there. People were running around planning schemes. We did not shut our eyes at night. That same night, they drafted my brother-in-law Moshe with a truck from our headquarters in order to evacuate the Russian wives of senior army captains who lived in Jonava.

On Monday morning, thousands of refugees from Kovno and nearby towns had already arrived in town. They came by vehicle or on foot. Wagon drivers or truck drivers escaped with their vehicles. We also did that. The following people came in our truck. Yisrael Namiot and his wife Yentl, Aunt Esther (her sons Elik and Shmaryahu escaped by bicycle previously) my mother Shula, my father Yisrael, my sisters Sarah and Feiga, my husband and I. Along the way we picked up Reuven Gurvich and Rivka Rubinovich and her children.

We arrived in Dvinsk through the air bombardments and running through trenches. The city was bustling with people, cars and wagons. The commotion was great, for the Germans did not let up their bombardment. We left there and arrived in the town of Kreslawka near the border. We were too late, for the border had been closed in the meantime. The following members of our family were killed in the bombardment: Shalom Lukman, his wife Chaya, their son Hershel and their young daughter, my aunt Sara Beila the seamstress and her husband Yankel Levitt.

We remained in Kreslawka for several days; however we did not succeed in crossing the border. We decided to return to Jonava. The Germans were already in Dvinsk. The Latvians warned us that in Dvinsk we would be liable for imprisonment. Nevertheless, we entered the city, and indeed we were imprisoned. The men were separated from the women. We were liberated after a few days in terrible prison conditions. We did not meet the men. We were informed that they were all shot.

We decided to walk to Jonava on foot. We hired wagons along the way in exchange for clothing and food. They sent us off after several kilometers. At times, we met Jews in towns, and found refuge for the night. Along the way we met Lyuba Lukman from the other side of the Viliya, with her daughter Feiga and two children. Feiga and her children were killed along the way, and Lyuba returned to Jonava, where she met her death with everyone else.

We arrived in Jonava at the end of July. The center of the town was consumed by fire. We met hundreds of men and women waiting for food distribution next to the cooperative on the road. Among them I saw Meirka Lukman, Itzik Suntochky, Kahansky, the Seniors, Moshel Beker and others. They told me that they had been expelled from their houses, which had been captured after the fire. They wandered around the gardens.

Our house remained intact. The German headquarters located itself in our house and that of Yisrael Namiot. They did not permit us to approach, so we passed over to the other side, to Lukman's house. This house was empty. The family of Itzik Sintuchky was also with us, for their house had gone up in flames. They gave us food, clothing and money. The next day I met Moshe Beker who told me that he was living in the carpentry shop along with the families of Moshe and Zusman Klotz, the owners of the carpentry shop.

My friends whom I met told me that a group of young women – Yocheved Shegansky, Batya Senior, Rivka and Yudit Ferber, Suntochky and Klachman – were serving the German headquarters and clearing weeds from the pavement. My brother- in-law in Kovno told me that my house in the middle of the ghetto in Slobodka was empty, and that I was invited to come. My mother-in-law and relatives with whom we had made the entire journey to the border and back advised me to go, and told me that they would follow after me. However, they all perished.

I traveled to Kovno and entered the ghetto. I came without any energy. I was in my seventh month of pregnancy. I rejoined my husband's family and lived together with them. A son was born to me. I worked in the brigade in the airport as well as in sewing. One day when I returned from work I did not find my son. He was taken and he perished in the children's aktion. I suffered until the ghetto was liquidated. I was taken to Stutthof, and then to other camps.

I was liberated by the Russians in 1945. I immediately returned to Vilna. I married Shlomo Drucker and we had two children.

I had received a nationalist education at home. I studied in the Tarbut School, was active in the Zionist youth organizations, and was attracted to the Land of Israel. We put in many requests but were not answered. Finally, in 1967, my husband, I, and our daughter Dorit arrived in Israel and settled in Neve Sharet.

The following people perished from my family: Father, Mother, my two sisters, my brother Moshe who arrived in Russia, was drafted to the front and died a heroic death. Our relatives Leizer Monosevich, his wife Merl and their children, Chaya the wife of Yoschek Monosevich with their three daughters and a son also perished.

[Page 186]

My Path of Tribulations

by Leah Helerman (Kronik), Melbourne

Translated by Jerrold Landau

Early in the morning of Sunday, June 22 we were awakened by the sound of airplanes flying through the blue skies of our town. We ran outside to the street and felt the fear that heralded the beginning of the war. Rumors spread that the Germans were approaching. People did not know what to do. The Russian guard brigade began to flee, and many of the Jews of Jonava joined them in order to find salvation in Russia. Those who owned horses loaded up some belongings and also fled. Where to run? Nobody knew the answer. Some ran with sacks to the train station or to the road to Wilkomir. Many ran to Lithuanian friends in nearby villages. It was necessary to flee for the front was on the other side of the Viliya in the area of Polygon, and many shells fell on the town. Fires broke out, and the entire town was burning. Many hid in cellars, and some people suffocated from the smoke and the heat.

My parents Leib and Rashel, my husband and child also decided to flee to a village, to a Lithuanian acquaintance who had been our customer for many years. It was a hot day. I had a sack over my shoulders and pushed our child in a stroller. My husband and parents were laden with sacks. We all set out in the direction of the village.

The way was filled with army people, and Jews – the old, women and children. All had one purpose: to quickly flee from the Germans to the extent that was possible. We arrived in the village. Our Lithuanian acquaintance received us with friendship and put us up for a few days. Special emissaries came to the village to warn people not to hide Jews, and to threaten with death anyone with whom a Jew would be found.

The farmers were frightened and tearfully told us that we must leave the village. We again fled with sacks on our shoulders, with the child in the stroller, and we continued to wander in the direction of Wilkomir. The cannons thundered and the airplanes roared above our heads as we ran to greet the unknown, left to the mercies of a bitter fate. Along the way a Jewish acquaintance informed us that we were near a Jewish village – Old Gustonys. We went there. My parents no longer had strength. They advised us to return to Jonava. My husband was still a young man, and I was afraid that he would be taken from me, so we decided to enter that settlement. We parted from my parents. They returned to Jonava and we returned to Old Gustonys.

The Jews of that place did not want to take us in, for the houses were filled with refugees. Embittered by this reception, we broke into one of the houses. There we met the Jonavers Shlupsky and his wife, Berman and his wife (from the Untershatz family), Menachem Mines and his wife and children. We remained there for about two weeks.

One week after we arrived, the Lithuanians came. They gathered all of the men and took them out as if to work – but in reality it was to be shot. The parting from our husbands was heartrending.

One week later, Lithuanian soldiers came on wagons and removed us from the village. We were certain that we were being taken to the forest to be shot to death, as had been done to the Jews of Jonava who remained there. To our surprise we saw that they took us to the road to Kovno. There, we entered the ghetto. This was on the Sabbath of September 27, 1941. One day earlier, approximately 10,000 Jews had been removed from the Kovno Ghetto to be murdered at the Ninth Fort. I remained in the Kovno ghetto with my child for about two years. I did not encounter anyone of my family there. All of them were murdered in Jonava. I passed two selections, in which the fate of life or death was hanging by a hair. Life was filled with fear and hunger.

In the ghetto I worked in the brigade that was taken daily to the airport in Aleksota. I went out almost naked, barefoot and starving. I held my stand for the urge to live was strong.

When they liquidated the Kovno Ghetto, they transferred my son and me to the Šanèiai Camp. There my situation improved. I worked in the warehouse of army fatigues, and I am not ashamed to state that I stole clothing from there in order to maintain my stand. However, this did not last for long.

One morning, as I was at work, the German murderers came and gathered all of the old people and children, including my only son Bentzele… I never saw him again. The rest were brought on transport trucks to Stutthof. There, the veritable hell began for us. Everything that we had endured to this time was like the Garden of Eden compared to this (excluding the fact that my husband and son were murdered). We were there for two weeks. They selected 500 strong women, including myself, and hauled us to Germany to dig trenches. We received food in order to sustain ourselves somehow. We slept in rags on straw mattresses. We did not have anywhere to wash. We were broken and crushed in body and spirit.

This continued until 1945. The war had already moved to German soil. As the Germans retreated, they continued to drag us along to the interior of Germany. This was in January, in the midst of the winter. We women marched in light clothing and in tattered, open shoes. Many froze along the way, and some were shot along the way. I was among the few who survived. This was due to some luck. The German commander, who had seen me working diligently at my tasks in the camp, had mercy on me and issued an order to give me closed, wooden shoes. These shoes saved me along the long journey, for we traversed dozens of kilometers in deep snow.

We were liberated on March 17, 1945. We were in an extermination camp on the preceding night. In the morning, when a few women left the bunkers, we noticed that the guards had disappeared. From afar we saw the Russian army marching in our direction. If they had tarried a few days longer, I would not have merited this. They quarantined us, for we were sick and infected with lice. They cut our hair and took us to the hospital. I remained there for a month. After that, we were transferred to a rehabilitation center. There, we regained our strength and energy.

This describes in brief the story of my life from 1941-1945. Today I live in Melbourne, Australia. I remarried, and I have a daughter whom I have already brought to the chupa (marriage canopy). Our family perished in Jonava. In addition to my father and my mother, there was my sister Ruchama Gertner, her husband Chona and their two children Lula and Efraim, Chaim Abramsom and his wife Shifra, Efraim Abramson, his wife Riva and their children Moshe and Pnina, Yosef Abramson and his wife, Leah the daughter of Chaim Abramson and her two children Moshe and Efraim.

[Page 188]

Thus was I Saved

by Lipa Berzin, Neve Sharet

Translated by Jerrold Landau

Lipa Berzin

Our family lived on Breizer Street, the street of the proletariat. My father Itzik, Liba Leah's,[2] floated barges on the waters of the Šventoji, Viliya and Neiman Rivers. In the winters, when the rivers froze, he was a porter. Our material situation was low, and our youth was not easy. In our family there was my mother Pesl, three brothers – me, Nachum-Izak and Melech, and our sister Miriam. Our small house was divided into two dwellings. Our family lived in one of them, which was 25 square meters. The family of my Uncle Nachum-Leizer lived in the second one. Father came home for Sabbaths and went to the synagogue.

We boys studied in Yavneh and our sister studied in the Yiddish school. When I concluded my studies in school, I went to study carpentry. My brother Nachum-Izak studied upholstering. At that time, I was active in the Young Chalutz. I moved to Kovno and worked in a furniture store until 1940. I was drafted to the Lithuanian Army. There were some Jonavers together with me in the Third Unit of the Artillery Brigade in Šanèiai: Zerach Goldman, Leibka Lukman from across the river, Shlomo Berzin the son of Uncle Yonah, and Leizka Stoliar (Krupnik).

When the Soviets arrived in Lithuania we were transferred to the barracks of the infantry unit in Vilna. When the war broke out our unit was in Polygon. The captains fled as the front approached. A Lithuanian sergeant took is in and told us: "Whoever wishes to return home – can arise and go; whoever wishes to come with me to Russia – follow me!" We were approximately 40 men. He led us by foot through Nemenèinë to the border. On the third day, June 24, we met up with three trucks with the flag of our unit from our headquarters. They took us in and we continued to the border. We arrived in the city of Plotzk in White Russia, and later in Wielkie Łuki. There we joined Russian units and entered into battle against the Germans. We fought with grenades, guns and Molotov cocktails. The Germans surrounded us and inflicted losses. We succeeded in escaping the siege in small groups. We swam across the Dvina (Daugava) River. We joined other Russian units, and in the midst of the battles we retreated to Kalinin.

We were sent to Gorky Blachna when the Lithuanian Division was set up. I joined unit 224 of the Artillery Brigade. With me there was my cousin Mottel Berzin, Yudel Baten, Notka Friedman, Shimon Strum and Motka Segal. The two latter ones were killed on the front. I was wounded in the battles near Nikolsk on the Orlov-Kursk Line. I was brought to the hospital in the city of Ulan Uda, where I remained for four months. From there I returned to my unit and continued to participate in the war until its end. We were then in Libau. There, we closed in on a concentration of Germans from units that had been defeated.

Chaim Wichov was also in our unit. He filled an important role with the Soviets in Jonava. In our unit, he served as the editor of the Lithuanian newspaper.

The command of the unit requested volunteers for a special mission. Chaim Wichov, who was not a combat soldier, was among the first to volunteer. He set out on his mission on a cold winter night in 1943, when the snow was one meter deep on the roads and in the fields. He did not return from this mission.

I was freed from the army on June 12, 1946, and I hastened to Jonava. I did not find anyone of my family. I found out that my father and brother were killed as they were floating a raft. My other brother perished along with the Lithuanian partisans. My sister Miriam and my mother were in the Kovno Ghetto. The British liberated them from the

Buchenwald concentration camp. From there, they went directly to the Land of Israel, and settled in Kiryat Motzkin. My sister married Yosef Pinkus.

When they were informed about me, they began to send me requests to come and join them. I presented their papers for 12 years and did not receive an exit permit. I only succeeded in 1967, and I arrived in Israel with my wife and two daughters. We settled in Neve Sharet, and I continue my career as a carpenter in the local factory. My wife works and the children are studying. We have finally come to peace.

Recorded by Y. B.

[Page 189]

We Fled from our Homes

by Chava Leah Kravchok, Neve Sharet

Translated by Jerrold Landau

Chava Leah Kravchok

On Sunday morning, my father Shevach Gutler traveled to Kovno as usual, to his work as a driver in a truck base. I went to my work as a bookkeeper in the headquarters of the wagon drivers. I began to sense the outbreak of war. A few drivers obtained two trucks in order to flee with their families. Father did not obtain a truck. He returned to Jonava, and we decided to escape on a wagon. He got in touch with Trotsky who promised to take us – that is my father, my mother Ethel, my brother Notel and my young sister Lyuba. The Trotsky family numbered four souls. He loaded all of our most vital belongings on the wagon, and we went by foot.

We left our home on the road, next to Petrosovich's home, on Monday June 23. Along the way to Wilkomir, about 15 kilometers from Jonava, we met David Monosevich and Adeskes with their families, who were traveling on a fire engine. They stopped and took us aboard along with our family, except for Mother, who remained with Trotsky to guard the belongings. We said that we would wait for her in Wilkomir.

I got a nervous breakdown from the air bombardment. I wept the entire time. There were many fires in Wilkomir at night due to the bombs and fires ignited by the Shaulists. Adeskes decided not to stop. We were already in Uteny [Uetna] on Tuesday. Thus we were separated from Mother. One of our relatives whom we met along the way told us that there was no point in advancing, for the Russians are not allowing anyone to cross the border. Since we traveled all night, we stopped for a short rest. There was a bombardment in the morning in which Adeskes' father-in-law was killed. This compelled David Monosevich to continue on immediately. My father and brother had gone to a neighboring home and had not yet returned. What could we do? They assured me that they would follow us to Dvinsk.

In Dvinsk, we rested in the Beis Midrash. After resting, we went to the border. There were thousands of people there, but they were not permitted to cross. We returned to the city and waited for our family for two days. The Jews of Dvinsk provided us with food. The front approached. We again approached the border near Zilupe. There we met the following people from Jonava: the brothers Chaim and Leibl Baten, Yerchamiel Garber, Hillel Epstein, Shlomo Ber Meirovich, the teacher Sarah Sherman, and the Dragachki and Droskin families.

We heard a strong explosion as we sat in a house in Zilope. There was a crash of two railway cars, one of which was carrying explosive material. We did not know what happened, and we thought that the Germans had shelled the railway station. We fled through the fields for a distance of five kilometers. There we were met by Latvians who took us into a school. We suspected that they wanted to murder us. David Monosevich and Yitzchak Droskin ran to the city to inform the police. They calmed them, for they were citizens who were interested in preserving the order, and they did not want people wandering around outside who might attract the attention of the German aviators.

We removed some of our belongings from the fire engine in order to make more room. Adeskes, his wife and two children, Monosevich, his wife and child, the four members of the Droskin family, my sister and I mounted the vehicle and traveled to the border. The place was full of bogs. We placed branches down in order that the vehicle could pass, but we got stuck in the mud. We descended from the vehicle and continued along our way in mud up to our knees. We arrived at the border. There was no guard there, and we crossed. We reached the town of Krasna in White Russia. The farmers gave us potatoes and milk. We rested and set out for the railroad station. The tracks were destroyed from the bombardment, and no trains were moving. Thus did we walk onward for two weeks through the roads and dirt paths in order to avoid bombardments. We traversed approximately 500 kilometers. Once we covered some ground with a truck that took us in.

At one of our stops we were thought to be spies. Our Lithuanian passports aroused suspicion. We spent a night in prison and were freed the next day. The police placed us on a train that was traveling to Gorky. We journeyed for approximately two weeks. We were stationary for longer than we traveled, for preference was given along the way to trains with soldiers and arms. Along the way, we lost David Manosovich and his wife, and the Dragachki and Adeskes families. Remaining were my sister and I, the Droskin family, Shlomo Ber Meirovich, Hillel Epstein, Moshe Monosevich, and the young Biarsky from the other side of the Viliya. Thus we arrived in the Chuvashian Autonomous Republic. We lost a few more along the way. The Droskin family, my sister and I arrived in Gorky. We were placed in a steamboat, and we traveled down the Volga to the city of Engels in the German Autonomous Republic. I worked there as an orderly in the hospital. The men worked in the army factory. The Germans received us with friendship. We did not lack food.

Winter drew near. We were half naked. One of us had the idea that we should perhaps travel to Tashkent, which was warmer. I was attracted to go there, for according to Biarsky, David Monosevich was also there. We abandoned our bread and went to search for crumbs. The tribulations began when we arrived there. Tashkent was overflowing with hundreds of thousands of refugees. People were lying around in crowds in all of the gardens and schools. Indeed we did not suffer from cold, but people were dying at every step from hunger. We were also starving.

We decided to travel to Samarkand. From there, we were sent to a sovkhoz. The situation there was no better, and we returned to Tashkent. There we met Yossel Monosevich, and David Monosevich and his wife. The men were drafted into the Lithuanian division of the army.

We women decided to return to the city of Engels, but we were not permitted to do so. We were transferred to the Osinovka Kolkhoz near Saratov. We worked in the fields. We did not suffer from hunger. We remained there until the end of the war. My sister and I returned to Vilna in December 1944.

As I have stated already, we lost our father and brother forever in Uteny. I was informed that Father, Mother and my brother had been seen in Wilkomir, but they all perished.

We had received a nationalist education in our home. I studied in the Tarbut School with the teachers Keidansky, Apatkina, Rosenberg, and others. When I returned from Russia, I had decided conclusively to travel to Israel. This was not so easy. I got married in the interim. Our dream was only realized in February 1969. My husband and I live and work in Neve Sharet, and are content.

Recorded by Y. B.

[Page 191]

In the Talons of the Enemy

by Meir Tsoref [(Goldshmidt)]

Translated by Jerrold Landau

This was a clear morning. I was with the brigade not far from Memel. There was to be a demonstration before the Lithuanians. Apparently, they already knew what was about to happen. Everything was grey. Suddenly we heard explosions, and after that our train was shelled.

When I arrived in Jonava, all the people of the town were already on their feet. Owners of wagons and cars set out on their way, hurrying to escape. My young wife was already waiting for me. In Kovno, the Lithuanians had already begun to perpetrate violence against the Jews even before the Germans arrived. Jonava was filled with Jewish refugees from Kovno. Mirka Lan, who was a high official in the city council, remained at her post and attempted to calm the situation by stating "This is a panic for nothing". Even though she saw that the Red Army was retreating she did not wish to believe this, and hoped for a miracle as would an observant Jew... for this situation does not make sense. They sang, "If there is to be a war tomorrow, we are already today prepared to maintain a stand..."

She tarried until the last minute, and along with her, those who had faith in Soviet Lithuania continued their guard...even though the true defenders were already on the roads in the direction of the interior of Russia. Precious time was wasted. This was also the case with the writer of these lines.

We set out on our journey in a group after we were freed from our jobs by Mirka Lan. We set out along with all of the other despairing pedestrians, chased up to the neck by the retreating Red Army and the Lithuanian Shaulists (riflemen), and under the fire of the German airplanes. The road was blocked by the Red Army. Shelling began. We saw our town go up in fire, burning day and night. Along with it, the years of childhood went up in flames, and our hearts were aching: our town is burning up completely, and we are holding hands without offering assistance...

We tarried as well on account of our friend who was in our group, the Yiddish actor Leibovich, who was wounded in his leg and was not able to proceed. Even though he begged us to leave him to die, we would not have considered fleeing for our lives, leaving him in agony. The Communist ethics did not teach us thus… We wound our way through towns and villages, pillaged shops and destroyed wells, as if an invisible evil hand was assisting the Angel of Death…

The first victims of the terrible slaughter appeared before our eyes: bodies of children hung from trees, strangled by their red Pioneer ties, wearing their white shirts as if they were dressed up for a school party. Their black hair showed that they belonged to those who wore the red Pioneer ties with love and joy, and for this they paid with their young lives…

The Unexpected Transpired

We sent our wives and children before us, and we men began to prepare the young victims for burial. However, we were not able to do so, for we were stopped by two Lithuanian murderers. We were certain that our end had come. However, apparently they were not so sure of themselves, or their guns did not have bullets which had been distributed to us on the first day of the war. Therefore, they brought us to a stable and locked us in from the outside. At night, we broke through and escaped. Our wives who had waited endlessly for us returned to us, and we were united once again. The shelling ceased. A frightening silence pervaded, and the heart foretold evil. Indeed, at the blink of an eye, like devils from hell, we were surrounded by the Germans on motorcycles, with rolled up sleeves, as butchers at their bloody work. The muzzles of their guns were pointed toward us, and once again we found ourselves about to be separated from the iniquitous, murderous world. As if to anger us, the air was filled with the pleasant aroma of the forests, and our lungs enjoyed this air, as if they wished to fill themselves up as much as possible for the final time, in order to enjoy an additional moment of life…

The unexpected took place. The commanding officer, after investigating our identity papers in which was written "Zydas" with large characters, permitted us to lower our hands. He caressed the heads of the children and gave them jam, cheese and sausages, and instructed us to travel on the road upon which the orderly German army was moving. He stressed that this was the Wehrmacht rather than the S.S.

I was not particularly expert in the difference. It is possible that those who preached on behalf of the Communist or nationalist idea, and directed one to die the death of the brave, were correct. However at that moment I was satisfied that we had hidden our Comsomol membership cards under a tree at the advice of our practical cousin Leibka "the bastard"…and we willingly accepted the gift of the enemy – the lives of myself and my wife, who was eventually to become the mother of our son. Even though we did not know what would take place in the future, our lungs were again able to breathe the aromatic air. The young conscience seeks an answer and comfort for what took place:

apparently not all of the Germans are devourers of Jews. There were four million Communists in Germany. We regained our faith in international solidarity. We started walking in the direction of Jonava.

We tarried in the Jewish village of Old Gustonys. There we found out the terrible truth of Jonava: the rape of the daughter of Kopeliansky, who went crazy; the mass murder that was perpetrated by the murderers Lyubka Zachar, Jan Pinkowski the Polish chimneysweeper and the Sabbath goy, and others. Even though the villagers fed us, gave us drink, and gave us refuge for the night, they requested that we leave the village, for the gentile mayor of the village threatened them that they would suffer for giving refuge to Communists. We understood this. It was easier to suffer for political sins than to suffer because one was born a Jew.

The Father Hides Communists and the Children Murder

We left through the forest before dawn. With a loaf of bread and cheese as provisions, we marched along a path in the thick of the forest, breathing the clear air, as if there were no murdering and pillaging Germans in Jonava. We were prepared to continue living in the forest that was full of secrets, far from the city and from death. However the droning of the black transport airplanes with the white swastikas, like black ravens, came to remind us that even here in the bosom of nature, the murderous fist was liable to catch up with us…

Without our noticing, suddenly the veteran Shaulist, Justyn the forester, who waved the yellow-green-red flag of Lithuania at all celebrations in Jonava, appeared before us. He calmed us and told us that we need not fear him, for he liked the Germans as much as the Russians. He told us, "Simtas velniai isejo ir dusimtai atejo" (one hundred first born of Satan left, and two hundred arrived). We were guests in his home for approximately a week. He gave us food and drink. We slept in the granary in order to avoid any mishap. He told us that, to his dismay, his children went to Jonava to take revenge on the Communists. He kept us with him until the danger passed, that is to say until the murderers would be sated with Jewish blood. This was a paradox – the father was hiding two young Communists while the murderous sons were raping and pillaging…

From him we heard the first accurate analysis of the situation since the beginning of the war: The Germans would lose the war, and their fate would be like that of Napoleon's army. However, like Napoleon, Hitler would also reach the gates of Moscow, and the war would last for four or five years, which we did not believe.

We were again Freed by our Enemies

From behind the brick kilns next to the road we heard the recognizable, blood-curdling shriek. Two Lithuanians, an adult and a youngster of about 14 years old, apparently a father and son, with wild flax-like hair and murderous catlike eyes, pointed their guns at us. From their stony, bloodthirsty gaze I realized that the end had come… It was strange – for subconsciously I looked around for Germans who might save us… The Lithuanian barked at me to strip out of my suit. Apparently, this attracted the murderer. I figured this out and answered him that he would have to strip my suit off himself. He did not shoot. He did not want to ruin such a suit with bullet holes and my blood… He did not dare come close. Suddenly, as in a fairy tale, a wagon appeared on the street with German soldiers. I decided to scream, and a few soldiers hastened with their weapons. The farmer and his son were at a loss and began to stutter in Lithuanian, "Zydy". We explained in clear German that he was about to rob us on our way home. They removed the guns from the Lithuanians, beat them soundly, and freed us. We were once again freed by our sworn enemies.

To our good fortune the German army was moving in an orderly fashion along the road, and we arrived in Kovno in peace. An elderly Christian stopped us near the first houses. We entered his house and he informed us that they were arresting all of the arriving Jews and taking them to the Seventh Fort. He took our packages from us, gave me a satchel and my wife a farmer's kerchief, took us across the river in his boat, and advised us to go only to the center of town.

In House Imprisonment

Our room was in the center of Meironiou Street. We would walk in Petrovka and Freedom Street as an Aryan couple in love, until we returned to our dwelling with pounding hearts. Before our eyes, Lithuanians passed by transporting groups of Jews with their hands on their heads, including children whose hands could not yet reach their heads… and our hearts were torn to pieces. We wished to shout out: Take me also with them, for I am also a Jew!... However, the desire to live was stronger. We huddled close to each other, as if this was a charm to prevent the tragic Jewish fate…

No evil came to our dwelling. The owner of the house was Chefetz, a woman's tailor. The hand of the hooligans had not reached there, since the house was in the region of the Lithuanian Bank, and the Germans had placed a unit there to protect the bank. The cook [of the unit] who alone knew of our existence would at times secretly bring us bread and leftover food. We were willing prisoners, for we could not appear in a store, and we did not have food cards. In the marketplace, we would have encountered attacks, imprisonment, pillage, and murderous beatings.

We found out about the terrible pogrom that the Lithuanians perpetrated against the Jews of Slobodka, without passing over any house. Children were murdered with the butts of the guns of the murderers. Later we found a Jewish house with the word

"Revenge!" written with blood on the wall. We also found out about the ineffective resistance mounted by the people who were lacking any weapons.

We remained thus for a few weeks as house prisoners, waiting to see what would transpire. We had no contact with the outside world except for the German cook who sustained us, until we were ordered by the gatekeeper, in the name of the German government, to move to Slobodka, which had been established as the living place of the Jews. Deliberately they did not use the term ghetto. They organized attacks in the center of the city in order to convince the Jews to make haste and move there. Thousands of Jews were snatched from their homes – men, women, and children – and not one of them returned… On the other hand, there was quiet in Slobodka, and Jews were even permitted to purchase something in the stores. Jews were "convinced" and began to load their belongings on baby strollers and other primitive means of transportation, as it was during the Exodus from Egypt – however in a different direction – from one exile to another that was called a "ghetto". This was a return to the middle ages in the middle of the 20th century. They did not imagine that what lay before them was worse than anything…

We Outsmarted them with regard to Members of the Family

The murderers crowded more than 30,000 people into an area where previously several thousand Jews had lived, themselves not with ample space. Nevertheless, everyone found friends, acquaintances, and a roof over their heads. I found my dear mother and the children in the Beis Midrash. My father and my young brother Hershele had been dragged by the Lithuanian murderers to the Seventh Fort. My brother Avraham was also with them, but my father told him to take the opportunity to escape. He succeeded, and returned to Mother in the Beis Midrash.

The joy of reuniting with members of the family did not last long. We lost them again, this time forever, in the first aktion that the Germans perpetrated one bright day when the men had been taken outside of the ghetto to backbreaking work. This was the first organized pogrom according to the German style. My brother Avraham and sister Asnat were with us that morning. When the German guards arrived they began to run to Mother, but the murderers prevented them. Thus we thwarted them. The family was united, and two more beds were set up in the small dwelling. We bore our mourning in the heart together. Together we traversed the thorny path until the end, with hunger, want and cold. We lacked the means to help each other. However when my brother succeeded in obtaining a loaf of bread, he hid it deep in his pants in order to split it with me. After he passed the inspection, it seemed that it ate up his insides slowly, without being sensed.

Despair overtook most of the dwellers of the ghetto. People began to avoid going out to work in the city. The Germans set up a Jewish police force whose task was to summon the people to work. Hunger pervaded in full force in the ghetto. No food was brought in. The ghetto dwellers did not even receive the minimum rations of prisoners. The ghetto was well guarded by the bloodthirsty Lithuanians. The few who went out to work in the city had to pass a strict inspection when they returned, and everything was taken from them – a piece of bread and a potato. Often, they would pay with their lives for attempting to bring in food products that they had obtained in exchange for clothing.

Wandering About in the Ghetto

Jordon, the short and luckless merchant from Aydkunen, became the lord over the fate of 35,000 people, according to the official count. The elder Dr. Elkes, appointed by the Germans as head of the Jews, had to appear before him and listen to his orders. Children suspected, like birds bearing secrets, that they would be among the first to perish. They ceased weeping, and refrained from appearing in the alleys of the ghetto. They lay quietly in secret corners, waiting with hungry eyes to see if their parents might bring them something to assuage the hunger – and even that for a brief period.

The echoes of gunshots were heard from some distance away day and night. Jews in the ghetto comforted themselves: the front is not far away, shortly they will be defeated like Napoleon and Haman – and the Jews would celebrate a new Purim. That which the newspapers were writing – that the battles were taking place in Smolensk, near Leningrad and Moscow – is a lie! One is not to believe the Germans. Such comforting thoughts filled the hearts of the suffering Jews of the ghetto. At that time, the marksmen at the Seventh and Ninth Forts were sowing death and reaping the lives of the Jews, who only yesterday had been among the ghetto dwellers. The rumor that was spread by the Germans before the first aktion that the Fuehrer had banned the shooting of Jews and that those who remained alive would have to work for the Germans, was very exciting and enhanced the words of comfort. The Jews took hold of this and transferred it from mouth to ear. With their own eyes they saw that food was being brought into the ghetto: bread, flour, sugar, grits, jam and even meat. Another proof: they began to register people and distribute work permits by profession – and especially food cards. It was said that they would even give money… the writer of these lines met secretly in the city with a Russian from Jonava, Kolka Semionov, a former member of Comsomol. From him I found out that excavators were working at the Ninth Fort, digging mass graves, and that they were bringing chlorine there…

The hatred of the Lithuanians toward us grew from day to day. Even children would look at you with an odd face and follow after any Jewish child. My wife was to become a mother, and this was considered a great crime according to German law, punishable by death. My dear, refined wife and I sat hungry, overtaken by despair, thinking about what to do. To remain in the ghetto meant death the next day. To escape from the ghetto meant death today. Of course we decided to wait until the next day. Even one additional day of life is worth something.

It is Yudka

One of the powers of the ghetto leadership entered our room to register the residents. To our surprise, this was our fellow townsman Yudka Zopovich. After a brief conversation, the two former political rivals reached an agreement about the need for resistance. From his mouth I learned that Mirka Lan was also in the ghetto. He further told me that Jews from Jonava were also being brought into the ghetto, and a bit of hope rose in our hearts. We had already mourned all of the Jews of Jonava… And if some still remained alive, perhaps there was someone from our family. And if death was decreed upon the Jews of the ghetto, why would the Germans be bringing in other Jews? Was there no more place in Girialka? A shadow of a doubt entered – perhaps the optimists were correct? And why was there a registration? They had already murdered many Jews without registration…

In order to prevent any disaster from occurring, Yudka Zopovich registered us under different names –Leon and Sonia Genes. We were no longer Communists, but rather construction workers, the profession of my father. The Germans had need of such. We went to build a new airport. In our following encounters, he informed me of his naïve deliberations, apparently logical, about how to evade punishment. According to the Germans we were all equal – Zionists and Communists. The death penalty would only come if we had the brazenness to give birth…

There are Still Lithuanians…

Death did not wait long for him. Indeed, a few Jews were brought from Jonava, who had been able to hide in villages. The police even arranged farmers' wagons to transport them to Kovno. These people were very satisfied to dispense with their Jewish guests, even though they maintained them for a fee. We were fortunate Jews, for we found relatives: my wife's mother, aunt, brothers and sisters. We also found out that her younger sister Yentele, tall, light haired, with a Polish manner of speaking, was hiding in Kovno as an Aryan. She worked in Kovno as a maid for the Lithuanian noblewoman Viktoria Krulitzkina. To us, this appeared like a fantastical unbelievable child's story in a nightmare. There are still Lithuanians who are willing to risk their lives to save a Jewish child?... We even succeeded to see her briefly from the other side of the wall. She was indeed going about as an "Aryan", arm in arm with her merciful woman on one bright Sunday. They were walking on the sidewalk, which was forbidden to Jews. She was well fed, dressed appropriately, proud, without the yellow badge. She had an artificial, broad smile… And on the other side of the fence – they were starving, wearing rags, sentenced to death – her mother, father, brothers and sister. Heaven forbid she should shed a tear… To cast a glance would likely sentence her and her savior to death. Someone in the family should survive to light a memorial candle.

What was going on in the heart of the young girl on the other side of the fence and in the heart of her mother on this side of the fence is known only to G-d and to themselves. It seemed that perhaps the girl would separate herself from the noblewoman run to the barbed wire fence, grab on to her tormented mother who suffers from hunger and want, kiss her with eyes wet with tears, and shout out, "My dear mother, I wish to die along with you, I no longer have the strength to listen to the jokes made by the drunken murderers at the expense of the slaughtered Jews and to pretend that I am happy along with them! I have no more strength to die 24 hours a day of the fear that they might find out that I am a Jewess!"…

There are no Bounds to the Degradation

However, the will to live and her responsibility to the good woman Krulitzkina, who was liable to pay for this with her life, prevented her from taking any steps out of despair. She continued to stroll as if nothing happened. An ordinary stroll near the place of the gathering of the members of the inferior race, as if – to differentiate[3] – in the zoological garden. The mother fainted after witnessing this strange sight. She was revived with difficulty. The hunger was so strong that she forgot anything, and had a thought about one thing only: food! The children looked with hungry eyes, like birds in a nest with wide open beaks, and requested with a whisper: "Mother, food!"… A neighbor said that near the fence there are farmer women walking around with bread. Mother took off her summer coat, ignored the danger of being shot without warning – as had already happened, for more than one person remained hung to the fence for desiring to obtain a loaf of bread – and ran to the fence, where a gentile woman with a loaf of bread was walking on the other side. The exchange took place. Mother hurried home without a coat. She was hiding something that informed the starving eyes that there would be a relief from the burning hunger pangs. Something to eat! The children were already swallowing their saliva… Mother is already at home, and perhaps there would be a loaf of fresh bread on the table. All of them sensed the sweet aroma, but the color appears suspicious. However in times like this who paid attention to the color. Everyone followed the knife that cut the soft bread… And nobody could believe their eyes. There are no bounds to the depravity of humankind! The baked bread consisted of cattle dung with straw, with a thin outer layer of dough…

The children did not want to pass up on the hope of silencing their hunger, so they lapped up the thin layer like an ice cream cone until they reach the stinking dung…

[Page 196]

The Large Scale Aktion

Then came the day which we had feared – the day of the large scale aktion.

Before dawn, they began to summon all living souls to the "Demokrato" (Democracy) square. What a frightful paradox! The square was surrounded by a chain of Lithuanian murderers with machine guns. In the center stood Germans who were directing who to the right and who to the left, like sheep. Nobody knew which would be better. Someone turned to go to the left with his mother. The Germans beat him and chased him back to the right. And vice versa. Yudka Zopovich ran among the rows advising people to separate themselves into small family groupings. We listened to his advice and turned to the right. Those to the left were surrounded by a fortified guard. They were dragged to a small ghetto, and from there, the next morning at dawn, to the Ninth Fort. The husband of my Aunt Esther, Uncle Shmuel Silber of Jonava, who was separated from his family and directed to the left, escaped at night and returned to the ghetto. He perished later in the city as he was searching for a hiding place for his children.

The terrifying echoes of the machine guns once again echoed in the air from the direction of the Ninth Fort. This was no longer a secret. Everyone began to look at death directly in the face, to breathe in its fresh poison into the lungs.

Eleven year old Itzik Bloch came back, covered with blood and without his underwear, bringing definitive proof. He had escaped from the pit. He told how they brought the people to the pit in groups and shot from all directions, after they forced them to strip out of their clothing… His mother shouted after him: Run! He ran, and felt a burning sensation in his shoulders. Overtaken by the fear of death, he continued to run until he lost his strength and fell into the bushes. Later, under cover of darkness, he dragged himself to the ghetto, and snuck inside over the fence, in a wounded state. Two other youths, Reuven Gorgel and Aharon Gafenovich, who hid as Christians in the nearby village and were eyewitnesses, later told in the ghetto about the atrocities that they had witnessed.

All of this put an end to any delusions about the fate of the ghetto dwellers.

In the meantime, another person was added to our family. My brother, who was traveling with a brigade in the region, met some Jewish men, one of them being my wife's father. He was brought into the ghetto with the assistance of Yudka Zopovich. We remained the only fortunate family who found the father of the children, after he had already been mourned. He was found – only to be later lost again – either in Auschwitz or in Dachau.

Life in the Shadow of Death

We slowly got used to living with the fear of death, but one must eat. One of the young girls, Yudit Berko, today my wife and then a 15 year old girl, was small and thin. Starving, she wandered near the fence like a bird in a cage. He young mind was not able to grasp what was taking place here; why on the other side of the fence there is everything – life, bread, song, and on this side of the fence – only hunger, torture and death… Like a bird in a cage, she attempted to stick her head through the wires of the fence. This is how it went. After her head – her thin body. The aroma of fresh bread from a nearby house attracted her like a magnet. She ignored the danger (we already endangered ourselves in order to eat at least once a week…) She opened the door and to her great surprise she received enough food for satiation, as much pork and bread as she could eat.

After she ate to satiation, she requested some food for her brothers, mother, and the newborn. Laden with bread, potatoes, onions, legumes, flour, and even milk for the mother who gave birth, she succeeded in returning to the ghetto. There was joy in the house. An angel from heaven… From then, she took with her whatever she could – socks, cloaks, shoes, and returned with bread and flour. Thus did she sustain the family. When she saw that the girl had succeeded, bold Aunt Gittel did likewise. She removed her patch and went to the marketplace as a farmer woman. She purchased whatever provisions she could find and smuggled them through the gate into the ghetto. We waited with pounding hearts. We gave her a sign when the guard moved aside from the corner of the gate where the barbed wire was cut and connected in a temporary fashion. Others did likewise and provisions, money and cigarettes began to flow into the ghetto.

There were even rolls. When a German appeared – everything disappeared as if it never was.

[Page 197]

Organized Resistance

We were already active in a circle of Communists: Eliusha Shmuelov, Ronit Rosenthal, Mirka Lan, Eidka Pilovnik, and Leizer Silber. The young writer Chaim Yellin had his own circle. Christians were in contact with the circles, and a united resistance front was formed. We found common language with Yudka Zopovich and his group consisting of Ika Greenberg and Moshe Levin. The latter was the head of the Jewish police in the ghetto. We nicknamed him Levin the Yellow. He and Yudka Zopovich utilized their role in the police and greatly assisted the groups of activists to unite them all – Zionists, Communists, Bundist, and ordinary Jews into an underground organization with the aim of battling the enemy.

The ghetto was overtaken by despair. Its dwellers cursed their lack of means and weapons. Hungry and worn out from hard work, fear, and worry about their relatives – they looked with respect upon those who, in their opinion, belonged to the partisan movement. They even wove tales about deeds of bravery. They assisted any emissary who broke from the ranks and intermixed with the Aryans on the sidewalk. They would hide such a person from the eyes of the German guards, and receive him with honor when he returned, as if he had the power to bring the redemption… Such emissaries came willingly. One would fail and ten others would come to present themselves for a mission fraught with danger.

Miriam Lan with members of the Anti-Fascist Organization in the Kovno Ghetto, from the History of the Underground by Tzvi Braun and Dov Levin

Such people included the following young women: the curly haired Shulamit Lerner, Rivka Uriash, Sania Goldshmidt, Maniek Holtzberg, Sara Katz, Eidka Pilovnik, Ronit Rosenthal and many others, who gave their lives in the efforts to obtain weapons and in conducting other missions…

Yankel Levi grew a moustache, and had the facial appearance of a typical Lithuanian. Rivka Uriash walked proudly in the free streets with her blond hair, and German captains attempted to engage her in conversation. At a critical moment, when she was in danger of being identified by a Lithuanian who knew her previously, she took hold of the arm of a German captain, and the Lithuanian did not dare approach.

Chaim Yellin became the driving force of the movement. Dima Galperin took the helm with deliberation and caution. Others performed their respective roles. A weekly hand-written bulletin was published, which passed on from hand to hand news from the front, collected in underground fashion. Discussions were conducted in secret places. Interesting lectures and evaluations were even heard from Dr. Walsnak. The organization set as its goal to support the masses – so that they should not lose the power of resistance, and that every quarter should dig for itself a well-camouflaged bunker. They assisted as much as possible anyone who dug a bunker. They transgressed the German commands. They set up a school for children. The teacher Rosenthal served as principal, even though the death penalty was in store for her because of this. Children sat on crates with rags. When a German inspection took place, the crates were overturned, as if the children were mending worn out clothes.

The Ghetto Police Assist

All of this was done with the knowledge of the chief of police and his assistant Yudka Zopovich. In contrast with other ghettos, the Jewish police in the Kovno ghetto placed itself, to the extent possible, at the disposal and service of the organization in the battle against the German murderers.

Hershel Levin of Jonava, a member of the Judenrat, also assisted the organization. At first we did not trust him, for he was freed from a Soviet prison by the Germans. However, later on he showed himself to be a dedicated activist in the ghetto underground, and added his blessings to the youth who went out to the forests: "Go and take revenge for our blood – an eye for an eye!"

Levin the Yellow and Yudka Zopovich would come to the gate when a group such as this was about to leave. There was a case where at a tense moment, S.S. investigators appeared. There were those who refused to disband. This would have left the driver, who had come with a forged passport, abandoned. Levin the Yellow hinted to Yudka Zopovich, who stated that everything was in order in the ghetto and that a brigade was waiting to drive into the forest to prepare firewood for the Wehrmacht… When they received permission, Moshe Levin, assisted by Yankel Werbovsky, began to urge on those going out, and with his own hands helped pack the sacks onto the truck. In the sacks there were guns, grenades and bullets.

The Germans apparently sensed that Jews were wandering about in the city. They set a reward for anyone who turned in a Jew – a kilogram of butter, a kilogram of sugar, and 500 marks. A hunt for Jews began. Even children began to follow after Jews. There were many victims from this hunt.

Eliusha Shmuelov was caught, tortured and shot at the Ninth Fort. However, we continued to seek contact with the activists in the city who opposed the Germans. The conditions for obtaining weapons and hiding them were easier in the city than in the ghetto. In the ghetto, the Germans found new means on a daily basis to torture the Jews, so that they would have no time to occupy themselves with anything other than searching for a morsel of bread. We had underground bunkers which were dug at night, and even a library and some weapons. We trained in those bunkers.

One morning that quarter was cut off and given over to the gentiles. We lost everything that we had toiled for. With that, the plans for defending the ghetto went down the drain, for what was left of the ghetto was indefensible. Every road was isolated, easy to seal off and ignite with fire. Nevertheless, we once again began to dig bunkers and underground conduits to use in the event of the liquidation of the ghetto. The ground was sandy, and everything was covered in sand.

Then an emissary from Moscow came to us as if from heaven. Her name was Alvina, a Jewish girl, and her real name was Gisa Glazer. She brought with her greetings from the free world that was at war. Her words encouraged us. From her mouth we learned that Leib Slomin, the son of the furniture manufacturer from Jonava Chaim Slomin, was located in the region of Jonava, and was organizing the farmers to battle against the occupation. We also found out that Zimans, the teacher of the Shalom Aleichem Gymnasium, is called Jurgis and stands at the head of the partisans in southern Lithuania in the region of Vilna, that the Jonaver Mendka Grun was shot to death when he parachuted out of an airplane in the region of Vilna, and that Avraham Yitzhak Mashkop the husband of the Jonaver Saraka Shapira, formerly the secretary of the Communist Party of Lithuania, perished near Ponovich (Panevĕþys).

The Departure from the Ghetto

We received orders to organize an exodus from the ghetto to the forests of Augustava. This seemed strange to me: without weapons, starving and wandering about an enemy area, where armed Shaulists swarm about everywhere – to walk for 300 kilometers! However Alvina was positive that there was a base with weapons and with experienced Soviet officials. Thus was she promised in Moscow. She believed them blindly. Later she committed suicide in Vilna by a bullet when the Germans exposed her with the help of a provocateur.

The situation in the ghetto was unbearable. The aktions continued. There was almost no possibility for any resistance. The Germans no longer trusted the Jewish police. They conducted the aktions themselves and also captured members of the organization. The leadership of the organization was therefore forced with a heavy heart to accept the plan. One hundred youths left the ghetto in the direction of Agustava. Of them, only two reached their destination: Nechemia Andlin and Shmuel Martkowsky, a refugee from Poland who studied in Jonava in the Yeshiva of Mendel Deutsch and later in Slobodka. After they roamed about the area for three days, they returned to the ghetto empty-handed… There was no base, no Soviets, no weapons. All the rest of those who went out were caught in groups by the Germans and imprisoned in the Ninth Fort for undertaking a special mission. They even succeeded in escaping from there, as we will see later.

After the failure with Augustava, Mirka Lan went to Slomin in the region of Jonava, and Chaim Yellin went to Zimans in the region of Vilna in order to obtain their agreement to accept partisans from Kovno in their ranks. Mirka Lan did not return. Chaim Yellin returned with the directive that every Jewish partisan must bring weapons with him – and not only for himself. This restricted the possibilities of sending out more groups to the forest. The Germans organized armed gangs of Lithuanians who guarded the routes that led to the forests. The organization found the means. With the assistance of a Lithuanian driver who worked for the German police, Jewish fighters, headed by Chaim Yellin, donned S.S. uniforms. In this way, groups of fighters were smuggled into the forests of Raudeniškiai. Among them was the Jonaver agronomist, my friend Chona Kagan, who testified about himself: "When you go out with a gun, your stature straightens". Even though he was able to tell about open anti-Semitism there as well, he was proud that he was able to take revenge on the murderers. These "brave souls" would flee for their lives without their pants when they heard the word "partisans"…

Jews in the ghetto collected these stories which were passed from mouth to ear with additions. They were proud of the deeds of their sons and daughters who smote Germans and Lithuanians. They even forgot that they were starving. The activists of the organization continued to arm groups of partisans with weapons. Chaim Yellin, the courageous leader of the organization, accompanied the fighters into the forest until he fell into the hands of the enemy.

Mass Escape from the Ninth Fort

After their defeat near Stalingrad, the Germans began to conceal the traces of their crimes. They opened up the mass graves, removed the bodies and burned them. The ashes were scattered on the fields by a special machine and mixed with the earth. All of this was done secretly. Jews of the ghetto, members of the organization who were captured on the way to Augustova, were occupied in this task, as were Jewish prisoners of war from the Soviet Army. It was clear to them what awaited them at the end of this job. The Germans were so certain of their victims that they did not even attempt to conceal this from them. When someone got sick, he was shot on the spot and burnt.

A group of youths from the organization did not lose their spirit, and planned an escape. We must bow our heads before this sublime courage and fortitude of these people who were sentenced to death. Through their own efforts, without any assistance, they organized, planed, prepared and successfully conducted a mass escape from the Ninth Fort, which was fenced in, well guarded, protected by natural obstacles, and in which 80,000 people had been murdered – mostly Jews from Kovno and its surrounding areas, as well as Jews from other lands. Some of the escapees infiltrated into the ghetto, and we hid them until they were sent to the forest in a truck as a brigade of workers going out to work in the provincial towns.

The Gestapo men flew into a rage. They surrounded the ghetto. The commander Kietel threatened to liquidate the ghetto if the escapees were not turned over to him. Even though the heads of the police knew everything, they denied everything vehemently. The Gestapo men were now doubly perplexed. Their secret will be exposed in public, and if they acknowledge that the escapees infiltrated the ghetto – it means that the ghetto was not guarded properly. Kietel did not follow through with his threat, but he later took revenge on the police. He shot Levin the Yellow in front of everyone. Other policemen, including the Zopovich brothers, were dragged to the Ninth Fort. There they were tortured harshly in order to force them to give over the locations of the bunkers where they hid the partisans, children and elderly. A member of the organization, Itzik Weiner, whom the Germans returned to the ghetto along with other policemen, told that once, after an inquisition, Yudka Zopovich was sent to a casemate with his ears cut off. While he was dripping blood he made everyone swear that nobody would dare give over anything about the ghetto fighters and the children even if he must pay with his life – and he ended his life with the singing of Hatikva. His brother Meir died along with him. There were those weak-hearted policemen who gave over the locations of the bunkers in which the children were hidden. These poor children were dragged to the Ninth Fort and murdered.

The Blackest Day of the Ghetto

That day is etched in the memory as the blackest day in the annals of the ghetto. The wild Ukrainian murderers, drunken with blood and liquor, were going from house to house armed with axes, hoes and other instruments of destruction, dragging the children who were looking with pleading eyes at the adults to save them, while the trained dogs attacked and gashed the desperate mothers who did not want to give over their children. There were buses with sealed windows from which burst forth the joyous tunes of Strauss and Wagner in order to muffle the screams of the young, guiltless victims who were leaving the ghetto on their final journey from which they would not return…

Our block was next to the fence. We were cut off from the center in an unexpected way, and we were unable to transfer the children to the bunkers that we had prepared for them. Since the murderers began their activities on the other side, we utilized the time to prepare improvised bunkers for the children and elderly. We dug a pit beneath the oven. The sandy ground was liable to cave in. We placed supports inside and removed the sand, so that no trace would remain. We did all of this in daylight. The German sentry who stood on the other side of the fence saw all of this, nodded his head, and did not turn us in. Perhaps he thought about his own children during those moments…

The fateful moment came to us as well. A mother who did not succeed in hiding her three year old child covered him in a rag and hung him on the wall as if this was a package. The German captain, for entertainment or as a test, whipped the package with a whip, and no scream was heard. When the "fortunate" mother took down the package after the murderers left, she saw a blue stripe immersed with blood along the length of the tender body of the child.

Two Germans and a Ukrainian with a hoe and a large dog entered our room. The dog could not tolerate the pungent smell of the material that we had spread on the floor, and he left. The German who was holding him on a leash followed after him. The Ukrainian attempted to open up the floor with the hoe that was in his hands. He apparently sensed the danger when he saw our metallic faces. I had a loaded pistol in my pocket, and I was determined not to give our child over cheaply. The Ukrainian also left. The second German continued to search for something, and he left. When the murderers were some distance away, we heard the stifled cry of our two year old child.

The Ghetto was effectively liquidated. Concentration camp guards were all over. It was clear to us that it was no longer possible to hide the children. A miracle does not occur twice. The organization set as its goal the saving the children that were still alive. They would be given to Germans. They were put to sleep and taken out to the fence, covered up as packages, when it was possible to do so. My wife succeeded in taking our child. She left him next to a monastery. A nun took the basket with the sleeping child and disappeared into the monastery.

The Gestapo set as its goal the breaking of all Jewish resistance. With the assistance of provocateurs, they succeeded in exposing the brave ghetto fighter, the young writer

Chaim Yellin. The organization suffered defeats. The best of its sons and daughters perished. Among them was my refined and noble life partner, who was connected with the ghetto underground – Sania Goldschmidt-Berko, as well as the weapon procurer Sara Katz.

Nobility in the Concentration Camp

We saw that the Germans were beginning to retreat. The front was approaching. We heard the echoes of gunfire. The ghetto was guarded zealously. It was impossible to establish contact with the outside. Most of our weapons were hidden in the city, and we had no possibility of defending ourselves. We attempted to hide in bunkers. The Germans bombarded the ghetto and ignited all of the ruins. We were hauled on closed wagons to "cultured" Germany, filled with concentration camps surrounded by barbed wire fences – to further suffering, backbreaking work, hunger, cold, epidemics and lice.

There too the battle for life continued. In the frightful conditions of the camp, where one person was prepared to snatch a piece of bread from his fellow, where the Germans brought their victims to the point of animalistic foraging, our Jonava friend Gershka Reibstein, the son of Baruch the butcher displayed exemplary nobility. On account of his trade, butchering, he was employed in the German army kitchen. There, he had opportunity to steal preserved food. He endangered his life, both in the place of stealing as well as in the camp inspections. Five women were indeed hanged for onions that were taken from the field and discovered during the camp inspections – what would have been in store for a loaf of bread made out of coarse flower and preserved food bearing the seal of the army? What he stole was not for himself, and not even for sale, but in order to sustain his friends. There was always a lineup of hungry people next to his hut – as perhaps Gershka might bring something… and his heart was anguished when he did not succeed in bringing something to distribute.

My shoes ripped, which in the camp meant certain death. The simplest cold could result in pneumonia and the crematorium… Gershka Reibstein stole cigarettes even though he did not smoke. He exchanged them with a German for a pair of wooden shoes and brought them to me: "Here they are, try them on to see that they do not pinch". We shared food. Thanks to Gershka, all of the members of the collective survived and did not lose their human form. We did not always assuage our hunger. How happy he was that I found my son, even though he did not find his family and children. He found out that his younger brother Izak fell at the front, and that his brother's wife and son remained in Russia. He gathered them, and traveled to the United States with them.

On the Ruins of Jonava

Here I am standing next to the Peleg, listening to the whisper of its cold waters. The echoes of the laughter of Jewish children on Sabbath afternoon walks are no longer heard. The Peleg streams along, as if its waters are whispering "Kel Malei Rachamim"[4]. The old watermill is falling over – slumbering as if under the curse of a sorcerer. Its large wooden wheel is rotting. The pipes are covered with spider webs. Mice run about undisturbed, staring with amazement at the strange visitor, as if to ask: "How did you get here? You should be in the World of Truth[5], like our miller Veps, like all the Jews…"

In the destroyed cemetery: Lipa Berzin, Chaim Aron, Chana Berzin

Here in the cemetery, denuded of its awe and respect – without the stone fence that separated between the living and the dead, without trees, without guarantors… The stones were destroyed and uprooted. Naked as a shorn sheep, as Jewish women in the camp… Only the grave of Rabbi Silman of blessed memory with its canopy still stands. And in a place of honor – an almost fresh grave. A simple board upon which is written with a chemical pencil: Here is buried the modest women Feiga Pogir.

She lived quietly, and died quietly… A quiet funeral – the final funeral… She was escorted to the grave by Uncle Eliahu and Aunt Freidl, whom fate had brought from Gorky to visit mother. They did not succeed in returning and their fate was like the fate of all the Jews of Jonava.

Bitter Worlds over Grandmother's Grave

Do you recall, dear Grandmother, how much you enjoyed going with my mother to a performance in the fire hall? There, they would usher you with great honor to the front bench. Dressed with the black shawls of Rosh Hashanah, you would cross the hall as if going to a Torah honor. You would be slightly embarrassed as they would stare at you and say: "Here are the mother and grandmother of the principal actor"…

Do you remember that you could not sleep after the play? You waited for me until late in the night in order to verify that indeed it was your grandmother who moved you to tears. You participated in his suffering and joy. You further told how your son Yisrael played King Solomon. Sarl Pogirsky herself came to your house and brought a present to the wise "king" for his wise decision.

Do you recall how you protected me from the anger of Father's belt – when I did not go to services, when I went on the Sabbath to a basketball game, and for other "sins" that were punishable by "lashes"[6]… You did not permit him to hurt the child, even though he sinned in some manner…

Do you remember how happy your heart was when a package arrived from America, and some of the clothes were appropriate for one of the children of my mother Sara? And the debates with Grandfather about important matters? Even though you did not know a great deal, you took it upon yourself to put Grandfather, the "philosopher from Ragožiai" in his place, and to debate with him with contrary arguments. Grandfather mocked your children and their Communist friends who worry about the entire world and do not wish to work for or worry about themselves, so how could they worry about others?... He further claimed that he saw Smetona[7] and not a president: "Why does he put them in jail and feed them for free? – He should gather them up, take them to the Russian border, and send them to taste the taste of Communism. Then they will come knocking at the doors and kiss the boots, asking to be permitted to enter again…"

You would claim on the contrary, how is it that Smetona is so good, and how could it be that the son of Chaim Kopiner is worse than him. Grandfather would answer: "Smetona gives bread and meat, and the son of Chaim Kopiner as well as Yankele Magid will give convulsions and not bread." You countered him that it was not Smetona who gives bread, but rather the farmer. He did not remain challenged, and answered with a wise smile: "Animal such as you! Indeed the farmer gives bread, but for Smetona he is prepared to plough the land with his nose and give bread, and Yankele Magid the "Zhid" would say – go plough yourself…" It was as if he was a prophet…

Do you remember how he used to curse the needle that it did not hasten to take in the thread, or when the thimble disappeared? On the other hand you saw him beaming with contentment when we went with him to Ragožiai, where every farmer recognized him and asked for his advice. As a true farmer, grandfather took a handful of earth, scattered it with his hands, and thereby determined whether or not the time for planting had arrived. As a true farmer he did not like lazy people – which were rabbis, Yeshiva students, and Communists.

And you, Grandmother, lectured mother that she was spoiling us by giving us the fresh cakes of Aunt Chaya every morning, even though she gave them to Mother at or below cost price. Indeed, you were correct, we swallowed the rolls and the cakes, but the bread which you baked we ate all week and broke our teeth. Nevertheless, it was good: the black bread that you baked for us – each of us had a loaf in accordance with our size – its taste for us was sweeter and better than a cake…

And the kvass[8] that you made from dry breadcrumbs or rotten apples – nothing went to waste. You were generous. To you, everyone was a "child of G-d". You cared about everyone. Even Friedka the Crazy found a place with you next to the oven to warm up, and a plate of soup with other food was always waiting for her. When the members of the household were not happy about this, you said: "What can be done? When everyone chases her away I have to take her in, as mercy on a human being". In the home, you were from "the House of Hillel"[9]. You related to everyone with trust and love.

On Sabbath eves, everything was prepared to greet the Sabbath Queen. The copper candlesticks were on the table next to the braided challas on the white tablecloth. They had been polished with ashes and lime, and were sparkling. The smell of gefilte fish, tzimmes and other Sabbath delicacies filled our whitewashed, low-ceilinged house. On the floor was sawdust that had been brought from "Madis" sawmill, spread out like a soft carpet. Everything was prepared by the diligent hands of your daughter Sarale, my mother, with Jewish expertise, like a true woman of valor, having inherited this from you… Covered with your Sabbath shawl, you would approach the chest of drawers, take out from the knot of your apron the coins that you had saved, and tarry by the charity box with awe, as if you were deliberating about to whom to give first – the Yeshiva of Ponovitch, the Yeshiva of Telz, or perhaps to Meir Baal Haness[10] – until you decided and put a 10 cent coin into each box with awe. The blue and white box of the Keren Kayemet with the Star of David and the map of the Land of Israel was closer to your heart than all of them, for this reminded you of our Matriarch Rachel who never ceased to weep for her children who were exiled and scattered across all the lands of the earth. We children were touched to our hearts that she did not cease weeping, and at times we forewent an ice cream and put a coin into the box. At the time of the blessing over the candles, you supplicated in the name of the patriarchs to Mother Rachel, as if you were speaking to Perl the shoemaker, Rosia the miller, or Sara-Leah the hat maker in simple Yiddish. Was it possible that Mother Rachel did not understand Yiddish…

You begged her to intercede for your grandchild, my brother Shlomoke, the pure lamb, who separated from the flock and went to her to the Holy Land, to its desolation, to dig up rocks and thorns – that she should protect him from snakes, scorpions, fever and the wild Arabs… And for your eldest daughter, my sister Malka, the pride of the family, who did not even have a wedding dowry, and for Eska, the pure dove as she was called in the family, and for Avrahamele, Hirshka, Itzele, Beilinka, Gitale, and Meirka of Uncle Elia, who was not so expert in his studies, but was expert at skating and basketball.

… And for your sons Yoel and Yisrael who wandered to far-off America, and for your son Itzik the "laggard" as he was nicknamed by the tailors, who was tall and of erect posture even though he was a blacksmith. This Itzik went to Birobidzhan, and from him there was not even a "dipped pen"[11]. However, "evil talk" spread that all of the Jonavers in Birobidzhan were put in jail. However, this did not make sense to you. Your Itzik is himself "righteous". You remembered how hard he worked to bring to your house a new pot, a potato peeler, and new dishes for the weekdays and the Sabbath. You were loath to use them, for they were as beautiful as your Passover dishes, which were stored all year in boxes in the closet, and only decorated the "royal" table on Passover. He brought you a new clock which adorned the chest of drawers. There was Uncle Shmuele the "joker", always in a good mood, who would laugh and bring laughter to everyone, even grandfather. The poor guy fell into a trap, married an evil woman and was forced to get divorced. This was the only bad incident in your extended family.

You also asked Mother Rachel to intercede for your daughter Friedka. You talked about her as if about an extraordinary beauty. She remained in Russia after the revolution, and was not short on tribulations.

And for your young daughters Esther and Rivka, who took it upon themselves to overturn the world and bring justice; whereas in the interim they spent some time in jails… And nevertheless – in your heart you agreed with them. Why not? G-d created his world with everyone equal – therefore why are there rich and poor? Indeed you helped them to hide illegal books and a flag even though you did not understand the benefits; however if your wise daughters were doing this, apparently this is the way it should be…

And later, in the year that was like a great festival for the Jews, the year before the outbreak of the war, in which every day passed with music and joy – you begged them quietly, and also my mother – that the joy should not cease…

It is difficult, so difficult to believe that all of this suddenly was lost, as if it was cut by a knife…

You believed like my parents and those of others with children with red ties and red membership cards of the Comsomol or the party, as if from above they knew how to redeem us from the murderous neighbor who already ruled over half of Europe – and the outcry of the Jews reached all the way to Jonava…

Even householders, storekeepers and merchants recited their verse after the nationalization: "Better Stalin with the key than Hitler with the head".

During the early days of the war, you looked at me as if begging for protection from the long barreled guns that I received from Mirka Lan.

No, dear Grandmother, I was not even able to protect myself. The gun had no bullets… And you, my grandmother, merited to die in your bed, in our home – and you have the last grave in the cemetery. You were the last one who merited attaining a Jewish burial – something that the six million Jews of Europe did not have. Rest in peace and calm, just as you were calm in your life.

[Page 204]

A Hymn of Jewish Faith
by Noach Stern

Translated by Jerrold Landau

What is needed to oppress the Jewish soul?
Hunger and Want? Life in fetters?
    (Within the barbed wire of the ghettos, with the last of the bodily strength
    Singing sublimely, the weakened body sings.)

What is needed to subdue the Hebrew pride –
Curses, spittle that is not cleaned up?
    (Even when the leaders are bent over from weakness and torment
    As a flame surrounds them, inside there is the bush of redemption[12])

What is needed to quiet and silence Jews?
False libels, mass death and destructions?
    (The Jew is not shaken even in the pyres of fire,
    As he awaits the end and concludes with "Echad"[13])

What is needed to cut Jews off from their homeland?
The distance and the wandering imprisonment of the exile?
    (Indeed, from the depths of the netherworld, in every generation,
    The living Hebrew never ceases to return.)

What is needed, to break apart and destroy Jews?
Inhuman torments, constant madness?
    (In the infernos of the world, rebellious fires burn,
    Ignited by partisans, and a storm spun.)

What is needed, what is needed to silence a Jew?
To make a Jew shrivel up, and to strangle him?
    The Hell of the German Amalek? The intrigues
    Of rulers clad in long coats, and sighs?

No, no, no, the Jew will not shrivel up and be cutoff!
He will not forget his essence, the Jew will not flee!
    Even in the pit of corpses, in the last filtering
    Of dust and air in the clods of the vault.[14]

The ground will bend, and the sand will strain
As anger and hope gesture from the grave
    And say to the enemy, who stares and shudders:
    –This is not the end!

Remember – this is not the end!

                (5706 / 1946)

Translator's Footnotes

The Shaulists were a Lithuanian squad that collaborated with the Germans. See http://en.wikipedia.org/wiki/Ypatingasis_bûrys. The term comes from the Lithuanian word for riflemen.

It was common in Eastern Europe to nickname people by the names of their mother, using the possessive. This would mean Itzik the son of Liba Leah.

"To differentiate" (Hebrew – Lehavdil) is an expression used to point out irony when juxtaposing two radically different thoughts. Here it is used ironically. It is also often used in a religious sense to separate a holy thought from a profane thought in the same sentence.

The prayer for the dead.

A traditional euphemism for the afterworld.

The term for lashes here, "malkut" is the same term used for the Biblical punishment of flagellation for transgressing various sins.

Antanas Smetona was the president of pre-war Lithuania. See http://www.president.lt/institution/istorija/1.

A fermented bread drink. See http://en.wikipedia.org/wiki/Kvass.

The House of Hillel (Hillel being a Talmudic sage) was known to be very accepting of everyone, whereas the House of Shammai was more strict and restrictive.

A charity for poor Torah scholars in the Land of Israel.

I assume that this means that he rarely, if ever, wrote letters.

A reference to the burning bush of Moses (the Sneh).

The last word of the first line of the Shema prayer – a reference to the recital of Shema at the moment of martyrdom.

A reference either to the grave, or to the gas chambers or mass burial graves of the Nazis.

[Page 206]

What I Endured – A Little of the Large Amount…

by Ala Abromovich–Dalitsisky

Translated by Jerrold Landau

The Second World War came as a most harsh, heavy blow to the Jews of Lithuania, including the Jews of my hometown of Jonava.

In the Hospital

I was in Kovno, in the Jewish Bikur Cholim Hospital, when the war overtook me. I was then a young woman, married to Tzvi Yafa of blessed memory, the son of the Yanova bookbinder, and in my fifth month of pregnancy. I entered the hospital on May 25, 1941 due to the kidney disease that afflicted me as a result of my pregnancy. I was cared for in the woman's clinic of Dr. Levitan, who was known throughout Lithuania, and my situation improved. My husband, family members, parents, brothers and sisters visited me often, and we were happy that my situation had improved and I would be able to return home in a week or two.

Before the outbreak of war, my mother came and decided to stay with her brother Chaim Levin for a few days and wait for me to take me home.

Early in the morning of June 22, 1941, we heard a fierce bombardment that shook the walls of the hospital. We did not know what this was about. Later, we found out that the Germans had bombed the Kovno airport and they were advancing to us without any opposition from the Russian Army that had conquered us in 1940. The Germans were already in Kovno by the afternoon. My mother came to me with great fear in her eyes and told me, "My daughter, the war has started. Woe to us and all the Jews. Who knows if we will ever see our family."

In the evening, I already heard that the Germans were speaking German with the nurses and doctors and commanding them to send the patients home quickly, for they themselves would need the hospital. A great commotion arose, and fear and depression overtook the Jewish patients. The hospitalized residents of Kovno did not even wait for their clothes to be brought to them from the wardrobe. They escaped home in their pajamas and clothes that their family had brought – some went on foot, some by vehicle, and some by stretcher. Their only wish was to be together with their family at this terrible time. Despite the fact that the hospital was owned by a Jewish institution, Russians and Lithuanians were also hospitalized there. Most of the staff of doctors and nurses were Jewish, and the helpers were mainly gentile women. They began to tell slander to the Germans and point by finger to any patient, doctor or nurse who was Jewish. The Jewish doctors and nurses disappeared from the hospital one after the other. Many were shot to death in the hospital yard. Many seriously ill people who could not leave on their own accord were also shot. The situation grew more serious from day to day. Only four of us patients, who could not leave on our own accord, were left: two older men and an older woman, all from various towns of Lithuania, and I – a young, weak, pale woman with my baby inside me, whom I could no longer hide. They transferred us to a small room so that we could be together – rather than to be with the gentiles. They barely brought us any food. The two older men died one after the other. Only the two unfortunate women remained. The Germans issued new orders each morning, which they posted in the lobby: a) it was forbidden for Jews to use any type of vehicle; b) it was forbidden for Jews to walk on the sidewalk. Instead, they must walk at the edges of the road; c) a yellow Star of David patch must be sewn on the chest of the outer garment, as well as firmly affixed onto the back. There were many other such decrees.

My mother would come daily from the back side of the building, where the morgue was located, and I would talk to her from the second floor. My heart died inside of me anew whenever I saw her distraught and weeping for her four children, grandchildren, and husband who remained in Yanova. I was the only one of her loved ones who remained, and I was in such a difficult situation. At that time, Mother lived next to the hospital with a family of Yanova natives who settled in Kovno after they had fled and left everything behind in Yanova. The proximity to the hospital made it possible for Mother to come to see me frequently. She would come to me when she saw that everything around her was quiet. The woman who was with me in the room was from the town of Šėta, not far from Jonava. She wept day and night over her children that were lost to her. One evening she began to laugh and speak things that did not make sense. She told me "My children are waiting for me outside. I am going to them." She suddenly got up, left the room, and disappeared. She never returned. I remained alone enveloped in fear, and was afraid to sleep at night.

[Page 207]

At that time, a Lithuanian woman, about 35 years old, who had worked together with Jewish physicians before the outbreak of the war and forged many friendly relations with them, was appointed as director of the hospital. One day, she entered my room, sat on my bed, and asked me from where I was, and whether I have family. I told her with weeping and tears that I want to go home to my family and my city of Yanova, and that I cannot continue to live alone there in the room. I asked her to permit me to leave the hospital. To my great surprise she took my hand, caressed it and told me, "You do not know anything, but I know that you no longer have anywhere to go. The Jews escaped from Yanova. Most of them were shot and killed. I have an uncle who lives not far from Yanova, and he told me about all the atrocities that overtook the Jews of Yanova. You are not fit to go. They will shoot you as soon as you leave here. I want you to give birth to your baby here under my protection, and then you will go to the ghetto that is being built for you in the nearby city of Viliampolė (Slobodka)."

I saw tears in her eyes. I put my head on her lap and wept. I realized from her words that my family is no longer in the city, and that my town that I had loved so much was destroyed. I have no house, no husband, no family. The only ones left were my Mother, the baby inside me, and I. How can I overcome everything? I cursed the day of my birth[1]. I cursed my life. I was overtaken by a longing to run to Yanova to see everything with my own eyes, for I was unable to believe what I had heard from the physician. At that time, the physician transferred me to a small room next to the bathroom (previously, it held the dirty laundry). The room had a window and a bed for me. The physician ordered me not to leave the room, so that they would not see me. A nurse who could be trusted would bring me food. I sat myself on the bed, looking out the window at the lovely landscape and the shining sun for days on end – but these were not for me! I would only go out to attend to my bodily needs when nobody would see me. The physician would visit me and bring me medicine. The nurse would leave me food for two or three days, for she worked in shifts. There were no other Jews in the hospital, and nobody saw or knew about me. The mice in the room did not allow me to sleep at night. I would sit at night afraid to fall asleep. Mother would come secretly in the morning to see me. This was the sum total of my life.

In the Ghetto

The physician director came to me on August 13 and told me that she could no longer hold me in the hospital. She added, "The Germans prepared a ghetto for you Jews, and all the Jews must be in the ghetto by August 15. Anyone who is found outside the ghetto will be shot to death." She gave me a letter of confirmation that I was on my way from the hospital to ghetto, so that nobody would hurt me. "Perhaps you will have good luck to arrive in the ghetto on foot," she told me and blessed me. I kissed her hand and said, "I will never forget you, for you were an angel for me. My entire life was in your hands."

I left the hospital, where I had been for almost three months. Mother was waiting for me outside. I was wearing a long, flowered robe that the physician had brought me, as well as men's size 42 shoes. I had no longer had any clothes in the hospital for a long time. We went along the route to the ghetto. We saw masses of Jews dragging bedding and household utensils. All were hurrying to the ghetto to get a dwelling. I walked with difficulty, for my legs were heavy from lying down so much. To our good fortune, nothing bad happened to us along the way. We entered the ghetto through an electrified barbed wire gate that was guarded by two Germans and Lithuanians who were armed. We made our way with heavy hearts. Where should we go? We were hungry, tired, dirty, penniless, without clothing, without food, and without a head of a family to worry about us. Who needs us at all? Finally, we went to my cousin, Chana, the eldest daughter of Shlomo the *shochet* of Jonava. She was married to Yaakov Shlomins of Plungė, who used to be a driver for the Kemach factory in Yanova. They had two children, a four year old boy and a five week old girl. She lived almost next to the gate on 4 Linkuvos Street in a small room that was formerly a kitchen. Her two brothers Leibel and David lived with her, and now my mother and I had come. There was not even any place to sit. She had an unparalleled good heart. She greeted us and said, "We will live together. What will be with us will also be with you." We slept on the floor in our clothes, without a blanket or pillow. Her husband Yaakov and her brothers would go out to work, and would bring a hundred grams of bread and thin soup, and at times other items that they purchased from their Lithuanian co–workers. From this, they would give my mother and me a small piece of bread and a cup of soup. I grew weaker from day to day. I could not stand on my feet. I lay down all day and waited to fall asleep and never wake up again. My mother would go out to the fields to find cabbage leaves or rotten carrots that were left behind by the Lithuanians after they left the suburb of Slobodka to go live in the fine houses of the Jews of Kovno, who had left their houses to go to the ghetto. It was inhuman for eight people to live in such a small room. The filth, lice, and lack of food began to affect us. We were in the yard for the entire day, and one could choke in the room at night due to lack of air.

[Page 208]

My mother went to the ghetto committee, where Jews sat and directed the life in the ghetto: dwellings, work, medical help, and deaths. There were all sorts of offices in this large home with many rooms. Of course, everything was conducted under the supervision of the Germans. Mother met a native of our town, who was a ghetto policeman, Meir Zopovich. He went with her to the dwelling office and helped her to obtain a dwelling on the same street, 25 Linkuvos. Meir went with us to that address and informed the owner that we would live there, and that he will not do anything bad to us. Meir did a great favor for us, for many serious incidents took place where the owner of the dwelling looked unfavorably on strangers who took a room from them. Despite the fact that our landlord was by nature a bad person, he was afraid of the presence of the policeman, and agreed. Meir Zopovich helped the landlord transfer our furniture to the other room, and we remained. We obtained a narrow bed and we were happy that we had our own place. After about a week, another six–person family came to us, and set up their beds without asking anything. There were now eight of us living in a small room. We became friends. They were quiet people – a couple, their three children, and an unmarried girl. We cooked outside, for the kitchen belonged to the landlord, and he did not allow us to enter. Mother brought the same leaves as usual. We cooked them in water. We were hungry all day. There was no place or no facilities to wash. The lice proliferated, and we found no solution to that. Hundreds of people died daily due to the unhygienic lifestyle and diseases that afflicted the ghetto, with no help available.

The Germans and Lithuanians would go through the streets daily to search for men for hard labor. Most of the Jews who went out to work, so to speak, did not return. They would take them directly to the fortress of the Ninth Fort and shoot them. The Germans knew that all types of communicable diseases, especially typhus, were liable to spread in the ghetto. In general, they were interested in liquidating excess people, for the crowding was great. The situation was terrible. We were allowed to be on the streets only until 7:00 p.m., and anyone transgressing this law would be shot on the spot. The windows were closed and covered with heavy cloth, so that no small ray of light would be seen. We thought that the light would give a sign to the enemy. New decrees were issued daily. People were taken out to be killed daily. Every morning, we heard the wild voices of the Germans who were breaking through the doors and snatching weak Jews for work. It was frightful and difficult to live. We were jealous of those the dead, who were hauled by the dozens to the cemetery in the ghetto by covered wagon hitched to thin, hungry horses.

Childbirth

There was a large building on Kriščiukaičio 101 with many rooms, in which people worked and studied for professions prior to the outbreak of the war. It was called "The Verkstatn". The Germans permitted this building to be turned into a hospital for the ghetto. They set up beds there, prepared a bit of medicine, and employed physicians. Most of them, who had worked in the Kovno hospital, were excellent doctors. They were headed by the well–known doctor, the surgeon Dr. Zachrin.

[Page 209]

Dr. Zachrin was one of the last to enter the ghetto, for the Germans used him for all sorts of complicated operations for which he was the only qualified person in Kovno. Dr. Zachrin helped greatly with operations, with receiving medicine from the Germans, and many other things. He directed the hospital, and was considered to be an important person in the ghetto.

The time for the birth approached, and I was afraid that it would take place at night, for it was forbidden to leave after 7:00 p.m., and the hospital was several kilometers away from us. My fear was not in vain, for my labor pains began at 10:30 p.m. I bit my lips until they bled. Mother stood next to me and wept. My neighbors had mercy upon me. We were not able to go out to summon a doctor, and how could we wait until morning? I wanted one thing: to die, and not to live, for I no longer thought about life, and death would certainly be my only redeemer. I told mother at 3:00 a.m., "We need to go to the hospital, or I will die of pain." I was afraid to scream, lest the Germans hear me. The neighbors said to me, "Ala, don't go, for the Germans will kill you on the way." However some strong force pulled me, a force that did not care, a force that impelled me to run specifically to death more quickly than to die of labor pains without medical assistance. I took Mother's hand and opened the door. The street was dark and quiet, like a cemetery. Suddenly, I sensed the strong ray of light from a flashlight lighting us out. I got scared and closed the door. However, I heard the voice of the German enemy, "Stop, come out immediately, or I will shoot." The neighbors in the room began to push me, "Go out immediately, we do not want to die because of you." I opened the door again, and we went out. We went in the direction of the gate, as German and Lithuanian guards with loaded guns approached us. The light of their flashlights fell upon us. When we stopped, the German asked me where I was going. I answered him, "To the hospital to give birth to a child." "Now?" he said, "Do you not know that it is forbidden for you to go on the street after 7:00 p.m." I responded, "Yes, I know, but I will die at home, and if I go out at night, I will also die: the second death will be quicker." He looked at me and asked, "Where is your husband?" I responded, "The Lithuanians killed him along with my entire family, and this woman is my mother." "Fine," he said, "go to your hospital to give birth. I will not do any harm to you. But along the way, you will certainly meet S.S. men or Lithuanians, and they will shoot you."

I thanked him greatly and we continued on the way. I was certain that a shot would be heard immediately and I would fall, but they turned around and walked toward the gate. We continued in the direction of the hospital. The way was long, with no road. The darkness was terrible, without any sign of human life. It was literally a city of ghosts. It seemed to us that we had already been walking for entire hours, but we still did not see the hospital gate. We stood every few minutes, for the pains did not permit me to walk. I thought that I would lose consciousness at any moment. Without Mother, I would certainly have fallen into the sand from the weakness that overtook me at all times. We stood next to a house, and I heard a child crying and the mother comforting it. I knocked slowly on the blind and said, "Good woman, tell me where the hospital is?" The woman began to curse me hysterically, "Go, you should die, who is coming in the middle of the night? You are crazy. I will not open for you." I begged again and again that she only tell me the direction, and she said, "Go about 100 more meters, and you will see a white wall with a white gate."

We continued with our last strength until we reached the white wall. We found the gate with difficulty and began to knock with all our might. The Jewish gatekeeper ran to the gate and spoke in German, "Immediately, immediately sirs, I will open." When he opened and saw us two women, he did not believe the sight of his eyes. Doctors and nurses gathered around us. They were all astonished that we had not met along the way any German or Lithuanian who swarm through the ghetto during the nights and shoot people for any small ray of light that can be seen in their windows. In my case, I went in peace from the road that has the gate through a long way. This was literally a wonder. It appeared that some supreme power had helped me. I told those gathered around, "Take me immediately to the birthing room." I recognized several doctors from Kovno who could not stop talking about the miracle that happened to me that night.

[Page 210]

After a short time, I gave birth to a daughter. This was on September 15. The baby was healthy, of full weight, and in good shape despite all the hell and hunger that I had endured during the past few months. I was happy that finally I was the mother of such a beautiful daughter, but from where would we get food for her once I left the hospital? I got an idea in my head. In the hospital, I received food and also a bit of milk. When I left after five days and came home, the bigger tribulations began, for I did not have anything to eat, or anything with which to nurse my daughter.

October came. It was cold and rainy outside. The rags that I called diapers, brought to me by my good neighbors to diaper my daughter, did not dry outside. I washed them without soap and lay upon them to sleep at night, so that my body would dry them. I called her Miriam, after my grandfather Manus, who had died a natural death. We ate the leaves, the leaves that Mother cooked with dirty well water. I swelled, and noticed that my little daughter was weakening, for we gave her as well the leaf–water with a bit of sugar. She would cry at night, and we had to carry her in our arms all night, so that the crying would not be heard outside and cause problems for our neighbors.

One morning, we saw through the window that many S.S. men with Lithuanians came to the ghetto and stood in the middle of our street, talking amongst themselves and scattering themselves out. There were many alleyways and roads on the other side of Linkuvos Street, and the crowding was very great. During the time that the men were at work, the S.S. surrounded all these alleys and sent out all the residents to Linkuvos Street. I stood next to the window with my daughter in my arms, and saw all this. Among them were several Yanova families who lived there. They also went out and stood in the street under the guard of the Lithuanians. I was surprised and asked, "Mother, where are they taking them?" At that moment, an armed Lithuanian noticed me. He ran to our house, banged on the shutter with his gun, and shouted, "Accursed you should be, frog, why are you looking, do you also want to go? – I will take you." I left the window in fear, and waited, trembling, for him to enter our house. He did not come, however, for the command was to take out all the residents on the other side of the street to death. They all went quietly without weeping, without screams – grandmothers, and mothers with their children. They were surrounded with S.S men and Lithuanians holding automatic rifles. Their steps receded, and the street became quiet again. We did not know where they had taken them. When the men returned from work in the evening, they did not find their wives and children. They sat down and tore out their hair. That night, we heard endless shots coming from the direction of the Ninth Fort killing station. They had brought all the victims there, and everything was clear and known…

The Death of Shlopochnik the Medic (Feldscher)

The residents of Yanova knew the Shlopochnik the medic (feldscher) very well. He had lived with his family on Vilna Street. He was our beloved doctor, for he healed us of all our illnesses. If a sick person had no money, he would also help.

During the latter years before the outbreak of the war, he moved to Kovno with his family. Mother and I met him in the ghetto. He was already bent and elderly, and he wept over his son who had been taken from the house by the Lithuanians, and had not yet returned.

He greeted us and began to cross the street. This was not far from the ghetto gate. Suddenly I noticed that a German said something to a Lithuanian and pointed out Shlopochnik. The Lithuanian lowered his gun and aimed it carefully. Suddenly, we heard a single shot, and Shlopochnik, who had not even noticed anything, fell dead, wallowing in his blood. The German began to shout and call, "Come, come, four Jews, and take your comrade!"

This is how the upright feldscher Shlopochnik died. He had healed sick people throughout his life. I was a witness to his death at the hands of the lowly murderers.

The Great *Aktion*

At the end of October 1941, the ghetto was in ferment. Notices were posted on all the tall buildings that everyone must come out to the ghetto square, called Demokratu Square at 5:00 a.m. All of the sick and elderly must be brought out along with the beds if they cannot walk on foot.

[Page 211]

Children and babies must also be brought, and the doors were to remain open, so that the Germans could check that nobody remained in the house. Anyone who transgressed this edict would be sentenced to death. This was signed by Oberscharführer Fritz Jordan.

We did not know the meaning of this, but we felt in the depths of our hearts that a terrible decree was about to be perpetrated in our ghetto.

We got up at 5:00 a.m. It was cold, and frost covered the road. I covered my daughter with all types of rags, so that she would be warm. We went out to Demokratu Square with the rest of our neighbors.

The Jews went out en masse. Family members were holding each other by the hands, so as not to lose each other. About 20,000 Jews gathered in the square, which was not large. The crowding was great. People lost track of family members. Throughout the entire day they shouted at people, called them all types of names, and searched their family members. We were frozen, and we shivered from cold. We did not know or see what was taking place in front of us. Only in the afternoon did we realize that we were approaching the specific place from where German voices, headed by the ghetto commander Jordan, were emanating. They were shouting: Right – Left! That means: life or death. The healthy young people were sent to the side of life, whereas those who came with their young children or with elderly parents were sent to the side of death. I saw half frozen people lying upon stretchers or pushed by the masses swarming from place to place. I saw a child of about 12 years old, whose face was covered with boils, whose face was red from the high fever, shivering in the cold. His poor parents covered him in clothes and wept. They took him out of his bed, and his verdict was sealed. I saw several Yanova families, such as: Nathan Rabinovich and his wife; Chaya Kapol and their pretty daughter Dina; Mosheke Glaz the violinist who used to give us enjoyment in Yanova with his violin. He was very tall, and I saw him standing with his wife Shifra Kagan the pianist; The Braun family from Breizer Street – Ethel with her two daughters Elka and Rachele, and their young children; Alter Kalutz with his wife and baby; the Zopovich brothers, who were policemen and kept the order of the masses. To my sorrow, not one of them remained alive.

We approached the *selektion* area. To our good fortune, my cousin David, the son of Shlomo the *shochet*, suddenly came before us. We went together. At least we should go with a man, so perhaps we would remain alive. When we came closer, we saw that Hershel (Tzvi) Levin was standing not far from the Gestapo. He was also my cousin. He worked in the ghetto council (Eltern Rat). Mother shouted to him, "Hershel, Hershel!" He noticed us. A Gestapo man sent us, without looking at us, to the bad side, to the side of death. At that moment, Tzvi ran to us and said, "Aunt, run quickly to the opposite side!" The Gestapo man who was already busy with others did not notice this, and we ran quickly to the other side. That is how we were saved. Many people who were standing on the good side saw that relatives, acquaintances and family members stood next to them – and they did not hesitate to bring them to the other side. In general, people did not know where to go: where is death and where is life was hidden from them. The Lithuanians who guarded us beat us mercilessly.

Suddenly, everything ended. We returned home to the ghetto at 6:00 p.m. frozen and hungry, without energy to live further. Our neighbors who had returned before us were tearing their hair and weeping: three people from the family did not return. My daughter Mirele was frozen and blue, with wet, frozen rags on her. I realized that her end was approaching. She did not even take a bit of warm water that I requested from our neighbors for her. She stopped breathing after a short time. Her life ended. A great pain, that I had never felt throughout my life, overtook my heart. I began to kiss her small, precious body. The girl, who through the six weeks of her life did not even taste a drop of warm milk or have a dry diaper, whose fate was to be born at that accursed time, was a sacrifice for me – for had it not been for her, I would have not been sick, and would therefore not have remained alive. Mother, who comforted me with her pleas, stood up on her feet with difficulty. She suddenly appeared about ten years older. Her granddaughter had been taken from her. We covered the baby with a clean, white sheet that we had brought from our neighbors, and placed her at the foot of our bed. We sat all night and waited for morning. The next morning, Mother went to the *Chevra Kadisha* (burial society) and requested that they come to take her. They said that they would be busy for several days, for Demokratu Square was full of people who had died during the *selektion* day.

[Page 212]

I ask humanity, where is justice? Is there anything in the world more terrible for a mother – to lie in one bed with her dead baby for four consecutive days? This is indeed what happened to me. I was this unfortunate mother. On the third day, there was already a bad smell in the house, but the *Chevra Kadisha* told us to bring her only the next evening. On the fourth day after her death, Mother and I took her to the ghetto cemetery. We waited until they buried her. They did not even put up a board or any marker. This is how they buried hundreds and thousands of Jews without any marker. Their only sin was that they were born Jews.

We returned home shaken and depressed, without a will to live on, full of bitterness at the wide world that was silent and took no interest in us. The next day, close to 30,000 Jews were hauled to the Ninth Fort and shot to death. This was the largest *aktion* that was perpetrated in the Kovno Ghetto!!!

Backbreaking Labor

I began to work at the airfield. We went out at 5:00 a.m. to walk to work, a distance of five or six kilometers. We worked at all types of tasks – we dug, hauled rocks and concrete, and built a bigger airfield. The work was very difficult for women. We received 100 grams of bread and weak soup daily. When we returned home at 9:00 p.m., we also received a hundred grams of bread and soup in the ghetto. I was very weak. Mother gave me hot soup and guarded me like the apple of her eye. After some time, I began to work in the lumber brigade. We worked very hard, but we were able to bring home a bundle of wood. One day, I left a bundle of wood for us, and the next day I would sell it and purchase a bit of margarine and potatoes. This strengthened me somewhat, and I was happy that Mother also had something to eat. We moved to a two– room dwelling. The entire family that lived there previously did not return from Demokratu Square other than one child, a young lad, who met us and cried and pleaded with us to come to live with him. We had a separate small room there to live.

Mother went out to near the gate every evening and waited for my arrival. I would hear her voice from afar, "Alinka, my child." I would enter, put down the bundle of wood, and we would walk home together. How good it was that mother was with me. She would put me to bed and feed me, as I would read to her in Hebrew and translate into Yiddish a book of Sholom Aleichem that I found in the new dwelling. Several times, I was on the threshold of parting from my mother. At one time I had to be sent to Riga, and another time to a different place from where I might not have ever returned, but some Supreme force protected me so that I should be together a bit longer with my beloved good mother.

My only friend from Yanova, who was in the ghetto with her husband, was Shoshana Rashkes and her husband Wolf. They lived in a small room, which was a kitchen, not far from us. I often visited them. We would all sit and talk with great longing about out city of Yanova, the dynamic youth, our Hashomer Hatzair movement, our family members about whom we knew nothing – perhaps they somehow are alive? Or perhaps they are not alive at all any more. She would feed me and give me packets for Mother. She endured a great deal. She was always my friend with a good, merciful heart, as was fitting for the intelligent daughter of Yehuda and Fruma Rashkes.

There were other Yanovers in the ghetto who lived not far from us: the three Dubiansky brothers and their father, their sister Chaya of blessed memory and her husband Nachum Blumberg, Miriam and Rachele the daughters of my uncle Yitzchak Levin. Miriam was the eldest, and she was there with her husband and young son Tzvikale. Tzvikale remained alive. His parents gave him over to a gentile woman, who saved him from a certain death. He lives in Kovno today. I had other relatives in the ghetto: my mother's brother Chaim Levin who lived in the ghetto with his son Tzvi Levin and daughter Rachele with her two children. These relatives helped us a bit with food. None of them survived except for Tzvi.

The Klooga Camp in Estonia

On October 26, 1943, after two and a quarter years of living in the ghetto, Gestapo men and Lithuanians came suddenly and began to go from house to house along with members of the Jewish police. The purpose was to gather people and send them to some unknown work place. They came to us as well, and permitted us to take a small bag of clothes or food. A wagon hitched to a horse waited for us outside. We put the suitcase on the wagon and walked behind the wagon. Several tens of other people followed after the wagon. I then saw the sisters Tzvia and Sara Wiker. They stood next to their house and asked us from afar where we were going.

[Page 213]

Trucks waited for us outside the city. We ascended and traveled along the route leading to the Kovno airfield. My heart predicted bad things. I was afraid of Mother's fate, and my fear was not in vain. When we arrived at the airfield, a terrifying scene unfolded before me. I saw that people had got off of the trucks that arrived before us, and the Gestapo was making an immediate *selektion*: men separate, young women separate, and children and babies along with older women. Mother did not understand what was happening. I understood that this was the end, that my mother would be taken from me. I began to cry hysterically. Mother comforted me, "My daughter, we will live together in the ghetto, this is not so bad, the main thing is that we will be together." I did not have the chance to explain what I was thinking. The Gestapo came immediately and told us to get off quickly. One of them hit Mother, who was holding on to me, with his hand, and began to drag her. I ran after him and shouted, "She is my mother, let us remain together!" Instead of a response, he gave me a sharp blow on my head with the stick in his hand and pushed me back. When I came to, I saw Mother as the German was helping her board the truck. The truck was full of young children and babies. I saw another Yanova resident, Yehudit Landman, the daughter of Shimshon–Elia the butcher, together with her. She was also an older woman, who had lost her children in the Kovno Ghetto. Both of them stood on the truck, as the Gestapo men every minute stuffed in another child who had been snatched from its mother's hands. The truck was filled, and it traveled off quickly. This was the last glance I had of my mother. I knew that this was the end of her life, as well as the end of the lives of the young children who were placed in her hands…

They pushed me behind along with other young women whose cries reached the heavens. They pulled out their hair and cried that they had taken their darling children from them, as I was crying because they took my devoted mother from me. The Germans beat us again and again to quiet us down, and pushed us onto a long transport train. We were crowded into the cars. When the car was closed, they locked the door with a bar. These were transport cars, which had been used previously to transport cows. The filth was great. There was straw on the floor. There were several loaves of bread and margarine in a corner, and a bucket to attend to our bodily needs. Every one of the women screamed and cried, calling out the name of their beloved children. We began to bang at the door, and we lost our energy. We fell onto the straw, each of us with our own agony. It was already dark at night, and we began to travel slowly. We traveled and stopped again and again. Every time we stopped, we waited for them to tell us to go out to the killing place. Every car had several steps upon which Ukrainians stood and guarded us. They spoke among themselves out loud, and we heard that they were taking us to be killed.

We travelled this way for seven days without the doors being opened. The air was full of the odor of feces and urine, for the bucket overflowed. We were filthy and hungry. We stopped in the forest on the seventh day, and they opened the doors under heavy guard. They permitted us to get some water to drink and to wash. This was a large bog, with frogs jumping around. We were so thirsty that we drank the brackish water. We breathed a bit of air, and they again brought us into the cars. We traveled for another three days, and we stopped in Estonia. They opened the doors, and many Gestapo men and women met us. They immediately began to whip us so that we would arrange in fives. Our legs were stiff, and our eyes could not tolerate the daylight. We arranged ourselves in fives with difficulty. Trucks then came to take some of the people to a variety of camps.

Of the 3,000 that we were when we left the Kovno Ghetto, only a few hundred remained. The brought us to a camp called Klooga in Estonia, known for its cruelty and hunger. There were already several thousand Jews from the Vilna Ghetto there, who had been brought there a half a year previously. The work was hard. I worked with concrete. Two women would drag rocks and concrete weighing 80 kilograms. We worked in the rain. We returned home soaked to the bone. The food was meager, for the person in charge of food sold our provisions and gave us small portions. Many people died. People looked like skeletons. They would burn the dead before our eyes. I got seriously weak, and I felt that I would not be able to manage for long. The punishment for any minor infraction was murderous blows. Once, I receive beatings with a thick stick on the back from the S.S. I thought that all my bones were dismembering. However, apparently, at times a person is able to endure a great deal. After nine months in Klooga, suddenly, many Gestapo people arrived, arranged us again into fives, and conducted a *selektion*. The weaker ones, myself included, were placed separately, and the rest were sent back to the blocks. We sat in the sand all day awaiting our fate. Toward evening, we were driven by truck to the port in Estonia, where they placed us on a ship. We set out on the Baltic Sea to Stutthof.

[Page 214]

Stutthof Concentration Camp

Stutthof was a transit camp as well as a death camp. Day and night, the tall chimneys spewed black smoke blended with the stinking odor of burning flesh. This was the flesh of Jews who were burned in the ovens day and night. Almost every day, they would remove us from the block and conduct a *selektion*. Every day, they took thousands of people to the gas chambers and then to the crematoria. Every day, thousands more arrived from all parts of Poland, Lithuania, Estonia, and Germany.

I met there a woman from Yanova, Ita Piklachik of blessed memory. I will remember this intelligent woman as long as I live. She died in the camp, as did her daughter. Her husband and son survived, and live in Israel. We were together for my entire time in Stutthof, and I was very happy that I had someone close to me who influenced me with her special spirit. We lay down all day in the sand. We received thin soup and a morsel of bread once day. At night we received a cup of black coffee. That was all. Lice devoured me.

Once I found out that women were demanded for work. I quickly ran to the gate. They took me for work along with many other women. We traveled to do agricultural work in Tiegenhoff[2], which was not far from Stutthof. Farmers lived there who had many cows as well as land. We helped them with all types of tasks. We received good, satisfying food. Aside from this, I ate fruits and vegetables such as carrots, beets, and apples. I felt my energy returning. We worked there for three months. The work ended, and we traveled back to Stutthof. I no longer found the people whom I had left behind. They were already different, appearing to us as living skeletons. The women would sit all day cleaning their clothing from lice, while we were clean at that time. Apparently, the S.S. were angry about this. They put us into other bunks, where the lice fell upon us with great fury. We became more and more broken with each passing day, and lost our human image.

Thus did time pass. *Selektions* took place every two days, and many diseases afflicted us, until the end of 1944 came. I heard that they required people for work in Dresden. I hurried to the gate, and they indeed took me there. Dresden is a large German city, the capital city of Saxony. We worked there in an armaments factory. I knew how to sew blankets. They gave me ten women and a work room with many dyed quilts that had been brought from Poland. These had been the property of Jews who perished. I had to cut them apart and sew blankets for the residents of the camp. For this, I received an extra portion of soup and bread.

In the middle of the night of February 13, 1945, we heard intermittent sirens and heavy bombing. These were the American and British bombers bombing the city of Dresden. We immediately went down to the shelter along with the S.S. people who were guarding us. We sat in the shelter for three days without food or water. The city turned into a cemetery, where 200,000 Germans were buried under the rubble. The upper story of the building in which we worked was damaged by a fiery attack. The sick people who remained there, more than 20 individuals, were burned alive. The buildings on both sides of the road were burning with leaping flames. The road, which was also on fire, burned the soles of our wooden clogs. We ran with our last strength. We left the city and sat by the banks of the river. The next day, we went out to work to clean the railway tracks. Our sentinels could not recognize the streets even though they were residents of Dresden. Everything was destroyed, without a path, without a road. We slept outside. It was very cold at night, and we almost froze completely.

With Failing Legs

A few weeks later, they loaded us on train wagons once again and we traveled to the border with Czechoslovakia. There, we continued on foot. Our clothes were completely torn, as were our shoes, which were tied with ropes. We walked 20 kilometers or more per day through the Sudeten Mountains. We would go to some village at night, and receive a few cooked potatoes or soup from the residents of the village. We slept outside, and at times in the barn of one of the residents.

[Page 215]

Many girls from Vilna and Kovno escaped along the way. As we passed through a forest and they noticed that the sentinels were not watching them, they would quickly slink into the forest and hide behind a large tree. There were a large number of girls. However, there was no place to hide for an extended period. They were forced to come out to beg for food in the villages. Then, the Gestapo men captured them and shot them. I knew that I had no place to escape. I only hoped that I would perhaps remain alive without escaping. Some sixth sense always guided me. Apparently, this was my good luck.

Many people who could not continue on would collapse along the way. A German sentinel would sit on a tree stump not far from the person, and wait until we would be a distance away. We would hear a shot, and the sentinel would return to us with his body. The collapsed person was already liquidated. Hundreds of gentiles who had worked in Dresden and endured the bombardments along with us were together with us. There were Poles, Ukrainians and even Germans who had been investigated by the Nazi guards and sent to the camps in Dresden. We Jews walked together, helped each other, and supported those who were especially weak.

The numbers dwindled day by day. Many escaped at any opportunity during the night or day. We continued to march through the months of March, and April. The nights were cold and wet. We slept on the wet ground, crowded one against the other. I felt that the cold was even penetrating my brain, and my consciousness was dwindling. I would get up and walk, lie down again, and walk again. Not every person could endure such conditions. Many women who could not get up in the morning were taken out to be killed by the S.S. As usual, we continued marching 20 or more kilometers each day from village to village. We heard bombing in the village that we had passed through just the day before. We later found out that every village that we passed through had fallen into Russian hands. However, our sentinels knew nothing and did not want to know.

They had no other order than to continue to haul us, so that we would not fall into Russian hands.

This was at the beginning of May. We passed through a small city and saw the picture of Hitler covered in black in the windows. There was no end to our joy, but we also knew that they would liquidate us at the last minute, just as the S.S. did in other places. Berlin had already fallen to the Russians, and Germany was already defeated. This was May 3, 1945. However, we still continued to walk with the S.S.

On May 8, we reached a village and slept in a large barn. The next morning, May 9, they got us up again to continue on. When we went out to the street, we saw a strange sight: The German army was traveling en masse with all types of vehicles, hurrying along and filling the entire road. Our sentinels told us to go into the meadow at the side of the road and continue. Suddenly, a German soldier in a passing truck threw us a jar of honey and shouted, "Now the sun will begin to shine for you too. The war is over!"

We stood astonished and did not dare to approach the jar despite our hunger. They also threw bread and cookies at us. However the S.S. men who guarded us stood there with pointed guns and told us that they would shoot anyone who lifted something off the ground. The German women took special revenge upon us. Each of them had fallen in love with one of the S.S. soldiers, and they would express their love publically. They would beat us with wild cruelty in order to demonstrate that they were loyal to the party and to Hitler.

Suddenly a car stopped before us, and a high ranking S.S. man came out and called to our sentinels. They hurried to him. He told them things that I understood clearly. He said, "Where are you going with these people, do you not know that the war has ended? You are S.S. men, get on some truck quickly and drive back to Germany quickly!"

Our sentinels remained with opened mouths and discussed amongst themselves. One gentile woman approached them and said, "What shall we do, where shall we go?" They answered her, "Run quickly to the village to ask for bread!" They quickly got on a stopped truck and traveled away. We were about ten Jewish women who remained alone from all the hundreds that we had at the beginning of our journey. We asked each other, "Has everything ended? Are we free?" We did not believe it. But when we saw that our sentinels had fled for their lives, we went away from the road and went deeper into the forest. We did not want anyone to see us, lest someone else would want to shoot a bullet at us.

[Page 216]
We sat down, and began to hug each other and weep bitterly. Has the war indeed ended, and we are free? Now what? Where should we go? We went through the forest.

The entire world was now beautiful in our eyes: the green forest, the grass, here is a small stream. We looked at its waters and saw our reflection – skeletons! Creased faces. No hair, since they shaved us because of the lice. And the rags that we were wearing. We screamed a hysterical scream, and were suddenly filled with might and courage. We entered the nearby village to ask for bread. The residents of the village gave us food and told us that Germans had lived in the next village, and they would certainly have escaped. We should go there to take their clothes and food. We went, and it was as they had said. We found abandoned houses, with old shoes, strange dresses, boxes of cans. We found wine in the cellar. We ate to satiation, and at night we went back to sleep in the same barn that we had left in the morning. We sat down and began to talk amongst ourselves. Suddenly the straw began to lift, and two Hungarian Jews who had been with us on the journey appeared before us. Their joy was boundless. We gave them some of the food that we had brought.

That night, we heard the sounds of half–tracks. In the morning we found out that those were soldiers of the Red Army who had entered Czechoslovakia. The American Army met the Russian Army there. We lived in that village for several weeks. The residents of the village, mainly Czechs, brought us food and clothing, and treated us well.

Return to Yanova

I slowly regained my energy. Then, I started longing for my town and my family. I hoped that someone might have survived. One month after the end of the war, I traveled to the railroad station along with six other women from Vilna and Kovno. We traveled for a month, for the train would travel for a day and stand for a week. I endured these tribulations as well.

We arrived in the city of Grodno in White Russia [Belarus]. I endured several weeks of interrogation from the Russians to find out whether I had been a kapo in the camp, whether I had beaten Jews or served the Germans. A big joke! When they found no stain on me, they gave me a certificate stating that I was permitted to go to Kovno and settle there.

When I arrived in Kovno, I found Nachum and Chaya Goldberg, and their baby Zisla there. They were happy to see me. They fed me, and I remained with them for some time. I found out from them that nobody from my family had survived. My family had perished in Dvinsk [Daugavpils], Latvia: my father, two brothers – one of them married with three young daughters, and my two sisters. My husband had died on the way to Kovno, as he was coming to see me when I was in the hospital. His parents had also perished.

I travelled to Yanova, for I could not overcome the inclination to see my city once more and then to leave it forever. From the Yanova railway station, I walked on foot for several kilometers. I passed places through which I had strolled in earlier years. I came to the city and barely recognized it. I arrived in the city and barely recognized it. Entire streets were destroyed. Our street, Kovno Road, was half destroyed. The other half, where we lived, remained. The house in which I had grown up was still there. I walked around the house and did not see anyone. The door was closed. We children had an invention – to pull it a bit, place our hand inside, reach the lock through the crack, and open the door. I could not restrain myself. I went up three steps, stuck out my hand, pulled the door, reached the lock, opened the door, and entered with trembling hands and clanging knees. There was nobody home. There was furniture – but not ours. A picture of the crucifix was hanging on the wall. I entered the dark bedroom, the kitchen, the dining room. I sat down and wept. The same house, the same walls, the same rooms, but where were my dear ones? They were lying dead in some unknown place. I do not recall how long I sat there immersed in my thoughts. Suddenly, the door opened and a woman entered. She looked at me with a murderous face. I recognized her. She was a Lithuanian woman who used to stand in the market selling candy, crucifixes, pins, and other small items. Her husband was missing a hand. Her sons assisted the Germans in taking control over the Jews. They fled to Germany when the earth began to burn beneath their feet at the end of the war.

[Page 217]

"Who are you who entered my house?" I heard her murderous voice.

"Do you not recognize me?" I answered. "You used to buy lemonade from my father. I lived in this house, and it is mine!"

Her face turned red.

"You will not take the house from me. I purchased it during the war and paid money for it."

I did not want to argue with her, for I had no energy for that, seeing her eyes full of hate and murder. I got up, crossed through the kitchen, and exited into the yard through the back door. I entered the stable where our good horse and cow whose milk I had drunk had lived. Everything was empty. She had sold everything, and had taken our house without purchasing it from anybody.

As I was walking through the street, gentiles looked at me and were literally afraid to approach me and talk to me. I found out that a woman named Ula, who had once been our assistant, lived in a Jewish house. She received me politely. She was very poor, and lived with her husband and two young daughters. I stayed with her for a week. I prepared the papers to get my house back. When I obtained it, I sold it to a gentile. I looked at my house for the last time. In this city, I had spent my lovely, pleasant childhood years along with my brothers, sisters, intelligent father who had given me Zionist and Hebrew education, and my finest mother who had been snatched away by a most cruel hand. Thus did I leave Yanova and curse it in my heart that it should burn from edge to edge. I traveled to Vilna.

I Could Not Remain in One Place

In the meantime, some of the Jews of Yanova who had escaped to Russia at the beginning of the war, as well as those who had returned from the Red Army and the concentration camps, returned to Vilna.

A family of Yanovers named Dragatzki lived on Truki Street: Shmuel Dragatzki of blessed memory with his two children and pregnant wife Leah, his brother Shlomo with his wife and two children, and their elderly mother. This house served as a guesthouse for anyone who came. All of them received food from Leah Dragatzki and a place to sleep. Sometimes, about twenty people slept there in all the rooms and on all the floors. Despite her pregnancy, nobody left in the morning without Leah giving them an omelet and a full breakfast. The Lukman family was another such family. Before the war, they lived on the other side of the Vylia. Their three children survived in Yanova: Moshe, Sarale and Ben–Zion, as well as their father. There too, everyone was provided with a place to sleep and food until they managed to organize themselves.

The summer passed. I could not stay in one place. I traveled from Vilna to Kovno – to the Blumberg house that was always filled with people who had returned from Russia and the camps. Everyone received food and a place to sleep. I searched for people who had perhaps met someone from my family. I found no rest. I met people who were together in the ghetto and concentration camps – each with their own gloomy history. I returned to Vilna and found some relatives of mine who had returned from Russia. This was Shaul Yudelevich, the son of David Eliya. He was a driver. He lived with his family and the family of his brother who had died in Russia. I lived together with them and was happy that I was among relatives who were concerned about me. After some time I met my present husband. We got married, and I began a new life. We had two sons, may they be well. When they got older, I would tell them about what happened to me, about my family, and about my Zionist education that had not faded throughout the entire twelve years that I lived in Russia.

We left Russia in 1957, at the first opportunity that was presented to us. We moved to Poland. From there, we made *aliya* to Israel in 1959.

I wish to point out that everything that I have written is only a small part of what I endured throughout four consecutive years. Each day had its own tribulations, and each camp had its own atrocities. I had the power and desire to live.

I hope that others who did not endure what I had, especially the young people, will read this and learn what their parents endured during the Second World War of 1941–1945. We will not forget the innocent blood of the Jews that was spilled. They were murdered only because they were Jews!

We will not forget and not forgive!

Translator's Footnotes

A reference to Job 3:1.

Nowy Dwór Gdański.

[Page 218]

The Shaulists[1] Were Worse than the Germans

by Shmuel Tepper (Ramat Hasharon)

Translated by Jerrold Landau

Uncaptioned. Shmuel Tepper

I was born in Yanova to my parents Abba and Chana. We lived in our private house on Kovno Street, on the other side of the city market in the direction of Keidaniai Street. My father was a builder by profession. His nickname was "Abba the Moler". Our economic situation was poor. We children were not spoiled, and we tasted the taste of poverty from our earliest youth.

Father was Orthodox and attempted to give us a Torah education. I studied in the Yavneh School, as well as in the Yeshiva of Mendel Teitz in Yanova. When I got older, they sent me to complete my studies in *Gemara* in the Yeshiva of Vilkomir [Ukmerge]. Considering our economic situation, I decided to leave the Yeshiva of Vilkomir, and to return to Yanova to begin to study the carpentry trade with Daniel Yankelovich. At that time, I was active in the Beitar organization, and I volunteered for activities on behalf of the Keren Kayemet LeYisrael [Jewish National Fund] and Keren HaYesod.

In 1933, I left my parents' home and moved to Kovno. There, I met my wife Sara, a native of Zasliai. I got married and continued working in carpentry as an employee in Shragovich's furniture factory. On the day of the outbreak of the war, June 22, my wife and I decided to escape to Russia. I, along with my wife and daughter Chana, left Kovno and walked in the direction of Yanova. We reached Yanova in the evening, and decided not to tarry, but rather to continue along our way to Vilkomir. The Germans were already there by the third day. The captains of the German Army gathered about 2,000 Jewish men from among the refugees, including me, and sent us to various jobs. Later, they freed us, ordering us to go back to our homes.

We returned to our home in Kovno. I lived in my home until July 15. On that day, we were given an order to move to the Slobodka Ghetto. While living in the ghetto, I worked at all types of backbreaking jobs at the Aleksotis Airport. Later, they transferred me to work at an army bakery in Šančiai.

In 1942, the Germans transported me along with three other Jews in an army truck to Polygon near Yanova in order to inspect the local bakery and remove the machinery. We arrived in Yanova. Of course, we saw no Jews. Yanova was Judenrein in Nazi terms. Along with the Germans, we entered a command of partisans and Shaulists that was set up in the home of Namiot on the Vylia. Suddenly, a Lithuanian from Yanova named Vansevicius, from the well–known murderers Vansevic and sons, who are to blame for the murder of hundreds of Jews, entered. When he noticed us, he shouted, "Look, here are "*Zydi*." He pointed his gun toward us vainly and said, "We finished with the Jews in Yanova, so how are you here?" The German captain who accompanied us approached him, smacked him on the cheek, and removed his weapons. He was not calmed. He ran to the second room, brought a gun, and pointed it at us. The German captain arrested him, and the rest of the German soldiers who were on the truck hurried in. They surrounded us and hauled us onto the truck. In the meantime, other partisans and Lithuanian ruffians gathered and demanded that they give over the Jews. The German soldiers protected us. The driver drove quickly and we left Yanova.

[Page 219]

I am relating this incident so that the future generations should know how cruel the Lithuanian partisans in Yanova were to us. It is funny to state that Hitler's soldiers defended us from them. We traveled to Polygon, removed all the machinery, and transferred it to a military bakery in Šančiai. I worked in this bakery with three other Jews until the final day, the day of the liquidation of the ghetto. One was Wulkan from Vienna, the second was the locksmith Yisrael Sandler from Kovno, and the third was Michael Papilski.

In the latter period, my wife worked in the Šančiai labor camp. On March 27, 1944, when my wife was at work, the Germans came and took my two daughters: Chana Gita who was born in Kovno in 1939, and Fruma Liba who was born in the Kovno Ghetto in February 1942. They were taken to their deaths along with the rest of the children.

On the day of the liquidation of the ghetto, the Germans took me to Stutthof with the rest of the survivors. I was taken out from there and was imprisoned in Camp number One of Kaufering–Landsberg, a sub–camp of Dachau. The women remained in Stutthof. I met my wife in Łodz. We went from Łodz to Munich. I finally arrived in Israel in 1948. Here, I live in the Lithuanian neighborhood of Ramat Hasharon. After the trials of absorption, I opened an independent carpentry shop.

We had a son and a daughter in Israel. My economic situation improved, and today I live a happy life.

The following family members died in Yanova: my sister Rivka and her husband Daniel Yankelovich; their son Chaim and their daughter who was married to the carpenter Landsman; and my step–brother Avraham Epstein, also a carpenter.

Written down by Yitzchak [Burstein].

Translator's Footnote
Lithuanian Riflemen's Union. See http://enc.tfode.com/Shaulists

In the Ghetto and the Camp

by Nachum Blumberg of Tel Aviv

Transcribed and adapted by Yitzchak Burstein

Translated by Daniella Thompson

In the Kovno Ghetto

At dawn on the morning following our arrival, we were sent to work in the Aleksotas[1] Airport. The head of all the brigades was Luria, who was later revealed to be a despicable man and a sadist. At the airport I met my sister Henia, who lived in Šančiai[2] after her marriage. She looked ghastly: thin, pale faced, dressed in a long caftan held together with rope. On the first day of the war–even before the Germans had arrived–her husband was called out by a Lithuanian officer, their neighbor, who drew his pistol and shot him to death. She was left with two little children aged nine and three. She lived in the ghetto in a small room on Krikshtshiukaichio[3] Street and was almost entirely destitute. In her early days there, she obeyed the occupying regime's orders and turned in her money and gold, leaving herself only 100 rubles. Since then she had been dependent on ration cards. I helped her with money and groceries.

The first task at the airport was to level the ground. The prisoners did this work with shovels and rakes, guarded by S.S. youth. They were dreadful types–did not allow anyone to straighten his back even for a minute. Whoever dared to raise his head and breathe a little air received blows to the head from the butts of their rifles. At the end of the day, they loaded the corpses of the prisoners who died at work onto platforms and shipped them back to the ghetto, so that the number of those returning would correspond to the number of those who came out.

After a week's work, it became clear to me that it would be impossible to survive in the face of this cruelty and running down the Aleksotas Hill for the pleasure of the S.S. men.

[Page 220]

One morning, upon our arrival at work, they announced, "Brickmasons, forward!" The men of the Dubiansky[4] family–father and three sons–stepped forward. When they returned, they related that they had worked at their trade, building airplane hangars. Their supervisors were German artisans, and they were treated well.

The next day, when the announcement was repeated, I also stepped forward. I worked in the same brigade with my father–in–law and brother–in–law. I received a bricklayer's trowel, level, and hammer. Each worker was assigned a length of six meters to complete. I watched to see how it was done. The German noticed it, approached me, and shouted, "Damned Jew, you're a baker, not a builder!" He hit my head with a plank, and I fell, covered with blood. I was ordered to get up. I claimed that my father had been a mason. "Then say so!" he replied and showed me how to work. Afterwards, he became my guardian angel and obtained groceries for me. Every now and then he would ask if I knew who had a gold ring. I ordered a ring from a goldsmith in the ghetto and brought it to him. He paid me in groceries and ordered rings for his friends as well. These were my first steps toward adaptation to the prevailing conditions so I could survive and obtain food for myself and for my sister and her children.

In the summer of 1942, after I became proficient at bricklaying, I approached Tzvi Levin, the Yanovan in the Ältestenrat,[5] and requested that the Dubianskys and I be transferred to small brigades working in the city, where conditions were better it as was possible to establish ties with the populace. Tzvi informed me that Luria did not want to let us go, and that there was only one way to dodge him: volunteer for work in Gaižiūnai,[6] felling trees along the sides of the railroad. The work would be hard, but it would last no more than a month. Furthermore, it would be in the environs of Yanova, a known area. There it would be possible to obtain groceries and bring them into the ghetto with no inspection. We accepted the suggestion and informed Luria. He was surprised, since only prisoners worked there, but gave his consent. We took with us clothes to barter for groceries.

I knew how to fell trees. The saws were very sharp. We worked at a slow tempo until 10 at night. The brigade's cook was the Yanovan Necham'ka Zisla, daughter of Chaim. Thanks to her, we didn't lack for food. I suggested to her that she have a word with the white–hatted German, who was known as a murderer, and recommend me for work in the bread bakery. The profits would be his. He consented. During roll call he called, "Baker, forward!" I stepped out of the line and was ordered to prepare wood for baking. Then he sent me to the village to obtain flour and baking supplies. I went to a Russian acquaintance, who was surprised to see me. I gave him clothes, and he provided me with the flour and all the other items. He heated the bathhouse, and I washed and shaved. The next morning he took me in his cart to the brigade's vicinity. I had flour, eggs, butter, ham, and honey, and several bottles of samogon[7] for the German, and also a bowl for mixing dough.

The Russian went to Nechama. She reported that I was liable to be shot. I stayed in the forest. Nechama was told to say to the German that a wheel had broken on the way owing to the heavy weight of the supplies, and that we brought liquor, eggs, butter, and honey for him. Having heard this, the German ordered me to begin baking immediately. It seems to me that I have never managed to bake bread as tasty as that one. Nechama brought the moonshine and the comestibles to the German, and he, the "White Hat," got so drunk that he didn't accompany the brigade to the forest the next day. Everybody was pleased. From the bread, the German had an income of 80 marks per day. He asked me to stay for the second month.

At the end of the month we returned to the ghetto. We brought groceries that we received in exchange for clothes. The truck entered with no inspection, as Hirschl Levin had promised. The only one who stayed behind was my brother Chaim, who had light work, and Nechama took care of his food. I distributed groceries to the women who had given me clothes to barter.

Having been registered by Luria for another month in the forest at the request of the "White Hat," I came down with lumbago and was given a week's leave by a doctor. In the meantime, Hirschl Levin arranged for me to work in Engineer Slonimsky's brigade–about 100 men who worked in the Šančiai barracks. There I continued to work in bricklaying with my relatives. I suggested to Slonimsky that he employ me in baking bread for the brigade–a kilo to each man, with the profits going to the overseer, the Wehrmacht man Brumkin [sp?]. The latter consented provided he received ten gold rubles a day.

[Page 221]

The money that the workers paid for the bread was used to buy gold in the ghetto, and the daily quota was met. Brumkin [sp?] sent me to Šančiai under guard. There I got in touch with a Lithuanian woman, Atkočiūnaite.[8] In exchange for clothes, she gave me flour, a dough–mixing bowl, and all that was required for baking. We agreed that I would bring her clothes for sale daily, and in exchange she would supply us with groceries. We smuggled the clothes from the ghetto on our bodies–a dangerous undertaking–and did the same while smuggling groceries into the ghetto. Each morning, my brigade comrades wrapped me in kerchiefs, sheets, tablecloths, and even blankets, and tied it all with ropes. This is how I, and others, smuggled items out of the ghetto.

Once, the woman asked that I provide her with a Karakul fur coat–for money, obviously, since it was impossible to smuggle the equivalent value in groceries into the ghetto. I found such a coat and sewed the money I received for it into my hat's lining. When we arrived at the ghetto's gate, we were told that thorough inspection was taking place. What to do?

I approached the policeman Yankele Verbovsky and sought his counsel. He advised me to come with him [to the gate] with the hat on my head, since we were usually required to remove our hats at the gate. I stepped toward him, and he slapped me on the cheek, grabbed my hat, shouted, "Runter mit der Mütze,"[9] and tossed it beyond the gate. This was how I managed to smuggle the proceeds from the sale of the fur coat.

All those who gave me clothes for barter were satisfied with the exchange. I purchased gold rings for emergencies. These I left with the woman or sewed into my pants.

One evening, as I arrived at the gate, I fell into the hands of the Lithuanian policeman Ratner. I had no groceries on me. During his search, he felt me and found the gold. I was subject to a death sentence. I whispered to him that the gold was for him; I would enter the police hut, get it out, and hand it to him. He agreed to it. I entered, plucked three buttons from my coat, wrapped two of them in paper and handed them to him stealthily. Fortunately for me, there were hundreds of people in line, pushing their way in. His hands were engaged in cracking a whip over the gatecrashers' heads. He had no time to inspect what I had given him. That's how I took my revenge on him. When I came home, my wife Chaya did not recognize me, so pale and terrified I was. After this incident, I put the rings in a builder's level. I worked in the brigade until the end of 1943.

Shochat from the Ältestenrat–a Jew from Memel–came to me once and said that it had been decided to build a shelter for the Ältestenrat. He wanted the Dubianskys and me to do it. It would be counted as brigade work, and they would authorize it on our documents. It was in a three–story house at 11 Biaro [sp?] Street. Chaim Dubiansky carried out an inspection and suggested digging a tunnel that would begin under the tank in the laundry room and lead to the garage. The shelter would be built under the garage's concrete floor. We were promised comestibles. I stipulated that space be guaranteed for my sister Henia and her two children. We worked at night. The earth was transferred to a garbage pit. The work lasted about a month. There were four rooms. The walls and the floor were lined with cork. The tunnel was 11 meters long. It was necessary to crawl while traversing it. Entry required the removal of the laundry tank.

One rainy day, close to the end of work, we sat down to eat when the door opened and Goecke[10] appeared with two S.S. men. "What are five strong men doing here?" I got up and reported that we were working. He saw the hole and the earth and believed us. This was fortunate, since the slightest suspicion would have carried a death sentence. As was revealed later, the digging of the shelter was prompted by radio bulletins from foreign sources, announcing that the mass murderer Goecke was due to arrive and liquidate the Kovno Ghetto. And indeed he came. In order to camouflage his intention, he appeared at first as beneficent and ordered groceries to be supplied to the ghetto to reassure the inhabitants.

At the conclusion of the work, we were ordered to a forced labor camp in Kėdainiai[11] under the command of Luria. This was done to blot the evidence of our work on the shelter. Knowing what awaited me there, I approached Luria and asked him to exempt me from it, as I was determined to escape the ghetto in order to survive as the sole witness of Yanova's Jewry. He refused, saying that he was responsible for me.

[Page 222]

In the Labor Camp

A week before the transfer to Kėdainiai, I told my sister Henia about it and offered to build a dummy wall, so the children could be hidden behind it. I built the wall in a few days. Then we were sent–about 300 persons–by train to Kėdainiai, near a village. We were put to work building an airport. With me were my brother Chaim, the Dubianskys with the father Chaim and the girl Etel'e, Mendel's daughter. Conditions were tolerable. We knew local peasants and bartered with them. We were guarded by Wehrmacht soldiers from Rommel's African army, who had come here for a respite from the fighting. They didn't treat us badly. We worked there for about a month. Then an order arrived from Goecke to form brigades of 100 men each and intensify security. This made us very apprehensive. We began to organize and looked for contacts with partisans to whom we could flee in time of peril. The camp's trustee was the German Jew Lehman, who had with him several Jewish policemen.

Lehman found out some details about the underground resistance. According to his instructions, we were employed in menial labor. One day, at the morning roll call, he asked, "Who is a baker here?" I raised my hand. He told me that he had a job for me and allowed me to take a helper. I chose Mendel Dubiansky. We were led under guard to the pilots' kitchen at the airport, where we were to repair a smoking stove by noon, or we'd be shot. Scared, we labored hard, looking for the source of the smoke. Meanwhile, the clock's hands inched forward.

Finally we discovered that the chimney on the floor below was broken, and this is what drew the smoke downward to the first floor. We repaired the chimney and were saved. The cook rejoiced. At that moment, the purser appeared. When he saw the stove burning properly and heard the cook praising us, he ordered us to follow him. He brought us to the food storeroom and filled two pails with sausage, honey, bread, and cheese. The guard accompanied us back to the camp. I knew a Lithuanian, Atkočiūnas,[12] who was a horse trainer. The guard was well disposed toward him, and when Atkočiūnas invited me, we went to him. I proposed a barter trade to him. Every day, the guard accompanied me to him. I brought clothes and returned with groceries.

My wife Chaya was employed in the workshop where the Wehrmarcht's linens were mended. The Lithuanian woman[13] offered to remove my wife from the camp. She said she had contact with partisans in the Melnik[114] forests. Their commander promised her that he would receive us. I must go there to negotiate. The guard allowed me to take a helper with me. I took my brother–in–law, Shmuel Dubiansky. I asked the woman to lead me to the partisans, while the guard was to wait at her place. We covered our Stars of David with sacks that we threw over our shoulders. When we reached the forest, the woman went off to the partisans and returned with their commander, a Pole by the name of Astreika. It turned out that we knew each other; he came from the Yanova area. He agreed to receive us. In exchange for receiving more people, he asked for payment in gold.

We returned to the camp. As we got nearer, we heard bitter wailing. We were told that cars had appeared in the morning, and Ukrainian S.S. men seized children and old people and led them to an unknown destination.

One child by the name of Zuckerman escaped through a window, lay down in a room, and covered himself in a sack. During roll call it was revealed that two children were missing: Etel'e Dubiansky and Zuckerman. The girl was found right away–she was hiding under some bedding in a tent. When dragged out, she wept and cried, "Grandfather, are you letting them take me?" From her words they understood that the grandfather was also in hiding. They found Chaim Dubiansky immediately and shot him on the spot. Only the boy Zuckerman was missing. The Ukrainians found him, dragged him by the legs, and killed him with their rifle butts. His father, seeing all this and hearing the cries of his second child, "Aba'le, save us!," lost his mind. Three women who returned from work and didn't find their children also went mad.

The *Aktion* was well organized and camouflaged from the start. Every day, the children received candy as proof of the good intentions toward them. After his daughter Etel'e was killed, Mendel Dubiansky had a serious seizure and died a few days later in the hospital. Thanks to the woman Vislitsky, who worked as a cook for Camp Commandant Menzel, we received from the latter permission to bury Mendel in the Kėdainiai Jewish cemetery. We wrote his name on a board and took our leave of him.

The camp commandant and the Wehrmacht guards kept us from work for three days and avoided meetings with Jews. They had always assured us that it was impossible that Jews were being exterminated–they were all alive in camps somewhere. Now they faced the evidence.

[Page 223]

We were under the shock of the tragic *Aktion*. We realized that our lives were also nearing a tragic end. The resistance group organized an act of sabotage at work. One day Margalit, from the Kovno Ghetto Ältestenrat, arrived and met with Lehman. Ten days following his visit, I returned to camp from work once with the impression that camp security was strict. I was too naïve. As I entered, a horrific scene was revealed to me: S.S. men were dragging a wounded Jew who was trying to extricate himself and shouted, "The sun is shining."

I didn't enter the huts but hid in a latrine hole. I waited until it was quiet again and tried to climb out but couldn't. My call was answered by Yerachmiel and Shmuel Dubiansky and some others, who pulled me out of the hole. In the hut they told me that Lehman had prepared a list of 15 people who belonged to the resistance group and disrupted order in the camp. The S.S. men who arrived found only six of them and therefore seized anyone they came across. The Jew I had encountered, Chayat, was one of those they captured. He was beaten on the head with a rifle butt, was in nervous shock, and screamed.

Those on the list who managed to hide decided to take revenge on Lehman. He lived with his wife in a special office. In the morning, before roll call, they lay in wait, wishing to grab him as he left his room. He noticed it, opened the door, and presented a letter from Margalit, stating that it was he, Margalit, who determined their fate, which was awaiting them any day. The ambush was removed; they left for work but did not return to camp.

Lehman waited a few days, and when one of them reappeared, he arrested him and notified the commandant that nine people were missing. The commandant contacted the Ghetto Ältestenrat, and they reported this to Goecke. The murderer Goecke came with a retinue to liquidate the camp. They took Lehman and drove to see the airport commander. The latter told them that the workers were industrious, and he needed them. This helped. But Goecke intended to instill terror in the camp, so he chose the six most beautiful girls and conducted them to a nearby copse, setting nearby ten laborers with shovels. He ordered the women to strip down to their briefs and lie down in a circle with their heads touching. Then he drew his pistol and shot a bullet in each of their heads. Among them were a mother and her daughter. The laborers were ordered to bury them.

Lehman announced at the camp that everyone should thank God for having remained alive, including Lehman himself. The entire camp had been earmarked for extermination and was saved thanks to the airport commander.

Thus life in the camp continued. The people who traveled to the Kovno Ghetto to fetch the weekly rations brought me a letter from my sister Henia. She told me that Margalit discovered that she had hidden her children and therefore wanted to send her to Raudondvaris. She believed that she would be killed there for not surrendering her children. I asked the woman Vislitsky to suggest to Camp Commandant Menzel that he send me to fetch the rations from the ghetto. I received permission and took along a supply of foods.

On arrival, I went straight to my sister. Her neighbors told me that she was at work. I waited for her. We hugged and wept. When we entered the room, it was quiet as a grave. I didn't dare to ask where the children were. She gave a sign, and from behind the dummy wall emerged two pale ghosts, a four–year–old boy called Ze'ev'ale and the ten– year–old Shlomo'le. Their joy at seeing their uncle bearing food was great but wordless. I cried in my heart. They asked me to stay with them. Henia asked if I could help overturn her banishment to Raudondvaris. I decided to go to Margalit's house and to ask my sister–in–law, Feine [sp.?] Goldshmid from Kovno, to influence him. I waited until she appeared at her house door. When she asked what I was doing there, I told her what I wanted. She advised me to vanish immediately, because if he saw me there I would be lost. He suspected everyone. She promised to plead for my sister. I returned and reassured my sister. She told me that our brother Chaim, who was in the ghetto, did not come to see her, and she was worried about his fate. Tearfully, we separated for the last time.

I went back to the camp in Kėdainiai and never saw the Kovno Ghetto again. In time, I revealed to several people in the camp–among them one Berkover (now in Israel)–that there was a way to contact the partisans. They receive all comers, but one must bring money and clothes so they can buy arms.

We organized a large group, but nothing came of it, for this reason: The Melnik forest partisans and their commander Astreika got drunk one holiday and were all captured. This was fortunate for us, as we could have been captured with them. I was determined not to remain in the camp, since the situation was becoming more perilous from day to day.

Remaining of our family were Shmuel and Yerachmiel Dubiansky, my wife Chaya, and I. They also agreed to flee. In recent days, I increased my contacts with the Lithuanian woman Atkočiūnaite[15] in the estate near Kėdainiai. All this happened in the presence of my German guard Hans. The woman didn't know my real name. I promised her that if she saved my wife, she would come into a large fortune that my relatives in America would send her after the war. She took this seriously. She would come to the airport workshop, stand next to my wife, and entreat her to come along with her.

[Page 224]

How We Extricated Ourselves From the Camp

I was ordered to go under guard to check the stoves in the guards' huts along the road. While I was cleaning a stove in one of the huts, I came upon a letter written in Russian and Yiddish.

The letter said that whoever was employed in repairing the stove should not hurry to finish the work but should leave his name. The next day I found a second letter expressing satisfaction in my being thus employed and telling me again to take my time. I told my family about it. This went on for several days. I also found some edibles there.

The guard Hans told me that he had received a letter from his mother. She was pleased to read in his letter that he had been guarding a Jew for eight months, and instructed him to treat him well, because anyone who harms a Jew will come to a bitter end. Hans also said that while he was in the guard hut, a telephone call was received from the Kovno Ghetto, announcing that soon the camp would be liquidated and everyone would be sent to Danzig. "Don't be afraid, I will travel with you."

The next day, as I came to work on the stoves, I found a letter informing me that the following day a cart would pass by with an old man crying "Eggs!" My task was to have the guard buy the eggs and put them in his hat while his rifle was on his shoulder. At that moment, he should be grabbed and flung into the cart.

On my return to the camp, I related all this and said that tomorrow we'd be working until noon and that we'd be shipped to Danzig. I took the gold cache out of the builder's level and distributed it among the family members. I instructed them to set upon their guard while they were being led to work, suffocate him, and flee to an unfinished house in the vicinity–I would come to get them there. I told my wife to show herself to the Lithuanian woman.

That day security was fortified, because the old "Ringer" and Yantke the tailor informed [the camp authorities] that many were planning to flee.

I went to work accompanied by the guard. As planned, an old peasant came by in a cart and proclaimed, "Eggs!" The German bought the eggs for a low price and didn't know where to put them. "In the hat," I suggested. He did so.

At that moment I grabbed him from behind, hurled him into the cart, and the peasant sat on his head. After some time the peasant asked me how he had treated me. When I said, "Very well," he freed the guard's head a little. "What have you done to me?" asked [the guard]. "All will be well," I answered. The rifle was taken from him. When we reached the edge of the forest, the partisan whistled, and several partisans appeared. They led the guard and me deep inside the forest and into a camouflaged trench. We sat there several hours. I reassured the guard that there was no danger to his life. They took me to another trench for questioning. The Russian interrogator gave me his hand, said I had acted like a hero, and thanked me for the "language" I had brought.

Among the partisans there were also a few Jews. Most were Russians. I was sent to ask the German if he would be willing to collaborate and brought him food. He was willing. I told the partisan commander about the imminent liquidation of the work camp, about my family members, about Atkočiūnaite, who was supposed to save them, and their current whereabouts. I asked for a cart.

We left at night, and at dawn we reached the vicinity of Melniki.[16] I walked toward Vincgalys.[17] An old peasant came toward me, leading a horse to pasture. I asked him where Atkočiūnas lived. He asked me, "Which one? Because there are two–one rich and the other poor." He pointed out the house of the poor one, and indeed its roof was thatched, as I had been informed in advance. Heart pounding, I approached it. I met an old woman. When I asked her about Atkočiūnas, she crossed herself and denied any knowledge. It occurred to me that perhaps a disaster had struck. She pointed to a house not far from there. Weak–kneed I went there, only to be directed to the previous house. Again she feigned ignorance.

[Page 225]

"And who lives opposite?" "One who cultivates our land." I went in to him and asked about Atkočiūnas. He asked who I was. "A Jew," I replied. "If so, then run away quickly. They are looking for you!" I took out ten gold rubles, gave them to him, and asked him to show me where to flee, and to come with me and point out a good hiding spot. He pointed out the nearby forest. The place was boggy and overgrown with weeds. I waded in the swamp up to my knees, fearing that my wife had been captured and shot. After walking quite a distance, I heard a voice as if from heaven: "Ponas Blumbergas" (Mr. Blumberg). I thought I was imagining it, but the voice called again. From a distance I saw a woman in a long coat waving her arms toward me. I approached and recognized Atkočiūnaite. She showed me the direction to the place where my wife was hiding with her own husband and children. It's hard to express my joy at that moment. We hugged and kissed. She related that informers brought the Germans to her house and pointed her out because she had hidden my wife.

Fortune smiled on my wife. When the Lithuanian woman extricated her from the workshop almost against her will, she refused to go to the former's house but hid in a rye field. When [the authorities] couldn't find her, they arrested the three children of the Lithuanian woman and told their mother that if my wife Chaya did not present herself, they would execute the eldest daughter. Her husband related the old informer's message that Chaya would come to no harm. Atkočiūnaite pleaded with her to leave her hiding place: "I wanted to save you, but your Jews are impeding me." Chaya responded that their daughter Vincenta[18] would not be killed–it was only a threat–and that she herself would not return. Having lost her trust in the Lithuanian woman, she went farther into the rye field. When the husband and wife returned home, their neighbors told them that their daughter had escaped from the Germans through the window after plying them with liquor. The Germans left, since they were to accompany the transport of Jews to Danzig.

Atkočiūnas searched for and found Chaya, told her what had happened, and communicated his decision to go to his mother in Melniki, fearing that the Germans might return. Chaya agreed on condition that she remain in the forest some distance from his mother's house. That's where I found her.

Now I asked Atkočiūnaite to guide us to Vilna. She agreed and went to get her husband and children, clothes and food. I warned her that if she informed on us, her fate would be like ours for hiding Jews.

In the evening she returned with groceries. We ate and started toward Vilna. At four in the morning we reached a lumber mill in the forest. This was the home of the Vaičiūnas family, with whom they were acquainted. They knocked on the window, entered, and told them that they were fleeing the Germans, who wanted to transport them to Germany, and that with them was a Polish family, husband and wife, who had escaped from a camp. They need a suitable place and would pay well. It was resolved that Chaya would reside with the Atkočiūnas family as a blond Aryan, and I would go into hiding. Vaičiūnas brought me to a hay barn. There was a dummy wall of hay and straw that he had prepared as a hiding place for himself. I hid there. They brought me breakfast. I spent about ten days there.

Once I saw through the cracks a group of Germans arriving in trucks and tanks. Chaya understood from what they were saying to each other that the front would soon be here. They advised the populace to take shelter in the forest. Chaya told me this. I came out of hiding and suggested to the host that we lead his cattle and sheep into the forest, where we would build them a pen and dig trenches for ourselves. He recognized that I was a Jew and turned to Atkočiūnas: "But your Pole is a little Jew!"

We Are Free

Many peasants assembled in the forest. Cannon battles began. The next morning, silence reigned. I came out of the trench to breathe some fresh air. Suddenly I saw a soldier with an automatic rifle. He shouted to me in Russian, "Hands up! Who are you?"

Seeing and hearing this, I became paralyzed with joy. Were we really saved? Was it not a dream? Ten soldiers and an officer surrounded me and ordered me to say who I was. Among other things, I told them that the Germans had entrenched themselves on the other side of the forest. We asked them to let us join them, but they refused, saying that the area was full of mines. At night the shooting continued, and in the morning the Russians were already there in their multitudes.

[Page 226]

The Soviet commander told me that in his unit there was one of "us." He was a Jew from Ukraine. He was amazed that I managed to survive. In Russia one hardly ever came across such a case–the inhabitants turned them in to the Germans.

The rumor spread through the forest that there was a Jew here who was rescued from the Nazis. The peasants began to bring food in the hope that I would save them from the Russian army. The Lithuanian newspapers spread rumors that the Soviets' treatment of the Lithuanians was atrocious.

I handed over all the gifts and edibles to Vaičiūnas as a mark of gratitude. I spent two more weeks with him until the front had moved away. With the Atkočiūnas family, we returned to Kėdainiai by a roundabout way. A Jew from Riga was the head of the city administration. I went to him and told him about the Atkočiūnas family that rescued us, asking him to find them good jobs. And, indeed, he did so. We spent several more days with them, gave them part of our money, and traveled by military truck to Kovno. We found accommodation in a private house. A few days later, I traveled to Yanova to look for the murderers and see to it that they would be properly punished.

My first encounter in Yanova was with the builder Vansevičius,[19] whose sons murdered [people], and he, too, did not stand idly by. His first question was where I had come from. I replied that I came from the real world. He consoled himself by arguing that it wasn't the end yet. The Germans were at Marijampolė, and their aircraft were still seen in the sky.

I went to Sreika, who later became chairman of the city council. He was a leftist and a good man. I told him about my meeting with Vansevičius and demanded punishment to the murderers. He promised to help. I slept at his house and the next day went to Army Intelligence. I informed them about the killers. For three days they received my testimony. Everything was written down. They took me to visit the prison so I could identify the murderers. There were about 60 prisoners there, among them many Lithuanian murderers from Skaroli, Bazilioniai[20]–Shaulists. I found there the sausage grocer Meldes, who shot and killed Judelevich, Judith Dragatzky's husband and his rival; the carter Simanis, who lived near "Medis"; the carpenter Gineika, who raped Boz's daughter and then shot her to death. For a long time I trailed Manginas. After several months, I found him in the rubber factory "Inkaras," beyond Slabodka. I denounced him to the police and met him face–to–face in prison. Full of rage, I fell upon him and thrashed him. He confessed to everything. In the end, this murderer got… only ten years in prison; others–even less. They are all walking about as free men in Yanova and Lithuania.

Yes, my dear Yanovans, you learned how we managed to dodge fate for three years and come out of hell alive.

My story was long, but I couldn't shorten it. Every step was full and connected to death. We prevailed through nerve, courage, and, trickery.

On both my mother's side and mine, we were a large family. Eight of us came out of Yanova, but only my wife and I survived.

Translator's Footnotes

The Hebrew text renders the name as Aleksoti.

Šančiai is a borough in Kovno. The Hebrew text renders the name as Shantzi.

The Hebrew text renders the street name as Krikshtshiukaite.

The Dubianskys were the narrator's in–laws.

The Ältestenrat was the official name of the Kovno Ghetto's Jewish Council of Elders. The Hebrew text uses the term "ghetto council."

The Hebrew text renders the name as Gaižūn.

Moonshine vodka.

The Hebrew text renders the name as Atektzeine.

Off with the hat!

Sturmführer Wilhelm Goecke, the ghetto commandant.

The Hebrew text renders the name Keidani.

The Hebrew text renders the name as Atketziunas.

Atkočiūnaite, presumably the horse trainer's wife.

The correct name and exact location of these forests have not been established.

In this and all subsequent mentions, the Hebrew text renders the name as Atkečiūnaine.

There is no such name on the map of the Kėdainiai area.

In the Hebrew text, the name is rendered as "Veinçalis" (in quotation marks).

In the Hebrew text, the name is rendered as Vintzota.

The Hebrew text renders the name as Vansevitz.

The Hebrew text renders the name as Bazilishok.

[Page 227]

From the Vale of Tears and the Valley of Murder

by Sinai Persky of Tel Aviv

Transcribed and adapted by Yitzchak Burstein

Translated by Daniella Thompson

Sinai Persky (Tel Aviv)

I was 14 when the war broke out. That day I was in the Lithuanian middle school,[1] where I continued my studies after graduating from the Tarbut School.

I am the son of Avraham and Frumel. Our house stood close to the Viliya,[2] on the left side of Road Street.[3] We had a billiard table that my father had acquired, a cafe[4] offering tasty meals that mother used to prepare, as well as beer and soft drinks. My father also erected bathing huts next to the river willows on the beach. We weren't very grand, but we lived the life of *ba'alei bayit*.[5] We were six souls, including my younger brother Chaim, my sister Miriam, and aunt Ita, who lived with us. We all studied at the Tarbut School. Our favorite teachers were Shaul Keidansky, Aptekina, and Manes. They planted in us the love for Hebrew and *Eretz Israel*.

During the Soviet period, the billiard room was used by the army, and father worked there as an employee. On Monday, when we saw the stream of refugees, we loaded a cart and set out on the road to Vilkomir. With us were my uncles Yiztchak and Hillel Perevoznik and their family members: Hillel's son Aizik and his two daughters, Sara and Miriam, and uncle Yitzchak's son, Tzvi. Our relative Heishel Kaper also joined us. His sons, Levi'ka and El'ka, were in hiding in Kovno to evade expulsion to Siberia.

We reached Luki [Lukšiai?] Mountain. There we met Yudel Katzenberg, who had fled before us on a bicycle. He told us that he was going back, since he found out that the Germans were already in Vilkomir and the road was cut off. When we heard this, we also turned back. For several days we sat at home. When the shooting increased and Yanova was already ablaze here and there, we found shelter in the cellar of Leizer Levin, who lived in the Vilkomisrky house on Kovno Street. Yiztchak Perevoznik lived in the second wing. When the fire spread, we all ran to the spring next to the watermill. We sought shelter from the shells in trenches that we dug. When conditions worsened and the danger increased, we ran to Vertigo Mountain and found a hiding place in a gorge. Hundreds of Yanovans were concentrated here. German soldiers who were in the vicinity warned us not to budge from the place, since the battles were escalating.

The first victim of the German bullets was Berl Gold: he tried to run across to the other side, was ordered to stop and didn't, was shot and died on the spot. On Saturday we returned to town. The center had become a bonfire. Remaining on the road by the Viliya were the bus station, the Namiot and Manosevich houses, and the house of Yosef Katzenberg. We spent the night here, and on Sunday morning our family set out with Heishel Kaper toward Kovno via the dirt road that passed by the brickworks.[6] The Perevozniks remained in Yanova. That evening we reached Slabodka[7] and found accommodations with an elderly woman of our acquaintance.

[Page 228]

The next day I went with Heishel Kaper to the Green Mountain[8], to my uncle Elchanan Perevoznik. Staying there were Heishel's two sons, Levi'ka and El'ka, and also Levi'ka Perevoznik. From there I frequently went to visit my family in Slabodka. I was blond, looked Aryan, and nobody bothered me. On July 2nd, the Lithuanians took Father and other Jews to clean the streets. Then they transferred everybody to the Seventh Fort.[9] A day later they took Mother there as well; and on July 5th they collected all the people who were staying at Elchanan Perevoznik's house–among them Heishel Kaper and his sons–and transferred them to the Seventh Fort. I was also among them.

There were hundreds of Jews there. Among those from Yanova I saw the raft operators, the Brezins, Alter Jog[10] and Chaim Yitzchak Vikar. The men were collected in one gulley, the women in another. I could not find my father any more, since groups were led from here every day to the Ninth Fort, where they were shot to death. In this vale of tears I spent three days. The men were forbidden to stand up. They were allowed only to lie down or to kneel. We were surrounded by Shaulists (members of the Lithuanian Rifle Union). They frequently ran amok and would start shooting the prostrate crowd with their rifles and machine guns.

Once a Jew got up. He had been a volunteer in the Lithuanian army, was disabled and decorated. He hurled a hysterical shout at them:

"Who are you shooting? I spilled my blood in battle for Lithuanian liberty–and you, the Lithuanians, are shooting us!"

This had some influence. Several hours later, Lithuanian officers arrived and ordered all former volunteers to report to them. My uncle hinted to me to run after them. I did so, but I lost them on the way and arrived at the gulley where the women were assembled. There I found my mother and also Elchanan Perevoznik's wife, Masha (formerly Burstein, a native of Aleksotas) with her children, Yanke'le and Shneye. We were all conducted to the Ninth Fort. For two days we wallowed there. They gave us something to eat. All of a sudden they started to let women and children go. I was also set free with my mother and aunt. We went to Slabodka. My little brother was there, and our younger sister was kept in hiding. The Kapers and Elchanan Perevoznik did not return from the Ninth Fort. The groups that were transferred from the Seventh Fort were the first victims.

From the ghetto I was compelled to go out and work at the airport. I worked as an "angel," which, in the language of the ghetto, was a kind of "saint for hire," replacing those who refused to go out to work. In the fall of 1943, we–mother, brother, sister, and I–were sent to camps in Estonia: my brother and I, to the KuremÃ¤e camp; mother and sister, to the Soski camp. Only in the fall of 1944 did I meet them again at the Stutthof camp.

My brother and I worked on the railroads, wondering from camp to camp. Conditions were appalling: we were naked and barefoot and suffered hunger and cold. In Stutthof I also met the Yanovan barber Lieberman and the two Khasid brothers. The latter were annihilated in Estonia.

At Stutthof I worked near the crematoria. With another Jew, I carried a stretcher full of embers for the burning ovens. Once, my eyes caught the sorrowful gaze of my mother and little sister, who stood far away by the barbed–wire fence. They were emaciated, very pale, and dressed in rags. I wept bitterly, but their tears were invisible to me. That was the last time I saw the souls who were dearest to me. One day, as I returned from work, I didn't find my younger brother. They had marched him with a group of children to the killing place. From there they did not return.

And in all those trials, all that I and we went through–I held on! My will to live was strong, because I was still young. I still knocked about other camps in Germany. The English liberated me in Bergen–Belsen. Since I was ill, I was taken to a hospital in Bergen. From there I was transferred to a hospital in the Soviet sector.

After I got well, I returned to Kovno. I stayed with Tevya Jaffe, who survived by fleeing Kovno Ghetto. In 1953, I married Mirka Levin of Yanova, and in 1969 I arrived in Israel with my wife and our two children.

Translator's Footnotes

The Hebrew text employs the term *progymnasium*, describing a school that goes only as high as the 10th grade.

The Neris River.

This was the St. Petersburg–Warsaw–Berlin road that passed through town.

The Hebrew word, *miznon*, is equivalent to *buffet*, a light eatery found in railway stations.

Homeowners.

This is a guess. The Hebrew word used, *malbenot*, is uncommon.

Vilijampolé.

A suburb of Kaunas.

The first concentration camp in Nazi–occupied territories after the beginning of the war with the Soviet Union. Five thousand Jews were killed here in the summer of 1941.

In the Hebrew text, the name is spelled to be pronounced as Yag.

[Page 229]

In the Path of Suffering

by [Sidney Iwens] Yeshaya Ivensky [USA]

Translated by Jerrold Landau

Same as *[Page 11 - English] and [Page 19 - Hebrew]*

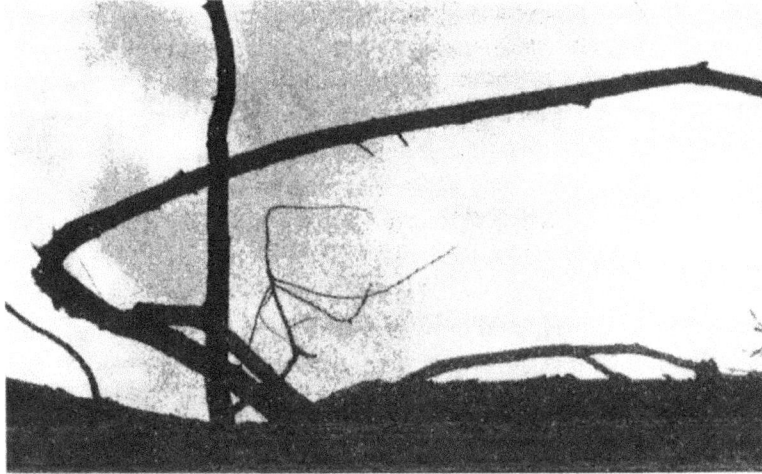

[Page 241]

With Jonava Townspeople on the Front and in the Hospital

by David Friedman of Vilna

Translated by Jerrold Landau

David Friedman

Hirshke Atkatz arrived at the front one day late. It was hard for him to walk, and he remained behind us. When he approached me, I asked him.

"Hirshke, what are you dragging with you on your back? What is in your sack? If there are extra things that are too heavy for you, discard them."

"What are you saying?! How can I discard the tools for fixing watches? How will I work after the war?" He did not merit thus. May his memory be a blessing.

Tall, thin Meir Pogir excelled among those who sang in our group. He also excelled in shooting. He was one of the better marksmen.

At the beginning of March 1943, we advanced in an attack, marching side by side. Suddenly he was hit by a bullet and was seriously wounded. He uttered a few words with difficulty: "Remove from my pocket photographs of Jonava as a memorial."

I was standing beside him like a stone, not knowing what to do. My hands were not listening to me. The command was heard: "Advance!"

Thus, with tears in my eyes, I left behind my dying friend. The command knows no mercy.

May his memory be blessed.

Moshe Goldschmid (Moshke the Potato) reached the rank of Division Commander in the army.

We were in a trench. Above us there was a barrage of shells. Nobody dared raise his head. Suddenly the information was received that the field kitchen arrived, and we should come to get food. Moshe collected the food utensils from everyone and prepared to go to get the food. I tried to stop him: "Wait a bit, perhaps the fire will abate". "I will somehow sneak through", he answered, "My soldiers do not need to starve".

Thus did he slither away, never to return.

May his memory be blessed.

In March 1943, we conducted a fierce battle against Hitler's soldiers. The cold was bitter. Mountains of snow piled up in the trenches. The shooting did not let up even for a moment. The nerves were tense. The German trenches were about a kilometer from us. The path was along hills and valleys.

After several days of battles, we, the group of soldiers, received permission to go to rest in the nearby village, three kilometers from the front. We were to return at 4:00 a.m. Of course there was almost no trace left of the village. We found a destroyed storehouse full of soldiers sitting and warming themselves next to bonfires.

Shmuel Schneider from Anykščiai and Bentze Rashkes were in our group. At 2:00 a.m. there was a heavy snowfall, and within a short period, everything was covered with snow. We were forced to move on with the clear knowledge that it would be easy for us to lose our way and fall into the hands of the Germans. Rashkes was determined to return no matter what. We attempted to convince him to wait until dawn. We did not succeed in convincing him. He went himself. At 4:00 a.m., I went along with Schneider. We walked slowly in the deep snow and got lost. Suddenly we saw a German guard from afar. To our good fortune, he did not notice us. We began to run back to the village from where we came. We only returned to our unit at 7:00 a.m. along with the field kitchen.

Bentzke Rashkes was not there. May his memory be a blessing.

Berko Aiker reached the rank of lieutenant. I was not in his unit. By chance I met him in our training division in Balciunai. He was at the hospital there, as was I. In June 1943 we traveled again to the front under his command. He quickly endeared himself to the soldiers, and everyone wanted to fight in his division at the front. However, when we arrived at the front, we separated, and I never saw him again.

He did not succeed in coming to the victory and the liberation. May his memory be blessed.

Wounded, I was brought to the front in the city of Yelcha. I immediately began to search for natives of our city. To my great joy, I found Shlomo Kanovich. We were together the whole time, and of course we discussed Jonava a great deal. We recalled all sorts of events that took place, and pondered a great deal about what was the fate of all those that remained, where are they, and whether they are still alive?

All of this transpired as enemy airplanes flew over Yelcha and the hospital day and night dropping bombs. We were together for a month. My wound healed and I returned to the front. I parted from him with tears in my eyes as we wished each other that we would meet in our city after the victory.

Kanovich is also living in Vilna today.

I was once again in the hospital in Ivanova. One week before July 21,1944, the commissar of the hospital came to me and said:

"You are the only one here from Lithuania. We have a tradition here of celebrating the date of the joining of each republic to the Soviet Union. Since Lithuania joined on July 21, I am hereby inviting you to appear and to tell us about that day. After that there will be a concert.

My response was that I was not used to making speeches, but I was prepared to play Lithuanian folk songs on a mandolin.

The celebration took place in the hospital. I played verses of Lithuanian folk songs. After the applause, I was asked to do an encore. I stated that I would play a Jewish dance, the Hora. I had never played with such enthusiasm. The chords of the mandolin trembled, and there were tears in my eyes. Again, there was a thunderous applause…

The soldier Shlomo Berzin – among those who perished

[Page 243]

My Activities in the Kovno Ghetto

by Tzvi Levin of Frunze, Russia

Translated by Jerrold Landau

During the years of the German occupation, 1941-1944
(A brief account.)

Hirsch Levin, one of the important organizers of the Jewish resistance movement in the Kovno Ghetto [1]

In December, 1941, with my initiative, I organized a clandestine meeting in the ghetto with the representative of the Communist underground (Galperin). At this meeting, the foundations for the united underground of the Kovno Ghetto were laid. Its members were Zionists and Communists.

Between 1942 and 1944, I was a member of the leadership of the underground organization. I carried out the following actions:

Through my initiative, at the beginning of 1942, a radio receiver that operated only through earphones was set up in the cellar of the ghetto pharmacy. News from the fronts was received through this radio throughout the duration of the ghetto period. The transmissions were recorded, transcribed, and distributed among the members of the underground and the ghetto population.

My father Chaim of blessed memory played an active role in the distribution of the news. He was burned in a bunker at the time of the liquidation of the ghetto.

I played an active role in the drafting of the Zionist youth, with the aim of transferring them to partisan camps in the forests.

I conducted a campaign to raise funds and obtain valuables inside the ghetto and outside of it, with the goal of purchasing weapons.

I played an active role in obtaining weapons from outside the ghetto, and I often personally smuggled weapons into the ghetto.

Through my initiative, Segalson, the director of the large workshops in the ghetto, organized a group of trustworthy individuals to transfer army coats, boots, underwear and other items of army clothing to the Jewish partisans. These items were stolen from the workshops where they were being prepared for the Wehrmacht.

I was the communications man between the leadership of the underground organization and the directors of the ghetto, who secretly helped the partisan movement in the ghetto a great deal.

I remained in constant contact with the "Matzok" (Merkaz Tzioni Vilijampolė, Kaunas - Zionist Center of Vilijampolė, Kaunas), and helped transfer young people of that organization to the partisan camps.

I provided revolvers to some members of the group of Jewish partisans who escaped from Fort Nine on December 25, 1943, and hid in the ghetto. Similarly, I hid in the ground a metal chest filled with gold teeth that had been extracted from murdered Jews, and that the partisans had taken with them during their escape. After the liberation of Kovno, the chest with the gold teeth was given over to Kotargna the dentist, who was then at the helm of the committee for assisting the surviving Jews.

[Page 244]

Through the means of the directors, I placed trustworthy Jews of our people in important tasks in the guarding of the ghetto. These people would carry out the directives of the united underground movement and Matzok, and thwarted the commands of the Germans.

One of these people was Yudel Zopovich from Jonava, who along with the Zionists Moshe Levin and Ika Grinberg of the ghetto guards helped the Jewish partisans leave the ghetto and smuggle weapons outside. Yudel Zopovich was tortured and shot to death at Fort Nine along with a group of Jewish guards, by Keitel, the infamous murderer of Jews. Witnesses related that Yudel Zopovich took a brave stand until his bitter end, and encouraged those who shared his fate.

At the end of March, 1944, after provocateurs informed the Gestapo about the roles that I played in the ghetto, Gestapo men, headed by Keitel, appeared at the ghetto council and demanded that they reveal my place and turn me over to their hands.

With the assistance of the underground organization, I escaped from the ghetto and hid in secret places and underground hideouts.

As I was told by those who had been among the directors of the ghetto, Keitel searched for me until the last day, and nicknamed me "Levin the leader of the gangs."

January 24, 1971

Translator's Footnotes

Hirsch is the Yiddish form of the Hebrew name Tzvi.

The Straight Path that We had to Follow

More on the activities of Tzvi Levin in the Kovno Ghetto

Translated by Jerrold Landau

One morning in August 1943 - as is related by Moshe Segalson, the director of the smithies - my friend Tzvi Levin, one of those close to the Altstenrat [1] of the Ghetto, entered my office in the smithy. He said that he must discuss a very urgent matter with me… "That which is being discussed here must remain a complete secret," he said. "I thought that you already knew about the new movement… A complete unity of all streams, from left to right, has been achieved. Our goal is to organize an armed mass whose task would be to conduct war against the bloodthirsty enemy… What we want from you is the following - first of all, to dress the men and women as needed; second, to collect money from the workers of the smithies"… "I thought about this a great deal, I took into account all the dangers and obstacles, but it was inconceivable that any obstacles and dangers should prevent the salvation of a portion of our young brothers and sisters. All of us must be prepared to give up our lives… This is the straight path (in the original: *wirdikste*, that is the honorable) that we must follow. I took everything into my conscience. This was solely for the benefit of the surviving the Jews of Lithuania, and for the benefit of the entire Jewish people. Every opportunity of resistance must be seized, especially when one is talking about a battle of honor"…

A meeting with Tzvi Levin and Chaim Yellin took place two days later in my house. They brought me the first request for 40 people… They told me that by the end of that year, they were to have 300-500 people going out (to the forests, to the partisans - the editor)… Everything was more or less ready a few days before the time. I informed Tzvi Levin.

Thus far was the testimony of Moshe Segalson.

Tzvi Levin played a very important role in the communication between of the council of elders (Altstenrat) in which he was the representative of the Revisionists, and the representatives of the underground.

At first, he joined the committee responsible for carrying out the transfer to the ghetto. Later, he was a member of the "communal council for salvation and resistance" of the underground organization in the Kovno Ghetto. Since he was one of the leaders of the Revisionists in Lithuania, he served as their delegate in Matzok (Zionist Council of Vilijampole, Kovno, or Center of Veteran Zionists of Kovno) around the time that he left the Soviet prison. Along with two other members of Matzok, he participated in long clandestine meetings with Irina Adamovich - the trustworthy and experienced contact woman with the Jewish underground of Poland, who was sent by the leadership of the FP'A (Fareinikte Partisaner Organizatzia - the united partisan organization of the Vilna ghetto). She recalled his name in her words of testimony.

Tzvi Levin was one of two representatives of Matzok who were appointed to conduct negotiations with the members of the"Anti-Fascist Organization" regarding joint activity and uniting the fighting forces in the ghetto. An agreement was signed and a joint command was formed to stand constantly at the helm of the activities. Tzvi Levin, one of the two signatories of the protocol of the agreement, was among those appointed.

[Page 245]

He was forced to disappear along with other activists of the organization when their arrest warrant became known. On April 4, 1944, members of the Altstenrat were arrested for failing to carry out the command of the Germans to arrest the Altstenrat member Tzvi Levin, who was among the finest of the AYK'L (General Jewish Fighter's Organization).

From the book "History of the Underground" by Tzvi A. Braun and Dov Levin, published by Yad Vashem.

Efraim Zilberman of the United States, who sees himself as a owing a debt of gratitude to Tzvi, wrote to use the following:

I have great satisfaction that when I escaped from the ghetto one week before its liquidation, I took Hirschel with me. We were in hiding for four weeks with a Lithuanian, about 14 kilometers from Kovno, not far from Kacergine. We were liberated together on August 1, 1944, when the Soviet Army reconquered Lithuania.

… While he was still a student, Hirschel stood at the head of the Revisionists in Jonava. Later, he served as the chairman of the Revisionist Party of Kovno. When the Soviets entered, he paid dearly for this. He was arrested and imprisoned in the Yellow Prison, and his family was deported to Siberia. When Hitler's armies entered, the Russians did not have a chance to take the pro-Lithuanian prisoners with them. Hirschel and other activists were freed from prison. His period of freedom was brief - only until the establishment of the ghetto. However, even when he was in the ghetto, he found no rest.

In the continuation of his words, Efraim Zilberman confirms the aforementioned words regarding Tzvi's many activities. He concludes by stating that we are permitted to be proud of this Jonaver.

Translator's Footnotes: The term for the Judenrat of Kovno.

With a Clear Conscience

In memory of Yehuda Zopovich

Translated by Jerrold Landau

… We conducted weapons training in the dwellings of the collective… Under the direction of the vice police chief of the ghetto, Yehuda Zopovich, who was appointed to the leadership corps in training - these are the words of testimony of one of the survivors of a partisan group who tells about the preparations for going out to the forest. Similarly, Yehuda played a central role in the ghetto police. He also played an active role in the "Communal Council" that was established for obtaining financing and property.

At the end of March 1944, 140 policemen were taken to Fort Nine for interrogation. After questioning, the acting chief Yehuda Zopovich and the police supervisor Ika Grinberg were brought for interrogation. They were ordered to reveal information about the ghetto, and in the process, they were beaten with deathly blows.

Yehuda was interrogated by the S.S. man Keitel, who was expert at dealing with ghetto liquidations and "taking care" of Jewish resistance movements. They were interrogated about the terrorists in the ghetto, arms caches, hiding places, etc. They were tortured harshly, but they withstood to the test.

When he and Ika were returned to their cell, they were beaten in a more serious fashion, and they were bleeding. Zopovich's head was broken. However, the interrogators did not obtain anything from their mouths. They stood with their stubbornness and were silent.

When the handsome Y. Zopovich was returned to his cell after the first interrogation, he appeared as a broken old man, and his friends barely recognized him. "Our youthful lives are lost," he told his friends, "Let us die as brave men and let us not expose the bunkers in which thousands of pure children are hiding. Let our consciences be pure before death." Then he sat among his friends and sang his beloved song, "A burning flame surrounds me."

He was murdered along with 40 other guards, including the entire cadre of commanders and his brother, police officer Meir.

The conduct of Moshe Levin, Ika Grinberg, Yehuda Zopovich, and their friends bore wings, and their names spread with reverence throughout the residents of the ghetto, who to that point had no appreciation for the police since they did not know about their activities behind the scenes.

From the book "History of the Underground" by Tzvi A. Braun and Dov Levin, regarding the fighting organization of the Jews of Kovno during the Second World War. Also from "The Book of Jewish Partisans," published by Sifriat Hapoalim, Volume I.

[Page 246]

People of Jonava in the Fight against the Nazis

by David Rubin

Translated by Jerrold Landau

Chuna the Partisan

Several of our townsfolk stood at the head of the underground organization of the Kovno Ghetto. They excelled in the organization and in battling against the Nazis.

The first, who was renowned for his bravery and organization talents, was Chuna Kagan. Weapons training activities took place in his dwelling. The weapons cache was located in his home. He was among those who accompanied the members of the ghetto to the partisan units in the Rodnitzki forests. He would return to the ghetto and continue in his publicity work on behalf of the struggle against the Nazis.

Meir Leib Goldschmidt (Tsoref) was a member of the leadership committee of the organization of ghetto fighters. He excelled in publicity in all circles of the fighting force. Exercises in weapons practice and partisan fighting took place in his home.

I also joined the underground through Meir Leib. I practiced with a Czech gun in his house.

His wife Sonia was also active. She moved to the Lithuanian side and dedicated herself to the saving of children and in procurement. She met her death through the bullets of the murderers as she was returning from a task of salvation.

One of the heads of the fighting organization was Miriam Lan, who headed a division of the underground organization. She went on many missions outside the ghetto. She maintained contact with the partisan heads in the forests of Augustova and Jonava, and endangered her life to save ghetto fighters. She participated in many actions against the Nazis, and joined the partisans in the forests of Rodnitzki.

Leib Solomin parachuted in from the Soviet Union to organize the partisans in Lithuania. He set himself up in the forest of Jonava and commanded the first partisan units that were established on Lithuanian soil. He participated in many activities in his war against the enemy, and inflicted many losses on the Nazis and their helpers. Solomin himself was seriously injured in battle, and remained handicapped throughout his life. It should be noted that he did not want to connect with the underground in the ghetto, and did not conduct joint activities with it.

Many others natives of our city excelled in the war against the Nazi enemy when serving in the Red Army.

We express our esteem and honor for the brave heroes who fought alone against the powerful, evil enemy, and fell in battle.

[Page 247]

Miriam Lan[1]

Translated by Jerrold Landau

A committee of six members stood at the helm of the "Anti Fascist Organization of the Kovno Ghetto". Miriam Lan of Jonava was one of them.

Miriam Lan was a Communist activist with underground experience. She joined one of the Communist groups that were set up and were active in the Kovno ghetto during the autumn and winter months of 1941.

During the attempts to forge connections with the partisan bases, Miriam Lan, as an activist of the "Anti Fascist Organization" was sent out to the forests of Jonava. The messenger did not return to the ghetto, and for a long time, her fate was unknown. Later it was verified that she joined the Solomin group (He was a Jewish paratrooper and partisan commander).

When the Russians entered Vilna, Miriam Lan was given a security mission: to take a stand along with two other people at the crossroads, to stop anyone entering the city, and to search after suspicious people…

Based on the book on Jewish partisans and the history of the underground.

[Page 247]

A Veteran Partisan and Commander

Translated by Jerrold Landau

In Memory of Shmerke Valonas[2]

His true name is not known to this day. Valonas was his nickname. He was born in Jonava, Lithuania in 1922. He escaped wounded from the Jewish area of Dvinsk (Daugavpils). He hid with farmers. Germans exposed him there. He defended himself and shot at them until he used up the last bullet in his gun. When his ammunition was finished, they captured him alive. The brought him into a house and put him under guard. After a few days, when his energy returned, he attacked the guard, felled him, and fled through the window. He hid once again with farmers. On account of his Aryan appearance, handsomeness, and fluent command of the Lithuanian language, they took him for a Lithuanian. Therefore, he received good and dedicated care. When he recovered from his wounds, he escaped from the German hospital. He arrived in the Kazian Forests and was accepted into the Lithuanian Brigade at the beginning of 1943. There he was appointed as the head of the division of the "Kostas Kalinoskas" brigade.

Shmerke was a veteran partisan and a commander. Valonas became famous already before he came to the forest.

Shmerke Valonas commanded a group that included four other Jews. When they went out to activities, they took along a certain gentile who related to Jews with denigration and curses. Their first action was the bombing of a train that was traveling toward the front. They destroyed it, along with many soldiers and heavy weapons, including tanks. They did not suffice themselves with this. They burnt down a large dairy that served as a supply base for a nearby German garrison. They sawed down forty telephone poles.

They encountered an ambush on the third night. Were it not for the leadership abilities of Valonas and the level-headedness of the fighters, probably none would have survived. After an exchange of bullets and fierce firing, they succeeded in breaking through a path for themselves. The only one who lost his resolve and did not even attempt to shoot was the gentile Savka, who acted as an observer on behalf of the command.

He was killed by the partisans from the Lithuanian unit when they attempted to confiscate his and his friends' weapons.

Based on the book of Jewish Partisans, volumes I and II, published by the Workers' Library, Kibbutz HaArtzi of Hashomer Hatzair.

[Page 248]

A Revolver – and a Pair of Tefillin

by Shmuel ben-Menachem (Deitz)

Translated by Jerrold Landau

The Yeshivas were disbanded when the Russians entered. My father Mendel, the Rosh Yeshiva, and I became shoemakers. We worked in Slobodka where Grandfather lived.

We hurried to Jonava when the war broke out. When the bombardment began, we hid in Itzka Zalonker's cellar. During a lull we were able to see what was taking place outside. We saw Rashkes leaving his yard and being caught by a German – the first German that I saw in my life. The town began to burn. All of Breizer Street was in flames.

We left Jonava and set out for Kovno. Along the way we stopped to sleep over in a bathhouse in a village. The nationalist Bendits, or the Lithuanian Nazis as we called them, came in the morning and chased us out of there.

We arrived in Slobodka. The young people, myself included, were arrested and brought to the synagogue in Kovno. Our first command was to raise our hands so that they could see our watches, which they removed from all of us. After three days without food we broke out. Since there were no guards, we escaped. We returned to our families in Slobodka.

Our area of residence was annexed to the ghetto. We set up a hiding place under a pile of wood in a storehouse in the yard. We thereby succeeded in getting through the first aktions.

My father and I worked as night guards in the airfield before the large aktion in October. When we returned through the gate in the morning, we did not succeed in hiding, and we were forced to stream toward the concentration field with the entire community. Our family was divided into separate groups. We were nine children. All of the family members were sent to the Ninth Fortress. I, my sister Chaya Fruma, and my youngest brother Yitzchak remained from the family as people fit for work.

The youth began to organize in the underground. I sold my sewing machine and purchased a revolver. I joined the organization of religious Zionist youth (The Brit Zion Organization" (AB"Z). At the head of the organization stood Avraham Melamed of

Slobodka, today a member of the Knesset[3] and Avraham Rapopski of Jonava, who lived in a religious commune in the ghetto without any family.

Later we began to dig hiding places. The commune dug the first hiding place. At the same time, we began to forge connections in order to go out to the forests. When the underground received information that an aktion was about to take place, we decided to send out several groups in different directions. After two days all of them, consisting of approximately 100 people, were arrested by the Gestapo, with the exception of one who succeeded in escaping.

The entire population was certain of a German victory, and therefore was active in giving over the enemies of the Germans into their hands. Collaboration between the Lithuanians and the Germans began to flourish when everyone became confident of a German victory. The gentile concluded that his neighbor would turn him in when the time came.

Then the underground began to operate.

We made attempts to connect with the Russians – the Starovirs who were residents of Shpinan. However, the Germans were following them so closely that any attempt to connect with them was futile.

We continued to train. The region of old Slobodka became separated from the ghetto. We had to uproot ourselves and crowd into the ghetto, but we decided to remain in the bunker with the hope that we would succeed in forging connections with the ghetto and enlist a trustworthy gentile to complete the unfinished structure atop the bunker.

To our sorrow, the Lithuanians exposed us due to our tracks in the snow. We had to uproot ourselves. At night, Yehuda Zopowitz reached us along with a group of police, giving us the weapons of the underground! (The policemen of the ghetto were almost all members of the underground). They took us out from the "burnt" bunker (which was exposed), and brought us peacefully, along with the moveable objects that remained after the Lithuanian pillaging following the exposure. This was the bunker of the Yeshiva.

[Page 249]

The bunker of the commune had been exposed a day previously. They transferred to our bunker that very night, and they transferred to the ghetto together with us.

I worked at shoemaking in one of the workshops of the German guards in Kovno. We maintained connections with the general underground, and began to organize for our exit to the forest.

I realized that I would not succeed in going out through the Zionist underground, who were discriminated against with respect to going out to the forest. Therefore I turned to the Communists and went out with them.

Recorded by Sh.[imeon] Noy

The following is the continuation of the story from the History of the Underground by Tzvi A. Baron and Dov Levin, published by Yad Vashem.

Shmuel Deitz was a member of the religious Irgun Brit Zion faction in the Kovno ghetto. He came into contact with the Communists after the childrens' aktion in order to join a group of fighters that went out to Kazlu-Ruda.

On May 4, 1944, Ira Berman returned to the ghetto and took two other people with him, Yerachmiel Berman and Shmuel Deitz. On the way, Ira fell into the hands of an ambush of Lithuanian police. His two friends succeeded in reaching a small partisan unit that was in the organizational phase. This was a group of fighters from the Kovno ghetto that called itself "Kochargin" and conducted joint activities with a local Soviet paratrooper brigade.

In June, Sh. Deitz was sent to the ghetto to bring new fighters. The third group, consisting of eight people, also stumbled into an ambush. All perished aside from Shmuel Deitz.

The following is Deitz' story about the second and third groups.

We went out on the Sabbath through the gate – I and Rachmilke Berman. Irka waited with Maria Laschinski – one of the most trustworthy of the Christian intermediaries who lived near the ghetto. I had two revolvers, one of which I had obtained from the Communists as a trade for my sewing machine. Rachmilka did not have a gun. The directive in the event of combat was that we were forbidden to use weapons within 100 meters of the ghetto fence. We slept in the Christian cemetery…

We set out for that aforementioned Christian woman on Sunday morning. Irina Berman[4] was there. She had a small gun and Yerachmiel took the parabellum gun. We set out on our way. They both walked together and I walked behind them out of caution. Along the route that day, the gentile recognized Yerachmiel and shouted: "Jews!". We hid in one of the groves and waited for about an hour until we saw that they were not pursuing us. We began to walk on a second rater road toward Garliava. When we passed near one of the houses in one of the villages, a 5-7 year old boy stood and shouted; "Bendiates!" I noticed that that house had a telephone connection. After we walked two more kilometers, a Lithuanian on a bicycle caught up with us. He placed the bicycle next to the telephone pole, as if to inflate the tires with air, but I noticed that he was following after the first two who were walking…

According to our agreed upon sign (a whistle), they left the path and waited for me between some bushes at the side of the road. I told them about what had happened, and we realized that the matter was very serious. Since there was no place to escape from there, we began to guard the area around and waited for what might happen. Yerachmiel was the commander. Nothing happened for an hour. We continued to advance in the direction of Garliava, and when we crossed the train tracks we saw that there were unusual preparations with armed people at the edge of the village. Strong and sustained fire was opened against us as we approached within 500 meters of Garliava.

We retreated and returned to the train tracks. Yerachmiel had lost his compass along the way. We ran for five kilometers into the forest and did not know how to leave. We saw a secondary road along our way and we went along it until we entered the village of Papliva on the Pliva River. Since we wished to find out where we were, Irina decided to endanger herself. She turned to the first farmer that she saw along the way. She presented herself as a student who had gone out on an excursion, and asked for directions to our destination. The gentile showed us the way, but after we went for about 500 meters, he caught up to us on his bicycle and apologized to use for showing us the wrong direction. We went along with him, and when we passed his house again, his wife and son were standing there. They invited us to sleep over with them, since the day was ending. His name was Antanas Kontziatis, a guardian of the forest.

[Page 250]

We had no choice. We entered his house, with the attitude of "let us honor him and suspect him". We set up the night into three watches, with each of us taking one watch.

After we went to sleep, the neighbors came to summon him, complaining that a wild animal was destroyed the field. Then we saw him take a hunting rifle and go out with them. We opened up the locks and waited for what was might happen. After some time he returned and went to sleep. We were calmed, and continued with our watchful guarding. In the morning after we ate, he hitched his wagon and took us to the main street. He would not even take a coin from us, even though we urged him to do so.

From there we continued on foot at the edge of the road in the same formation (I remained 500 meters behind them). We were about seven kilometers from the village in which we were supposed to forge connections with the partisans. Lula Berman was there (Irina's sister). A truck with Lithuanian guards caught us, and stopped when it reached the first two. At that moment I saw that Rachmilke aimed his rifle and shot them. They caught Irka after a struggle. Rachmilke escaped to the other side of the road. I was afraid that they would comb the forest into which Rachmilke fled. I fled to the other side of the road, and entered into the forest to a depth of several kilometers. I waited for three hours, and when I saw that they were not pursuing me, I returned to the main road and continued to go on the road until I reached the village of Pazliai. I knew that we were supposed to meet at the fifth house on the left of the road. However, when I reached the village, I found out that there were two entrances and two houses. I waited a bit in order to identify the correct house. Suddenly a 17 year old girl came out of the Lithuanian village, looked at me and asked me if I knew an actor by the name of Berman. I realized that she was searching for me. She brought me to the nearby grove… I met Yerachmiel Berman in the grove who told me that he fled and arrived through a side road. We went to the house of the contact at night fall, where several partisans and Irka's sister Lula were waiting for us. We slept in that house. Then they took us to the nearby forest (several kilometers from Kozlu-Ruda). There I met Meir Silber. The partisans did not wish to keep him. They claimed that he was not able to be a partisan. There were several other Jews there, who came to us in a non-organized fashion. I remained there for about a month. Pechkis, who had been the police chief during the Russian era, was the commander, and he was still in a state of getting organized. Therefore, there were not yet any actual actions. We obtained food from the area. One day I received an order from Pechkis to return to the ghetto to bring more people. They sent Meir Silber with me to return to the ghetto. Before that, we took his personal weapons from him.

We set out in the morning. We continued along the main path and walked along the railway tracks. We passed close to the path upon which we had the incident with the bicycle rider. We saw a new wagon approaching with a man in uniform inside. Meir said to me, "This is one of the forest guards", but I recognized that this was the police chief himself. At that point, he was already very close and there was no point in escaping from him. He stopped next to us, pointed his gun and asked, "Where are you going?" I responded that we were going to our relatives in the village. He said, "Wait!" At the moment that he jumped off the wagon I pointed my gun and pulled the trigger. Aside from the sound of the trigger, I did not hear anything. The bullet was a dud. When the police chief saw the gun he decided to back off. Since my gun did not work, we both escaped into the nearby forest. I lost Meir Silber when we entered the forest, and to this day I do not know what happened to him. I looked for him, for he had no weapons (I had six bullets). However, I did not find him. I saw on the map that I could exit to the main road through the forest. When I exited to the road a volley of bullets rained upon me. I heard "Here he is" in Lithuanian. I crawled away as the bullets were flying over my heads. After 200 meters I entered a hole and disguised myself with branches. I exchanged the bullet in my gun and waited for what was to come.

The police combed the forest and one of the policemen came within four meters of me. I realized that he was going as if a demon was compelling him, as if someone was saying, "You will not harm me, and I will not harm you". The tip of my gun followed him until he disappeared from my eyes.

I later came to Miria Leshchinski, and he signaled the ghetto. I entered the ghetto that night and they told me that they would tell me when they would give me some people (this was a few weeks before the liquidation of the ghetto). I went to the bunker of the Communists at their underground headquarters which was near the Christian cemetery on Bruliu Street. Along the way I met two captains of the ordnungsdienst, Arnstam and Grossman. They wanted to capture me, but I managed

[Page 251]

to escape from them. One day I received a command to return to the underground. I was given eight more people. Now there were orders (in contrast to the previous ones) to go only at night. We did not have any more weapons.

Traveling at night was difficult from a practical perspective. We worked according to the well-known policy: We took a person in every village who accompanied us to the next village. In one village, after we took one of the gentiles, someone apparently alerted the local police. We heard people running and shouting in Lithuanian, "Hands up." Since this was an ambush, we spontaneously dispersed into the wheat fields. I heard intermittent shots, and to this day, I do not know what happened to the rest of the youths. I lay down for two days in the wheat, for I knew that they were searching for us in the area. I had a gun and a pair of tefillin (Before I went out, I had an argument with Dimka Galperin, who did not permit me to take tefillin and a watch with Hebrew letters. Nevertheless, I took the tefillin).

I decided not to return to the partisans, but rather to go to the farmer Antanas Konchaitis in Paplivia. I called him outside and told him the entire truth. He told me that he had realized this already at our first meeting, for I was wearing worn out boots and riding pants, and the gun in my pocket stuck out from them. One of the reasons that I decided not to return to the partisan unit was that they did not agree that I could bring my sister and three year old brother to the forest, whereas this gentile had promised to bring them from the ghetto. He brought me to the forest which he guarded and put me in a hiding place that he had made to hide the meat and wheat from the eyes of the Germans. One week later he went to the ghetto and got in touch with the "Lafa" factory. There he told my sister to prepare herself, for he would come to get her in a week. When he came two weeks later, the ghetto was in flames.

[Page 251]

The Stubborn Starovirs

Translated by Jerrold Landau

"Leib Solomin", who was appointed in August 1942 by the central committee of the Lithuanian Communist Party in Moscow as the "secretary of the underground faction of the Kovno city and region", parachuted into that region along with a group of young Lithuanian Communists. They set up a partisan base in the forest around Jonava.

Solomin's partisan brigade functioned under relatively easy conditions. The population in the villages around Jonava was almost all Russian, and Communist influence in this region had always been strong. When the Germans entered, the Lithuanian nationalists took revenge on these Germans and perpetrated a slaughter. There was barely a house which was not affected by such deeds of slaughter. The majority of these Russians were from the Starovir sect, which was a religious sect in Russia. They were known as a stubborn people, and the Lithuanian atrocities did not subdue them. On the contrary, they rejoiced at every opportunity for revenge, and they willingly helped the partisans who appeared in the region. They also resisted the enticement to turn in Solomin in exchange for 60,000 marks.

(From the History of the Underground by Tzvi A. Braun and Dov Levin, published by Yad Vashem, page 256.)

[Page 252]

Illegal Mail in the Kovno Ghetto

by Efraim Silberman

Translated by Jerrold Landau

After a series of aktions in the Kovno ghetto in the fall of 1941, culminating in the large aktion of October 28, life began to return to its usual course. Many worried about the fate of their dear ones in the ghettoes of Vilna and Siauliai. Word of aktions came from those places as well. The details were not known, for mail connections were forbidden to Jews. Unconfirmed rumors arrived from time to time. The council of elders of the Kovno Ghetto began to search for ways of maintaining a connection with Jews in other cities, first and foremost Vilna and Siauliai. This was no simple matter, and fraught with great danger.

At that time, I worked in the group that was putting up bunks and doing other work in the Kovno railway station. One day when I returned from work, I was summoned to come to the general secretary of the council of elders, the lawyer Yisrael Bernstein. He explained to me the importance of setting up an illegal postal connection between the ghetto and Jews of other cities. Since I worked in the train station, He wanted me to try to get in touch with one of the railway officials who could be trusted, so that mail could be transferred from the Kovno Ghetto to the ghettoes of Vilna and Siauliai, and mail could be brought in return. I promised to look into the matter.

It took a month until I succeeded in finding an honest and trustworthy railway official who would take it upon himself to transfer the mail every ten days. I came to the council of elders with the news. I informed them that the matter was arranged and that letters could be prepared. Thus did the illegal postal connection begin in the Kovno Ghetto in December 1941.

I received two sacks of small letters from the council – to the council and individuals in the ghettos of Vilna and Siauliai. I hid the mail as I went out to work, and set out for the railway station with a feeling of pride that this day I was engaged in an important task for the benefit of the ghetto. I met the aforementioned railway official at exactly noon. I gave him the sacks and we agreed that he would bring mail from there in another ten days.

I waited for that day impatiently. Indeed, at the set day and hour, the railway official approached me and quickly gave me letters from the Siauliai ghetto and sacks of letters from the Vilna Ghetto. He informed me that he could not transfer mail to Siauliai due to technical difficulties. I waited impatiently for the end of the work day. I returned to the group in the ghetto with satisfaction. I went straight to the council and gave the mail to Y. Bernstein.

The lawyer Chaikin and another official Yuter were also occupied in postal matters. We continued exchanging letters between the Kovno Ghetto and the Vilna Ghetto for six months.

One day, when I brought sacks of mail with me, the middleman did not appear. I decided to not bring the letters back to the ghetto for fear of a stringent investigation. I hid the sack in the shed in which I worked, with the hope that the intermediary would appear the next day. He did not appear, but when I went to get the sack, I did not find it.

I arrived in the ghetto in the evening full of despair, and I informed the council men about the disappearance of the sack. Y. Bernstein sighed and said: "We must wait a few days to see what will happen." He attempted to calm me. The next day when I returned to work, a Jewish policeman approached me and told me that I was summoned to come to Serbovitch. Yosef Kaspi-Serbovitch was the only Jew in Kovno who worked as a steward with the Gestapo. He was the chief of the ghetto guard.

It was clear to me that the sack fell into the hands of the Gestapo. As it later became clear, the sack was discovered by a German driver and was turned over to the station police, who transferred it to the Gestapo.

When I entered into Serbovitch's office, I immediately saw the letters on his desk. He asked if I had hidden the letters in the shed. I answered him, "Yes". He informed me that he had been ordered to arrest me, and that the councilmen would also be arrested for conducting illegal activities.

[Page 253]

I answered him that the mail was my private initiative and that the content of the letters was solely family matters. I told him that if he were to imprison me, I would never see my wife and children again.

My words made some impression upon him. He said, "I will do what I can." He told me that the councilmen were guilty, but that he could not change the command of the Gestapo. He must arrest me.

He brought me to the confinement room. After a few hours, a Jewish policeman brought me to the council. There I was brought in to a special meeting of the entire council headed by Dr. Elkes. Serbovitch was also there, who received a written affidavit about the entire matter of the letters. I must confess that the steward Serbovitch related to the matter with a Jewish heart. The deliberations lasted until 5:00 a.m. In order to mitigate the seriousness of the matter and to prevent innocent people from becoming victims, I took full responsibility upon myself. The affidavit stated that I gathered and transferred the letters with my own initiative, and the councilmen did not know anything about this.

After the meeting, Dr. Elkes approached me, took my hand and said, "You performed a holy task for the ghetto. You acted with honor and pride. I will do everything in my power for you."

I parted from them all, and the policeman returned me to the confinement room. From there I was taken to the Gestapo early in the morning by a Lithuanian policeman. When I left the ghetto I had the feeling that I would never again see my family or the ghetto.

When I was brought into the Gestapo office, I saw the murderer Rauka next to the table. Serbovitch was also there, who pointed me out as the letter man. Rauka looked at me with his murderous eyes and aid, "Are you the bearer of the letters?" I did not answer him. Rauka ordered the Lithuanian policeman to take me to the Yellow Prison on Mitzkovitch Street. Serbovitch gave me a pitying glance and disappeared into another room.

A half an hour later I was already sitting in cell 54 in the Yellow Prison. I met five other Jews there who told me that a "cleansing" of the Jewish prisoners was conducted every ten days. They were brought to the Ninth Fortress. It was a rare occurrence that a Jewish prisoner was sent back to the ghetto. This did not improve my spirits. The five prisoners were very depressed and starving. They received scanty food rations, and they were forbidden from receiving food packets.

The first night in jail passed without sleep. I recalled all of those occasions when I looked death in the eye. I had the feeling that no more miracles would take place with me. I did not believe that the council of elders would be able to do anything for me.

The next night, the iron gate was opened, and I was surprised to see the lawyers Bernstein and Chaikin, as well as Yuter. Our meeting was emotional. I understood that with their imprisonment, the matter had become very serious. The only one who had not lost hope was Bernstein, who placed his hope in Dr. Elkes who said he would go the next day to deal with our matter with the Kovno Gestapo commander Jager.

Eight days passed in jail. On the seventh day, three of the five who were in jail at the time of my imprisonment were taken out. The inspector said that they were taken out for interrogation. However, they did not return to their cells. Six of us remained in our cells. We feared the awaited "cleansing". We were afraid of every rustle of the door.

One day the jailer gave me a note. He commanded me to read it and to destroy it. With trembling hands I opened the note and read.

"Remain calm. We are doing everything for you. There is hope that you will all return to the ghetto."

When several days passed without a "cleansing", we began to hope that perhaps a miracle would occur.

Thirty difficult days passed in the jail cell. We received no additional information about our fate. Then the heavy door slowly opened, and the jailer read a letter with the names of the four of us. He commanded us to take our belongings and follow him. Our hearts were trembling. We were standing in the long corridor. I asked the jailer, "Where are they taking us?" "I don't know", was his answer. When we entered the jail office, the official told us that we would return to the ghetto that day.

We kissed each other with tears in our eyes. At that moment we all felt that the Slobodka Ghetto enclosed with its barbed wire fences was for us – freedom.

(From "From the Last Destruction), Munich, December 1948. Edited by Y. Kaplan.

[Page 254]

I Was a Partisan for Three Years

by Zalman Rochman

Translated by Jerrold Landau

I was born in Vievisin 1914 to my parents Michael and Feiga Ribel. We moved to Jonava in 1916. We lived in the Alley of the Marketplace (the Alley of the Rabbi), opposite Rickless' house, in the house of Ovadia. Father was a wagon driver, who brought merchandise to shopkeepers. The floor of the house was made of red loam. We would sprinkle yellow sand on it in honor of the Sabbath.

I studied along with my brothers Yehoshua and Aharon in Yavneh with the teachers Preis, Alter Kagan and others. Later I moved to the Yeshiva in the Kloiz of the Peddlers. From there, I went to the Ohel Moshe Yeshiva in Slobodka. In Jonava I also studied in the cheder of Yankel the vinegar maker.

In the days before Passover, I would work in the matzo bakery in the evenings so that I could purchase clothing and continue with my studies. I continued thus until 1929. Our sister Sarale, who worked in the store of Meir Goldschmid, helped us with our tuition expenses. My brother Aharon, who studied in the Knesset Yisrael Yeshiva in Slobodka, excelled at his studies. However, since it was difficult for both of us to continue, I decided to learn a trade.

I Became an Upholsterer

I began to work in upholstering with Mottel Gurvitch. I worked there for three years without a break, but I left there as a first class tradesman. This also saved my life in the ghetto. Therefore, I love my trade, and I continue with it here in the Land.

I went to work as an upholsterer with Koppel Reznik. I earned a good living and assisted my family.

After I completed my service in the Lithuanian army in 1936, I moved to Shaty [Shat/Seta] and opened up an upholstery shop, and later a furniture shop. The Soviets took my workshop and store from me in 1940.

In 1940, when businessmen, manufacturers, Zionists and activists started to be exiled to Siberia, I fled to the town of Pastovys about 100 kilometers from Vilna, along with my wife Rachel, who had come there from Kovno for our wedding about two months previously.

When the war broke out, we set out on a journey along with all of my wife's family members, with the aim of going deep into White Russia. However, since the Germans caught up to us, we decided to return to Pastovys

Miracles During our Flight

Along the way we had to pass through the town of Krivichi. Our troubles began there. The Poles arrested us, put us in jail, and tortured us, beat us, and pulled out our hair, thinking that we were Communists. We deflected this accusation by showing them our Tallises and Tefillin. The next day they informed us that the men would be shot and the women would remain in jail. However, the captain of those Poles sufficed himself with the booty that had come into their hands – our wagons and all of our belongings. He brought us into a house and promised us to come the next morning to take us out of the town on the condition that I would give him my gold watch. Thus it was – he kept his promise.

We continued along our way to Pastovys along with other family. We stumbled upon three gentiles who told us that we were Communists and therefore were guilty of death. However, they were apparently afraid of us, for we were a large group. Along the way, German captains passed by us. We saw that the gentiles stopped them and pointed us out to them. They returned, blocked off our route and asked us who we were. We told them. They gave chocolate to the girls and told us to hurry up, for the Germans must pass. This was miracle number two for us.

[Page 255]

They Searched For Me

We returned to Pastovys. The Germans came in the evening and took my wife's grandfather and uncles. They did not enter the room in which I was sleeping. They were taken out the next day to be murdered. We found this out a half a year later.

Three months after we arrived, the Jewish Street was turned into a ghetto. Three families lived in one room. We were taken out to forced labor every day. We were divided for work amongst the farmers. I worked in pressing hay, cutting trees, cleaning streets, and other such tasks.

Once a Polish policeman came and asked about me. The workers advised me to leave. I wanted to move to a ghetto in a different town. I went to ask the advice of the Jewish council and it became clear that they were looking for a professional. They told me that that the district representative issued an order to repair the seat of his car. They sent for a cobbler, but he did not know how to complete the repair. The representative threatened that if the repair were not completed within a few days, he would kill 100 Jews. Indeed, I completed the repair to the satisfaction of the representative, and the decree was cancelled. The representative instructed that I be sent to the forestry enterprise, where I was given three square meters of firewood, worth a large amount.

A short time later, a command reached the Jewish council that I must open an upholstery shop outside the ghetto, where I was to work for the Christian population who would be sent there by the authorities. Five elderly and weak Jews worked with me. They were sent by the Jewish council in order to complete the quota of 60% employment in the ghetto.

To the Partisan Gatherings

One day a Pole came to me, took me aside, and told me that he had met several times with Jewish partisans. I begged him to help me get in touch with them. He came back about a month later and brought a letter in Yiddish from the partisans Michaelicha and his brother Zalman Friedman of Dolginov. They requested that I act kindly with the bearer of the letter and organize youth and weapons to send to agreed places outside the city. From there they would be brought to the forests. The situation was not easy; nevertheless we succeeded in organizing groups and sending them to the designated places. They reached their destination.

I received the final letter from them in October 1942, which stated that I was to arrange an additional group and come along with it, since they had heard the news that the Pastovys ghetto was about to be liquidated. We were told to bring as many weapons as we could. We obtained weapons from the locals in exchange for objects and gold. I kept the matter secret. I only told my wife and family members the night before we were to leave the ghetto.

We were a group of 42 people. All of the men were armed. The Jewish ghetto police did not want to let us leave. They kept one girl behind. We threatened to open fire, and the ghetto would suffer from this. Then he let us all leave the ghetto in small groups. Outside we removed our yellow patches, and went to the gathering place. The Jewish partisans were waiting for us there. They took us in wagons for a distance of 20 kilometers from the ghetto. We remained for two days in an empty village near the seashore at Naroshetz, in the Nivra Forests. From there we were taken to the gathering places of the partisans. The men joined various groups, and the women, elderly and children were to be smuggled across the border into Russia. My wife and her parents remained with me.

The partisans were mainly Russians – prisoners who escaped or soldiers who had gotten lost. They were about 10% Jewish. The commander of the unit was Markov, a teacher and Communist from Zhebenchian. We obtained weapons by sudden attacks on the Germans, or searches in the villages. We also thereby obtained our food.

Once we went to the village of Sloboda, near the town of Dunilovichi. The commander told us to enter the house of one of the farmers and to find the guns that he had. We entered the house at night. We were three Jews: Nachman, Kopel, and I. We demanded that he give us his guns. He denied that he had any weapons. We took him out to the yard, tied him up in a rope, and lowered him into the cold water of the well; but he did not admit to anything. When we raised him up he told us that he had already given the weapons to another unit, and that a stranger was staying with him who is liable to report the entire matter to the Germans, and that he would be punished. We entered the house and woke up the man. The two partisans from Pastovys who were with me interrogated him. He was an anti-Semitic priest. We took his gun from him and brought him with us. Along the way he was asked to confess how he tortured the Jews of the ghetto. He admitted his atrocities hoping that we would set him free. However, we decided to kill him. We tied him to a tree and shot him.

[Page 256]

At the beginning of 1943, the Germans brought in garrisons to fight against the partisans and they surrounded the forests. A command was issued to scatter about into small groups to escape the trap. I was in a group of 15 Russian partisans. My wife was in a different group. Once our group stumbled upon a guard of Germans, Lithuanians and Ukrainians. A few members of our group fell in battle. I and seven Russians were left. That night we met in a region that contained a large group of partisans. The next morning Markov commanded us to move 300 kilometers to the east, to the region of the cities of Vitebsk and Plock. We went there in wagons and set up a fortress for ourselves in the forest for five or six months. Our group at that place had about 200 Jewish fighters, in addition to groups of old people, women and children who worked at various supporting services.

The Commissar Jurgis and the Captain Mendel Grun

During the months that we were in the new place, a Lithuanian unit was set up from a Lithuanian division that was parachuted in. The commander was Kazimir and his second in command was a Jew who was nicknamed Jurgis. This was Ziman, the editor of the Tiesa newspaper in Vilna. He came to my commander and requested that I be transferred to the Lithuanian unit. I was sent to the city of Dokszyce where I participated in some battles.

The Commissar Jurgis once asked me to accompany him to greet some new partisans who were about to be parachuted in. They lit bonfires in an open field as a sign that they had arrived by parachute. He spoke to me in Yiddish along the way. Only then did I realize that he was a Jew. From among the partisans that were parachuted in I recognized a youth from Jonava, Mendel Grun, whose parents lived in the market square. He was wearing captain fatigues. We were together in the group for approximately three months.

One night we were sent out to a specific action. There were five other Lithuanians and two women with us. We stumbled into a German garrison along the way. We stopped at a distance of approximately 100 meters from them. We asked who was there. They answered in Lithuanian: "A Lithuanian guard". We responded in Lithuanian that that we are also Lithuanian guards. We agreed to put down our weapons, and the two sides met. Since we were more numerous than them and we were well armed, we surrounded them and took them to our command as prisoners. After an interrogation it became clear that they had conducted joint activities with the Germans. After we kept them in prison for three weeks, we took them and gave them over to the appropriate authorities.

As time went on we were commanded to move westward, to our former gathering area. There I met my wife, but we were forced to separate because I had to continue along with my unit.

Once Mendel Grun told me that he wanted to organize a group of partisans to go to Vilna, a distance of 100 kilometers, in order to bring Jews out from the ghetto to the forests. I was invited to join. I refused, and also advised him to put off this plan for the time being, for it was fraught with great danger. He did not listed to my advice, and set out with a group of 20 people. Along the way, they ran into German army units. A battle broke out, and he did not return from there. Another Jew and four Lithuanians were killed. The rest fled and returned to us.

Our main activity was to place dynamite on the railway tracks upon which army trains passed with weapons for the front. We also destroyed shipments of wheat and meat that the farmers sent as a tax to the occupying authorities.

When I returned to the place where my wife was, I found approximately 500 Jews – men, women and children from the from towns of the area: Kornitsa, Dunilovitchi, Pastovys, and Eišiškes. I asked Commissar Jurgis (Ziman) to form a Jewish unit. He pushed off my request and turned the matter over to Commander Kazimir. The commander answered my request, and asked me to organize men and women from among the refugees, to furnish them with arms, and to appoint a Lithuanian Jew as their commander. The commander was Shapostineitis of Mariampol, a former member of the Maccabee. His second in command was Tovia Gelfer of Vilna (today in Ramat Gan). I remained in my unit.

[Page 257]

The Jewish unit conducted successful actions, and the Lithuanians were satisfied. As time went on, we organized small groups of Jewish partisans who went out to Vilna to bring Jewish youths from the ghetto to the forests to join the aforementioned group of Mendel Grun. Yosef Gluzman of Kovno arrived in the first group. When he arrived, he was put at the head of a 12 person group which conducted various operations.

We Did not Believe that the Liberation was Drawing Near

At the end of 1943, the Germans once again surrounded our forests. We again dispersed into small groups. Yosef Gluzman went with his group in the direction of the railway track near the village of Sloboda. Battles broke out there in which many groups of partisans took part. They attempted to sever the track. I was also in one of the groups. At night I met Yosef Gluzman. He advised me to go in the direction of the region that was abandoned by the Germans. I advised him to join our group and not to go in the direction which he advised. He did not agree, and we parted. I and my group found refuge with a Byelorussian family whom we knew, who told us to go in a different direction in which there were no German guards. We thereby succeeded in breaking through the siege and returning to our place. We heard echoes of shots along the way. This was an exchange of fire between the Gluzman group and the Germans. The entire group, which consisted only of Jews, was killed in battle.

We arrived in the village of Zazaria in 1944. A farmer told us that Soviet army units were two kilometres away. We did not believe that the liberation was so close. I went in the direction that the farmer showed me, and we encountered a soldier of the Red Army. When we came to his unit, we told them that we were partisans.

I cannot describe in words joy at this meeting.

One of them accompanied us to a base where Jewish refugees were gathering. When we appeared there, and they saw the Red Army soldier, they burst out in tears of joy, as if they saw the Messiah. Some people fainted.

Our task as partisans had ended. A command was issued the entire unit should go into one of the towns of the region and impose order until the arrival of the regular army.

Kazan was in my area. We remained there for 15 days. Many people joined units of the regular army. Many others were liberated, including me. I met my wife, and we traveled to her town. We remained there for three months. From there we moved to Vilna. In 1946 we arrived in Lodz, and from there we went to Stettin on the way to Germany. We went to the French occupation zone and then to the American zone.

In 1949, I, my wife and four year old child arrived in Israel. We settled in Raanana, and I resumed my occupation of upholstering.

As I look back, it is hard for me to believe that my wife and I spent three years as partisans.

Now we merited and arrived in Israel. We returned to normal life, which was our reward for everything that we had endured.

Translator's Footnotes

There is a footnote in the text here: See the article of M.[eir] Tsoref. Page 197.

According to all of the signs and according to what was told by Y. Ivensky, See "In the Path of Suffering", page 235 – Valonas is Namiot. The editor.

The Israeli parliament.

The name has appeared in three different forms in the preceding paragraphs. Ira, Irka (which would be a diminutive of Ira), and Irina.

[Page 258]

Marching Song

by Noach Stern

Translated by Jerrold Landau

Set the agony afar,
Pick the pace
Go forward – with a foot on the clod of earth – oh valiant Hebrew.
Lad and youth,
Without fear or trepidation,
Go the thoughts of anger and rebellion.

We were orphaned
By a nation that no longer had mercy,
The captives of our people sunk into the depths.
But as long as we have not been annihilated
We will yet take revenge for the nation,
We will bear the banner of our battle aloft.

Set the agony afar,
Come, oh drum, and beat,
And summon the ancient might to awaken.
Cut through the storm,
And raise the flag,
Until dawn like thunder will bring freedom.

5703 / 1943

[Page 259]

With Jonavers in Exile in Siberia
by Yitzchak Ben-David (Burstein)
Translated by Jerrold Landau

On the Sabbath of June 14, 1941, I left the house in which I lived on Uzaska Street in Kovno in order to go to work at the office on the Green Mountain near Petrovska. I walked in the middle of the free sidewalk. I was surprised to suddenly see dozens of army and civilian trucks laden with moveable objects, men, women and children, traveling in the direction of the train station accompanied by Soviet vehicles. All sorts of explanations of this matter came to my mind.

I arrived at the office. The Jonavers Rachel Levin, Tovia Kolbiansky (the son of Moshe and Rachel) and the director Shimon Merbiansky also worked there. It was through the latter that I was hired as chief accountant after I transferred to the Kemach factory where I continued my service for some time after the war.

Something was about to Transpire

An oppressive atmosphere pervaded the office. Everyone sensed that something was about to happen. I attempted to get in touch by telephone with my family in Jonava, but was not successful. Rumors spread that Jewish families were being sent to Siberia. I waited impatiently for the end of work. I hurried home to my sister Miriam Levin, with whom I lived for the final six months.

Two people were waiting for me at the entrance: The Comsomol member Leizke the Yellow, and a strange man who was a representative of the N.K.V.D. I was ordered to raise my hands. They searched my pockets, and searched through all of my personal belongings in my room. They informed me that I was a prisoner, and that they were bringing me to the train station in Jonava in order to reunite with my family along the way to Siberia.

My sister arrived in the meantime, and when she found out what was happening, she was smitten a second time. The first strike was that her husband Tzvi Levin was imprisoned when the Russians came to Kovno. He was held in the Yellow Prison, and she remained with two young children and with no means of livelihood aside from payments for the room and food. We parted without knowing if we would ever see each other again.

Meir Wolfovich lived downstairs in the house. He was the youngest son of Leiba, and studied in the gymnasium. We were put into a taxi and brought to Jonava, directly to the train station. I did not know at the time that my father was lying in bed sick. We passed by the Kemach. I requested that we stop so that I could pick up some personal belongings. They summoned Greenblatt who brought me suits, boots, coats and shoes. I had placed these there at the time the Soviets entered.

Family Meeting on a Cattle Car

The train station bustled like a hive with hundreds and thousands of people. A long chain of transport or cattle cars stood on the tracks. There were two Soviet guards next to each car. We were greeted by the N.K.V.D. official, my acquaintance and fellow townsman Shmuel Wichov. He seemingly apologized and said,

"Yitzchak, you will see that for you it will be better, for what will our fate bring? For the war is approaching." We were brought to the car of Jonavers. A guard opened the lock and the latch and brought us up to the train car. Shmuel Chernman and Dr. Mordechai Wolfovich fell on my neck and kissed me. They poured vodka and said, "Drink, and it will be okay for you!" I emptied the cup. I looked around – and what did I see? In a corner on one of the shelves, my poor mother was sitting in agony. Father remained sick in the house, and who knew if she would see him again. Her daughters remained in Kovno, and what would be their fate? As she sat immersed in thoughts about the fate of the family members, suddenly her only son appeared as an angel from heaven! She hugged and kissed me with silent weeping. My sister Leah and her husband Dov Segalovsky with their year old child Uza surrounded me, as well as the other Jonavers in the train: Malka and Avraham Jochovsky, Batya (Perevoznik) and Nissan Goldshmidt, who had gotten married that year, Yochel and Shmuel Chernman, Teibel and Leiba Wolfovich with their daughter Bunia and sons Mordechai, Meir, and Tzvi with his wife Batya (Namiot), Moshel Monosevich (Greenberg), as well as a few people from Wilkomir, and some Lithuanian families, primarily teachers from the Gymnasia.

We accommodated ourselves in a crowded fashion on two levels of planks, and set out for our long journey. The lavatory was in the middle, next to the back wall, behind a thin partition. Disgusting odors filled the air of the train wagon. Anyone who could, would control themselves, and try to use the "facilities" during the night. The ventilation was insufficient: two small windows with metal grilles on the front wall.

Losses Along the Way

We spent the first night in the station, waiting for other people from the area. In the morning, I saw through the window the wagon driver Itzka transporting my father to the station. I was quite emotional, and followed after them. I saw father get out and speak to the officials. Apparently he wanted to join his family members. He was arrested by a sentry as he attempted to walk toward the railway car. Father became pale and emotional, as he was forced to return. He entered the station, and disappeared from my eyes forever. The train set out toward Vilna. Our eyes were fixed to the landscape, going toward darkness and uncertainty: What would happen in the future? We were together in our tribulation. Our modest desire was that we not be separated, as it would be easier to bear the tribulations of exile together. A Russian adage states: at a time of trouble – open your gates wide.

We heard knocks on the door on the first night after midnight. A Lithuanian teacher was taken out and disappeared in the darkness of the night. We all trembled from fear about what was to come. A half an hour later, there was another knock, and a second Lithuanian teacher was taken out. We attempted to calm ourselves that these people were taken for interrogation, since they belonged to the Tautininkai nationalist party. After a few hours of quiet, it seemed that we heard knocks again. This time, a voice from outside ordered Tzvi Wolfovich to prepare to leave the railway car in ten minutes. The perplexity of the rest of us grew. During the first two nights, Berl Segalovski, Avraham Jochovski, and Nissan Goldschmidt left us –all of them young members of Beitar and the Revisionists who had gotten married that year. Nissan and Tzvi perished in the Reshety confinement camp in the region of Krasnoyarskaya in Siberia. Shmuel Chernman and Leiba Wolfovich were later taken from us. Three of us men remained: Dr. Mordechai Wolfovich, Yechiel Kerem of Wilkomir and I – with tense nerves. A deep mourning overtook all of us. Many questions drilled through the head: Where would the men be taken? Where were we being taken to? We did not want to utter the word Siberia on our lips – for a certain death from hunger and cold would await us there.

Stops Along the Way

The train moved along slowly. We wrote letters and scattered them along the tracks with a request to take them to a mailbox. We crossed the border into White Russia. At the first stop, we were ordered to choose three men to bring food, accompanied by a guard. I and two others exited the train. We breathed the fresh air into our chest. People who were simply dressed stared at us in curiosity. Sights such as this were not strange to them from previous years… We were informed that one of the trains that had just passed was full of men. I deduced from this that the men who had been taken from us were on that train. I found out that our train consisted of 20 cars – 18 for prisoners, a car for medical staff, and a car for N.K.V.D. workers. We received soup, meat and rolls according to the ration of 500 grams for an adult and 300 grams for a child. We returned to the train. We ate with an appetite, for it had been five days since we had eaten warm food.

Before we arrived at the Orsha Station, I found out that the war had broken out. The Lithuanians counted on a German victory and rejoiced that they would be able to return home shortly. We remain oppressed, for our hatred of the German Hitlerists was greater than our hatred of the current enemy.

The city of Orsha was a large railway junction. We stopped on a side track and once again left to bring food. We did not succeed in getting newspapers, for many people used the paper to smoke "makhorka". We also filled up a bucket of "kipiatok" (hot water) and returned to the wagon with food; however we had no news to tell. Only as we continued our journey did I succeed in obtaining some sort of newspaper from which I learned that the situation on the fronts was not bright. Lithuanian cities were being abandoned, and battles were being fought near Minsk. I thought a great deal about the fate of our dear ones who were left behind.

Far from the Front

Our train crossed the border from Europe to Asia at the beginning of July. We entered the Ural Mountains, at the Plada manufacturing region. One morning we stopped at a remote stop. The guards permitted us to go out for a few hours. Anyone who has never been imprisoned cannot imagine the extent of the joy that we all felt. We burst out and approached a small pond. The women did laundry, and the men and children bathed. We breathed clear air far from the front, and approximately 2,500 kilometers from our Jonava.

When we returned to the car, the guards did not close the door. They were sure that nobody would escape. The tension let up somewhat. We left the door slightly open and breathed easily. We found out from the guards that we were being taken to Siberia.

We moved slowly, for the railway tracks were full of trains with soldiers, arms and supplies. We arrived in Novosibirsk, the capital of Siberia on July 8. This was a giant station, the largest and most important on the Trans-Siberian Line. The station bustled with throngs of people. The pressure of the war could be felt. Our train left the Trans-Siberian Line and turned southward, toward the capital city of the Altai Krai, Barnau From there we traveled along thick pine forests toward the city of Biysk. This city resembled a large village. If it was already decreed upon us that we must be in Siberia, we would have been content to remain in that place. But that is not what fate had in mind.

On Trucks to an Undesirable Place

We were ordered to remove all of our luggage, and we were informed that trucks would come to take us to kolkhozes and sovkhozes in the area. In the meantime, the N.K.V.D. men approached us and conducted an additional search of our belongings. A Finnish knife that was a souvenir from my visit to Helsinki, pictures, and other things were taken from me. The trucks then arrived. The representatives of the farms understood the "living merchandise", our muscles. They searched for families that were not caring for children. We fell prey to the representative of the Karpovsky Sovkhoz of the region of Soloneshnoye, Rodkov the medic, who served as a physician and a veterinarian.

We loaded up our luggage and went out in a caravan of ten trucks. We crossed a bridge over the Ob River. Other trucks set out to other sovkhozes of the area. We crossed the Katony River in ferries. We spent the night in a youth hostel in one of the villages. When we reached the final village on the dry plain, the drivers filled up with petroleum in preparation for the venture into the mountainous region. A sudden rainfall dampened the roads. The wheels got stuck and began to sink in the mud. We were forced to return to our hostel in the village below. We returned soaked, except for the elderly and children who sat in the drivers' cabins.

We set out on our way again in the afternoon. This time, we succeeded in reaching the summit of the mountain. A wide, mountainous plateau spread out before our eyes. It was completely empty and filled with grass at the height of a person. There was no living soul, except for our caravan. We fell asleep. When I woke up it was dark. The people in the trucks slept, but the drivers snuck away and went to the village of Berezovka among the clefts of rocks to sleep.

This was at the edge of the Soloneshnoye region, occupying an area of 100 by 80 kilometers. Through the years this region became my second home. I worked there for 15 years. I crossed its length and width, without permission to leave it.

We continued on our multi-faceted journey along the tortuous mountains. Throughout the entire time, the following thoughts never left our minds: Where are they taking us? What awaits us – a human life or a dog's life? We arrived in a remote and desolate village of Lyotyevo. This was a large town of wealthy people before the revolution. Later they were exiled from there, and a large area was left abandoned. During the mid 1950s, a tractor and combine station was built there to work the land according to Khrushchev's plan. I was then appointed as the chief bookkeeper. The town grew and even succeeded in getting electricity. In the interim we continued our journey and arrived in the Madbadivka Farms – one of the five units that comprised the Karpovsky Sovkhoz. Those traveling in the first truck were designated for that sovkhoz.

They remained there at the crossroads. Most of them were Jews from Wilkomir, such as the Peltz, Yaffa, Chait, Riklansky, Janovsky, and Zaks families. The rest were Lithuanians. Of course, I wanted to remain there at the crossroads, where automobile connections were possible, but the reality was otherwise. We would also have preferred that all of the Jonavers remain together in one place, but blind fate also thwarted that desire.

Once again we ascended mountains and glided down trails until we arrived at the farm. The women and children were put up in the hall, and the men and unmarried women in empty granaries. The Jonavers were split up along the way: the Wolfovich family went to Pashchanka Farm to work in cutting trees and transporting them to the sawmill. In the morning, there was once again a thorough search of our belongings. We asked for permission to heat up the bath house so that we could wash up from the filth of the journey. When everything was ready and we prepared ourselves for our bath, we received a command from the director, the crafty Vizinsky, that we must report immediately to work. All of our pleading was for naught. The time was pressing. We must weed the fields and provide food to the front.

Work in the Heat during the Hot Season

We set out to the fields, a journey of five or six kilometers with the brigadier at the head. The following people were in the group: Yochel Chernman, Batya Goldshmidt, Malka Jochovsky, Moshel Monosevich and my sister Leah. The brigadier showed us the field which we were to weed. I was appointed as supervisor and was told that I was permitted not to work, and that I would receive four rubles per day. The quota for each person was four dunams. The field was filled with thistles and wild grass, to the point where it was hard to make out the oats. The women were equipped with parasols and gloves to protect them from the great heat and the prickly thorns. We had a measure of water. The women were immersed in worry, as were the men.

Yochel advised that we rest every ten minutes. They lay down on the soft mat of grass and chatted as if they had come for a vacation. When I advised them to get up for work, all of them spoke up at once: "Look at him, how dedicated he is to the Soviet government..." The sun set and we had only cleared one dunam instead of 10 hectares (20 dunams). The area was indeed clear. Thus passed two days

I had the opportunity to chat with a group of female workers, natives of the farm. They explained to me how they met the quotas. They would cut down the heads of the thistles with a scythe, and not concern themselves if they also cut down oats... We also attempted this method, but with our hands, for the use of tools was forbidden. I requested from the work director that I be transferred to another job. I was sent to work in preparing fodder for the winter.

I worked hard. The heat was great. Drops of sweat rolled down from my face and my body, which was half naked. There was a pail of cold water next to me. I would drink it with thirst. We built up the heap in the middle of the valley. When the base reached a height of two meters, a worker ascended and began to bind the fodder, which I then placed in the heap. As it grew higher, I exchanged the pitchfork for a longer one, which reached four meters in length. The work became more difficult and backbreaking. Our hands trembled, however, we made sure to bind the fodder well so that it would be properly preserved.

My Value Increased

From the first days of my work in that area, my name appeared on the chart of honor as a Stachonovich who fulfilled his quota by 200%. Of course this was not correct, but management wanted to set somebody up as an example so that others would increase their energy in their work. My bread ration was increased to 700 grams. The local residents treated me with honor, and I was appointed as the head of the group. Discipline was standardized and if anyone acted lazy, I would attack him with a fundamental, juicy Russian curse. This increased my value even more.

One day I received an invitation to appear in the main office of the central farm. I was freed from work, and I walked the ten kilometers by foot. The director received me politely, and invited me for a meal at his house. He treated me to vodka and a modest meal. Then he asked me to become the accounting director of the Komsomolskaya Farm. I agreed on the condition that he would give my family and me an appropriate dwelling. I was promised this, and two weeks later, I moved my mother, my sister and her daughter Uza to the new dwelling. It had a small corridor with a dirt floor. The room itself was nine square meters, with an oven and a shelf for sleeping and suitcases. This was a Garden of Eden compared to the previous conditions.

As I have stated earlier, the farm consisted of seven houses compressed into a narrow valley. Everything was neglected and abandoned on account of the casualness of the local people, and also of course due to the lack of working hands – for most of the men had been drafted into the army. We barely received any food provisions aside from bread.

We decided to purchase a cow at any price. The price for the cow, "Burka" was 1000 rubles, a dinner jacket, dresses, pillow cases and sheets. We concluded the sale successfully at the end of August 1941. "Burka" sustained us throughout the war years and after.

A man with a prison outfit, a Star of David and wooden shoes, holding a document or a book

Meeting with my Sister

I wrote to my sister in the Land of Israel at the time that I arrived. I received a telegram from the Land about one month later, stating that money and a letter were on their way. In the letter we found out that my sister Miriam with her two children were also in Siberia, near Biysk, approximately 200 kilometers from us. Rachel was in the city of Slogorod, also in the Altai Krai. Our joy could not be measured. However we also grieved over father's fate. Only after four years did we find out that he perished in the Stutthof Camp. I immediately wrote to my sisters with the addresses that I received.

the Wolfovich and Chernman families. Despite the shortage of physicians, the N.K.V.D. did not permit Dr. Mordechai [Wolfovich] to work at his profession. Only after much intercession was he permitted to move to the central town of Soloneshnoye and be appointed as a physician in the regional infirmary.

Being Uprooted – and Order within Disorder

In the spring of 1942 rumors spread that we would be transferred to the Yakutia in the Far East. We had nothing to lose. The situation was intolerable, with food shortages, inadequate housing and crowding. The issue of firewood was even more pressing. We had to travel on a difficult path of 15 kilometers in order to cut trees – and there was a shortage of horses and oxen. Nevertheless, we had fears about what was waiting for us in the east, a distance of about 2,000-3,000 kilometers away. Indeed, the Wolfovich family and Masha Namiot (five people), and Batya Goldshmidt (nee Perevoznik) were taken to Yakutia in the month of June. Remaining in our place were our family, Yochel Chernman, and Malka and Avraham Jochovsky in Parshchinka. Avraham was freed by mistake at the time of the liberation of the Poles from internment camps.

The war continued on and the situation became more serious. All of the work was done by women, children and the elderly. The death rate among the flocks of cattle, sheep and horses increased due to the lack of fodder. The veterinarian invited me to accompany him in his inspection of the cattle flocks in order to help him care for them. My task was to surround the head of each calf and hold it tight as the injection was given. After the operation we would drink the spirits that were designated for the care of the sheep, and refresh ourselves with black bread, onions, and grains of salt that were designated for the cattle.

My director was exchanged and the new director watched the newspapers closely. There was a great competition among us on this subject. There were no radio receivers, for they had been confiscated at the outbreak of the war. We received all of our news from the newspaper, which came four days late.

Throughout this entire time we barely had any news about what was transpiring in the Jewish world. However, bitter thoughts bothered us and gnawed at the heart. Mother had one "meal offering" that remained for her a refuge from all of the searches and confiscations. For her the Sabbath was a source of inspiration. She would pray and weep, while this was a regular workday for the rest of the family. In 1943, Mother and our sisters decided to arrange a Passover Seder. There was a great deal of planning. With difficulty, we managed to obtain a bit of dark rye flour. We baked matzos whose appearance was of the darkness of Egypt and Siberia. The meal was simple but festive. Everything was in small portions, but in good taste. We invited several guests who came: the Krikin widow, the Yaffa sisters and Chait from Wilkomir who came from the central farm. We ate, discussed, and talked not about the Exodus from Egypt, but about our travails here in the mountains of Siberia.

In 1942, we found out about the location of Berl Segalovsky, the husband of Leah, who was in an internment camp near the main railway line in the Krasnoyarsk region; and Yosef Dushnitzky, the husband of Rachel, in the region of Archangelsk. Their situation was difficult, and we saw it as our duty to send them food packages. We were receiving packages in growing quantities from our sister Sara in the Land. These permitted us to support our dear ones in the internment camps, as well as easing our own situation. These packages contained clothing, thread, soap, tea and coffee – all items that could not be purchased with gold.

We had good fortune and we were able to obtain butter and honey. We also obtained onions, garlic and tobacco in necessary quantities. Our sisters brought the packages to Soloneshnoye or to Biysk, and they sent them by mail.

The Struggle for Existence

In the winter of 1944, I was transferred to the main office of the central farm as a statistical bookkeeper, and finally as a replacement for the chief bookkeeper. We received a large dwelling. The connection with Biysk was relatively easy, and our sovkhoz had three trucks. The trip in them took eight hours, whereas it would have taken three days by horse. I was close to the upper class of the sovkhoz, and I was able to obtain all types of favors. Miriam and Rachel worked in cleaning hides, sawing wood and clearing snow. In the summer, Miriam was appointed as a shepherd. Despite her fear, she went out to the sheep pasture, a distance of five kilometers from home. She would sound a bell to scare away the wolves. As she worked she would collect twigs for firewood, and she would return home in the evening with a load of wood on her shoulders.

The director later appointed her as the central cashier. Rachel continued on with the farm work. This enabled her to have some free time on occasion and travel to Biysk in order to send packages. She was our "foreign minister".

Leah and mother were occupied with housework: caring for the four children, cooking, and laundry. In addition they tended to the cow, the chickens and the vegetable garden of the size of four dunams. The work in the garden was Mother's duty, and she did it with diligence, love and success. The carrots, beets and onions were first class. Aside from this, we had a potato field on the mountain slope, a distance of two kilometers from the farm. I would turn over the ground for two weeks during the month of May – before and after work, and on the day of rest. My sisters came to assist me. This was backbreaking work, but fulfilling, for the field supplied us with potatoes for the winter season. In the final months of the winter, when the supply diminished, I was forced to travel to the town of Solonovka, approximately 35 kilometers away in order to purchase approximately 300 kilograms of potatoes for food and planting, in return for various belongings. The negotiations would last for hours, for we had to go to many houses in order to obtain the necessary quantities. At this time, we would also purchase tobacco, and sometimes also wheat.

I Almost Lost my Life

On one such journey I almost lost my life. I traveled with a Russian refugee from Leningrad. The cold was more than minus 40 degrees. We reached the forest and went to sleep in the guesthouse of the sovkhoz. The negotiations lasted until the afternoon. We set out on our return journey. We wound our way atop the mountain on foot with a sleigh laden with 250 kilograms of wheat. The cold increased, burned our faces and made breathing difficult. We met a caravan that was passing near us; not in the set direction, but rather toward the higher altitudes of the mountain. They called and gestured to us from afar, but we did not understand anything and continued onward. We journeyed some distance, and suddenly before us was a flood of water and snow, and the path disappeared. We tried to cross the obstacle, but the sleigh sunk deeper and deeper. The horse escaped from the harness. We remained immersed in water, snow and fierce cold. I did not lose consciousness. From the sleigh, I jumped onto the horse from behind and attempted to place him back in the harness. However, the horse balked at the harness and fell into the water. My felt boots filled with water. The situation became serious. We had to rush, to leave behind the sleigh, to leave the water on the back of the horse and hurry to an inhabited place, for there was danger that my feet would freeze. I poured out the water from my boots, but they remained damp. He rode on the horse and I went by foot in order to warm up. Among the clefts of rock we found a broken and abandoned house. We collected twigs and lit the furnace, but it did not help. The cold worsened and I felt that my boots were frozen. We continued in the direction of the sovkhoz, a distance of seven kilometers. The journey was difficult, and the snow reached a height of a half meter. I moved with all my might. The lenses of my glasses were covered with mist inside and with snow on the outside, and I followed after the horse and its rider with difficulty. The Russian offered me the horse, but my instincts told me not to rest and to continue to move.

After a two hour journey, with my boots turned to pillars of ice and being barely able to feel my feet, I notice a light flickering in a window from afar. Here was the awaited settlement! We were saved! I called to the Russian. We entered the house and I called to mistress of the house, whom I knew: "Oksania, save me! My feet are frozen!" Her brother, a strong, aging man, advised me to lie beneath the burning furnace. He put my feet inside in order to melt the boots. It was only after a half an hour that I was able to remove the boots. I was fortunate, for only two toes of my right foot were still frozen. I scrubbed them with cold water. I was unable to sleep due to the great sensitivity and pain in my toes. I groaned silently. The gentile also did not sleep, for he was concerned that the wheat would disappear. As for me, my sole interest was about my frozen toes.

The owner of the house went out with us early in the morning in order to help free the sleigh. We equipped ourselves with axes and poles. When we reached the place, we found a frozen pond, sparkling with colors in the first rays of sunlight; however we did not see the sleigh. Suddenly we saw something sticking out of the ice. This was the front, high part of the sleigh. We were encouraged. We cut the ice with axes and dug out the sacks of wheat. We dragged the sacks to a dry place. We freed the sleigh with the help of ropes. We loaded the sacks, harnessed up, and continued on our journey. After this event I was laid up for a month. The medic tended to me with dedication and later I was able to resume my work.

Concern for Fodder and Fire Wood

Good news began to come from the fronts, which kindled the hope for liberation and return from where we came. The motto on the internal front was "to work harder" for the soldiers on the front. Aside from the office work, we also had to work in the fields, to prepare animal feed, fodder and silage for the herds of cattle and flocks of sheep. We went out to work with three wagons hitched to horses, and collected the fodder into piles. We would return home at around noon. During that season, there was a great deal of rain on the Altai Mountains. We needed to make use of the clear days. When I would urge the girls to arise from their rest and return to work, they would sing me the following ditty: "Witnesses from Above / the rain and precipitation / enough to soak everything / and we will be free from work." However, when they worked, they worked diligently.

I also had to concern myself with fodder for our cow. I did this on my days of rest. I would go out with a sickle to cut the soft grass. My sisters would go out to help me collect the fodder.

We also had to assist in bringing in the harvest in the autumn. To do this, we would go out to the farms for a week and sleep in the fields. As winter approached we had to prepare reserves of wood. If you got an ox or a horse on the day of rest, you could collect only enough for two weeks. However it was not always possible to obtain these animals and sleighs, despite the will to assist. The weather was also not always appropriate, for there was great cold and snowstorms. This was a battle for existence. You would go out in the morning and return at night frozen, tired and hungry, but with a sense of satisfaction as you looked at the sleigh laden with birch wood – fuel for two weeks.

We had to ascend the summit of the mountain, clear the snow near the trees, and use the axe. However, the first blow would not penetrate on account of the cold. Slowly we would overcome the tall birch. I would load the branches with their leaves on the sleigh. The foliage dragging behind served as a brake during the descent from the mountain. Below we would cut the branches, saw the trunk into short blocks, and tie them to the sleigh with ropes. I would walk on foot, for the cold penetrated the bones. At times the load would overturn along the way, and we would have to reload everything. This was my lot and fate for days and years.

The Difference Between the Russian and Jewish Mentality

At times I pondered the difference between the Russian and Jewish mentality. The men were at the front, and who knew if they were still alive. At home there was want and backbreaking work – so what reasons were there to rejoice?! The Jew in this situation was immersed in worry and agony. When we arrived we purchased a bottle of fine wine that we found in the store. My sisters hid it away for the day of the liberation of Berl or Yosef. The Russian women behaved otherwise. Almost every two weeks some mistress arranged a celebration and invited guests. For days before, she would prepare beer from honey and hops. There would be small portions of food, but the drink was aplenty, and the party was accompanied by song and dance until dawn. There were times when we prepared the fodder for our private cows together according to the timing of the cycle from one party to the next. With the passage of time I began to understand them: life was difficult, there were many worries, and one needed to give salvation to the soul.

On the day when the chairman of the economic cooperative would return from Biysk with a large barrel of liquor, which happened no more than once every three months, the saleswoman would arrange a party. I was always among the guests. The saleswoman had stocks of white flour, meat and butter, and we would eat to our fill, since we were generally always hungry. They would replace the bottles of liquor that were taken from the barrel with water.

We Also Drank

At the end of 1942, Avraham Jochovsky was transferred from Parshchinka to Solonovka, and after that to the city of Biysk. Only Yochel Chernman remained in the place, childless and forlorn. She devoted all of her energy to collecting food in order to send it to Shmuel who was imprisoned in the Reshety internment camp. She would carry the packages on her shoulders to the post office in the town of Soloneshnoye, a distance of 35 kilometers through winding upgrades in the mountains. She would tarry with us for rest. I tried to convince her to take care of her health, but she did not listen to me. She weakened in 1944 and moved to us in order to get medical assistance. She took ill in the spring of 1945. We cared for her for more than a month. The women Chait, Levi and Yaffa from Wilkomir assisted us. We arranged a rotation to stay with her during the nights, but it did not help. She died, and we buried her in the Russian cemetery in the town of Karpovo. Shmuel Chernman was freed from the internment camp and came to us. He stayed with us for about a week, received the "inheritance" left to him by his late wife Yochel, and moved to Biysk. He got married there, got a job, and remains there to this day.

In January 1946 we received a telegram that Yosef Dushnitzky, the husband of my sister Rachel, was freed from his internment camp. The joy in our house cannot be described. He arrived emaciated and pale, but he recovered. The director wanted to appoint him as an official in the office, but he refused and went to work in a smithy. We invited guests, and finished off together the bottle of wine that we had saved for this purpose from 1941.

The issue of sending packages troubled us greatly, with the concern for a permit and travel to Biysk. However, in February 1945, Leah received a permit and moved with her daughter Uza to Biysk. From that time, it became easier for us to send packages.

Time and Emotions Did their Work

In the winter of 1941, refugees who evacuated Leningrad and Moscow came to us in the sovkhoz. Among them there were two young, educated women with children. One of them, Galina Michaelova, was appointed as my office assistant. I will admit that the local women were not attractive to my heart. They lost their femininity because of the difficult work. In addition, they were simple, with a low, provincial level of intelligence. Suddenly an intelligent, young, pleasant woman appeared before me, with bright eyes and hair, cute dimples and a pleasant smile…

At first, of course, we maintained a business relationship. It was appropriate to keep my distance. However time and emotions did their work: a 35 year old bachelor falls in love like a young man! A cautious approach, a light caress, and many compliments. A quick kiss. She became friendly with my sisters and family. It was pleasant to chat with her. She understood our spirit. Her mother remained in Moscow. Her husband, an engineer, was in the Kolima region of Siberia. Because of his legal status, she did not say whether or not he had been sent to hard labor. She corresponded only with her mother.

With the passage of time we became further connected with intimate relationships. She remained in my place as the director of accounting when I moved to work in the central farm. Every Saturday after work I would walk by foot through the mountain paths, a distance of 5 kilometers, to visit my beloved. I would pick aromatic flowers along the way and give them to the mistress of the house, who accepted them with thanks and love. Galina had a sweet voice. She would sing folk songs, and she accompanied her songs with the guitar. She tried to make my day of rest pleasant with drink, food, and an abundance of expressions of love.

The Bright Star Disappeared

In 1944, a command was issued that all of the residents of Moscow must return to their places by a specific date. Otherwise, they would lose their rights of residency there. She had a dilemma, to remain in the remote mountains according to the pull of her heart, or to return to the capital city according to healthy logic. The push to return came from my advice. She corresponded with me for years. I knew her as a talented musician. Her songs that were dedicated to me were songs of truth and earnestness, and every letter was a virtual hymn. In 1947 I received a telegram from her from Novosibirsk in which she stated that she was traveling to Kolima and wanted to see me very much. She would be waiting in the train station. This was something impossible: to receive a leave from work, a permit, and transportation, would take more than a week. In the meantime, I would miss the train. With this, the contact was severed. A bright star had appeared suddenly in my sky in the darkness of my night, and disappeared into the horizon…

In the summer of 1944, after the liberation of Kovno, my sister Sara in the Land received a letter from Tzvi Levin, who was the sole survivor of his entire family. He was of course interested in the fate of Miriam, the children and the rest of the family. In the subsequent letters he wrote that he had received a position as the fuel director in Kovno. His supervisor was Eliezer Kagan from Jonava. Tzvi wanted to come to us to take Miriam and the children with him. However fate was otherwise. One dark night they knocked on his door, conducted a search, arrested him, and sent him to far off Ural. We waited in vain for letters. After some time they wrote to us that he was imprisoned, and they did not know way. A dark melancholy overtook the residents of our house and the question tormented us: "Why, to where, and for what?!" Finally, after a few months, the awaited letter arrived from Tzvi. He said that he was in the coal mines in the Sverdlovsk region and was waiting to be freed. He requested food packages.

The War Ended

It was Sunday morning, May 10, 1945. I traveled to cut branches to make a fence around our vegetable garden. The twigs of the old fence were used for firewood. I wound my way behind the wagon, immersed in thoughts. Suddenly I heard the shouting of a woman from among the rocks.

"What is it, miss?" my voice echoed through the mountains.

"I have just heard that the war ended," she shouted to me with an emotional voice.

Thus is it was in the far off mountains. Without a telephone or a radio, news traveled with the speed of lightning. I hastened back to inform the community and my family of this news. On the farm there was tumult and emotion. People left work and gathered together. I tarried a bit and returned to my journey.

On the journey I was engrossed in all types of visions: we were liberated, and we could go home. Those who were imprisoned in internment camps would follow behind us. We are again in Jonava and Kovno. How good and pleasant will it be for brethren to dwell together. But all of this was a dream... while awake. We later had reason to sense that it was not the time to engage in false hope.

In the evening, when I returned home, the joy and exultation was great. Honey and liquor were placed on the table. We gathered together, drank, sang and danced.

After the war, the supervision by the N.K.V.D. became more intense. Was it decreed upon us that we must remain in this place for eternity?

Joy came to our house in April 1947. Tzvi Levin was liberated and came to us – pale and emaciated, but healthy and whole. Mother and his wife Miriam took good care of him, so that he would return to his strength and recover from the suffering of the internment camp. He arrived on an official passport and was permitted to travel anywhere he wanted, but his wife and children were not allowed to leave the region. We found out that the N.K.V.D. was going to confiscate our passports, and we made sure to thwart them. We spoke to acquaintances who transported him that very evening – the day before the N.K.V.D. was to come – to the town of Solonovky, 35 kilometers away. From there he traveled by truck to Biysk, and from there by train to Moscow and Vilna.

My Family Members Leave Me

On June 15, 1947, two months after Tzvi's liberation, we once again had good news. Berl Segalovsky returned to his wife Leah and her daughter Uza in Biysk after six years of backbreaking labor in the taiga of the Krasnoyarsk Region. He also came to us and told us that he survived thanks to the food packages that we provided him. He assisted us in preparing fodder for our cow. He stayed with us for about a month and then decided to return to Biysk and from there to Vilna. After he would establish himself he would bring his wife and daughter. In September of that year I confided with Director Vardnikov, who was a proper man, that he should allow me to transfer my mother to Biysk to be with her daughter Leah, where her life would be easier, even without an official permit from the N.K.V.D. He gave me his agreement. On account of the rain that began to fall, the trucks only reached the Madovdivka Farm. I was forced to seat her on a calf and transport her there through mountains and mud. This was her final journey of her wanderings, and she was 75 years old. From Madovdivka, they took her straight to Biysk by truck.

That autumn, Leah secretly obtained train tickets without her neighbors knowing, and she left Biysk and the Altai Krai permanently along with her daughter and mother. Then came the turn of Miriam and her children. She requested permission from the N.K.V.D. to move to Biysk. The pretext was the education of her son. The requested permit arrived. I bid farewell to Miriam and her children. I was like a father to them during the war. From Biysk they set out directly to Vilna. Rachel and her family also went there from Novosibirsk.

I Remained Alone – But Not Alone

I was the only one left of all the Jonavers in the exile in the Soloneshnoye region of the Altai Mountains. I was connected to family life – a wife, without the bonds of a marriage ceremony. After Galina Michaelova of Moscow left the sovkhoz, other women attempted to take her place. Among them, Zoya Konstantinova Gromka of Leningrad stood out. She was 27 years old with an eight year old child. Her husband, an army captain on the front, married another woman and cut off contact with her. Zoya moved to my house and assisted me in conducting our private farm: Burka the cow, the ducks, the chickens and the vegetable garden.

In 1948, I was appointed as the accounting supervisor of 40 kolkhozes, and we had to move to the central town. My salary was lower than that in the sovkhoz, where I also had received all types of provisions. Here, I was like a synagogue mouse…[1]

I wandered from one kolkhoz to the next, most of the time by vehicle, but sometimes on foot, a distance of 40 kilometers. I worked in that position for two years. I saw the people of the kolkhozes at work, in their houses, and in their times of joy. I knew that their lives were not easy at all. As a result of this, they related to their work with indifference. After all the inspections, I reported the findings to the director of the kolkhoz. A general meeting would then be called, and I, Yitzchak the son of David, preached words of reproof to the local Ivans.

I returned to my office after each inspection. Zoya, who worked as a secretary in the financial office of the director of the region, would type my report with a typewriter. It would then be discussed by the local council.

In the months of August and September I was busy, along with other officials, in the preparation of fodder for the horses that were owned by our office. We would put up huts out of branches and straw, similar to tents. We lived in them. We cut the grass with sickles. I would cut for our own cow at night until midnight, and also in the morning. In addition, we had to work at various communal endeavors, such as removing the ice from the channel that brought water to the hydroelectric plant, so that there would be no interruption of the flow of electricity.

I was dismissed from my job in 1950. I was satisfied with this, for I was tired of the sleeping over, the journeys and the walking to strange places on snowy, muddy and icy days and during snowstorms, when the river water rose and I could only cross by lying on my horse who swam across the water, with the danger that we might be swept away by the current.

Later I found out that that the first secretary of the party in the region was opposed that I – the spoiler of rights and from the bourgeois class – should be the inspector of kolkhozes and find out too much about what was doing with them and what their situation was, which was evident at every inspection.

New Places of Work

I was accepted as the accounting director of the restaurant of the consumers' union. My economic situation improved. My salary increased significantly, for the restaurant exceeded its plans by 150% each month, and we received gratuities. I was able to receive my food provisions and eat at low prices.

Before that there were many thefts. There was no such event throughout the two years that I worked there. I conducted audits. I spoke earnestly to the staff, urging them to fulfill their duties and thereby profit. Indeed thus it was. Their salary increased, and they were satisfied. The sudden inspections of the N.K.V.D. were in vain. From that time, they would send me out for an inspection at any incidence of corruption in the region. Since I had worked in the sovkhoz for seven years, it was not hard for me to uncover any cunning tactics. Workers of the sovkhoz, who were jealous of the drunks and thieves, would come to my assistance and provide me with information. The source of the theft was the excess that was hoarded by the keepers of the warehouses. They would take that to the black market.

At the end of 1952, I was appointed as chief accounting director of the new tractor station in the town of Lyutayevo, approximately 40 kilometers from the regional town along the way to Biysk. This was during the year that Khrushchev decided the scope of labor.

At that time, the N.K.V.D. began to follow us more closely, because no small number of people like us uprooted themselves from their places of exile and escaped back to Lithuania. Among them were my mother and sisters. Therefore I wrote to my family in an indirect manner. They searched after them in Vilna, and Leah was imprisoned twice. Finally they became disgusted with the entire matter, and they moved to the city of Frunze in Kirgizia: the Levin, Dushnitzky and Segalovsky families – 11 souls – led by mother. All of this was made possible by the assistance that was provided to us by our sister Sara in Israel.

I Went a Bit Further Afield

We had to move to the designated location, Lyutayevo, before the October holiday. We loaded our belongings and the cow on a truck. Zoya was next to the driver and I was on top. We set out on the journey in the snow and cold. We arrived at midnight. The head of the office set us up in our dwelling. After about a month we moved to a new office, whose walls and floor were full of cracks due to the hasty construction. Wind would blow through the cracks. Zoya got a cold and a cough, but she continued to work in order to make up the balance sheet. I had to travel to the city of Barnaul and give it over to the chief director of 200 tractor stations in the Altai Krai. A small crack was opened for me, and I began to go a bit further afield.

I found out about the events of the world from the following newspapers: the Altai Truth, Pravda, and Izvestia. From them I found out about the War of Independence and the State of Israel. The articles were brief, but supportive of Israel.

I digested the news. I did not have anyone with whom to discuss the events. I would reconstruct them in my mind in my bed at night.

My first stop in Biysk was at the home of our fellow native, Avraham Jochovsky. At night I knocked on his door, which was locked with seven locks. The joy of our meeting was great. After a meal and glasses of liquor, we sat and chatted until dawn. The topic was the Land of Israel. He knew much more than I.

I was a regular guest of the Abramovich family in Barnaul. There, I would listen to the radio and hear the news from Jews about the Jewish State.

When I returned, I was occupied and immersed in the small town reality, with its problems that had become my problems. There was no small number of negative characters who came to the region among the volunteers. Some squandered the money that they had received in advance and attempted to escape. I had an additional job – to pursue the wanderers and initiate legal proceedings to have the money returned.

As time went on, they built a two room house for me. The economic conditions improved. I received a salary of 1,200 rubles and Zoya received 600 rubles. We continued to maintain our own auxiliary farm. We would prepare fodder and bring it with a tractor.

The year was 1953, the year of the Doctors' Plot[2]. The atmosphere was very tense and oppressive. Many people were fired from their jobs at that time. I do not know to this day how I succeeded in retaining my high position.

In Siberia. 1. Yitzchak Burstein, 2. Miriam Burstein. 3. Zoya

Visit to Frunze

In 1954 I took a two month leave and received permission to travel to Frunze to visit my mother and sisters. I traveled with Zoya. This was not an easy journey at all. We traveled by truck and trains. We sat on our suitcases for about ten hours until we found a place in the cargo cars of the train, which were nicknamed "the joyful train" by people. Many youth were traveling on it. The doors of the cars were open. They sat with their feet outside and sang songs accompanied by accordions and mandolins. Then we transferred to another train and arrived in Frunze at midnight. Berl Segalovsky, Tzvi Levin and Yosef Dushnitzky with their children greeted us. The joy was great. The city was adorned with greenery. We stopped next to a wooden house with electric lights, with a large apple orchard beside it. Everything seemed to me like a summer dream. There was Mother; there were my sisters with their sons and daughters whom I had cared for. All of them greeted me with great warmth.

We spent a month in Frunze. We walked through its streets. We visited its markets that were full of fruit, vegetables, watermelons and food items about which we could only dream in Siberia.

(Continued on page 273)

[Page 272]

The first letter that arrived from Tzvi Levin after the liberation of Kovno by the Russians (abridged).

Kovno, August 19, 1944

I do not know how to begin. I lack words. From all of our large family only I remain… Some perished in the ghetto and others were hauled to Germany. I survived by a miracle.

I found out five months ago that the Gestapo was plotting to arrest me because I was involved with smuggling young Jews to partisan units in the forests of the area. I succeeded in escaping from the ghetto, and I hid with farmers in the villages of the region as well as in Kovno.

It is a sufficiently gloomy picture. Of the 38,000 Jews who were concentrated in the Kovno Ghetto, only about 500 survived. The ghetto was burnt and bombed by the Nazis.

Now, about my last hope, what is the fate of Miriam and my two children? If they are alive, you certainly have contact with them. Please tell me the entire truth, good or bad.

Please answer quickly

Yours

Hirsch Levin

The story of the photocopy:

… My first visit in the Land was with my childhood friend Shimon Zak in Jerusalem.

During the conversation he turned to me and said:

"Did you find the picture of the opening of the University which was hanging on the wall of your room in Jonava?"

"No, and no. Everything was lost."

"After 40 years from the founding of the University, I saw that exact picture in a photographer store window display on Ben Yehuda Street."

We went there.

The photographer showed us two pictures and said.

"My father took this picture. I will not give up the large picture under any circumstances, but you can have the small one."

I paid some money and took it as a souvenir.

And here it is before you.

Yitzchak B. is noted in the center of the photograph (*See the top of page 275)*

The photograph mentioned on the previous page
The first letter of Yitzchak Burstein from Siberia to his sister Sara in Israel (abridged)

20/-/ [illegible]

Комсомольская Ферма
10 августа 1941 г.

Дорогой дядя, дорогая сестра Сара и муж [illegible]!

Я пишу вам это письмо с Сибири, Алтайского края. Мы здесь прибыли 10 июля с.г. и выехали из Яноgo экстренным эшелоном 17 июня. Со мною находится мамаша, Леа с Азинькой. Мы все здоровы, работаем и живем. Отец при нашего выезде был болен и поэтому остался дома, в данном случае мы очень довольны этим, потому что, эта длинная поездка 5000 клм. повлияла бы очень плохо за его здоровье. Утром перед нашим отъездом, он все таки прибыл на станцию, с намерением чтобы с нами в месте поехать, и понятно что я просил начальника эшелона не разрешить ему соединиться с нами. Он остался одиноким дома и Гене будет присматривать за ним. Кроме того остались Хацке Сегаловская и жена Милец и понятно, что они позаботятся за ним. Берель как и другие мужчины поехали другим поездом и пока не знаем где они. С ним в месте находятся из Яновских, Лейба Вульфович, Аврам Жуковский, Нисон Гольдштейн, Гирш Фульфович, Шмуел Чернеман и многие из Яновских литовцев. Мэри [illegible] с Иозефом выехали с Ковно 14 июня и я тогда еще работал на моей службе в Ковне. Утром зашел к ним и никого не заставил дома. Вечером я поехал в Янову и там не пришлось с ними повидаться. 16 июня будучи на Яновской станции передали нам что Мэри удалось повидаться с ними на Ковенской станции. Мэри с ребятами как видно осталась на месте в Ковне с Хаимом. Гирша как видно тоже выехал. Мы находимся как уже выше указал в Алтайских горах, 130 клм. от желез. дор. станц. Бийск это будет на южном направлении от города Новосибирска. Мы все Яновцы находимся в ферме Большой-Тихе Карповского Совхоза, а именно жены Н. Гольдштейн (бывшая Перевозник, дочь [illegible] Перевозника) Жуковского, Чернемана. Не далеко отсюда на ферме Лес-Участок этого совхоза живем Тайбе, Моте, [illegible] и Меер Вульфович в месте с женою и Гиршем (бывшая Маша Наккот которая работала в [illegible] конторе). Еще в некоторых фермах этого совхоза живут большие части Вилькомирская колония, а именно — старший Криуг с женой, фамилия Яновск, Грац, Заке, Палец, Шапиро, Рикланский. Я все время работал на сено-уборке отличился в моей работе и вот с 10 августа меня назначили бухгалтером Комсомольской фермы этого совхоза. Я получаю особую квартиру и через несколько дней переедут ко мне мамаша, Леа и Азинька.

Original letter in Russian

August 10, 1941
Komsomolsk Farm (Siberia)
To my dear ones.

We reached here on July 10. We left Jonava on a "special train" on June 17. With me are Mother, Leah and her daughter Uza. We are healthy and working. Father was ill and remained at home. Dov Segalovsky along with other men traveled on a different train in a different direction. Along with him were Aryeh and Tzvi Wolfovich, Avraham Jochovsky, Nissan Goldshmidt and Shmuel Chernman. Rachel and Yosef Dushnitzky were "taken" from Jonava on June 14. I went to their house in the evening and found it closed. Miriam Levin and her children apparently remained in Kovno. We are located 130 kilometers from the train station of the city of Biysk. We and almost all of the Jonavers are located in the Karpova Sovkhoz. These include: Batya Goldshmidt (nee Perevoznik), Malka Jochovsky, Yochel Chernman, Mordechai, Bunia, Teibl and Meir Wolfovich, and Masha Namiot, the wife of Tzvi Wolfovich.

… I am concerned that Father and perhaps Miriam and her children remained under Nazi rule… I understand that neither you nor we can get in touch with Father. We will wait until Hitler is defeated at the end of the war.

Shalom,
Your brother Yitzchak

Jonavers in Vilna and in Israel. In Vilna – taking leave of Yitzchak Burstein:
Chaya Leah Druker (Monosevich), Shlomo Druker, Shlomo Ber Meirovich, Leizer Glazer, David Friedman and his wife, Avraham Jochovsky, Batya Namiot, Yitzchak, the wife of Shlomo Ber, Rivka Simchovich, Batya Goldshmidt-Perevoznik, Malka Jochovsky.

In Israel at the wedding of the daughter of Nachum Blumberg.

The First postcard that arrived in the Land from Miriam Levin-Burstein from Siberia

Realshoz, October 15, 1941
To my dear ones:

I am with my children Shlomo and Yehoshua in a settlement for wood-chopping in the Altai forests, Troitsky region. We are healthy and well. I have not seen Tzvi for more than a year, since he was imprisoned, and there is no news from him. Yitzchak and Leah with her family were also deported, but we do not know where they are. Rachel and her family were also deported. Father remains ill in Jonava. Our friend "Meistans" we do not see (Editor: an innuendo that there is no meat). "Fiana" (that is milk) we receive on occasion.

Please let me know the address of family members if you know them.
Peace to you
Your sister Miriam

[Page 273][3]

We liked Frunze. We returned to our place and requested a permit to move to Frunze. In October 1955, we set out on a journey in a truck belonging to the tractor station.
Farewell to the Altai Mountains

When the truck ascended the final snowy peak, before gliding down to the desert, I asked the driver to stop. I went out and shouted out in a strong low voice:

"Farewell to you, Altai Mountains! Thank you for the bad and the good!"

After 15 years of ascending and descending the Altai Mountains I remained alive, healthy and whole, and I succeeded in reuniting with my family – that is why I felt the duty to do what I did.

We remained in Biysk for two days with Jochovsky and met Chernman, who in the interim had remarried.

From there we traveled to Barnaul. We stayed with the Wolfovich family. The mistress of the house Teibl was no longer alive, but I found a Jonavan atmosphere. We shared memories with Leiba, Mordechai and Bunia.

We finally arrived in Frunze. Mother had obtained for us a room with a kitchenette, 12 square meters in area. I found work in the Ministry of Building, and continued to work there for approximately ten years.
The Voice of Israel and the Voice of Comfort

Here I heard for the first time, after 15 years, Kol Yisrael (the Israel radio station) in Yiddish. This was at 8:00 p.m.. On most days I went into my mother's room at 9:00 p.m., set the channel, and listened to the voice of our homeland for 15 minutes. In this manner I absorbed the news of Israel every evening for ten years. In May 1964, my sister Sara in Israel subscribed me to "Kol Haam", which was permitted to be distributed in Russia until the Six Day War. Communism disseminated in the Hebrew Language was less untouchable for me. I also read between the lines. The newspaper broadened my knowledge of the Hebrew Language.

Nechama Lifschitz came to Frunze. I purchased a ticket and went to listen to Yiddish folksongs in the theater after a hiatus of 15 years. I will never forget that evening. When I saw the hall full of Jews applauding enthusiastically, the impression on me was very great. I wept. I was unable to stem the tears. The second time she came to us she was brazen enough to sing a Hebrew song. The thunderous applause roared through the air for several minutes.

Acclimatizing to Frunze

There were approximately 5,000 Jews in Frunze at the time, including approximately 30 families from Lithuania. There was also a small synagogue in a residential dwelling. After my mother passed away in 1964 I got to know almost all of the worshippers, since I went twice a day for 11 months to say Kaddish.

I must admit that anyone who wished to go to worship or to circumcise his son was not bothered by the Soviet authorities. Nevertheless, I must also state that the Star of David that was hanging at the entrance of the courtyard of the House of Worship suddenly disappeared, and in 1964, the recitation of "Next Year in Jerusalem" after Yom Kippur ceased in accordance with a directive from the government authorities for religious matters. Apparently this was in reaction to the wave of national awakening of the Jews.

I became acclimatized to Frunze. I had a fruit garden that required care. Berl Segalovsky and I dedicated each Sunday, the official day of rest, to that end. We were not short of firewood. We also plastered our own walls. It was impossible to hire professionals for such work due to our low salaries.

The three families from Jonava – Burstein, Segalovsky and Levin – lived as neighbors, with Mother at the head. On Sabbath eves we would sit at the table, covered with a white tablecloth, adorned with candles. I would recite Kiddush in father's tune – of course with aberrations and dissonance.

In the winter of 1957, my wife's son, who concluded his studies, arrived from Novosibirsk with his wife and stayed with us. We lived together in a 12 square meter room: we on the bed and they on the floor. In 1960 I enlarged the dwelling to 20 square meters. I knocked down the wall with my own hands, and dug the excavation and poured the foundation myself. Similarly, I did all the painting and glasswork. I was assisted by other builders and by a friend for other work. I received the building materials from the ministry for a cheap price.

Family Meeting

Sara came to Moscow in the summer of 1963 in order to visit Mother and the family. She was not permitted to travel to Frunze. We had no choice but to go to her in Moscow. I arrived by airplane and was put up with acquaintances. Mother and my sisters traveled by train for three exhausting days through the Kazakhstan desert ("The Desert of Famine") in excruciating heat. I rented a large room in a national hotel in the suburbs for them. I met my sister, and we traveled by taxi to meet the rest of the family in their hotel. My sister Rachel and her daughter also came from Kovno for the family gathering.

We remained in Moscow for a week. We went every evening to mother in the hotel, ate together and discussed memories. The day of parting arrived. Mother wept silently, as if she suspected that this was her final meeting with Sara. We returned to Frunze by airplane – a five hour flight. This was mother's last journey. She died in May 1964. A few days before her death she adjured me to attempt to leave Russia, to go to the Land and to gather together all of the members of the family.

Parting from my Friends and from my Girlfriend

The day arrived, November 11, 1965, and I was on a railway car from Frunze to Vilna, on my way to the Land. All of the members of the family from Frunze, my girlfriend Zoya, her son Boris with his wife and daughter, friends and acquaintances – all came to see me off. My sister Miriam was with me in the train. She accompanied me to Vilna. Many hoped to see me again in the Land. My girlfriend Zoya wept bitterly, for this parting would be forever. After twenty years she remained alone, broken and ill. She was a proud and upright woman. She did not want to burden me, for this contradicted her personality. Members of my family and Zoya accompanied me to the nearby station. There were warm kisses, and the train departed.

An elderly woman. *(Translator's comment – likely Yitzchak's mother.)*

[Page 275]

Pictures of my Life Passed Before Me

I lay on my bed on the upper berth and immersed myself in thoughts. Pictures of the film of my life passed before my eyes: My native village of Kaplice, at the Carlebach Gymnasium in Kovno. Classes were conducted in German, but Hebrew studies occupied many hours. Rabbi Yudel "The Yellow", who knew the entire Gemara clearly, taught me various sections of it. The days of the German occupation – when I received Russian lessons from the teacher Libshin. I concluded the gymnasium in 1922, at the age of 17 and a half. We moved to Jonava. My communal activities were cut off in 1923 when I was accepted as a student at the upper level school in Vienna. There as well I was active in the Zionist Hechaver student organization, and was later appointed as secretary of the organization. (The chairman was Binyamin Aktzin, today the rector of the University of Haifa.) In 1925 I was among the three delegates who were selected by the organization to participate in the opening ceremonies of the [Hebrew] University in Jerusalem in 1925. I visited the Nahalel in the valley, which had been settled very shortly before, with its residents living in bunks; the winepress of Rishon Letzion where I was treated with cellared wine; I spent an evening in the Casino nightclub in tiny Tel Aviv, whose foundations are embedded in the sea.

Then there was the festive celebration, conducted with great emotion: Before my eyes were the great ones and spiritual leaders of the nation (see the photo after page 272).

I was once again in Jonava. I continued my variegated activities, and I assisted Father in his business.

I fell in love with Rosa Kagan, the beautiful brunette with modest "sex appeal", a scion of a good family and a cultured girl. Only a tremor in the corner of her upper lip gave expression to her hidden desires, to the modest beginning of motion on the volcano. I courted her for two years. The only thing that was lacking was a formal engagement. Suddenly events took their course – and we parted. We remained friends. My heart always aches for the fact that she did not succeed in her life, by going after the fiancé of her youth.

I was also unlucky. Out of my great despair I fell into the arms of a married woman, a demonic woman with blue eyes, with an overflowing and immodest sex drive, lacking discreteness. I was attracted to her because there were no other options, based on the adage "and she will rule over you". Her family life was stormy. I attempted to calm her with intimate relations, and I spoke to her heart for her to desist, but she did what she wanted. After some time she again snared me with her spread-out spider web. This stolen love lasted for ten years. Stolen waters might become sweet. The end of this era came only at the time of the arrival of the Russians…

How pleasant it is to remember events of childhood, youth, and young adulthood!

I Again Boarded the Train

The train arrived in Vilna. Miriam and I stayed with our sister Leah. I met the survivors of Jonava, and spent a week with my sister Rachel in Kovno. When I returned, the Jonavers arranged a farewell party for me at the home of Mrs. Namiot. Leizka the Yellow turned to me and said:

"Yitzchak, do you remember when I, as a Comsomol member in Jonava, went to Kovno in order to send you to exile in Siberia? This time I will accompany you and seat you in a train that will take you to the Land. He said it and did it. The next evening, at the time of parting at the train station, he came to the fore from the side, grabbed me in his strong arms, and brought me up to the train. The train was taking me and Shlomo Levin, the son of my sister Miriam, to Minsk. From there I would go to Moscow on my own. After much toil, which is a story in its own right, I ascended the threshold of the Embassy of Israel. Behold, I was in the lobby of the embassy. Nobody was there. On the small table there was an abundance of periodicals and brochures. Everything was in Hebrew. Was this a dream or reality? I forgot the reason that I had came and immersed myself in reading. Nobody came. There was a bizarre quiet.

I knocked on one of the doors and entered. An embassy employee greeted me and asked me to sit down. He clarified for me that the address of the embassy was written in my passport. He advised me to fly by airplane but I preferred to travel to Warsaw by train, and then to go to Vienna via Czechoslovakia. On December 23, [1965] I arrived in Lod on an El Al airplane.

[Page 276]

15 Years and One Day

by Batya Goldshmidt (nee Perevoznik), Petach Tikva

Translated by Jerrold Landau

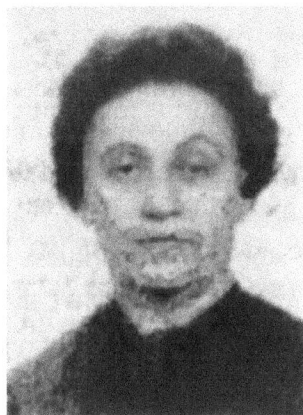

Batya Perevoznik Goldshmidt

I Struggled and Succeeded
15 Years in the Siberian Taiga

I was young when the Soviets arrived in Lithuania. I had not yet turned 20. My father Hillel was a dedicated Zionist. I studied in Tarbut and continued in the Hebrew Real Gymnasium in Kovno. I was active in Beitar, and my entire outlook was directed to the Land of Israel.

Our brick kiln, which was owned in partnership with my Uncle David Yitzchak, was nationalized immediately after the proclamation of the Soviet guard. We were left bereft of an economic base.

I decided to leave home and to get married to my childhood friend Nissan Goldshmidt, an official with Segalovsky, whose enterprise was also nationalized. I got a job with the thought of beginning a quiet life appropriate to the times. However, this was not to be my fate.

Late at night on June 14, 1941, we were awakened to the sound of knocking on our door. To our question, "Who is there?", someone declared in Russian, "Open up, we are from the N.K.V.D.". Two of them broke into our small room with pointed guns, accompanied by Reuven Vidzky of the Comsomol Youth. They conducted a thorough search and ordered us to prepare for a journey within 20 minutes. We were permitted to take up to 100 kilograms of belongings. In the darkness of the night, we were hauled to the train station in a truck, accompanied by soldiers. We were forbidden to bid farewell to our parents and relatives. We were brought into a transport car, the doors were closed with bars and locks, and a Soviet guard guarded us.

At a young age, lacking in experience, innocent of wrongdoing, and suddenly I bore the mark of a criminal. Why and for what reason? Where were we going? Large question marks floated before my eyes. I was broken. My world darkened upon me. I wept bitterly and screamed, "Mother!".

The next day, my mother, father, brothers and sisters appeared. They stood at a distance. They were not permitted to approach. Through the mesh window I could see them weeping as they peered into the cage in which the bird, the apple of their eye, was imprisoned.

The next day, at one of the stops in the darkness of the night, they knocked on the door and asked for Nissan. He was ordered to leave the train. Thus my lad, with whom I had hoped to share my fate in the new exile, was cut off from me. I never saw him again. He perished in the Rashuty Camp in 1942. I remained alone, alone as is written in the Book of Job, "A fire of G-d has fallen from heaven and burned the flocks and lads and consumed them, and I remain alone…"

Yitzchak [Ben-David (Burstein)] already wrote about the tribulations of the journey and my life in the Altai Mountains throughout the year. I will not repeat it.

I will describe in brief what transpired with me in the far-off, frigid Yakutsk region.

At times, a person needs to be stronger than iron if he wishes to continue to live and to come to better days.

Members of Beitar of Jonava: Levi Perevoznik, Nissan Goldshmidt, Yehudit Ferber, Dina Kapol, Yocheved Kahansky, Batya Senior, Moshe Namiot, Batya Perevoznik, Tzvi Suntochky, Babilsky, Biarsky, Yaakov Kapol.

The Siberian winter in the endless forests. Batya writes about her daily routine.

Batya Goldshmidt among the woodchoppers of Yakutsk in Siberia.
1.　Batya. 2. Shimon Shapira of Wilkomir.

The expanses of the endless forests and the woodchoppers. 1. Batya.

Batya at work, and measuring rations.

Batya at work and on a break

[Page 277]

In August 1942, we received a command from the N.K.V.D. that all of the families who do not have small children should prepare to leave the Karpova Sovkhoz. Wagons hitched to horses were sent. We loaded our belongings, and walked on foot to the city of Biysk, accompanied by the N.K.V.D. guards who were riding on horses. The Wolfovich family and Masha Namiot were with me. The journey lasted for three days. In Biysk we learned that we would be taken to the region of the Arctic Ocean, to the Tiksi point on the Lena River, a journey of 4,000 kilometers. We proceeded to Barnaul and Novosibirsk on open transport trucks, and from there, we boarded the Trans-Siberian railway. After a week of travel we arrived at the Osterovo railway station. From there we continued in trucks on an uncharted route through mountains and valleys, for hundreds of kilometers until the water mill on the Angara River. There, they loaded us like cattle and sheep upon transport barges, and after three days we arrived in a place not far from the port of Mukhtuya (Lensk) on the Lena River.

We transferred to a larger ship, and after we traversed more than 1,000 kilometers in a seven day journey along the downstream of the Lena, we arrived at the port of Olekminsk.

We, a group of four families numbering ten souls, were put up in a room of 12 square meters. The day after our arrival, we went out to work in the taiga that extends the length of the Lena River. Our work was to prepare firewood for the ships. We received portions of bread according to rations. Since we were not used to this type of work under these conditions, we did not reach the quota, and were starving for bread. The cold was minus 40, and it exhausted our strength.

As I was at the threshold of despair, I recalled the admonitions of Yitzchak [Burstein] who was our work director at the time we worked in the fields of the Altai Mountains. If you wish to remain alive you must work well, and whoever acts otherwise will have a bitter end. These words were spoken in the heat of an argument with Yochel Chernman, and her end is known. Thus did I act. I never refused to perform all of the work that was imposed upon me – the backbreaking labor of men. I withstood the test. I had to do so, for I had no relative, no redeemer, and no packages from abroad.

I was transferred to Berezova, also on the Lena, at the end of 1942. There I worked in setting up barges. We would roll tree trunks to the water, and I would ascend the blocks of wood and tie them together. We would tie them six rows high. The barges on the Viliya seemed as toys in contrast to the barges that we prepared. I was the only Jewess there. The Lithuanians there were in the same "Specifraslanska" situation as I was.

In the autumn we took down the storehouses that served as our residences, loaded them on barges and floated them down the river to a place that was called Delgey. We re-erected our houses in the vast forests with our own hands. Two Jewish families from Wilkomir joined us (Shimon Shapira and his wife, today in Neve Sharet, and the Krem family).

I continued working at cutting down trees, making barges, and other backbreaking work until 1948. I became an accomplished professional. In 1947 I received a government prize for dedicated work during the wartime years.

We again packed up and moved 200 kilometers further to opposite the city of Olekminsk. I continued my work of tree cutting in the winter and producing barges during the summer. The system of food ration cards was revoked, and the situation in that region improved.

I was appointed to head staff in 1952. I breathed easily. A heavy burden had been lifted from my shoulders. My job was to allocate the workplaces and to register the quotas. The shortage of workers was made up with political prisoners who were freed after serving their sentences in the prison camps of the Kolyma Peninsula. Without any way to continue their journey home during the winter season when the only means of exit from this area of Siberia was by boat, they tarried with us in order to earn some money before continuing onward. These people were a part of our staff during the long winter.

During the well-known Doctors' Plot of Stalin in 1953, I was suddenly fired from my "high office" as an official in the forest, and sent back to physical labor, which I continued until June 1956.

That year, thanks to my government prize, I was informed that my designation of "Specifraslanska" was removed from me, along with all types of restrictions. I received an identity card with the Hebrew designation, and I was permitted to move throughout all of Russia, with the exception of Soviet Lithuania and an area of 100 kilometers around the capital cities of the Soviet republics.

I seized the opportunity and left the Yakutsk Region. Despite the ban, I went to Vilna. Shmuel Balnik (today in Ramat Hanasi, Bat Yam), a member of the party, with a high government position in the milk combine (like Tnuva), set me up with work and assisted me in registering with the Vilna police as a resident with full rights.

I did not find any members of my family. I immediately began to take interest in immigrating to the Land. I fought for this right for 12 years, and I only received my permit in 1969.

I spent 15 years of my youth in the taiga of the Yakutsk Region, in conditions of terrible cold, fierce snow storms, freezing fog, malnourishment, and backbreaking work which was the work of men. I, the sole Jewess, strode through endless forests up to my knees in deep snow in the winter and in the ice cold water of the Lena in the summer, working together with men, the vast majority of whom were criminals, thieves and murderers – and all of this in order to come to better days.

180 months, which are 6480 days and nights – without a relative or a redeemer! Days and nights filled with tribulations, frustrations, delusions and desires of a young soul; days and nights of lack of sleep and fear of the N.K.V.D. who wanted to capture me in their net and embrace me with a life of danger, slander and causing harm to others. Then they would treat me with a "candy".

My conscience remains clear. I struggled with them and succeeded.

[Page 278]

One Day in the Siberian Taiga

by Batya Goldshmidt-Perevoznik

Translated by Jerrold Landau

In the vast forests, in the desolation of the snow, white prevails. Walls of grey tree branches, adorned with piles of snow, close in from both sides. On the fourth side is the vast span, covered with a white desert, sparkling like ice in the dim light of the moon. This is at the banks of the gigantic Lena River, spreading out below our feet – the silence and splendor of the works of creation.

In this open region, in this ice, an altar was prepared for me upon which I offered my energies and my youth.

The chimneys of the barracks which house us "Specifraslanskas" stuck up skyward. There were about 20 other small wooden huts for the rest of the workers. The chimneys spewed smoke.

It was 5:00 a.m. The early risers had already lit the large oven and were warming the soup, prepared from the previous day. During the night, the strong cold penetrated into the barracks. The windows were covered with a layer of thick ice that was beginning to melt.

I woke up. I breathed in the cold air and tarried in getting up. I had not slept enough. However, the hunger was gnawing at the stomach and the head, and I involuntarily crawled out from beneath the warm blanket.

The light of the dim lantern spread its shadows around. Along the length of the walls were twelve wooden shelves, one meter wide each. These were the wooden beds, called the "nars". Beside each such bed, attached to the wall, was a wooden shelf. This was the food corner. The passage between the beds was half a meter, and beneath them
– all of one's property: suitcases and sacks from the parental home.

The iron oven with its tin pipes reaching up to the chimney was already burning, red from the fire. The wooden beds hung down from the ceiling on both sides of it, and above it were the tattered clothes that were hung up the previous evening while they were still wet, and now they were dry. A small pull, and my patched pants made out of cotton and my pupikia[4] were in my hands, warm and dry. I slid into them, took a few cups of soup and bread, sipped a cup of tea – and already the gigantic bell (brought from some church), hanging on the pillar in the middle of the field was pealing and breaking the silence. It was time to go out to work. I tarried a bit. Immediately the barrack supervisors castigated me with shouting and curses:

"Hurry, daughter of a bitch, lest you be late for work."

It was still dark outside. Only the stars were shining above, as if they were blessing those going out. How beautiful and frightful was the world around. We went out on foot into the recesses of the sleepy forest. Snow fell at night. The paths were covered and disappeared. Again we dug a new furrow through the cover of snow. We marched through the darkness for an hour. We got hot. The sweat rolled down from under the headgear on the forehead and dripped onto the eyes. The fog was heavy. The minus 50 degrees cold weighed down upon us.

We reached the place of the cutting. We spread out two by two in all directions of the wide area. I and my work partner, a Lithuanian gentile, approached one of the silent trees whose foliage was still enveloped in darkness. We quickly removed the pile of snow around its roots until we got to the layer of frozen ground. I used the axe to slowly chop chips of the trunk until the appropriate depth. Then I moved to the other side and used the saw. We kneeled on our knees or stood bent over, monotonously pulled the saw, and cut this gigantic tree with a humming sound. A small groan was heard. We jumped to the side. The pine tree slowly leaned downward. One more minute, and the giant fell over, raising a flurry of snow. Now we cut the branches with axes, gathered them into a pile, and lit them. The trunk was cut according to the standard measurements. Our quota was eight cubic meters, which was made up by 30-40 trees.

Lunchtime approached. We removed the piece of frozen bread from our sacks and placed it on a wooden twig next to the bonfire to toast it. We also melted snow in a cup. The water boiled and the tea was ready. After an hour of rest, we returned to work.

It was 4:45 in the afternoon. The work was registered by an official of the office. They signed the document – and the fate of the quota of bread and of life was decreed upon you. We cast a glance around, there had been a forest and now there was a dead field. It was time to return "home". The light was dimming. The sun disappeared behind the treetops. The cold deepened. The pants, pupikia, felt boots and gloves were damp from sweat and the deep snow. I quickened my pace, and in my head there was one thought: hot soup and fresh bread.

When we arrived at the small field we hastened into line at the small store in order to receive our ration of bread: 600-800 grams. Once a month we also received other provisions: a kilogram of sugar, two kilograms of grits, 700 grams of butter, a small bag of tea and two small bags of machorka for smoking. When there was no butter we would receive a kilogram of horse meat in lieu of each 100 grams.

We removed our work clothes when we entered the barracks. Everything was hung to dry. The oven was lit, and the elderly people and children who had remained there had already prepared their meals. We snatched our places near the oven. Whoever was unable to cook their meal had their pot pushed to the side. It was now the turn of the people of the forest.

The meal was ready. I devoured my "delicacies" but I did not have the feeling of satiation. I arrived hungry and remained hungry. There was no radio or newspapers, and all sorts of rumors were spread. Everyone jumped in and said what he wanted. The Lithuanians spread fabricated stories about the German victories. The gnawing in the heart grew. Aside from these stories, we heard words of argument, strife and slander.

It was 9:00 p.m. I hastened to my bed, fell asleep and dreamed about food, love, and days and years gone by.

Tomorrow is another day of work. One of thousands like it.

Translator's Footnotes

Similar to the English expression, "poor as a church mouse".

See http://en.wikipedia.org/wiki/Doctors'_plot

Page 273 is missing in the NYPL scans (Page 275 was repeated twice in error).

I am not sure of the meaning of this term – although I expect it is some form of long underwear (the word pupik, Yiddish and Slavic for navel or abdomen, is present).

[Page 280]

To Those who are Making the Effort
- Be Strong and of Good Courage!
Translated by Jerrold Landau

"Let us Remember" - this is the name of the 50-page booklet that was published by the Geulim School of Bat Yam, which adopted the community of Jonava for itself.

The teacher Riva Shalovich, the organizer of the adoption activities, tells:

"I was raised with the stories and memories, as my late mother used to tell and describe, so that to me, Jonava became a living and well-known town, even though I only spent the first two years of my life there."

The commemoration ceremony was organized on the 9th of Tevet, 5730 (1970). The occasion was particularly impressive and very moving. The guests - including many Jonava natives - felt anew the experiences of those days, and could not stop the emotions that came to the fore.

The ceremony left a great impression even upon the students who played an active part in or witnessed the proceedings, to the point where they were able to identify with the fate of the people of the town. This is expressed through their impressions:

"I felt literally as one of the survivors of Jonava. Tears began to flow from my eyes," writes Rivka Shami.

Chaya Loberbaum also testifies to this, "I felt as if I was in that town of Jonava and participated in all the experiences... The identification filled my entire essence... This evening imparted a great deal to me and to all those who were present."

The rests of the students in the booklet confirm this.

On the memorial day on the 9th of Tevet 5731 (1971), the memorial corner, that is the perpetuation room, in which the students invested a great deal of work and dedication, was opened.

The ceremony began with the words of the school principal Rachel Angel. Then, Menachem Levin and Yitzchak Burstein spoke. A representative of Yad Vashem also spoke.

The ceremony. The banner at the top reads, "I have made a vow to remember everything. To remember, speak and not forget.

חדר-הנצחה
לקהילת „ינובה" שבליטא

The Perpetuation Room of the Community of Jonava of Lithuania

At the memorial in the Geulim School of Bat Yam, which adopted our town of Jonava. The dais: Zeev Ofek, Y[itzchak]. Burstein, Rabbi Aryeh Lifshitz, the representative of Yad Vashem, principal Rachel Angel, teacher Riva Shalovich - a Jonava native, the daughter of Yentl Solomin, teacher Maoz Shefi.}

Jonava natives and the parents of the students

The female students presenting a performance about the fate of the Jews of Jonava.}

Students of the school at a play on the memorial day

The students listening to the words of Zeev Ofek. Next to him is the principal Rachel Angel

[Page 281]

Many students participated in the performance. They gave expression to their identification in skits, words, and song. Actor Meir Tsoref [Goldshmidt] read an excerpt from Holocaust literature.

This was a ceremony of unity that left a strong impression on all the participants.

On top of all this, we express our esteem and thanks to the efforts of those who led and carried out the adoption efforts - the teachers and students together.

For strengthening our hands - let your hands be strengthened!

A Small Room that Contains So Much
by Riva Shalovich from "Nir", the publication of the students of the school.
Translated by Jerrold Landau

A large group gathered from various places in the Land. They came especially to participate in a memorial evening for the general Holocaust Day, and to open a perpetuation room for the community of Jonava of Lithuania that was wiped out in the Holocaust.

It was obvious that the evening was very precious to everyone. Many years have passed since then, but the memory of the town with all its personalities and people is etched upon the hearts of everyone as a living picture. The gathering evoked memories of youth that ended in pain and great sadness.

The perpetuation room was opened for visitors. The small room includes so much in it - a full world of the life that once was. I looked at the faces of the visitors. Emotion overtook them. They were searching for faces and childhood landscapes that they recognized in the pictures. Stories and trivia were dredged up from the recesses of the past. It was hard to leave the place.

One felt that one was situated in a corner of communion with the destroyed home of one's parents; a corner that is the connecting link between that generation that witnessed the events of the Holocaust with its own flesh and the younger generation that grew up free and secure -- children who attempted to the best of their ability to understand the magnitude of the tragedy, and to feel the pain of the nation.

The adults feel gratitude toward the following generation who are learning to recognize the Jewish towns of the European Diaspora by delving into stories of the life in the town.

Let this be their comfort, and it is no small comfort, for all those who lost their dear ones and for those who survived the Nazi inferno.

By Riva Shalovich,

[Page 281]

Impressions...
by Riva Shalovich
Translated by Jerrold Landau

... I was deeply impressed by the perpetuation room, as if we had been in that community of Jonava (Elana Zavdon).

... We heard the sounds of weeping from among the audience present at the ceremony. Our tears also choked our throats. It was only with great difficulty that we held them back. Our part in the ceremony came. We ascended the stage with the feeling that we were part of those people. I must admit that we did not fully understand the meaning of the word "Holocaust"; but after we had heard from the natives of the town what had happened to that community and its people, our hearts were filled with feelings of honor and understanding for them, and for all the people of the Jewish communities who were overtaken by the Nazi destruction.

(Yitzchak Levi)

From the impressions of the students present at the perpetuation ceremony, from the same publication.

[Page 282]

Children in front of a picture of the town

The memorial ceremony opened a wound that may not heal. Perhaps? Is it possible to forget?

The burning question: How could such an atrocity have taken place?

The drama club of our school put on a performance of a chapter of lives of the children in the ghetto, which brought us to tears. It was obvious that memories were brought forth in the hearts of the audience. I attempted to control my tears, with the prayer in my heart that such a Holocaust never be repeated, that we will never again have to weep over communities of Israel.

Orli Mendelson, a grade 8 student.

On the 9th of Tevet 5732 (1972), we gathered together to recall the victims of the Holocaust, as is our custom.

The ceremony began with the reading of *Yizkor*, and the recital of *Kaddish* and *Kel Maleh Rachamim*[1].

Mr. Shani spoke in the name of Yad Vashem. The editor of the book of Jonava, Shimon Noy, spoke about unique stories of the Jews of the town, the youth, and expression of resistance[2].

The actor Meir Tsoref [Goldshmidt] read sections of the book of Jonava and described some of his personal wartime experiences. His words were spoken in Yiddish and were directed primarily to the new immigrants.

The dramatic club of the school, under the direction of Ruth Lifschitz, presented skits of the life of the children in the ghetto. The material of the skits was culled from the books "The Children of Mapu Street," and "There are no Butterflies Here."

The meeting between the youth who grew up in the Land and did not know the terrors of the ghetto with the natives of the town blew a spirit of support and hope into all those present.

With this, we fulfill the commandment: Remember, and do not forget! We also emphasize that such a Holocaust will never take place again.

Riva Shalovich, the coordinator of the adoption effort.

Translator's Footnotes

Kel Maleh Rachamim is the Jewish prayer for the dead. *Kaddish* is a doxology recited in memory of the deceased. *Yizkor* is a memorial prayer.

Evidently, resistance efforts to the anti-Semitism of the Holocaust.

[Page 283]

In Memory of the Fallen

Yitzchak Pogirsky
by Dr. Shimon Zak from the book "Banim" ("Sons")
Translated by Jerrold Landau

We were both born in Jonava, and we were approximately the same age. I knew Yitzchak (Itzel) already from his childhood, even though we did not study in the same school, for, in accordance with the will of his father, he received a more religious education that I was given.

When we returned to Jonava at the end of 1921 after the expulsion, I met Yitzchak in Kovno as a student of the Real Hebrew Gymnasium. In 1922, we were both accepted to the medical school of the Lithuanian University. The friendship between us strengthened. We sat on the same school bench for two years, always did our practical work in the same group, and prepared for exams together. In 1924, he decided to continue his studies in France. We met again in Strasbourg. He moved to Paris in 1926, where he completed his studies.

When I returned to Lithuania in 1932, I found that Yitzchak had established a family in the interim, and served as a physician in the Lithuanian Army.

Yitzchak, with a wife and two children

He made *aliya* with his family to the Land in 1933. I made *aliya* in 1934. He remained in Tel Aviv, and I joined a Kibbutz. We met on occasion, and I always enjoyed my encounters with my old friend.

In 1941, fate brought us together once again. We were drafted into the British Army as physicians. Yitzchak was sent to Egypt, and I was sent to Sudan and Ethiopia. In 1943, I received the news that Yitzchak was no longer alive. He had fallen in October, 1942…

The following are some of his personality traits, as are guarded in my memory. First of all, he was particular and diligent. If he set times to study, nothing could move him from his learning. He had internal integrity. He would carry through to completion anything that he believed in. He was exacting in fulfilling the commandment of "the produce of the Land." Despite the fact that he was well off, tall, strong and handsome, he did not desire to stand out and did not take any pride in doing so.

The strand of his life was snuffed out in his prime, when he was only in his early 40s.

May his memory be a blessing.

[Page 284]

Yerubaal and Hillel Lavie, Rachel Zisla

Published by Ein Harod

Translated by Jerrold Landau

Yerubaal Lavie

Hillel Lavie   Yerubaal Lavie

Yerubaal, the son of Rachel (nee Zisla) and Shlomo Lavie-Levkovitz, was born on the 1st of Tammuz 5684 (1924). He was born, raised and educated in Ein Harod. He was orphaned from his mother during his childhood. He was modest in his deportment and upright and of pure heart in his way of life. From his childhood, he was known as being responsible and dedicated to any matter to which he was given responsibility. When he left school, he participated in farm work and the course of life. He was active in local defense activities. His regular work was in the shed. He enlisted in the Hebrew Brigade of the British Army in the latter part of 1944. His stops included Sarafand[1], Egypt, Italy, Austria, Belgium, Holland, and France. When he returned from the army, he joyfully returned to the work of the farm and the realities of life at home. He was employed as an orchard worker. In the latter, turbulent period, he found his role in defense, and dedicated himself to this with his full energy and strength. He became known as a competent leader and filled his role of company commander with responsibility. On the 8th of Adar II, 5708 (1948), he hurried the reinforcements to assist his friends in the Battle of Gilboa and fell.

Hillel Lavie

Hillel the son of Rachel and Shlomo was born in Ein Harod on 11 Av, 5689 (1929). His mother died when he was a year and three months old.

From his childhood, he stood out from among his friends in his independence and storied spirit. With the passage of time, when he set out with his classmates from the school and entered the farm along with his friends, he naturally became the center of the group, and the instigator of the spiritual and social activities of his friends.

He chose work in the home garden as his regular occupation.

With the outbreak of the disturbances and the war, he immediately played an active role, at first among the local ranks and later as a leader and trainer of youths and adults. He participated in the Battle of Gilboa in which his older brother fell. Then, he was sent to a national course for leaders. On the night of the invasion, he volunteered to go from the course to the incursion unit of the Palmach in the Negev, and participated in all of its daring activities.

He set out in a convoy of jeeps to bring help to Kfar Darom on June 6, 1948, after the first ceasefire. On his return from the village, on 7 Sivan, 5708 (1948), he was hit by an Egyptian shell.

His body was brought to burial in the soil of Ein Harod on the first anniversary of his death.

This Was His Mother

Hillel was born to a mother - oh, what can one say about this mother? Wellspring of love flowed from her to all that surrounded her. With all these, she was able to keep the depths of the wellsprings of her love for her children…

In one of the letters that she wrote to the father of her children when he was away from home for a few days, we find a praise for Hillel ---------"Now I think, how great is the power of the children, as I think of Hillel, I feel that all the chambers of my heart are filled with light, joy, and love. It seems to me as if the light of the sun and the chirping of the birds exist only in the merit of children. Everything is wonderful in its beauty and goodness…"

We called him Hillel. She said that our oldest son is called Yerubaal. "He will destroy the idols[2], and he will be the heir to your fighting spirit… This one will be my heir, like Hillel the Elder in Jewish tradition; he will seek peace, calm, and love."

This was the mother of our children.

Father

Translator's Footnotes

A town in pre-war Palestine, near Ramle. A large British army base was located there.

An additional name given to the judge Gideon. The name means "He who fights with Baal."

[Page 285]

Mordechai Herman
by Shoshana and Gershon Vilan
Translated by Jerrold Landau

Lieutenant Mordechai Herman

Lieutenant Mordechai Herman, the son of Chaviva (nee Persky) and Yeshayahu, fell in the area of the Suez Canal on the 4th of Elul 5729 (August 18, 1969).}

I first met Motti at the beginning of 1964, when I came to lead the Hachorshim Brigade of Hashomer Hatzair in Ramat Gan. I met a unique youth, central and active.

Motti loved nature, and especially living beings, very much. He visited the Negba on the Feast of First Fruits of 5724 (1964)[1]. That entire day, Motti was filled with excitement about the horse races. He wandered around the stable, visited the horse, and inspected it from head to hoof.

Finally, the competition itself came. Motti galloped on a horse with blazing eyes - on the grass at the center of the Kibbutz. Our truck was waiting, and the driver was blowing the horn (in order to return to Ramat Gan). The travelers were already seated and ready for the journey - all of them, except for Motti. He could not part from the horse. "Go, I will return myself," he shouted to us.

His great knowledge of agriculture astounded me at the time. He took interest in crops, irrigation, machinery and tractors a long time before he began his studies in Hadera.

With his love of nature, he was an ideal member of the youth group.

Motti studied in Hadera for three years.

I only followed him during the first period, at the beginning of his path there. I felt that the period of time in the agricultural school was an important milestone for Motti along the path toward independence and adulthood.

I visited the school twice. I chatted with Motti's advisors. I recall his many stories of his status and his feelings toward the school and the group - how he operated the mechanical equipment for plowing and the equipment in the garage, how he worked as the operator of agricultural implements for the farmers of Hadera. Motti indeed found his place in that school, despite the fact that he had uprooted himself from Ramat Gan, his friends, and even in pushing off his army service.

The connection between us continued even after I returned to Negba. On occasion, on Sabbaths, Motti would come to visit us, bringing some of his friends along. I will admit that each visit left a unique feeling with us.

I remember Motti as a soldier in army fatigues and high army boots, standing in the darkness and stubbornly entering the children's room to take a glance at his sleeping baby. This seemed slightly strange to us, but it was so true to his nature! The older daughter already knew his name and remembered him from visit to visit.

[Page 286]

There were also meetings in the field, several kilometers from the farm. Motti would appear in the field and come to me. I was not at home, and he went to search for me in the field, full of happiness and a smile. He would give me professional advice on the tractor and on cultivation. He was full of joy and faith in life, all exclamation marks with no questions.

My final meeting with Motti was after he completed his course as an armor officer. A mature officer sat next to me, a lad in whom the Israel Defense Forces had placed great responsibility. We exchanged impressions on Sinai and the Suez Canal. Motti told us about his plans in the army. We parted, and he entered his white "Saab", started it and set out on his way. Shosha, who was standing next to me, said, "See, we knew a land and now he has grown up. Did you ever believe that your "wild" Motti would become a captain?"

Motti had a deep sense of volunteerism: to forge forward, to do, to help, to succeed, to prove himself. How proud was he of his deeds during the Six Day War in Kibbutz

Haon, when he took an ambulance and transported wounded people himself, even though he was only a lad in national service.

It seemed that there were no bounds to his wellspring of energy... However ... however ... Motti is no more; Motti, with whom we were so connected and whom we liked so much, who was so full of youthful plans: flourishing, laughter, and renewal. The heart refused, the logic contradicts, but the reality screams out.

Translator's Footnotes

Shavuot.

Eliahu Hagalili (Galanreichik)
Translated by Jerrold Landau

He was born in 1913 in Vilna and was raised in Jonava. He made aliya in 1933. He fell in the War of Independence, in the Western Galilee in the area of Nahariya, on June 27, 1948.

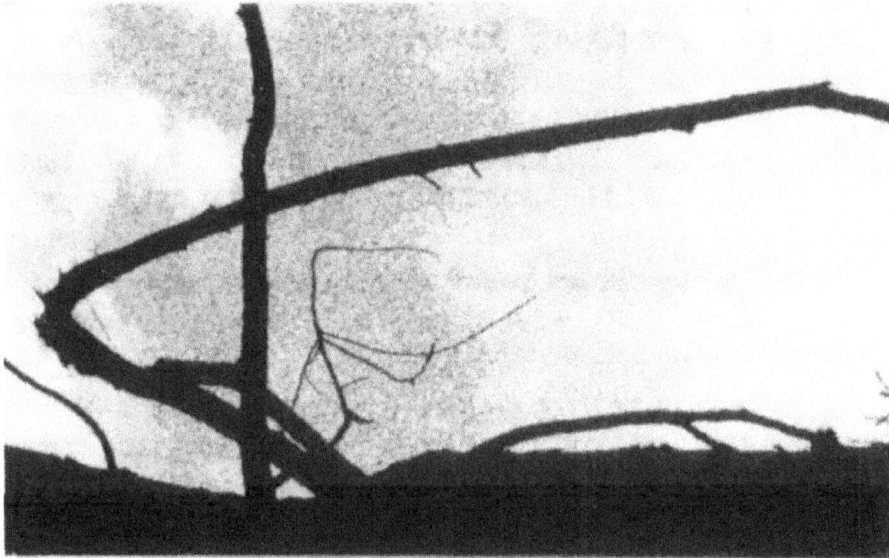

A barren tree

[Page 287]

Jonava

[Page 289]

A Backward Glance

[Page 291]

Our Big–City Shtetl

by Yisrael Yaakov Pagir (United States)

Translated by Jerrold Landau

Yisrael Yaakov Pagir

Our native city, the playground of our childhood, the beginning of our experience of the world, the city in which we were born. In our young minds, from the passing years, from the Dizzy Mountain – Yanova, I see you. You remain etched in my memory.

Your houses spread out from Keidaini Street until the endless highway, from our clear, running, flowing Vilya River until the cemetery mountain. Some of our Yanovers also lived on the other side, first Velvel Fromer and later Shneur Sesitzky, the Kozianer Rabbi. Ferries driven by long ropes connected the other side to our native city. The ferry floated majestically back and forth, always transporting and bringing new customers.

I see your streets and alleyways, your schools and *Beis Midrashes*, your *kloizes* and Hassidic *shtibels*, and – on the other hand – the Russian Church and graveyard not far from the [Jewish] cemetery, as well as the Catholic Church in the middle of our Jewish city, where the Christian folk from the surrounding villages used to gather for their religious services to request good upon themselves. On their holidays, the Jewish shopkeepers of the Yanova market waited for the village folk to come to make their purchases, so that they could earn their livelihoods.

I heard the bells ringing from their churches / On Fridays before candle lighting, I heard the synagogue caller summon everyone to the synagogue with all his might / I witnessed your weddings, and heard your musicians play as the bride and groom were led to the *chupa* [wedding canopy] near the *kloiz* / and I witnessed the joyous parents on the wedding day of their children, as everything was adorned with gladness.

[Page 292]

I witnessed your funerals and heard the eulogies and recitation of Psalms. The Talmud Torah students would call out "Your steps should be before Him" as they walked behind the coffin. The *shamash* would clang the *pushka* [charity box] and call out "Charity saves from death." I witnessed your Simchas Torah festivals with Jewish joy and heartfelt gladness / and I witnessed and felt the fear of a pogrom that was perpetrated upon our city with terror and suffering.

Yanova! I saw your youth defend Jewish lives. They prepared well for a pogrom, and twenty Jewish youth sat with non–empty hands at each of the eight synagogues and *kloizes* / And because of this, the evil gentiles from the surrounding villages forgot about the designated day / No gentile came to Yanova that day even for medical purposes / Nobody saw a gentile / Our city became almost completely Jewish:

The miller and the bread maker
Even the woodchopper
Furriers and the smiths
All were dear Jews.
Shlomo the shaver and barber
Leizer the chimneysweep
Bentze the deaf sentry
Izik Segalovsky – who had one son and eleven daughters.

The finest beauties of our city with Jewish charm, everyone had a beautiful daughter of Zion. Itzik Dembo the carver and Itzik the tinsmith / who knew how to crawl nimbly upon roofs / they were the heads of the fire command / and other Jewish lads, who together formed the Jewish fire brigade.

Keidainer Street

It should have been called the Russian Street, because only Russian residents lived there, with large gardens, orchards with fruit trees, and flowers with a variety of fine colors that, with their beauty, beautified the old, small houses that barely had the energy to stand. Only one house on the street was a beautiful one – the one in which the *pristov* [police chief] lived. In that same courtyard was a "women's gathering place" where the majority of the girls were our Jewish daughter from well–to–do parents, 14–15 years old, speaking Russian amongst themselves, dressed in white aprons and black dresses, with combed heads and intertwined long braids. Such beauties one cannot find, encounter, or see in today's modern world. It was only our Jewish daughters who were so charming, our own Yanovers.

Whoever has not seen our Keidainer Street on the holy Sabbath Day in the summer months has never seen beauty. The street was long, straight, and unpaved. There were three steps leading up to the sidewalk, and cherry trees were planted on both sides in the front row. The cherry trees were blossoming in the warm spring, and the entire, straight street was decorated with white blossoms. As the cherries grew, the trees turned green and then red. Such a stroll on that street would lead past the water mill, which milled flour for the Sabbath *challos*. A narrow path between thick trees wound toward the Dizzy Mountain.

[Page 293]

A forest and a field with shadows of trees, fresh air and the usual aroma of pine trees, and the smell of strawberry gardens refreshed and brought joy to everybody's hearts. Upon that mountain, everybody fulfilled the Sabbath need for joy and beauty that they were seeking.

Bashful brides and grooms, who were afraid of the evil eye – the bride would stroll on Keidainer Street with her girlfriends, and the groom would walk in the same direction with his friends. When the groom encountered the bride on that stroll / he took her by her hand / the embarrassed friends followed the bride and groom / and there was joy and mirth. The young, bashful, Yanover boys on Breizer Street who wanted to guard their eyes from women / ran away or fled / however, one could find the beloved girl with her beloved lad on Dizzy Mountain / and the lovers did not have to wait long or hope fruitlessly / everyone was glad with the Sabbath joy / until one had to return home toward evening.

On the other hand, there were also idealistic youth in Yanova, who were seeking some sort of human accomplishment.

Dizzy Mountain was the best place for the Yanova parties to gather. The pine forest disguised everything. Our Talmud Torah teacher Yachnovitz delivered a speech to all the Jewish parties at a gathering in the forest. I was a member of the S. S. youth[1] along with Shmuelke Brandwein, the son of the Kaplitzer teacher, and Davidka, who worked in Chaim Levin's optical shop. They did not drive us away. Guards were placed to warn if the police were coming. In total, there were six policemen and one police chief in Yanova, but we did manage to put up proclamations with red ink. The guards were to give a signal that we had to separate into small groups. This is how the day of joy for everyone on Dizzy Mountain passed.

When the sun began to get lower upon Dizzy Mountain and the shadows of the trees got longer, everyone set out for home. Everyone could see Yanova from the top of the mountain. The golden sun lit up all the roofs with its last rays /

Whether the house was low or high /

Whether the house was straight or crooked /

The sun lit up everything.

Keidainer Street witnessed the nicest parade. The Jewish youth escorted their Sabbath, dressed up and admirable. Their way home led through Breizer Street, and this was possibly the nicest thing that Breizer Street had ever witnessed – the Jewish youth in their element…

Happy is the eye that saw all this[2].

Translator's Footnotes

This is not the S.S. that is notorious from Nazi times, but rather a pre–war youth movement.

This is actually a quote from the Yom Kippur *Musaf* service, after reminiscing about the Yom Kippur Temple service.

[Page 294]

Productivity, Cultural, and Innovations

by Efraim Zilberman (America)

Translated by Jerrold Landau

Efraim Zilberman

Jonava was one of the most important and well-rooted Jewish communities in Lithuania. Throughout the 19th century, it quickly developed into a large Jewish settlement on the lovely banks of the Vylia, 30 kilometers northeast of the capital Kovno. As a child I recall how the older generation used to mention with anguish the "great fire" which afflicted the town in 1905. The fire destroyed the entire town in one night. Not long passed before new brick houses and six fine, large Beis Midrashes were built in place of the old wooden houses. Already before the First World War, the population reached 5,000 souls, of which 3,500 were Jews.

In 1915, the Jews of Jonava experienced the decree of the Czarist authorities: in 48 hours they must leave their homes along with all of the Jews of the Kovno Gubernia. The Jews wandered out to various cities in Czarist Russia. Some paused in Vilna and returned to the town immediately after the Germans marched in. After the end of the war in 1918, the rest of the Jews who had gone deep into Russia returned to their Jonava. The rabbi of the town, Rabbi Chaim Yitzchak Silman returned along with important activists of the time such as Reb Abba Pogirsky, Chaim Levin, Shmerl Stern, Yaakov Gloz, and A. Abramson. They began to rebuild Jewish societal life. The Talmud Torah was renovated. It was led by the veteran Hebrew teacher of Jonava Shaul Keidansky. A small Yeshiva was founded, as was a charitable fund for Jewish artisans and shopkeepers which later developed into a large Jewish public bank. A Bikur Cholim (organization for visiting the sick), Linat Tzedek (organization for providing lodging to wayfarers), and other such institutions were founded. Jewish life began to pulsate again in Jonava. Jews also had a majority in the city council. For several years, the mayor of Jonava was the honorable communal activist Reb Chaim Levin.

[Page 295]

Jonava was especially known for its large number of Jewish artisans and laborers. The well-developed center of the Jewish furniture factories in Jonava with their dozens of Jewish carpenters produced modern furniture for all of Lithuania. "Jonaver furniture" was a known item. There were large Jewish sawmills and brick kilns there. Jonava also had a large Jewish match factory called "Oran" and several modern rolling mills in which many Jewish people were employed. Jonava had a "Smith Street" where there were dozens of Jewish smithies which produced worked metals and special light wagons for the Lithuanian marketplace. In addition, Jonava had dozens of Jewish tailors, shoemakers, quilters, tin workers, locksmiths, belt makers, furriers and potters. Jewish hands made all types of things in the town. On account of the Vylia, Jonava also had a large number of barges. Jewish toilers earned their livelihood by binding together and driving the barges. Even the Jonava Jewish wagon drivers and coach drivers were known throughout Lithuania. The town also had a lively, temperamental youth with right and left leaning organizations. The Zionist movement was led with enthusiasm by the veteran Zionist Moshe Ivensky, particularly the years 1923-1925. Many people also immigrated to America and Africa. Jonava also had good sports clubs – Maccabee and Hapoel.

A Maccabee march in the Girialkac Forest

[Page 297]

Our Parental Home

[Page 298]

Smiths (1911): Moshe Ritz (Moshe Feiga–Leah's), Yisrael Pagir, Tevka, Shlomo (son
of David Elia the coachman)

[Page 299]

My Incarnations

by Yisrael Yaakov Pagir

Translated by Jerrold Landau

Woe, woe, roll the blacksmith
Roll does he well
His stall and metal limbs
Set the blood on fire
(From the Iliad)

My father, who knew some Torah and worshipped three times a day, understood the prayers. He would sit at the table between *Mincha* and *Maariv* in the Karebelgikshen Kloiz on Breizer Street, and listen to the rabbi's sermons. He earned his livelihood as a tailor, not as successful as Naftali the tailor and his son, from among our Jewish brethren – but for the gentile acquaintances from the surrounding villages, he was a very good tailor, for he did not charge too much for the pieces of fur that the gentile brought for a fur coat. If the fur coat turned out long or wide, then father was the best craftsman. My mother was an exquisitely beautiful woman, always with a nice kerchief covering her beautiful curly head of black hair. Hardened and tired, she would bring bread home for the nine children, one more beautiful than the other. She knew how to pray and recite the petitions[1] – which was a great wonder. Yose the tailor did not want his wife to go to worship at the *kloiz*, and stand next to the *zogerke*[2] and help her with her groaning. He did not allow her to go to the *kloiz*, where she would not know how to worship from her own *siddur* [prayer book]. He taught her and I always wondered.

My Father and his Customs

When he would come home from the *kloiz*, he would tell all the news that he heard, as well as what he had learned at the table. We children were amazed at Father who knew about everything. Once when somebody asked him to remove a half of a strip of fur from a fur coat, he said to Mother with a sigh and a groan: "You know? Three types of Jews do not get the World To Come: Rabbis, who live off the accounts of others; shopkeepers, who use false weights and measures; and tailors, who steal the remnants and sell them to others – and the gentile[3] immediately asks, 'If it is not allowed, why do you steal?'"

"I do not steal for myself. I steal for perhaps a pair of winter boots for you… For bread, I earn, but for boots I must steal, and lose my World To Come… (A tailor's accounting, from my father's treasury). Feiga, what would you say if you had no money? Look at your five sons, each one of them is worth as if a treasure from a thief, a dowry of 300 rubles. Do you have no less than 1,500 rubles? We also have four daughters, such beautiful daughters with a sparkle in their eyes, they would be grabbed up from you, with a kiss on the hand, for 150 rubles cash and a 150 promissory note. We would only require 500 rubles. Subtract the 500 rubles from the 1500 rubles, and you will be left with 900 rubles. Show me one wealthy man on Breizer Street who has ready cash?"

My father was very concerned to find trades for his five sons, from which they could earn livelihoods, and would not be at different stations of life from each other and have jealousy and hatred. He set up my eldest brother with our neighbor, Archik the rope maker. With regard to me, on account of my learning and writing, he felt I would be suitable as a rabbi. What about the third one? He would be a tailor. The fourth one, who eats bread like an athlete, would be a shoemaker. The fifth one would be a clockmaker or a smith.

[Page 300]

"What do you say Feiga? Do you like my plan?" My mother said, "They should grow up in good health. We will then see."

The Fire and the Beginning of My War

It was a miracle from heaven – our house was spared from the flames. Was this due to the merit of Shimon the teacher? Or perhaps due to the merit of wet blankets on the roof, that Father had moistened with cold water that the five boys had fetched. Or perhaps in the merit of the wind that blew toward the Viliya. Father's wealth remained with a roof over the head. When the sun shone, it was a roof, and when it was raining, it was a sieve; however, as long as it did not rain, it was not so bad. It would have been worse, Heaven forbid, if the house had burnt down. The intelligent fire victims who lived as neighbors, who did not lose anything, had clear thinking, and if the flames were to affect them, they would find a place in the Talmud Torah. Each family took over one corner. The children whose rooms had not burned down were the most unfortunate. To their dismay, they had to go to *cheder*. However, the over 100 children who went to the Talmud Torah either remained free as a bird or became workers, earning ten kopecks a day fetching bricks. I also started to work at transporting the bricks from one place to another. It did not take long for the skin of my finger to become worn down. I escaped to my home and left behind my work. Father bandaged my finger.

"If you were looking for the reason for the work, listen to me, "Father said to me, "We do not know when the Talmud Torah will open. In the meantime, go to the *Yeshiva* or the *Beis Midrash* and study *Gemara*. You will indeed become a rabbi."

I immediately responded that I did not wish to become a rabbi.

"So, working is better? Look at your finger. You still have a few years until your Bar Mitzvah. Even if you will be a poor tailor, some *Gemara* will not hurt."

I went to the *Beis Midrash*, mourning and distraught. I went to the table where the children were studying with the rabbi. One was shouting louder than the other.

"What do you want to say, son?"

"Father sent me to study *Gemara*."

"What have you studied until now?

"I studied in the Talmud Torah."

"With gentiles?"

"No, with Jews," I answered in anger, even though he was a teacher. He did understand, though, that he should not ask any more. He tested me in Bible. He realized that I knew Bible well. He opened up a *Gemara*, and said, "Show what you know?" I read the *Gemara* with understanding, but without the *Gemara* melody. The children laughed, but the rabbi said that I was a good vessel that one must fill with *Gemara*. I sat down at the greasy table and pined for my teacher Yachnovitz who moved away after the fire. I wanted to complete the lesson, so I reviewed the *Gemara* without spirit and without feeling. I studied in the *Yeshiva* until my *Bar Mitzvah*. The day after My *Bar Mitzvah*, I no longer wanted go to the *Yeshiva*. My father stated, "We do not abandon things in the middle. It is only a few months until Rosh Hashanah. The old year will end. When the new year comes, on the intermediate days of Sukkot we will think it through and discuss what next." There was nothing I could do, one must obey Father. On the intermediate days of Sukkot, the directors of the *Yeshiva*, Yankel the vinegar maker and Shalom Keidainer claimed to my father, "A boy who knows how to learn must learn." They discussed my situation – if I would study in the *Beis Midrash* under the supervision of the Vilkomirer Parush during the winter, I could go to the Slabodka yeshiva in the summer. Then Father asked me, "What do you say?" I responded briefly and sharply:

[Page 301]

"I do not want either Slabodka or the *Beis Midrash*. If you send me to study worldly subjects, I would go to the ends of the world and do everything. If you would permit me, I would study a trade. If I must go to the *Beis Midrash* to study, which I do not want to do, I will escape at the first opportunity."

My Father's Plans

This is what I promised. Good or bad, the winter passed. When the summer came and the gentiles had no time to bring work, Father had no work. He decided that after the Sabbath he would walk to a village that he was familiar with to seek a bit of work. I waited for this. On Sunday morning, Father set out for the village. Instead of going to the *Beis Midrash*, I set out to seek work, and I found work: helping a turner move the runner by foot, polishing wooden oak legs of a table or furniture. I earned a zloty a day, and worked for the week. Father returned on Friday afternoon, and Mother did not tell him. On Sunday morning in the *kloiz*, he found out that his darling had left the *Yeshiva*. Father went to the turner, and summoned me home. Father gave me a lecture – what kind of a thief was I from him, I am throwing a way a life of honor, for I was destined to receive rabbinic ordination.

"A wealthy Jew would come to the *Yeshiva*, who would want to marry off his daughter and would want a son–in–law who was a rabbi. You would receive 100 rubles as a dowry, and a several years of support, and you would live a life of good fortune. And you want to throw everything away and become a tailor, a tradesman. You want to be a poor man like me?"

When my father concluded his lecture, I responded:

"I recall that you have said that a rabbi does not get the World To Come, and a shopkeeper is a thief, and now you want me to become a rabbi, and to be the son–in– law of a wealthy shopkeeper and be supported from stolen goods, from dishonest weights and measures? I am certain that a wealthy householder who has a thousand rubles for a dowry could find better sons–in–law than poor lads, unless the bride is so ugly that one cannot look at her, or if she has a blemish on her eye."

I Become a Tailor

My mother began to laugh at my lecture. Father became angry:

"You want to become a tailor? I will not teach you. I will not teach a lad who is able to write and study, and become party to such a crime. Go to Leizer the

[Page 302]

tailor. When I was a lad, I worked for him. Tell him that you are my darling, and that you want to become a tailor.

I won the first battle, and, as an arrow shot from a bow, I hurried to Leizer. He asked me to sit down. He gave me a thimble, as well as a needle with a bit of cloth and a thread, so that I could learn how to hold a needle in my hand. I worked with Leizer the tailor until the intermediate days of Sukkot. I was not happy to work with him, and I was not able to get accustomed to the tailoring witticisms.

In Pilvinski's Shop

As Father requested, from that day and onward I had to pay something toward shoes and clothing, and Leizer refused to pay. Father told me to seek another type of job. I was happy, and I accepted a position with the shopkeeper Pilvinski. His shop was across the way from the Polish church, along the way to the barracks, right where the Russian girls and boys used to come in the winter to stroll and choose brides or grooms.

I did not work that hard, but it was enjoyable. I enjoyed very much when, on the long winter evenings, Leib Granewitz, the tall lawyer Alter, and others would come in with the Hatzefira newspaper, and we would have full debates about Jewish problems and the anti–Semitism of the Russian regime. I would sit and listen in a corner, so that they would not see me. Pilvinski did not look for any work for me. I had great enjoyment as I learned more things about the world, more than I did in the *Beis Midrash*, and furthermore, I earned a ruble a week in salary. Granewitz and Yankel were Zionists, and they wanted Pilvinski to purchase a *shekel*[4], but he was stingy. Aside from them, sometimes Melechke the hunchback would come in with two others to request money for the Bund. Pilvinski would give them 15 kopecks. They wanted Pilvinski to register his name, but he refused this honor. Melechke the hunchback signed. A bit later, youths from important Jewish families would come in to request money for the S.S. Pilvinski gave them nothing and almost chased them out. His wife asked:

"Does it make sense? You give 15 kopecks to someone who you do not know? To the youths – and I know them all – you give nothing?"

"The other I do not know. I am afraid of him. These ones I know. They are fine children, and they will not do anything to me."

My first year of working passed for better or for worse, but I felt as if I was a free person. On the intermediate days of Sukkot, I spoke to the boss. I had worked well for him, and I asked for a raise in salary. He understood that I was correct, and he was very happy with me; however, he could hire a Bar Mitzvah boy for a ruble a week for the work that he required. I was now a very shamed youth, and I had to go to seek work. My father completely refused to get involved with my work situation.

"You do not want to obey. Do as you wish."

[Page 303]

I had an idea: to go to Avchik Pagirsky in his metal business and ask for work. I would go to ask before I went to eat lunch at home, so if I was fortunate, I could announce the good news at home. As I passed by Hane Matel's three story brick house and took a look, my breath was taken away. I read the sign with large Russian words, and my heart pounded like a hammer. Crossing the street, near Lazer Levi Itzik's I cast a glance to see if Pilvinski's customers were there. I took a deep breath, and went by the street with hasty steps, went up the three steps in one breath, and entered the dwelling and stood at the door. Something glared in my eyes: the gold and silver samovars sparkled on the opposite shelf like mirrors. People were all around. Gentiles collected cash boxes. They shook and put the boxes near their ears to hear the clanging. I reviewed what I was preparing to say. When Sherl Pagirsky asked, "What do you want, lad?" I do not know what I answered... I answered the other questions as follows:

"Where did you work? Can you write?" I responded that I could read and write Yiddish and Russian, and could do arithmetic.

"Where did you study?"

"In the Talmud Torah."

"Do you want to work tomorrow? What is your name?"

"Yisraelke."

"You are already a big lad, we will call you Yisrael. If you work for a few weeks, I will tell you what I will pay you. Do you want the money every week?"

"I do not need money. My mother requires that she can come to request it when she needs it."

"You are a good boy toward your mother: Come, I will show you. When you come tomorrow, you will go to Avraham, and work with him."

I exited, going through the iron doors to the yard: iron, iron, iron and steel in the paved yard. Near the windows there was iron. It was a world of iron.

"This lad will help you. His name is Yisrael."

I looked at Avraham and wondered who called him Avraham? Just as they named me Yisrael, Avrahamele would have fit him better, a minute little thing. After that I found his appropriate name, Avrahamele the Little Pepper. I did not walk home, but ran. I opened the door and said that I was an apprentice with Avchik Pagirsky in his iron workshop. What should I say? I said it over and over again. During the week, my lunch was farfel stew with sour cream, blueberries and white sour cream. Father helped Mother make the meal for me... I still recall the taste today. I left in the morning as Yisraelke and came back at noon as Yisrael, and my father remembered well what had to be done. My employment at Avchik Pagirsky's iron workshop was an honor. Aside from earning my salary of two rubles a week, I felt as if I was living in the Garden of Eden. Furthermore, at home, my younger brothers and sisters looked upon me with awe, and even my father said that it worked out for the best.

Working in the yard with Avrahamele and Kachel Zaflatz the cart man was enough to laugh. In the evening, when the brouhaha with the customers of the day ended, and we were involved with filling the orders or the requests that came by mail and packing them up to send them to the metal merchants in the surrounding cities, they called me to go with the older people to remove the tools and iron products from their tall shoulders. I especially liked doing this for Freidele due to her refined mannerisms and her beauty. Everyone had the same opinion. I do not follow the Jewish custom of not stating a person's praise in front of him. I do not say – I write, and when I write, I believe it is permitted by all opinions.

[Page 304]

As I am dwelling on the memorials from that period, it is appropriate to mention Ronka Das and Shulka, as well as Alter Miche's, the fine person and wagon driver, as well as Michel Kapusta, his wife, and their horse. There were to some extent examples of those whom the Yanover Jews in that trade were jealous of, for they also were involved in working with Avchik Pagirsky. Then, something took place that turned my life in the direction of a completely happy life.

I Prepare for a Higher Level

Then a day came when Avrahamele the Pepper committed a wrongdoing. I am not completely sure about what happened, or whether it was only a mishap. Mende Tzemach's arrived with a gentile to purchase some iron for a wheel. His order was estimated at ten pounds extra, and the gentile unfortunately paid. Forty extra kopecks were taken, and Avrahamele and Mende divided the stolen money at 20 kopecks a person. I noticed that a gentile already paid for the iron and placed it in his wagon. When Sherl Pagirsky noticed that Mende was with the gentile, she asked him to carry the iron back and lay it on the scale. It was ten pounds less than what the gentile had paid for. Sherl returned the 40 kopecks. She told him that they had tricked him. She told Mende that he must no longer come with customers to trick them, and to Avraham she said, "You must not do this anymore, for you will have a bad end."

One fine day, whatever the reasons were, the goodhearted Sherl Pagirsky expelled Avraham from the yard, and even closed the door behind him herself and said:

"You shall never set foot in this yard again." To me she started to say:

"You can come without him. You do not need him. Karel will help you. I feel a great pain, but I felt I had to issue the punishment for dishonesty." The preparation for a higher role was a great thing for me. The improvement could be seen in that when written orders arrived, nobody had to stand with me to check and adjust the weights. I did everything. The fact that I could read and write Yiddish, Russian, and even Hebrew also came in handy, for many metal shopkeepers used a Hebraic style in writing their orders. Hebrew letters used to even be written by the metal shopkeepers, and Moshe Mishelevitz knew the language well.

The summer passed, and Avraham used to go to work at floating the barges on the Viliya and even on the Neman. However, it got cold after Sukkot, and Avraham was no great hero. Avraham and Bayla were in great need, and several of their children helped.

[Page 305]

Sherl Bluma's gave a raise of a half ruble a week for each child, and according to the calculations, there were already seven. When Avraham got married to Bayla, he was earning three rubles a week, and when he lost his job, he was earning 6.5 rubles a week. This was the calculation.

When I came to the yard one Sunday morning during the month of *Cheshvan*, Avraham was already there, dressed in his work clothes. He was standing and crying, and also…

Finally I Decide to Become a Smith

I felt the tragedy of not having work in my hand. I realized for myself that I had no way other than to study to become a smith. A carpenter who makes furniture earns well. A smith also earns well, due to the fact that Pagirsky takes in all the goods that smiths produce, purchases them, and sends them to all the cities. I knew that Moshe Feiga Leah's and Mota the Smith, Hirsh the son–in–law of Ben–Zion were seeking a worker. I immediately set out to find out who would be prepared to teach me the work. Yisrael became a smith, and then he was back to Yisraelke. I understood that this was a major step, and I assured myself by making a condition: 100 rubles a year with food. I was certain that eating at home would not happen, and I would even be sleeping in the smithy. It was my desire and aim to become independent, and to earn my living through honest work.

My father felt that the sky was falling in Breizer Street. Such an honorable job I was throwing away, and I was throwing away the learning and writing into the mud! Why would a smith need to study and write? My father did not speak to me for a few months. On account of a battle with a competitor, I had to leave my position. I began working with Moshe Ritz. Since Moshe Ritz was a sick man, I was the full–fledged second in command. We sent all types of hinges to Vilna. I worked and was the manager with six helpers. I wrote the letters, the addresses, and the accounts. I worked until 8:00 p.m., and then conducted the correspondence in my house.

As an 18 year old, I was already earning seven rubles a week. My father made a request of me when my sister was about to get married, and I had to give a contribution of 100 rubles. I gave my mother three rubles a week, kept one ruble for myself, one ruble was put in the bank for me by my boss – or two rubles a week when I earned more.

I Follow the Tide to America

When all the young lads started to go to America, Moshe Ritz took me on as a partner, with 40% for me and 60% for him. I was not going to go to America, because for me, America was here. Unexpectedly, on a Thursday night in the month of February, Yidl the mailman brought me a ship ticket to America. I went to the eye doctor in Kovno on Friday morning. On Saturday, I visited my acquaintances, and on Sunday morning, I set out on the trip. I snuck across the border. On March 1, 1913, we I arrived at Ellis Island near New York on the Fatherland Ship. I arrived in the city of Pittsburg as a 19 year old on March 4, 2013 as they were swearing in President Woodrow Wilson.

[Page 306]

I tinkered around for a week, and then realized that I must begin to think about work, if I wished to get work in a smithy. How would a Jew come to a smith? A gentile is a smith. A Jew is either a peddler or a tailor. I did not want to hear about such things. The work that I was interested in must lead me to self–sufficiency. That was what I wanted. One cannot get rich from working, and there was no hope to move up from work – so my cousin told me.

My cousin found an announcement in the newspaper that someone was looking for smiths in a place where they made locomotives for the railway. I was happy. In the morning, I went on the tram with my cousin as my guide and interpreter. We arrived at the factory, and they directed us to the blacksmith's shop – as it was called in America. They opened the door for us, and we entered hell: fiery flames, clanging hammers, the smiths – gigantically tall, large, hefty men, and I looked like a child next to them. The foreman explained to us courteously that here, they must have people who understand the language, and they must be able to know the signals since one does not hear what is spoken. He told me to come back when I understand the English Language, most probably in a few years. He extended his hand, and told me in German *auf wiedersehen.*

I obtained work in a German factory where they did work for buildings – iron steps for the tall buildings. I was the only Jew among 25 German employees. They spoke English and German – and what Jew does not know German?

After working for a few years, I asked my foreman with whom I worked whether there was a possibility for me to get to understand the plans by which he worked, and whether I could ever work as he does? The Germans were very good machinists, he told me. If I want to become a very good worker, and wish to understand the plans and work on the plans as he did and perhaps even better, I must understand the language in which the plans were written. This would take me approximately three years.

I Bless the Day When I Become a Smith

In the winter of 1916, my friend from Yanova, the son of Leizer the chimneysweep, invited me to come to his wedding. The war was in progress, and I had not received any letter from my loved ones. I decided to accept the invitation, and I went to the wedding in Boston. This was the best thing that I could have done, for during the three years that I had been in the large industrial city of Pittsburg, I had never seen the moon, and the sun shone as if through a cloud, on account of the smoke from the large iron factories.

I decided then that I was not going to return to Pittsburg, so long as I could get a job. I got the job in which I am still working now, after 51= years. A few years later, I found out that he was from the same town as my mother, Kaplice, and he knew my mother, my father, and my grandfather. This had no connection to my employment there. My employment was a result of my abilities.

[Page 307]

I married my wife, who was beautiful even among the beautiful. We have three children. We gave them the best education. One son is a doctor and a teacher of the English language. Our daughter is an educated chemist and works as a librarian for chemistry books in the New York Public Library. One son is a musician, with a Master's Degree in music. He tells me, "Pa you earn your living from hard work, and I make a living playing."

I did not come out of work with wealth. I bless the day when I became a smith in Yanova, and I am full of happiness as I state: The work of my hands is splendorous.

Translator's Footnotes

Techinos – special woman's prayers.

The woman who leads the women in prayers in the women's section of the synagogue.

Here, the derogatory term sheigetz is used.

Token of membership in the Zionist organization.

My Life Stopovers

by Mari Winton (Moshe Vinitzky)

Translated by Jerrold Landau

Moshe Vinitzky

Our house, in which our parents lived and where I spent my childhood years, was located on Kovner Street, on the right side in the direction of Keidainer Street. The house was made of bricks and plastered with white lime. It was large and roomy enough for the entire family. There was a large fruit orchard near the house, and a smithy nearby.

We were known in Yanova as the family of Yuda Pesach's. My father, Pesach of blessed memory, was a pious Jew, but not fanatical. He was a good tradesman, and worked in the smithy together with his brother Yoel. They were master tradesmen, and they used to manufacture carriages and sleds that were not made to order. In the yard there were various spare parts from manufacturers, and my father used to sell them to the landowners from the region. He would also send merchandise to Zasliai and other towns.

My mother Chana, may G–d avenge her blood (murdered by the Germans) was much more pious than father. She was strict with kashruth. She was calm and good natured. Our family consisted of three sisters: Chaya Sarale, Esther and Moshel; and three brothers: Moshe (Mari), Berl, and Yudel. Father's earnings were sufficient for food and clothing for the family, and they sent the children to study in the cheders and yeshivas of Yanova.

In our house–workshop, we had one cow, and some hens and geese.

[Page 308]

Mother took care of them. We children used to love leading the cow to the field, going all around Stepan's pasture around Dizzy Mountain in Josefka.

I studied in the *cheder* of Yisrael–Ber on the highway. Later, I studied in the Yanover Yeshiva of Yudel Gurfinkel, who was called the Yellow Rosh Yeshiva teacher. Still later, I studied in the Ramailis Yeshiva in Vilna, on the Jewish street opposite the synagogue of the Vilna Gaon. In that *Yeshiva*, we studied Hebrew, *Gemara*, as well as Russian. I studied everything diligently. At that time, I felt an inner striving toward knowledge and culture. Unfortunately, this was interrupted by the outbreak of the First World War. I also had an inclination toward music. I studied music with Reuvke Baron. When the Jews were driven out of Yanova in 1915, we all started packing. In that process, my mandolin broke. That marked the end of my musical dream.

After packing up our belongings in a rented wagon, we set out in the direction of Zasliai on the eve of *Shavuot*. The edict of deportation did not apply to Zasliai, which belonged to the Vilna Gubernia. There, we lodged temporarily with our relative Yosef Burstein. A short time later, we traveled by train in freight wagons to Chernigov, Ukraine, and from there further on to Vitebsk. We remained there until the end of the war, when the Germans permitted us to return to Yanova. In the interim, I set myself up with work in "Zemelnia–Soyuz" in Gomel.

In 1918, I hatched a plan to set out on my own to Yanova. At that time, I belonged to the Youth Home. I stole my way in a train that transported Latvian refugees to Latvia. I did not have any documents. I hid for several nights in the buffers of the train cars. In Yanova, I found that our house was in ruins. The floor had caved in, and the entire yard was overgrown with tall grass. I went to consult with the Jewish policeman, Yisrael Stein. He advised me to travel to my relatives in Wilkomir, the Resnick family. After a brief consultation, they purchased my tickets to travel to Dvinsk, and from there, back to my parents. Beyond Dvinsk, I snuck over the German–Russian front, and arrived at my parents in Vitebsk. Hearing that I had been in Yanova, my sister Chaya– Sara stole across the border and once again went there, where she fainted from terror.

In 1919, the entire family returned to Yanova in a legal fashion. We renovated the house and workshop, and my father returned to his old work of smithing. Later, since I had already been in larger cities in Russia, Yanova was not alluring to me, and I decided to emigrate to America, where we had many relatives from both father's and mother's sides. I first traveled to Berlin. An aunt of mine lived there, mother's sister Esther Makel, who had gotten married and lived there. I lived with them for some time until I received the needed papers from my uncle in America, who had married my aunt.

My uncle owned a 150 acre tobacco farm in Connecticut. I worked at the tobacco plantation and earned very well. My sole desire at that time was to bring over the entire family to America. I sent papers to my sister Esther and brother Berl. My sister Moshel came a bit later. In the meantime, my father died, and my youngest brother Yudel took over father's trade and thereby supported his family. We succeeded in bringing over our mother, but, after a short time, she decided to return to Yanova. She missed the remaining children in Yanova, to whom she was deeply connected. In 1935, our youngest brother Yudel came to America, along with his wife Tzipora Shaham whom he had married in the interim, and their two children. My sister Chaya–Sarale, who had married Aharon Segal, remained in Yanova. He was the founder of the movie theater of Yanova. We did not succeed in bringing them over, for they did not pay attention to my documents of request.

Right: Y[israel]. Pagir in 1919.
Left: Y[israel]. Pagir in the American Army, 1918.

Sitting in the middle: Yudel, Feiga (nee Shaham), Esther, and Morris Vinitzky–Winton.
Below: the pictures of Grandfather and Grandmother – Yehuda and Faya Vinitzky.
In Yanova, they raised four families (3 brothers and 2 sisters)[2], and today in America,
they number more than 200.

At a corner of the Smiths Lane and the Old Street – Opnik's smithy: Ben–Zion,
Avraham–Yitzchak (Mitzka), Mordechai, Yaakov, Fruma: The Brezin girls. The third
house belongs to Alta the Milk Woman.

Feiga (Shaham), Berl and Yudel Vinitzky

Yoska the Crazy.

[Page 309]

My mother Chana, my sister Chaya–Sarale, her husband Aharon Segal, and their three sons Moshe, Mordechai, and Chaim were among my relatives who were murdered.

My former tobacco farm is still called "Winton Park" after my name, and the street is called Winton Road[3]. Our family in America now consists of over 100 people. Most of them live in the city of Hartford. The nationalist education that we received in our youth has not worn off to this day. We are still Zionists, and work toward the upbuilding and strengthening of Israel. I travel to Israel every two years and stay with friends and Yanovers for an entire four months. One brother, Yudel, who is an active Revisionist[4] is giving up his business and desires to settle in Israel.

Translator's Footnotes

Vav is a letter of the Hebrew alphabet, with the 'v' sound (or 'w' sound when transliterated into English).

The math does not add up in this sentence, but the discrepancy is likely due to the sister who was murdered in the Holocaust (see continuation of story).

One can find a Winton Road and Winton Park in East Windsor Connecticut, near the Connecticut River north of Hartford.

A follower of the Revisionist Zionism of Jabotinsky.

Through America to Israel
by Tzipora Winton (nee Shaham)
Translated by Jerrold Landau

Yudel and Tzipora [Shaham Winton]

Our family was well–known. My father Shaya Shaham was a scholar, who knew how to study *Gemara* well, and also knew Hebrew well. For this, he can thank his education that he received in his home from his father Avraham–Yitzchak the Shochet [ritual slaughterer]. My father was a good–natured man. He loved societal work. He was traditional and observant, but not fanatical. He was a convinced Zionist, and was active in the Keren Kayemet [Jewish National Fund] and Keren Hayesod. He made sure to transmit the education that he received from Grandfather down to his own children.

[Page 310]

Avraham–Yitzchak [Shaham] the Shochet.

My mother Geneshe was an exquisite Jewish mother. She was calm, peaceful, quiet, and dedicated with love and life to her family, her husband, and the education of her children.

We were four children: two sisters Sonia and Feiga[1], and the brothers Yosef and David. We all received a nationalistic education, and were active in Young Zion, Young Socialists, and Maccabee. We received our education in the *cheders*, the Talmud Torah, and later in the Tarbut School.

Veteran Yanova Residents

Incidentally I wish to note that my grandmother Rivka–Buna's ancestors (from my father's side) stem from an important family from Portugal. After the expulsion of the Jews from Portugal[2], their ancestors settled in France. They later moved to Lithuania and settled in Wilkomir. After their marriage, they settled in Yanova toward the end of 1799 or the beginning of 1800. This proves that we were veteran Yanova residents. My mother had four brothers and four sisters. In time, all of them emigrated to America, except for my mother and her brother Mottel who remained in Yanova. They were destined to be murdered by Hitler's murderous bands together with father.

From far–off America, memories of my childhood years swim around in my head. I always marvel at the calm of our town, especially in the early morning hours at sunrise. In the summer, the sun was always high on the horizon at 4:00 a.m., as the entire town was still in deep sleep. Only the shepherds who used to collect the cows and the goats in the pasture, as well as the tired women who brought the cows and goats to the collection point disturbed the early morning calm.

We Were Driven Out

The happy period of my youth continued until the outbreak of the First World War. My father was drafted into the army, and sent to Vilna and later to the deep interior of Russia. My mother remained alone with her four children.

One early morning, a division of Cossacks appeared in Yanova, appearing like a whirlwind through the streets. They held lances and spears in their hands, which they used to spear the challos that the women in the market kept in troughs to sell. We children stood in amazement at their dexterity, as we were full of fear.

On the eve of Shavuot of 1915, we found announcements posted that all the Jews must leave Yanova within 24 hours. One cannot imagine the extent of the misfortune that befell our town. People did not know where to go and run. People hired farmers with horses and wagons. They sold their goods and traveled to Kaisiadorys (Kashedar) and Zasliai. We contacted the Russian landowner Stepan, who owned many fields around Dizzy Mountain, and who knew my mother well. He sent two horses with drivers, and helped us sell a few valises, and we set off in the direction of the town of Zasliai. Along the way, we passed through the Boda Forests, which had been burnt down, seemingly by German agents. The Cossacks who were lodging in the surrounding area ordered us to put out the fire, and threatened us with whips. No amount of begging helped us, and we set off.

[Page 311]

Thousands of refugees gathered in Zasliai. All of the houses, kloizes, and streets were overflowing. There was no place to lodge. People were in the fields. They set up kitchens, and cooked and ate in the open field. Since there was a railway station in Zasliai, people would enter the arriving trains and travel to wherever the train was going. We traveled to Poltava in Ukraine. There, we encountered a variety of tribulations – first, the 1917 Revolution, followed by several regimes: Red, White, in the pinnacle of the murderers Denikin, Kolchak, and Petliura. The Germans were also there for a brief period. After a full seven years of suffering, hunger and terror, we succeeded in coming home. We arrived in Yanova in 1921.

My first impression when I arrived from the city of Poltava was unexpected. The houses seemed small and low, and the streets were small. Slowly, we got accustomed to things, and began to lead a normal life.

In Maccabee and Young Hechalutz

Once, at an encounter with Ephraim Silberman, who was at the time a football player in the Kovno Maccabee, we decided to found a Maccabee club in Yanova. Leibl Zisla, who incidentally served as the first chairman, Shlomo–Ber Merovich, Velve Kerzner, and others joined us. I was among the first Maccabeeists. Being in Maccabee and hearing the frequent lectures about Israel from Yanosevich, Ivensky, the teacher Shaul Keidiansky and others, I decided to enter Young Hechalutz. This was in 1924. When I was 18 years old, I was accepted as a *Chalutza* [Zionist pioneer], and went through *Hqchshara* in Memel. I returned home when *aliya* to Israel was temporarily halted. In the interim, I met my future husband Yehuda Vinitzky, also from Yanova. We got married, and that is how my pioneering ideals were buried.

To Israel via America

My husband Yudel also had nationalistic tendencies. He was a member of Maccabee, and was active in the Revisionist Party. After four years of family life, enriched by two children, the large Vinitzky family in America – primarily the oldest brother Moshe, invited us to come to them.

In 1935, we obtained papers and we set out. My family expanded in America. All three daughters and our son got married, and our family expanded with grandchildren. Everyone is living a happy life. Yudel and I remained alone. At this point, the pioneering feeling of our youth was reawakened, and we are contemplating settling in Israel among our Yanova friends and Jews.

Translator's Footnotes

Feiga is the Yiddish form of Tzipora.
In 1497.

[Page 313]

Characters and Personalities

[Page 315]

The Excommunication Declared by Rabbi Silman

by Frank Sirek (America)
Translated by Jerrold Landau

As is known, the Czarist regime drove out all the Jews from the Kovno Guberniya at the outset of the First World War. This also included all the Jews of Yanova. Those who did not travel deep into Russia, but rather stayed in the Vilna Guberniya, returned to their homes as soon as the Germans took over Yanova.

People were separated from their homes for more than a year. They had liquidated their sources of livelihood and workshops, and the issue of livelihood was very difficult. The smuggling business developed during the years 1915–1917. It was called by the name "*malina*" and its practitioners were known as "*malinashchikes*." The chief *malinashchikes* were the Shapira brothers – Shmerka, Binka, and Avrhahmka, the Girshevitz brothers accompanied by "the Turks" Izak Nachumevich and the small "Stinkes." The main smuggling material was grain, which was smuggled to the Vilna Guberniya, where there was a famine and where the German authorities perpetrated great persecutions. Therefore, almost all of the grain storehouses were emptied, and Izak Segalovski's mill could not produce the required quota of what to provide the city bakers with bread. In one word, hunger threatened the population of Yanova.

The rabbi called a meeting of the householders, and it was decided to forbid the export of grain. Anyone who did not obey the ban would be placed into excommunication. Nothing helped, and the householders and the rabbi decided to declare an excommunication. The entire community was summoned together in the old kloiz. Black candles were lit and the text of the excommunication was read. Rabbi Silman then threatened that if anyone violates the ban, it will not only take effect on that person, but also on future generations.

Some time passed. Some people were deterred, but the more daring people began to supervise the smuggling. In the marketplace in town, in the *kloizes* between *mincha* and *maariv*, at the group of Psalms reciters – there was only one topic of discussion — the excommunication and those who disobeyed it. They would point with their fingers and show that so and so is disregarding the ban and is smuggling that which the world requires. The more heretical people did not pay attention to it. The observant people and the masses of ordinary people, especially the wives, followed the warning to obey. They saw G–d's punitive hand in every small issue and tribulation.

It happened that Falka the son of the smith died, as did Shlomo Kadish's son. Shmerke Moshe Tzvia's got an illness in his feet. The horse of one of the *malinashchikes* died. Lastly, Sirek was murdered by a murderer while on the way. The believers understood the need to obey the ban, and saw the dark hand of G–d's punishment.

[Page 316]

At this point, the opponents of Rabbi Silman at that time began to complain about the rabbi and the householders who were his adherents: That is, how could the rabbi be so daring as to place a ban of excommunication upon his flock?! He must clarify himself well, or remove his excommunication. The old communal battle once again flared up.

When Rabbi Silman died before his time many years later, people in the community whispered that he fell victim to the demons set loose by the ban of excommunication that he had issued. Even his adherents did not agree with the tactical means used by that scholar, in invoking such a cruel means as a ban of excommunication.

Rabbi Silman the Stringent
by Frank Sirek (America)
Translated by Jerrold Landau

The following is an event that took place:

After the First World War, almost every resident of Yanova owned a cow as a protection against hunger. Our Yanovers looked like residents of some large village when they used to get up very early on summer mornings, and the women took out the cows and accompanied them down the highway to the shepherd at the collecting point. Cows and calves would gather from all streets and alleyways, accompanied by Jews and Jewesses with sleepy faces. The picture was very pastoral. The cow was the chief source of livelihood for the middle class. People would sell milk, and manufacture cheese and butter for themselves, their family and for sale. Moshe the Smith (Baron), who lived near the Vinitzkys did this. He had two cows — a mother, and a daughter. The mother was a rare example, a record breaker. She produced six pots of milk a day, and supported the large family in an honorable fashion. On an early winter morning, when the cow was giving birth, to everyone's surprise she gave birth to twins – two calves in one stroke. In the early morning, when I was in bed, my mother came to me and told me about the wonder – that Moshe the Smith's cow gave birth to two calves. I responded that I had read in some holy book that this was a danger, similar to the case when a hen begins to crow.

Mother went to Moshe the Smith and told him about my suspicion. In order to verify the accuracy of the stories, Moshe the Smith went to Rabbi Silman to ask for advice and guidance. As soon as the rabbi heard the story, he issued a decision that the cow must be slaughtered. Moshe complained and begged that the rabbi have mercy and repeal the verdict. A trifle? A family of six or seven people earn their livelihood from her. If the verdict has been issued from the rabbi's mouth, it is difficult to change it. A scream came, the wife arrived with weeping and pleading. Rabbi Silman, who was always stringent, finally understood the pressure on the desperate family. He peered into the books. Wrinkling his brow, he saw that a misfortune might overtake him, Heaven forbid. After a great deal of self–reflection, he finally changed his original verdict, and ordered that the cow be sold in this case. Even the lighter verdict fell upon the head of Moshe the Smith like thunder. Is it a trifle? It was a record breaking that had supported the family for many years, and now their source of livelihood would be lost all at once. However, in the small towns in those days, Jews believed strongly that a verdict from a rabbi was like a verdict form heaven. With a heavy heart, Reb Moshe finally had to part from his cow, and sold her.

[Page 317]

In the town, people later told that a similar case occurred in a different town, and the question was posed to the rabbi of Zasliai. The Zasliai rabbi did not make such a big deal about it. He heard the story and issued a verdict: go home in good health, and continue to milk your cow.

Heard and edited by Yitzchak Burstein

A Series of Personalities
by David Friedman of Vilna
Translated by Jerrold Landau

David Friedman

My dear Jonavers, I present to you a gallery of Jonava personalities with all of their foibles and comical sides. I do not mean, Heaven forbid, to poke fun at them, but rather to mention them as a memorial. What person does not have his foibles? People understood this, and conducted themselves properly in public, as well as within their own realities.

Rebbes
"Hirshe the Teletze"

Our rebbe was called Hirshe the Teletze. He was the eighth son of Chaim the Teletze. The source of his nickname is unclear. Apparently, it was inherited through several generations. That rabbi had a foible of taking naps and sleeping. He learned a few lines with us, and once again dozed off. We would take a stick or a stone and give a hard bang on the table. He would wake up in a great fright. Forgetting where we were, he began to teach the verses of *Chumash* from the beginning. A few minutes later, he would doze off again and begin to snore. Apparently, he was only able to afford very meager meals from his earnings as a rebbe, and he would enjoy his sleep before his meals.

He was very prone to anger. He would shout and administer beatings more than teach. He would speak into his large beard, and it was very difficult to understand him. His wife died in his latter years. Since it says in the verse[1], a man should not be without a wife, he decided to marry for a second time. If he was already getting married, why not take a young wife? He indeed found such a young widow. She made a condition, however, that he must give her a promissory note of 1,000 *Litai*. So as not to struggle with the evil inclination, it is better to write a promissory note and to get a young wife for the house.

He sobered up a few weeks later, and realized that the young woman had taken advantage of the older man by demanding a 1,000 *Litai* promissory note. He demanded the promissory note in return. He did not retrieve the promissory note, but he did get a bill of divorce.

The Rebbe Yose-Ber

He was called Yose-Ber, or the Kaplitzer Rebbe. His *cheder* was in his private dwelling. This was a house with many occupations – a conglomerate in miniature format. Yose-Ber would conduct class with his students. His wife would occupy herself with the hen business. She would purchase live hens, slaughter them, and sell them already plucked. An elderly Jew who worked as a gaiter stuffer lived in a second room in the house. In the same room, the gaiter stuffer's wife would bake bread for sale.

Aside from studying, Yose-Ber's students had an additional special job. They had to help Yose-Ber's wife catch the hens to slaughter. For us, this was the best activity. We would chase the hens over the table. They would jump into the window, and the feathers would fall all over the room. The noise was so loud, and the attention to the work was so minimal, that Rebbe Yose-Ber would always get involved in the matter and send us home.

The Recluse

The biggest mischief-makers in the town would learn in his *cheder*, such as Yoshke Girshevich, Lipke Cherneman, Lielke and Motke Joselovich and others. The greatest delight of the students was the *shacharit* service before beginning their studies. When the recluse would stand for *Shmone Esrei* and sway back and forth in devotion, the students took advantage of that time, and during those moments, the *cheder* looked like a madhouse. The students did as their hearts desired. They would bang on the tables with their hands and with sticks. During the winter, they would roll a snowball and bring it into the *cheder*. At Purim, they would shoot large keys stuffed with matches, which would explode with a loud bang. One could become deaf from the explosion. In addition, we would shoot at our rebbe's long *kapote* with toy guns.

[Page 319]

Once, after such a *Shmone Esrei*, when we broke sticks and conducted such a concert over the tables and benches, the recluse was at *Oseh Shalom*[2], pacing a few steps back, when somebody suddenly threw something. He grabbed the stick from the perpetrator, and snatched it from his hands. It was some sort of a sporting match: the recluse from one side, and on the other side the students who had moved aside. As we were talking together, we tossed the stick once more. The recluse fell on the floor with his feet upward, and we all quickly turned toward the door.

The Hiltzerner Rav[3] (Fleishman)

The era of the *cheders* ended. Modern schools were founded. Yavne was one such school. Aside from the modern teachers, there were still some of the typical rebbes. One of them was the "Hiltzerner Rav" whom we also called by another nickname, "G-d is Atzig.[4]" The Hiltzerner Rav read Hebrew poorly. Instead of saying "*Hashem oz leamo yiten*"[5], he would say, "*Hashem aiz leamo yiten*"[6] The group of jokers from amongst the students would translate "*Hashem Eiz*" as "G-d is a goat," and the nickname took hold.

In his later years, he became preacher who traveled from town to town. Once, he arrived in a town on the very day when the 500th anniversary of Vytautas the Great[7] was being celebrated. Gatherings took place everywhere, and, as well, the rabbis sermonized about the issues of the day in the *kloizes*. The Hiltzerner Rav began to deliver a sermon in that town. His words began as follows, "Five hundred years ago, Vinchuk the Great died, may it be for many years[8]. Everyone burst out in laughter, and the gathering ended.

The Enchanted Craft at the Prayer Leader's Podium in the *Beis Midrash*

a.

Several people served as prayer leaders: Kremer, Furmans, Kirzner, Schmid, Buchalter. Meshel Ivensky, who had a fine voice, also wanted to bestow his cantorial skills upon the congregation. He had a beard like a very pious Jews. However, the *gabbai* always invalidated him from being a prayer leader; there was one small thing, he was a freethinker, and therefore, they spread gossip about him that he had a fondness for married women. In invalidating him, the *gabbai* meant, but was not bold enough to actually say… Meshel Ivensky had some connection with money and credit in the People's Bank… And that is why he was able to benefit us with his fine tenor.

[Page 320]

b.

When Pesach the furrier engaged in cantorializing in the *kloiz*, everything was quite cozy. The primary coziness came on *Simchat Torah*, when they took advantage of his cantorial skills. First, they would give him a cup of liquor, and he would get the courage to go up to the podium with self assurance, as if to clip and shave. Pesach the furrier used to begin high, with a festival tune. However, Tevchik Jaffa the photographer sat behind him, and, as if to incite, he would break out in a weekday melody. He did not have a tuning fork, the noise reverberated in his head, and it was very easy for him to move over to a false tone. Laughter and a racket broke out in the *kloiz*. Thus did the group of jokers take advantage of him. Others would tie him to a lectern with a towel, while still others would bombard him with wet towels. The feeling of a veritable *Simchat Torah* pervaded in the *kloiz*.

c.

The *kloiz* had two strong competitors – not, Heaven forbid with regard to livelihood, but rather for the sake of Heaven – that is, with regards to cantorializing. These were Yankel-Leib Landsman the carpenter and Yosel Levin the smith. As was the custom, Yankel-Leib the wealthy man had more access to the podium than Yosel the Smith.

One Friday night, when Yankel-Leib was preparing to don his *tallis* and begin to sing *Lechu Neranena*[9], the group of jokers headed by Tevche Jaffa, began to incite a rebellion and spur on Yossele the smith.

"Well, why do you let him lead you by the nose? He is indeed a wealthy man, but everyone is equal before G-d. Why must he always lead the services, and you not?"

Before Yankel-Leib got started, Yossel the smith was standing at the podium, and singing out "*Lechu Neranena Lashem*" in a loud voice.

The next morning, during the time of the reading of the Torah, a group was standing in the synagogue yard, discussing both competitors. Some supported one side, and others supported the other. One of the jokers shouted out:

"Reb Yankel-Leib, being a smith who bangs all week with an anvil, was so embarrassed yesterday before the entire congregation? An unacceptable shame!"

Yankel-Leib shouted out, "What do you want from a cold smith. He knows how to forge shoes for a horse, but with respect to leading the services, he is no good."

"Reb Yankel-Leib," called out Yossel the smith, "Perhaps you are better with smithing together the rendition of the festival service, but with regard to the Sabbath rendition, I am ten times…"

Everyone laughed, and continued to incite them on.

Berele the Goat and his Assistant

They would call him Berele the Tzig [Goat]: Berele because he was short and lean, the goat – because he had a stretched out form and a small, pointy beard on his chin, and therefore, he would bleat like a goat during his prayers. He was occupied with various trades. He was the *shamash* [beadle] in the synagogue, and he taught *Chumash* to children with obtuse minds. He conducted lotteries for miscellaneous objects, such as a large, 10 kilogram pike, old candlesticks and other sundries.

[Page 321]

G-d had endowed him with an abundance of children, and in order to earn a livelihood, he would go to the villages announcing that a famous cantor was to come. He would post notices in the local *kloizes* that the famous cantor would be conducting services. Eventually it became clear that the famous cantor would not appear. On Friday night, he would bleat out the services with his cantorial rendition. On Saturday morning, they would promise to pay him for not leading the services.

Berele the goat had an assistant, a deputy *shamash*. He was a former Cantonist[10] who served Nikolai for a full 25 years. That deputy *shamash* also had the role of the summoner to the synagogue. He was tall and thin, with a large, thick beard that he never combed. He would run through the streets of Jonava like a Czarist general on Friday at candle lighting time, shouting, "Go to the synagogue!" A group would follow him from behind, and help him shout, "Go to the synagogue!", and throw prickly burrs at him. At the end of the march, he would look like a shield of burrs.

Mottel Salanter

a.

At one time, he was a shoemaker. He had a double name: Mottel Salanter, or Mottel Glaz. Later, he became a fisherman in a *sadovnik*[11]. He also occupied himself with matchmaking. What did he not do to earn a living? He was a prankster. He was always cheerful and at ease, and jokes would always issue forth from him. He would tell about his attempts at matchmaking. He proposed a match for a small-town lad with a young girl who lived with her parents in a village. He was not that appropriate according to the rules of matchmaking. He indeed pushed the match through, but the villager was not able to come up with the matchmaking fee before the wedding. The villager did not hurry to pay his obligation. Later, when he requested of him the fee, the villager took out a package of Czarist money that was no longer valid currency and said, "Here, you have your matchmaking money." The matchmaker looked at the money, looked at the villager, and thought, "He must be out of his mind."

"Why are you staring at me?" called out the villager, "am I guilty for the fact that you have delayed proposing a match for ten full years."

With a lowered head, the newly minted matchmaker left after his first failure.

b.

He once proposed a match for a girl with a coachman. The parents were willing, but the girl was stubborn, saying that she was not interested.

"Why?" they asked her.

"What will I do if his horse dies?"

c.

He proposed a match for Meirke the Miller, who was not all that astute, with an older girl from a village. The match went through, and the wedding was to be celebrated. The wedding ceremony was to take place in the synagogue courtyard. For the young people, this was immensely surprising – that is – Meirke the miller is going to the wedding canopy! The group crawled over the surrounding rooftops, and when Meirka recited "*Harei at*"[12], brooms and wet cloths were tossed from the rooftops. The groom did not maintain his composure. He went forth from the wedding canopy and chased after the crowd with curses.

[Page 322]

That same Meirka took on the task of painting the *kloiz*. As the rabbi of Jonava was walking by the synagogue, he made a comment about his work.

"Rabbi, you understand this type of work like a rooster understands noodles. And in general, rabbi, a fool does not understand half the work."

Dvora Leah the Reciter[13]

Dvora Leah sat in the women's gallery of the synagogue on Yom Kippur, surrounded by a group of women who unfortunately could not read. She served as the reciter for them. The old women reminded her together:

"Dear Dvora Leah, do not forget to remind us when we are supposed to begin to weep."

Dvora Leah the reciter was very pious. She had two daughters, Michle and Itke, both old maids. She was not well disposed toward Itke. One day, after an argument with Itke, she summoned all the women to the synagogue. When the crowd came to pray, she went up to the Holy Ark, knocked on its door, and started to recite:

"Good morning, dear G-d. Your servant Dvora Leah is standing before you and I beg of you: Give us a good groom for Michle, for she is unfortunately a girl getting on in years. For Itke – a malady, for I have had years of suffering from her.

An Example of Stinginess

Reb Mende Tzemach's, may he forgive me, was very stingy. When they constructed the sidewalks in Jonava and every householder was required to plaster his own segment at his own expense, Reb Mende Tzemach's got to work. He would stand with a broom in his hand and refuse to permit anyone to walk on his sidewalk, lest they wear it out, Heaven forbid.

Fanning the Evil Eye

Feiga Kriger of Breizer Street owned a goat from goatland. Jonava had never seen such an udder as this goat possessed. When Feiga would walk her goat, a group would run behind her and shout, "Feiga, the goat has a large udder." Feiga was afraid of the evil eye, and therefore fanned the goat ten times to ward off the evil eye.

A Glutton and Exaggerator

Reb Moshe David Mauer, the former Stirnik[14], had an open house. Better guests would always come to them. His wife Sara-Batya was a wonderful cook, and the guests would always have good food, such as a good roasted duck or gefilte fish. The problem was that Moshe David was a healthy man, tall, thick, and therefore had a hearty appetite. Their restaurant fed him in a legal and illegal manner. When Sara-Batya would leave the house, Reb Moshe David would go to the oven, snatch a freshly roasted duck or a freshly stuffed fish, and quickly wolf it down. He would wash his beard and moustache, take a few *Litai* and place them on the shelf. Sara-Batya would return, go to the oven, and notice that a duck was missing.

[Page 323]

"Moshe David, who ate the duck?"

"A little while ago, a guest came who was a glutton. The money is over there."

Moshe David, like his brother Avraham the Stirnik, were both known as exaggerators. When one of them would tell a story in an exaggerated fashion, he would immediately call the other brother as a witness. And when the second would pester someone, the first brother would help him. They would tell stories about travelling in America. Reb Moshe David tells:

"When I went to America, I befriended someone on the ship. It was Friday during the day. We were sitting together in the coach and travelling for such a long time that the Sabbath began to approach. Tell me my friend: Before we travel home, let us travel to the *kloiz*, and you will see how fine and beautiful our *kloizes* are. We entered the *kloiz*, and my friend began to whisper to some people, and then I heard that they had called me up for *maftir*[15]. The *bima* was so far away that I had to sit in the coach and drive. If you do not believe me, ask my brother Avraham." He called to Avraham:

"You will all believe me about the 'American thief.' A fine thing happened to me in America. Immediately after arriving there, my friend said: 'Get up, Avraham, I want to show you an America style *mikva* [ritual bath], without the Jonava mud.' I will no longer punish myself. I went to the *mikva*, and saw a veritable sea before my eyes, and I jumped in without fear. I knew how to swim well as a Stirnik. I used to swim back and forth across the Vylia, and this to me was like a piece of sugar cake. I decided to take a swim in the *mikva*. I started to swim, fathom after fathom, and then I noticed that I can no longer see the shore. My hands and feet became shaky, and the thought came to my mind that I might drown in the *mikva*, Heaven forbid. Suddenly, a miracle took place. I noticed an island in the middle of the *mikva*. I grabbed onto its shore with both hands and was saved. Is this not true, Moshe David? You saw this yourself."

Someone who Made Calculations

When the policeman, the *labas*[16] would give Mote Flaks a ticket for failing to clean the street, bringing with it a fine of ten *Litai* or three days in jail, Reb Mote Flaks would calculate that it was cheaper to sit for the three days. He would send his sister's husband, who worked for him in the grain warehouse, and earned a small salary.

An Overheard Conversation

Dr. Ran, the chief physician of the Jonava hospital, became a good friend of the administrator Glaz. They were once sitting during a break and conversing. Dr. Ran called out: "My wife is young, and only wants to have a good time. Here in Jonava, she is lonely. She likes to go on vacation in Kovno. She goes to the theater, and she goes to the opera. You understand, this costs me a lot of money."

[Page 324]

The administrator Glaz with the long beard answered him.

"On the other hand, my wife is old and sick, and does not let me enjoy life. I no longer want to save money. Sir Doctor, do you know what? You are a bit miserly, as is my wife. Your wife wants to live it up, as do I. Let us make an exchange, and we will both gain."

A Wealthy Man – A Haughty Man

a.

Reb Leibe Wolfovich states:

"Today, I picked up a new suit for my Meir (14 years old), from Meirke the tailor (44 years old).

b.

"Itzke!" (Referring to Yitzchak Burstein.) "Did you see my Hershele?"

It Does Not Pay to Exchange

One Friday night after services, I was walking with Reb Leibe from the large Beis Midrash. We were walking and chatting. He was talking his heart out to me, and, as usual, he began with his well-known expression:

"Did you hear, beloved brother? When I lived as a youth with my parents in Taraker Kretshme (the village of Trakai between Koplice and Siesikai), I recall that I went around to the villages all day, but not to make purchases. Did you hear, beloved brother? I was a very poor person, and I toiled hard. I would carry a calf on my shoulders from the village to Tarak, where I would slaughter it and sell its meat in town. I would return home only on Fridays. Mother would prepare for the Sabbath. She would spread a thick, linen tablecloth over the table, and put out the brass candlesticks. She would make thick noodles from coarse meal for food. Did you hear? Then I began to sense the pleasure of the Sabbath. And what is it like today? In my home, today is like yesterday, and tomorrow is like the next day. There is no difference between the weekdays and the Sabbath. The fine, white tablecloth is on the table every day. We have a good lunch every day of the week, beloved brother, and I get no enjoyment from the Sabbath of today."

After such a lecture, I worked up my brazenness, and said:

"Reb Leibe, it is not all that difficult to return to your former lifestyle. If you agree, I will arrange for it. I will talk to Yose the Tzimmes or old Shlomo Itze's to arrange an exchange with you, at least on a trial basis for one year. It could very well be that after a good Sabbath, they will want to go back to the impoverished Sabbath."

"Truth be told, Davidke, the exchange does not interest me. Let things stay as they currently are."

Translator's Footnotes

This is not actually a biblical verse, but rather a halachic statement.

Near the end of *Shmone Esrei*.

Literally "The wooden rabbi.".

G-d is a goat.

G-d gives might to his nation.

Lithuanian Jews often pronounce the short 'o' vowel as 'ai'. Literally, the verse would now mean, "G-d gives a goat to his nation.".

See http://en.wikipedia.org/wiki/Vytautas

A traditional greeting for a long life.

The first words of the Friday night service.

See http://en.wikipedia.org/wiki/Cantonist.

I am unsure of the meaning of the term 'Sadovnik'.

The first words of the betrothal phrase recited by the groom at a wedding ceremony.

A "Reciter" (*Zogerke*) is a woman who informally assists the women in the women's section of the synagogue with the recital of the prayers.

A log driver who accompanies logs down the river to market.

The concluding Torah honor (*aliya*) on Sabbaths and festivals. The person who gets this aliya also reads the *haftarah* (prophetic portion).

In Lithuanian, *labas* means "good,"i.e., the good policeman.

[Page 325]

Areh Yankel

by Yisrael Yaakov Pogir
Translated by Jerrold Landau

Like his ancestors, he lived on Breizer Street. His wealth consisted of a house that was given over as an inheritance from generation to generation, until Areh Yankel received it. The house stood across the street from the new, fine building of the Talmud Torah.

G–d blessed him with a young, beautiful daughter – with a head of black, curly hair, smiling lips and eyes as beautiful as diamonds: Rashe–Etl. Her nickname was Rashetke Areh Yankel's. She knew how to hold her own. In addition to her traits – tall and beautiful – she also procured a machine to knit socks. She would nimbly move the machine back and forth. She would put the raw materials for a sock into the opening of the machine, and a sock would slowly grow. She would remove the sock, put it down, and begin a second one. That is how Rashetke produced socks.

In the winter, when the streets were full of snow, Areh Yankel's window was covered with frost and ice, nobody could see in. However, when summer came and Rashetke opened the window, the noise from the sock machine and her singing attracted everyone's attention, and all the passers–by peered into Rashetke's window. They would also see Areh Yankele with his horse. Areh Yankel was recognized and known on account of his horse.

Areh Yankel was already getting old, and he could no longer be a wagon driver. His grey, pointy, sparse beard and his pipe that was always on his lips also looked old, as if they had been passed down as an inheritance from generation to generation. When he had to answer or talk to his horse, his worn–down teeth bit down on his pipe, so it would not fall out. Then, his words would be uttered in anger. However, Heaven forbid, Areh Yankel was not prone to anger. He was a good person, who was content with his lot.

Areh Yankel's Sources of Livelihood

He worshipped with the first *minyan*. After that it seemed as if he was grabbing at his heart as he hitched up his horse and waited near his house. Perhaps something would come of it. A neighbor might have not paid his rent, or might have joked around with a female neighbor, and then would have to move to a different house. Such things happened even in Yanova, and one would have to transport the baggage: a pair of benches, a three–legged table, a dismantled bed with a bit of straw – that still looked very important when all bundled up on the cart; a heavy kettle which one would use for the Sabbath tea and cake, still filled with water; a few clay pots, at times a samovar – but one does not put a samovar in Areh Yankel's wagon, but rather carries it by hand, for it is too large. Then one would summon Areh Yankel and hire him. This was always a good source of income.

In the event that a day was not so lucky, Areh Yankel sat down on the three boards of his wagon, took the reins and drove off to Keidainer Street, near the cemetery on the way to Varnepke. That was where there was a hill with the golden sand that was light in the eyes. He filled the wagon with the fresh, yellow sand, sat down in the wagon, and picked up the reins. The horse did not take offense. The way was hilly. It would relax a bit, until it returned to Breizer Street. On the weekdays, there were not too many people interested in the yellow, sandy merchandise, except for the women who were searching for bargains – two shovelfuls of fresh, yellow sand for a kopeck. On the other hand, on Friday, the eve of the Sabbath, Areh Yankel never had enough sand for all his customers. What is the wonder? When my father was about to leave his tailor shop on the eve of the Sabbath, he covered the new machine with a white tablecloth and swept the room. He then sprinkled the black floor with the yellow sand. When the mother blessed the candles, and sat down to relax, she would give a blessing to Areh Yankel: May Areh Yankel live long, and the yellow sand be a light in the eyes.

[Page 326]

Our town had many fine traits, but it was lacking one thing: Even in Yanova one could not live forever, and therefore we had a *Chevra Kadisha* [burial society] with *shamashim* and pallbearers, who fulfilled the adage, "we will carry you with our hands…" The *Chevra Kadisha*, with Yankel Henech as the *Gabbai* [trustee], then decided that the pallbearers must fast on all the fast days of Mondays and Thursdays in order for them to perform their service. They must also not leave the synagogue or *kloiz* on days that Psalms are recited. But for those who are only interested in eating, but have no time for the "lift up your hands"[1] – for such people, being a pallbearer is like a blessing in vain. The *Chevra Kadisha* decided that Yanova must have a single casket platform, and no banging should take place. There also must be a horse with a rider – therefore we have Areh Yankel.

From that time, Areh Yankel did not harness his horse immediately after the first *minyan*. Instead, he would wash his horse and give it some soup, so that it would look, so to speak, like a proper person. He would then wait until after the second *minyan* to make sure that nobody would come to him with any news. Only then would Areh

Yankel go out to search for customers with baggage, or to collect sand. And if something happened with the neighbors and they had to receive a "blessing"[2] they would say that G–d should make it that Areh Yankel would soon come with his horse and cart, and take a walk through Keidainer Street... Nothing more was needed...

Areh Yankel Brings Rashetke to the Wedding Canopy [*Chupa*]

On Saturday night after *Vayiten Lach*[3], nobody wished Areh Yankel a good week. He would walk alone. He would go ahead, and people would walk slowly so as to avoid chasing him. If he approached, people would flee. Rashetke was cheerless, and she stopped singing even the sad songs of longing. All of the lads who were shoemakers, tailors, smiths, and furriers were running off to America. Who remains? The damaged goods. They were not good finds. Therefore, things got more serious for her. She would sit there manufacturing socks, waiting for a widower, or she too would have to run to America, and escape from what? From the sock machine? She had just recently acquired it.

However G–d is a father. G–d prepared for Rashetke Leizer Micha's (Katz), a fine lad. He would help his elderly father as a wagon driver. He was drafted as a soldier in the Russian Army. Now, he had returned on leave. He was visiting with his brother, the most honorable wagon driver in Yanova, Alter Micha's (Katz). He noticed Rashetke, tall and beautiful, knitting socks like an angel. He truly fell in love with her.

The few weeks of furlough passed, and he had to return to serve the Russians. Leizerke promised that he would he would come from Slizovo, he would travel here with musicians from Keidaini, to the Karabelnikshe Kloiz for the *chupa*.

Rashetke sat at the open window, and the machine was still nimbly and slowly knitting socks. She sang her songs louder, and her songs sounded more beautiful. The joy became greater with the approach of her groom's discharge.

On a summer Friday afternoon of *Shabbat Nachamu*, the in–laws of Breizer Street went to the reception for Leizerke Micha's, and the Keidainer musicians led Rashetke to the *chupa*. No bride went to the chupa with such pride as did Rashetke. She held herself high, her beautiful head of hair with her white slippers. When an in–law murmured with jealousy, "Such luck... they are leading the bride to childbirth with musicians," Rashetke does not even hear, and she is circling around the groom with joy. A new Areh Yankel, a middle class in–law, led his daughter to the *chupa* with a candle in his hands, as well as his pipe.

After *Shabbat Nachamu*, a different picture was seen near Areh Yankel's house. A different girl was sitting in Rashetke's window, knitting socks and singing new songs.

Two horses were standing like lions opposite Areh Yankel's door, and two wagons were hitched up. The middle class wagon driver left the house with a whip and a smile, and slowly closed the door.

Areh Yankel stood in the alleyway with his horse and wagon, talking to his neighbor Shlomo Itze. From there, Areh Yankel went out to the sandy way as he held the reins. Shlomo Itze was among the customers for the sandy merchandise.

A man standing in front of a horse hitched to a wagon, with a house in the background.

Translator's Footnotes

A verse that is customarily recited prior to washing hands before eating. Its recital is not an obligation.

The meaning here is the opposite (i.e. the quotes indicate an irony): referring to a curse.

A set of prayers following the evening service at the conclusion of Shabbat.

With his own Traits
by Yitzchak
Translated by Jerrold Landau
Leibe the Wagon Water

They lived on the Highway Street not far from the Vilya, in the house of the Wolk family. He was of average height, docile and chubby. She was smaller, but not thinner. Both moved about with difficulty, while at the same time, vibrant in mind. I would say that they were a pair from G–d. She was from the Wolk family, and remained an old maid, and was gaining in years and intelligence. As G–d runs things, she was sent a match from heaven from some Lithuanian town. They remained childless, but they took care of each other. I do not know how they earned their livelihood. It was said that the relatives from America supported them. They would always walk arm in arm, mainly at the banks of the Vilya. They would walk slowly, pondering G–d's world, explaining to each other their logical explanation of all goings–on.

The husband and wife walking hand in hand by the bank of the Vilya, with two wagons in the air

One summer afternoon, when the water in the Vilya was quite dried out, they suddenly stood still and looked up. Before their eyes was a picture, like rafts taking off in flight, which seemed, like a trick, to be full of sand. They seemed as if they wanted to offer some advice, and Leibe thought of his own invention: "Chasia," he said, "one can bring a wagon with water, and it will float up in the air." Scoffers overheard him, and from then on, he was referred to as "Leibe the Wagon Water."

The Fine Singer.

Uncaptioned.

Yose the Tzimmes

He was a water carrier by trade. (There was no water system in Yanova in those days.) Who did not know him? He was of average height, slender build, with a half– long pointy beard and a moustache. He wore a long, torn *kapote* [frock], with large, crooked boots. He wore a rope as a belt around his *kapote*. He carried the semicircular pole with the two tin pails on his shoulders.

It is said that his name came to him because when he was carrying the water on Friday, every mistress of the house would treat him with a plate of *tzimmes*. He had many customers, and on that day he ate a world of *tzimmes*, as he was not willing to refuse his customers.

Yanova inherited a motto from him: Yanova is a city where there are many householders, but when it comes to carrying water, one turns only to Yose the Tzimmes.

He was no great scholar, but here he hit the mark.

The Fine Singer

He himself was not a resident of Yanova, but since he was always travelling, and he visited our city several times throughout the year, he belonged to the Yanova landscape. He had a short beard, a moustache, and yellow teeth. He wore a long kapote and boots, and on top, a katelak hat. His face was dark brown due to the wind, sun and frost. He was an eternal wanderer, unemployed, a character similar to the gallery of characters in the dance of the beggars in Anski's "The Dybbuk." He was also knowledgeable in the black characters[1]– *chumash*, Bible, and *gemara*. His special calling was in reciting rhymes. If someone asked him to recite a rhyme about Yitzchak or Moshe, he would produce a set of rhymes about the name for 10–15 minutes. Then he would stop, and would be given a payment so he would calm down.

[Page 330]

Shachke

Who did not know him – the average height, thin lad who suffered from a nervous disease? He would wander about the streets all day with his right hand smacking his right cheek. Eventually, that cheek sprouted a large, black spot. He would shout "doloi" with every smack on the cheek.

Later, his parents bought him a bicycle so that his hands would be occupied and he would stop hitting himself. Within a few weeks, he learnt how to ride. He would hold the handlebars with one hand, and continue with his "profession" with the other hand. I would often stop him, and discuss with him that he should better spend his time reading books, and to forget about it. He was very understanding, and heard me out. He looked at me with intelligent eyes and smiled, and answered with a smack on his face and a shout of "Doloi Itzka."

Mainly at gatherings, when discussions were heard between Yanovers on street corners, he became more agitated and would smack himself and shout "doloi" even more. When the Soviets arrived, the custom was that there were gatherings every day with orchestras singing "Long live Stalin." When the agitators approached him, he would be the first to shout "Doloi Stalin," even during the time of Nikita Khrushchev[2]. The police would arrest him. Later, when they realized his illness, they never charged him.

Lozer Poleit

Who did not know the night guard who guarded Pogirsky's iron enterprise as well as Pogirsky's daughter Masha Granewicz's business for a generation? Later, when the house was taken over by Hershel Koper, he also guarded his fashion business. Who does not recall the small, thin, refined man with a small, grey beard and a moustache, with red eyebrows, inflamed from lack of sleep, with a cane in his hand and a small dog as a partner in the guarding?

The people of the night knew him better, because he would rarely be seen during the day. If the notion of honesty and decency exists, Lozer was the embodiment of this notion. He did not require any special clocks to regulate himself. His consciousness controlled him, and it never happened that he took a nap while he was carrying out his duties.

We, the youth, who also filled certain roles as night watchmen and wandered around until the late hours of the night, often encountered him.

He knew all of the night secrets: who was walking with whom on side lanes, and whose wife committed an impropriety with a young man at night. If you found him at his post, walking around Pogirsky's business until Chaishel Koper's he would stop you and share with you the latest secrets from the center of town: nighttime secrets and minor intrigues that he had noticed.

He was murdered along with all the others.

Translator's Footnotes

I.e. the printed word.

Nikita Kruschchev became the head of the Communist Party of Ukraine in 1937, well before he became the Premier of the Soviet Union.

[Page 331]

A Gallery of Personalities

by Meir Tzoref (Goldshmid), Tel Aviv

Translated by Jerrold Landau

Uncaptioned. Apparently Meir Tzoref

Yankel Shimshon Glass the Hassid, Mosheke Odoskes, Lentshinke, Hirshe A Shnaps, Der Shul Rufer (the synagogue summoner), Sachke, Alter and Libe-Chana Reines, Shleimtze the Ox, and Serl Ruk Zich.

Yankel-Shimshon Glass – He was tall with a handsome black beard and black eyes. He spoke with his proper Jonaver accent, sharply pronouncing "shin" like "samech", which people from Jonava, as from other towns in Lithuania, were not able to pronounce. He was the chairman of Bikur Cholim (the Society for the Visiting of the Sick), and also a veteran officer of the Yavneh School, even though he had no children. It is no wonder that his wife, a "Kvake"[1], used to always go around with her head bound in a cloth as she groaned…

There were even rumors that he carried on a secret love with the "Figurner" nurse. His "Kvake" indeed used to often throw him out, and according to her, he was "on duty" every night in the hospital; however no open disgrace ever took place.

He worshipped in the Hassidic shtibel, which, unlike other kloizes, had no almemar (bima) and no second story for women, but rather a small room with a few windows for the women. Their mode of prayer included "Veyatzmach Purkanei Vekarev Meshichei" in the Kaddish[2]. In general, they worshipped like all the Jews in the kloizes and Beis Midrashes of that time. On Simchat Torah, they would go out with the Torah scrolls to the courtyards, and crawl upon the tables to dance, and we children would enjoy and truly rejoice in celebrating a Simchat Torah with such joyous Jews, in contrast to the High Holy Days with their Al Chets …[3]

[Page 332]

In that same Bikur Cholim, Moshe Odoskes worked as a male nurse. He was involved with and was in love with the daughter of Alter the wagon driver, or better stated – with one of his daughters. Alter the wagon driver had daughters almost like Tevye the milkman[4], but in Jonava, this was scarcely current merchandise, so they sat and waited for their saviors…

Alter himself was an observant Jew. On his wagon the children were not beaten with whips if they came to get a ride. On the contrary, when he had a "good day" – that is he had livelihood for himself and the horse, he would take a full wagon of children and, with a cantorial melody, bring them to his home opposite the synagogue courtyard, and sometimes they would turn onto another street. Indeed, children would wait for him to finish his hard workday: They would notice a smile under his dark gray beard and a cantorial hum under his moustache, without even asking – we're off – a jump onto the long wagon, crowding in, taking up as small a place as possible so that there would remain room for other children. Alter did not like those "well placed" children who had no concern for others once they were aboard. They all bounced down on a stone sidewalk, and when someone was ready to jump, they would make room for him.

Mosheke Odoskes indeed got married to one of Alter's daughters. There were even rumors that he carried on a love affair with Gitke the crazy woman before she went crazy. Others wanted to say that it was indeed because he had led her on, promised to marry her and broke his promise, that she lost her mind… On the other hand, others claimed that he threw her out already after she had gone crazy, for what would he do with a crazy wife? She was not even all that crazy. All she would do would be to talk to herself while she moved her hands to see her watch for she was afraid of missing an important date.

As it were, Mosheke Odoskes was the chief of the voluntary fire brigade, and an honorable citizen of Jonava. During wartime, he was in the Lithuanian division of the Red Army. He stumbled during a conversation with a comrade of the camp. He said: "Were we to have required the 'large' and 'small' moustaches while we were resting in our mother's wombs, we would today be sitting in our homes…"

Shortly thereafter, he was arrested and sent to a camp in Siberia. He was liberated and rehabilitated after Stalin's death. He died of a heart attack in Vilna shortly after he was freed.

Jonava was patient with its crazies. One of them, Lentshinke, used to awaken the residents in the middle of the night with terrible cries of "fire, it's burning!" We heard a mysterious sound come from him to warn the Jews that they should not rest or sleep with folded arms in the face of the terrible fire that was awaiting the Jews of Jonava and the entire Jewish people. However, nobody paid any attention to his shouting. When the Christian residents complained about him, they bound him up and sent him to Kalvarija. Jewish householders offered guarantees about him that it would be peaceful. They redeemed him from the insane asylum, and once again he started continuing with his cries of "fire". They did not give him over even when he beat the teacher Optekina with his cane during a hysterical attack. The writer of these lines as well, as a youth, got a hole in the head from his "crazy man's" cane. The lovely nurse joked that this would go away by the time of my wedding, and now with an open head the Torah could penetrate quicker…

[Page 333]

Jonaver Jews were known as lovers of good food, as well as people who would not refuse a drink. At every opportunity they would indeed have a snack of the wrappers of the lungs at Perski's, a roasted duck at Shule's, and fresh gefilte fish, well peppered with the taste of the Garden of Eden. Authentically, this was given the name of a "drola" in official language. The Lithuanians even used to say: "Eisme Fas Perski Padarisme Drola".

Jews were not professional drunks, except for one, about whom nobody knew from where he had come, or anything about him. He stood by himself, alone. He would come to services, but he would not receive any aliyas.

He was called Hirshe A "Shnaps" and later Hirshe "Chandzhe"… At first, he was ashamed of his drunkenness. People would get angry with him and throw stones at him. Children or ordinary scoffers, who loved to joke with one another, would shout after him: Hirshe, ahem", implying a cough after a quick swig of whiskey. Later he switched to denatured alcohol, or as we used to call it "chandzhe", for economic reasons or for its strength. Then he no longer cared if we shouted after him Hirshe Chandzhe. The children left him alone when they saw that he did not react. When the priest would preach to the believers during the Sunday mass about their drinking, he would give an example about how the Jews conduct themselves: "They do not drink and they do not slaughter themselves with knives," a din from the audience could be heard: "One indeed drinks!," referring to Hirshe A Schnaps.

There was also a strange Jew in Jonava known as "The Shul Caller". He was tall and slender with a long, wild, pointy beard. He wore a tall hat. He looked like a

Cossack. Children would indeed be afraid of falling into his hands when they would crawl into the attic of the synagogue to catch pigeons. He was a former cantonist[5] and remained without a family. As children, we would indeed hear his slightly hoarse voice: "Get into the bath!" On Friday at the time of candle lighting, we would hear the same melody: "Go to the synagogue!" He would go as far as Segalovski's mill and announce the beginning of the Holy Sabbath with a long whistle.

[Page 334]

Mende "Di Kop Her" (The Head of Hair)}

Since we are already talking about Jonaver crazies, we must mention one more. The popular proverb states: "No crazy person beats his own head". Jonava was an exception.

Sachke the crazy (this was a short form of Yissachar), or "Sachke Dalai" used to slap himself on the cheeks and shout: "Dalai, Smetana!"[6] The aforementioned was a smart youth. With understanding, the Smetana situation could be attributed to his illness, and nobody caused him any trouble when he shouted out "Smetana Dalai". People only begged of him that he should not shout out in the streets during a national holiday when guests come. He once shouted out "Soviet Dalai" before the Soviets. They beat him and scared him to the extent that he stopped shouting "Dalai", and other such bad curse words.

That tailors are pranksters is known, but Naftali the tailor stood out over all of them. Bursting into the "Popular Shearing and Iron Workshop" was dangerous for an ordinary human. They immediately grabbed his by his weak point and lay him on the plates…

Thus was Naftali the tailor described by a regular customer, a fine Jew, Alter, husband of Liba-Chana Reines, coming home with a new suit. His wife Liba used to bake onion pastries. Connoisseurs used to come from all corners of the city to purchase the fresh, tasty onion pastries. She would not pry them loose from the oven. She would stick the spade into the hot oven as if it was the eve of a festival… He, Alter, would come to her with a clean, new suit. He would cautiously and politely ask: "Nu, Liba, take a look, how does the new suit fit?" And she looked in the oven and answered: "I see already that it is undone"…

In Jonava there was a furrier and hat maker who was called Shlomo Itza, or with the nickname "Shleimetze the Ox". He was tall and looked comical as he sold a hat that looked like toy in his large hands. It was said that his own wife gave him the nickname "ox". When he traveled to a fair in the city with a hand wagon, he lay down on the way to rest. He took off his large shoes, put them down with the toes facing the direction of Shat (Seta) and fell asleep. Someone who was passing by, as a joke, turned the shoes, pointing the toes toward Jonava. Our Shleimtze, instead of going to fair in Shat, returned to Jonava, and said, "See, all cities look the same!"… until his wife finally informed him, and gave him the nickname "ox".

She was tiny, thin, and an expert in selling. Without her – a handsome face would have had his large hands… She was known as "Serl Ruk Zich" (Serl the Pusher). She received the nickname from the honeymoon following the wedding, when they lived in a room constructed from boards, where any rustle could be heard from the neighboring rooms, and the intimate nighttime conversations would be discussed over the plates… Thus came the name, indeed without embarrassment… We knew all this from the frequent fights with their competitor, the furrier Pesach from Kovarsk and especially his wife Sara Lea the furrier over a peasant who was a customer in the market. The gentile enjoyed watching the two Jews fighting over him, and at home he sharpened the bloody ax for both of them together…

Translator's Footnotes

Seemingly meaning a 'croaker' or a 'quacker'.

These words in Kaddish are indicative of the Nusach Sephard or Hassidic mode of prayer, in opposition to the Ashkenazic mode of prayer that was more common in Lithuania.

Al Chet is the term for the confessional litany of Yom Kippur.

Tevye the milkman, of Fiddler on the Roof fame, had five daughters.

A cantonist was a Jewish man who had served his 25 year stint in the Russian army, often starting as young as twelve.

Bedrich Smetana (1824 - 1884), held an important place in the development of musical nationalism in his native Bohemia. http://www.naxos.com/composer/smetana.htm He played an active role in the reawakening of Czech culture that followed the Austrian defeat by Napoleon III. http://w3.rz-berlin.mpg.de/cmp/smetana.html. Perhaps the Lithuanians and/or Russians favored his music and its anti-Napoleonic nationalism, and Jews in Jonava were fearful that Sachke would bring the government's ire upon the entire Jewish community.

[Page 335]

Episodes and Events
by Ella Daltitsky (Abramovitch) of Tel Aviv
Translated by Jerrold Landau

Ella Daltitsky

1.

Who does not remember Alter the Water Carrier? He used to carry water from the well with poles for Alter the Baker, "Alter Liba–Chana–Reines–Lieberman," as well as for Yudel Betman, who was a great scoffer. To earn his living, Alter the Water Carrier also had a second profession – transporting deceased people to the cemetery with a horse. Yudel Betman once turned to him and said, "Alter, you take too much – a whole three Lit to transport a deceased person. This is terrible. You will not be rewarded by G–d." Alter responded, "If Jews would die more often, I would indeed be able to charge less. However, the way Jews tend to die, I must charge more."

Alter with his water buckets.

2.

Shlomo Itche Furman. He was tall, with red, constantly inflamed eyes. He was a hat maker by trade, and lived on Kovner Street.

Once, on a winter Friday night, after dinner, his wife Sara went out to chat with a neighbor. Meanwhile, Shlomo Itche lay down on the sofa to take a nap. The door remained open. Frode the crazy person seized the opportunity, entered the house and lay down in Sara's bed. She covered herself up and slept with a comfortable snore. In the meantime, Shlomo Itche woke up from his nap, got undressed, went into the bedroom, lay down in bed, and began to wake Sara. "Sara, move over, Sarale, move closer to me," he whispered. However, "Sara" snored. When his requests and caresses did not help, and "Sara" did not awaken, he lifted the blanker and saw Frode with her grey bun of hair. He jumped out of bed in great terror, barefoot and in his long johns, and shouted, "Save me. Frode is lying in bed beside Sara."

[Page 336]

3.

That same Shlomo Itche purchased potatoes in the market during the winter. His wife Sara was standing at his side. They spoke only Lithuanian with the farmer. Shlomo Itche shouted out to Sara in Lithuanian, "*Sara, Padak Meisa Greit Padak Meisa.*" He wanted her to give him the sack (*Meishe* is a sack in Lithuanian). Of course, our Yanovers gave him a nickname, "Sara Rok–Zich" and "Sara Padak Meisa."

4.

A Jew named Spivak lived in Yanova. He was a baker by trade. Since he did not earn any livelihood in Yanova, and had a sick wife and two children, he would go to Kovno. There, he would bake various bagels and buns, and bring them to the market in Yanova every Wednesday. He looked like a gentile and also spoke a good Lithuanian. He would sit in the market at a table full of bagels and buns, and shout in Lithuanian, "*Panai Nie Pirki Fas Zidus, Pirkiti Fas Mania*" ("Do not by from Jews, buy from me"). Of course, he was the target of many curses.

5.

A son was born to Mendel the *Rosh Yeshiva* [Yeshiva Head]. Since he had many children, he named them after rabbis and pious Jews. He was lacking a name for that child. Gershon Kagan was at the circumcision, among the gilded householders. He turned to him and asked him to recommend a name. The wise Gershon did not ponder for long. He said, 'The best name for him is Gana" (That is "Enough" in Lithuanian).

6.

A young tailor named David–Izika lived in Yanova. He was also called "Der Grizik" (The Hoary). A poor man from a different town came to him to ask for a donation. It was a frosty winter day. David Izik's wife gave him a glass of hot tea so he could warm himself up. The poor man took a sip and shouted, "Why do you give me your hot tea? Do you want me to not see Der Grizik?" Then David Izik came and grabbed the poor man without him knowing that it was David Izik. He took him by the collar and threw him outside into the snow.

7.

Moshe Aharon the chimneysweep had three sons. He loved playing cards, and he would play with his sons. As he was sitting and playing, one of his sons called out, "Father, when you do not have an ace, you will already be lying in the ground with me."

8.

There was a butcher Moshke with the nickname "Di Bande." He was a very tall young man with very shortsighted eyes. He was a large eater by nature. When he would go visit acquaintances, he would sit down immediately and start to eat the food that was already on the table. His wife Freidel, who gave birth very often, had an excess of milk for suckling. Every evening she would produce two glasses of milk and put it in a saucer. Her husband Moshke would come very late from the slaughterhouse. When he found the milk in the saucer, he would drink it with a roll.

Avraham Yitzchak Abramovitch

Two Poems
by Avraham Yitzchak Abramovitch
Translated by Jerrold Landau

With the tune: Laugh, Laugh, Friends.

(1)

In Jonava there were many automobiles

They do not rip, they do not bite.

They live very quietly.

They meet together in the morning, very fine and elegant.

They kiss each other , they grab each other's necks, they push together the hands.

Chorus:

Laugh, laugh, laugh, friends! Laugh all together!

For the lie regarding this is very big.

For in Jonava

Such has never taken place.

(2)

They sit calmly making calculations, they make no commotion.

They live very well, like a brother with a brother

They have no chairs, and they do not bang on the tables

Heaven forbid, one should never know of a theft.
Chorus:
Laugh, laugh, laugh, friends…

(3)

They get along with the passengers, very refined, very fine
They travel away immediately, as he sits inside
They wish him best wishes for Kovno
They bid him farewell and tip their hats.
Chorus:
Laugh, laugh, laugh, friends.

(4)

They do not drink liquor, and make no schnapps
They are indeed Jonavers, and there is no joke
Nobody is guilty in the American Bendrova
She will certainly believe my frequent words.
Chorus:
Laugh, laugh, laugh, friends

[Page 338]

To the tune of : A Jew has a wife

(1)

Sunday, all ten automobiles travel out
People come around cheerless
As in the dirges of Tisha B'Av
Chorus:
A Jew has a little car
He has problems with it
A bill comes to him
It should serve as an atonement.

(2)

Monday it travels well
They come in dozens
The crumb is already lost.
Chorus:
The Jew has a little car…

(3)

Tuesday, everyone known
Is a day of good fortune
There are no passengers
They may raise a lament.
Chorus:
The Jew has a little car…

(4)

Wednesday everyone pays with promissory notes
This is no joke
For tribulations, one goes to gamblers (mania)
To have a good schnapps.
Chorus:
The Jew has a little car…

(5)

Thursday, travelling
The autos are full
Underneath, a wheel breaks
Nevertheless, the guardhouse stands and shouts.
Chorus:
The Jew has a little car…

(6)

Friday is the eve of the Sabbath
I have everything in the ground [perhaps: in hell]
I prefer to go back
To the wagon with the house
Chorus:
The Jew has a little car…

(7)

The Sabbath, it is quiet, there is no tararum
Sunday, again Avraham–Yitzchak
Will create a new song
With a new rhyme
Sunday: The Jew has a little car…

Translated by Ella Dolticki–Abrahmovitch

Meita the Baker
by Frank Sirek
Translated by Jerrold Landau

Thursday evening in the small towns, as is known, was a dark and worrisome evening for women. A trifle, one prepared for the Sabbath. One had to make the challa. One had to prepare flour, yeast, eggs, and raisins, make the dough, and prepare the oven. One had to let it stand until dawn, then warm the dough, kneed it, roll it, braid it, light the oven, and place the challa in the oven. Now you can imagine what the evening must have been like for Meita the baker (Levin), who baked challa and bread not only for herself, but for a large part of the city.

One day, on a winter Friday, our Meita woke up before dawn, hastened out of bed, lit the kerosene lamp, and went quickly to the dough which was already beginning to hang over the edges of the wooden boards. In her great haste, she forgot to put on her dress. She was wearing her thick, cotton bloomers with a slit in the rear, in railroad fashion. The oven flickered with large flames of fire, as if holy spirits were blowing beneath it. One could hear Meita knocking and panting, as she conducted her holy work in honor of the Sabbath. Meita moved the hole-filled dough from the boards, cut it with a knife, tossed it onto round boards, sprinkled it with white flour, beat under the dough with her hands, kneaded and rolled it, twisted it, braided one side into the other, tossed the dough into forms, spread it on the bottom and on the top. The work was conducted with such ecstasy that she could have been, of course not literally, the High Priest engaged in the holy service in the tabernacle.

Early in the morning when the darkness had not yet abated, the table was already covered with boards laden with various baked goods in various shapes and flavors. The fire in the oven was already dying down, and the flames were calming down, and the top of the large Russian oven had already darkened. The only thing left to do was to clean out the ashes and place down the challas. Suddenly, she realized: "Oy vey. I don't have any pomele[1]." She did not think for long. She ran out the back door and off she went to the nearby market. Outside, it was the gray of early morning. The zealous woman was wearing her bloomers. She did not even notice that she was running with her cotton pants… She bought the pomele and ran home. Then she noticed that someone on his way to the first Minyan was looking at her and smiling. She then recalled that people were also laughing at the market. Then she realized what had happened: she had forgotten her dress, and she appeared in the street in pants. As she arrived at her home, young jokers laughed at her out loud and made merriment. She ran into the house with her head covered in shame.

[Page 340]

Word of that episode spread throughout Jonava that Sabbath, and the jokers of Jonava nicknamed her from then on, "Meita the Baker with a Crack in her Underpants", or for short "With a Crack".

Told over by Yitzchak Burstein

Translator's Footnote

A baker's mop for cleaning out an oven.

[Page 340]

One Relates
by Sara Burstein
Translated by Jerrold Landau

1.

It is told that Reb Moshe David Mehr was once a guest of his daughter Reizel in Kovno, and she invited him to see a film. It was the manner of Reb Moshe David to have a good sleep in the movie theater. He woke up in the middle of the film and saw before him a wide river with clean banks. "Oy, a curse on me!" he shouted out loud. "The rafts have floated away."

2.

Reb Moshe David was never able to choose a collar for his neck – he was so fat, thick, and burly. Once, as he was entering the city while driving rafts to Kovno, he went with his brother Avraham to search for an appropriate collar in the Kovno shops. He stood in a shop, tried and tried, and could not choose. Avraham called out to him: purchase two collars and you will "*tzuzamenshvrteven*" them. (The formal meaning is from the water jargon, binding together two parts of a raft).

3.

It was said that once, Reb Moshe–David went to Nafcholin the tailor to sew a costume. Moshe–David took off his coat and the joker Reb Naftali and his son Meir came to the workplace to take a measurement... Naftali, with his glasses on the tip of his nose, appeared from behind, fastened the edge of the measuring tape to the pants, and Meir told him to wind the tape around his body. As he was measuring, Reb Naftali shouted to his son: "Meir! Where are you?" "Papa, wait a while, I will come soon," responded the joker Meir.

[Page 343]

"Labas" the Lithuanian Policeman
by Yerachmiel Garber
Translated by Jerrold Landau

He would take off his blue police cap with the Lithuanian sheaves for everyone, irrespective of age or pedigree, and weakly say "*Labas*" (good morning). It was remarkable that he enjoyed it very much when someone grabbed on to his *Labas*, and responded to him with a *Labas*. The Jonaver jokers caught on to that weakness, and gave him the nickname "The Labas."

A great change took place in the psychology of the Jonava householders, as soon as that new policeman appeared in Jonava, to the point where they could not be recognized. Suddenly, they had respect for brooms, burins, and spades. Those tools became the most esteemed and important. Jonaver householders had the opportunity to chat about work politics and local news, not only in the kloiz, but also while going around the area near the house. Some sort of secret power took place there. Early every morning, after the *shacharit* service, everyone hurried after every straw and scrap of paper. Even the women took part in the work, armed with knives in their hands. They would sit on their knees and cut up every blade of grass that sprouted up between the cobblestones.

Who has seen how Jonaver laborers went out from their "palaces" at the end of the winter, when the first warm sun rays appeared, armed with all types of tools, declaring a war against the layer of ice and dirt that accumulated during the long winter. Now you will understand why they were coronated with the nickname "Jonaver ruffians." I recall the scene when my father, may G–d avenge his blood, would go out with a sharp hatchet and a pickaxe, to declare a war of annihilation against the layer of ice. The dull thumping and banging of the pickaxe cutting apart the ice could be heard and seen through the Jonaver streets on such a spring morning. This does not mean, Heaven forbid, that the Jonavers had a special sense of cleanliness. No, my dear ones, this was all, unfortunately, under duress. The main guilty party was indeed the "Labas." He caused the sweat, and therefore the curses that the Jonavers sent his way when he arrived in the town. He would go through the Jonaver streets and alleyways from dawn till dusk, terrorizing everyone. He would sprout up everywhere where one unfortunately would encounter him. He would always find something that another person would not notice. One would always notice that he could not pass by indifferently if a piece of straw or a forlorn piece of grass in the pavement was sticking out, or if the side of the cobblestone was not cleaned appropriately. What upset him most was the dirty, unchopped ice in the spring, or puddles of dirty water in the autumn. He would consider such things as a terrible infraction of the rule books. He had some sort of sixth sense of a bloodhound as he spots the guilty person at the place of the infraction, and he seldom made a mistake.

A policeman in a cap, standing in front of the town, giving a salute.

When the "Labas " used to exit the house of the person who committed the infraction, that person would be certain that the penalty would arrive in the form of a ticket. There were various levels of penalties. The penalty would be very high when the "Labas " would utter his beloved words "*Tamsta Vadinasi*." From the gradience and intensity of the tone, one would already know how many Lit would be on the ticket. The first time, one would sigh, cry, and pay. When he appeared again a few days later, and some straw would fall down as if to cause a vexation, and the Jonaver householders would realize that the issue would have no end, some would decide that it is better to sacrifice oneself and discharge the penalty by going to jail. A person would go there for an entire day, so he would take along food, *tallis*, *tefillin*, and a small book of Psalms. He would then return exonerated.

With the sanitary inspections and accompanying fines, Jonavers suffered from the "Labas " who never tired. He would consider it to be a godly injustice if the Jonaver carpenters, smiths, or shopkeepers disturbed the holy peace on Sunday. Whereas the former policemen used to spend the day resting in their homes, the "Labas " ran around through the streets, searching for anyone violating the holiness of the day. He searched for the Jews who cunningly violated the laws of the state and engaged in commerce or general labor in the workshops.

At the same times, the Jews of Jonava were also correct. As it was supposed to be, they rested on the Sabbath, as God had commanded. Two days to observe was too much! One must have a livelihood for one's wife and children! Where is the justice? For him,

[Page 345]

the dedicated protector of the law, this made no difference. With his exceptional senses, he would sense and hear from afar every bang of a hammer in the master workshops on Kovno and Breizer Streets, and the smithies on Smith Lane. He would hear the voices of customers in the shops and stores. On such a Sunday, unlike any other day of the week, he would morph into a fierce form of a Sherlock Holmes spy. He knew all the back entrances to the shops, carpentry workshops, and wig salon. As if to vex, he would always catch the violator, even behind the closed doors of the wig salon, or the rear door of the shop or carpentry shop. The accused guilty person would always be certain of a good "earning" for the Sabbath.

The Jewish citizens of Jonava began to search for a cure for their affliction. They indeed found one. They gathered a group of young people, of course with payment, to follow the steps of "Labas." The group would loudly announce the arrival of the peril. The group of youths thanked God and the "Labas." They made pocketfuls of money that day, for the cinema, lemonade, or confectionary. It was indeed a general mobilization of the youth that day. They could not play or bathe, but it was worth it. My father Yitzchak Aharon and his brother David, who were turners and supplied material to the carpenters, could also not allow themselves the luxury of two days of rest. They hired me, and I performed my duty honestly for an entire day. I sounded an alarm as the peril threatened, as the "Labas" with his blue cap appeared from afar.

Under the Germans, the "Labas" was expected to enforce the law. However, he related well to the unfortunate Jews. Nachum Blumberg relates that when the *"Labas"* accompanied the wagons that ran from Jonava to the Kovno Ghetto, he displayed great courage. When they asked to stop the wagons to purchase water to drink or food, he fulfilled the requests willingly. In general, he was a friendly man.

Noach the Roof Layer

by Yerachmiel Garber (Tel Aviv)
Translated by Jerrold Landau

On Shul Gasse, opposite Shlomo the Shochet's house, there was a small, wooden house with a large garden. Noach lived there with his wife Hinda, who diligently tended to the vegetables in the garden.

Since the wooden houses of Jonava were mainly covered with shingles, people had to go to Noach the Roof Layer.

He was a quiet man. He would mutter about how much the work would cost, not looking his customer in the eye. His work was reliable.

He had a grey beard and a pale face. He would wear a black cap, and he would often look towards the sky with his eyes. Therefore, the jokers gave him the nickname "the sky wanderer." Some sort of tear emanated from his eyes.

Young householders – in honor of their father–in–law and mother–in–law – used to go to the Large *Beis Midrash*, at least on the Sabbath, to worship a bit and to catch a conversation or tell a joke. But this was not sufficient. There were various sorts of pastimes: tying together the *tallises* of two people absorbed in their prayers, confusing the prayer leader regarding the correct tune, mocking somebody.

[Page 346]

Tossing a wet handkerchief at Noach at the right time – this was the chief act. When the moment came – everybody knew. Noach's place was a bench at the back on the right. When the cantor ended the *Shmone Esrei*: "He Who makes peace on high…" Noach would become very agitated. He would jump up from his place and shout out his own version: "He will make war and destroy Israel, and let us say Amen." He would be very pale, shake his head and tremble. At that moment of ecstasy, when he did not notice what was going on around him, someone would toss a wet handkerchief at him from behind. The tosser would then go to retrieve it.

Noach the Sky Wanderer had the type of end that he had requested for everybody: he was murdered along with the other worshippers.

Where is Father
by Rachel Dushnitzky
Translated by Jerrold Landau

Rabbi Menachem–Mendel Teitz, the Rosh Yeshiva [Yeshiva Head] of Or Noga in Jonava, had lots of children. His livelihood was not so good.

However, on the Sabbath after the cholent, Reb Mendel would go for a walk on the streets of Jonava, dressed in his long, black, silk *kapote*. His light brown, long beard and *peyos* would sparkle with the Sabbath enjoyment. Nobody would be equal to him. A bunch of children with their *peyos* and *streimels* would accompany him on both sides.

As is the custom of children, they would ask him questions. Menachem–Mendel would answer them all calmly, bending down to the right and left.

As they passed Pogirsky's house, where a large poodle guarded the entrance, the small youngster asked a silly question, "Daddy, does a dog have a father?"

"Yes my dear," was the answer.

"Daddy, is Reb Avchik Pogirsky the father of Pogirsky's dog?"

The jokers caught on to this.

[Page 347]

My First Year Working at Filvinsky's
by Yisrael Yaakov Pogir
Translated by Jerrold Landau

For a thirteen year old boy, being an assistant[1] was an honorable profession – something of a trifle!

After Sukkot, when I went after services to Velvel Filvinsky, he treated me to a glass of tea. First he taught me how to make a glass of tea: one puts in a third of concentrated tea essense, a third milk and then fills it with hot water. The dwelling was on the second story. On the first day, I made eight glasses of tea! One went up and down on the steps.

Once I was silly and made it the opposite way – first the water, and the essence at the end. He noticed it and did not drink it, and I had to bring him another glass of tea.

Once I opened the door angrily with a glass of tea in my hand. He closed the door with great anger and gave me a smack on the hands. The saucer remained but the glass fell victim. I returned and brought another glass of tea; but he continued on with his anger and told me that today's glass of tea would cost me dearly. The wonder is that in carrying 8 glasses of tea for 300 days, I only broke one glass.

When did the day of a 13-year-old assistant end? In short, I did not study the Code of Jewish Law. I had to wait until Filvinsky closed the business. However, Filvinsky waited until Elazar Levi Itzik's (Yudelevich) closed his business. I would go to take a look every few minutes to see whether Eliezer Levi Itzik's[2] closed the lamps. Perhaps he was waiting for Filvinsky? In the meantime, I sat there until approximately 10:00 p.m. No customers came. Therefore, I was happy when Leib Gronevich, Alter the lawyer with his powerful voice, Moshe Itzik and other businessmen came to converse.

During the evenings, I waited. I used to sit in the corner on a sack of sugar and listen. They talked about the Governmental Duma, Hamelitz, and Jewish tribulations. Today I think about the stories that they used to tell! They laughed so much. Were I to have known this then, I would have collected the Jonaver humor, and I would have sweetened it today. Alter always had the last word. Since he talked loudly, he won all the debates. My boss had candies and nuts, but he never treated his guests who sustained him. He finally let out a smile…

A day came when an agent from "good things" for the Krasna market arrived. Before the Julians arrived, the Barishnies came to search for sons-in-law and vice versa.

The events took place before the Polish church, right in the place where Filvinsky was sitting[3].

[Page 348]

The agent came in the evening and left his merchandise, various types of sweets. Immediately thereafter came the humorous customers who talked about G-d and his Messiah, about trees and stones. They were the experts about the candies. They continued sampling and ate up his entire stock. The agent shouted that they ate everything up. I quickly fled home, cursing all the businessmen. If G-d desires, I would not longer be an assistant[1]. Eating a Vilna Jew out of his livelihood? Such businessmen I could not tolerate.

Every Monday was market day. As Filvinsky waited to sell and not to purchase, his business began after midday. In the evening after the commotion, Filvinsky sat down to count the hard tens, the silver 20 kopecks, the guilders – and tie up the packages. He handed me a heavy load:

"Go off to Sarel Blume's (Pogirsky), give her the 85 rubles and small change, and ask her for a full hundred. She owes me 15 rubles to pay a promissory note.

For her I would never lend, even if I had to go hungry; and for him I had to shamefully borrow, all for a ruble a week!

Sarel Blume's gave me a hundred ruble bill and told me not to lose it. I brought him the money. First I had to go to Moshe Tzvia's (Lukman) in the hotel, find Yankel Asher's and ask whether he was travelling the next day to Kovno with the coach. Then I had to take the hundred ruble bill and trudge on to the businessman who was traveling to Kovno, telling him to take the money to koznochistova and pay the Filvinsky's debt.

On Monday evening, I did not have to wait for Elazar Levi Itzike's to close his business. When I returned home, Lozer's (Elazar's) business had already long been closed...

Translator's Footnotes

The word here is "Prikozhik'.

This style of name, appearing several times in this chapter, was common in those days. A person would be nicknamed for his mother or father, with the possessive form applying to the parent names. In this case, the father was Itzik, so the man was called Itzik's.

'Julians' would be Russian slang for 'boys', and 'Barishnies' for 'girls'. This cryptic paragraph is obviously describing some matchmaking that was going on in this store.

From the Series of Folk Songs
Prepared by Elchanan Katzenerg and Yitzchak Dembo
Translated by Jerrold Landau

Our dear rabbi, oy vey
A mother cries out such,
What has happened with her daughter
Thursday morning, another family has fled
It was slippery, oy vey, she is lying prostrate,
And the little hill ran off.
That is what she knows. Dear rabbi, imagine
How her belly has become swollen…
And there is nothing to laugh about that,
How did all these things happen to my daughter!
The rabbi heard this out and decided
The Sabbath was approaching, one must prepare for the Sabbath…
[Page 349]
(About Zelik Kapol)
A fashion store, following after fashion, fashion, fashion
They arrested him, and brought him to the commandant.
They took him for a very fine person
And therefore he punishes him
His brother hears, it will not right
If he does not send in the fine.
Couplets It is now a new time
Everyone goes with a short shuffle
The young and the old now are dancing
Mother and Father are dancing
Even Mitka and Agata
Grandmother is also jumping with her feet.
(Ch. Katzenberg)
Where are you going, away from me.
You lovely Maccabeist?
Where are you going, away from me,
You terrible one, that you are? —
To the Land of Israel, my love
I want to be a pioneer there.

My love, adios, you my dear.

(H. Levin)

Between Dizzy Mountain and Viliya River

Is a town, large and high;

And there in the small Jonaver Valley

The large and small play football.

(L. Stern)

"Hakoach" came to us

To play football –

Jews with blessed feet

Shooters of a goal.

Everyone is an expert

A master of the trade,

Everyone shoots goals.

They have a lot.

It is over in a short time.

One day in all –

The last few goals

Were scored by the L.P.L.S.

[Page 350]

They should reciprocate

And answer with a goal

But it is not their luck –

With football.

They wanted, very, very much

To shoot a goal in the goal post, in the goal post.

But we can help them laugh,

For they don't understand football issues

And they cannot shoot goal after goal

(Composed by Notinger in 1925 and sung by the Jonava ball players.}

There was a city in Lithuania

It is situated in a valley

It is difficult to travel there with a train –

Therefore, they have a car

A carpentry shop on every corner

They work – tables and benches;

So that there will be what to sit on

When they come to the tavern…
Oy, oy oy, only in Jonava,
A city of carpenters, ducks, and Yeshiva students, oy, oy
Only in Jonava does one make a drawl
Until the day
The eyes were on Jonava
With girls everywhere
One passed by along the waist,
The other – for two…
They are waiting for a match
Literally without limit;
One wants a genius from Kletzk,
The other, a red commander…
Oy oy, oy, only…
There is a war in the world
One struggles for fuel
The lamps run dry,
Punished, unfortunately, from G–d,
But it still is Jonava
Far from a yokel;
They find something else instead of kerosene
And put it into the lamp.
Oy, oy, oy…
Given over by Miriam and Sinai Persky

[Page 351]

Nicknames
Translated by Jerrold Landau

(According to the alphabet)

Jonaver Buraliakes (ruffians), *Beni–Zuskes, ganovim* (thieves), *Zhulikes* (crooks), *Chalalech*

From Lita Buch, Yiddish, given over by Sudarskin in America

{Translator's note: This is a list of Yiddish or slag terms used as nicknames. I transliterated the original, and translated those that I could, putting the translation in parentheses.}

Oybershter (G–d), *Eibiker Kavalier* (eternal Cavalier), *Indik* (turkey), *Ochs* (ox), *Aho*

Bande (gang), *Baal–Guf* (Fatso), *Bas, Blinde* (Blind), *Balshevikes* (Bolshevik), *Balerina* (Ballerina), *Bulbe* (Potato), *Bok* (He Goat), *Bushlen* (Storks), *Bul*

Gimpel[1], *Greizik* (Grey haired), *Grobachka* (Fatso), *Geller* (Yellow)

Dos (This)

Hotz, Hoicher (Tall), *Hoiker* (Hunchback), *Hinerchaper* (Chicken Snatcher), *Himel–Dreier* (Sky Wanderer), *Hiltzerner Rav* (Wooden Rabbi)

Vagen Vasser (Wagon Water), *Vaz* (Vase)

Zhulik (Crook)

Chalulim (Profane Ones), *Chazirim* (Pigs)

Terk (Turk), *Trante* (Rag), *Teletze* (Heifer), *Tuchle* (Stale), *Tumtum* (Person of indeterminate sex), *Troide, Tshigun*

Ya Nia Tshlavek

Lord (lord), *Lipele, Lachterne*

Mamzer (Bastard), *Matei, Matamid*

Neger (Negro), *Nem An*

Seske, Samures, Sneitshukes, Smaktshe (Sucker), *Skrizale*

Feigele (Bird or Homosexual), *Pudele* (Poodle), *Feiem* (Fairy), *Pak Geld* (Bundle of Money), *Puterbande* (Band of Butter), *Ferdganav* (Horse Thief), *Perler* (Pearler), *Padak Meise, Frentke Kravetz, Pustines* (Idle Ones), *Presole, Poilisher* (Polish), *Pas– Pas, Patshukes, Pitem*

Tzap (He Goat), *Tzig* (Goat), *Tzimes* (Vegetable stew), *Tzigeiner* (Gypsy), *Tzande*

Karn in Drerd (Rye in the Ground), *Konsuli* (Consul), *Kapitan* (Captain), *Koze*, *Kozak* (Cossack), *Kot*, *Kophar* (Head of Hair), *Krume Kop* (Crooked Head), *Kop Tzapke* (Goat Head), *Krupnik* (Barley Soup), *Kazak* (Cossack), *Kurtzer* (Shorty), *Kapuste* (Cabbage), *Kishkenik* (Gut Person), *Kotzapes* (Nicknames), *Kutkelach*, *Krishzelikes*, *Kololinke*, *Konke*.

Rok Zich, *Rodel*

Schvalb (Swallow), *Schvartzer* (Dark One), *Shvitzer* (Braggart), *Schnaps* (Liquor), *Shveshke*, *Shalos–Seudos* (Third Sabbath Meal), *Schnarch* (Snore), *Shisenberg*, *Shafaya*

Translator's Footnote

A surname. Evidently from the story by Isaac Bashevis Singer, Gimpel the Fool.

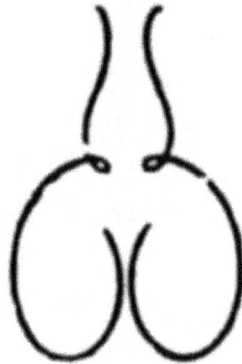

[Page 352]

Our Talmud Torah
by Yisrael Yaakov Pogir
Translated by Jerrold Landau

Our Jewish children of Jonava, who were born in the time when the *Haskala* (Enlightenment) and Zionism pervaded our hometown, were of the most fortunate and perhaps among the first whose way of life was brightened by a fundamental education. Aside from studying Torah and religion, they also studied general knowledge and good deeds.

At the beginning of the 20ᵗʰ century, a fine, beautiful building was built on a large tract of land on Breizer Street. There were two classrooms on each side of the corridor. One could play, be marked, and sting one's hand. The floors in all the rooms were very smooth.

From one side of the fence, across the way from Areh Yankel's alleyway, there was a door for bringing in wood for heating. At the other side, next to Chana Eizik's well, there was a door for exiting to the yard. The key was with Nese the Goat, who cleaned the classrooms and lit the ovens in the wintertime before the children and teachers arrived.

Cheders and Melamdim

The new term in the *cheders* began twice a year, after Passover and after Sukkot. During the intermediate days of the festival – was there any income from tuition? One was certain that G–d would provide. Others were worried.

The new friends would speak the praises of their previous rebbes. One would say that Reb Shmaya the Angry would bite his beard when he got angry / and we pinched him with pranks. A second one would say: My rebbe Shimon David would, for every little thing / would drum my ear with a shalshelet melody[1] / until tears would come out of the eyes / therefore my right ear grew longer. The third would say: My rebbe, Yisrael David the Shochet [ritual slaughterer] of Shul Gasse, would often stick me with his pointer / "Recite it already, nu". The lesson had not yet crashed through my head. The fourth said: My rebbe, Reb Yankel, numbered *aleph*, *beis*, *gimel*, *daled* and whipped / Everything about this I remember well and always know. That which I need to remember and know – I do not know today. However, the beating I remember. The students that remained from the previous term, shook their heads and uttered in a cheerless tone, "You too will not lick honey from our rebbe" / The rebbe prepared a new stick.

My friend's father did not work on Chol Hamoed. He swayed at the table and said, "You know, my child, you have already grown. It is time to begin to learn about Judaism." He opened a Siddur, and said, "Recite my child, *kometz aleph* is oh." When I repeated it, a kopeck fell upon the table with a clang. My mother, brother, and sister said that an angel from heaven threw the kopeck at me. My father said to me that if I learn well, the angel would always throw kopecks at me.

On the morning after Passover, his[2] mother took his hand and led him to Reb Yisrael David the teacher on Breizer Street. He was nicknamed Yisrael David the Kitten: because when he studied with young children, he would say to them lovingly, "Come, recite, kitten." For the second term, his mother took him to Reb Yankel the Chumash teacher.

[Page 353]

The *cheder* was on an alleyway between Shul Gasse and Kovner Gasse, not far from the synagogue courtyard. Older children would go to that *cheder*: the Terks, Yisraelke and Meirke, the son of Shlomo Kadish the wagon driver, Avremke Lipe's and Motke, the son of Yisrael the bricklayer, and a few others. All of them studied *Chumash* together out loud. My friend said that he did not know why the rebbe grabbed the stick. The older students were running around the table, and the rebbe was running after them, until they went through the door and fled into the street. Later, when they came into the *cheder* one by one, the rebbe, Reb Yankel, grabbed each one by the ears, and twisted the ears with a *shalshelet* tune. They shouted to the heights of the heavens. My friend cannot forget that picture.

The second term, in the winter, had finally passed. On Chol Hamoed Pesach, his father tested him and decided that my friend would go in the *cheder* of Reb Shmuel Leizer, the *Chumash* teacher on Breizer Street. Reb Shmuel Leizer had a pleasant disposition, and was hard to anger. He was nearsighted. When he opened the *Chumash*, he had to put it up to his nose to see what he was looking for. Fortunately, he knew the entire *Chumash* by heart. My friend was astounded by the erudition of his rebbe. If a student made a mistake, he would hear it immediately and correct it. The rebbe may not have seen well, but he did hear well.

When I remember Reb Shmuel Leizer the teacher, I am always in doubt as to whether he was engraving monuments in his teaching, or vice versa. He could do it both ways: cut the Hebrew letters with sharp knives in wood, and also impart them to the students.

The libel spread about teachers, that they became teachers because they could not do any other job, is not true. He saw himself how Reb Shmuel Leizer and Reb Yankel, both *Chumash* teachers, did things very well.

The day came – it was either Chanukah, Tu B'Shvat, Purim, or simply a day of good tidings – Reb Yankel the teacher brought a package of Stambul (Istanbul) Tobacco and put it on the table near Shmuel Leizer. Reb Shmuel Leizer wanted to take a look as one would with a package of Stambul Tobacco. Since he was nearsighted, he raised the package of tobacco to his eyes. He smelled the pleasant aroma of the tobacco with his nose, and immediately said, "Reb Yankel, you know, one must make the blessing 'He who revives souls'." They inspected the package of tobacco from all sides, and both agreed where it should be cut. The nearsighted Shmuel Leizer cut the package of tobacco with a sharp knife. After the slaughter, they came upon a plan to make a fair division. They gathered two smooth lids and found a Hoshana branch [willow beaten on Hoshana Rabba]. They bound it together with a thread. The branch hung down, and they tied it together from every side with three strands of invalidated *tzitzis* [ritual fringes that were no longer valid for use] so that it would all be bound together. They put the two bundles of half–package tobacco down on the contraption. Then they moved the golden strands of tobacco with trembling hands from one side to the other, until they came to agreement that they had split it fairly. Finally, they cast lots as to who will get the "stamp" and who will get the "seal". My friend was studying *Chumash*. In the interim, he learnt how to build a scale. He was astonished at the abilities of the rebbes.

[Page 354]

When the first two Talmud Torah rooms were ready, the teachers Reb Yankel, Reb Shmuel Leizer, and the *aleph–beit* teacher Reb Yisrael David, moved to the new Talmud Torah building with all their students.

In the New Building

The day came when Shmerl Moshe Itzik's or Shmerl Stern arrived in the *cheder* with a well–dressed guest. They went through the rooms and walked through the yard, looking around. They talked to the rebbe, Reb Shmuel Leizer, and left. The same guest came the following day. He was wearing an overcoat. He hung up his hat, removed his overcoat, and put on a fine, silk yarmulke. A table with a stool was brought to the middle of the room. The table was covered with a green sheet of paper. A pen, ink, a blotter, and a large and small bell were brought to the table. He rang the small bell. All the children became silent. He stood up at the table, acted as the teacher, and told us how things would work.

The teacher divided up all the students of the Talmud Torah into three classes. All the beginners went to the first class with Yisrael David as the teacher. All the students who knew Hebrew well but were beginners in *Chumash* went to the second class. That class had the largest number of students. I was among them. They got the new teachers. The older students and those above Bar Mitzvah went to the third class, with Reb Shmuel Leizer as the teacher. That class had the smallest number of students.

The teacher placed all the students from the second class along the wall with a *Chumash* for each pair, and said, "We will divide our class into the first class and the second class. When the first class is learning, the second class will write. I will recite twice from *Bereshit*, until *Vayehi Erev Vayehi Boker*[3], and translated it into Yiddish. I want you to listen well. Each oen of you will recite over what I have translated. Those that can recite it will be in the first class. Those that cannot recite it well will be in the second class."

The teacher recited the first verse, and translated it, "In the beginning, G–d created the heavens and the earth." Each child had to go to the middle of the room and repeat the translation out loud. Those who recited well went to one side of the room. Those that did not succeed went to the other side. All of those who had never studied *Chumash* translated well. Almost all of those who had learned and translated according to the old style did not succeed.[4]

Within a few days, a wagon laden with *skameiks*[5] arrived at the *cheder*.

Whomever did not see the beauty of the first days when the teacher entered the class and greeted us with "good morning", with the students responding "good morning", and the teacher going through the entire class and saying "sit in your seats" – has never seen beauty before. The change from the *cheder* atmosphere to the classroom atmosphere was the greatest encouragement for the students, and the nicest thing they had ever seen.

[Page 355]

The teacher Shimon the son of Gershon Landres from Bobryiusk was a fine personality. He had a fine, well–groomed beard, which gave him a distinguished appearance. He walked smoothly, talked clearly, and did not smoke cigarettes or a pipe.

The punishments for infractions were not offensive, and did not hurt the feelings of the children. The punishment for hurting one's fellow was that the guilty student received three or six raps over the hand with the ruler for the infraction. According to the teacher's judgment, the punishment for not paying attention was standing in the corner with the face to the wall for a half an hour or more, losing the rights to participate in the great Purim play, sitting in the classroom and writing 20 lines of translation or 100 times the final *Fey* or *Tzadi*, or remaining in the classroom after everyone went home. The students loved the teacher – this was the bottom line.

I recall my sins today. The teacher gave me a "2". Since this was the first "2", I begged the teacher to not record the sin. This did not help.

I received the "2" because I dared raise my hand to hit a friend. This branded me for life. "A person who raises a hand is considered wicked," is what the teacher responded to my pleas. I recall this sharp and clear.

Our teacher obtained the best text book, the "*Beit Hasefer*" [School], which was in four parts. The first part contained the first three Torah portions: *Bereishit*, *Noach*, and *Lech Lecha*. The second part contained all five *Chumashim* of the Torah. The third part contained the Tanach [Bible] : Joshua, Judges, I and I Samuel, I and II Kings. The fourth part contained the earlier and latter prophets. Every Hebrew word was translated into Yiddish, with the source or the root, the grammatical person and tenses. Every page had a written letter of the *aleph–beit* for a daily lesson, and a few lines of *Chumash*. Thus, the book made it easy to learn and remember the language. Since the language is the key to knowing the Jewish Torah, the teacher dedicated the greatest part of the class time to studying the language – the Holy Tongue. He requested that we speak amongst ourselves in Hebrew: "You will know how to write Yiddish when you know the Holy Tongue."

The Bells Ring, and Rumors

The seekers of wrongdoing of Jonava began to spread rumors that the teacher does not pray, and that they believe he eats non–kosher food. How can it be that bells ring in a Talmud Torah? And they were certain that the Talmud Torah children do not wear *tzitzis*.

A day came. The teacher was learning with the class, and the students of the other class were writing. Yankel the vinegar maker and Slalom Keidianer, the spies, entered, went to the children and began to search. The teacher saw this and said, "Are you checking for their *tzitzis*? I will show you their *tzitzis*!" He invited a child with a torn cloak. "You are wearing a warm fur? – With that cloak, he will freeze; He will get sick and die, and you are looking for *tzitzis*!" He brought forth another child and took off the cloak – without a hem over his body! And you are searching for *tzitzis*? – If you bring him a pair of boots, and for him a warm cloak with a hem – I myself will put the *tzitzis* on them.

[Page 356]

Take the *tzitzis* and go. Do not dare to come without what they need!" They heard about the spies in Jonava – and the city of Jonava was joyous and glad...

The teacher immediately put up a notice on the door of the entrance. Aside from the trustees, nobody is permitted to enter without permission from the teacher. It was signed Shimon the son of Gershon Landres of Bobruisk.

The conclusion of the episode of the spies was a good one. Our young Jonaver Jewish women gathered together and founded a society for providing clothes to those in need [*Chevra Malbish Arumim*].

Within a few weeks, four women brought two large roles of cloth for pants and two roles of black cloth for outfits. Every student received a piece of grey cloth for pants and a piece of black cloth for an outfit. Each one could give it over to be sewn. The *Malbish Arumim* Society would pay for those who cannot pay. Those who needed boots would order boots, and the *Malbish Arumim* Society would pay a few weeks later. When everyone's clothes were ready, the Talmud Torah students were all dressed up in new, warm clothes, new boots, and black caps. The teacher arranged the students in rows of four, and they marched through Breizer Street like true soldiers – those on duty in front and the teacher on the side. This was the finest parade that I remember from my young days, aside from the march of the bride and groom to the *chupa* [marriage canopy] near the *kloiz*.

A rumor spread that there were students in the Jonava Talmud Torah who were hungry. They checked this out and decided that all orphans and children of those in need who do not have enough to eat – would have breakfast every morning except for Saturday. Yeshaya brought from Meite the Baker two bagels or cakes for 15 children. They ate breakfast before the teacher arrived. Many children were jealous of the orphans, who ate such fresh rolls and cakes, while they ate a morsel of dry bread.

Purim and Examinations

The holiday of Purim arrived. The leaders were Itzik the cutter (Dembo), Leib Granevich, and the lad Yankel Weitzstein. They chose children who could sing, and they practiced *Shoshanat Yaakov*[6] and other songs of Zion.

The Purim evening was conducted in the *Beis Midrash*. The majority of Jonava Jews were present, and the *Beis Midrash* was packed.

After the successful Purim evening, the teacher decided to conduct and open examination for the Jews of Jonava who supported the Talmud Torah.

The first to come was Shmuel Leib Burik. He went through the rooms, looked through the books, and put on his glasses and asked us to write *Aavha*. The students were confused, for they had never heard of such a word. Shmuel Leib said: "*Ahava raa Avatanu*" and the teacher said, "*Ahava raba ahavtanu*"[7]. Shmuel Leib was very insulted and we heard very strong words. He grabbed his cane and wanted to escape, but the teacher held him back. Shmerl Moshe Itzik's and another few came. Few parents came.

No more open examinations were called. Rumors spread through Jonava that the Talmud Torah children were able to learn better than even the Kaplitzer Yosi–Ber Brandweiss' students. The two other classrooms were ready.

[Page 357]

Another wagon of new *skameiks* arrived. The teacher brought in another young teacher from Bobruisk. He was a fine, tall lad with a head of curly hair. His name was Jachnovich. The teacher Shimon the son of Gershon gathered his second class into the new room, and Jachnovich took over the teacher's classroom with new students who had grown up well, forming a true third class. Shmuel Leizer's very few students formed the fourth class.

The first class with their teacher began to speak Hebrew among themselves. The true wealthy householders started to send their children to the Talmud Torah. They even agreed to make the same clothes for their children. Even Binemke Pogirsky sewed the same clothes with a cap, and sat on the same *skameik* as I did.

The fathers of the children shouted that the wealthy people wanted to take over the Talmud Torah. They want to pay, and the poor do not, so the teacher will dedicate himself to teaching the wealthy children. They listened to their outcry, and it was decided that the students who pay should come after the Talmud Torah students go home, and the teacher would teach them until 6:00. Then the teachers let out a great, bitter outcry that teachers who were not true *melamdim* were coming to our city, and were taking away the morsel of bread from the mouths of the true *melamdim*. This did not work well, and they gave in. Many fathers wanted to also include the poor families, for they too were not wealthy. This was perhaps the first time in our hometown when wealth was a deficit, and those who were wealthy were jealous of the poor.

Once, at services in the *Beis Midrash* on the Sabbath, the teacher with the householders approached the table of the common folk and looked for Talmud Torah students from the common folk. They found a student from the first class who had learnt for a year, and had studied the first section of "*Beit HaSefer.*" He knew Hebrew well, and knew many words of the Holy Tongue. They examined him, and he recited a half page of Hebrew, as easily as water flows down a mountain. My friend had studied the second section of "*Beit HaSefer,*" and was studying the Torah portion of *Vayigash*. He translated a half a page. The teacher moved on to *Bamidbar*, and my friend was also able to understand *Bamidbar*, for they studied the Holy Tongue, and they would understand any section. The teacher Shimon the son of Gershon left with the examiners and was proud of his students, who knew what they were studying.

New Teachers and A New Outcry

When we came to the Talmud Torah classroom after Sukkot, we found that the teacher Jachnovich had brought two new teachers. One, named Choshev, was from near Bobruisk. He took over Jachnovich's class, and Jachnovich took over Shimon the son of Gershon Landres' class. I have forgotten the name of the second teacher. He took the place of Reb Shmuel Leizer to teach the beginners. A Jewish girl from Jonava, who graduated from the Peterburg Russian University, was given an hour to teach the Russian language to the third class. Later, they decided to send the students to the Russian school to learn Russian for a half day.

[Page 358]

When we 12 children arrived at that school, they told us to stay home until we would receive a permit from the governor. It took a few weeks for the permit for us to study Russian arrived. When we came, they sat us in the front, near the wall. When the teacher started the Russian lesson with the new lads, he said that whomever had an old book should give it to the *Yevreis* [Jews], and he would receive a new one. He knew how to do this well, calming us and ensuring that nobody would hurt us.

We were about ten years old at that time. The complaint came anew regarding the Talmud Torah: they are taking Jewish children who were sent there to study Torah, and sending to a Russian school where they would become apostates. The bitter words against the Talmud Torah were because they were teaching a Jewish boy to write a Russian address – and one must not do this. However, the fathers of the students knew better, stating that the Talmud Torah teachers and leaders were more pious, honorable and useful than even Shalom Keidianer, whose daughter knows Russian much better than Yiddish, and can write and teach the Russian language.

Our classrooms were always tidy, orderly, and clean. They brought pictures of the great people of our generation. Every room was decorated with those pictures. Dr. Herzl's picture, with the long, black beard, hung among them. All the leaders of the Talmud Torah, including Shmerl Stern and Komberg, who would always come to Talmud Torah meetings, arrived. All the classes took place, and the teacher Jachnovich delivered a eulogy for Dr. Herzl. He addressed all the students of all classes, saying that the children should recite Yizkor for the leader of the generation throughout their lives, and asking every student to write a story about Dr. Herzl. Every story will be read in front of the class. The best story will win a prize. A cantor recited the memorial, and everyone sung *Hatikvah*.

Our Talmud Torah Celebrations

We sang songs of Zion once a week. All the classes gathered together. In Jonava, there was somebody without a son–in–law on support. The son–in–law had married a girl from Jonava, and was involved in the cantorial arts. He would come often to teach singing.

Lag B'Omer was a true festival. We would go to the forest, every class with their teacher. We would march two in a row, like soldiers. We would march through Keidianer Street, passing by the cemetery. We reached the sandy hill, which we would ascend. We would play various games. The winner would receive toys, which were brought by Shmerl Stern: rubber balls and other such things. The teacher brought candies. The children brought delicacies to eat during the day. No celebration in the Talmud Torah would take place without Shmerl, Moshe Itzik's.

Then the day came… It seemed that the dear Talmud Torah students were good children. However, the inclination of man is evil from his youth[8]. The Holy Sabbath is a day of rest. One worships, eats, plays, hurries to the meadows, and to the Dizzy Mountain.

In the middle of the joyous, lively playing, we suddenly realized: It was two o'clock. We had to go to cheder – in the summer to recite the chapter of *Pirkei Avot*, and in the winter *Barchi Nafshi* with all the *Shir Hamaalot* Psalms. The children were enthusiastic as a flame of fire for the chapters and for the *Barchi Nafshi*. They wanted to uproot them, and rip them out of all the prayer books, so that could be free… The older children conferred together, raised their hands and swore… We are not going to *cheder* on the Sabbath. Not everyone was able to keep the secret, for the fathers found out. They had to go, but a few did not go, I among them. On Sunday morning, the teachers Jachnovich and Choshev were the judges. They said that we were correct, we should not study on the Sabbath. We must go an entire day Friday, and then be free. We did not want to give up the half day on Friday. We would prefer to go on. We had to go on the Sabbath to recite the despised chapter and the cold *Barchi Nafshi*.

[Page 359]

We students felt that the teachers hated going to *cheder* even more than the children. However, it was an inviolable rule from our ancestors. They did not shame us strikers, but it was bitter enough that we had to go on the Sabbath, for on the Sabbath, the householders would come to look over the Talmud Torah and examine the students. And Shmerl Moshe Itzik's, what did he do on the Sabbath?

Shmerl Moshe Itzik's or Shmerl Stern

He was a communal activist who gave so much of his time for the upkeep of the Jonava Talmud Torah. He would fill in if a teacher was sick. He would come a few times a week to check if everything is in order. During the many years that I was a student at the Talmud Torah, there was nobody who did as much as he did for the welfare of the students and the teachers. It is a rare individual who would give over so much for the welfare of the public.

Shmerl Stern

I mention Shmerl with awe and honor. When I mention the teachers who taught us and lit up our world – Shimon the son of Gershon Landres of Bobruisk, Jachnovich the second teacher, and Choshev the third — Shmerl Stern is always included.

[Page 360]

On a hot summer day, when the sun shone from the heights of the Jonaver sky, the first shout of "Fire! Yisrael the Tzigelnik's house is burning" was heard. The Talmud Torah students ran home, and the men of Jonava ran to the fire with buckets of water. The hot wind blew the fire and within three hours from the first fire alarm, the entire town was on fire. The hot coals fell here and there. The black chimneys looked like gravestones over the Jewish houses of Jonava that were still standing. The Jonava Talmud Torah was not burnt, but the lights in the Talmud Torah were extinguished, and the institution was destroyed. It was used as a shelter for many families.

When I came to the Talmud Torah the next morning and saw our teacher, I saw the battle that took place for a bit of floor space in our classrooms. People tried to grab a larger floor space in the corners. The *skameiks* marked the borders. Children sat on the sacks – the wealth saved from the fire. They were all partners in driving me out: they were afraid of a new enemy. They did not need any guests there, so I had to go to the

Beis Midrash. As I recall, these neighbors were in the Talmud Torah for a few years. One thing I do not know: How did the Jonava Talmud Torah become a jail, and who were the jailkeepers who took over two rooms, and dissociated themselves from the unwanted neighbors. The windows of our Jachnovich's classroom were sealed with iron grates for the prisoners, and the other room was for soldiers from the convoy. The unfortunate neighbors lived in the other two rooms, that they had taken over on the day after the fire.

One day, the Talmud Torah rooms, which became a jail after the Jonava fire, had their iron grates removed from the windows, and turned into a house of worship. A "Tiferet Bachurim" group was founded in Jonava under the influence of Yankel the vinegar maker and Shalom Keidianer.

There was a long table with two long benches. The young lads sat and Yankel the vinegar maker studied the Abridged Code of Jewish Law with them. There was a Holy Ark with three decorated Torah scrolls on the eastern wall. There was a podium for the prayer leader and a lectern for Reb Shalom Keidianer, the leader of the Tiferet Bachurim. There was a table in the middle of the room for the reading of the holy Torah, and for the distribution of *aliyas* and honors. It was a veritable holy place. It seems that all the holy places survived the fire as if by a miracle: the old *Beis Midrash*, the large, beautiful *Beis Midrash*, and the Frachtfule Shul on Shul Hoif all remained. The Korobelniksher Kloiz on Breizer Street remained whole, and the Hassidic Shtibel also did not burn. Only the old *kloiz* burnt down, but a new one was built.

Aside from this, the other classrooms were occupied by the unwanted neighbors as if it were a poorhouse.

Around 1909, rumors spread that the Jonava Talmud Torah was being revised with the teacher Shaul Kiediansky.

I often saw him passing by on the way to the Talmud Torah. Due to his outward appearance and his proud gait, he looked like our teachers Choshev and Jachnovich from before the fire. Within a brief time, I heard that another teacher was coming to the classroom. That teacher was already a Jonaver by birth, from a prominent Jonava family, Yosi–Meir Itzikovich. His father Yankel Asher's, a tall Jew, used to go around every Thursday before the Sabbath with his big basket to collect challah for Kiddush for those who could not buy or bake it. On Friday, he would divide it up among those in need, and who lacked bread to eat during the week. His son became a teacher in our Jonava Talmud Torah. He was a son–in–law of Moshe Keidianer, who owned a carpentry shop near the Viliya. Pogirsky's neighbor, my friend's brother, a student of the revived Talmud Torah, already wrote and spoke the Holy Tongue, just like the good, old times. A third teacher came to the Talmud Torah. The sound of the Talmud Torah students began to be heard on Breizer Street. When my friend went to America, the correspondence with his brother was in the Holy Tongue. His Bar Mitzvah letter from his brother was full of expressions from the Hebrew of the Jonava Talmud Torah.

[Page 361]

The Hebrew letters floated back and forth over the Atlantic until the second conflagration of the First World War, and the expulsion of the Jews of Lithuania.

Translator's Footnotes

A *shalshelet* is a cantillation trop with an elongated melody. See https://en.wikipedia.org/wiki/Shalshelet

The story changes from first person to third person here, seemingly to generalize.

The first chapter of Genesis.

I did not transpose the Yiddish translation here word for word, but it is clear that the new style looked at the entire verse as one unit, whereas the old style translated phrase by phrase, so that the translation did not match proper sentence structure (i.e. In the beginning, Created, G–d, the Heavens…"

Skameik means bench in Russian. This is evidently a type of bench.

Lily of Jacob, a Purim hymn.

The latter phrase is part of the morning prayers. The former phrase is a corrupted pronunciation of it.

Genesis 6:5.

On Separate Paths
by Y. Y. Pogir
Translated by Jerrold Landau

We were three friends, born on the same Breizer Street.

Each one of us prepared to earn a living through work. Alke Ozvolk became a gaiter stitcher. Yisraelka Pogir, the son of Yosa the tailor, finally became a smith. Meirka Fridel's, an orphan, could not prepare himself for a trade. He went onto the water to float the barges.

In 1913, on a snowy Sunday morning, we three friends, 18–year–old lads, set out for America. We stole across the border, traveled by ship, and arrived at Ellis Island, the island of tears. There, we separated.

We often wrote letters to each other. The debates about our ideals branched out. I remained a supporter of Poalei Zion, and am active in Poale Zion work with my wife to this day.

The following is from Meirka's letter from New York in 1915, to me in Pittsburgh:

"… You write to me that you are now a Poalei Zionist. I congratulate you for your new ideal. I am somewhat against that ideal.

… What have the Zionists done to this point? And if they will indeed accomplish, can we take light from them, for they do not know how to fight. They will be too small in number. However, Socialism is here for all people, and Socialism must come.

Zionism today is merely an idea, and not for everybody. Only for a small number. It presents a fine fantasy with empty hope. However, if you honestly believe in it, I wish you success.

As it is, I am a big against it. But this is not so much because that the Poalei Zion supporters in New York are now like Socialists…"

From your dear brother,

Meir Petershein

[Page 362]

My Native Village of Siesikai
by Shmuel Balnik
Translated by Jerrold Landau

Shmuel Balnik

As in the fog of a spring dawn, my small hometown, where I spent my childhood, is revealed and crystallized before my eyes. It stands like a discarded pearl on some intersection, between forests, fields, fruit orchards, and deep lakes. Memories are awakened. For me today, this is only a cemetery, a desolate desert, from which I escaped with closed eyes.

The village of Siesikai is located 35 kilometers northeast of Jonava, near Tarakai–Bukonys–Gustonys, which goes to the town of Seta in the winter[1].

Siesikai is surrounded on the east side, which leads to Vilkomir (22 kilometers), by two large lakes. From the other side, leading to the town of Pogir (12 kilometers), it is surrounded by forests and small farms. In the south, leading to the village of Taujenai, it is surrounded by large forests of oak, firs, and alders. These were the Gruzer and Kikuner forests, where I worked for many years as a driver for Jewish forestry merchants.

On the north side, there were many fruit orchards, such as the Heifer and Pasader orchards. I would travel to Jonava through two main routes: on was via Tarakai and Pageležiai, and then via the highway. The second was via Tarakai–Kaplice (the native town of the Bursteins and Wolfowitzes), and Mateikiškiai. The village was built in the year 1534. It burnt down and was rebuilt several times. One building always remained intact – the church. It was known for its massive stones, and its artistic style both inside and outside.

According to legend, there were two Siesikai brothers during the time of Vitas the Great, who came with their horses and wagons and brought a large stone. They built a hut on the location of the church and said that they wish to remain there until a house of worship for Jesus is built there, and the stone would be the base of the foundation. The founding of the town followed. It was especially known during the years of Lithuanian independence. The courtyard of the Lithuanian president Antanas Smetona[2] was not far from the town (10 kilometers away). This was the Uzgirish courtyard, in which he was born in the village of Terpeikiai.

[Page 363]

He would stop in Siesikai during the summer, when he traveled to the courtyard. Every time, he would visit the small synagogue to have a chat with the local elderly Jews. The 400th anniversary of the church was celebrated in in 1935. During his speech, the president mentioned the local Jewish residents of the town who had settled in the region and lived in peace and contentment with the Lithuanians.

Connections with Jonava

The reader should not wonder why this book, which is dedicated to the holy memory of the heroic Jewry of Jonava, describes the lives and tragic destruction of the Jewish community of the village of Siesikai. The memory of my village with its scant thirty Jewish families was connected with the life of the nearby larger Jewish community of Jonava. It is sufficient to mention that the rabbi of Jonava, Rabbi Chaim– Yitzchak Silman of blessed memory, would come to our synagogue in Siesikai to give sermons and teach Torah. He met his wife there, the daughter of the honorable Reb Ben–Zion Bin, the spiritual leader of the town. In the later years, when he occupied the honorable rabbinical seat of Jonava and became well–known, he would come twice a year, on Shabbat HaGadol and Shabbat Shuva, to worship with us and deliver sermons. His sermons were full of Torah, moral lessons, and life wisdom. These would serve for the Jews of our town as way setters for the entire year. He would boast about his holy community of Jonava, where Torah and work were bound together.

Siesiker Jews did not own houses, distilleries, or factories. The most important source of their livelihood was the wheat business: Abba Sulski, chaim Perlstein, Yonah Katz, and others. In the summer, they did business with fruit. They would lease the fruit orchards from the surrounding landowners. In the autumn, they would bring the apples to the Jonava train station with a wagon. The Jonava fruit traders would then purchase the fruit and export it in wagons to Germany. The Siesikers would purchase cattle for the Jonava butchers Izik Nachimovich, Shlomo Judelovich – or, as the Siesikers called them in short form: Izka the Butcher, Shlomo the Maskver. When the local farmer had cattle to sell, he would turn to the local merchants to tell the Jonaver businessmen to come. It was considered humiliating to sell in Vilkomir, even if the price was higher. The local Jews would also purchase furs for the Jonaver merchants.

There were also several shopkeepers who maintained small shops. The would obtain the merchandise from the Jonaver wholesalers Liber Farber, Meir Goldschmid, and others. The forest machines used on an annual basis, which would be placed in the autumn in the forest department in Kovno, were sold in the Siesiker region and exploited via the Kemach factory in Jonava (Inhaber, Burtein, Wolfovich).

As has been stated earlier, I worked in all the forests as an employee (called a *Shafer*) for the aforementioned firm for many years. I was also given the responsibility by the firm to concern myself with providing the small synagogue with firewood, which was unused the entire year. All together, the connections that bound us to the Jonava community were very deep. When a Jew of Siesikai would travel with horse and wagon to Kovno, Jonava would be the first stop. When farmers of Siesikai would fight with each other, the victor would claim that he "drowned" like a Jewish wagon driver or butcher from Jonava. On the other hand, when a gentile fought with a Jew in the village, he would shout, "This is not Jonava for you!"

[Page 364]

We mention such a curiosity: Itzik Jozefs of blessed memory, who was a quiet, poor, intelligent person, but also an ignoramus[3]. He came to the landowner Daugiala to request that he lease him the orchard with the fruit of the season. The landowner said to him, "Unfortunately, I cannot lease it to you, for you Jews murdered our god." Itzik did not think long, and answered, "My master the landowner, it was not the Jews of Siesikai, but rather the Jews of Jonava, who did this." He was so certain of the power of the Jonavers that he had no fear of the great landowner, who owned more than half of the houses in the town in which the Jews lived.

There were close connections between the Siesikers and Jonavers, for example between the Jonaver Wenders and Perevozhniks, the Farber family with the Jonava Farbers and Dragatzkis, the Meltz family with the Jonaver Lukmans, etc.

Living in Harmony

In general, the Jews of Siesikai lived in harmony, like one large family. There was barely any jealousy or hatred, for everyone was on the same social level.

There were no parties and organizations in the town. However, they were all warm, nationalistically inclined Jews and Zionists, who would place money in the blue box (the Jewish National Fund). They youth strove for culture, and they decided to found a library.

Its first founders were Sara Bin (Balnik) together with Morris Orlin (today in Africa). It was not so simple to do this. However, thanks to all the forestry merchants and their drivers would lodge in the home of Yaakov Bin of blessed memory. Sara indeed used the opportunity and approached the guests. Egoz from Vilna, Swirsky from Kovno, Yonah Katz of blessed memory, and Tanchum Burstein of blessed memory assisted with money. The youth then had a fine library and a place to meet for lectures and entertainment. In the later years, Rachel Orlin of blessed memory, the mother of the aforementioned Morris Orlin, gave over her entire dwelling to the older youths for that purpose. We all called her Bubbe Rachel, and honored her greatly. We saw with our eyes how she would sit in the corner of her dwelling, with photos of her four sons and daughter who immigrated to Africa on the table. Next to every photo was a charity box for the Jewish National Fund.

A wedding in Siesikai (1933). The groom was Moshe, and the bride was Fruma

The founders of the library with the societal activist Moshe Orlin before his departure for South Africa. In the photo: The Bin sisters from Siesikai, Wender, and Lukman from Jonava

Bentze the Siesiker. On the right is his daughter Rebbetzin Silman

Jews of Siesikai meeting the Episcopal from Panevežys, 1935. Greeting him – Meir Felisher. Standing nearby, Bentze Levin

Siesikai

[Page 365]

One of the modern cultural activists was the Zionist Meir Fleisher. He came from the town of Vilkaviškis, and founded a sawmill here – the first large enterprise. A year after the arrival of the Soviet Army, he was deported to Siberia as a Zionist and bourgeoisie. Today, he lives in Kovno, and strives to come to Israel.

Since there was no material basis for the older youth, with the passage of time the youth emigrated, primarily to Africa. About twenty people settled in the city of Johannesburg. They especially came from the large families blessed with many children, such as the Bin, Orlin, and Balnik families. I state with happiness that when I was in Johannesburg in 1969, I found a Siesiker society with over 200 members, most of whom had never been in the town. The warm, good, Jewish character traits and national faithfulness of their parents in the Siesikai of old was given over to them as a heritage. Their children donate and do a great deal for Israel, especially from the Magen David Adom. The former Bin sisters, today Sara Balnik, Helen Salken, Munia Balnik, Alta Orlin, Teiba Orlin, and others are active in that sense. All Siesikers take part in funding the various campaigns for Israel.

Unfortunately, the older generation is passing away, and I met them only on the gravestones of the cemetery there. These included my two brothers of blessed memory.

The picture from 26 years ago swims before my eyes, how I returned from the front at the end of the war and took a look at the destroyed town of Siesikai. I alone had escaped from there to Soviet Russia at the beginning of the war, and not one Jew survived. I read a frightful document, in which the police chief from Siesikai, Zaremba may his name be blotted out, shared with the police force of Vilkomir the fact that Siesikai was Judenrein. That is when I made my decision that my foot should not be found on Lithuanian soil, which was soaked with Jewish blood spilled by the Lithuanian executioners. I fought for ten years, bringing papers to the Interior Ministry every year, to be permitted to leave. In 1966, I finally merited to come to the homeland here in Israel with my wife and two daughters.

The Destruction of Siesikai Jewry

In the last 5–6 years before the outbreak of the Second World War, when Hitlerism spread and overtook one country after another, the Jews of Siesikai lived very mundane lives, occupied with their day to day livelihood and with the words from the letters from the children who had spread out through the world. With all the things happening to to the Jews, they began to recite Psalms more intensely. This was the only weapon in their hands. This was the situation when Hitler grabbed Memel and Poland. The older Jews would say that they would survive this new Haman.

[Page 366]

Nothing was requested when the Soviets entered Lithuania. Nobody was wealthy, and nobody mixed into politics. It was only darker to live, for the Jews had cast off the small stores. Shortly before the outbreak of the war, 21 families with 70 individuals lived in Siesikai. As we determined after the war, based on testimonies and documents, on the second or third day of the war, on June 23–24 1941, many Jews of the town who had gotten married in the big cities returned to the town. Many Jonavers came with their families, including Liber and Yudel Farber, Yaakov Bin, Meir Wender, and others. So many people came, just as happened during the First World War, when people felt it would be easier and calmer to spend the wartime period in a small town. However, a few days later, some of them, including Meir Wender and Bin, returned to Jonava. The farmers immediately displayed their murderous faces, and Jews were unable to purchase anything. Only a few helped, and it is appropriate to mention to mention such Lithuanians as Imbras and Andrei Talalas. However, the majority, including those with whom we had grown up, stole, murdered, and mocked. The Jews sat in their houses in shock, torn from the world.

On the 9th or 10th day of the war, a loaded tank arrived from Kovno, headed by 10 bandits, and brought a command from Maiar Impulavicus, who lives today in America, about clearing Siesikai from Soviet agents and other anti–German elements. They brought with them seven bound Russian youths from Russian village of Manteik. The

Lithuanian bandits, who came together with the town bandits such as Klatinas, Sokolovski, Karaliunas, and others, broke into the Jewish houses and snatched 27 Jews, among them my two brothers, and the children of Korobelnik, Grazutis, and Meltz. The strong Jews such as Yankel and Avraham–Ber, as well as Moshe Levin and his family (the son of the former *shochet*), Liber and Yudel Farber from Jonava, were driven to a grove two kilometers from the town, with spades, and order to dig pits. They were brutally beaten and murdered. Everyone in town heard the shots. The cry from the mothers and families made the bandits happy. After their work, they drank and celebrated wildly the entire night.

On Friday afternoon, September 1, 1941, all the Jews were dragged out of the houses, and brought to the small, wooden synagogue. They were not allowed to take anything along. They were already shadows of people. Those who witnessed it said that the older people, especially the women, led the children by the hands, for they could not go themselves. They were held up in the synagogue the entire night without water. Nobody was allowed to leave. On Saturday morning, about 20 wagons set out with four people in each wagon, bound by the hands. They were transported to Vilkomir, and murdered in the Pivaner Forest on September 5, 1941 by the Lithuanian executioners, may their names and memories be blotted out.

More than 12,000 Jews were murdered in the Pivaner Forest near Vilkomir. A memorial stands there today, and Jews come once a year to visit the grave of their ancestors. In accordance with my request and the request of the parents of the 7 murdered Russians, the 27 people shot near our town were exhumed in 1964, two years before my departure from Lithuania.

[Page 367]

When they were exhumed, many looked as they did when they were alive, for the ground was wet and sandy.

The bodies of the 27 Jews and 7 Russians were brought to the military cemetery in Vilkomir and buried with a ceremony. The inscription says, "Here lies Soviet citizens murdered by the Nazis."

During the night when they placed all the Jews in to the synagogue, as I have written earlier, the young Jewish lad Elke Meltz succeeded in escaping and hiding in the forest of the area until the beginning of 1944. As the liberation approached, the local farmers found him in the forest and cruelly murdered him.

Meir Fleisher's wife Devora and her brother Berl hid with farmer acquaintances for several months. At the end, the farmers turned them in to the police. They were transported to the Pivaner Forest near Vilkomir and shot together with two other Jews of Vilkomir. Chaim Baran and Dr. Yeshayahu Rabinovitch also hid with farmer near Siesikai.

As we later learned, only Lithuanians participated in all the aktions against the Jews in Siesikai, the area, and Vilkomir. After the war, many of the murderers of Siesiker and Jonaver Jews were tried by the Soviet courts. Among them were Klatinas, Karalaunas, Maldaikis, Zamachkas, and many others. I took part in and provided materials for many of the trials. Many of those sentenced served their time and now live free in their place. Many succeeded in escaping with the Germans, included the murderers Gipas, Talalas, and others, and today are living free in America.

From all Siesiker Jews, Meir Fleisher (today in Kovno, Lithuania), and the writer of these lines survive – that is 2 out of 70 people. In short, this is the story of the tragic death of the Jews of my hometown of Siesikai, including my beloved mother Chaya, brothers Yitzchak, Rafael, Yechezkel, and Aryeh, and sisters Dvora and Sara.

These lines were written in their memory.

[Page 368]

Three Events from the Year 1902

… Regarding a political gathering of 100 people in a forest near Jonava, with a n unrolled red banner upon which revolutionary words are described in "Fasli Izvestiz" (October 22, 1902):

"The Bund – the speaker said – worries as a father does for his children, even in such a hole as Jonava. Given over to the Bund (the speaker turned to the incoming representative from the center), he must not forget us Jonavers when he will call the Jewish workers to revolution: Wherever he calls us to, we will go, even unto death."

The same issue (August 22, 1902) describes a characteristic case of the delaying of the reading [of the Torah] by the workers in the same Jonava, and regarding a matter to which the workers had no direct connection, only it was handled with simple justice and propriety:

A police chief battered the Jew Yankel Roker. The family of the beaten man demanded from the "Fani" (Russians) of the city that they bring a doctor to Kovno to conduct a trial against the murderous police chief. The "Fani" refused for fear of starting up with the police chief. The workers and the family of Yankel Roker came to the synagogue. They did not allow the Torah reading to proceed, as they demanded a trial against the police chief. This led to a large fight in the synagogue itself, and also on the street. The workers came to a Kovno hospital and also were in the street. The workers brought a doctor from Kovno, took the beaten man to a Kovno hospital, and conducted a trial against the police chief.

…The householders in Kiediani hired hooligans to beat and terrorize the "statshkenikes." Of course, the police were on the side of the householders. The Kiedianers called the Jonavers for help: A large group of healthy workers arrived from Jonava. It was dark in town. The doors and gates were closed out of fear. In the evening, with the Oriondik and the Satniks were out to the street together with the hooligans, they were beaten so badly that they fled in a bloody state. We had taught the hooligans well.

(From the book "Lita" published in 1951 in America, edited by Dr. Mendel Sodarski.

Translator's Footnotes

The first two towns are close to Siesikai. The others are not. I suspect that this is referring to a railway line.

See https://en.wikipedia.org/wiki/Antanas_Smetona

Am Haaretz implies an ignoramus in religious knowledge. Thus, one can be intelligent in worldly affairs, but also an ignoramus.

[Page 372]

Untitled Poem
by Batya Perlstein
Translated by Jerrold Landau

She was 87 when she wrote this.

My husband and my children

We were so devoted and dedicated;

They so tragically killed you,

Woe is my life.

My dear ones, they prodded you

To the slaughter, like a flock of sheep;

Nothing matters to me,

And I get no sleep at night.

Your crying and shouting

Should have split the heavens;

The murderers had no compassion –

Not on the young, and not on the old.

Regarding your final end

I know nothing about

Where you rest in your eternal sleep

And where your holy bones lie.

They snatched old and young,

And prodded them through the streets;

And with your blood and tears

They washed them.

They beat you

With sticks and whips;

That end should quickly come to

The Lithuanians and the Germans.

My lovely, little Yosef Hirsch,

They probably buried you alive;

Nobody is left behind,

Alas, for your grandmother.

My famous beauty Eta–Rivkale

Your well–known wisdom
We wait to see a speedy
Revenge on your murderers.
Not clear, not meaningful,
I have already written a complete poem,
Only singing and weeping –
Only the pain in the heart
Remains behind for me.

[Page 373]

At the Large Mass Grave
by Efraim Zilberman
Translated by Jerrold Landau

The entire town was in flames already on the second day of the war. Jonava was fiercely bombarded by the German air force. Battles between the Soviets and the Germans also took place in the town. The first victims of the war in town were 70 Jews who were hiding in a cellar that was bombarded.

Several hundred Jews went to Russia along with the Soviet Army as it retreated from Jonava. Jonava was already occupied by the Germans on June 26, the fourth day of the war. Hundreds of Jonava Jews who were hiding in the fields and forests around the town because of the bombardment began to return. Most of them no longer found their houses, for they had been burnt down or destroyed by the bombardment. In the entire town, only the houses around the new market, a few houses on Kovner and Breizer Streets, and the entire Keidianer Street remained. Over 2,500 Jews lived in Jonava when the Germans occupied Lithuania. Two or three families had to live in a single room. The Great Synagogue, the *Beis Midrash* and the old Talmud Torah were also packed with Jews. Many Jews lived in the stables and villages around Jonava. Approximately 150 Jews lived in the nearby Jewish village "Old Gustonys" 8 kilometers from town.

The Lithuanian partisans from Jonava immediately took up their arms to terrorize the Jewish population. They would break into the Jewish houses with the pretext of searching for weapons, and they would steal all the best items. Hundreds of Jews, young and old, were taken daily by the Lithuanian partisans to various jobs, such as cleaning the grass from the streets of the town, and other difficult jobs. The partisans would beat them harshly while working. Every day, several men would not return from work. The partisans would take them behind the town and shoot them. That is what the Lithuanian bandits did to the honorable elderly teacher and social activist Shaul Keidianski and his two sons.

In the third week of the occupation, an edict came that the Jews must wear yellow patches. A few days later, the Lithuanian partisan headquarters of the town sent a summons to the Jonava rabbi, Rabbi Nachum Baruch Ginsberg, demanding that the Jews of Jonava raise a hefty sum of money and give it to them within three days. If the sum is raised, no Jews would be shot, and a ghetto would be established in town. That same day, the rabbi called a meeting with the Jonava communal activists and decided that the Jews of Jonava would be unable to raise the amount. The wealthy Jews had traveled with the Bolsheviks to Russia during the week prior to the war. The rabbi went to the partisan headquarters to beg that they reduce the contribution. In response, the Jonaver Rabbi and several other householders were arrested as hostages. If the amount would not be raised, they would be shot. The Jonaver rabbi negotiated with the chief of the partisans to be permitted to travel to the Kovno Rabbi for one day, who would help raise the sum of money. The Jonaver Rabbi was taken to Kovno, accompanied by two partisans. The Jewish activists in Kovno, headed by Rabbi Shapira, brought the Jonaver rabbi a large sum of money that very day. The rabbi returned to town under the accompaniment of the partisans and gave over the money to the partisan headquarters. The Jews of the town also collected a large sum of money, gold, and valuables, and gave them over the partisan headquarters on time. The rabbi was freed along with the other hostages, and the Jewish population believed that they had been saved.

[Page 374]

Three days later, on August 1, 1941, armed Lithuanian partisans took 500 young Jewish men, apparently for only a few days of work. They took them all via the Wilkomir Highway to the Giralka Grove one kilometer behind the town, opposite the Jewish Kemach mill, and shot them all. Now, almost only women, children, and old men remained in town. It was already clear to everyone that the contribution that they paid did not help at all. This was only a method for the Lithuanians to extort money from their Jewish neighbors. The fate of the surviving Jews already looked hopeless, until ——

A few families hid in the forests and with Christians around Jonava. News of this reached the partisan headquarters. Placards with a warning to the Christian population not to hide Jews appeared in town. The reward for turning in a hidden Jew would be the weight of the Jew in pork or sugar.

On August 13, 1941, all the remaining Jews in town together with the rabbi were taken to that same Giralka grove, where large pits were already prepared. They were all horribly shot there. Giralka grove near Jonava became the mass grave of the Jonava Jews.

As has already been stated earlier, approximately 150 Jews employed in agricultural work remained in "Old Gustonys" near Jonava. Thanks to this, those few Jews were able to temporarily prolong their lives until they would harvest the grain from the fields. When the liquidation of the Jews of the town took place, several partisans came to the Jewish village with a prepared list, and took away four men and one women, including the well–known activist Moshe Ivenski, and shot them in Giralka along with all the rest of the Jonavers on that day.

At the beginning of September 1941, all the Jews from "Old Gustonys" were brought to the large Kazarma yard in Jonava. The Jews gathered, and were to be taken to the Kovno Ghetto. With this, the Jews were hoping for a miracle. The Lithuanian partisan headquarters also posted placards announcing that the Jews in hiding could report to the large Kazarma yard, and nothing would happen to them. They would be taken with the remaining Jews to the Kovno Ghetto. Several families who had been hiding in the surrounding forests and with Christians who refused to continue to hide the Jews also gathered in Kazarma.

The Jews were held in Kazarma for three weeks under strict supervision by the partisans. The Jews already lost hope that they would be taken to Kovno. On October 3rd, the Jews were informed that everyone would be taken to Kovno very early the next morning. That same day, they took the best objects and money from everybody. The Jews did not believe at all that they would be taken to the Kovno Ghetto. They believed that they would be taken to the Giralka Grove the next day, for their "final journey" …. The last, close to 180, Jonaver Jews spent a sleepless night. At dawn on October 4th, when the armed partisans led the 180 Jews to the highway in the direction of Kovno, the Jews felt lighter, and had a bit of hope.

[Page 375]

With the ordinance to bring the Jews of Jonava to the Kovno ghetto specifically that day, October 4, the Gestapo had calculated that the "aktion of the small ghetto" would be taking place in Kovno that day, and the Jonaver Jews would be murdered in the Ninth Fort together with the Jews brought in from the "Small Ghetto."

Thanks to the fact that the journey by foot from Jonava to Kovno took more than half a day, the Jews of Jonava arrived in Kovno after the aktion of the Small Ghetto. The 180 Jews from Jonava were not taken to the Ninth Fort, but were left in the Kovno Ghetto. A large portion of the group of Jonava Jews were murdered on October 28th, 1941 during the "Large Aktion" in the Kovno Ghetto. After the Children's Aktion in the Kovno Ghetto (March 28, 1944), the Germans in the Ninth Fort collected a group of 50 men from the arrested Jewish ghetto policemen, and transported them to the Giralka Grove in Jonava, where they were ordered to bury the dead bodies of the murdered Jonava Jews. When the policemen finished their work, they were also murdered.

At the end of the summer of 1944, when Jonava was liberated by the Russians, I visited my former hometown. The entire town looked to me like a large cemetery. I regarded every Lithuanian whom I encountered as a murderer. I also went to the large mass grave in the Giralka Grove – mounds of earth overgrown with grass. Such mass graves are what remains of the renowned Lithuanian Jewry – and such a grave remains also from the old Jewish community of Jonava.

Copied over from "From the Last Destruction," Munich, December 1948, edited by Y. Kaplan.

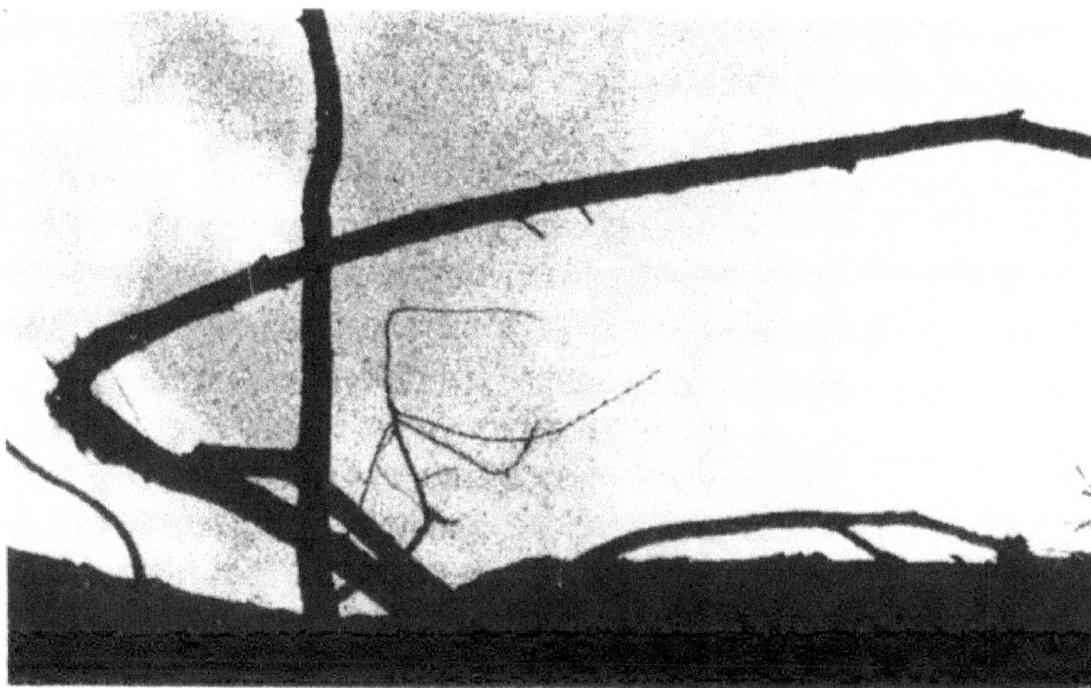

A barren tree

[Page 376]

The Beginning of the Destruction
by Reizl David (Rashkes) of the United States
Translated by Jerrold Landau

Reizl David (Rashkes)

As an eyewitness, I will attempt to describe here the beginning of the destruction of Jonava on June 23-24, 1941.

Jonava was one of the army camps of Lithuania. The camp named Poligon was located five kilometers south of the town. When the Russians conquered Lithuania in 1940, they fortified this camp further with tanks and cannons. The Poligon Camp overlooked two large bridges over the Vylia. In Poligon, the Russians demonstrated their greatest opposition to the Germans. I say "Russians" for the Lithuanians immediately turned into collaborators with the Germans.

The opposition lasted for one day and one night.

On Sunday, June 22, toward morning, the roaring of airplanes at a high altitude was heard in Kovno. The airplanes innocently looked like tiny birds, flying calmly at the beginning of a lovely summer morning.

However, suddenly, those innocent birds began to drop bombs on Kovno (at that time, I was living in Kovno). People ran outside to see what was going on, but it became known immediately that these were German airplanes. The war had also reached Lithuania.

We Escaped from Kovno

My brother who lived in Kovno, Ben-Zion Rashkes of blessed memory, immediately arrived with packed suitcases. People ran back and forth without knowing where to flee, what to do, how to save themselves – the confusion was great. We also ran, but we knew to where we were escaping: home to Jonava, in order to be together with Father, Mother and our sister; to be together with our closest, most beloved relatives, whatever may happen.

Hundreds of Jews escaped. Gentiles, of course, did not escape. We fled via the mountain road. The roads were overloaded. Nobody knew how far they would succeed in reaching during their escape. Everyone ran with great fear in their eyes and with large packages on their shoulders and in their hands. However, they were unable to drag all those bundles for a long period; and the roads were filled with abandoned suitcases, with their contents scattered. Gentile farmers stood in the fields at the side of the road and waited for these treasures, as if they fell from the sky, and grabbed them immediately. However, nobody cared about this, because we only thought that if we were to survive, we would also have belongings.

My brother saw a wagon driven by the Manoshovitzes and loaded up all our bags onto it. He also sat on the wagon, and we never saw him again.

The Russian Army was also in a state of confusion. Soldiers went by foot or traveled on tanks or vehicles without knowing where they were going. We saw them driving in opposite directions, with frightened eyes. They did not know how to answer the questions we asked them. The generals fled first and left the soldiers to their own devices.

We traveled for a full day. In the evening, we reached to a point next to the wooden bridge over the Vylia near Jonava. The bridge was already broken and bombed out, for the Germans had bombed there too. My dear father and sister Rachel were already standing there waiting for us on the banks of the river. Gentile farmers would transport people across the river in boats (of course in exchange for payment). Gentile women joined them in the boats in order to collect the belongings that the Jews had abandoned due to being unable to carry them further. On the other side of the Vylia, that is in Jonava, my dear, beloved mother was standing there waiting for us. This image is etched in my heart forever. She was happy through the tears of her eyes. Simultaneously, a great fear was expressed through her beautiful cherry-like eyes: What would be the end of her endangered chicks?

[Page 377]

Jews ran to and fro: "Tell me, Jews, to where are you escaping? Perhaps we will escape along with you!" The response was: "We also do not know. We were in the train station but the train did not arrive. Thousands of refugees were sitting there waiting for the train, including Jews from Poland who came to Lithuania in order to save themselves from the German, may his name and memory be blotted out. Then we ran to Wilkomir Road. The Germans bombed the roads. Many people were killed."

In the Snares

We remained in Jonava. After one night, the cannons began to shoot over our heads. From one side, the Germans were behind Keidiani Street, and from the other side, the Russians from Poligon. We remained in the middle, as if in a trap.

Then, the Lithuanians began to act in a wanton fashion. They gathered in the bell tower of the church and shot with machine guns at the Jews who were running to seek refuge from the cannons. The young fascist Lithuanians also shot from the progymnasium at their Jewish fellow townsfolk, with whom they had lived in harmony until this time. The good neighbors turned into great, deadly enemies within a moment.

We fled from our house the Street of the Road to the parents of my sister's husband, The Goldmans (who owned a furniture factory). They lived on the Street of the Synagogue. Why did we specifically go to them? Perhaps because their house was close to the synagogue courtyard – who knows? We hid in a pit that was quickly dug by the men in the yard of their house. My father and mother did not want to leave their house under any circumstance, for the house was filled with all types of food provisions that they had stockpiled throughout the year, since the time of the Russian regime (for the Russians would send the foodstuffs to Russia). The household economy had been firmly established for many years already, and leaving the house would leave everything ownerless – something that the gentiles were awaiting.

In the morning, as we were lying in the pit, we heard a knock on the opening to the pit. We opened the wooden door, and saw Father standing pale. It was difficult to recognize him. With a trembling voice he asked that we give him a jar of honey. When we peered out from the pit, we saw a German in green fatigues. We had taken from the house jars of honey and jam, and other foodstuffs that we would be able to live on – as Mother said when she gave them to us. She promised to bring the rest the next morning, when she and Father would come to us. They said that during the day, they would not be suspected of leaving the house. These unfortunate people were na?ve: they had faith in human beings – they might come to pillage at night, but during the day, they thought, the gentiles would be embarrassed…

We gave Father a jar of honey and asked him if the house is still whole, and why do Mother and he not join us. Father answered quickly, with a trembling voice, "Mother is making coffee for the Germans," and he quickly disappeared with the German.

Jonava in Flames

In the meantime, the bombardments increased. A shell damaged the synagogue. It seemed to us that it fell next to our pit. We peered out with our heads and saw that a large portion of the synagogue was missing. We could not continue to remain in the pit, for Jonava was already in flames by the afternoon. We already felt the heat of the fire in our pit, and the smoke penetrated inside. When we exited the pit it seemed that the Street of the Road, upon which our house stood, Kovno Street, Breizer Street, and Vilna Street were all burning. We ran to the Vylia River. At that time, the Lithuanians were shooting at us from their hiding places with machine guns. We miraculously reached the shrubs behind the bathhouse. Some gentiles also fled there with us, for the cannons did not discriminate, and they too were in danger. The gentiles were very friendly to us during those moments, but as soon as the bombardment stopped, they no longer knew us. It was already impossible to run back; therefore we dug as deeply as possible into the ground so that the bullets and shells that were literally flying over our heads would not hurt us. During the bombardment, Monas Klibensky the carpenter got up suddenly and said that he thinks that he did not lock his back door, and he started to go. His son- in-law Avraka Unterschatz dragged him back to the ground with his foot. His daughter Feiga began to weep and pleaded, "Father, where are you going? Everything is burning." However Monas apparently foresaw the Holocaust and his nerves weakened. He again got up and said that he thinks that he forgot to close the windows. He felt it necessary to go to find out. Avraka once again dragged him to the ground, covered him with his body, and did not let him get up.

{*Unnumbered page after 377*. Photo: Jonava in flames. (The houses of Granovich and Zopovich in the foreground.)}

[Page 378]

I saw the wife of Avraham the *shochet* lying there with my friend Feigcha, Berele the youngest of the children, and Hirshka. I did not see the daughters Rachel and Rivka, nor Avraham the *shochet*.

I lay down and wept, for nobody saw Father and Mother anywhere. Anyone we asked was not able to say anything, and I suspected that they all knew something but did not want to tell us. Father and Mother had remained with the Germans. Only G-d knows what they endured on that dark night. What did the Germans do to them? How can I live without Mother and without Father, heaven forbid? How is it possible?

The sight of Jonava that night was terrifying: a frightening sky, very red, and all of Jonava engulfed in flames like hell.

The shells flew over our head with greater strength. We were already able to tell if a shell was falling closer to or farther from where we were. Every time that a cannon was shot and its scream was heard above us, a gentile would be able to determine where the bullet was. (The bullets fell far away, whereas the shells rained upon us.) He would say, "A shell has fallen at a distance of ten feet, now a shell has fallen at a distance of five feet." He was right, apparently, for we did no hear him speak anymore. The cannons quieted somewhat, and at sunrise they were almost completely silent. Then, when we began to arise and get up, we saw dead bodies lying near us. We did not realize that we had been lying beside dead bodies all night.

We looked up to see whether Jonava was still burning, and we saw thick smoke bursting forth to the sky. We ran back to the house of the parents of the husband of my sister Rachel. The house was still whole, almost the only one in the entire alley. The Jewish hospital opposite the Goldman's house was burnt. The ill people were lying burnt in the iron beds.

Running About

We did not yet know what had happened to our parents. It was dangerous for women to leave the house. I sat and prayed to G-d, and the door at the side of the house opened. They entered quickly, short of breath, sweaty and panting – first Father and then Mother. The joy was great. We hugged, kissed, and all wept from joy. Once again, we were all united with an eternal connection. Mother was wearing only a dress, and Father a cloak and pants. They could not salvage any more of their property. Father told us what had happened to them. When they were left alone in the large house, they were unable to sleep at night. Father went out to the yard and dug a deep pit as a refuge from the shells. Father said that the shells were flying very low between the houses. Not a living soul was seen on our street (the Street of the Road). The appearance was terrifying, like a city of ghosts. Only shadows were seen here and there sneaking into the abandoned houses and pillaging, even in the midst of the bombardment. Therefore, Father and Mother were very afraid to remain in the house, lest the pillaging gentiles kill them. They then decided to escape to us, to the Goldmans. However, before they had time to pack various valuables, they heard knocking on the door. It was still dark. Father approached the door with trembling steps and asked who was knocking. They answered in German, "Open the door, Jew!" With great fear, father opened the door. A group of 30 German soldiers broke into the house. Apparently, these were the first soldiers -- scouts. The commander ordered Father to go through all the rooms with them, then to the cellar and the storehouses in the courtyard, and even the pit that Father had dug in the yard – all this in order to check that no Russians were hiding there. Then the commander ordered to bring water. Father brought them pails of water from the well that was in the cellar. They all washed up. As per their order, Mother brought them towels and underwear so that they can change. Then they ordered Mother to make them coffee and give them something to eat. The Germans drank from the cups from the fine dishware set that belonged to my sister. Then they put the dishes into their backpacks along with many other valuables, such as the silver candlesticks, the silver cups, silver boxes, and other such items. Then one of the Germans asked Father if he had any honey, for he loved honey. Since Father was naîve and innocent, he told the German that his daughter had taken the honey with her. That is why they came to us to get the honey. All of this took place under the rain of shells, as Jonava was already burning and almost the entire Street of the Road was in flames. The Germans did not permit my parents to escape from the fire and bullets until our house was bombed and began to burn. In the meantime, they saw other Jews, who before had apparently been hiding in the cellars. They also ran. Among them were Gitel Klotz and Zusman Klotz, our maternal cousins. Suddenly shots were fired from some place behind the fleeing Germans. The Germans captured Father, Zusman Klotz and other men whose names I do not know, and stood them against a burning wall in order to shoot them, out of suspicion that they had been shooting at the Germans. They would have been killed within another second, but suddenly two Lithuanians with guns in their hands burst forth from behind the burning wall. They were searching for a refuge from the fire. The Germans caught them and shot them, and freed the Jewish men. The Jewish men continued to escape toward us, but they could not run through the Street of the Synagogue because everything around was burning. Burning houses became shaky, and the streets were filled with ruins and fire. All of Jonava was one large ruin. They ran to a place where it was still somewhat possible to save oneself from the hell, and they came to the brick kiln. They lay down all night. In the morning, when the shelling ended, they ran to us.

[Page 379]

Dangers Lurk

Father stood on his feet and said, "We do not have time now to speak a great deal. Let us go out to see what the situation is." He told my sister Rachel and I to not dare to go outside. We accompanied him to the rabbi of the town, Rabbi Ginzburg, who was apparently leaving some hiding place. We surrounded him with questions, "Rabbi, what will be?" His fine face was pale, and his appearance had changed greatly. He spoke in choppy words, with tears choking his throat: "We have to be careful with security. G-d will help. Jews, we must be strong." He himself was wailing like a baby. Everyone was weeping. We returned home in order to hide from the dangers that began to stalk us.

After a few hours, Father returned with a darkened face. He told us, "An entire group of Jews was burned in Liber Farber's basement." Father was the first one to open the iron door of the cellar – burnt skeletons were resting on the door. The first skeleton was the largest, and they realized that it was of Meir Wunder. The door of the cellar locked itself on them, and they were unable to exit and save themselves from the fire.

"Our house," Father said, "and the streets in general are unrecognizable, for the destruction was great and went to the foundations. Here and there, smoke was coming out of the ruins." Father recognized the lot in which our house had stood from the pit that he had dug. Father noted, "A smart cat hides in a pit, but I locked our cat in the house. Perhaps it too was hiding in the pit…"

In the meantime, the Jews began to search for food, for a morsel of bread. Hunger pervaded the city. One Jewish bakery that by chance remained intact at the end of Kovno Street was taken over by gentiles who chased out the former owners and baked bread for he gentiles. Jews stood and stuck out their hands for a morsel of bread, and the gentiles chased them away, saying, "Go ask the Communists. They will give you bread." My sister risked her life and left the hiding place. A gentile acquaintance gave her a piece of bread and told her, "Hide and do not go outside. They are plotting to rape the young women of Jonava." The Jews of Jonava began to feel that danger was waiting for them not only from the Germans, but also from their Lithuanian neighbors.

There used to be a pharmacy in our house in which a gentile woman had worked as a cashier. We were good friends. Father came running to me with fear in his eyes and told me that this woman was looking for me, and of course, she was not planning to do anything good to me. She had become an important leader and immediately began to threaten the Jews of Jonava. With his clear sense, Father suspected that a great danger was awaiting me, his youngest daughter: The gentiles were wandering around looking for Jewish girls to rape. When I later was in the Kovno Ghetto, a group of Jonava woman arrived.

[Page 380]

One of them was Chanka Rabinovich who told me that the *shkotzim* forcefully put young Jewish girls into a barn and tortured hem to death.

Return to Kovno

Father immediately decided that I was to return to Kovno. "There, the gentiles do not know you," he said with a trembling voice. He was about to part from his beloved daughter for who knows how long, perhaps forever. Mother was overtaken by convulsions, and Father began to plead with Mother to calm down. "This is the only way," he claimed. As has been said, we, that is my husband and I (I got married only a few months before to Wolf David from Kretingen near Memel), parted also from my sister Rachel, from my brother-in-law Yitzchak Goldman, and from the entire Goldman family, none of whom survived. The Goldmans had five sons and a daughter Batya. The sons were Yitzchak the eldest, Mordechai, Zerach, and two twins whose names I do not recall.

Father said that we must escape back to Kovno via the old path, for he realized that a large army would be passing through the main road, and that we would be safer on the old road that begins on the descent of Kovno Road, for it is an inferior road. That is indeed the way it was, as my wise father had known. Many refugees returned to Kovno. The refugees were from all over Lithuania and also from Poland, who had come to Lithuania a year earlier when the Germans entered Poland. They wanted to reach some safe place, perhaps to Russia, but they had remained in Jonava. We, a full camp, went back to Jonava. All of the family and many other Jonavers accompanied us to the brick kiln. Father pleaded to everyone to refrain from making this public farewell procession, for this might end badly, heaven forbid. Nevertheless, everyone wanted to give us a farewell blessing. Taibl, Rachka Jalinowitz' mother, hugged me, kissed me, and wished me good fortune. I asked her, "Where is Rachka?" and she answered: "Hiding."

This was the last time that I saw my family and that I set foot on the ground of Jonava, my dear birthplace with its dear, heartwarming Jews, may their memory be a blessing, may G-d avenge their blood.

[Page 382]

The Last Day
by Yerachmiel Garber of Neve Sharet
Translated by Jerrold Landau

Yerachmiel Garber

In the morning of Monday, June 23, I went as usual to my workplace in the Oren match factory. The war had begun, but the work had to take place no matter what. In any case – where was Jonava and where was the front? We were given spades and told to dig protective ditches. Some of the diggers were immersed in thoughts, some tried to joke that there was no need for ditches. The jokers trusted that the Soviets would not let Hitler reach Jonava.

Suddenly, the noise of autos reached our ears. We put down the spades and ran to the road to snatch a glance. We saw the Red Army trucks covered in green branches, such as *Sukkot* covered with *Sechach*[1]. The faces of the soldiers were black with dust. We only saw white teeth and glittering eyes. We suddenly heard the sound of thunder, but the skies were clear without any clouds at all. It seems that this was the echo of an artillery battle. Everyone's face became serious. People were immersed in thought.

I did not return to the spade. I hastened to town to see what was going on. It was the same town, but unrecognizable. We felt hasty movement. Everyone's face was serious and perplexed, as if they were seeking a refuge from a crazy situation. Hundreds of people were running on the ascent of the road. Others turned toward the wooden fence. Refugees from Kovno turned in that direction. I turned toward the bridge with large steps. It seemed as if Jews were gathering here for Tashlich[2], however we heard no prayers, but rather conversations between Jonavers and Kovnoites who were astounded at the situation. I could not understand, what was with them? Did they take leave of their senses – to run by foot from Kovno?

Among those who were coming, I met a lad who was an acquaintance, Shliten. I had studied together with him in ORT[3]. We turned aside, and I asked,

"Oh, what is taking place here?"

"Don't ask questions," he responded, "lift up your feet and get out of here as fast as you can. The Germans are already in Kovno."

I was still rolling my eyes, but the seriousness of the situation penetrated my consciousness. I returned home. I met friends along the way, and we decided to leave Jonava for a brief time and to go to Wilkomir, with the belief that the Germans would quickly receive a deathly blow from the Soviet Army…

I ran to my friend Hershe-Yankel Stein. I heard shrieks and screams next to the house, as if during a funeral. Taibl Katzav was taking leave of her son, who was about to leave on his bicycle. This was strange in my eyes: is this how one weeps for a living person? He told me that he and his friends were setting out on their bicycle, and that they would wait for me. I ran home quickly. I met Uncle David, who had moved in with us with his family until the storm would pass. I told my parents about my plan, and they accepted it with understanding. They gave me several rubles, and I went out of the house without even taking leave. We did not grasp the seriousness of the situation, that we would never see each other again.

As we passed by the post office, we ran into young Lithuanians who were looking at us with a bitter smile and gnashing their teeth. We were on the ascent to the mountain. The entire way was strewn with people and wagons. The wagon drivers loaded their belongings and families, and fled for their lives. We passed under the railway crossing. Suddenly, airplanes appeared low above our heads. They shot at us and dropped bombs. We were lying in the ditches at the side of the road. We were not injured. We continued to move. Bad thoughts went through the head. It seemed that we were separating ourselves from Jonava. The journey was not easy, even though we were young and healthy. The repeated running back and forth to search for a hiding place in the ditches drained our strength. The enemy did not stop sending his airplanes at us, shooting at the refugees. Along the way, we lost some people and met up with others until we reached Wilkomir.

It was night. It was dark. The Germans shot shiny bullets that looked like stars from the airplanes. In Wilkomir, I met Mosheke Goldschmid of Jonava immersed in worries: There was a puncture in his tire. I helped him with the repair, and we prepared for the journey. It was only possible to move at night. The question was, in what direction. Some advised to go to Vilna, the capital of Lithuania. It would not be easily captured by the Germans. There, they would break their teeth. Others felt that we should go toward Zarasai (Ezrani) at the Latvian border. I supported this, and the group agreed.

We travelled all night. At dawn, the airplanes appeared again, and everything repeated from the day before. At times, we ran to the ditches. The breaks between the air attacks continued to shorten. We turned away from the road, went up to the side road, and lay in the grass to rest. An army truck stopped next to us. We wanted to have a conversation with them, but they did not know Russian. One person succeeded in asking what was happening in Jonava. The response was: In Jonava – the Germans.

This oppressed us, and we did not ask further.

Translator's Footnotes

A *Sukka* (plural *Sukkot*) is the tabernacle of the holiday of *Sukkot*, and *Sechach* is the foliage covering of the *Sukka*.

A ceremony that takes place near a river or body of water on Rosh Hashanah.

Organization of Rehabilitation through Training, that ran (and continues to run) various trade schools within some Jewish communities.

[Page 384]

Fortunate to Remain Alive
by Leah Drucker (Monosevich) [Tel Aviv]
Translated by Jerrold Landau

{Translator's note: This Yiddish article is equivalent with the corresponding Hebrew article on page 185. The Yiddish version has a few extra incidental details which were not included in the Hebrew. The English translation is from the Hebrew version only.}

[Page 387]

We Were Saved from the Talons of the Murderers
by Tuvia Garber [Tel Aviv] [1]
Translated by Jerrold Landau

Before the outbreak of the war, I worked in the carpentry shop of Koppel Reznik and his sons, which was nationalized as Government Carpentry Shop Number One. The director of the factory was the former worker Ankodinov.

On Sunday, the day of the outbreak of the war, all of the workers were gathered together. They gravity of the situation was described, and the workers assigned a rotation for guarding. I guarded the carpentry shop on Sunday night and Monday. At night, we heard the roar of airplanes that were flying to bombard the Polygon.

On Monday morning, when Jonava was full of refugees who fled from Kovno and other towns, the mood in the town was oppressive, and nobody thought about going to work. The refugees said that there had been many murders and attacks against Jews by the Lithuanian population in Kovno.

Our family, consisting of my father Melech Garber, my mother Yudes, my brothers Chaim and Hershel, my sisters Henia, Batya and Gittel and I, decided to escape to Russia. We spoke to our friend Shabtai Droskin, who owned a horse and wagon. We set out along with them in the direction of Wilkomir [Ukmerge]. We naively believed that we would be able to return easily from there. We did not believe that the Soviet Army would retreat so quickly. We left Jonava on Monday at 6:00 in the evening. We loaded a few belongings on the wagon, and we all walked behind it on fit. When we reached the Kemach factory, I and my cousin Zamka Droskin decided to run to the railroad station where we might catch a train going in the direction of the border. Along the way we met many people from Jonava and Kovno returning from there who told us that there is no hope at all with a train.

On Tuesday morning, June 24, we arrived in Wilkomir, tired and crushed. Along the way, we endured bombardment and shooting from airplanes. The highway had been full of retreating Russian military battalions. A terrifying panic pervaded the city. Many Jews had already fled. We traveled to the edge of the city and wanted to rest. The city was heavily bombarded that night, so we continued on but we continued in the direction of Utënai. Along the way, army battalions shot at us from the forests. Utënai was also heavily bombarded and destroyed. Most of the Jews who had decided to escape were already no longer in the city. We traveled quickly through the city and stopped to rest in the grove outside the city. After a brief rest, we traveled on and reached Airënai. The Shaulist partisans shot at us from the church in the center of the city, but they did not hit us, thank G–d. Two Russian tanks shot at the church tower and destroyed it. As we passed through villages, there were farmers who brought us food and water. Along the way, we ran into Shaulists who threatened us with arms and ordered us to return. We were frightened when they told us that the Germans had blocked our way. Many of the Jewish refugees believed them and returned along the way that they came. We were not influenced by their words. We continued to travel quickly. We caught a lost horse along the way, harnessed it to our wagon, and continued onward.

[Page 388]

We reached Dvinsk (Daugavpils) early in the morning. When the people of Dvinsk saw the masses of refugees, they also took up the wandering staff and set out along the way. We had just left the city when we saw German airplanes bombing the bridges and blocking the routes. We stopped in a village near the town of Dagda. A farmer gave us food and refused to take money. We rested there for a few days. Father approached the nearby town of Dagda to assess the situation. When my father and I arrived there, we noticed the policemen escaping from the town. We quickly returned and decided to escape to the border. Within a few days we arrived at the town of Zhivich next to the border. Thousands of refugees waited there for permission to cross. When we reached there, we received permits, and entered the Soviet Union.

We split up on the other side of the border. Our family of eight traveled by train deep into Russia. Uncle Shabtai Droskin and his family traveled on their horse wagon. We reached a kolkhoz called "The Second Five Year Plan" in the Mordovian Autonomous Republic.

I was drafted into the Lithuanian division of the army on February 7, 1942. My parents and the rest of my family remained in the kolkhoz. I fought in the army from

1942 until the end of 1943. I was badly wounded on August 10 of that year. I was evacuated to the Otkorsk area in the area of Sartov. There, they amputated my left hand. I returned to my family in the kolkhoz in November. We returned to Vilna after the war.

Uncle Shabtai Droskin and his family arrived by wagon to the Tatar Autonomous Republic, and at the end of the war they returned to Lithuania. To our good fortune, nobody in the family was killed.

I presented my papers to travel to Israel in 1969. I received my permit. I arrived in Israel with my wife and two children in 1970.

Recorded by Y. B.

Translator's Footnote

The two chapters on pages 387 and 395 have equivalent chapters in the Hebrew section. Since the Yiddish provided more detail, I have retranslated them. My suspicion is that all these duplicated articles were originally written in Yiddish, and then rendered into Hebrew in a somewhat more concise fashion.

[Page 389]

My Way of Suffering

by Leah Helerman (Kronik) [Melbourne, Australia]
Translated by Jerrold Landau
My Way of Suffering
Same as on page 186 of the original book

We Fled from the Home

by Chana–Leah Gutler (Kravchok) [Tel Aviv]
Translated by Jerrold Landau
We Fled from the Home
Same as on page 189 of the original book

[Page 395]

Thus Was I Saved

by Lipa Berzin [Tel Aviv] [1]
Translated by Jerrold Landau

Lipa Berzin

Our family lived on Breizer Street, the street of the proletariat. My father Itzik, Liba Leah's, was a water–man, who floated barges on the waters of the Šventoji, Viliya and Neiman Rivers. In the winters, when the rivers froze, he was a porter. Needless to say, our material situation was difficult, and our youth was not easy. Our family consisted of my mother Pesl of blessed memory, three brothers – me, Nachum–Izak and Melech, and our sister Miriam. Our small, wooden house was divided into two dwellings. Our family lived in one of them, which was 25 square meters. The family of my Uncle Nachum–Leizer lived in the second one. Father was a pious Jew, but not a fanatic. When he was not busy with barges, he would go to the synagogue during the week. He would always come home for Sabbaths and went to the synagogue. He had his customary seat there, and he would always take us children with him.

Mother was pious, and observed kashruth meticulously, making sure to never mix dairy and meat. On Friday night, the table was covered with a white tablecloth and brass candlesticks. Mother would put a kerchief over her head and bless the Sabbath candles.

The food was entirely different during the week, but the Sabbath meal consisted of fish, meat, soup, and tzimes. We boys studied in Yavneh and our sister studied in the Yiddish school. When I concluded my studies in school, I went to study carpentry. With this, I would be able to help my parents materially. My brother Nachum–Izak studied upholstery.

At that time, I was active in the Young Chalutz. Having studied carpentry, I moved to Kovno and worked in Stragweitze's furniture factory until 1940. I was drafted to the Lithuanian Army. There were some Jonavers together with me in the Third Unit of the Artillery Brigade in ŠanÉiai: Zerach Goldman, Leibka Lukman from across the river, Shlomo Berzin the son of Uncle Yonah, and Leizka Stoliar (Krupnik).

When the Soviets arrived in Lithuania, we were transferred to the barracks of the infantry unit in Vilna, near Stadion. Our unit was in Polygon when the war broke out. The captains fled as the front approached. A Lithuanian sergeant took is in and told us: "Whoever wishes to return home – can arise and go; whoever wishes to come with me to Russia – follow me!" We were approximately 40 men. He led us by foot through NemenÉinë to the border. On Tuesday, June 24, we met up with three trucks with the flag of our unit from our headquarters. They took us aboard the trucks and we continued to the border. We arrived in the city of Plotzk in White Russia, and later in Wielkie Luki. There we joined Russian units and entered into battle against the Germans. We fought with hand grenades, guns and Molotov cocktails. The Germans

[Page 396]

approached us with tanks. They surrounded us. We were behind and they were ahead. We unfortunately suffered great losses. We succeeded in escaping the siege in small groups. We swam across the Dvina (Daugava) River. We joined other Russian units, and in the midst of the battles we retreated to Kalinin.

We were sent to the front at Gorky Blachna when the Lithuanian Division was set up. I joined unit 224 of the Artillery Brigade. With me there was my cousin Mottel Berzin, Yudel Baten, Notka Friedman, Shimon Strum and Motka Segal. The two latter ones were killed on the front. I was wounded in the battles near Nikolsk on the Orlov– Kursk Line. I was brought to the hospital in the city of Ulan Uda, where I remained for four months. From there I returned to my unit and continued to participate in the war until its end. We were then in Libau. There, we closed in on a concentration of Germans from units that had been defeated.

Chaim Wichov was also in our unit. He filled an important role with the Soviets in Jonava. In our unit, he served as the editor of the Lithuanian newspaper "BVayevi Listak."

The command of the unit requested volunteers for a special mission. Chaim Wichov, who was not a combat soldier, was among the first to volunteer. He set out on his mission on a cold winter night in 1943, when the snow was one meter deep on the roads and in the fields. He did not return from this mission.

I was freed from the army on June 12, 1946, and I hastened to Jonava. I did not find anyone of my family. I found out that my father and brother were killed as they were floating a raft. My other brother was killed by the Lithuanian partisans. My sister Miriam and my mother were in the Kovno Ghetto. The British liberated them from the Buchenwald concentration camp. From there, they went directly to the Land of Israel, and settled in Kiryat Motzkin. My sister married Yosef Pinkus.

When they were informed about me, they began to send me requests to come and join them. I presented their papers for 12 years and did not receive an exit permit. I only succeeded in 1967, and I arrived in Israel with my wife and two daughters. We settled in Neve Sharet, and I continue my original trade as a carpenter in the local factory. My wife works and the children are studying. We have finally come to peace.

Recorded and written by Y. B.

Translator's Footnote

The two chapters on pages 387 and 395 have equivalent chapters in the Hebrew section. ...dish provided more detail, I have retranslated them. My suspicion is that all these articles were originally writte͟n , and then rendered into Hebrew in a somewhat m fashion.

[Page 397]

I Was With Them At Night
by R. Spigler (Mankovski), Melbourne
Translated by Jerrold Landau

R. Spigler

I had already been in the ghetto for six weeks. I lost my first husband on the second day of the war. On June 24, I was left with a sick mother, and old grandmother, and two dear, sweet daughters; eight–year–old Pesele, and five–year–old Esele.

I cannot describe with a pen nor in words the want and the hunger. However, Jews always had faith in the most terrible moments. Suddenly there was a cause for joy in the ghetto: they gave out potatoes for the families without husbands. It was Friday, September 26. My smart, good mother comforted me:

"Do not worry. We will cook potatoes, and the war will end."

My dear children imagined the finest fantasies about how good it will be when their mother brings the potatoes…

I went out to Linkauer Street and stood in line. The line was colossal. Thousands of unfortunate people pushed and cursed with various curse words. We had to stay there an entire day. However, I did have to stay. I collapsed from hunger, but I must bring a few potatoes for my dear ones.

Suddenly, a painful terror appeared on everyone's face. We, the unfortunate ones, saw the bloodthirsty vampires, the indescribable Lithuanian murderers, running with guns in their hands, chasing everyone away from the line, roaring like wild tigers, and issuing beatings.

I immediately ran to my children, to my little home. However, how great was my pain when they beat me and did not let me go: "Cursed ones, you will all be shot like dogs!" They prodded me into a yard. I looked through a crack and saw how they were taking people away without measure.

They stated pretext that the Jews had shot a commandant. Hours passed. They asked the unfortunate people who had a husband or a son – and they let them alone in the meantime. It was enough for those left behind to be still alive. They collected a large number of victims, and sent them to the Ninth Fort to be killed. They gave up their pure souls there.

Finally, I was in Stuthauf for a few months, and then on the death march. Everything was unbelievable and beyond comprehension. I will never forget anything that I endured. I was with them at night, and in the day, I must live for the future. Everything will have to be described in iron so people will know. Immediately after the war in 1945, I wrote two notebooks. There was someone from Israel with us in the camp, and he took them from me. I have a copy. Once, I read it to my children. More I cannot do.

You would not believe the experiences I went through. I myself cannot believe them…

[Page 398]

Songs from the Ghetto
Translated by Jerrold Landau

Many songs were composed in the ghetto. Here is a song about patronage. I know the melody.

Given over by Ella Dolsachki–Abramovich

(1)

At the Inspector Columns entered the ghetto at night
Of tired, languishing Jews.
Mottel, and Yudel are running quickly
To show the inspector their pants, their shoes.
Give me a furlough, give me one quick
Look at my pants, and see my shoes.

Chorus

It is not your fortune to be free,
To the group of quilters you must go.
No furlough. Do not talk about one.
The full quota must be met tomorrow.

(2)

At the same inspector stands a woman
She requests a furlough, the heart gives out.
Therefore, however, the inspector does not let her free.
She also attempts to shed a tear.

Give me a furlough, I am so tired.
Have pity, you are a Jew.

Chorus

It is not your fortune…

[Page 399]
(3)

At the Doctor

Dvorale runs to the doctor
Her nose is well bound with a kerchief.
Dear Herr Doctor, give me a furlough for a day
The white cap will take a beating
I have sat to rest on the grass
He came and he beat my nose.

Chorus

It is not your fortune…
White cap – a German
Who beats strongly.

Comes a Madame to the same Herr Doctor
She is not certain of the reason for the Flug–Platz [1]
Her eyes glisten, her lips like blood
She turns to Herr Doctor, and asks in Russian:
"Kvaas Ya Yavilas Sievodnia Opiat,
Deitia Manie Orloig Na Dnei Dvadtzet Piet." [2]

Chorus

Yes, you have luck, you are free.
You have received a furlough for this
With such eyes, lips and teeth.
You certainly cannot go to the Flug–Platz.

Translator's Footnotes

An aircraft workshop.

Evidently a request for a furlough.

[Page 400]

With the People of Jonava on the Front and in the Hospital
by Dovid Friedman of Vilna
Translated by Jerrold Landau
With the People of Jonava on the Front and in the Hospital
Same as on page 186 of the original book

[Page 402]

My Activities in the Kovno Ghetto
by Tzvi Levin of Frunze, Russia
Translated by Jerrold Landau

During the years of the German occupation, 1941-1944
(A brief account.)

Hirsch Levin, one of the important organizers of the Jewish resistance movement of the Kovno Ghetto.

In December, 1941, with my initiative, I organized a clandestine meeting in the ghetto with the representative of the Communist underground (Galperin). At this meeting, the foundations for the united underground of the Kovno Ghetto were laid. Its members were Zionists and Communists.

Between 1942 and 1944, I was a member of the leadership of the underground organization. I carried out the following actions:

Through my initiative, at the beginning of 1942, a radio receiver that operated only through earphones was set up in the cellar of the ghetto pharmacy. News from the fronts was received through this radio throughout the duration of the ghetto period. The transmissions were recorded, transcribed, and distributed among the members of the underground and the ghetto population.

My father Chaim of blessed memory played an active role in the distribution of the news. He was burned in a bunker at the time of the liquidation of the ghetto.

I played an active role in the drafting of the Zionist youth, with the aim of transferring them to partisan camps in the forests.

I conducted a campaign to raise funds and obtain valuables inside the ghetto and outside of it, with the goal of purchasing weapons.

I played an active role in obtaining weapons from outside the ghetto, and I often personally smuggled weapons into the ghetto.

Through my initiative, Segalson, the director of the large workshops in the ghetto, organized a group of trustworthy individuals to transfer army coats, boots, underwear and other items of army clothing to the Jewish partisans. These items were stolen from the workshops where they were being prepared for the Wehrmacht.

I was the communications man between the leadership of the underground organization and the directors of the ghetto, who secretly helped the partisan movement in the ghetto a great deal.

I remained in constant contact with the "Matzok" (Merkaz Tzioni Vilijampolė, Kaunas - Zionist Center of Vilijampolė, Kaunas), and helped transfer young people of that organization to the partisan camps.

I provided revolvers to some members of the group of Jewish partisans who escaped from Fort Nine on December 25, 1943, and hid in the ghetto. Similarly, I hid in the ground a metal chest filled with gold teeth that had been extracted from murdered Jews, and that the partisans had taken with them during their escape. After the liberation of Kovno, the chest with the gold teeth was given over to Kotargna the dentist, who was then at the helm of the committee for assisting the surviving Jews.

[Page 403]

Through the means of the directors, I placed trustworthy Jews of our people in important tasks in the guarding of the ghetto. These people would carry out the directives of the united underground movement and Matzok, and thwarted the commands of the Germans.

One of these people was Yudel Zopovich from Jonava, who along with the Zionists Moshe Levin and Ika Grinberg of the ghetto guards helped the Jewish partisans leave the ghetto and smuggle weapons outside. Yudel Zopovich was tortured and shot to death at Fort Nine along with a group of Jewish guards, by Keitel, the infamous murderer of Jews. Witnesses related that Yudel Zopovich took a brave stand until his bitter end, and encouraged those who shared his fate.

At the end of March, 1944, after provocateurs informed the Gestapo about the roles that I played in the ghetto, Gestapo men, headed by Keitel, appeared at the ghetto council and demanded that they reveal my place and turn me over to their hands.

With the assistance of the underground organization, I escaped from the ghetto and hid in secret places and underground hideouts.

As I was told by those who had been among the directors of the ghetto, Keitel searched for me until the last day, and nicknamed me "Levin the leader of the gangs."

January 24, 1971

Translator's Footnotes

Hirsch is the Yiddish form of the Hebrew name Tzvi.

[Page 404]

Illegal Mail in the Kovno Ghetto
by Efraim Zilberman
Translated by Jerrold Landau
Illegal Mail in the Kovno Ghetto
Same as on page 252 of the original book

[Page 408]

Two Good Friends
by Yitzchak [Ben–David (Burstein)]
Translated by Jerrold Landau

In memory of Greenblatt and Shalputer, with whom I worked in the Kemach factory from 1925 until 1940, and who both lived there.

I met Greenblatt in 1957 in Vilna, when I visited there from the city of Frunze [1]. He worked as a mechanic in a large milk facility. This is what he told me about the last days in Jonava.

Already on Sunday, June 22, 1942, Yona Shalputer decided to leave Jonava to rejoin his parents who lived in the small town of Wysaky–Dwor [Aukštdvaris]. He talked with a Russian farmer from the village of Sponėnai, asking him to take him there with a carriage. As we later found out, the farmer attacked him along the way, took him to a large forest "Di Budes," murdered him in cold blood, and stole his bit of money and belongings.

Greenblatt decided to hide with a farmer he knew well, Peterosevich, apparently his friend from the other side of the Viliya near the village of Skaruliai. When he got there, he told him his wish. Peterosevich said nothing about hiding him. He only hinted that he should not be afraid of death in the village to which he is going. He hinted that the shooting lasts only for a minute. Hearing the "intelligent" speech of his friend the farmer, he decided to leave at once.

He set out along the banks of the Viliya in the direction of Vilna. The march lasted for three days. He hid in the thick willows on the banks of the river. He travelled at night. The hunger afflicted him. During the day, he would go out when he saw people and ask them for food.

Twice, he encountered people who apparently wanted to help him and went to bring him products. When they delayed, he was suspicious of them, and he quickly fled. One elderly woman along the way helped him and brought him a basket full of various products. This allowed him to sustain himself along the way.

On the third day in the evening, he came to a water mill on the Viliya about 20 kilometers from Vilna. After dark, when he noticed that the owner was in the mill alone, he emerged from hiding, summoned his courage, and approached the miller. He was a 60–year–old Pole who made a good impression by his outward appearance. He told him the truth, that he was a Jew from Jonava, and was a miller by trade. He asked him to hide him from the Germans, and he would work for him for free, with only the expectation of food. The miller decided that he would only work during the night shift, for many farmers from the area come during the day, and many eyes could cause harm. He looked like an Arian. At that time, he was blond, with blue eyes. However, they decided not to risk him working during the day.

[Page 409]

He hid with that Pole for over three years. He worked in the mill at night, and slept during the day. Together with the Pole, they dug a pit as a bunker deep in the ground under the canal that transported the water to the large wheel. There, in the dark, damp pit, he slept and sat until the night came, and he could breathe fresh air during the night shift. He said that large cats lived with him. They slept near him and kept him warm.

The Pole had three sons, all of whom were in the forests as partisans fighting for Poland. The father did not tell them the truth, for he did not trust them. A few times, the German S.S. men came at night to search for partisans, and he had to hide.

When the Russians arrived, the miller set out into the city. His conditions were not unbearable, but he ended his period of living with that Pole. Greenblatt died in 1966 in Vilna of natural causes, and at a good age.

Yona Shaputer and Greenblatt were both the embodiment of decency and cooperation. They were dedicated members of the Young Zion movement. They had national sensibilities, and were given over to the Land of Israel and the Jewish people.

May their memories be a blessing!

The Young Zion movement in Jonava, at the conclusion of its fifth year of
existence, Passover 5686 – 1926.

A share of the Jewish Colonial Trust from 1901 in the name of Batia Tartak
(Perlstein). See page 90.}

Translator's Footnote

Frunze was the name of Bishkek, capital of Kyrgyzstan, between 1926 and 1991.

[Page 411]

List of Those Killed
Translated by Jerrold Landau
May the memory of the martyrs of Jonava be perpetuated forever on these pages.

[Page 412]

A memorial plaque

In eternal memory

For the martyrs of the community of Jonava (near Kovno, Lithuania),

may G-d avenge their blood

Who were murdered and perished at the hands of the Germans

And the Lithuanians, may their names be blotted out

In the year 5701, 1941

The memorial day

Their holy memory will not depart from the midst of us forever

May their souls be bound in the bonds of eternal life

The natives and survivors of the community of Jonava in Israel and the Diaspora

[Page 413]

{Translator's note: the list of names start here. I am rendering it here in a table (the table form is not used in the book), so as to facilitate its entry into an Excel spreadsheet for the JewishGen necrology project. In the comments, I will mention the start of a new page in the Yizkor book. If the unnamed children are broken down as males or females, or include an unnamed wife as well, I added comments in the Comments field in addition to the number in the Unnamed Children column. If there is no additional information, they are just recorded in the Unnamed Children column. In some cases, there are both named and unnamed children. In those cases, the unnamed children are recorded in the Unnamed Children column, and the named children are recorded in their own rows. In some cases, there was some confusion as to whether the first names Abba or Ema refer to real first names, or to 'father' and 'mother'. In cases where I believe that such confusion exists, I made a note in the Comments field.}

	Surname	First name	Family Relationship		Comments
1	ABRAMOVICH	Avraham Yitzchak			
1	ABRAMOVICH	Rivka	Avraham Yitzchak's wife		
1	ABRAMOVICH	Zelig	Son of Avraham Yitzchak and Rivka	3	Wife and 3 unnamed children
1	ABRAMOVICH	Wolf	Son of Avraham Yitzchak and Rivka		
1	ABRAMOVICH	Sara	Daughter of Avraham Yitzchak and Rivka		
1	ABRAMOVICH	Yankel	Son of Avraham Yitzchak and Rivka		
1	ABRAMOVICH	Malka	Yankel's wife		
1	ABRAMOVICH	Chaya	Daughter of Yankel and Malka		
1	ABRAMOVICH	Dina	Daughter of Yankel and Malka		
1	ABRAMOVICH	Nachum	Son of Yankel and Malka		
2	ABRAMSON	Chaim		2	Unclear if the unnamed children are of Chaim and Shifra, or of Leah
2	ABRAMSON	Shifra	Chaim's wife		
2	ABRAMSON	Efraim	Son of Chaim and Shifra		
2	ABRAMSON	Rivka	Wife of Efraim		
2	ABRAMSON	Moshe	Son of Efraim and Rivka		
2	ABRAMSON	Pnina	Daughter of Efraim and Rivka		
2	ABRAMSON	Yosef	Son of Chaim and Shifra		
2	ABRAMSON	Sheina	Yosef's wife		Nee ENTES
2	ABRAMSON	Leah	Daughter of Chaim and Shifra		
3		Avraham			The Zeeika

					(Footnote in text here: We apologize that we were not able to determine the full names of a few of the victims, and are forced to identify them by their nicknames.)
4	ADLER	Meir		2	
4	ADLER	Musia	Meir's wife		
5	UNTERSHATZ	Rachel			
5	UNTERSHATZ	Moshe	Son of Rachel		
5	UNTERSHATZ	Aner			
5	UNTERSHATZ	Tzipora	Aner's wife		Nee KULBIANSKY
5	UNTERSHATZ	Shmuel	Son of Aner and Tzipora		
5	UNTERSHATZ	Tzvi	Son of Aner and Tzipora		
5	UNTERSHATZ	Ben-Zion	Son of Aner and Tzipora		
6	OPNITZKY	Leib			
6	OPNITZKY	Sheina	Leib's wife		
6	OPNITZKY	Abba	Son of Leib and Sheina	2	Includes wife and 2 children
6	OPNITZKY	Ezriel	Son of Leib and Sheina		
6	OPNITZKY	Pesia	Ezriel's wife	2	Nee DEMBO
6	OPNITZKY	Eliahu	Son of Leib and Sheina		
6	OPNITZKY	Eiba	Eliahu's son		
6	OPNITZKY	Urik	Eliahu's son		
7	OPNITZKY	Tzvi			
7	OPNITZKY	Malka	Tzvi's wife	2	Nee SOLSKY
8	OPNIK	Mordechai			
8	OPNIK	Fruma	Mordechai's wife		
8	OPNIK	Yaakov	Son of Mordechai and Fruma		

8	OPNIK	Reizl	Fruma's wife	3	
8	OPNIK	Ben-Zion	Son of Mordechai and Fruma		
8	OPNIK	Chaya	Ben-Zion's wife		
8	OPNIK	Avraham Yitzchak	Son of Mordechai and Fruma		And his wife
8	OPNIK	Yosef	Son of Avraham Yitzchak		
9	IVENSKY	Moshe			
9	IVENSKY	Mina	Moshe's wife		
9	IVENSKY	Nechama	Daughter of Moshe and Mina		
9	IVENSKY	Reuven	Son of Moshe and Mina		
10	IZRAELSON	Baruch			
10	IZRAELSON	Chana	Daughter of Baruch		
10	IZRAELSON	Esther	Daughter of Baruch		
11	ITZIKOVICH	Mordechai			
11	ITZIKOVICH	Leah	Mordechai's wife	2	
12	INTRILIGITER	Chaya			
12	INTRILIGITER	Yosef	Chaya's husband	2	
13	ITZIKOVICH	Asher			
13	ITZIKOVICH	Menucha	Asher's wife	2	
14	ITZIKOVICH	Gershon			
14	ITZIKOVICH	Alter	Gershon's son		
14	ITZIKOVICH	Yosef	Gershon's son		
14	ITZIKOVICH	Seril	Gershon's daughter		
15	AIKER	Yudel			And his wife
15	AIKER	Sara	Yudel's daughter		
15	AIKER	Yosef Moshe			
15	AIKER	Chana Etel	Yosef Moshe's wife		
15	AIKER	Chava	Daughter of Yosef Moshe and Chana Etel		
16		Alter			The pot maker.

					Includes his wife.
16		Chana	Alter the pot maker's daughter	3	Includes her husband (unnamed), and 3 unnamed children.
17	ARONSON	Elimelech			
17	ARONSON	Rachel	Elimelech's wife		
17	ARONSON	Reuven	Son of Elimelech and Rachel		
18		Archik			The Linik and his wife
19	BOZ	Yisrael			
19	BOZ	Serel	Yisrael's wife		
19	BOZ	Lipsha	Daughter of Yisrael and Serel		
19	BOZ	Miriam	Daughter of Yisrael and Serel		
19	BOZ	Golda	Daughter of Yisrael and Serel		
19	BOZ	Yudit	Daughter of Yisrael and Serel		
19	BOZ	Etel	Daughter of Yisrael and Serel		
20	BOILSKY	Hershel			
20	BOILSKY	Breina	Hershel's wife	2	Nee REIBSTEIN
21		Bomash			The doctor and his wife
22	BURSTEIN	David			
23	BATEN	Itzik		2	His wife and 2 unnamed sons
23	BATEN	Bayla	Itzik's daughter		{top of page 414}
24	BATEN	Zusia			
24	BATEN	Sheva	Zusia's wife		
24	BATEN	Alter	Son of Zusia and Sheva		
24	BATEN	Avraham	Son of Zusia and Sheva		

25	BATEN	Yudel			
25	BATEN	Yentl	Yudel's wife	3	
25	BATEN	Yitzchak	Probably Yudel's father (although might be Yentl's father)		Is called "grandfather Yitzchak"
25	BATEN	Liba	Yitzchak's wife		
26	BLUMBERG	Moshe			
26	BLUMBERG	Chaya	Moshe's wife		
26	BLUMBERG	Yerachmiel	Probably Moshe and Chaya's son		
26	BLUMBERG	Henna	Probably Yerachmiel's wife		
26	BLUMBERG	Zavele	Probably Yerachmiel and Chaya's son		
26	BLUMBERG	Shlomole	Probably Yerachmiel and Chaya's son		
27	BEILIN	Yirmiyahu			
27	BEILIN	Tova	Yirmiyahu's wife		
27	BEILIN	Moshe	Son of Yirmiyahu and Tova		
28	BARON	Eliezer			
28	BARON	Rachel	Eliezer's wife		Nee ALTA
28	BARON	Shalom			Probably a child of Eliezer and Rachel
28	BARON	Pesach			Probably a child of Eliezer and Rachel
28	BARON	Chaim			Either a child or a grandchild of Eliezer and Rachel
28	BARON	Moshe			Either a child or a grandchild of Eliezer and Rachel
29	BARON	Chaim Notl			
29	BARON	Shmuel			
29	BARON	Raya			

29	BARON	Elka			
29	BARON	Nachum			
29	BARON	Reizl			
29	BARON	Moshe			
29	BARON	Reizl			
29	BARON	Yonah			
29	BARON	Shmuel			
29	BARON	Chaya			
30	BARON	Hirshka			
31	BARON	Chaya			
32	BARON	Puah			
32	BARON	Betzalel	Puah's husband		Last name may be different
33	BARON	Sara			
33	BARON	Moshe	Sara's husband		Last name may be different
34	BARON	Michael			
34	BARON	Nesa	Michael's wife		
34	BARON	Aida	Daughter of Michael and Nesa		
35	BARON	Moshe			
35	BARON	Tzvia	Moshe's wife		
35	BARON	Taibl	Daughter of Moshe and Tzvia		
35	BARON	Sara	Daughter of Moshe and Tzvia		
35	BARON	Yaakov	Son of Moshe and Tzvia		
35	BARON	Reizl	Daughter of Moshe and Tzvia		
36	BRONZNIK	Moshe			
36	BRONZNIK	Yonah			
36	BRONZNIK	Shoshana			
36	BRONZNIK	Yetta			
37	BERZIN	Yonah			
37	BERZIN	Rachel	Yonah's wife		

37	BERZIN	Dvorah	Daughter of Yonah and Rachel		
37	BERZIN	Rivka	Daughter of Yonah and Rachel		
37	BERZIN	Yankel	Son of Yonah and Rachel		
38	BERZIN	Yitzchak			
38	BERZIN	Nachum Izak	Yitzchak's son		
38	BERZIN	Melech	Yitzchak's son		
39	BERZIN	Nachum Leizer			
39	BERZIN	Zlata	Nachum Leizer's wife	1	An unnamed son
39	BERZIN	Miriam	Daughter of Nachum Leizer and Zlata		
39	BERZIN	Aharon	Son of Nachum Leizer and Zlata		
39	BERZIN	Vloka	Son of Nachum Leizer and Zlata		
39	BERZIN	Lipka	Son of Nachum Leizer and Zlata		
39	BERZIN	Chaya	Aharon's wife	3	
40	BERZIN	Shmuel Yankel			
40	BERZIN	Tzila	Shmuel Yankel's wife	2	
40	BERZIN	Yosef	Son of Shmuel Yankel and Tzila		
41	BRAZNIKOV	Yaakov			
41	BRAZNIKOV	Chaya	Yaakov's wife		Nee BERZIN
41	BRAZNIKOV	Zalman	Son of Yaakov and Chaya		
41	BRAZNIKOV	Aidel	Daughter of Yaakov and Chaya		
42	GUTLER	Shevach			
42	GUTLER	Ethel	Shevach's wife		
42	GUTLER	Notel	Son of Shevach and Ethel		
43	GOLD	Berl			

43	GOLD	Chaya	Berl's wife		
43	GOLD	Sara	Daughter of Berl and Chaya		
43	GOLD	David	Son of Berl and Chaya		
44	GOLDMAN	Abba			
44	GOLDMAN	Yudit	Abba's wife	2	An unnamed son and daughter
45	GOLDMAN	Esther			Neta's sister
45	GOLDMAN	Leizer	Esther's husband	4	Surname may be different
46	GOLDMAN	Gittel			
46	GOLDMAN	Bayla	Gittel's daughter		
47	GOLDMAN	Hirsh			
47	GOLDMAN	Henna	Hirsh's wife	4	
48	GOLDMAN	Yitzchak			
48	GOLDMAN	Rachel			Nee RASHKES
49	GOLDMAN	Yisrael			
49	GOLDMAN	Lyuba	Yisrael's wife	3	
50	GOLDMAN	Moshe			{top of page 415}
50	GOLDMAN	Yache	Moshe's wife	2	
51	GOLDMAN	Notel			
51	GOLDMAN	Breina	Notel's wife		
51	GOLDMAN	Abake	Son of Notel and Breina		
51	GOLDMAN	Rivka	Daughter of Notel and Breina		
52	GOLDSTEIN	Yisrael			
52	GOLDSTEIN	Alta	Yisrael's wife	4	Nee KAGAN, 3 unnamed sons and 1 daughter
53	GOLDSHMID	Chaim			
53	GOLDSHMID	Gittel	Chaim's wife		
53	GOLDSHMID	Devorah	Daughter of Chaim and Gittel		
54	GOLDSHMID	Chaim Shimon			
54	GOLDSHMID	Sara	Chaim Shimon's wife		

54	GOLDSHMID	Malka	Daughter of Chaim Shimon and Sara		And her husband Berl
54	GOLDSHMID	Tzipora	Daughter of Chaim Shimon and Sara		
55	GOLDSHMID	Tzvi			
55	GOLDSHMID	Yitzchak	Tzvi's brother		
55	GOLDCHMID	Bela	Tzvi's sister		
55	GOLDSHMID	Ita	Tzvi's sister		
56	GOLDSHMID	Meir			
56	GOLDSHMID	Liba	Meir's daughter		
56	GOLDSHMID	Tzarka	Meir's daughter		
56	GOLDSHMID	Eliezer	Meir's son		
56	GOLDSHMID	Bayla	Eliezer's wife		Pharmacist
56	GOLDSHMID	Chana	Meir's daughter		
57	GURVICH	Mottel			
57	GURVICH	Pesia	Mottel's wife		
57	GURVICH	Yitzchak	Son of Mottel and Pesia		
57	GURVICH	Pinchas	Son of Mottel and Pesia		
57	GURVICH	Beni	Son of Mottel and Pesia		
58	GORDON	Leib			
58	GORDON	Leiba	Leib's wife		
58	GORDON	Yosef	Son of Leib and Leiba		
58	GORDON	Sheina	Daughter of Leib and Leiba		
59	GORFEIN	Menachem Mendel			
59	GORFEIN	Asher	Son of Menachem Mendel		
60	GINZBURG	David			And his two sisters
60	GINZBURG	Malka	David's wife		
61	GIS	Michael			
61	GIS	Batya			
61	GIS	Avraham			
62	GELBROIT				
62	GELBROIT	Chana	Mr. Gelbroit's wife		
62	GELBROIT	Shimon	Mr. Gelbroit and Chana's		

			son		
62	GELBROIT	Yosef	Mr. Gelbroit's and Chana's son		
63	GLAZ	Mordechai			
63	GLAZ	Feiga	Mordechai's wife	2	
64	GLAZ	Moshe			The violinist and his parents
65	GLAZ	Shimshon			
66	GLAZER				The midwife
67	GLAZER	Minda			Aunt Gittel
67	GLAZER	Chana Pesl	Minda's daughter		
68	GALINSKY				
69	GELFER	Zelig			
69	GELFER	Liba	Zelig's wife	3	Nee DASNIK
70	GANIS	Binyamin			
70	GANIS	Miriam	Binyamin's wife		
70	GANIS	Fruma	Daughter of Binyamin and Miriam		And her grandparents
71	GARBER	Yitzchak Aharon			
71	GARBER	Michla	Yitzchak Aharon's wife		
71	GARBER	Yacha	Daughter of Yitzchak Aharon and Michla		
71	GARBER	David	Son of Yitzchak Aharon and Michla		
71	GARBER	Sara	David's wife		
71	GARBER	Yosef	Son of Yitzchak Aharon and Michla		
72	GRODSKI	Chana			
72	GRODSKI	Sheina			
72	GRODSKI	Mina			
72	GRODSKI	Chaim			
72	GRODSKI	Pesach			

72	GRODSKI	Yosef			
73	GRUN	Sara			
73	GRUN	Matla			
73	GRUN	Chaim			
74	GROSSMAN	Pinchas			
74	GROSSMAN	Chaya	Pinchas' wife		
74	GROSSMAN	Eliezer	Son of Pinchas and Chaya		
75	GERTNER	Chuna			
75	GERTNER	Ruchama	Chuna's wife		Nee KRONIK
75	GERTNER	Lola	Daughter of Chuna and Ruchama		
75	GERTNER	Efraim	Son of Chuna and Ruchama		
76	GREENBLATT	Leib			
76	GREENBLATT	Eidel	Leib's wife		
76	GREENBLATT	Gedalya	Son of Leib and Eidel		
77	GREENBERG	Elimelech		2	And his wife
77	GREENBERG	Eidel	Elimelech's daughter		
77	GREENBERG	Kalman	Elimelech's son		
77	GREENBERG	Riva	Elimelech's daughter		
78	DABOL	Alter			
78	DABOL	Itta	Alter's wife		
78	DABOL	Chana	Daughter of Alter and Itta		
78	DABOL	David	Son of Alter and Itta		
79	DOBIANSKY	Eliahu			
79	DOBIANSKY	Vichna	Eliahu's wife		
79	DOBIANSKY	Nathan	Son of Eliahu and Vichna		
79	DOBIANSKY	Vluka	Son of Eliahu and Vichna		
79	DOBIANSKY	Berl	Son of Eliahu and Vichna		{top of page 416}
79	DOBIANSKY	Yaakov	Son of Eliahu and Vichna		
79	DOBIANSKY	Doba	Daughter of Eliahu and Vichna		
80	DOBIANSKY	Chaim			
80	DOBIANSKY	Eidel	Chaim's wife		
80	DOBIANSKY	Mendel	Son of Chaim and Eidel		
80	DOBIANSKY	Hinda	Mendel's wife	2	Nee PERLSTEIN

80	DOBIANSKY	Yerachmi el	Son of Chaim and Eidel		
80	DOBIANSKY	Miriam	Yerachmiel's wife		Nee SHEGANSKY
80	DOBIANSKY	Shmuel	Son of Chaim and Eidel		
80	DOBIANSKY	Rivka	Shmuel's wife		Nee ATKETZ
81	DODAK				And his wife
81	DODAK	Rachel Leah	Daughter of Mr. and Mrs. Dodak		
81	DODAK	Yosef	Son of Mr. and Mrs. Dodak	2	Wife and 2 unnamed children
82	DAVIDOVICH	Hirsh			
82	DAVIDOVICH	Dosya			
82	DAVIDOVICH	Yisrael			
82	DAVIDOVICH	Rachel			
82	DAVIDOVICH	Michka			
83	DAVIDOVICH	Chuna Itzik			
83	DAVIDOVICH	Leah	Chuna Itzik's wife		
83	DAVIDOVICH	Rivka	Daughter of Chuna Itzik and Leah		
83	DAVIDOVICH	Vichna	Daughter of Chuna Itzik and Leah		
83	DAVIDOVICH	Chana	Daughter of Chuna Itzik and Leah		
83	DAVIDOVICH	Shlomo Yaakov	Son of Chuna Itzik and Leah		
83	DAVIDOVICH	Yosef	Son of Chuna Itzik and Leah		
84	DAVIDOVICH	Yechiel			
84	DAVIDOVICH	Leah	Yechiel's wife		
84	DAVIDOVICH	Moshe Tzvi	Son of Yechiel and Leah		
85	DEZENT	Avraham			
85	DEZENT	Feiga	Avraham's wife		

86	DEZENT	Mendel			
87	DEITZ	Menachem Mendel			
87	DEITZ	Tzeitl	Menachem Mendel's wife		
87	DEITZ	Yosef Chaim	Son of Menachem Mendel and Tzeitl		
87	DEITZ	Moshe	Son of Menachem Mendel and Tzeitl		
87	DEITZ	Yaakov	Son of Menachem Mendel and Tzeitl		
87	DEITZ	Yitzchak	Son of Menachem Mendel and Tzeitl		
87	DEITZ	Fruma	Daughter of Menachem Mendel and Tzeitl		
87	DEITZ	Perl	Daughter of Menachem Mendel and Tzeitl		
87	DEITZ	Taiba	Daughter of Menachem Mendel and Tzeitl		
87	DEITZ	Sara	Daughter of Menachem Mendel and Tzeitl		
88	DEMBO	Yitzchak			
88	DEMBO	Rivka	Yitzchak's wife		
88	DEMBO	Moshe	Son of Yitzchak and Rivka		
88	DEMBO	Yaakov	Son of Yitzchak and Rivka		
89	DASNIK	Rivl		2	Wife and 2 unnamed children
89	DASNIK	Elimelech	Rivl's son		
90	DROSKIN	Efraim			
90	DROSKIN	Batya	Efraim's wife		
90	DROSKIN	Yosef	Son of Efraim and Batya		
90	DROSKIN	Elka	Daughter of Efraim and Batya		
90	DROSKIN	Rachel	Daughter of Efraim and Batya		
91	DROSKIN	Reuvel			

91	DROSKIN	Batya	Reuvel's wife		
91	DROSKIN	Yitzchak	Son of Reuvel and Batya		
92	HONIGMAN	Efraim			And his wife
92	HONIGMAN	Henna	Efraim's daughter		
93	HEIMAN	Shaya Leib			
94		Hirshka			The Yellow
94		Feiga	Hirshka the Yellow's daughter		
95	HENDLER	Bentza			And his wife
96		Hertz			The carpenter
96		Alta	Wife of Hertz the carpenter		
96		Pesia	Daughter of Hertz and Alta		
97	WOLK	Avraham Yitzchak			
97	WOLK	Batya	Avraham Yitzchak's wife		
97	WOLK	Rivka	Daughter of Avraham Yitzchak and Batya		
97	WOLK	Moshe	Son of Avraham Yitzchak and Yaakov		
97	WOLK	Yaakov	Son of Avraham Yitzchak and Yaakov		
98	VIDZKY	Mottel			
98	VIDZKY	Ethel	Mottel's wife		
98	VIDZKY	Reuven	Son of Mottel and Ethel		
98	VIDZKY	Shlomo	Son of Mottel and Ethel		
99	WEILER	Alter			
100	WEINER	Menashe			
100	WEINER	Genia	Menashe's wife		
100	WEINER	Tzipa Leah	Menashe's sister	2	
100	WEINER	Yudit	Menashe's sister		And her husband Mr. Shakhnovich
101	WILK	Pesach			
101	WILK	Sara Leah	Pesach's wife	1	Unnamed

					daughter
101	WILK	Menachem	Son of Sara Leah and Pesach		
102	VILKOMIRSKY	Mira			
102	VILKOMIRSKY	Lula	Mira's daughter		
103	VINITZKY	Chana			
104	WUNDER	Yisrael			
104	WUNDER	Shmuel	Yisrael's son		
105	WUNDER	Meir			
105	WUNDER	Freda	Meir's wife		
105	WUNDER	Chaya	Daughter of Meir and Freda		
106		Veps		1	The miller, his wife and a child
107	WOLFE	Avraham Yitzchak			
107	WOLFE	Rivka	Avraham Yitzchak's wife		
107	WOLFE	Elka	Daughter of Avraham Yitzchak and Rivka		
108	VALCHOKOVSKY	Nathan			
108	VALCHOKOVSKY	Sheina	Nathan's wife		
109	JOCHOVSKY	Bayla			{top of page 417}
109	JOCHOVSKY	Sheina			
109	JOCHOVSKY	Itta			
110	JOCHOVSKY	Meir			
110	JOCHOVSKY	Chaya	Meir's wife		Nee PERLSTEIN
110	JOCHOVSKY	Rachel Esther	Daughter of Meir and Chaya		
110	JOCHOVSKY	Nachum	Son of Meir and Chaya		
111	JOCHOVSKY	Alter			
111	JOCHOVSKY	Chaya Sara	Alter's wife		
112	ZOPOVICH	Meir			And his mother
112	ZOPOVICH	Yudel	Meir's brother		
113	SILBER	Alter		3	Wife and 3 unnamed children

114	SILBER	Pesach			And his wife
114	SILBER	Moshe	Pesach's son		
114	SILBER	Tzvi	Pesach's son		
114	SILBER	Sara	Pesach's daughter		
114	ZLONKER	Sheina			
114	ZLONKER	Yitzchak	Sheina's son		
114	ZLONKER	Tzvika	Yitzchak's wife		Nee BERZIN
114	ZLONKER	Chaya	Sheina's daughter		
114	ZLONKER	Chana	Sheina's daughter		
115	ZELMANOVICH	Chaim			(Kfiner) and his wife
115	ZELMANOVICH	Yosef	Chaim's son		
116	ZELMANOVICH	Chaim Nachum			
116	ZELMANOVICH	Leah	Chaim Nachum's wife		
116	ZELMANOVICH	Yitzchak	Son of Chaim Nachum and Leah		
116	ZELMANOVICH	Reuven	Son of Chaim Nachum and Leah		
116	ZELMANOVICH	Zamka	Son of Chain Nachum and Leah		
117	ZELMANOVICH	Yekutiel		3	And his wife, 2 unnamed sons and a daughter
118	ZELMANOVICH	Reuven			
118	ZELMANOVICH	Ethel		2	Nee BATEN
119	ZANDMAN	Batya			
119	ZANDMAN	Feiga			
120	ZAK	Moshe			
120	ZAK	Feiga	Moshe's wife		
120	URLOVICH	Mina	Daughter of Moshe and Feiga Zak		And her husband Mr. Urlovich
120	URLOVICH	Rivka	Mina's daughter		
121	ZAKS	Leib			
121	ZAKS	Chasia	Leib's wife		

122	KHAVELS	Wolf			
122	KHAVELS	Miriam	Wolf's wife		Nee NACHMANOVICH
123	KHASID	Mrs.		1	1 unnamed daughter
123	KHASID	Yisrael	Son of Mrs. Khasid		
123	KHASID	Alter	Son of Mrs. Khasid		
124	KHANOCH	Avraham			
124	KHANOCH	Aida	Avraham's wife		Nee KULBIANSKY
124	KHANOCH	Ben-Zion	Son of Avraham and Aida		
125	TEITELBAUM	Moshe			
125	TEITELBAUM	Ethel	Moshe's wife		
125	TEITELBAUM	Yerachmiel	Son of Moshe and Ethel		
125	TEITELBAUM	Rivka	Yerachmiel's wife		Nee SESITZKY
125	TEITELBAUM	Shneur	Son of Yerachmiel and Rivka		
125	TEITELBAUM	Yonah	Son of Yerachmiel and Rivka		
126	TAFFER	Alter			
126	TAFFER	Alta	Alter's wife	5	
127	TARTEK	Chaya			
128	YAG	Alter			
129		Yudel			The Shochet and his wife
130	YUDELEVICH	Zelig			And his wife
130	YUDELEVICH	Reuven	Zelig's son		
130	YUDELEVICH	Moshe	Zelig's son		
130	YUDELEVICH	Sara	Zelig's daughter		
130	YUDELEVICH	Shmuel	Zelig's son		
131	YUDELEVICH	Yudit		2	Nee BERZIN
132	YUDELEVICH	Shlomo			
132	YUDELEVICH	Chaya	Shlomo's wife		
133	YUDELEVICH	Zadok	Son of Shlomo and Chaya		

133	YUDELEVICH	Yudit	Zadok's wife	2	
134		Yudka		1	The Consul, his wife and an unnamed child
135	JOSEFS	Chaim			And his wife
135	JOSEFS	Hershel	Chaim's son		
135	JOSEFS	Moshe	Chaim's son		
135	JOSEFS	Chana	Moshe's daughter		
135	JOSEFS	Henka	Moshe's daughter		
136	YUTER	Feivel			
136	YUTER	Ala	Feivel's wife		
136	YUTER	Hershka	Son of Feivel and Ala		
136	YUTER	Bayla	Daugher of Feivel and Ala		
136	YUTER	Chana	Daughter of Feivel and Ala	2	Her husband and 2 unnamed daughters
137	YONENSON	Emma			Possibly "mother"
137	YONENSON	Leiber	Son of Emma		
138	JONAS	Yehoshua		1	His wife and 1 unnamed son
139	JONAS	Mr.		2	His wife and 2 unnamed children
140	JOSELOVICH	Feiva		2	His wife and 2 unnamed children
141	JOSELOVICH	Mr.			
141	JOSELOVICH	Tzipa	Mr. Joselovich's wife		{top of page 418}
142	JALINOVICH	Moshe			
142	JALINOVICH	Taibl	Moshe's wife		
142	JALINOVICH	Rachel	Daughter of Moshe and Taibl		
142	JALINOVICH	Yaakov	Son of Moshe and Taibl		
143		Yentke		2	Kapusta, her husband and 2 unnamed children
144	JANUSOVICH	Reiza			

144	ROSENBERG	Liba	Reiza's daughter		
144	JANUSOVICH	Nathan	Reiza's son		
144	JANUSOVICH	Hinda	Nathan's wife		Nee SHOHAM
144	JANUSOVICH	Tzipora	Reiza's daughter		
144	JANUSOVICH	Chemda	Reiza's daughter		
144	JANUSOVICH	Leah	Reiza's daughter		
145	YANKELOVICH	Daniel			
145	YANKELOVICH	Rivka	Daniel's wife	1	Nee TAFFER
145	YANKELOVICH	Chaim	Son of Daniel and Rivka		
146		Yankel		2	The butcher, his wife and 2 children.
147	YAFFA	Moshe			
147	YAFFA	Chaim	Moshe's son		
147	YAFFA	Tamara	Chaim's wife	2	
148	KAGAN	Alter			
148	KAGAN	Liba Chana	Alter's wife		Nee STERN
148	KAGAN	Chaya	Daughter of Alter and Liba Chana		
148	KAGAN	Sara	Daughter of Alter and Liba Chana		
148	KAGAN	Pesia	Daughter of Alter and Liba Chana		
148	KAGAN	Rivka	Daughter of Alter and Liba Chana		
149	KAGAN	Chaim			The pharmacist
149	KAGAN	Dvosha	Chaim's wife		
149	KAGAN	Roza	Daughter of Chaim and Dvosha		
150	KAGAN	Mr.		1	Valder (probably a forester), 1 unnamed daughter
151	KAHANSKY	Yisrael			
151	KAHANSKY	Sara	Yisrael's wife		
151	KAHANSKY	Yocheved	Daughter of Yisrael and		

			Sara		
151	KAHANSKY	Gita	Daugher of Yisrael and Sara		
152	KATZ	Aida			
152	KATZ	Yasha	Aida's husband		
153	KATZ	Rasha Ethel			
153	KATZ	Yosef	Rasha Ethel's son		
154	LAN	Hirsh			And his wife
154	LAN	Mordechai	Hirsh's son		
155	LOIT	Lozer			And his wife
155	LOIT	Meir	Lozer's son		
155	LOIT	Miriam	Lozer's daughter		
156	LOIT	Leizer			
156	LOIT	Rashel	Leizer's wife		
156	LOIT	Yitzchak	Son of Leizer and Rashel		
157	LEVIN	Eliezer			
157	LEVIN	Sheina Tzipa	Eliezer's wife		
158	LEVIN	Emma			(may mean Mother (i.e. Ema) Levin
158	LEVIN	Binyamin	Son of Emma		
158	LEVIN	Freda	Daughter of Emma		
158	LEVIN	Roza	Daughter of Emma		
159	LEVIN	Chaya			
159	LEVIN	Yitzchak			
159	LEVIN	Chana	Yitzchak's wife		
160	LEVIN	Chaim			
160	BILBOTZKY	Sheina	Chaim's daughter		Nee LEVIN
160	BILBOTZKY	Yudel	Sheina's son		
160	BILBOTZKY	Naomi	Sheina's daughter		
160	TRASPOLSKY	Rachel	Chaim's daughter		Nee LEVIN
160	TRASPOLSKY	Dov	Rachel's son		
160	TRASPOLSKY	Elya	Rachel's son		

160	KAIROVSKY	Feicha	Chaim's daughter		Nee LEVIN
160	KAIROVSKY	Benik	Feicha's son		
161	LEVIN	Yosef			
161	LEVIN	Leah	Yosef's wife		
161	LEVIN	Golda	Daughter of Yosef and Leah		
161	LEVIN	Mordechai	Son of Yosef and Leah		
161	LEVIN	Feivel	Son of Yosef and Leah		
162	LEVIN	Yitzchak			
162	LEVIN	Reizl	Yitzchak's wife		
162	LEVIN	Rachel	Daughter of Yitzchak and Reizl		
163	LEVIN	Meir Moshe		2	His wife and 2 unnamed children
164	LEVIN	Nachum			
164	LEVIN	Ethel	Nachum's wife		
164	LEVIN	Nechama	Daughter of Nachum and Ethel		
164	LEVIN	Miriam	Daughter of Nachum and Ethel		
165	LEVITZ	Mottel			
165	LEVITZ	Liba	Mottel's wife		
165	LEVITZ	Chaim Moshe	Son of Mottel and Liba		
165	LEVITZ	Sheindel	Chaim Moshe's wife	2	
165	LEVITZ	Hinda	Daugher of Mottel and Liba		
165	LEVITZ	Mina	Daughter of Mottel and Liba		
165	LEVITZ	Feivka	Son of Mottel and Liba		
165	LEVITZ	Feiga	Daughter of Mottel and Liba		
166	LOPIANSKY	Yudel			
166	LOPIANSKY	Sara	Yudel's wife		Nee NACHUMOVICH
166	LOPIANSKY	Peretz	Son of Yudel and Sara		
166	LOPIANSKY	Eliahu	Son of Yudel and Sara		
167	LUKMAN	David			

167	LUKMAN	Aryeh			
167	LUKMAN	Feiga			
167	LUKMAN	Hershel			
167	LUKMAN	Yitzchak			
168	LUKMAN	Yitzchak			The Bul
168	LUKMAN	Peska	Yitzchak's wife		
169	LUKMAN	Shalom			
169	LUKMAN	Chaya		2	
170	LIBER	A.			
170	LIBER	Batya	Mr. A. Liber's wife		Nee OPNIK
170	LIBER	Yisrael	Son of A. Liber and Batya		
171	LIBERMAN	Mr.		2	{top of page 419} the barber, his wife and 2 unnamed children
172	LIBERMAN	Mottel			
172	LIBERMAN	Sara	Mottel's wife	2	Nee DASNIK
173	LEICHTER	Itel			
174	LINDA	Mr.		1	The blacksmith, his wife and an unnamed daughter
175	LINDA	Tzvi			
175	LINDA	Mosel	Tzvi's wife		
175	LINDA	Moshe	Son of Tzvi and Mosel		
176	LIPSHITZ	Avraham			The shochet
176	LIPSHITZ	Ethel	Avraham's wife		
176	LIPSHITZ	Rachel	Daughter of Avraham and Ethel		
176	LIPSHITZ	Tzipora	Daughter of Avraham and Ethel		
176	LIPSHITZ	Rivka	Daughter of Avraham and Ethel		
176	LIPSHITZ	Heshel	Son of Avraham and Ethel		
176	LIPSHITZ	Berl	Son of Avraham and Ethel		
177	LANDMAN	Abba			And his wife

177	LANDMAN	David	Abba's son		
177	LANDMAN	Menashe	Abba's son		
177	LANDMAN	Sheina	Abba's daughter		
177	LANDMAN	Miriam	Abba's daughter		
177	LANDMAN	Ethel	Abba's daughter		
178	LANDMAN	Mr.		2	Wood engraver, his wife and 2 unnamed children
179	LANTZMAN	Chana			
179	LANTZMAN	Menashe			
179	LANTZMAN	Abba			
179	LANTZMAN	Rivka			
179	LANTZMAN	Pesl			
180	LEFFER	Mr.			And his wife
180	LEFFER	Chana	Daughter of Mr. Leffer		
181		Meir		4	Maker of furniture polish, his wife and 4 unnamed children
182	MOVSHOVICH	Berl		1	his wife and an unnamed daughter
182	MOVSHOVICH	Yankel	Berl's son		
182	MOVSHOVICH	Leah	Berl's daughter		
183	MONITZ	Yosef			
183	MONITZ	Alter	Yosef's son		
184	MIASNIK	Yankel			
184	MIASNIK	Chaya	Yankel's wife	1	Unnamed son
184	MIASNIK	Shifra	Daughter of Yankel and Chaya		
184	MIASNIK	Bayla	Daughter of Yankel and Chaya		
185	MILNER	Yitzchak		1	The builder, his wife and an unnamed daughter
185	MILNER	Shmuel	Yitzchak's son		

185	MILNER	Efraim	Yitzchak's son		
186	MILTZ	Henna			
186	MILTZ	Manka	Henna's son		
186	MILTZ	Abba Yaakov			Perhaps "father Yaakov"
187	MILSTEIN	Yaakov			
187	MILSTEIN	Grunia			
188	MINES	Menachem			
188	MINES	Freidel	Menachem's wife		Nee GOLD
189	MINES	Pesach			
189	MINES	Dvora	Pesach's wife		
190	MECHNIK	Hillel			
190	MECHNIK	Chana	Hillel's wife		Nee ZOPOVICH
191	MECHNIK	Moshe Michka			
192	MELAMEDOVICH	Mr.			
192	MELAMODOVICH	Miriam	Mr. Melamedovich's wife		Nee LEVIN
193	MANOSOVICH	Dvora			
194	MANOSOVICH	Hirsh			
194	MANOSOVICH	Chaya Sheina	Hirsh's wife		
195	MANOSOVICH	Yisrael			
195	MANOSOVTCH	Shula	Yisrael's wife		
195	MANOSOVICH	Feiga	Daughter of Yisrael and Shula		
195	MANOSOVICH	Sara	Daughter of Yisrael and Shula		
195	MANOSOVICH	Moshe	Son of Yisrael and Shula		
195	MANOSOVICH	Eliezer	Son of Yisrael and Shula		
195	MANOSOVICH	Miriam	Eliezer's wife		Nee WILD
195	MANOSOVICH	Yosef	Son of Yisrael and Shula		
195	MANOSOVICH	Chaya		4	3 unnamed daughters and 1 unnamed son

196	MAR	Eliahu			
196	MAR	Yaakov	Eliahu's son		
196	MAR	Katriel	Eliahu's son		
196	MAR	Pesach	Eliahu's son		
197	MAR	Sara Batya			
197	MAR	Chava		1	her husband Chaim and an unnamed son
198	MERBIANSKY	Shimon			
198	MERBIANSKY	Miriam	Shimon's wife	1	1 unnamed daughter
198	MERBIANSKY	Moshe	Son of Shimon and Miriam		
199	MARGOLIS	Shlomo			
199	MARGOLIS	Sara	Shlomo's wife		
199	MARGOLIS	Perl	Daughter of Sara and Shlomo		
199	MARGOLIS	Aryeh	Son of Sara and Shlomo		
199	MARGOLIS	Reuven	Son of Sara and Shlomo		
199	MARGOLIS	Batya	Daughter of Sara and Shlomo		
199	MARGOLIS	Mina	Daughter of Sara and Shlomo		
199	MARGOLIS	David	Son of Sara and Shlomo		
200	RECHA'S	Moshe			The miller (Recha's means that he was known as the 'son of Recha' rather than being a formal last name.)
200	RECHA'S	Rachel		1	{top of page 420} 1 unnamed son
201	NOVIKHOVICH	Yitzchak			
201	NOVIKHOVICH	Gnesia	Daughter of Yitzchak		
202	NACHUMOVICH	Izak			

202	NACHUMOVICH	Rivka	Izak's wife		
202	NACHUMOVICH	Meir	Son of Izak and Rivka		
203		Nachumke		2	The tailor, his wife and 2 unnamed daughters
204	NAMIOT	Yisrael			
204	NAMIOT	Yentl	Yisrael's wife		
204	NAMIOT	Eliahu	Son of Yisrael and Yentl		
204	NAMIOT	Shmaryahu	Son of Yisrael and Yentl		
204	NAMIOT	Esther	Daughter of Yisrael and Yentl		
205	SEGAL	Aharon			
205	SEGAL	Chaya Sara	Aharon's wife		Nee VINITZKY
205	SEGAL	Moshe	Son of Aharon and Chaya Sara		
205	SEGAL	Chaim	Son of Aharon and Chaya Sara		
206	SEGALOVSKY	Chaicha			
206	SEGALOVSKY	Ethel	Chaicha's daughter		
207	SOLSKY	Abba		4	His wife and 4 daughters
208	SOLSKY	Zelda			
208	SOLSKY	Moshe	Zelda's son		
209	STOLLER	Shlomo			And his wife
209	STOLLER	Shifra	Shlomo's daughter		
209	STOLLER	Sara	Shlomo's daughter		
209	STOLLER	Shmuel	Shlomo's son		
209	STOLLER	Avraham Leib	Shlomo's son		
209	STOLLER	Leizer	Shlomo's son		
210	SILMAN	Chana Leah			The Rebbetzin
210	SINTOCHKY	Yitzchak			

210	SINTOCHKY	Aidel	Yitzchak's wife	1	1 unnamed son
210	SINTOCHKY	Rachel	Daughter of Yitzchak and Aidel		
210	SINTOCHKY	Yentl	Daughter of Yitzchak and Aidel		
210	SINTOCHKY	Tzvi	Son of Yitzchak and Aidel		
211	SINTOCHKY	Mendel			
211	SINTOCHKY	Alta	Mendel's wife	1	Unnamed son
211	SINTOCHKY	Leibka	Son of Mendel and Alta		
212	SINKA				The Sinka family
213	SLOMIN	Shlomo Nota			
213	SLOMIN	Chaim Moshe	Son of Shlomo Nota		
214	SLIBKIN	Chaya		1	
215	SANDLER	Mina			
216	SENIOR	Chaim			
216	SENIOR	Reshil	Chaim's wife		
217	SENIOR	Naftali			
217	SENIOR	Meir	Naftali's son		
217	SENIOR	Sheina	Meir's wife		
217	SENIOR	Tovia	Naftali's daughter		
217	SENIOR	China	Tovia's wife		
217	SENIOR	Batya	Naftali's daughter		
217	SENIOR	Rivka	Naftali's daughter		
218	SESITZKY	Berl			
218	SESITZKY	Chana	Berl's wife		
218	SESITZKY	Sachka	Son of Berl and Chana		
218	SESITZKY	Yachka	Daughter of Berl and Chana	3	Her husband Leivka
218	SESITZKY	Zeev			And his father and mother
218	SESITZKY	Pesl	Zeev's wife	2	Nee KIRZNER
219		Ovadya			The tailor and his wife

220	EPSTEIN	Chaya Dina			
220	EPSTEIN	Wolf	Son of Chaya Dina		
220	EPSTEIN	Sonia	Wolf's wife	2	
221	PALAN	Abba			Probably referring to 'the father' – i.e. the father of the following two
221	PALAN	Bayla			
221	PALAN	Sheina			
222	PALTZ	Fruma			
222	PALTZ	Mottel			
222	PALTZ	Sara			
223	POGIRSKY	David			
223	POGIRSKY	Maya	David's wife		
224	POGIR	Alka			
224	POGIR	Sara	Alka's wife		
224	POGIR	Reuven	Son of Alka and Sara		
224	POGIR	Lyuba	Daughter of Alka and Sara		
225	POGIR	Freda			
225	POGIR	Lyuba	Daughter of Freda		
226	POZITZER	Yaakov			
226	POZITZER	Chasia	Yaakov's wife		
226	POZITZER	Ethel	Daughter of Yaakov and Chasia		
226	POZITZER	Aryeh	Son of Yaakov and Chasia		
227	FURMAN	Shlomo			
227	FURMAN	Sara	Shlomo's wife	2	2 unnamed daughters
228	PETRIKANSKY	Perla			
229	PIMSTEIN	Malka Breina			
229	PIMSTEIN		Malka Breina's son	2	Name not provided. With his

				wife and 2 unnamed children.
230	PLAKS	Mota		
230	PLAKS	Chana		
231	FELDMAN	Freda		{top of page 421}
231	FELDMAN	Chaim	Seemingly Freda's husband	
231	FELDMAN	Chasia	Daughter of Chaim and Freda	
231	FELDMAN	Nechama	Daughter of Chaim and Freda	
232	FLEISHMAN	Mottel		
232	FLEISHMAN	Ethel		
233	PLAKSER	Zamka		
233	PLAKSER	Tzvia	Zamka's wife	2	Nee WUNDER
233	PRAKT	Efraim		2 unnamed sisters
234	FERBER	Leiber		
234	FERBER	Ethel	Leiber's wife	
234	FERBER	Rivka	Daughter of Leiber and Ethel	
234	FERBER	Moshe	Son of Leiber and Ethel	
234	FERBER	Yudit	Daughter of Leiber and Ethel	
234	FERBER	Rafael	Son of Leiber and Ethel	
235	FERBER	Miriam		
235	FERBER	Yehuda	Son of Miriam	
236	PEREVOZNIK	Itta		
237	PEREVOZNIK	Hillel		
237	PEREVOZNIK	Chaviva	Hillel's wife	
237	PEREVOZNIK	Izak	Son of Hillel and Chaviva	
237	PEREVOZNIK	Sara	Daughter of Hillel and Chaviva	
237	PEREVOZNIK	Miriam	Daughter of Hillel and Chaviva	
238	PEREVOZNIK	David Yitzchak		

238	PEREVOZNIK	Chaviva	David Yitzchak's wife		
238	PEREVOZNIK	Tzvi	Son of David Yitzchak and Chaviva		
238	PEREVOZNIK	Levi	Son of David Yitzchak and Chaviva		
238	PEREVOZNIK	Elchanan	Son of David Yitzchak and Chaviva		
238	PEREVOZNIK	Masha	Elchanan's wife		
238	PEREVOZNIK	Yaakov	Son of Elchanan and Masha		
238	PEREVOZNIK	Sinai	Son of Elchanan and Masha		
239	FRIED	Chatzkel			And his wife
239	FRIED	Moshe	Chatzkel's son		
240	FRIEDBURG	Gershon			
240	FRIEDBURG	Reizl	Gershon's wife		
241	FRIEDLAND	Moshe			
241	FRIEDLAND	Lina	Moshe's wife		
242	FRIEDMAN	Abba			May mean 'father'
242	FRIEDMAN	China	Abba's wife		
242	FRIEDMAN	Eliahu	Son of Abba and China		
242	FRIEDMAN	Lipaka	Son of Abba and China		
242	FRIEDMAN	Bayla Yachna	Daughter of Abba and China		
243	FRIEDMAN	Tzvi			
243	FRIEDMAN	Alta	Tzvi's wife		
243	FRIEDMAN	Reuven	Son of Tzvi and Alta		
243	FRIEDMAN	Hirshka	Son of Tzvi and Alta		
243	FRIEDMAN	Bayla	Hirshka's wife		
244	FRIEDMAN	Shmerl			
244	FRIEDMAN	Ethel	Shmerl's wife		
244	FRIEDMAN	Leibka	Son of Shmerl and Ethel		
245	PERLSTEIN	Chaim			
246	FRANK	Berl			
246	FRANK	Ethel	Berl's wife	2	Nee GARBER, one unnamed son and

					one unnamed daughter
247	PERCHIK	Elimelech			
247	PERCHIK	Sheina	Elimelech's wife		Nee FRIEDLAND
248	ZIBOL			1	(Taffer) his wife and unnamed son
249	CHERNIAK	Yosef			
250	CHERNMAN	Mr.			
250	CHERNMAN	Bayla	Mr. Chernman's wife		
251	KAPER	Heshel			
251	KAPER	Levi	Heshel's son		
251	KAPER	Eliahu	Heshel's son		
252	KOBLANSKY	Nachum			And his wife
252	KOBLANSKY	Sheina	Nachum's daughter		
253	KULBIANSKY	Yosef			
253	KULBIANSKY	Dova	Yosef's wife		Nee OPNITZKY
253	KULBIANSKY	Chaya	Daughter of Yosef and Dova		
254	KULBIANSKY	Mashel			And his mother
254	KULBIANSKY	Rachel	Mashel's wife		Nee KAGAN
254	KULBIANSKY	Tovia	Daughter of Mashel and Rachel		
255	KOPILIANSKY	Binyamin		2	His wife and 2 unnamed children
256	KOPILIANSKY	Matka			
257	KOPILIANSKY	Moshe			
257	KOPILIANSKY	Leah	Moshe's wife	2	
258	KUSHILEVITZ	Yefim			
259	KEIDANSKY	Shaul			
259	KEIDANSKY	Sara	Shaul's wife		
259	KEIDANSKY	Reuven	Son of Shaul and Sara		
259	KEIDANSKY	Emanuel	Son of Shaul and Sara		
259	KEIDANSKY	Chana	Daughter of Shaul and Sara		
259	KEIDANSKY	Tziona	Daughter of Shaul and Sara		

259	KEIDANSKY	Ilya	Son of Shaul and Sara		
260	KEIDANSKY	Shlomo			
260	KEIDANSKY	Gittel	Shlomo's wife		
260	KEIDANSKY	Feiga Rashka	Daughter of Shlomo and Gittel		
260	KEIDANSKY	Pesa Mina	Daughter of Shlomo and Gittel		
260	KEIDANSKY	Moshe Ben-Zion	Son of Shlomo and Gittel		
261	KERZNER	Zeev			And his parents
262	KLOTZ	Zusman			
262	KLOTZ	Gittel	Zusman's wife		Nee LEICHTER
263	KLIBANSKY	Monish			
263	KLIBANSKY	Dina	Monish's wife		
263	KLIBANSKY	Yosef	Son of Monish and Dina		
263	KLIBANSKY	Yaakov	Son of Monish and Dina		
263	KLIBANSKY	Roda	Daughter of Monish and Dina		{top of page 422}
264	KLEIN	Mr.			
264	KLEIN	Leah	Mr. Klein's wife		
264	KLEIN	Perl	Daughter of Mr. and Leah Klein		
265	KALINSKY	Abba			
266	KAPOL	Chaya			
266	KAPOL	Yaakov	Chaya's son		
266	KAPOL	Dina	Chaya's daughter		
267	KNIPER	Chaim			
268	KAPLAN	Gronia			
269	KAPLAN	Chana	Daughter of Moshe Tzion	1	1 unnamed son
269	KAPLAN	Zalman	Chana's son		
270	KAPLAN	Shmuel			
270	KAPLAN	Recha Itl	Shmuel's wife		
270	KAPLAN	Zalman	Son of Shmuel and Recha Itl		
270	KAPLAN	Yerachmi	Son of Shmuel and Recha		

		el	Itl		
271	KATZENBERG	Elchanan			
271	KATZENBERG	Sara	Elchanan's wife		Nee BARRON
271	KATZENBERG	Pesach	Son of Elchanan and Sara		
272	KATZENBERG	Yosef			
272	KATZENBERG	Chana	Yosef's wife		
272	KATZENBERG	Yudel	Son of Yosef and Chana		
272	KATZENBERG	Osnat	Daughter of Yosef and Chana		
273	KATZENBERG	Ezriel		1	His wife and 1 unnamed daughter
274	KRAM	Yosef			
274	KRAM	Sheina	Yosef's wife		
275	KRAM	Leib		1	His wife and 1 unnamed daughter
276	KRABTZKY	Berl			
276	KRABTZKY	Sara	Berl's wife		
276	KRABTZKY	Yitzchak	Son of Berl and Sara		
277	KRABTZKY	Naomi			
277	KRABTZKY	Taiba	Naomi's daughter		
277	KRABTZKY	Yudel	Naomi's son		
278	KRONIK	Leib			
278	KRONIK	Rashel	Leib's wife		
279	KREMENITZKY	Yisrael			And his wife
279	KREMENITZKY	Pesach	Son of Yisrael		
280	RAM	Yosef			(Magagozin)
280	RAM	Alta	Yosef's wife		
280	RAM	David	Son of Yosef and Alta		
280	RAM	Moshe	Son of Yosef and Alta		
280	RAM	Mirka	Daughter of Yosef and Alta		
280	RAM	Sheinka	Daughter of Yosef and Alta		
280	RAM	Mina	Daughter of Yosef and Alta		
280	RAM	Dina	Daughter of Yosef and Alta		
281	RAN	Grygory		1	His wife and 1 unnamed child

282	RABINER	Heshel			
282	RABINER	Chaya Tzipa	Heshel's wife		Nee REIBSTEIN
283	RUBIN	Nachum			
283	RUBIN	Fruma	Nachum's wife		
283	RUBIN	Nisan	Son of Nachum and Fruma		
283	RUBIN	Berl	Son of Nachum and Fruma		
283	RUBIN	Henech	Son of Nachum and Fruma		
283	RUBIN	Rasha	Daughter of Nachum and Fruma		
283	RUBIN	Yehuda Izak	Son of Nachum and Fruma		
284	RUBINOVICH	Leib			
285	RUBINOVICH	Nathan			
285	RUBINOVICH	Chaya	Leib's wife		
285	RUBINOVICH	Yosef	Son of Leib and Chaya		
285	RUBINOVICH	Henna	Daughter of Leib and Chaya		
286	ROSENBERG				The teacher
286	ROSENBERG	Zlata	Mr. Rosenberg's wife		Nee YASINOVICH
286	ROSENBERG	Yosef	Son of Mr. and Zlata Rosenberg		
286	ROSENBERG	Leah	Daughter of Mr. and Zlata Rosenberg		
287	REZNIK	Koppel			
287	REZNIK	Abba	Koppel's son		
287	REZNIK	Tzvi	Koppel's son		
287	REZNIK	Yitzchak	Koppel's son		
288	RIBEL	Hirsh			
288	RIBEL	Meir Rutis			
289	REIBSTEIN	Baruch			
289	REIBSTEIN	Batya	Baruch's wife		
289	REIBSTEIN	Izak	Son of Baruch and Batya		
290	REIBSTEIN	Yeshayahu			

290	REIBSTEIN	Sara Leah	Yeshayahu's wife	1	
291	REIBSTEIN	Shachna			
291	REIBSTEIN	Shifra	Shachna's wife	1	
292	RIKLESS	Mr.			
292	RIKLESS	Sara Reizl	Mr. Rikless' wife	1	
292	RIKLESS	Yudit	Daughter of Mr. and Sara Reizl Rikless		
292	RIKLESS	Yaakov	Son of Mr. and Sara Reizl Rikless		
292	RIKLESS	Mina	Yaakov's wife		Nee YUDELEVICH
292	RIKLESS	Shimon	Son of Yaakov and Mina		
292	RIKLESS	Yisrael	Son of Yaakov and Mina		
292	RIKLESS	Rivka	Daughter of Yaakov and Mina		
292	RIKLESS	Chaim	Son of Mr. and Sara Reizl Rikless		
292	RIKLESS	Nachum Ber	Son of Mr. and Sara Reizl Rikless		
292	RIKLESS	Yonina	Nachum Ber's wife	2	
293	RIKLESS	Chaim			
293	RIKLESS	Sara	Chaim's wife	3	2 unnamed sons and 1 unnamed daughter
294	RIKLESS	Mordechai			
294	RIKLESS	Mina	Mordechai's wife	3	
295	RIKLESS	Sara			And her husband Binyamin
296	RIKLIANSKY	Yosef			{Top of page 423}
296	RIKLIANSKY	Chana Reshil	Yosef's wife		
296	RIKLIANSKY	Shlomole	Son of Yosef and Chana Reshil		

297	RIKLIANSKY	Yisrael			
297	RIKLIANSKY	Reshil	Yisrael's wife		
297	RIKLIANSKY	Sara Leah	Daughter of Yisrael and Reshil		
298	RASHKES	Yehuda Leib			
298	RASHKES	Fruma	Yehuda Leib's wife		Nee KARO
298	RASHKES	Rachel	Son of Yehuda Leib and Fruma		
299	SHABTAI'S			1	Surname may be a nickname rather than formal surname. His wife and 1 unnamed child
300	SHOHAM	Yeshayahu			
300	SHOHAM	Dovel	Yeshayahu's wife		
300	SHOHAM	Shaul	Son of Yeshayahu and Dovel		
300	SHOHAM	Esther	Shaul's wife		
300	SHOHAM	Dvora	Daughter of Yeshayahu and Dovel		
300	SHOHAM	Necha	Daughter of Yeshayahu and Dovel		
301	SHULHEIFER	Mr.			
301	SHULHEIFER	Reshil	Mr. Shulheifer's wife	2	
302	SHACHOR	Henna			
303	SHACHOR	Golda			
304	SHACHOR	Yerachmiel			
304	SHACHOR	Dvora	Yerachmiel's wife		
304	SHACHOR	Pesach	Son of Yerachmiel and Dvora		
304	SHACHOR	Chana	Daughter of Yerachmiel and Dvora		
304	SHACHOR	Sara	Daughter of Yerachmiel and		

			Dvora		
304	SHACHOR	Muska	Daughter of Yerachmiel and Dvora		
304	SHACHOR	Leah	Daughter of Yerachmiel and Dvora		
305	STEIN	Yisrael			
305	STEIN	Taibl	Yisrael's wife		
305	STEIN	Chaya	Daughter of Yisrael and Taibl		
305	STEIN	Shoshana	Daughter of Yisrael and Taibl		
305	STEIN	Hersh Henkl	Son of Yisrael and Taibl		
306	STEIN	Nota			
306	STEIN	Musia	Nota's wife		
307	STEINBACH	Moshe			
308	STEINBACH	Tzipa			
309	STRUM	Moshe Yitzchak			
309	STRUM	Golda	Moshe Yitzchak's wife	2	Nee FRIEDMAN
309	STERN	Menda			
309	STERN	Chaya	Menda's wife		
309	STERN	Eliezer	Son of Menda and Chaya		
309	STERN	Chaviva	Daughter of Menda and Chaya		
310	STERN	Shmerl			
310	STERN	Bayla	Shmerl's wife		
310	STERN	Aryeh	Son of Shmerl and Bayla		
310	STERN	Chana	Aryeh's wife		Nee SESITZKY
311	SIMKOVICH	Chaim			
311	SIMKOVICH	Chaya	Chaim's wife		
311	SIMKOVICH	Nathan	Son of Chaim and Chaya		
312	SHLOMOVICH	Meir			
312	SHLOMOVICH	Taiba	Meir's wife		
312	SHLOMOVICH	Rachel	Daughter of Meir and Taiba		

312	SHLOMOVICH	Batya	Daughter of Meir and Taiba		
313	SHLUPSKY	Zeev			
313	SHLUPSKY	Malka	Zeev's wife		
314	SHELTOPER	Yonah			
315	SHLOMINS	Yaakov			
315	SHLOMINS	Chana	Yaakov's wife	2	Nee MARGOLIS
316	SHPILANSKY	Mila			
316	SHPILANSKY	Chaya	Mila's wife		
316	SHPILANSKY	Pessa	Daughter of Mila and Chaya		
316	SHPILANSKY	Yaakov	Son of Mila and Chaya		
317	SHAPIRA	Bina			
317	SHAPIRA	Bayla Chaya	Bina's wife	3	
318	SHAPIRA	Sinai			
319	SHARSHAB	Alta		3	
320	SHAPIRA	Moshe			
320	SHAPIRA	Feivel	Moshe's son		
320	SHAPIRA	Shmerl	Moshe's son		
320	SHAPIRA	Anya	Shmerl's wife	2	

[Page 424]

The list is long, and is certainly not complete.
This page is dedicated to filling in missing names.
[Page 425]

The Few of the Many
Of our Townsfolk who Fought on the Fronts
and Fell in Battle
Translated by Jerrold Landau

ATKATZ	Hirshka
ATKATZ	Zuska
IKER	Berka
BIARSKY	Nachum
BERZIN	Shlomo
BEREZNIKOV	Henech
BEREZNIKOV	Yankel
GOLDSHMID	Moshe
GUREVICH	Reuven
GRUN	Mendel
GREENBERG	Yaakov
DABOL	Yitzchak
DODAK	Motka
DROSKIN	Zuska
VICHOV	Chaim
WUNDER	Tzvi
KHASID	Yitzchak
JAG	Kadish
JAG	Shimon
LEVIN	Moshe
LUKMAN	Hirshka
MAGID	Yankel
MONOSOVICH	Moshe

MILNER	Yisrael
SEGAL	Motka
NAMIOT	Elka
NAMIOT	Shmerka (Valonas)
POGIR	Meir
FEIN	Abba
KOLBITZKY	Moshe
KLOTZ	Zalman
KLOTZ	Tzemach
RASHKES	Ben-Zion
STRUM	Moshe
STRUM	Shalom
STRUM	Shimon

Honor to their memory

[Page 427]

Jonaver Organization in New York
by Efraim Silberman
Translated by Jerrold Landau

The Jonaver Organization in New York was founded in 1906. It was the only such organization in all of America. Even though many Jonavers were scattered across various cities in America, they did not organize themselves into an organization.

The founders of the Jonaver Organization were: the brothers Moshe and Yosef Wunder, Izak Tambank, Sam Weinstein, Nathan Strom and others. They are now all long gone.

In the years before the First World War and also in the later years of the 1920s and 1930s, when the massive immigration of European Jewry to America took place, many Jonaver Jews also immigrated and took part in the organization. Then, the organization had over 250 members.

The Jonaver Organization conducted various activities in the realm of social and societal assistance. It helped both the Jews in Jonava, and the newly arrived Jonaver Jews.

Managing committee of the Jonaver Organization in New York: From right to left and from top to bottom – Meir Podison, Alchik Cohen, Benny Davis, Max Weinik, Efraim Silberman, Morris Goldberg, Louis Feterman.}

{Page 428}

After the First World War, in the 1920s, the organization purchased a house in Jonava on Shul Gasse, where the first Jewish hospital in Jonava was erected. On the eve of Passover, the organization conducted a Maos Chittin[1] campaign. The collected money would be sent to the rabbi of Jonava to distribute to the local needy families.

In America, the organization help the newly arrived Jonaver Jews become involved in the social, cultural and societal life in the country – for example, in obtaining a dwelling, work, a loan through the charitable fund that was created, etc.

The Jonaver Organization of New York acquired land in the Beth Israel Cemetery. The former cemetery, Mount Carmel, was already filled with Jonavers.

Unfortunately, today the organization in New York has a completely different appearance. It no longer has the inspiration and no longer draws nourishment from the succulent Jewish life of Jonava. The Jonaver Jews suffered the same tragic fate as all the Jewish residents of Lithuania during the era of destruction of the Second World War.

Today, the organization has approximately 50 members, who are already old and weak. The meetings of the organization, which take place once every two months, are poorly attended. The managing committee makes an effort to maintain the organization and conduct its activities. It collects donations from its members for the benefit of the funds in the State of Israel. The organization gave a large contribution to the Jonaver natives in Israel for the publication of the Yizkor Book of Jonava.

The managing committee of the organization consists of the following members: Moshe Goldberg – chairman, Leib Feterman – vice chairman, Efraim Silberman – financial secretary, Y. Jablokov – business secretary, and Benny Wilensky – protocol secretary.

The secretary, Moshe Goldberg, the son of Abba the bricklayer, was born in Jonava in 1886. He lived on Shul Gasse, across from the Hassidic Shtibel. He left Jonava in 1903. When he arrived in New York, he quickly joined the Jonaver Organization and became an active member. He held various offices at that time. At first he became the protocol secretary, and later the vice chairman. For the past 18 years, Moshe Goldberg has been the chairman of the Jonaver Organization.

Y. Y. Pogir speaks at a reception for Jonavers in the hall of the Organization of Lithuanian Jews in Tel Aviv

With Efraim Silberman in Israel: Mordechai Rashkes, Rabbi Lipschitz' wife, Yitzchak B.[Burstein], Rabbi Lipschitz, Moshe Bar, Dina and Daniel Rickless, Golda Sirek, Khasid and his wife

Moshe Bar, Dr. Shimon Zack, E. Silberman, Yitzchak [Burstein], Freda Shochet of blessed memory, Sara Burstein

The crowd in the hall of the Organization of Lithuanian Natives

Efraim is No More!

At the conclusion of the printing of this book, we received the tragic news that Efraim Silberman passed away on August 7 in New York.

He was one of the initiators and prime movers of the publication of the Jonaver memorial book. He helped actualize this, both with material and moral support. Unfortunately, he did not live to see the day, which is now rapidly approaching.

During the past three years, endless correspondence was exchanged between Tel Aviv and New York, in which he encouraged us, advised us, and sent checks from the Jonaver Organization and other Jonavers. In his answer to our last letter, in which we informed him that we had a deficit, he asked his wife Lena as one of his last wishes, while already on his deathbed, to send us one thousand dollars.

Efraim was born in Jonava in 1904 into a nationalist and honorable family. He studied in cheders and in the Talmud Torah. He was active in Maccabee and Zionist organization in Jonava and later in Siauliai. He endured the Nazi occupation in the Kovno ghetto. He lost his own 5 year old son. He and his wife Lena survived and were saved through great miracles.

When he was living in Germany after the war, he took part in writing articles about the Kovno Ghetto in the journal "From the Last Destruction".

He threw in his lot with America in 1948. From the first day, he was chosen as the secretary of the Jonaver Organization in New York, which consisted of 120 members. He worked for the Israeli funds and encouraged cultural activity.

He came to visit Israel and prepared to settle there permanently.

It was not to be.

He left behind a widow and a son.

Honor and respect.

The audience at the meeting with Y. Pogir, 1971

Translator's Footnotes

Literally "money for wheat" – a term for charity given to the needy prior to Passover so that they would be able to obtain matzos and other Passover supplies.

Glimpses at Janova
by Miriam Zakhary (Lomiansky-Wulf)

"Happy, happy unreturnable period of childhood – how can one not love and not cherish reminiscences of it." Tolstoy

Janova – the schtetel where I was born to Abe and Lea Lomiansky, a schtetel like all other schtetlech in Lithuania. Geologically, climatically architecturally these schtetlech were all alike. Their social make–up was so similar, that if you were familiar with one, you knew them all. This is true if you look at them objectively. Should one, however, begin to reminisce subjectively, many an outstanding feature – physical, as well as social begin to emerge, thus forming an unforgettable array of impressions, obviously everlasting…

Janova lay sprawled out on the banks of the river Vilya, the second largest in Lithuania. It was carefully etched by nature, and gracefully enveloped by green forests and gently–rolling hills. It had a lengthy cobble–stoned street with many shorter ones crossing it; its chausee or highway connected it with Kovno, with Vilkomere and many other small towns and villages. The railway, connecting Warsaw – Kovno – Vilno, ran through Janova all the way to Moscow. All these attributes, aided by the many industries in Janova, helped its development, supported nonetheless, by the hard– working, valiant people who populated it.

The river yielded the fish, which the fishermen caught prior to the Sabbath or any other holiday, so that he housewife could have it fresh and still breathing its last, when she brought home in order to make the famous "Gefilte Fish". During the summers we bathed in the river's clear, fresh waters, often in the nude – women separated from the men by quite a distance; this pleasure – at times interrupted by mischievous boys peeking through the bank bushes, for curiosity's sake... The frozen waters in the winter served as a skating rink for many a youngster; when solidly–frozen, the rock–hard ice could carry the horse–pulled transport sleighs all the way to Kovno (some thirty viorst); this practice was eventually abandoned after several unfortunate accidents, resulting in the drowning of several persons. Then there was the ferry, or 'parom', which ferried people and goods across from one bank the other. How we loved to ride it when we were small!

[Page 6 - English]

The forests supplied the lumber, enabling the foundation a brand of merchants called the 'Wald Sochrim'. The more affluent among them built two famous lumber and flour mills. A well–known Swedish financier by the name of Kruger opened a match factory there, eventually taken over by a group of Janover business men... What industries for a small town! The railroad carried steel product to various corners of the country, as well as to other lands. The textile business prospered, supplying its inhabitants, as well as those of adjacent villages. No less an occupation of importance was that of the coachman, the so–called 'Baal–Hagole', who taxied the passengers from Janova to Kovno and vice versa. Even the automobile could not supplant this much cheaper transportation – horse and buggy. And what about the artisans? The shoemakers, bakers, cabinet makers and the like – all had their place in this little society. All had a living to eke out and tradition to adhere to! And last, but not least, Janova became famous for its bevy of beautiful girls, particularly raised in this wholesome environment. Did not the family *Segalovsky* have eleven beauties, all one in one, each prettier than the other?

I recall the less fortunate – the poor, the demented – some begging, some roaming the streets. The demented were not put away either out of negligence or out of compassion. Such were the poor '*Yoshke* der Meshugener' who, even though he was meek, galloped around in circles, gathering around him–

Beautiful girls

Yoshke der Meshugener

[Page 7 - English]

self youngsters, indulging them with obscenities. There was 'Chasia with the Pack', a gentle woman, who with all her might clung to her last vestiges of ownership – her bundle of 'schmates', which she carried around incessantly; and should anyone have tried to take it from her she would yell at the top of her voice!… Each one of these unfortunates had a story in their past, which contributed to their mental and physical deterioration. The good people of Janova thought it best to have them around, perhaps, to remind themselves that the borderline between dementia and normalcy is often narrow. Quite a figure was cut by the 'Chimney Sweeper', tall and black from the soot he gathered when cleaning the chimneys. Proudly and seriously he paraded through the streets, like a peacock, his gear over his shoulder.

Irresistibly I look back upon this Janova, the schtetel of my childhood, recalling the touching expression of the great Tolstoy, who so aptly said: "Happy, happy, unreturnable period of childhood – how can one not love and not cherish reminiscences of it!" And so I cherish these memories of my childhood, which were eventually interrupted by World War One. Gone were the happy, careless days; the summer retreats to 'Datches', to the green forests, which held a mysterious fascination; the hammock swinging, the berry picking. How wondrous it was to watch nature flourish in its full summer glory; to milk a cow by the gracious consent of the peasant woman; to listen to the birds and the bees, and watch the cattle return home from the pasture! Or watch the peasants work in the fields! Summers gone, fall and winter had its own diversions and beauty to admire. Finally, the school days arrived, and from its very inception I became a dedicated student.

The market day in the week was an occasion of great interest to all. The streets would be crowded with horse–drawn wagons, laden with the produce of the good earth, brought in by the villages; on winter days the wagons were substituted by sleighs; the outside stalls in the market had to be warmed by coal–burning pots, often hidden under the women's skirts… The cackling of the hens, the crowing of the roosters, the neighing of the horses – all these sounds intermingled with the various spoken tongues: Lithuanian, Russian, Polish, Yiddish and even German. While bargaining, each tried to outshout the other; the shopkeepers shrieked at the top of their voices, trying to entice the shoppers to come in and buy their ware. On that day the populace was suddenly shaken out of its routine, out of its peaceful pursuits. What fun it was to walk through the crowded streets, peek here and there, listen to the folk's arguments and bargaining – all of this in spite of parental objections and cautioning: after all this was a possibility of being stampeded by a horse, or

,perhaps, even be carried away by a gypsy? The exodus of these weekly 'invaders' began toward sundown, leaving streets littered and dirty. This chaotic mess was rapidly cleared in order to return to normalcy. Many a drunk still lingered around the inns, unable to move, much to the chagrin of the innkeepers. Eventually, they too would leave, and another day, another week was to follow; on and on...

Our traditional holidays left an indelible impression. There was the Sabbath, ushered in by Friday night's candle lighting and Kiddush; the going to the synagogue by the elders on the following morning; the inevitable 'Shabos Shikse' present to light the fire on the Sabbath day; the 'tcholent' and the 'Havdole' stand out in my memory. The High Holidays, or 'Yomim Neroim' were awaited with awe and fear of judgement. Whereas, the Passover, ushered in by spring, was joyous and gay. The pre–Passover spring cleaning, the matzo baking (with us young girls pitching in for the poor) – it all aided an aura of unusual activity. The traditional meals in accordance with each holiday – we loved it all. Especially the afternoon teas with our relatives – the *Katz* and *Goldstein* families. My younger sister *Shifra* (aleha hashalom) and I devised an act, imitating the organ grinder with his monkey, who occasionally came to town to entertain the youngsters. Much to mother's delight and pride, those present laughed at this childish indulgence either out of politeness or, perhaps, true amusement!

[Page 8 - English]

In the community relationship the responsibility of the rich, or the ones materially secure, was to care for the poor and afflicted. Many a good woman – my own mother (aleha hashalom) included – would carry a cooked meal to the less fortunate ones, and this in the wee hours of the morning, so that no one should notice this act of charity.

The first World War interrupted this secure existence, exiling us far into the Ukraine from 1915 to 1919. I began my study in the Gymnasia. Father and mother made ends meet by teaching Hebrew, until such time as they could again reestablish themselves in the Russian business world. Then came the Revolution, the pogroms, our miraculous escape, and subsequent return to our beloved Janova. How well I remember this fateful, lengthy trek home by freight train, the only then available transportation; finally, upon our arrival, we were met by none other than *Leiba Vulfowitch*, who was eventually to become my brother–in–law. Our return was likened to an ascension from 'Tchias Hameisim', for in Janova there were rumors that we had perished in the pogroms. By the grace of Fate we were spared – a miracle attributed by dear mother to the 'Zchus' of her forefathers, the learned Rabbis: Reb *Kalmon Levin*, the rabbi of the Dvinsker Pletzer, her father; and the great Goen, *Reb Ryuvele*, the Mstislaver, the chief Rabbi of Dvinsk, mother's grandfather. These personal reflections to illustrate the deep influence the Talmudists of those days had on their kin and society at large.

We were, finally, again in our own home, among our people, much to our delight after suffering as refugees. (Of course, this cannot be compared with the inhuman suffering and eventual extermination during the Second World War). We found our many friends and relatives upon our return. Many succeeded financially, others have not done so well during the then German occupation. Father and mother, involved in business again found it imperative that we children continue our education. We were sent to Kovno to Gymnasia, as Janova did not have one. Many of our friends followed suit, and many were already there. Learning was great and came easy, but rooming and boarding had its shortcomings. In compensation, our returns home for vacations were more than welcome. Here the group of boys and girls, dispersed among the various schools, were united again by their common interests. Our minds, enriched by studies, were open to interchange of ideas and discussion.

[Page 9 - English]

We were also a fund–loving group and held many 'vecherinkes' in the *Burstein–Vulfowitch* factory or in private homes. Much desired were the outings by boat down the Vilya. Down the stream we'd row on Saturday afternoons to a nearby village, and upon arrival there, would feast on black bread, cheese, milk and freshly–churned sour cream and butter. These milk products never tasted better. Thus, our young appetites, ravished by hunger, were satisfied; refreshed by rest and fresh air, we could continue back home, upstream. Guiltily making our way home, we were strongly reprimanded by our pious parents (may they rest in peace) for having committed 'Chilul Hashabos'.

Memories of these wonderful, adolescent years full of hope, romance and love of life! The world was in trouble; the war and revolution had taken their toll of victims; the Polish–Lithuanian war was raging, unrest was brewing, but we were not aware of anything, that is we youngsters. Our touch with the outside world consisted of an occasional walk up the chausse's on Saturday afternoons to the railroad station to meet people from the outside world passing through. What a thrill! A whiff of adventure beckoning to us from somewhere mysterious and unknown; a desire to see how others live, to partake of the cultures of other countries! And so it was meted out to me. *Vulfowitche's* younger brother *Charles*, who was visiting his family (after having spent a few years in U.S.A.) and I met and were married shortly thereafter. For my traditional wedding my friends brought in flowers galore from the nearby villages; I walked down the flowered aisle with much hope and desire for a bright future. The much–coveted big world and the U.S.A. were awaiting me, and so were wifely duties, motherhood etc…

The last time I saw Janova was upon my return there in 1928 with my little boy. Little did I know that this was to be the last time I were to see my loving devoted parents, my relatives and friends. What a warm reception from everyone, including the whole townspeople! Never to repeat itself, but never to be forgotten!

I have cherished these memories throughout my lifetime. They have given me strength and courage. I have carried the ethico–traditional values, by which my parents lived in my heart and mind, adopting them to the American way of life. I have formed a gallery of pictures to which I occasionally retreat. And there I see our schtetel Janova with its homes somewhat shrunk and withered, after having traveled in the big, big world. I trot its cobble–stoned streets in my dreams, viewing our corner house, the shops, the market place; I see the "Schwindel Barg", the Vilya, the luscious forests. But most and foremost, the people – poor and rich; courageous and proud; some bent with sorrow and overwork, some enjoying and reaping the good things of life. It is all engraved in my memory!… Many have gone to Eternity naturally, by the grace of the All– mighty; most of them (my dear parents included) have perished through the stark madness of a maniac, who threw the world into chaos, suffering and destruction. Our Janova is wiped off the map, its demise along with that of its people; the beloved schtetel is no longer…

But those who survived, and who loved her, gallantly carryon her ideals, the ideals of their fathers and fore– fathers in the new home, the beloved land of Israel. This ancient, new homeland of ours is giving refuge to all who seek it. No longer do we have to live in 'Galuth' and be subjugated to foreign cultures and governments. Our own culture is flourishing, newly emerged, enriched by the wisdom of our Book and our sages. Indeed, it must be the 'Zchus' of the past and present generations which have created the living miracle of Israel. Its valiant, courageous people is fighting for its survival and peace, peace above all! If we have not perished by innumerable persecutions throughout history as a people, we will, no doubt, survive as a nation. This legacy for survival was passed on to us by Janova, her life and the entire Jewish people!

[Page 10 - English]

Mende di Kop Hoor

[Page 11 - English] [Page 19 - Hebrew]

Beginning, Growth and Destruction
by Itzchak Judelevitch (Jerusalem)

Janova was a small town, inhabited by some 4,000 people, located north east of Kovna. The town was situated on the main highway, on the crossroads of the railroad, the highway and the river which connected it with both Russia and Germany. Janova sat on the banks of the Vilia river (Nerys, in Lithuanian) – a wide body of water which starts north east of Vilna and has its outlet in the Nieman river in Kovna. The railroad trains from Liboi on the Baltic Sea would pass through on a high steel bridge east of the city on their way to Romani in the south of Russia. A wooden ferry boat connected both sides of the St. Petersburg–Warsaw highway. This ferry crossed the width of the river from bank to bank and transported people and vehicles. When a new bridge was built for the railroad, the country–wide traffic transferred to the old bridge and the ferry remained for the sole use of the internal traffic of the city.

Favorable Conditions

Janova was surrounded by high hills and thick forests. These, together with the stretches of green fields, lawn–covered squares ad gardens, nestled between the river banks, united to form a magnificent landscape where the townspeople – and especially the youth – found delightful excursion spots on weekends and holidays.

Janova, which was founded at the beginning of the 17th century, is named for kind Jan–Saveski. Several hundreds of years ago there was a small Jewish community in the Christian village Skarull, which lies on the left bank of the Vilia, and even to this day remnants of a Jewish cemetery are to be found there. At the end of the 18th century, the Jewish community began to concentrate on the right bank of the river, on the lands of the nobleman Kosakovski.

The whole little village, with its cobble–stoned, crisscross streets and market place, was inhabited by Jews; on the outskirts of the village, on two unpaved streets, the Gentiles lived in wooden houses, surrounded by fruit trees and vegetable gardens. The wider street, which faced the Jewish cemetery and the water–mill, led into the road to Kidani, and, indeed, it was called Kidani Street. It served as a promenade spot on Saturdays for the population.

The natural and geographical characteristics of the city gave it many sources of income. The rich forests provided plentiful lumber – raw material for the manufacture of furniture and for the building trade and a major item of export to Germany. This provided a source of income for many lumber dealers, lumber–jacks and handlers of wood. The sight of bonfires on the floats drifting through the dark and the sound of singing in the stillness of the night was typical of the dynamic character of Janova. On the convenient roads many people found employment as chauffeurs, transporting people to Kovna, Vilkomir and to the railway station outside the city. The vehicles of these chauffeurs and those of the farmers and landlords in the vicinity provided the foundation for many local trades; smithery, tannery, wagon–making etc.

[Page 12 - English]

The city was the center for a large rural population in the neighborhood – Poles Lithuanians who had become assimilated to the Poles, minor noblemen and farmers, "Starobriadcy", old–fashioned Russians whom the Communities transferred from distant places etc. These people provided a source of income for shopkeepers and tradesmen as: tailors, shoemakers etc. Twice weekly there were market days at which time the streets would become impassibly filed with wagons of the farmers and their families. The shouts of the bargaining, the grunting of the pigs and the neighing of the horses could be heard from every corner of the town; and in the late hours of the night the singing of the drunkards from the beerhalls would bellow forth. The stores would become crowded with customers and the tradesmen would be swamped with work.

A Special Type of Jewish Personality

Unlike most of the Lithuanian towns, Janova was economically and demographically well established. A special type of personality developed in this atmosphere – healthy specimens of masculine strength who lived by the sweat of their brow – people who attended the synagogue on Saturday and did strenuous physical labor on week days, who knew how to deal with the neighborhood rowdies – whether it was just "innocent boisterousness" of drunkards on market days of actual attempts at rioting bearing a deeper significance, there was also a wealthier sector of the population, people of education and culture; among them those who were educated in the modern sense – successful in business and concerned with community affairs.

The older generation devoted their time to local, traditional community affairs as: poor relief (Maot Hittim), synagogue building, religious school, community property, public bath etc. The younger generation embarked upon greater ideological horizons: political parties, youth movements, culture clubs etc. When turbulence was felt in Russian politics and in Russian Jewry, Janova did not lag behind the other great centers of population. In the early years of the Revolution, at the beginning of the century, the town had "representatives" of all the revolutionary parties and the stock market (on Bulvar Street) hummed with excited discussions until the late hours of the evening. In the period between both World Wars, the community life was divided in to two extremes, Zionism and leftist Yiddishism which tended toward communism. However, they were both engaged in constructive activities, they put up schools, established evening courses and libraries and they collected moneys for more distant objectives – for Zionist funds on the one hand and for communistic causes on the other.

[Page 13 - English]

The many possibilities to learn different vocations in Janova persuaded the Central Committee of Pioneers (Hechalutz) to channel groups of "halutzing" there and with the initiative of the local Zionist youth, a Pioneer Center (Beit Halutz) was founded which provided a home for the visitors and a center of Eretz–Yisrael spirit and culture.

There were seven synagogues in various parts of the town which served as centers for the traditional, spiritual needs of the community. They also served as meeting–halls in times of emergency. The largest of these were the "Beit Knesset Hagadol" and the "Beit Medrash Hagadol". These buildings were located in one large fenced–off area and nearby, outside the fence, was the small synagogue "Shtiebel" of the Habad Hasidim – a simple modest building, so suited to an intimate circle of people who were primarily concerned with their own social relationships. There were also other little synagogues, the "Kloiz" of the peddlers, the "Kloiz" of the stone cutters (this proves that in years gone by stone– cutting and peddling were important sources of income for the community). There were also "Kloizlach" of smiths, drivers etc.

Several Catastrophes

In the history of the town there were several serious catastrophes which served to signify special dates, as: after the first fire (1894), after the second fire (1905). In these fires, especially the second, almost the whole town was consumed and the community was left homeless, practically naked and impoverished. During such crises the very positive character of the community was revealed. On the morrow they started to rebuild the town and on the mounds of ashes put up pretty stucco houses, some of which even boasted of an "architectural style".

At the beginning of the first World War the town was shaken by an army order which decreed the evacuation of all Jews from the town. Part of the community wandered off to the far corners of Russia and many did not return. The rest concentrated in Vilna and the surrounding territory and returned after the German conquest. At the end of the War Janova embarked upon a program of social and economic development. The town's character changed from traditionally provincial to modern. The drivers exchanged their horse–drawn carts for automobiles and workshops became factories. The youth began to feel a need for the secondary schools and universities which were located in nearby Kovno. The development of the community and the improvement in the communication lines to Kovno made that city even more important to the town of Janova and, many inhabitants moved to Kovno and the little town lost its social and cultural independence.

[Page 14 - English]

At the end of the 19th century emigration from Janova started with the majority heading for the U.S.A. and South Africa. The current of emigration varied in accordance with the pace of the general emigration of Jews from Russia. Between both World Wars the movement of emigrants to Israel started. Almost half of the first pioneering group "Ahva" which left Lithuania immediately after the first World War was made up of youths from Janova. This group formed the basis for several settlements in Israel.

The emigrants maintained their ties with Janova; they supported needy relatives and even gave generous assistance to public projects. Groups of Janovites can be found all over the world and in Israel too – the remnants of the Janova community.

The Trees in Stormy Nights Whisper

The invasion of Lithuania by the Germans during the second World War – at the end of 1941 – wrought havoc on the town and its fate was the same as that of other Lithuanian towns: a small part of the Jewish population succeeded in escaping to Russia. Many were tortured to death by the Lithuanians in the very first weeks of the invasion, with the encouragement of the Germans. And on that day of horrors – 13 August 1941 – the rest died – a death of martyrs – in mass trench graves in the Gurelka woods. Some 150 Jews who escaped to a neighboring Jewish village "Der Alter Gostinetz" were later transferred to the barracks of Janova and from there to the ghetto in Kovno where they met the same fate as their brethren.

And so nothing was left of Jewish Janova; in place of the town – just heap of ruins. The only memorial to the age–old community is the cemetery with its desecrated tombstones. And only the tall trees whisper in the stormy night and tell about the birth, growth and destruction of a Jewish community, about her toil and the fate of thousands of men, women and children who were so mercilessly tortured by their treacherous neighbors – and their blood drenches the land which betrayed them.

The water carrier

[Page 15 - English] [Page 229 - Hebrew]

My Years of Agony
by Jesaiah Ivensky (U.S.A.)

The Three planes were flying high in formation. Silvery looking in the clear sky, they seemed majestic in their slow and unwavering course. Suddenly, delicate puffs of smoke materialized all around them – antiaircraft shells bursting. These were German planes, and so we knew, the war had caught up with us. It had arrived here in Janova that summer morning – on Sunday, June 22, 1941.

My family – Father, Mother, my brother, sister and I, spent most of the first day of war digging trenches in the garden. We expected to be bombed, but the only act of war which we witnessed that day, was a dog–fight, far off in the distance, between a German and a

Russian plane.

The first refugees appeared on Monday morning. They came from Kovno in small groups, but eventually this flow of people developed into a mighty stream. Although we had no definite news, we never doubted that the Germans were advancing rapidly, and would soon be in Janova. I heard that the government cooperative had received orders to distribute food–stuffs to the population, and to destroy whatever they were unable to distribute.

Some of the refugees passing through Janova told very disturbing stories – already parts of Kovno were burning, and a big battle around Kovno was expected.

By Monday afternoon, many were also leaving Janova, and the exodus increased by the minute. However, even then we did not realize the full extent of the Russian debacle. Our vague impression was that the Red Army had met with some reverses, and that the Germans were advancing. Since our town was strategically located by the Vilya and the Sventoji rivers, major battles would be fought around Janova. The general feeling lacked any permanence. We would have to leave town for a short time, but eventually the Red Army would recover from the shock of the German surprise attack, and would then throw the Germans back…

[Page 16 - English]

An Avenue of Flaming Hell

My family, like most Jews in town, got ready to leave. Joscik, the Geguziner, a relative of ours, stopped at our house, and we loaded a few valuable articles and food on one of his horse drawn wagons. It would be necessary to travel by foot, so we decided to meet later, on the highway (soshei) to Vilkomir.

As the day wore on, more and more people took to the road. By five or six o'clock, when my family left, Janova was beginning to look like a ghost town. An ominous stillness was settling over the city. As I left the place where I had been born seventeen years before, the familiar houses and streets took on an unreal quality. The stillness seemed heavy, as if before a storm, pregnant with the approaching disaster. It was only when we reached the "Soshei" to Vilkomir, that we realized what the true situation was.

The highway was clogged up with refugees and the fleeing disorganized Red Army. In their haste to escape the Germans, the people did not stop in Janova. They bypassed the town, continued their journey directly from Kovno to Vilkomir, crossing the Vilya over the steel bridge, avoiding our town, so as to gain time.

The highway was in utter chaos. Because the road was an arterial link connecting Kovno with Dvinsk, and running northeast, it was constantly under the attack of German planes. Worst of all were the stukas, diving low, with their awesome scream, and machine guns blazing. A few of them were enough to throw the multitude into panic.

A routine repeated itself again and again. It always began with the rapidly approaching planes. Alarm spread over the highway, and everyone ran for cover. Explosions of death and terror rained from the sky. While vehicles burned, the screams of wounded and dying men and horses were heard. The highway – an avenue of flaming hell. Suddenly it was quiet. The planes have left. People are returning to the road to continue their weary march, until once again, the planes will approach rapidly…

In one of the attacks my relative *Jankl Abramowitz* was wounded.

Sometime during the nighty linking Monday to Tuesday, we passed Vilkomir, about 38 km. from Janova. The town appeared to be empty. Glass was strewn all over from the looted store windows. I was barefoot, and had some trouble avoiding the glass. I had thrown away my shoes 10 km. from Janova, after developing a blister on my heel.

We rested for a few hours in a small forest behind the town and early before sunrise on Tuesday, (June 24) we proceeded along the highway towards Utena. In the beginning, we made considerable progress, but as soon as the sun rose, the German planes resumed their harassment. The terror repeated itself: the mad run to find a hiding place, the scream of the diving bombers. The hysterical chatter of machine guns – the exploding bombs.

As the day progressed, the attacks seemed to become more and more ferocious and frequent. We often passed the bodies of civilians and soldiers. Sometimes a whole line of people, who had taken cover in the ditch – the machine gun bullets had caught them as they hugged the wrong side of the ditch.

[Page 17 - English]

The Russian soldiers were completely disorganized and many of them were already without weapons and shoes. Burned out vehicles were everywhere, surrounded by refugees – tired and hungry, with the vast fear and panic enveloping everything like a dark cloud.

We Separated

For my mother and my sister, *Nechamah* (13 yr,), it became harder and harder to walk, but they suffered silently and kept up with us. The distance from Vilkomir to Utena, is about 60–65 km. and as we continued it became harder to make progress.

A few people were lucky enough to manage to get on a truck, but there were very few of them.

By midday on Tuesday, at one point there was hardly any interruption between one wave of planes leavings, and anther arriving. It was then, with all of us running with fear in indisputable command, that I was separated from my family. We were scattered behind some trees during a very intense bombardment of a bridge spanning a small river which we had to cross. I was with Ruvke, my brother, the rest of the family was a little farther, and all of a sudden I could not find them. Somebody said that they had gone ahead, looking for us. We hurried across the bridge, but meanwhile a rumor spread that the Germans were only 2 km. behind us, and everyone who had any strength left ran like mad. I never saw my parents and sister again. I found out after the war that my parents, like many other Janova Jews, turned back when the Germans caught up with them.

"Oifn Altn Gostinec" was a small Jewish village about 8 km. from Janova, and my father felt that the village was safer than the town. My family therefore together with another 150 Jews stayed in that village. On *August 13th 1941* all the Jews of Janova were taken out to Geralka woods and killed. At the same time, Lithuanian police arrived at "Altn Gostinec" with a ready–made list, and took away my father, three more men and one woman. They were also brought to Geralka, and shot together with the rest of the Janova Jews.

In the beginning of September, the Jews from "Altn Gostinec", among whom my mother and sister were included, were brought to Janova and kept in the "Kazarme". After about three weeks these last Jews from Janova were brought to the Kovno Ghetto. My mother and sister were killed in the big Kovno Akcija, on October 28, 1941.

My brother and I continued on our way to Utena. We were exhausted and our legs were swollen, numb with fatigue. There was only one thought pushing us on: escape the Germans. The German army seemed to be right behind us. We found food once in a while in half–burned army trucks, and so we kept pushing on. Often we would fall in with friends from Janova, lose them and meet other Janover, but we never lost sight of each other.

Somewhere on the road – "DVINSK" that city in Latvia, on the river Dvina, and bordering on Lithuania and White Russia, transformed itself into a glowing beacon of hope. To reach Dvinsk became to all of us on the road synonymous with reaching safety. Every kilometer closer to the goal – to Dvinsk, became a kilometer closer to the goal – to deliverance, and one kept hearing constantly: "How much farther to Dvinsk yet?" 100 km. then 90 km. – 80 – 60 — …

[Page 18 - English]

Sometimes during the night between Tuesday and Wednesday we crossed Utena. After resting there a few hours we continued ahead.

It was now Wednesday, June 25. The next big town was Zarasai, about 50 km. from Utena. The only thing that still kept us moving, was the frightful terror which was like a terrible beast on our heels. The highway now was not so crowded and sometimes the road would become quite empty, almost deserted – an indication that the Germans were right behind us, and the stillness then was more ominous than the explosion of bombs.

"Some Sport"

Meanwhile, many of the Russian soldiers were in no better position than we were. They were also treated in no way better by their luckier comrades who passed by in trucks. I could often see Russian soldiers, barefooted and looking like scarecrows, trying to hitch a ride. They would stand in the road, in the path of an approaching truck, until the last possible moment. The truck never stopped. But, even more heartless, was when one of these soldiers would grasp onto the rear of a truck, trying to get in, but the soldiers inside would start hitting him on his knuckles with their rifle butts until he'd fall off on the highway, like a sack of potatoes.

Zarasai is very close to the Latvian border, and Dvinsk is about 20 kilometers away. We reached Zarasai late in the afternoon. The city seemed deserted. Glass was strewn all over the streets from the broken windows. The setting sun, mirrored in one of the lakes, looked all aglow, flaming and vast, beautiful and terrible at the same time.

We arrived at Dvinsk Wednesday night together with the *Polans*, *Palec*, *Marevjanski* and others, but we were not allowed to cross the bridge leading into the city, because it was being used by the Red Army.

When we at last reached the railroad station on Thursday morning, it was obvious that the Germans would be there shortly. The streets were deserted, but the station was filled with people, all trying to get onto a train, to get away.

Incredibly, we managed to get on a freight train. When at last, the train left the Dvinsk railway station we all felt a wave of relief, it seemed that we were saved.

The train stopped after 4–3 km., and there seemed to be a lot of shooting going on all around. We could hear explosions nearby and assumed that the train was being attacked by planes. None of us in the closed car stirred from our places to look for shelter outside. We had all reached the end of our endurance, and by this time my feet and legs were so swollen that any movement meant agony.

The shooting continued for quite some time (an hour or two), and at times I even drifted off to sleep. Suddenly it became quiet. The door was opened from the outside, and there in the doorway stood German soldiers pointing guns at us.

We were guarded until late afternoon, and then ordered to return to the city of Dvinsk. It was getting dark and the city was on fire. Our group was all from Janova. We had stuck together since the day before when we first arrived at Dvinsk, and now we found an abandoned basement and waited anxiously what was to follow.

[Page 19 - English]

We stayed in that basement until Sunday, June 29. On that morning notices appeared on the walls, fences, etc., informing the populace that all Jewish males were to appear at the market place. Any Jew who failed to report would be punished by death.

After all the Jews assembled, we were marched down to the prison year, where for the next several hours, we went through a frightening and humiliating experience which was later to become quite commonplace, but at that time was like a wild nightmare. The Germans made, what they called, some sport.

Eventually, my brother and some other boys who were very young were allowed to leave, but we were all herded into the prison, jammed 15 or 16 in a small cell.

The Gate of Death

Wednesday, July 9, we were not let out from our cell on the 3rd (top) floor, but we could hear people being moved from the lower floors early in the morning. We could also hear what sounded like shots, but assumed that it was the backfiring of truck engines. Eventually, our cell was opened, and we on the last half of the third floor were herded down to the basement, where we were made to stop, and told to empty our pockets of all our personal belongings. So it was that we were passing through two mounds of belongings, at least two feet high, running parallel to both walls of the hallway.

When we were taken out in the yard, we were towards the end of a long column of men, divided up into groups of 21, each group guarded separately. We were moving ahead very slowly. Every few minutes the iron gate at the other end of the yard would open and the group next in line would be led in the park adjoining the prison yard. There was now absolutely no doubt. We were being killed, all of us, systematically and orderly. Every time a group was led through the gate, the shooting was heard, loud and clear, the following group was given shovels, and so it went on. We knew then that each group, before being shot, had to cover with ground, the bodies of the previous group.

As the day progressed, it became very hot. The sky was clear and the sun was like a fiery ball. I was sweating profusely, and the line was moving ever so slowly, but inevitably, ever closer did we approach the gate. That iron gate represented to me the end, death.

Except for the continuous sound of shooting, there was no sound, we were all very quiet. I could see he steady stream of traffic on the highway, spectators watching. Since the road at this point was much higher than the prison walls, German officers with their girlfriends could watch the drama like in an amphitheater.

There were then quite a lot of Janover in Dvinsker prison — all of us who tried to escape and were stuck here. Many had actually made it to the Russian border but were not allowed to cross into Russia, and returned to Dvinsk. That morning when we were herded down from our cells, many of us Janover instinctively gravitated together, so that in our group there were quite a few Janover, among them *Shmulke Palec* and *Froike Millner*. Now, as we were slowly approaching the end, I felt so very thankful to be with people I knew. I remember thinking "at least *Ruvke* is in town, he might survive", and "it would have been so much harder to die among strangers".

[Page 20 - English]

We said goodbye to each other, but could hardly talk because of the choking feeling, the lump in one's throat that each of us felt. One man suggested that we should try to kill a few Germans before dying. The idea was abandoned when another man called attention to the Jewish women and children who lived in town, "Think of what the Germans will do to them then". Everything was too sudden, too fantastic to consider logically. Rather certain thoughts passed by. We were seeing this event, this thing that was happening to us as something singular. "The Germans are enraged because they believe that the Jews have burned Dvinsk", and this was some sort of a pogrom.

It was close to noon by the time the group before us was marched through the gate. We were the next in line, and behind us there were only perhaps 300 still alive. Waiting there for the gate to open for us, with the last seconds of life ticking away, I was conscious of the profound and unique experience I was going through, and the thought recurred to me again and again, "If only I could tell somebody about this".

At last the gate opened. The SS man who came out discussed something with our guards, and we were given an order to turn around! We were marched back to the prison together with the rest of the column that was waiting in line behind us. It seemed like a miracle, there was a glimmer of hope.

A few hours later we were all marched out again, passed through the "gate of death", and found ourselves in the park. We were divided into two parts. The people of the one group had to run around over freshly filled up trenches and trample down the ground. We, the other group received shovels and were made to dig fresh trenches. It was very clear – they had run out of ditches and we were digging our own graves.

It was a scene of horror. I could see several carts with dead people, a few hundred feet away. The guards, now mostly Latvian, were extremely cruel. They beat us with sticks and abused us with words. A young German dressed only in shorts and sandals was walking around us. While whistling a tune, "roll out the barrels", he would put the pistol to the head of some Jew and kill him with one shot. In this playful manner, he killed quite a few people. He stopped next to *Froike Millner*, but Froike started to beg him to let him live yet a while, and he went to somebody else. Some people were trying to save themselves, but it was like a drowning man grasping for a straw. A middle–aged man tried to explain to a guard that he was a German officer during the first war; *Shmulke Palec* said that he was actually a Russian soldier, but the answer to everything was just, "but you are a Jew" and an extra beating on the head. Townspeople were quietly watching from behind a wire fence.

[Page 21 - English]

Under a Pile of Blankets

After we were through with our "work", we were taken back to the basement of the prison. The cells were left open and we could mingle in the hallway. Many were saying "Vidui" (the prayer before death), but otherwise people seemed to be calm. Four of us, *Shmulke Palec, Frolike Millner, myself and Chaim Kuritsky* from Utena, decided to try to hide some place, although it seemed hopeless to find a hiding place in that small part of the prison to which we had access. But then we noticed a room, rather larger than the other cells, which was also unlocked. This seemed to have served as a supply room and it contained all kinds of odds and ends.

We knew that we could not lose anything, tomorrow at sunrise we would be shot anyway. We found a few blankets in a corner. We crawled in between some boxes, put the blankets on top of us, and made it look as if we were a pile of blankets.

The next morning, July 10th, as soon as it became light, it was just as we expected. We could hear very plainly how the people were being chased out from the cells, the shooting, the screaming, the drunken guards beating and abusing the helpless people.

When the shooting stopped, we could hear the guards searching the cells. A few people attempted to hide. They were found and beaten mercilessly before being shot. Then they came into our room and made a thorough search. At one point a guard actually stepped on us, however we hardly breathed, and were not discovered.

We stayed in the same place the whole day. We knew that we were the only four still alive of the thousands of Jews who had been here only a day before. We could hear the guards, and often one would come into our room, looking for something. In the evening, new Jews were brought into the cells.

It was on Friday morning that we were caught. One of us must have moved while a guard was rummaging through the room. We ran through the hallways of the vast prison in a frenzy of fear. Eventually we were cornered, beaten with heavy ropes, and then thrown into one of the cells. From the way the guards talked, I realized that they were taking it for granted that we were of the people that had been brought here the night before. I found out that these were all Jews, and were all kept in the basement cells. Most of them were people who had reached the Russian border, but were not allowed to cross the frontier, and so turned back. There were many Janover among them. *Israel Namjot* with his two sons, *Elke* and *Shmerke, Hirsjankale Stein, Hirsale Lukman* with his uncle *Manishewitz. Hirsale Lukman* told me that not far from the border his parents were both killed and his brother,

Shmerke, was badly wounded in one of the airplane attacks.

Most of the people did not believe what we told them about the events of the last few days.

The Babies Were Aware of the Terror

For the next several weeks there was a different pattern to the killing of the Jews. Every few days the people of certain cells were taken out and shot. Other cells were left alone. Most of us Janover were in one cell, because we claimed that we were carpenters. At one time, some Germans came looking for ten young boys for work. Among them were *Hirsjankale Stein* both *Namjot* brothers and *Froike Millner.* As *Smerke Namjot* told me later: They were taken to a cemetery and told to dig ten graves for German soldiers who had died from wounds. After the job was finished they were told that they, the Jews, would also have to die. The Germans started to shoot them. They all started to run and *Smerke*, with another boy from Dvinsk, although both were badly wounded, managed to escape. They hid out, and weeks later we met them in the ghetto. Mr. Namjot himself was also taken out from our cell one morning and killed.

[Page 22 - English]

One cell had been designated for those of us wo had been wounded during the attacks on the highway. These people, many of whom were in excruciating pain, were spared for the first few weeks. However, they were given no medical attention, and so were left to bear the torment of their festering wounds, in the stench of rotting flesh, eventually to be killed anyway; thus, the Germans managed to use even that which we worshipped above all – life—to inflict greater suffering.

On July 23rd, the Jews who were still alive, about 80 of us, were transferred to what was to form the Dvinsker Ghetto. This so-called ghetto was actually the half burned out ruins of what was known as the Griver side of the Dvinsk Fortress (citadel). This was one long semi-circular structure, touching at one end the Dvina River, and after completing the half circle, reaching the river again.

Most of the building was burned out from the recent fighting. The ruins that were left standing became the home (albeit for a short time) for many thousands of people. For the next several weeks there was a steady influx of new people coming into the ghetto. They were all assembled here – the Jews from Dvinsk, from the towns and villages in the area and the refugees from Lithuania. Here in the ghetto I found my brother *Ruvke,* who had been working all this time ion a German kitchen with another boy from Janova, *Peiske.* There were also quite a few other Janover, *Peishe* There were also quite a few other Janover. *Smerke Lukman* had recovered from his injuries and was here, as well as other

Janover whose names I cannot recollect. Before the ghetto was established, many Janover women and children turned back towards home. They were either killed on the way, or when they reached Janova.

All in all, by early August approximately 12,000 to 14,000 Jews had assembled. The conditions were terrible. There was only one water faucet, and very few toilet facilities. The Germans, however, began to alleviate our overcrowded conditions all too quickly. Within several days they started the "akcijas", and from then on the process of thinning out the ghetto population was a continuous one.

During the month of August, there were many akcijas, during which probably two thirds of the Jews were killed. There were variations in the way in which akcijas were conducted, but the following is very typical of most.

By about 6:00 in the afternoon, most people who worked would have returned. Suddenly, we would be ordered to assemble in the yard. Everyone ran. Families, friends, would keep together. The people formed one long line stretching hundreds of feet, surrounded by many guards. There, in the beginning of the line, a group of S.D. ("Sicherheits Dienst") would already be at work, conducting the selection. As they passed by each person they divided up the people – those to die to the left, those who were to live,
-- to the right.

[Page 23 - English]

The faces of the S.D. officers expressed an unlimited capacity for sadism. It was these men, bearing S.S death-skull insignias and other Nazi symbols, coming closer and closer – ever closer – it was as if death itself was approaching.

A certificate that one worked meant he right side and life, and in the beginning, even the families of workers were sent to the right. But with every akcja the test became harder, so that not only were the families of workers sent to the left, but workers themselves needed very special certificates to stay alive. But always, whatever the test, at a given akcja, when the S.D. officer was standing next to you, regardless what credentials you had, if he did not like you, or if he thought you had looked at him with insolence or disrespect – you were sent to the left, to death.

The misery, the terror! One time, during a selection, it started to rain. There, on the left side, those destined to die had to wait for hours, standing quietly in the rain. I saw people in columns waiting for death many times, but I can never forget the children in the rain… The babies held in their mothers' arms and the rain coming down. The babies, though too young to really understand, yet, aware of the extraordinary terror, whimpering softly, but not daring to cry aloud, and the mothers comforting them, patting the wet hair…

In one of these akcijas, on August 19, my brother *Ruvke* was taken away. By the time I came back from work, he was already gone, and I never saw him again.

Liquidation of a Ghetto

There were no mass killings in September or October, and again many people started to hope that perhaps we would be allowed to live, but then came November, and with it the biggest akcja. It was not only the biggest, but also the most cruel. On November 5th, we all knew that an akcja was beginning. The guards around the ghetto were tripled and a fence was built to divide the ghetto. Only the people who had special red certificates were put in one part, and everyone else was put in the other. The next two days, the 6th and the 7th, nothing much happened, except that no one was allowed to leave the ghetto for work, and the lace was swarming with police. We knew exactly what was going to happen: We who had no red certificates would be killed in memory of the Bolshevik revolution.

The actual selection and removal of the victims from the ghetto occurred on November 7th, 8th and 9th. Approximately three thousand people, including many with red certificates, were then taken away.

Incredibly, I survived again by hiding myself with two other fellows. We were hidden from Nov. 5th, to Nov. 10th, under a roof. I left my hiding place several times, during the first two days, and was with the people who were later to die. When it was all over the guards made a very thorough search, and almost caught us, but we were fortunate.

During that time we found out, that the Jews in the town of Breslau, in White Russia, were comparatively free. Here in Dvinsk about 90% of us were already dead, and the rest of us expected the same fate sooner or later, and so some people who had the means, escaped to Breslau. Among them were also *Smerke Namjot Smerke Lukman and Shmulke Palec.* The only Janover left then in Dvinsk were myself, *Mr. Manisehwitz* and his nephew, *Hirsale Lukman.* The two of them lived together like father and son, and were probably closer than many parents were to their children. A few days after the big Akcja I got a job as a painter, and our whole group of about 20 workers were "kazernirt". Our group was transferred to live in the Citadel, and we lived close to the Germans for whom we worked.

[Page 24 - English]

The Citadel, consisting of many buildings, hospitals and other facilities, surrounded by a thick wall – was like a separate city, situated a couple of kilometers from Dvinsk. It was completely occupied by German soldiers.

Life was much easier here for our small group, and we had more freedom to move around. I would often visit *Manisehwitz and Hirsale Lukman* at the ghetto and heled them with what I could. I was always touched by the tender relationship the two of them had.

One day in December, the ghetto was completely sealed off. No one was allowed in or out, due to an epidemic, we were told.

For about three months we had no idea of what was going on in the ghetto, although we lived less than one kilometer away. The dark, foreboding structure, saturated with so much misery and death was always on my mind.

In early spring the ghetto was again opened and I had a chance to see my two Janover at the ghetto.

That winter, the Jews in the sealed off ghetto went through inhuman suffering. They had to subsist on so little food, that almost everyone I saw was either completely emaciated or swollen up.

For the next several weeks additional people from the ghetto were "kazernirt" and taken to live either in the city or the Citadel. On May 1st 1942 the ghetto was liquidated. As I found out later, the police came during the day and ordered the people out. The people knew very well that it would be their last trip, and so many of them refused to go. They were shot on the spot. The other people were taken a few kilometers away to a forest and killed there. Later that afternoon I was watching from across the rive the victims, killed in the ghetto, were being buried.

About 600 people were killed that time, among whom were *Manisehewitz and Hirsale.* There were now left in Dvinsk abut 400-450 Jews alive, of whom about 180 lived at the citadel (Krepest).

Even the Enemies of the Nazis were not Our Friends

I continued working as a painter, and life went on. We, the young ones decided that we would not sell our lives cheaply, and tried to look for a way out. We kept on making plans, changing them, and making other plans. We could escape easily enough at that time, but what then? With the front-line hundreds of kilometers away and the native population hostile, how long could we survive on the outside? Later on rumors were heard of Russian partisans in forests and swamps Southwest of Dvinsk, but we had no way of knowing if this was true.

Meanwhile, we made every effort to acquire arms at whatever cost or sacrifice. In spite of many difficulties, we were eventually successful. In fact, by the spring of 1043, virtually all of the young people in the citadel had in their possession some kind of weapon
– pistol or revolver and even some German grenades. The side arms we usually brought from civilians, whom we came in contact with during work, and for which we aid exorbitant prices. The grenades were usually discovered in the pockets of German uniforms. Some of my friends worked at sorting uniforms of the soldiers who were killed at the front. Various other German objects were "organized" at a tremendous risk. Money obtained for these objects (such as seal-skin jackets, destined for the Russian front)

enabled us to buy both arms and food.

[Page 25 - English]

By the spring of 1943 my friends and I were constantly preoccupied with escape, but the difficulties still seemed unsurmountable. Getting out of Dunaburg was at that time quite simple, but we were all cognizant of the inevitability of getting caught after a few days. Some of the difficulties which we often discussed were quite obvious. The native population was very hostile to Jews, and the few who did not hate us knew that to help a Jew could mean death, while informing on a Jew meant a reward. The front line was hundreds of miles away and the war might last for years. We had absolutely no experience with firearms or with the art of survival in the country. At all times, we knew there would be no second chance. To be caught meant death. We were unable to visualize how it would be once we got away. How would we go about food and shelter, or how long would it take until a farmer would give us up for a reward?

There were a lot of Russian prisoners of war in the citadel as well as Ukrainians who were now part of the German army. We got to know some of the prisoners, and it seemed logical that our chances for survival would be enhanced if we escaped together. They were experienced soldiers, and more importantly – the populace in this area (which was mostly Russian) was much more sympathetic to Russians than to us. It was, however, not so simple. A few events took place at about this time (early 1943) which left us not only disillusioned, but extremely cautious. We just had no friends, and *even the enemies of the Nazis were not our friends.* This was proven to us over and over again. We were at this time less strictly guarded than the prisoners of war.

The first incident was the escape of several prisoners with the help of *Gutke Jachnin.* Once they had used him to break out, and the prisoners had gotten the arms from Gutke, along with everything else he had – they abandoned him. After two days, he came back to us. Luckily, due to our covering up, his absence was not discovered by the Germans.

The second incident ended in much more tragedy. Four girls between the ages of 17 and 20 escaped with four prisoners of war, whom they had helped break out by sawing through the steel bars of a window in the P.O.W. compound. The girls also returned after several days. The P.O.W.s had made use of them, and then discarded them like dirty rags. Left defenseless the girls could see no alternative, and came back to the citadel whereupon they were promptly taken by the Germans to the prison and shot.

These incidents left us feeling very bitter. As the summer of 1943 wore on, and opportunities for escape failed to materialize, I often tried to visualize the end. We now had guns and did not feel quite as helpless as we had in the beginning of the war. While I had no illusions concerning our chances against the Germans, if nothing else – the dream of being able to make the hated Nazis pay dearly for our lives were comforting. The idea of dying while fighting it out to the very end surrounded by our close ones seemed not unattractive: Of course the hope was always there that in the final moment there might still be a remote chance to get away. So as not to be caught unprepared one of us always kept watch at night. He was to give the alarm in case the police were to come.

[Page 26 - English]

We Escaped to the Partisans

It was almost the end of the summer when an opportunity suddenly presented itself to us. Ton September 10, 1943 three of us, *Motke K.* from Anikst, *Berke K.* from Dunaburg and myself along with another even Russian prisoners of war and Ukrainians escaped from the Dunaburg citadel. Marching for two days with virtually no rest, we reached the partisan village of Babily. Although it was only about 100 km. it might well have been a different continent. The area stretching for miles and known as the "White Forest" was completely under the control of the partisans. Antonov's "otrijad" of the Shirokov brigade maintained its command post at Babily. Life at this time in the village was quite cheerful. The peasants paid taxes to the partisans, the Red Army was advancing on the Western front, and every Saturday night there were dances at the command post. It was something that I did not dare to expect even in my wildest dreams. Even so, the three of us were very unhappy. For one thing, the poison of anti-Semitism had spread here too. We were hated, distrusted and discriminated against; Thus, our guns were taken away. We kept thinking about our friends and the Jews of Dunaburg – such a short distance from us, who were suffering helplessly waiting for death. Unhappy as we were with the general attitude toward us, the threat of imminent death was not hanging over our heads. It was because of our anxiety over the fate of the Dunaburg Jews, that we kept on pressuring Commander Antonov and Komisar Gusev, to give us the assignment of bringing Jews from Dvinsk to the partisans. Eventually we succeeded in convincing the Commander. I received the task to go, accompanied by five other partisans. We were supposed to reach a certain forest about 25 km. from Dunaburg, where my escort was to stay while I was to reach the citadel myself. I was to get all the Russians I could, but I had explicit orders to take only the Jews who had guns. I was then to bring all the people back to Babily.

As it happened, the head of our group terminated the operation after we had marched about halfway to our destination. The whole partisan area was being surrounded by Germans, so he decided that it would be much too dangerous to continue, and we returned to Babily. The so-called blockade of "Bielaja" had begun.

I was disappointed, but then there was not too much time to worry about our friends at

Dvinsk. The Germans were tightening the noose around our area, and our situation became very serious. For reasons, which probably had to do with the retreat of their troops from the Eastern front, the Germans decided to clear out the partisans in Western White Russia at whatever cost. This they commenced doing in a very thorough manner indeed in the fall of 1943. The action was conducted in several stages; First, the whole areas was surrounded and quarantined, in a sense. Next, the villages and suspicious areas in the forests were bombed by the Luftwaffe. Finally – combing the forests and swamps and destroying the partisans.

[Page 27 - English]

As it turned out by the first stage of the operation the magnitude of the German effort was apparent to the partisan commanders. A decision was then made that it should be up to the commander of each otrijad to choose how best to weather the storm. There were two choices – to retreat to the East or to try to survive the German onslaught in the familiar forests and swamps. Most groups did sneak away to the East during the first and second stages; But our group, Antonov's, stayed, and we were in for it.

It was very bad. The night we left the camp was truly memorable. The commander made a speech about the night and the forest being the ally of the partisans, while the Germans were only a few kilometers away. There was last minute packing and frantic preparations for the abandonment of the camp.

From then on our otrijad was on the run. Never more than a step ahead of the Germans. The worst was always that we, the Jews, at all times were unsure of our own future – the hatred and distrust towards us could always be felt. At times I met Jewish members of other otrijads and heard many details of the persecution of Jews in the partisan movement.

Humiliating Event

I met *Smerke Namjot* one misty dawn, while I was on guard duty. It was much like a dream. Here was Smerke, a dear friend of mine from the same class in "Tarbut", suddenly to materialize between the trees with a group of partisans. With only enough time to exchange a few excited words and a quiet embrace he was gone again. Surely it was a dream. *Smerke* was a member of the "Lithuanian Brigade". This brigade was the envy of us all. Since the Russians wanted to prove that there were Lithuanians fighting the Germans, the brigade was cared for in a very special way. They were equipped with the best arms and provided an abundance of food. Even so, most of the members of the Lithuanian brigade were either Jews or Communists who had escaped previously to Russia, and were now sent to fight with the brigade.

I later found out that *Smerke* was killed shortly afterward – not by Germans, but by other Russian partisans. Smerke would not give up his sub-machine gun (a weapon which was much coveted) when demanded to, and so being only a Jew, he was killed.

Meanwhile, things were getting worse. The Germans, forming giant human chains, combed through every corner of the area. It was then that the most humiliating event took place. Under the excuse that the whole Otriad was being broken up into small groups, its seven Jews were cast away. The rest of the Otriad, however, remained intact. Luckily, I got my revolver and compass back.

We had no idea where we were, enveloped by total darkness in the unfamiliar forest. The stillness of then night was pierced only by the terrifying sound of German voices. Trudging on in an easterly direction, we reached a clearing and a concealed German out post. *Motke, Chaim* and I managed to escape the hail of machine gun bullets, however we lost the rest of our group.

[Page 28 - English]

The following day, Wednesday October 13, was one long nightmare. Early dawn found us in a swamp amongst several hundreds of partisans from several Otriads, including Antonov's. We were caught in a crossfire. People were dying all around us. *Chaim* was hit in the head and died instantly. The din of exploding shells, the evil hiss of flame throwers, whistling of bullets, and the overall stench of burning dynamite powder – made it all a large inferno. But the picture, which always comes to my mind when I think of this battle, is that of the partisan lying doubled up badly wounded and continually begging –"Brothers, please finish me off – please".

Again Alone

After the survivors of the initial entrapment reached meager cover offered by the trees, they formed small groups and tried to survive as best they could. Again *Motke* and I found ourselves alone. We spent the whole day dodging bullets, struggling through the swamps, and at times actually seeing the Germans in our pursuit in straight lines with their dogs sniffing after us. Evening eventually brought some respite. We continued running for several days. We met with other partisans on several occasions, but met with hostility when they realized we were Jews. Our physical condition had deteriorated by then. Legs swollen, feet bleeding, and with little food to sustain us we determined to break through the encirclement and reach our friends in Dvinsk. There we planned to get arms and organize our own partisan group.

Roads were out of the question. The compass was our only guide. I expected that a Northwestern direction would bring us to the river Dvina, which then would lead into Dinaburg.

As miraculous as it seems, a week later, we actually reached Dvinsk. After we managed to get out of the cauldron in the forest, our journey progressed very satisfactorily. Concealing ourselves during the day, we marched only at night. As the days passed, and everything seemed to work like clockwork, our spirits rose considerably. We were overcome with a feeling of confidence, and near exhilaration. We learned a great deal about the art of survival the last couple of months, and suddenly it seemed quite simple. We found out how to get food, how to hide and rest during the day, and with only a compass to guide us, we seemed to find our way through forests, swamps, and fields. While marching, a lot of time was spent making excited plans for our future "Jewish Partisan Otriad".

After some anxious moments, crossing the well-guarded bridge over the Dvina, we reached Dvinsk without any mishaps. Our October 22nd we managed to slip into the citadel unnoticed.

All of our plans, however, came to naught. After only a few days we heard very disquieting rumors, and took special precautions. On October 28th, 1943, the Jewish quarters were surrounded, and the people were taken away.

Actually, things did not run so smoothly. This last roundup of Jews was not unexpected, and when the police arrived, we were ready. There was much shooting, and often fighting. Motke and I were hidden at that time in an attic, and could follow the drama unfolding itself on the square below through a crack in the roof.

[Page 29 - English]

It was a scene all too familiar, taking place with some variations all over Europe in hundreds of towns and villages. There they were, the columns of Jews with the few belongings, looking s pitiful and helpless. Surrounded on all sides by the gun toting Nazis. they had to wait so long, while the area was being searched for the ones who escaped. Every once in a while, a Jew was brought to the column after his hiding place was discovered. They were beated, and made to join the rest. I could see Dovidke Bleier, a friend of mine, being chased. He pulled out his gun, in which I knew he had only three bullets. Firing twice at his pursuers, he killed himself with the last bullet.

Although they were only a few hundred Jews in the citadel at this time, many of us escaped. By now we had no more illusions, and many Jews with guns in their hands forced their way through the police lines when our quarters were originally surrounded. There were others, who – rather than be taken by the Germans – killed their close ones and themselves.

A Silvery Beam in the Darkness

We were actually in a very dangerous situation, since the building we were hiding in was occupied by German soldiers, and sooner or later we would have been discovered. Therefore, as soon as it got dark, we sneaked out and made our way to another hiding place, in which the *Guterman* family was hiding out, This was also an attic however its only entrance was through the roof. There was no door to it, thus it was a fairly good hiding place.

We stayed together for a week before we found out through a German soldier that Jews were again officially working for the Germans. It seemed like a German trick. Many Jews had run away, but it was almost winter, and the people, some of whom were not young, did not know how to survive the winter on the run. Now the Germans allowed the Jews to work and gave them food. A total of twenty-six Jews gave themselves up. Among them was the Guterman family.

Motke and I stayed in our hiding place, but were in contact with the Jews, who provided us with food. We had to decide what to do, and it was not an easy decision. We could go back to the same area in the forest, but we were not sure if any partisans were left there. It was now winter. Where would we get food? We saw all the villages in the area being bombed to the ground. Meanwhile we heard that a ghetto exited in the city of Shauliai, in Lithuania, and the Jews there were treated in a most humane way. However, we were very reluctant to go back into another ghetto.

And so the time passed. In fact, the whole month of November passed without our taking any action. And then, on December 4, 1943, the last Jews of Dunaburg, the 26, were rounded u and taken away. A young boy, (*Maxie*) managed to escape, and came to tell us about it.

As far as we knew, we were the only Jews still alive in Dvinsk. Tortured as we were by hunger, cold and the terror of being discovered, the days passed very slowly. We spent a lot of time talking, and that helped us endure the endless hours. My life in Janova seemed so far away, like a half-forgotten dream. The events since we left home personified the fact that we were always just a jump ahead of the angel of death. Motke's escape from Anikst in all the minute details – of how many of his formerly Lithuanian friends took part in the killing of the Anikter Jews, and how he, Motke, after being shot and covered with earth in a common grave, had managed to survive. Although seriously wounded, he dug his way out of his own grave, and after wandering a couple of months, which was an odyssey of superhuman effort and suffering, he eventually reached the ghetto of Dvinsk.

[Page 30 - English]

We often discussed our Jewish destiny. The suffering, the pain we have to endure, and everyone herding us down like wild beasts. It was not only the Germans – the Lithuanians,

Ukrainians Hungarians, Rumanians – all were murdering us. Even the Russians and Poles, we were enemies of the Germans. They too were our enemies.

But like a far-away silvery beam, the thought of Israel would pass through my mind. Surely we will die in this war there seemed no hope for us. But the handful of chalutzim in Israel will survive. They will build a new life and a safe-haven. Surely after all this it will have to be our own Jewish Homeland, and there was much comfort in the thought.

We were now completely alone, without ties. There were no more Jews in Dvinsk. We had no food or water, and we could not get away, because the gates of the citadel were now guarded day and night.

In a Freight Train to Shauliai

We spent a whole week without tasting food or water, and we were desperate. I realized how true it is that thirst is so much harder to endure than hunger.

By Saturday, December 11, we knew that we could not continue in this condition much longer, and would have to take some action. We knew of a German soldier, who tended the horses in his unit, and therefore had his own room at the stable. We decided to take a chance and ask him for help. He was indeed a "good" German, and was ready to help us get out from the citadel. He also told us that *Shmulke Palec* had been hiding out in the stable for the last week, and had just left with the hope of catching a freight train for Shauliai. Little Maxl decided to stay with the German, who promised him that by intermingling him with Russian refugees, the German would be able to save him.

Shmulke Palec from Janova had run away from Dunaburg (Dvinsk) to Breslau (White Russia), in the fall of 2941. When the Jews in that town were killed in 1942, he escaped t another town, but it was at a time when the Jews were being systematically eliminated and he soon had to run again. He managed to escape from about half a dozen different such actions, and in early spring of 1943, Shmulke returned to Dunaburg.

By sheer luck Motke and I caught the freight train, that was going from the front line to Radvilisik, and from there to Germany. We were on our way.

The train ride, lasting more than a night, was not only very difficult, but truly dangerous. First we were worried that we jumped onto the wrong train, but after passing Rokiskis we knew that we were moving in the right direction. Early in the trip we became very much aware of the bitter cold in the open freight car.

[Page 31 - English]

So while the train moved, we jumped almost constantly, to keep ourselves warm. The stops at the stations seemed to become longer and longer, as our train, moving empty from the front, stopped to let off heavily loaded trains to roar by to the fighting front.

The cars of our train were inspected several times, and at least once it was done quite thoroughly. Through the open doorway, the inside of each car was brightly illuminated by a lantern. Luckily, we were not caught; whenever the train stopped we flattened ourselves against the wall, right next to the door, and while the beam of the lantern searched through the car, it missed that little spot right next to the door. Towards morning, we stopped at a quite sizable station, which we thought might already be Radvilishkis. Not being sure, I jumped out to reconnoiter. I found out that we were a long way off yet. While trying to get back into the car, I was challenged by a Lithuanian security guard. Somehow, I convinced him, (in Lithuanian), that I was a Lithuanian worker trying to get back home for Sunday. After assuring him that I would never try to get on a freight train, he let me go. When the train started to move again, I managed to jump back into the car unobserved. It was at Panevezys, however, that we spent the most anguishing hour. After our train stopped at the station, we realized that there was another freight next to ours also waiting. Without even seeing much, we knew exactly what the cargo consisted of. We could hear very clearly the clamoring of little children for water. There was no doubt about it: it was a freight train loaded with Jews, packed like sardines on the way to a final destination, the nature of which we could well imagine. The wailing of children, anxious voices of mother and the coarse cursing of guards – all added up to a picture that was only too clear.

By the time the train reached Radviliskis, it was about 10 o'clock Sunday morning. From here the train was turning South to Germany, and we knew that we would have to go the 20 km. from here by foot.

We jumped out unobserved, and found the way to Shauliai, although neither Motke nor I had ever been to this part of the country.

Walking was hard, as we hadn't used our legs for six weeks. But it was a bright sunny day, that Sunday December 12, and in the evening, as planned, we arrived at Shauliai. After very careful questioning we found the Ghetto. It was guarded by Rumanian S.S., and enclosed by a barbed wire fence. We therefore waited until we saw a Jewish police aid, who helped us slip inside.

An Unexpected Incident in the Forest

In Shauliai the people were still very much affected by recent events. In October, about one half of the ghetto (known as the "Kavkaz" part) had been taken away, and the people were all pressed together in the part called "Traku". The really tragic event took place on November 5th. All the children, except for those few who managed to hide, as well as the old and sick people, were rounded up and sent away to their death, around 850 of them. The Ghetto was shocked and overcome with grief. And when we arrived five weeks later, the horror of the "Children Action" was still on everybody's mind.

Motke and I were assigned to a room where another six people already lived.

[Page 32 - English]

Crowded though we were, living eight to a room, to us it seemed almost luxury.

The ghetto, which contained at that time about 5—6,000 people, was organized by the Germans in such a way that most of the internal operations were in Jewish hands (a number of books have been published about ghetto Shauliai). I was surprised to find that some people actually expected to survive the war, bleak as the mood of the people was at the time.

On December 25, S*hmulke Palec* arrived in Shauliai. He had started out the same day that we did, but he was forced to turn back a number of times by unfavorable conditions. We were very glad to see him and immediately started making plans for the future. Each of us now had a gun and I also had a compass. Come spring we would be ready to leave. We also got acquainted with quite a few of the young people who were planning their escape or some other forms of resistance, and hoped to coordinate our efforts.

Winter was passing. The news from the war fronts sounded very encouraging and we were eagerly awaiting warm weather when we could escape to the forest and freedom.

When spring at last arrived, our plans, however, ran into a snag. Shmulke and I went sent to work in the forest, while Motke had to stay in the Ghetto, in this way our small group was suddenly split up. Our party which consisted of seventeen men was sent to cut trees for shipment to Germany. The forest was some distance away from Shauliai and we lived right there in a house of a farmer, guarded by two S.S. guards (Rumanian). Quite suddenly I lost all contact with Motke and the Ghetto.

The work, though rather hard, was quite enjoyable. We received plentiful food from the farmers, and to be so close to nature was invigorating. While marching to and from work we often sang Hebrew songs, a favorite of ours – a Zionist marching son introduced to our group by *Yankale Feinberg.* The guards, of course, understood nothing.

Weeks passed, and spring was slipping away. The Russians were advancing, and I was bursting with impatience to be back at the Ghetto, so as to complete our plans for escape.

As incident occurred which put an abrupt end to our sojourn at the forest. It was a late afternoon in the end of June. We were marching from work; as usual while passing through the small gorge in the forest, we were in single file with one guard in the front and the other in the back of the column. Suddenly there was a hail of bullets, machine guns were firing away at us from all sides. At the first sound of firing I threw myself to the ground. I could see the guard (I was very close to the front of the column) writhing in pain, crying for his mother – he was badly wounded. Cries of pain could be heard from the other people who were hurt. The firing stopped after a short time and the cries of pain by the wounded only accentuated the strange stillness after the din of firing. Carefully I lifted my head and saw armed men approaching. "Friends, what are you doing, we are Jews", I yelled. "So what if you are Jews, you work for the Germans", one of them retorted. After finishing with a bullet the wounded guard, they realized that the other guard managed to escape.

Three Jews were wounded, and one (*Lurie?)* very seriously in the stomach.

[Page 33 - English]

The partisans (they obviously were Red partisans) gave first aid to our wounded, and after a fruitless short search or the escaped guard, disappeared. We managed to bring our wounded back to the house where we stayed. The one who was hit in the stomach screamed for hours and then died during the night. When we were brought back to the ghetto, people wanted to know why we did not join the partisans. The fact was that the partisans did not act as if they would have welcomed us and though they did administer first aid as if they would have welcomed us and though they did administer first aid to our wounded, they were rather hostile to us. Of course, in our case (myself and Smulke) our friend Motke and our guns were at the ghetto. In general, I felt little affection for those so- called partisans. The conditions for the ambush were perfect: Ideal terrain, enough manpower, automatic weapons and unsuspecting victims (the S.S. were there to stop us from escaping, partisans were not expected in that area). Yet, they let an SS man escape, and in getting the other one they hit three of us Jews.

A Bitter Experiment to Escape

Now that the three of us were reunited, nothing seemed to stand in the way of our escape. We decided next night to get out through the loosely guarded fence. That evening, Motke informed L., who was the coordinator of whatever resistance there was to be in the ghetto. L. advised us to wait a few more days until Sunday, when we would be able to get out from the ghetto through the "Frankel" factory, and therefore almost without any risk at all. He also suggested that we enlarge our group by taking also some more fellows from the ghetto. We agreed to that plan. It seemed though, that there in Shauliai, our luck had run out; two days later the ghetto was surrounded, instead of the few guards, the ghetto was all of a sudden studded with heavily armed SS including machine guns. No one was allowed to go to work, but people who have for months – or even years – worked and lived in outlaying work camps were brought back to the ghetto.

For the next several days we ran around as if caught in a trap. The word was that we will all be shipped to Germany. We talked to a lot of guys trying to formulate some plan; we were determined not to go to Germany. During this period, there were still quite a few who escaped from the ghetto, but somehow all our plans seemed to misfire. At last we decided to scale the fence in a certain spot, regardless of the danger.

Motke and I were approaching the spot by separate streets. Suddenly the chief of the

Jewish Judenrat, Pariser, was in front of me. Things the next few seconds happened very fast, and before I knew it, he pulled out the gun from my pocket. It was always assumed afterwards that my undoing was due to an informer. At any rate, at this point Pariser became quite hysterical, yelling and pointing the loaded gun at me. I started to run and he waving the gun ran after me. It developed into a wild chase through densely crowded streets with a dozen Jewish policemen trying to catch me. Eventually I was cornered and thrown in solitary confinement. Through the efforts of L. and others, Pariser did not turn me over to the Germans, but I was shipped out to Germany with the very first transport. Motke, meanwhile, was caught while trying to climb over the fence and was put in the same transport.

[Page 34 - English]

The trip to Germany took several days, and I spent most of the time brooding over the fiasco with my gun, There was, though, this consolation – we were at least together, Motke and I.

Hard Work, Starvation and Harassment

Camp Stutthoff was truly hell on earth, a mad man's nightmare. I stayed there a very short time. On the second day after our arrival, a kapo, who was a few men short, approached our column. He counted out 5 of us, and I was the fifth. We were taken away. Motke, who was next in line, stayed, and that was the last time I saw my friend until after the war.

We were loaded up in freight cars, right away, and shipped deep into Germany.

Again, the voyage lasted 4—5 days. At last we arrived, and were unloaded at the village of Kaufering, not far from the town of Landsberg, in Bavarija. Only a few kilometers away was our new "home" – Dachau camp No. 2 (the main camp of Dachau was actually far away, but we belong administratively to it).

When we first arrived, construction of the camp was just being finished. The huts were constructed from a synthetic fiber which was like cardboard, and all other facilities were very primitive. There were about two thousand and I became one of the inmates. We were almost exclusively from Shauliai and Kaunas. One pleasant surprise was that among the people from Kaunas, I met a few Janover, the brothers *Meir Leib* and *Abraham Goldsmidt* and the brothers *Reibstein*.

The combination of hard work, starvation, and general harassment made our lives miserable. The worst was probably the 3—4 roll calls every day which sometimes lasted for hours. It was, however, with the arrival of fall that our misery became truly too much for a human being to endure. From the first brutal scream of "aufstehen" four o'clock in the morning, until late evening, we were tormented with no relief. Cold and hungry, shivering in our scant wet rags, every day was a journey through hell. During the rainy season, our clothes were very often still wet in the morning, not getting a chance to dry during our few hours of sleep. And so it was, that even though our camp could boast of no gas-chamber, nor crematorium, the death rate soared.

I tried different methods of making life a little more tolerable. I even made up a little game with myself. In my mind, I would on the same date live through the events of the previous year in an attempt to make myself forget the present. In this way on September 12, 1944, I relived the experiences of that day in '43'; how we had reached the village of Babily, the partisan headquarters; the relief of those first moments of arrival; the wild, joyous shooting in the air, the partisan officers galloping on horses in their colorful dress; the joy of meeting other Jews in the otrjad, and the smell of fresh hay where we slept. And even later dodging bullets, when in our abandonment, we were surrounded by Germans – even these seemed comforting in comparison to the present.

Meanwhile, more people were brought to our camp: Polish Jews from Lodz, Jews from Czechoslovakia and Jews from Hungary.

Above all this, the Angel of Death seemed to reign supreme. Friends, I talked to, unpresuming, were dead a few days later. Hunger – the yearning for food became the overriding passion, and I could think of little else. We talked and dreamed of food constantly.

[Page 35 - English]

Much has been written about German Concentration camps, the suffering and the desperate struggle for life. Particularly concerning the tendency of this environment to expose and nurture the very base and despicable element of human nature. Some were completely unscrupulous in their struggle for survival, and I have seen much of this.

But, I have also seen much of the good in human beings, which manifested itself even in the camps. People often endangered their own lives in their effort to help friends.

I often reflect that the very fact that I am alive today, is probably due, in no small part, to selfless acts of many individuals. Certainly, the Janover in camp were a great help to me, as well as some who were friends of shorter duration.

In spite of everything, most of us never lost our dignity as human beings. We would not allow ourselves to show any weakness to our tormenters. I can remember watching our guard smoking – and what wouldn't have given for a few puffs of a cigarette! – but when the guard threw the butt away, I would not pick it up. I would ache with desire for that butt, but I would not give the German the satisfaction of seeing me in this position.

Somehow I Survived

By December, I had been in the camp or 5 months. Despite the influx of additional arrivals, the population of the camp was cut by the ever-increasing death rate to a very low level. The authorities then decided to close our camp (No. 2) completely, and we – who were still alive – were divided up among the camps in the vicinity, camp No. 11 and camp No. 1.

I was transferred to camp No. 11 and lie, or what passed in camp for life was here the same as camp No. 2.

Somehow I survived that bleak winter. With the coming of spring, our hopes were raised by the news from the fronts. The Americans were getting ever closer.

I was by then so weak, that just to talk to my friends was an effort. My strength was giving out.

Towards the end of April, we were rounded up and evacuated from camp No. 11. We were marched for several days with very little food. I was getting constantly weaker; my feet and legs were swollen and it seemed that I had come to the end. When we arrived at camp Allach, the people who were sick were told that they could stay here. I fully realized that an admission of sickness in a situation like this meant death. At this point, I did not care anymore – I stayed at Allach. But time had run out on the Germans. Within hours the SS guards of our camp disappeared. Shooting was going on between the retreating the retreating Germans and advancing Americans (an artillery shell hit the hospital). I was at this point so weak that I lost all concept of time. Hours passed or days, but at one point I looked at the gate and saw tall and fresh looking soldiers in olive drab uniforms. They seemed somewhat bewildered as the inmates of the camp moving quietly in single file and

– looking like scare-crows – passed by them and one by one kissed their hands. They were Americans. It was April 30, 1945. I survived the war.

INDEX

A

Aaronson, 288
Abake, 87
Aberka, 337
Ablaz, 17
Abli, 237

Abramovich, 64, 66, 79, 85, 86, 148, 231, 318, 319,
    321, 322, 326, 347, 533, 710
ABRAMOVICH, 721
Abramovitch, 268, 638, 642
Abramowitz, 781
Abramsom, 407
Abramson, 68, 302, 360, 407, 584
ABRAMSON, 721
Abromovich–Dalitsisky, 438
Achber, 354
Adamovich, 489
Adeskes, 411, 412, 413
ADLER, 722
Aharon, 641
Aho, 74
Aiker, 97, 112, 307, 483
AIKER, 723
Aktzin, 544
Aleichem, 36, 37, 149, 274, 448
Almog, 189
Alta, 725
Alta the Milk Woman, 600
Alter, 87, 632
Alter the potter, 108
Andlin, 427
Angel, 559, 562, 564
Ankodinov, 701
Antes, 210, 302, 362
Antokolski, 241, 261
Antonov, 792, 793, 794
Apatkina, 62, 83, 91, 354, 413
Aptekina, 475
Aptkina, 346
Arlozoroff, 189
Arnstam, 501
Aron, 431
Aronovsky, 82
Aronson, 330, 331
Aronson, 724
Aryeh, 39
Ash, 37
Asher's, 655

Astreika, 467, 469
Atkatz, 214, 314, 315, 319, 321, 347, 482
Atkatz, 759
Atketz, 732
Atkočiūnaite, 464, 471, 472
Atkočiūnas, 466, 471, 472, 473
Avraham the mason, 98, 99
Avraham the potter, 168
Avrahamovich, 17
Avraka, 286
Avram, 310

B

Babilsky, 549
Baker, 11
Balnik, 8, 17, 554, 674, 677, 679
Balsher, 100, 101, 102, 114, 115, 117
Bankkutsher, 307
Bar, 763, 764
Baran, 682
Baron, 53, 54, 56, 61, 67, 77, 81, 84, 90, 93, 214,
    306, 311, 323, 347, 498, 598, 611
Baron, 725, 726
Barron, 10, 213
Barron, 753
Baruch, 330
Baten, 307, 312, 314, 316, 319, 322, 337, 409, 412,
    706
BATEN, 724, 725, 736
Batten, 211, 213, 214
Bauer, 87
BEILIN, 725
Beker, 67, 403
Ben David, 29, 295
Ben-David, 8, 16, 265
Ben–David (Burstein)], 716
Benkkutzer, 116
Ben-Menachem, 289
Ben–Netz, 239
Ben-Pazi, 165, 280
Bentza, 257
Bentza the deaf, the night guard, 20
Bentze the deaf sentry, 580
Bentzke the butcher, 116
Ben-Yehuda, 15, 186
Ber, 215, 298, 305, 538, 598, 614, 681
Berele the goat, 617
Berele the Tzig [Goat], 617
Bereznikov, 74
Bereznikov, 759
Berger, 103
Berko, 423

Berkover, 469

Berl S, 62

Berlin (Bar-Ilan), 154

Berman, 388, 406, 498, 499, 500

Bernstein, 312, 503, 504, 505

Berzin, 16, 305, 306, 318, 319, 322, 331, 347, 408, 409, 431, 484, 705, 706

Berzin, 726, 727, 736, 737, 759

Beten, 93

Betman, 638

Bialik, 36, 276, 285, 340, 355

Biarsky, 413, 549

Biarsky, 759

Bilbotzky, 740

Bin, 11, 675, 677, 678, 679, 680

Bina, 200

Binyamin P, 63

Bleier, 795

Bleiman, 211

Bliatzkin, 257

Bloch, 422

Bluma, 594

Bluma The Golden, 99

Bluma The Thief, 99

Blumberg, 14, 15, 67, 68, 71, 143, 186, 189, 198, 199, 209, 211, 214, 284, 302, 312, 314, 317, 327, 383, 389, 390, 393, 395, 396, 449, 457, 462, 471, 539, 651

Blumberg, 725

Blumbergs, 198

Blume, 655

Blume's, 655

Blusher, 361

Boilsky, 724

Bolnik, 10

Boz, 306, 473

Boz, 724

Bracanski, 100

Brandwein, 21, 133, 134, 581

Brandweiss, 667

Bransteter, 36

Braudes, 277

Braun, 231, 262, 424, 447, 489, 491, 502

Braznikov, 727

Brechkis, 143

Brezin, 600

Brezins, 476

Breznat, 362

Breznikov, 321

Briman, 362

Broides, 36, 260

Bronznik, 164, 180

Bronznik, 726

Brumkin, 464

Buch, 659

Buchalter, 615

Bulnik, 62, 67

Bumash, 362

Burik, 666

Burstein, 6, 8, 9, 10, 11, 12, 14, 16, 39, 46, 53, 55, 60, 61, 67, 70, 81, 83, 84, 89, 128, 130, 142, 211, 231, 236, 270, 296, 298, 302, 305, 312, 314, 328, 345, 347, 353, 360, 362, 364, 461, 462, 475, 477, 515, 534, 536, 538, 540, 542, 548, 553, 559, 562, 598, 612, 621, 646, 647, 677, 763, 764, 772

Burstein, 724

Bursteins, 198, 675

Burtein, 676

Buz, 68, 345, 347

C

Cain, 277

Carlebach, 31, 187

Carmi, 301, 323

Caro, 155

Chagall, 261

Chaikin, 504, 505

Chaim the Teletze, 613

Chait, 519, 522, 527

Chana the partisan, 16

Chandzhe, 634

Charif, 154

Charna, 187, 188

Chasia with the Pack, 770

Chasid, 77, 85, 92

Chayat, 468

Chefetz, 417

Chein, 299

Chermoni, 195

Cherneman, 614

CHERNIAK, 751

Chernman, 363, 516, 517, 519, 522, 526, 527, 538, 541, 553

CHERNMAN, 751

Chernoff, 261

Chernovitz, 302

Chernowitz, 134

Chizka's, 241

Cholim, 633

Chone the potter, 129

Choshev, 668, 669, 670, 671

Cohen, 23, 110, 220, 222, 277, 761

D

Dabol, 99

Dabol, 731, 759

Daltisisky-Abramovich, 14

Daltitsky, 148, 638
Dans, 66
Das, 593
Dasnik, 730, 733, 742
Daugiala, 676
David, 379, 690, 697
Davidovich, 52, 56, 69, 72, 285, 302, 314, 315, 321,
     347, 361, 364
Davidovich, 732
Davidovitch, 123
Davidson, 15, 239
Davis, 761
Deitz, 15, 109, 289, 359, 496, 498
Deitz, 733
Dembo, 20, 54, 55, 56, 77, 90, 92, 156, 215, 299,
     302, 316, 321, 340, 580, 656, 666
Dembo, 722, 733
Denikin, 606
Deutsch, 427
Dezent, 99, 103
Dezent, 732, 733
Dickens, 36
Dimant, 192
Dobianski, 384, 386, 389, 390, 393, 394, 395
Dobiansky, 56, 68, 70, 77, 80, 92, 213, 288, 299, 312,
     317, 330, 331, 333
Dobiansky, 731, 732
Dochovsky, 337
Dodak, 732, 759
Dodi, 76
Dolgatz, 385, 388, 391, 395
Dolitzki, 36
Dolsachki, 710
Dolticki–Abrahmovitch, 644
Donat, 211
Dragachki, 118, 306, 412, 413
Dragatsky, 63
Dragatzki, 151, 457
Dragatzkis, 676
Dragatzky, 66, 72, 87, 473
Dragatzkys, 87
Dreyfus, 285
Drogetzky, 299
Droskin, 74, 400, 401, 412, 413, 701, 702, 703
Droskin, 733, 734, 759
Drucker, 402, 403, 701
Druker, 538
Dubiansky, 449, 462, 463, 465, 466, 467, 468, 469
Dubinsky, 234
Dudak, 67, 74, 101, 102, 103, 116
Dulgatz, 104
Dushnitzky, 523, 527, 532, 534, 538, 653
Dv"Sh (David The Son Of Shlomo), 131
Dvora Leah The Reciter, 619

E

Egoz, 677
Eidl, 368
Eisenstat, 238
Eizik, 661
Elazar's, 655
Elia, 99, 164, 586
Elia The Butcher, 450
Elia The Fisherman, 99
Eliash, 200
Eliot, 36, 277
Elkes, 419, 504, 505
Elkind, 189
Elyashiv, 154
Entes, 362
Epstein, 14, 53, 55, 62, 73, 82, 84, 86, 90, 101, 102,
     103, 117, 167, 210, 213, 214, 237, 298, 307, 312,
     316, 362, 412, 413, 461
Epstein, 748
Evans, 36

F

Fancevich, 92
Farber, 87, 167, 302, 378, 384, 385, 676, 680, 681,
     696
Farbers, 676
Fein, 307, 388
Fein, 760
Feinberg, 288, 799
Feiska, 87
Feldberg, 111, 348
Feldman, 749
Feldstein, 226
Feliks, 69, 71
Felisher, 679
Felkser, 80
Ferber, 403, 549
Ferber, 749
Feterman, 761, 762
Filvinsky, 654, 655
Flaks, 60, 620
Fleischman, 385
Fleisher, 679, 681, 682
Fleishman, 749
Frakt, 53, 54, 55, 91, 298
Frank, 750
Freidel The Deaf, 281
Fridel's, 673
Fridland, 54, 59, 61, 80, 81
Fridman, 74, 79, 80, 84, 87
Fried, 88, 302, 330, 347
Fried, 750
Friedburg, 750

Friedland, 210, 330, 331, 338, 347
Friedland, 750, 751
Friedman, 16, 214, 215, 231, 298, 299, 305, 306,
    307, 310, 311, 312, 313, 317, 318, 321, 322, 323,
    326, 331, 332, 333, 337, 345, 356, 363, 389, 409,
    482, 509, 538, 612, 706, 713
Friedman, 750, 757
Fromer, 579
Frumer, 19
Furman, 639
Furman, 748
Furmans, 615

G

Gafenovich, 422
Galanreichik, 577
Galinsky, 330, 331, 332, 345, 347
Galinsky, 730
Galperin, 425, 485, 501, 714
Ganis, 730
Gans, 112, 319
Gaon, 240
Garb, 361
Garber, 15, 17, 69, 78, 92, 288, 380, 400, 412, 648,
    652, 698, 701
Garber, 730, 750
Garnow (Zlunker), 197
Gazit, 243
Gazit (Zisla), 193, 242
Gelbroit, 729, 730
Gelfer, 511
Gelfer, 730
Gelgiser, 164
Genes, 420
Gerber, 322, 338
Germanisky, 44
Gershke The "Bas, 113
Gershovich, 74, 87, 93
Gershoviches, 66
Gertner, 407
Gertner, 731
Giladi, 260
Gineika, 387, 388, 473
Ginsberg, 686
Ginzberg, 71, 93, 100, 109, 162, 241, 289
Ginzburg, 377, 385, 386, 389, 391, 695
Ginzburg, 729
Gipas, 682
Girshevich, 614
Girshevitz, 609
Gis, 729
Glass, 632

Glaz, 317, 318, 319, 321, 322, 361, 364, 447, 617,
    620, 621
Glaz, 730
Glazer, 102, 111, 117, 214, 302, 317, 321, 426, 538
Glazer, 730
Glinsky, 319
Gloz, 584
Gluzman, 512
Goecke, 465, 466, 468, 474
Gold, 180, 315, 476
GOLD, 727, 728, 744
Goldberg, 11, 80, 205, 262, 332, 455, 761, 762
Goldfaden, 137, 149
Goldman, 48, 151, 158, 298, 313, 321, 363, 374, 376,
    379, 409, 694, 697, 706
Goldman, 728
Goldmans, 692
Gold-Mines, 314
Goldschmid, 180, 274, 382, 483, 507, 676, 699
Goldschmidt, 168, 171, 492, 516, 517, 522
Goldschmidt-Berko, 430
Goldshmid, 10, 14, 15, 16, 18, 54, 56, 59, 60, 61, 62,
    70, 80, 81, 83, 84, 90, 169, 171, 235, 274, 362,
    388, 469, 632
Goldshmid, 728, 729, 759
Goldshmidt, 211, 215, 302, 305, 307, 310, 311, 312,
    328, 337, 344, 345, 347, 354, 414, 425, 516, 517, 519,
    522, 538, 547, 549, 550, 556, 565, 568
Goldsmidt, 801
Goldsmith, 33, 39, 159, 207
Goldstein, 280, 283, 364, 771
Goldstein, 728
Golombek, 200
Goloskos, 200
Gordin, 37, 38, 39
Gordon, 68, 154, 161, 235, 285
Gordon, 729
Gorfein, 8, 14, 21, 24, 52, 77, 79, 80, 85, 94, 125,
    302, 330, 331, 332, 333, 338, 343, 345, 352
Gorfein, 729
Gorfein Noy, 127
Gorfinkel, 40, 191, 220
Gorgel, 422
Gorki, 285
Graber, 112
Grabersky, 178
Granevich, 49, 80, 81, 341, 344, 352, 355, 666
Granewicz, 631
Granewitz, 591
Granovich, 167, 302, 375, 693
Granvich, 360
Grazutis, 681
Greenberg, 424, 516
Greenberg, 731, 759

Greenblatt, 17, 314, 315, 516, 716, 717
GREENBLATT, 731
Grigaliunas, 385, 386, 387, 391, 392
Grinberg, 486, 490, 715
Grinblat, 67
Grinblatt, 211
Gringold, 171
Grishovich, 305
Grodski, 110, 234
GRODSKI, 730, 731
Grodsky, 80, 213, 289, 330, 331, 332, 338, 345, 348
Gromka, 531
Gronevich, 654
Grossman, 67, 210, 214, 231, 312, 314, 316, 317,
    318, 322, 325, 337, 501
GROSSMAN, 731
Grun, 79, 426, 510, 511, 512
GRUN, 731, 759
Grundman, 70, 84
GUREVICH, 759
Gurfinkel, 598
Gurvich, 231, 305, 306, 310, 318, 319, 321, 337, 347,
    402
GURVICH, 729
Gurvitch, 507
Gurwitz, 149
Gusev, 792
Guterman, 796
Gutler, 17, 411, 704
GUTLER, 727
Guttman, 214

H

Habima, 262
Hagalili, 577
Handler, 74, 87
Hans, 470
Harel, 192
Hautriner, 105
Heiman, 74, 193, 318, 321, 344, 354
HEIMAN, 734
Helerman, 704
Hencha, 62
Hendler, 263
HENDLER, 734
Henech, 624
Herman, 16, 574
Hershkovitz, 192
Herzl, 93, 132, 155, 269, 270, 285, 668
Heshel, 237
Hiltzerner Rav, 615
Hirshbein, 309
Hirshe "Chandzhe", 634

Hirshe A "Shnaps, 634
Hirshe A Schnaps, 634
Hirshe The Teletze, 613
Hirshkan, 37
Hitler, 435, 698
Holtzberg, 425
HONIGMAN, 734
Horowitz, 354
Horwitz, 157
Huberman, 134, 261

I

IKER, 759
Ilinevits, 179
Impulavicus, 680
Inhaber, 676
Intriligator, 73, 156, 210
INTRILIGITER, 723
Intriligitor, 302
Ish-Shalom, 205
Israëls, 261
Itchikovich, 302
Itza, 636
Itza The "Bul", 98
Itze, 626
Itzele The Bul, 289
Itze's, 622
Itzik, 592, 654
Itzik The Tinsmith, 20
Itzike's, 655
Itzikovich, 87, 671
ITZIKOVICH, 723
Itziks, 89
Itzik's, 654, 663, 667, 669, 670
Itzka "Bul", 87
Itzkovich, 66, 318, 322
Ivenksy, 360
Ivenski, 103, 688
Ivensky, 15, 17, 70, 205, 210, 211, 214, 215, 265,
    267, 268, 270, 271, 272, 285, 298, 302, 310, 311,
    314, 315, 327, 328, 364, 479, 513, 584, 606, 615,
    616, 779
IVENSKY, 723
Iwens, 16, 17, 479
Izraelson, 361
IZRAELSON, 723

J

Jablokov, 762
Jabotinski, 98
Jachnin, 791
Jachnovich, 667, 668, 669, 670, 671
Jaffa, 616

Jaffe, 478
JAG, 759
Jalinovich, 6, 179, 322, 323, 330, 331, 332, 333, 338, 345
JALINOVICH, 738
Jalinowitz, 126, 379, 697
Janosevitch, 44, 123
Janosovich, 242
Janovsky, 519
Janusevich, 327, 354
Janusovich, 221, 315
JANUSOVICH, 738, 739
Jerome, 36
Jochovsky, 235, 289, 298, 312, 386, 516, 519, 522, 526, 533, 538, 541
JOCHOVSKY, 735
Jog, 476
JONAS, 738
Jonashevich, 186
Jordan, 446
Jordon, 419
Josef the baker, 104
Josefs, 231, 313, 318, 321, 326, 330, 331, 345
JOSEFS, 738
Joselevich, 284
Joselovich, 186, 191, 200, 327, 335, 342, 355, 614
JOSELOVICH, 738
Joselovitch, 44
Jozefs, 676
Judelevich, 201, 229, 231, 234, 473
Judelevitch, 41, 43, 774
Judelovich, 676
Jurgis, 426, 510, 511
Jurman, 321
Justyn the forester, 416

K

Kadish, 610, 662
Kagan, 9, 10, 15, 18, 53, 54, 55, 71, 74, 80, 84, 87, 176, 231, 244, 245, 256, 289, 301, 302, 310, 312, 313, 324, 342, 348, 349, 354, 356, 385, 386, 389, 391, 427, 447, 491, 507, 529, 545, 640
KAGAN, 728, 739, 751
Kahansky, 403, 549
KAHANSKY, 739, 740
KAIROVSKY, 741
Kalinski, 101
KALINSKY, 752
Kalutz, 447
Kamber, 173
Kaminska, 37
Kaminsky, 92
Kanan, 16

Kandinsky, 261
Kanovich, 484
Kaper, 235, 298, 307, 312, 337, 360, 476
KAPER, 751
Kapers, 477
Kapiner, 74
Kaplan, 53, 60, 62, 65, 84, 189, 211, 214, 317, 506, 689
KAPLAN, 752
Kapliansky, 74
Kapol, 62, 88, 93, 108, 447, 549, 656
KAPOL, 752
Kapusta, 593
Karalaunas, 682
Karaliunas, 681
Kark, 200
KARO, 756
Kasparowicz, 391
Katz, 56, 68, 89, 93, 101, 175, 176, 183, 211, 302, 303, 304, 306, 317, 318, 362, 425, 430, 625, 675, 677, 771
KATZ, 740
Katzav, 85, 86, 232, 318, 322, 381, 699
Katzenberg, 37, 63, 66, 73, 83, 202, 288, 299, 310, 323, 330, 331, 476, 656
KATZENBERG, 753
Katzenerg, 656
Kaufman, 200
Kaufmann, 241, 243, 261
Kazansky, 80, 319, 321
Kazimir, 510, 511
Kazlauskas, 386
Keidainer, 580, 589
Keidanski, 31, 113, 225, 229, 302
Keidansky, 235, 343, 345, 346, 347, 353, 354, 355, 385, 413, 475, 584
KEIDANSKY, 751, 752
Keidianer, 665, 668, 671
Keidianski, 173, 686
Keidiansky, 70, 606
Keitel, 486, 487, 490, 715
Kerem, 517
Kerzner, 54, 91, 361, 606
KERZNER, 752
KHANOCH, 737
Khasid, 159, 207, 213, 288, 318, 322, 330, 332, 356, 477, 763
KHASID, 737, 759
KHAVELS, 737
Khermoni, 15
Khrushchev, 518, 630
Kiediansky, 671
Kietel, 428
Kirzner, 211, 298, 314, 321, 615

KIRZNER, 747

Klachman, 79, 317, 403

Klatinas, 681, 682

Klein, 261

KLEIN, 752

Klibanski, 231

Klibansky, 59, 61, 63, 77, 80, 81, 213, 214, 235, 298, 306, 307, 312, 314, 316, 319, 322, 323, 330, 331, 332, 337, 338, 345, 355, 363

KLIBANSKY, 752

Klibensky, 375, 693

Klotz, 71, 74, 78, 211, 313, 314, 315, 319, 328, 363, 377, 395, 403, 695

KLOTZ, 752, 760

KNIPER, 752

KOBLANSKY, 751

Kobliansky, 87, 92

Kochavi, 225

Kolbansky, 361

Kolbianski, 302

Kolbiansky, 23, 71, 78, 92, 105, 342, 355, 363, 515

KOLBITZKY, 760

Kolchak, 606

Kolka, 200

Kolkovski, 394, 395

Komberg, 668

Konchaitis, 501

Konsky, 330

Kontziatis, 499

Kook, 165

Kopans, 100, 108

Kopel, 94, 510

Kopeliansky, 416

Koper, 52, 54, 61, 81, 82, 85, 631

Kopilansky, 92

KOPILIANSKY, 751

Kopiner, 432

Koplovich, 189

Korobelnik, 681

Korolenko, 229, 236

Kosakovski, 775

Koshlevich, 356

Kosiksik, 229

Koskowska, 22

Kotargna, 486, 714

Kotkas, 101

Kotler, 77, 85, 86, 318, 322

Kozanovsky, 363

Krabitzky, 331

KRABTZKY, 753

KRAM, 753

Kramerman, 362

Kravchok, 16, 17, 411, 704

Kravitz, 103

Krechmer, 241

Krem, 554

Kremenitzin, 56, 77, 79, 93, 101, 331, 333

KREMENITZKY, 753

Kremer, 615

Kretzmer, 386, 388

Kriger, 88, 619

Krikin, 522, 523

Kronick, 214, 314

Kronik, 81, 315, 405, 704

KRONIK, 731, 753

Kruger, 768

Krulitzkina, 420, 421

Krupnik, 409, 706

Kulbiansky, 15, 18, 211

KULBIANSKY, 722, 737, 751

Kulcianski, 248, 252, 253, 254, 255

Kulvianski, 243, 246, 248, 249, 250, 251, 254, 255

Kulviansky, 247, 258, 260, 261

Kuritsky, 786

Kursik, 364

Kursikishik, 204

Kursk, 229, 232

Kurskisik, 317

Kursnik, 10

Kushilevich, 323

KUSHILEVITZ, 751

L

Labas, 119, 149, 157

Labas" the Lithuanian Policeman, 648

Lamiansky, 263, 264

Lan, 16, 414, 420, 424, 427, 435, 492, 493

LAN, 740

Landau, 19, 22, 24, 29, 33, 40, 42, 46, 75, 96, 122, 123, 125, 128, 143, 148, 152, 154, 159, 161, 164, 165, 172, 175, 178, 179, 184, 186, 193, 195, 197, 198, 202, 207, 220, 223, 225, 227, 232, 235, 237, 257, 258, 265, 270, 274, 276, 278, 280, 283, 284, 288, 289,291, 295, 296, 298, 301, 327, 338, 340, 341, 359, 360, 365, 370, 372, 380, 383, 400, 402, 405, 408, 411, 414, 436, 438, 459, 479, 482, 485, 488, 490, 491, 493, 494, 496, 502, 503, 507, 514, 515, 547, 556, 559, 566, 567, 569, 571, 574, 577, 578, 583, 587, 597, 603, 609, 611, 612, 623, 627, 632, 638, 642, 645, 647, 648, 652, 653, 654, 656, 659, 661, 673, 674, 684, 686, 690, 698, 701, 704, 705, 708, 710, 713, 716, 719, 759, 761

Lande, 93

Landman, 81, 91, 104, 312, 363, 450

LANDMAN, 742, 743

Landres, 664, 666, 668, 670

Landsberg, 189

Landsman, 228, 318, 461, 616
Lantzman, 84, 305, 306, 312, 317, 319, 321, 322, 323, 347
LANTZMAN, 743
Laschinski, 498
Lavie, 16, 186, 190, 201, 219, 256, 571, 572
Lavie-Levkovitz, 571
Leah, 293, 594
Leah B, 82
LEFFER, 743
Lehman, 192, 466, 467, 468
Leib, 103, 104, 801
Leibka "the bastard", 415
Leibke the "bastard, 119
Leibke the Bastard, 118
Leibovich, 414
LEICHTER, 742, 752
Leizer, 20, 74, 408, 590, 591, 662, 663, 667, 705
Leizer the chimneysweep, 580, 596
Leizka the Gingi, 298
Leizka the Yellow, 545
Leizke the Yellow, 515
Lenin, 285
Lentshinke, 632, 634
Lerner, 425
Leshchinski, 501
Leshnitzer, 262
Letzion, 544
Levi, 425, 528, 567
Levich, 333
Levin, 10, 15, 16, 17, 21, 53, 54, 55, 60, 65, 66, 68, 80, 81, 83, 84, 88, 89, 165, 166, 194, 198, 203, 204, 210, 211, 212, 232, 298, 300, 302, 305, 306, 312, 314, 315, 317, 328, 344, 345, 355, 361, 362, 363, 365, 370, 391, 424, 425, 426, 438, 447, 449, 463, 464, 476, 478, 485, 486, 487, 488, 489, 490, 491, 498, 502, 515, 529, 530, 532, 534, 535, 538, 540, 542, 545, 559, 581, 584, 616, 645, 657, 679, 681, 713, 715, 771
LEVIN, 740, 741, 744, 759
Levin the leader of the gangs, 715
Levin the Yellow, 424, 425, 428
Levins, 198
Levinski, 111
Levinsky, 289
Levinson, 36
Levit, 99
Levitan, 438
Levitt, 74, 94, 402
Levitz, 39, 215, 299, 310, 312, 331, 388
LEVITZ, 741
Levkovich, 201
LIBER, 742
Liberman, 63, 64, 261

LIBERMAN, 742
Libermann, 261
Libertal, 52, 314, 315
Libshin, 544
Lichtenstein, 173, 359
Lieberman, 638
Liebermann, 241
Lifschitz, 330, 332, 345, 542, 568
Lifshitz, 562
Lilienbaum, 36
Lin, 10, 15, 179, 232, 361
Lin (Jalinovich or Ilinevits), 179
LINDA, 742
Lipe's, 662
Lipschitz, 10, 52, 80, 763
Lipshitz, 10
LIPSHITZ, 742
Loberbaum, 559
LOIT, 740
Lomianski, 161, 204, 210, 234
Lomiansky, 14, 18, 54, 59, 61, 80, 81, 299, 310, 344, 355, 361, 362, 767
Lomiansky-Wulf, 9, 14, 17, 767
Lon, 117
Lopianski, 71
Lopiansky, 305, 360
LOPIANSKY, 741
Lozer Poleit, 631
Lozer's, 655
Lukman, 66, 72, 80, 151, 402, 403, 409, 457, 655, 678, 706, 786, 787, 789
LUKMAN, 741, 742, 759
Lukmans, 676
Luria, 462, 463, 464, 466

M

Magid, 432
MAGID, 759
Magin, 117
Makel, 598
Maldaikis, 682
Maneh, 355
Manes, 475
Mangin, 388, 391
Manginas, 473
Manisehewitz, 790
Manisehwitz, 789
Manishewitz, 786
Mankovski, 708
Manosevich, 476
Manosovich, 73, 87, 413
MANOSOVICH, 744
MANOSOVTCH, 744

Mar, 15, 98, 101, 102, 296, 297
MAR, 745
Marevjanski, 783
Margalit, 467, 468, 469
Margolis, 110, 347
MARGOLIS, 745, 758
Markov, 509, 510
Markusevich, 257
Martkowsky, 427
Marx, 285
Mashkop, 426
Matei, 110, 659
Mateikiškiai, 675
Matel, 592
Mauer, 619
Mazolis, 388
Mechnik, 298, 306, 307, 312, 323, 337
MECHNIK, 744
Mehr, 647
Meidanek, 36
Meir, 109, 126, 157, 490
Meir the bath attendant, 108, 109
Meirke the miller, 618
Meirke the Miller, 618
Meirke the tailor, 621
Meirovich, 15, 52, 74, 231, 298, 305, 317, 319, 323,
     356, 412, 413, 538
Meirovitch, 215, 357
Meirson, 241
Melamed, 496
MELAMEDOVICH, 744
MELAMODOVICH, 744
Meldes, 473
Melechke the hunchback, 591
Meltz, 676, 681
Menachem, 359
Mendel, 359
Mendel the shoemaker, 368
Mendele, 285
Mendelson, 568
Meniuk, 92
Menzel, 467, 468
Merbianski, 302
Merbiansky, 515
MERBIANSKY, 745
Merovich, 606
MIASNIK, 743
Michaelova, 528, 531
Miche, 593
Millner, 785, 786, 787
Milner, 101, 107, 307
MILNER, 743, 744, 760
MILSTEIN, 744
Miltz, 53, 62

MILTZ, 744
Minde, 100
Mines, 70, 71, 204, 210, 211, 328, 354, 356, 357,
     364, 395, 406
MINES, 744
Mintz, 15, 186, 201, 220
Mishelevitz, 594
Modigliani, 261
Moirer, 325
Mongin, 92
Monitz, 200, 214, 230, 231, 302, 316, 317, 318, 319,
     321, 323, 325
MONITZ, 743
Monosevich, 402, 404, 411, 412, 413, 516, 519, 538, 701
MONOSOVICH, 759
Morr, 62, 72, 74, 156, 210, 211, 312
Moshe, 69
Mosheke "The Stale, 295
Mota the Smith, 594
Motnik, 360
Mottel the smith, 100
Movshovich, 14, 362
MOVSHOVICH, 743
Movshowitz, 152, 153
Mratchk, 15
Munitz, 72
Murbiansky, 67

                         N

Nachimovich, 676
Nachman, 510
NACHMANOVICH, 737
Nachum, 74, 389
Nachumevich, 609
Nachumovich, 231
NACHUMOVICH, 741, 745, 746
Nachumovitch, 39
Nafcholin the tailor, 647
Naftali, 90, 237, 293, 297, 368, 587, 636, 647
Naftali the tailor, 368
Namiot, 66, 67, 73, 84, 186, 187, 188, 189, 190, 199,
     200, 209, 218, 402, 403, 460, 476, 513, 516, 522, 538,
     545, 549, 553
NAMIOT, 746, 760
Namjot, 786, 787, 789, 793
Napoleon, 419
Nemlich, 243
Nikolevitch, 40
Noach the Roof Layer, 652
Noach the roofer, 107
Nobichovich, 323
Nochimovich, 52, 55, 56, 66, 77, 80, 81, 85, 86, 87,
     156, 299, 331, 335, 336

Nota, 69
Notinger, 657
Novichovich, 77, 81
Novickovich, 291
Novikhovich, 307
NOVIKHOVICH, 745
Novokhovich, 238
Noy, 8, 10, 14, 52, 120, 125, 332, 333, 338, 352, 498, 568
Noy [(Gorfein)], 8
Nuchimovich, 306, 307, 310, 318
Nusoviches, 72

O

O.[pnitsky], 210
Odoskes, 102, 632, 633
of Pogirsky, 653
Ofek, 9, 10, 356, 562, 564
Opanik, 299
Opanitzki, 153
Opanitzky, 43, 310
Opnik, 52, 82, 92, 310, 319, 322, 330, 331, 332, 338, 345, 355, 356, 600
OPNIK, 722, 723, 742
Opnitsky, 15, 209, 210, 211, 212, 215, 218
Opnitsky-Taub, 212
Opnitzky, 6, 65, 68, 90, 103, 186, 187, 190, 198, 199, 201, 202, 233, 235, 299, 312, 314, 330, 339, 360, 362, 363, 364, 385, 386
OPNITZKY, 722, 751
Optekina, 634
Optnitzky, 362
Orlin, 677, 678, 679
Ovadyah, 293
Ovadyah the tailor, 293
Ozvolk, 673

P

Pagir, 293, 578, 586, 587, 599
Pagirsky, 592, 593, 594
PALAN, 748
Palec, 783, 785, 786, 789, 797, 799
PALTZ, 748
Pandre, 72, 95
Panirsky, 10
Papilski, 460
Pariser, 801
Pass, 167
Pechkis, 500
Pechman, 276
Perchik, 77, 83, 86, 231, 313, 317, 318, 321, 322, 323, 326, 331, 333, 347
PERCHIK, 751

Peretz, 129, 155, 199, 220, 226
Peretz the tailor, 129
Perevozhniks, 676
Perevoznik, 10, 16, 18, 52, 66, 73, 74, 77, 231, 302, 313, 318, 319, 322, 326, 476, 477, 516, 522, 538, 547, 549, 556
PEREVOZNIK, 749, 750
Perevozniks, 476
Perlstein, 15, 17, 56, 68, 149, 184, 185, 230, 231, 232, 306, 317, 319, 321, 328, 331, 332, 338, 347, 390, 675, 684, 718
PERLSTEIN, 731, 735, 750
Persky, 16, 66, 73, 74, 475, 574, 658
Pesach, 23, 662
Pesach the furrier, 616
Petarosovich, 231
Peterosevich, 716
Petershein, 673
Petliura, 606
Petrikansky, 71
PETRIKANSKY, 748
Petrosovich, 67, 73, 411
Piklachik, 451
Pilovnik, 424, 425
Pilvinski, 591, 592
Pimstein, 78, 92, 321
PIMSTEIN, 748
Pinkovski, 385, 387
Pinkovski the fireman, 389
Pinkovsky, 104
Pinkowski, 416
Pinkus, 410, 707
Pinski, 37
Pinta, 257
Pisarro, 261
Pitkovsky, 225
Pitkowsky, 126
PLAKS, 749
Plakser, 330, 345, 363
PLAKSER, 749
Plasker, 319
Podison, 761
Pogir, 14, 16, 17, 18, 19, 30, 79, 89, 107, 431, 482, 623, 654, 661, 673, 763, 766
POGIR, 748, 760
Pogirski, 302
Pogirsky, 16, 53, 54, 55, 60, 63, 64, 70, 81, 84, 87, 89, 91, 102, 103, 167, 198, 203, 210, 211, 362, 363, 432, 569, 584, 631, 653, 655, 667, 671
POGIRSKY, 748
Pogirsy-Epstein, 62
Polans, 783
Portnoy, 86, 318, 319, 323, 331
Pozitzer, 385

POZITZER, 748
Praboznik, 101
Prakt, 211, 306, 310, 311, 314
PRAKT, 749
Preis, 507
Puzitzer, 66

R

Rabiner, 305, 306, 322
RABINER, 754
Rabinovich, 343, 378, 447, 696
Rabinovitch, 682
Rabinovitz, 240
Radkinson, 239
Rafael the Shamash, 130
Ralis, 274
Ralys, 34
RAM, 753
Ran, 302, 360, 361, 620
RAN, 753
Rapopski, 497
Rashkes, 9, 10, 14, 17, 71, 77, 80, 149, 154, 345,
    360, 364, 372, 449, 483, 496, 690, 691, 763
RASHKES, 728, 756, 760
Ratner, 465
Ratzker, 199
Rauka, 505
Raziel, 40
Reb Shmuel Leizer, 663, 664, 668
Reb Yankel, 663
Reb Yisrael David, 663
Recha the miller, 107
RECHA'S, 745
Reibstein, 52, 77, 305, 318, 322, 331, 332, 333, 338,
    430, 801
REIBSTEIN, 724, 754, 755
Reiles, 23
Reilis, 362
Reima, 385, 386, 387, 388, 389, 390, 391, 392, 393,
    394, 395
Reima the Lithuanian, 385
Reines, 632, 636, 638
Reping, 215, 299, 310, 312, 337
Resnick, 211, 314, 317, 598
Reuven the, 113
Reznik, 94, 337, 363, 400, 507, 701
REZNIK, 754
Ribel, 507
Rickless, 230, 288, 507, 763
Ricklis, 74, 92
Rickliss-Perlstein, 185
Riklansky, 52, 519

Rikless, 10, 13, 15, 99, 184, 227, 228, 230, 231, 298,
    313, 318, 319, 320, 321, 322, 323, 325, 326, 337
RIKLESS, 755
Rikliansky, 69, 84, 214, 306, 312, 361
RIKLIANSKY, 755, 756
Riklis, 68, 93
Ritz, 30, 586, 594, 595
Rivka–Buna, 605
Rochman, 507
Rodkov the medic, 518
Roker, 683
Rommel, 206, 466
Rosenberg, 70, 72, 124, 302, 343, 346, 347, 354,
    384, 413
ROSENBERG, 739, 754
Rosenberg-Janusovich, 302
Rosenson, 40
Rosenthal, 344, 424, 425
Rozenson, 154
Rubin, 14, 15, 161, 162, 163, 302, 362, 364, 491
RUBIN, 754
Rubinovich, 402
RUBINOVICH, 754
Rubinstein, 83
Rufer, 632
Runik, 158
Ryuvele, 771

S

Sachke, 632
Sachke Dalai, 635
Sachke the crazy, 635
Sack, 302, 320, 321, 344
Sadeh, 189
Sadler, 343
Saker, 283, 284, 340
Saker (Sirek), 10
Salanter, 617
Salkan, 11
Salken, 679
Saltuper, 62, 67, 84
Sandler, 53, 62, 70, 210, 211, 317, 343, 346, 347,
    354, 362, 460
SANDLER, 747
Sandman, 231
Sanel, 305
Sarig, 326
Saveski, 775
Savka, 494
Schmid, 615
Schneider, 483
Schneor, 95
Schwabbe, 31

Sefarim, 110
Seforim, 36, 149, 241
Segal, 56, 78, 237, 238, 409, 599, 602, 706
SEGAL, 746, 760
Segalovski, 210, 211, 609, 635
Segalovsky, 6, 10, 20, 47, 53, 61, 62, 63, 65, 66, 69, 80, 198, 235, 298, 307, 310, 311, 333, 337, 344, 347, 361, 363, 517, 523, 529, 532, 534, 538, 542, 547, 580, 768
SEGALOVSKY, 746
Segalson, 486, 488, 714
Seker (Sirek), 287
Semionov, 419
Senior, 403, 549
SENIOR, 747
Serbovitch, 504, 505
Sereni, 224
Sesitsky, 67, 84, 87, 91, 315
Sesitzki, 211, 388
Sesitzky, 19, 198, 211, 285, 314, 322, 347, 579
SESITZKY, 737, 747, 757
Shabses, 103
Shabtai, 52, 74, 85, 86, 307, 310, 318, 322
SHABTAI'S, 756
Shachke, 630
Shachor, 62, 69, 70, 77, 81, 299, 302, 306, 307, 310, 311, 318, 319, 328, 330, 331, 332, 333, 345, 347
SHACHOR, 756, 757
Shaham, 599, 600, 601, 603, 604
Shakhnovich, 734
Shalovich, 559, 562, 566, 567, 568
Shalovitz, 9
Shalputer, 716
Shaltuper, 314, 315
Shami, 559
Shamir, 122
Shanel, 321
Shani, 568
Shapira, 15, 18, 66, 77, 78, 82, 103, 178, 181, 215, 235, 298, 299, 306, 307, 312, 322, 330, 331, 332, 333, 337, 338, 345, 363, 385, 388, 389, 395, 426, 522, 550, 554, 609, 687
SHAPIRA, 758
Shapiro, 237, 352
Shaposhnik, 80
Shapostineitis, 511
Shaputer, 717
Sharshab, 112
Shaultufer, 17
Shava, 274
Shaw, 36
Shefi, 562
Shegansky, 403
SHEGANSKY, 732

Sheinyuk, 354
SHELTOPER, 758
Sherman, 412
Shimkovitz, 211
Shimon, 160, 228, 280, 281, 283, 293, 294, 332, 588, 664, 668
Shimon David, 661
Shimon Elia the butcher, 113
Shimon the teacher, 105
Shimshon, 364, 450
Shleimtze the Ox, 632
Shlimovich, 52
Shliomovich, 315
Shlomins, 441
SHLOMINS, 758
Shlomo (of David-Elia the Karetnik), 30
Shlomo the barber, 20
Shlomo the shaver and barber, 580
Shlomo the Shochet, 93
SHLOMOVICH, 757, 758
Shlomovitz, 180, 237
Shlopochnik, 446
Shlopochnik the medic, 445
Shlupsky, 88, 406
SHLUPSKY, 758
Shmaya the Angry, 661
Shmuelov, 424, 426
Shnaps, 632
Shneid, 85
Shneider, 159, 207
Shneour, 31, 32, 95
Shochat, 465
Shochet, 764
shoemaker Taffer, 104
Shoham, 10, 186, 213, 214, 298, 302, 307, 316, 317
SHOHAM, 739, 756
Sholem the Balagole, 14
Sholem, the Wagon Driver, 27
Shoub, 87, 104, 105, 111, 289
Shpilansky, 71, 315
SHPILANSKY, 758
Shragovich, 231, 460
Shtern, 244
Shugas, 386
Shukstaliski, 200
Shulka, 593
Silber, 103, 422, 424, 500
SILBER, 735, 736
Silberman, 90, 229, 307, 310, 312, 344, 503, 606, 761, 762, 763, 764, 765
Silman, 47, 65, 66, 91, 99, 109, 111, 155, 156, 162, 164, 199, 240, 257, 258, 348, 350, 351, 359, 364, 431, 584, 609, 610, 611, 675, 678
SILMAN, 746

Simanis, 388, 473
Simchovich, 538
Simkovich, 77, 330, 331
SIMKOVICH, 757
Singer, 660
SINKA, 747
SINTOCHKY, 746, 747
Sintuchky, 403
Sirek, 10, 15, 52, 156, 269, 283, 284, 314, 315, 340,
    361, 609, 610, 611, 645, 763
Sirek (Sakar), 15
Sirkin, 313, 325
Skarolski, 22
Sliagris, 385, 387, 392, 393, 394
SLIBKIN, 747
Slomin, 78, 210, 211, 302, 363, 426
SLOMIN, 747
Slonimsky, 464
Sluman, 69
Smetana, 262, 385, 387, 637
Smetona, 120, 432, 675, 683
Smolenskin, 36
Snunit-Zelmanovich, 74
Sobieski, 22
Sodarski, 683
Sodarsky, 23
Sofer, 16
Sokolovski, 681
Solomin, 231, 492, 493, 502, 562
Solomon, 9, 11
Soloveichik, 186
Soloveitchik, 123, 327
Soloveitchik (Janosevitch), 123
Soloviov, 113
Solski, 210, 211
Solsky, 14, 52, 60, 62, 68, 73, 82, 84, 85, 152, 314,
    362, 388
SOLSKY, 722, 746
Soutine, 261
Spector, 154
Spigler, 708
Spigler-Mankovsky, 17
Spivak, 640
Squire, 220
Sreika, 473
Stalin, 435
Stein, 213, 214, 215, 223, 302, 317, 381, 598, 699,
    786, 787
STEIN, 757
STEINBACH, 757
Steinkert, 74
Stepan, 605
Stern, 14, 15, 17, 42, 52, 54, 56, 68, 70, 87, 91, 156,
    160, 175, 176, 177, 205, 210, 225, 226, 231, 260,

272, 276, 278, 298, 302, 306, 310, 317, 325, 342,
    354, 356, 360, 364, 385, 388, 436, 514, 584, 657,
    663, 668, 669, 670
STERN, 739, 757
Sternberg, 103
Stoliar, 409, 706
Stoller, 52, 80, 330, 332, 345
STOLLER, 746
Strauch, 261
Strom, 761
Struk, 241, 243, 261
Strum, 90, 317, 318, 321, 322, 409, 706
STRUM, 757, 760
Sulski, 675
Sulsky, 310, 345, 347
Suntochky, 73, 74, 78, 403, 549
Swirsky, 677

                              T

Tabachovich, 347, 353
Tabchovich, 345
TAFFER, 737, 739
Taibl, 379
Tal, 103
Talalas, 680, 682
Tallat–Kelpša, 263
Tambank, 761
Tartak, 17, 185, 718
TARTEK, 737
Tauba, 15, 202, 204, 209
Tauba (Opnitzky), 202
Tauber, 363
Teitelbaum, 52, 77, 85, 86, 91, 231, 317, 318, 321,
    322, 325
TEITELBAUM, 737
Teitz, 459, 653
Teper, 86
Tepper, 459
Terks, 662
Tevka, 30, 586
The Shul Caller, 634
Thompson, 168, 293, 396, 462, 475
Tilmun, 291
Toibe, 281
Toleda, 293
Tolstoy, 285
Tovia, 92
TRASPOLSKY, 740
Trivish, 314
Trotsky, 411
Troyush, 211
Tschernoff, 249
Tshernikovsky, 276, 355

Tsoref, 414, 492, 513, 565, 568
Twain, 36
Tzemach, 88, 593, 619
Tzimes, 202
Tzion, 17
Tzipa, 89
Tzon, 402
Tzoref, 10, 14, 96, 159, 168, 171, 632
Tzoref (Goldshmid), 96
Tzoref, formerly Goldschmidt, 171
Tzur, 134
Tzvi, 318, 331
Tzvia, 331, 610
Tzvia's, 655

U

Ulpasky, 77, 318, 322, 331, 333, 339
Unterschatz, 59, 61, 63, 80, 81, 83, 214, 215, 257, 375, 693
Untershatz, 286, 298, 299, 302, 305, 306, 310, 312, 314, 315, 331, 333, 337, 338, 344, 347, 406
UNTERSHATZ, 722
Uriash, 425
URLOVICH, 736

V

Vaičiūnas, 472, 473
Vaitokunas, 34
Valchokovsky, 302, 360, 361, 364, 386, 389, 391
VALCHOKOVSKY, 735
Valchokowski, 111
Valdiva, 386
Valonas, 494, 513
Valshchiaus, 386
Vansevic, 460
Vansevicius, 460
Vansevičius, 473
Vansovich, 386, 388
Vansovitch, 98
Vardnikov, 530
Veps, 331, 333, 338, 431
Verbovsky, 464
Vicho, 361
VICHOV, 759
Vidtzky, 310
Vidutzky, 88
Vidzky, 547
VIDZKY, 734
Vikar, 476
Vilan, 574
Vilkomirsky, 84, 302, 323, 331, 333, 345, 347
VILKOMIRSKY, 735
Vinchuk the Great, 615

Vinitsky, 16
Vinitzky, 11, 314, 337, 597, 600, 601, 606
VINITZKY, 735, 746
Vinitzkys, 611
Vintman, 16
Vinton, 11
Vintshevsky, 15
Vislitsky, 467, 468
Vitas the Great, 675
Vizinsky, 519
Voves, 18
Vulfowitch, 771, 772
Vulfowitche, 772
Vytautas, 385, 388, 622
Vytautas the Great, 615

W

Walinchius, 111
Walsnak, 425
Wanglass, 239
Wansovich, 385
Wasgal, 69
Weichko, 103
WEILER, 734
Weiner, 6, 214, 273, 299, 310, 314, 315, 317, 327, 363, 428
WEINER, 734
Weinik, 761
Weinstein, 761
Weitzman, 198
Weitzstein, 70, 149, 156, 203, 362, 666
Wender, 78, 87, 678, 680
Wenders, 676
Werbovsky, 426
Wichov, 409, 516, 707
Wiener, 44, 46, 52, 62, 81, 84, 93, 361
Wiker, 449
WILD, 744
Wilensky, 762
WILK, 734, 735
Wilkomirsky, 80, 84, 88
Wilks, 386
Winchevsky, 23, 238
Winik, 361
Winitzky, 84, 93
Winton, 597, 600, 603
Wolchokovsky, 71, 149
Wolf, 241
WOLFE, 735
Wolfovich, 67, 68, 71, 78, 80, 81, 82, 94, 102, 235, 298, 299, 302, 305, 312, 356, 361, 515, 516, 517, 519, 522, 538, 541, 553, 621, 676
Wolfovich-Burstein, 72

Wolfowitzes, 675
Wolk, 210, 321, 347, 363, 627
WOLK, 734
Wulkan, 460
Wunder, 235, 378, 385, 696, 761
WUNDER, 735, 749, 759

Y

Yaakov, 280, 283
Yachnovitz, 581, 589
Yachnowitz, 21
Yafa, 438
Yaffa, 62, 74, 77, 78, 79, 82, 85, 86, 112, 151, 231, 298, 302, 312, 318, 322, 345, 347, 519, 522, 527
YAFFA, 739
YAG, 737
Yakov, 159
Yalinovich, 90
Yankel, 202, 280, 507, 591, 623, 624, 625, 626, 661, 663
Yankel the Blacksmith, 14
Yankel the Chumash teacher, 662
Yankel the vinegar maker, 109, 110, 280, 507, 589, 665, 671
Yankele, 623
Yankele Stein, 78
Yankelevich, 363
Yankelovich, 459, 461
YANKELOVICH, 739
Yannai, 242
Yanosevich, 33, 606
Yantke the tailor, 470
Yasi-Kanczeker the blacksmith, 129
YASINOVICH, 754
Yatkonski from Kovno, 302
Yechiel, 257
Yechiel the potter, 107, 108
Yehi Or, 239
Yellin, 424, 425, 427, 430, 488
Yenta with the goat, 105
Yerucham, 240
Yeshayahu Ivensky, 16
Yisrael, 228
Yisrael David, 664
Yisrael David the Kitten, 662
Yisrael David the Shochet, 661
Yitzchak, 70, 171, 180, 351, 627, 644
Yitzchak B, 305, 310
Yitzchak B., 314
Yitzchak the Shochet, 16, 603
Yonatan, 78
YONENSON, 738
Yose the tailor, 587

Yose the Tzimmes, 622, 629
Yose-Ber, 614
Yosef the cobbler, 72
Yosef the tailor, 170
Yoselovich, 341, 354
Yoshke der Meshugener, 768, 769
Yoska (the Schwalb), 319
Yoska the Crazy, 601
Yoske the Bird, 100
Yossel the Shochet, 130
Yossel the shoemaker, 129
Yudel, 199
Yudel "The Yellow", 544
Yudelevich, 52, 63, 66, 77, 79, 80, 86, 87, 98, 103, 117, 151, 313, 318, 319, 321, 322, 330, 332, 338, 457, 654
YUDELEVICH, 737, 738, 755
Yudfas, 82, 86
Yuter, 504, 505
YUTER, 738

Z

Zabara, 240
Zachar, 97, 104, 416
Zachrin, 443
Zack, 211, 215, 764
Zacks, 210
Zaflatz, 593
Zak, 53, 54, 80, 84, 89, 172, 175, 231, 272, 535, 569
ZAK, 736
Zakhary, 9, 14, 767
Zaks, 519
ZAKS, 736
Zalonker, 496
Zamachkas, 682
Zandman, 54, 90, 299, 319, 321, 331, 340
ZANDMAN, 736
Zangwill, 36
Zaremba, 680
Zeidel, 354, 355
Zelmanovich, 103, 307
ZELMANOVICH, 736
Zelonker, 56
Zians, 362
ZIBOL, 751
Zich, 632
Zilber, 87
Zilberman, 11, 16, 18, 489, 583, 686, 716
Ziman, 62, 117, 510, 511
Zimans, 426
Zimrani, 9, 341
Zisele, 245

Zisla, 15, 186, 193, 198, 199, 200, 201, 203, 204,
    209, 211, 215, 217, 218, 219, 222, 233, 298, 299,
    306, 327, 341, 344, 362, 395, 463, 571, 606
Zisla (Lavie), 256
Zisla-Gazit, 40, 191
Zisla-Levin, 201
Zlata, 293
Zlonker, 316, 317, 322

ZLONKER, 736
Zochovsky, 214
Zopovich, 52, 62, 306, 330, 337, 345, 375, 395, 420,
    422, 424, 425, 428, 442, 447, 486, 490, 693, 715
ZOPOVICH, 735, 744
Zopowitz, 497
Zuchovsky, 61, 68, 71, 83, 84, 87, 149
Zuckerman, 467